Multicultural School Psychology Competencies

A Practical Guide

Danielle Martines
Montclair State University

Los Angeles • London • New Delhi • Singapore

For information:

SAGE Publications, Inc.
2455 Teller Road
Thousand Oaks,
   California 91320
E-mail: order@sagepub.com

SAGE Publications Ltd.
1 Oliver's Yard
55 City Road
London EC1Y 1SP
United Kingdom

SAGE Publications India Pvt. Ltd.
B 1/I 1 Mohan Cooperative
   Industrial Area
Mathura Road, New Delhi 110 044
India

SAGE Publications Asia-Pacific Pte. Ltd.
33 Pekin Street #02-01
Far East Square
Singapore 048763

Printed in the United States of America

Library of Congress Cataloging-in-Publication Data

Martines, Danielle.
Multicultural school psychology competencies: a practical guide/Danielle Martines.
   p. cm.
Includes bibliographical references and index.
ISBN 978-1-4129-0514-5 (pbk.)
   1. School psychologists. 2. Minority students—Counseling of. I. Title.

LB3013.6.M365 2008
371.4—dc22   2007049059

This book is printed on acid-free paper.

08   09   10   11   12   11   10   9   8   7   6   5   4   3   2   1

Acquisitions Editor:	Kassie Graves
Editorial Assistant:	Veronica K. Novak
Production Editor:	Catherine M. Chilton
Copy Editor:	Susan Jarvis
Typesetter:	C&M Digitals (P) Ltd.
Proofreader:	Annette R. Van Deusen
Indexer:	Jeanne R. Busemeyer
Cover Designer:	Gail Buschman
Marketing Manager:	Carmel Schrire

Contents

Foreword

Multicultural School Psychology Competencies is a timely and valuable professional guidebook that is an excellent resource for the preparation of multicultural competencies and skill development of school psychologists-in-training or in practice, educators, school counselors, and other practitioners providing services to culturally and linguistically diverse (CLD) children and adolescents. The original meaning of multicultural education has gradually evolved from a traditional view of exposing students in teacher education programs to generic issues of cultural diversity, enrichment, and pedagogy in the learning environment to a multidimensional perspective that encompasses the academic development of a set of multicultural competencies.

Competencies specific to school psychologists cover foundational knowledge in multicultural theories and research in education and counseling; functional skills in practice domains such as cross-cultural consultation, bilingual assessment, and culturally sensitive interventions; and application of ethical and professional practice when providing services to children of racial/cultural and linguistic diversity and their families in the school setting. Essentially, a more in-depth and broader understanding of multiculturalism has emerged in the field of school psychology. Thus the academic preparation of school psychologists and clinicians in multicultural competencies is a critical aspect of professional identity and professional development.

The best practice approach provided in this guidebook is based on multicultural theoretical, research, and ethical premises, and is extended to a compilation of supplemental resources, instruments, and materials that are readily accessible to the practitioner and for training purposes. Consistent with training needs in the development of multicultural competencies in school psychology, this resource is comprehensive in scope yet practical, and is focused on the attainment, integration, and application of specific skills that will ultimately benefit CLD children and youth in the schools.

The guidebook is divided into four parts, each centering on essential practical resources for cultural competence in important domains such as multicultural assessment, assessment of multicultural intelligences, clinical assessment in a multicultural context, academic assessment, and consultations with teachers. It also includes a unique chapter on writing psychological and educational reports for CLD clients. A special section provides a comprehensive review and clinical suggestions for acculturation issues, bilingual education, prejudice reduction, and giftedness.

In this book, Dr. Danielle Martines brings together her extensive experiences as a trilingual multicultural school psychologist and her scholarly professional expertise as a researcher and educator. It is her hope that by providing students and practitioners with critical resources and solutions on multicultural school psychology practices, she can encourage sound clinical practice and advocacy for child and adolescent populations of varied ethnicities, cultures, and languages. That hope is clearly realized by this unique resource book.

Giselle B. Esquivel, Psy.D., ABPP, FAASP
Professor
School Psychology Program
Division of Psychological and Educational Services
Graduate School of Education
Fordham University

Preface

Why a Practical Guide in Multicultural School Psychology Competencies?

A review of the literature in the human service professions has continually encouraged multicultural competency training for mental health and behavioral science practitioners in order to enable them to better understand and intervene for the racial/ethnic and culturally and linguistically diverse children and adults they service (Canino & Spurlock, 2000; Cuellar & Paniagua, 2000; Gopaul-McNicol & Brice-Baker, 1998). Consequently, it has been documented that many professionals have struggled with fears of cultural malpractice, which may be attributed to poor multicultural competency training (Allison, Echemendia, & Robinson, 1996).

In view of this training obligation and requirement, as well as the increase in the diversity of children and adolescents in schools (Banks, 2002), there is a considerable need for a practical culture-sensitive informational text that is specifically compiled and easily accessible for the multicultural competency preparation of practitioners working with varied children and youth in schools and other educational settings.

Correspondingly, graduate students in educational training programs should have access to a comprehensive volume of applied-focused cultural competencies in school psychology and other related areas. To date, useful multicultural applications aimed at practice-based school psychology have not been collected into a specific volume for the student, the university trainer, or the practitioner. A general guidebook that will direct school psychologists in training and practice (and be helpful to counselors, educators and students in non-traditional forms of mental health) to current research-based approaches and provide accessibility to resource materials that can facilitate clinical multicultural practice is currently unavailable. The aspiration of this practical guide is to achieve this objective.

I first became aware of this nearly two decades ago as a practicing trilingual school psychologist on the Committee for Special Education for the Board of Education in New York City. If only, I mused, there was available a general text that would guide the practitioner or student to appropriate cultural methods as well as provide direction and examples for the various functions of multicultural school psychology practice. I soon found that I was not alone in my musing. Over the years, many of my colleagues practicing and teaching school psychology in New York, New Jersey, Connecticut, New Mexico, Oregon, and Arizona, and my graduate students, voiced the same opinion. It was difficult, they argued, to search for current articles and several research and theory books in order to obtain guidance as to the appropriate steps to take when servicing immigrant and U.S.-born children from diverse racial/ethnic cultures and languages. What were the necessary multicultural competency steps to take in assessment, second language acquisition evaluation and bilingual placement; consultation with diverse teachers and families; and prejudice issues that affected all school personnel? After decades of practice within school systems and mental health clinics, and as an academic, I know first hand that this query wish list continues to date!

This book, *Multicultural School Psychology Competencies: A Practical Guide*, is devoted to serving this need. It is a practice-based guide for the multicultural competency skill development of school psychologists-in-training and in practice, as well as educators, school counselors, and other mental health practitioners. The guide can be used as in-service or continuing education for the practitioner, in group workshop or individual (self-monitored) learning formats, or as part of a graduate-level course to prepare students as school psychologists or in related educational and mental health fields. For the university trainer, the guidebook can be used for several courses that require focus on multicultural school practices (e.g., school psychology practicum, one-year final internship seminar, school-based consultation practicum, therapeutic interventions in the schools, and as a general tool in assessment courses). The text can also be helpful to trainers of counselors and social workers as part of an overall introduction to multicultural school competency training.

The guidebook is divided into four parts and provides an instructional array of helpful "hands-on" checklists, suggested readings and literature reviews, and guided steps to take in various practice-based situations.

Part I provides the foundations for an understanding of the critical multicultural issues in school psychology. This introductory chapter presents a framework for the development of multicultural school psychology competencies. The information covered includes an overview of multicultural issues, recommended multicultural competencies, an introduction to cultural identity, and a look at acculturation. The chapter concludes with recommendation for the self-assessment of multicultural awareness, knowledge, and skills, and a discussion on instruments to assess cross-cultural competencies.

Part II is dedicated to the varied professional domains of the practice of multicultural assessment. The included chapters focus on multicultural assessment, assessment of multiple intelligences, academic assessment, clinical assessment in a multicultural context, and personality and behavioral assessment. This part concludes with a special chapter on writing psychological and educational reports for culturally and linguistically diverse clients.

Part III provides a compilation of practical multicultural competencies for school-based consultation. Two chapters titled "Consultations and Interventions Involving Teachers" and "Multicultural Competencies for Parental Training Programs" present reviews of consultation models as well as practical applications on the three levels of cross-cultural competencies: multicultural awareness; knowledge; and skills for consulting with teachers, parents, and schools. A special section is devoted to resistance in consultation.

Part IV comprises special topics in multicultural psychology that were chosen because of their importance in the field of school psychology. The aim of this section is to provide school practitioners with updated information and practice-based applications on a selection of culture-sensitive designated topics. Included are chapters on acculturation (cultural identity; racial/ethnic identity development; the acculturation process; and assessment of acculturation); the language barrier (factors affecting the learning of a second languages; distinctive factors of ELL and bilingual assessment; language factors in consultation and interventions; guidelines on the use of interpreters and types of bilingual education programs); prejudice reduction (causes of prejudice; biracial/multiracial identity development; lesbian, gay, and bisexual identity development; religiosity, lesbian/gay/bisexuality and racial/ethnic identity development; a Latino case of religious/sexual identity conflict; racial ethnic identity and prejudice assessment; prejudice reduction programs and teacher collaboration and teamwork approaches; and school-based prejudice reduction interventions). The final chapter, "Giftedness and Diverse Students," is included in this special topic section because of the rarity of focus in many training programs on giftedness and racial/ethnic, culturally diverse students in school settings.

References

Allison, K. W., Echemendia, R., Crawford, I., & Robinson, W. L. (1996). Predicting cultural competence: Implications for practice and training. *Professional Psychology: Research and Practice, 27,* 386–393.

Banks, J. A. (2002). *An introduction to multicultural education.* Boston: Allyn & Bacon.

Canino, I. A., & Spurlock, J. (2000). *Culturally diverse children and adolescents: Assessment, diagnosis, and treatment* (2nd ed.). New York: Guilford Press.

Cuellar, I., & Paniagua, F. A. (Eds.). (2000). *Handbook of multicultural mental health.* San Diego, CA: Academic Press.

Gopaul-McNicol, S., & Brice Baker, J. (1998). *Cross-cultural practice: Assessment, treatment, and training.* New York: John Wiley & Sons.

Acknowledgments

I wish to acknowledge and thank the many individuals who have encouraged me enthusiastically in the preparation of this book.

I am fortunate to have had two editors. I am grateful to Art Pompino, who was the first to acknowledge my vision for a multicultural school competencies guidebook; and I also thank his successor, Kassie Graves, for her continued support and advice. In addition, my gratitude goes to Veronica Novak for her speedy editing and consulting.

A particular note of appreciation is extended to my contributing co-authors, Pablo Fernandez Berrocal (University of Malaga, Spain), for sharing some of his work on culture and emotional intelligence in one of our chapters, and Sara Nahari (Queens College, New York), for compressing her multicultural school psychology expertise into two of the text's chapters.

I am very indebted to the various reviewers—Sharon Blackwell Jones, University of Georgia; Larry C. Loesch, University of Florida; Josie De Los Santos, University of Texas, Pan American; Janinie M. Jones, University of Washington; Amy M Rees-Turyn, Lewis and Clark College; and Kwong-Liem Karl Kwan, University of Missouri—for their invaluable commentaries and suggestions, which were put to good use and helped to make this volume more informative. Finally, a special thank you to Giselle Esquivel, my long-time mentor and colleague for her continual encouragement.

And, naturally, family and good friends who took the time to listen to all the twist and turns of each chapter, the fate of deadlines and their accompanying stressors. For this kind patience, I thank my brother Peter Francis Bracey, Rafaela Delgado Flores, and Diane and Bill Amison Loring.

—Danielle Martines

PART I

Multicultural
School Competencies

1

Introduction to Multicultural School Competencies

Developing Multicultural Competencies

Perhaps the fact that it is no longer necessary to explain why multiculturalism is an important concept in psychology and education demonstrates its lengthy and dusty trail to success. It is evident that the study of culture is not a novel idea. In the professions of counseling psychology, mental health, and education, culture and its relationship to sound practice in these fields have been studied for decades. School counseling services have been in effect since the mid-1960s and the need for multicultural competent counselors was recognized even then. Some fifteen years later, a position paper from the Education and Training Committee of the American Psychological Association's (APA) Division 17 (Counseling Psychology) produced various definitions of multiculturalism (Sue, Bernier, et al., 1982). The 1990s brought about the concept of counselor self-bias and the recognition that self-bias was a basic constituent of efficacious counseling. A larger concern is that psychology has been described as "Eurocentric" due to its historical and educational development. Multiculturalism in psychological practice has not been adopted easily within the teaching establishment.

Many researchers and practitioners have stressed the need for cross-cultural training (Canino & Spurlock, 2000; Gopaul-McNicol & Brice-Baker, 1998; Sue, Arrendondo, & McDavis, 1992; Plummer, 1998). Until recently, with the exception of a few researchers, school psychology was not as productive as it might have been in this cross-cultural undertaking and appears to have initiated a drive to "catch up" within the last decade or so, with numerous publications focusing on culture-based suggestions and guidelines (Ingraham & Meyers, 2000; Rogers et al., 1999; Rogers, 2000; Sheridan, 2000; Martens, 1993). It is now deemed vital for school psychologists to adhere to "culturally sensitive" ethnical and professional responsibilities. Recommendations have been made for school psychologists to service racial/ethnic and culturally and linguistically diverse (CLD) children and their families based on the American Psychological Association's (APA) Division 16 Taskforce on Cross-Cultural School Psychology Competencies and by guidelines established by APA's Division 17 for multicultural counseling proficiency for psychologists in the year 2000 (Rogers et al., 1999).

Most importantly, a recognized major challenge for the field of school psychology is the ethnic minority underrepresentation among the ranks of CLD school psychologists (Merrell, Ervin, & Gimpel, 2006). In order to meet the needs of the youths serviced in schools, changes in the field are recommended that will bring about an increase in the number of ethnic CLD school psychologists. One suggested way of tackling this issue is to ensure efforts are made to recruit and retain CLD school psychologists at all levels, from practitioners to administrators, as well as university trainers (Merrell et al., 2006; Sheridan & Gutkin, 2000). The National Association of School Psychologists (NASP) also considers an increase in the proportion of CLD school psychologists to be pivotal to the profession of school psychology in order to progress cultural and linguistic services in schools (Merrell et al., 2006). A positive response to this need will enhance the practices that are already in place in schools regarding culturally responsive service delivery (Curtis, Hunley, Walker, & Baker, 1999).

Racial/ethnic identity development, acculturation, and cultural psychology are major constructs that demonstrate how the profession has advanced in the last few decades. These constructs have been identified as differentially applicable to the diversity of the various racial and ethnic groups in the United States. The research on acculturation and racial/ethnic identity views the acculturative and racial/ethnic identity process as different for each racial/ethnic person (see Carter, 2005; Helms, 1994; Phinney, 1996; Sodowsky & Maestas, 2000). As a result of these distinctions, it is important for school psychologists to be aware that there are individual differences within racial/ethnic groups and that similar groups can be culturally and linguistically diverse.

As underscored in the various chapters of this book, school psychologists working with diverse groups of children in the United States will encounter children who are recently arrived, first-generation immigrants, and second- or third-generation settlers. Consequently, each child will have a specific family, educational, and language history. Some racial/ethnic and culturally and linguistically diverse groups in the United States have been citizens for centuries, while others have been here for only decades. In addition, it is important to note that the commonly used term "minority group" is associated with those individuals from lower socioeconomic status, education, and political power. This term is used interchangeably with various racial/ethnic groups which, because of their physical or cultural background, have been marked by the dominant culture/society as undesirable, and thus have been treated unjustly. Accordingly, Native Americans (including American Indians, Eskimos, and Aleuts), African Americans, Latino Americans, Asian Americans and Pacific Islanders are considered minority groups, as well as other racial/ethnic groups which have at some time immigrated to the United States and experienced unfair treatment.

In the multicultural literature, the term "ethnicity" is used to refer to a specific group of people who have the same social and cultural beliefs. Contrary to common belief, race is not a biological category that divides and labels different groups as a result of distinctive innate biological traits (U.S. Department of Health and Human Services, 2001). However, race has also been defined as having both biological and hereditary components (Ponterotto & Casas, 1991). The following explanation aids to clarify further the issue of race as a biological grouping:

> The visible physical traits associated with race, such as hair and skin color, are defined by a tiny fraction of our genes, and they do not reliably differentiate between the social categories of race. As more is learned about the 30,000 genes of the human genome, variations between groups are being identified, such as in genes that code for the enzymes active in drug metabolism. While such information may prove to have clinical utility, it is important to note that these variations cannot be used to distinguish groups from one another as they are outweighed by overwhelming genetic similarities across so-called racial groups. (Paabo, 2001, cited in U.S. Department of Health and Human Services, 2001, p. 7)

It is helpful to remember that the genetic analysis of different ethnic groups has resulted in compelling evidence that there are greater genetic variations within than there are across racial groups (U.S. Department of Health and Human Services, 2001). With reference to culture, Helms and Tallyrand (1997) explain culture as "race, ethnic, cultural and socioeconomic conditions of socializations." Different cultures "classify people into racial groups according to a set of characteristics that are socially significant" (U.S. Department of Health and Human Services, 2001, p. 9).

In actual practice, the knowledge of these different terms assists the practitioner to better understand important variables that must be considered when servicing children from racially, ethnically, culturally, and linguistically diverse backgrounds, whether settled in the United States for a decade or for a century or more. Hence the term "culturally and linguistically diverse," or CLD, can encompass children from various racial, ethnic, and cultural groups, all of whom may speak different native languages and/or may have acquired bilingual proficiency or remained monolingual. For the purposes of this guidebook, the term CLD is employed to identify children and youth from all racial/ethnic, culturally, and linguistically diverse groups in the United States. From this perspective, the term should therefore prompt school psychologists to be alert to the racial and ethnic identity, cultural history, and language acquisition of the particular students they service.

With these cultural perspectives and responsibilities in view, this guidebook is a compilation of straightforward references to some of the most compelling multicultural issues (and practice-based techniques) in school psychology practice. It is addressed to the questioning practitioner, the student in training, the university trainer, and other education and mental health professionals. The intent for school practitioners is to augment their awareness and knowledge of what is currently obligatory for culturally ethical and professional practice in schools. Subsequent chapters will address the majority of the multicultural issues noted in depth here. The ensuing review of multicultural issues and competencies is provided as groundwork for the more extensive discussions in the rest of this book. Suggested readings are listed at the end of each chapter in annotated bibliographies. Where feasible, checklists and instruments have been reproduced and/or information for obtaining them has been included in the reference sections. Lastly, an additional special ambition of this guidebook is to act as a proactive vehicle for increasing the numbers of racial/ethnic CLD school psychologists in our schools.

Brief Historical Review of Multiculturalism

This concise review of critical multicultural issues is aimed at increasing school psychologists' historical awareness of the "multicultural movement" in education and psychology, as well as providing a foundation for multicultural school psychology competencies.

Definition of Multiculturalism

Over the last few decades, various researchers have defined multicultural competency (Atkinson, Morton, & Sue, 1998; Pedersen, 1987, 1985; Sue et al., 1992; Sue et al., 1999; Sue, 1998). Recently, Sue and colleagues (1999) defined multiculturalism as including a broad *melange* of differences among people that ultimately tends to hinder communication and comprehension. These differences are: race, gender, sexual orientation, competence, incapacity, religion, and rank. To these we can add: age, language, ethnic educational/ vocational viewpoints, disciplinary norms, ethnic-perceived normal and abnormal behaviors, family constellation, and extended family members. Reynolds (2000) gives another definition: "Multiculturalism is about understanding ourselves and others who are different from us . . . at its core [it is] about people and relationships. And all relationships are about discovering our commonalities, our cultural differences, and our personal uniqueness" (p. 111).

These definitions can be applied to both sociological and psychological contexts, and serve as a stepping stone toward the understanding and recognition of various cultural groups. For school psychologists, multiculturalism is now a professional quest leading to more advanced standards and competencies for best practice.

Multicultural Education

Another important issue that is automatically connected to multiculturalism is education. Educators began using the expression "multicultural education" in the 1970s. Marshall (2002) defines multicultural education as "a vision of schooling based on the democratic ideas of justice and equality." Marshall points out that scholars from Canada, England, France, Australia, and South Africa are studying what multicultural education means for the teaching-learning process. In the United States, scholars studying multicultural education agree that traditional schooling is a thing of the past, advocating restructuring within the areas of teaching styles, techniques, curriculum, and interpersonal interactions (Marshall, 2002).

As the ethnic composition of the United States continued to diversify, the prospect that more educators needed to work with diverse student populations quickly became a reality in the classroom. To date, researchers have observed a continuing need for multicultural educators in the United States (Banks, 2002; Kim & Atkinson, 2002; Kim, Yang, Atkinson, Wolfe, & Hong, 2001; Ladson-Billings, 2001; Ramos-Sanchez, Atkinson, & Fraga, 1999; Sue et al., 1999). Multicultural education is now assumed to be an essential component of an educator's repertoire (Banks, 2002; Gollnick & Chinn, 2006; Ladson-Billings, 2001). Some university training programs have incorporated multicultural education courses in their curricula. Furthermore, numerous texts have been published on multicultural instructional strategies for teachers that serve to increase teachers' cultural awareness, their culturally sensitive knowledge, and the development of adequate skills for servicing diverse ethnic groups. Additionally, knowledge of teaching strategies for racial/ethnic CLD students is considered an integral part of teachers' necessary skills as a result of multicultural education advocacy and the influx of literature available in this instructional area (Banks, 2002; Nieto, 1999; Gay, 2000). School psychologists are encouraged to acquire knowledge in multicultural education instructional techniques so as to be prepared to offer classroom assistance to teachers through collaborative school-based consultation (see Chapter 8 on consultation).

Cross-Cultural Psychology

At the same time, it is anticipated that school psychologists-in-training will be trained to observe, discern, and discuss racial/ethnic CLD students' problems with the required cultural sensibilities and expertise essential for making placement decisions (see NASP standards on multicultural competencies— www.nasp.org). When did this all start? Historically, the more demographic changes occurred in the United States, the more it was noted that teachers, children, parents, and even patients could not be treated exactly alike—that is, utilizing the same Eurocentric methods in counseling, psychotherapy, education, and even vocational training (Canino & Spurlock, 2000).

Psychotherapists, psychiatrists, social workers, and psychologists began to notice the lack of response to treatment and the high drop out rate of their diverse ethnic clients (Atkinson, Bui, & Mori, 2001; Canino & Spurlock, 2000; Sue, 1999). Thus the continued efficacy of psychotherapy was a growing concern that in turn impacted on interventions and resulted in the establishment of the APA Division 12 Task Force (Promotion and Dissemination of Psychological Procedures), which authorized the investigation of Empirically Supported Treatments (ESTs). A succession of reports from the Task Force concerning psychotherapy emerged by the mid-1990s. These have been criticized from both theoretical and experimental standpoints. Most importantly, it has been suggested that EST criteria ignore client, therapist, and relationship variables. Atkinson et al. (2000), Doyle (1998), and Sue (1999) have also proposed that ESTs fall short of checking for ethnic/cultural factors. Furthermore, Sue (1999) has recapitulated the "Eurocentric" quandary, pointing out that multiculturalists have to defend their stance. Most likely, accentuation on EST will have a harmful outcome on school psychology training if this force is left unconstrained.

Gopaul-McNicol and Brice-Baker (1998) point out that cross-cultural psychology has a lengthy history that should not be considered specific to the culture of the United States. These practitioners highlight that as long as people are "racially, linguistically, culturally, religiously, and politically different" throughout the world, there will be challenges for any practicing clinician. Educators, mental health practitioners, and school psychologists must appreciate these differences, and also be aware that prejudicial sentiments are prevalent—especially when a leading culture perceives the values, traditions, belief systems, and religions of other ethnic groups to be inferior to their own. Moreover, immigrant groups have been known to assimilate better when their culture was similar to that of the dominant majority population of the United States (Ponterotto, Casas, Suzuki, & Alexander, 1995).

In spite of the fact that as far back as the 1950s there were therapists advocating culturally sensitive therapy, it was not until the early 1980s that Sue (1981) and Pedersen (1985) were nationally recognized as cross-cultural counseling promoters. Both Sue and Pedersen appealed to the counseling profession to improve clinical effectiveness with culturally diverse clients by providing the counseling profession with guidelines on how to attain multicultural competencies (see their landmark work in Sue, 1981; and Pedersen, 1985). Pedersen addressed the need for counseling practitioners to develop cultural awareness, knowledge, and skills for servicing diverse ethnic groups. Thus the counseling profession convinced the fields of psychiatry and educational, vocational, and school psychology to adopt a multicultural perspective in psycho-educational assessment, treatment, and intervention practices. Correspondingly, the *Diagnostic and Statistical Manual of Mental Disorders IV* (DSM-IV) and the DSM-IV-TR, a psychiatric diagnostic tool, now include culture and gender cautions—a big step forward from the more instituted psychiatric approach to treatment (American Psychological Association, 1994). However, the precautionary notations do not include suggestions for diagnosis.

Fortunately, there have been encouraging developments in the field of mental health. Recently, the U.S. Department of Health and Human Services' Office of the Surgeon General (2001) released a report, *Mental Health: Culture, Race and Ethnicity*, that underlines four important themes:

- Culture is important in mental health. This includes emotional anguish, manifestation of symptoms, various stressors, the specific utilization of services and the particular response to treatment.
- There needs to be consideration of the inequalities that subsist in the welfare of African Americans, Asian Americans, Latinos, and Native Americans which may place these ethnic groups at risk of mental health problems. However, these should not ignore the fact that these inequalities are mainly due to the lack of available services and/or the economic difficulties that impede affordability of services.
- Culturally focused treatment is now considered helpful.

- It is recognized that there is insufficient research regarding mental health issues, on the effects of prejudice, and in the analysis of the results of cultural competency in servicing various ethnic groups (U.S. Dept. of Health and Human Services, 2001).

Interestingly, when studied in aggregate, the major racial/ethnic groups are made up of long-standing U.S. citizens, and each is included as having specific racial/ethnic special mental health needs.

It can be said with confidence that school psychologists servicing the schools of this century and the next will be confronted with children and youth that manifest clusters of symptoms associated with mental illness. Today, schools are no longer solely educational institutions through which children learn: they are increasingly legally responsible for assessing, diagnosing, and treating children and youth with emotional disturbances that can range from mild behavioral disruptions to more severe antisocial, oppositional, and aggressive behavior disorders. In addition, schools are responsible for monitoring children and adolescents with depressive symptoms. The multicultural school psychologist is responsible for acquiring knowledge of the different *idioms of distress* by which different cultures express, experience, and cope with feelings of distress, in addition to knowledge of the different *culture-bound* syndromes which are more commonly manifested in certain cultures (U.S. Department of Health and Human Services, 2001).

Obstacles to Multiculturalism

In the 1990s and the twenty-first century, multiculturalism—which currently delineates all cultures residing in the United States—is known as the "fourth force in counseling" psychology (Pedersen, 1991, 1992). The concept of "multiculturalism," and the equally used and similar term "diversity," have been linked to "such labels as affirmative action, quotas, civil rights, discrimination, reverse discrimination, racism, sexism, anti-White, political correctness, and many other emotion-arousing terms" (Sue et al., 1998, p. 2). Unfortunately, this varied mix of conceptualizations pertaining to multiculturalism has often resulted in dire political actions and interpersonal confrontations that led to counterproductive outcomes (see Sue et al., 1998 for a detailed explanation of multiculturalism and its effects on U.S. society).

Clearly, there have been repeated obstacles to multiculturalism that block any intended progress. Ramirez (1991) describes three major impediments to a healthy multicultural environment: the urgency to assimilate; racial prejudice;

and oppression/persecution. Gopaul-McNicol & Brice-Baker (1998) give a detailed explanation for each of these barriers:

> *Assimilation*—Numerous ethnic groups experience the pressure to adopt the values and beliefs of the dominant culture. Noncompliance results in punishable and implicit consequences—such as the blockage of access to programs that are beneficial for growth in the community.

> *Prejudice*—The dominant group impedes the progress of different ethnic groups via economic, social, and political structures that isolate and reject various ethnic groups' legal rights and opposing equal opportunity (Aponte & Van Deusen, 1981).

> *Oppression*—Power misused against minority ethnic groups to impede their collaboration in the pursuits of the dominant culture.

Regrettably, these barriers tend to form an endless cycle, experienced worldwide and devastating to immigrant racial/ethnic groups, including those groups which have assimilated over the centuries. Furthermore, the barriers may continue to obstruct, as observed by several researchers of cross-cultural psychology. The U.S. Census Bureau estimates that by the year 2050, the Anglo ancestry population will *not* be the numerical majority. School psychologists will find that more than half of their clients come from backgrounds that are racial/ethnic culturally and linguistically diverse. Knowledge of ethnic group difficulties in dealing with assimilation, oppression, and prejudice are competencies that a school psychologist should make it a point to learn. Chapter 12 provides a detailed review of the issues in prejudice and suggestions for best school psychology practice.

Cross-Cultural Training

As a result of these obstructions to multiculturalism, and in an effort to encourage appropriate interventions for diverse populations, guidelines for cross-cultural competency training in counseling and mental health are now available—in particular, through the works of Bernal and Padilla (1982), Rogers, Close Conoley, Ponterotto, and Wiese (1992), Sue, Arredondo, and McDavis (1992), and Barona, Santos de Barona, Flores, and Gutierrez (1990). A culturally competent psychologist should adhere to the recommended guidelines and recognize that their own beliefs, attitudes, and values may influence their service to racial/ethnic CLD children and parents. Likewise, "training should allow them to recognize the limits of their skills and refer the client to receive more appropriate resources" (Gopaul-McNicol & Brice-Baker, 1998, p. 143). With respect to training, psychologists should also be able to identify the basis of any distress frequently observed in cultural differences and understand how such differences can be perceived or brought out in therapy (Gopaul-McNicol & Brice-Baker, 1998).

Although much has been accomplished, at some point in the future it is hoped that university training programs will move toward a stronger approach to multicultural school psychology competency training (Bernal & Padilla, 1982). Only a few multicultural courses are offered in most university training programs at present, and this is even less the case for future school psychologists (Banks, 2002; Ladson-Billings, 2001; Reynolds, 1995). Multicultural diagnostic approaches such as bilingual and informal/alternative assessments, culturally appropriate interventions, and consultation are beginning to surface—not without inevitable disinclination—in school psychology training programs, but these are left to the discretion of the university trainer and are often not perceived as part of core requirements (Gopaul-McNicol & Brice-Baker, 1998). Frequently, as Gopaul-McNicol and Brice-Baker (1998) point out, universities have failed to successfully hire trainers qualified to teach multicultural competencies and practical interventions. Chapter 6 provides suggestions for university-level training in multicultural school-based consultation.

Why the Need for Multicultural Competent School Psychologists?

Obviously, there is abundant literature emphasizing the need for cross-cultural training for psychotherapists, counselors (Gopaul-McNicol & Brice-Baker, 1998; Sue, Arrendondo, & McDavis, 1992; Sue et al., 1998) and for multicultural teacher education (Artiles, Trent, Hoffman-Kipp, & Lopez-Torres, 2000; Banks, 2002). Some literature has reviewed the need for cross-cultural considerations in consultation (Ingraham & Meyers, 2000; Sheridan, 2000; Henning-Stout & Meyers, 2000). However, as already mentioned, the literature has been rather scarce regarding the practical training of competent multicultural school psychologists. School psychologists working in schools, agencies, clinics, and hospitals will inevitably be asked to provide services to educators, parents, administrators, and even medical professionals from diverse backgrounds. Training at the graduate school level has mainly focused on the acquisition of skills in assessment, consultation, and interventions. In this regard, school psychologists-in-training are educated in consultation methods and techniques that accentuate suitable communication, interactive skills, and interventions; however, these programs fail to incorporate culturally appropriate competencies that would result in more constructive consultation. Disappointingly, it is this lack of awareness of and knowledge about cultural issues that frequently limits the school psychologist from providing effective services to teachers, students, and parents. This is further exacerbated by the fact that, despite more than two decades of counselor educators advocating multicultural training at the university level, only one or two courses are offered in most universities—let alone in a school psychology curriculum (Banks & McGee-Banks, 1995; Rosenfield & Gravois, 1998).

Consequently, a graduate student taking a specific school psychology core course may not have prior multicultural knowledge, much less skills. If this suspected deficit is not addressed, the varied training and practicum experience will continue to focus on assessment, consultation, and interventions from a traditional perspective, leaving the graduate student with little knowledge of and competence in working with cross-culturally diverse consultee-teachers and racial/ethnic CLD children and their families. Given these issues, it is the ambition of this text to provide a practical reference aid for certain competency areas that may have been overlooked.

Developing Multicultural School Competencies

It is therefore important that trainers of prospective school psychologists adopt methods of teaching assessment, consultation, and school-based interventions that will increase students' cultural sensitivity as well as their culture-specific knowledge and skills (Behring, Cabello, Kushida, & Murguia, 2000; Canino & Spurlock, 2000; Ingraham & Meyers, 2000; Martines, 2003; Rogers, 2000; Rogers & Lopez, 2002; Sue, Arrendondo & McDavis, 1992). Consequently, practicing school psychologists are ethically responsible for developing professional multicultural expertise (see NASP Multicultural Competency Standards online; APA Guidelines on Multicultural Education, Training, Research, Practice, and Organizational Change for Psychologists, 2003).

Given the professional guidelines and the prolific literature produced by researchers and practitioners on multicultural training, it would seem that if multicultural training is not offered in school psychology programs, prospective school psychologists-in-training should insist on this training and seek advice from the directors and instructors in their programs. The current and projected demographics on the increase of culturally diverse populations are sufficient evidence and reason to petition for this need. It can be considered the school psychologist's role to demand proper training. Of its own accord, this is a form of advocacy.

Recommended Multicultural Competencies

Regardless of whether or not school practitioners devote the majority of their time to assessment or consultation, Sue et al. (1992) propose a methodical schema that lists three major multicultural counseling competencies:

- *awareness*—the ability to have an awareness of one's own biases, assumptions, and values;
- *knowledge* (on a higher scale of competency)— possessing an understanding of the worldview of the culturally and linguistically diverse client; and
- *skills*—the competencies required to implement appropriate intervention and strategies.

In 1981, Sue outlined instructional goals for cross-cultural competencies for psychologists. Although not precisely intended for school psychologists *per se*, they exemplify a core competency groundwork that can be modified for the multicultural school psychologist and for this text's unique purpose. Moreover, other researchers and practitioners have endorsed these principles (Gopaul-McNicol & Brice-Baker, 1998). The following describes each of the guidelines.

Attitudinal competencies—This relates to the psychologist's knowledge about his/her ethnic heritage. It implies being knowledgeable about one's ethnic norms, values, and traditions as well as other relevant practices. In many cases, a psychologist may be bicultural—such as a psychologist with roots in Europe or Asia as well as the United States. Such a bicultural background should be acknowledged and appreciated. Any significant differences in practices between the two cultures should be noted as well as any evolved attitudinal/traditional changes.

Biases—A psychologist should be self-introspective of his/her own biases. The recognition of such will aid in establishing a "comfort zone" with ethnic differences. This involves overcoming prejudice and stereotyping, and recognizing that clients will have substantially different cultural values and beliefs that may be in conflict with the psychologist's own. In particular cases, a psychologist may have to refer her/his client to another practitioner of more appropriate ethnicity as a result of insufficient knowledge or failure to reach a comfort zone (Midgett & Meggert, 1991).

Knowledge competencies—Knowledge at the school level would have a comprehensive level of competency that requires the psychologist to have a thorough comprehension of various cultures as well as of the various racial ethnic identity models—an understanding of the society of minority groups—such as how societal structures relate to various ethnic groups (i.e., institutional barriers that force the outnumbered ethnic client by court-ordered school desegregation, affirmative-action policies, gender-regulated organizational regulations, or federal documentation procedures that clash with a particular culture's norms and practices).

Skills competencies—The ability to apply culture-based knowledge to solve ethnic-specific cases and select effective culturally sensitive interventions and consultation services. Skill competencies refers to the capability of the psychologist to put into operation the professional knowledge learned to resolve clinical cases, mainly by selecting successful intervention strategies.

When discussing multicultural school psychology competencies, it is best to focus on the daily school-based responsibilities of the profession. Some of the daily activities are conducting psychological and educational assessments, engaging in consultations with teachers, developing interventions for students' behavioral problems, attending placement decision multidisciplinary conferences, and formulating legal documents that ensure appropriate special education placement. Although these are the most common duties of the practitioner, there are numerous others (e.g., working with interpreters, identifying acculturative stressors in immigrant children and youth, implementing appropriate interventions, and involvement in community-based interventions for parental training in assessed domains of needs). Obviously, all of these varied professional duties cannot be serviced optimally without the compulsory multicultural competencies for best practices in school psychology.

Below are listed those domains of school psychology competency which are presented in this guidebook and which cover most of the daily responsibilities of the practitioner, all of which are aimed at developing multicultural competencies within each critical domain listed.

- multicultural assessment (of diverse racial/ethnic CLD children and youth);
- alternative/informal assessment methods;
- acculturation and cultural identity/racial/ethnic identity development);
- English language learners (ELL) (assessment of second language);
- school-based consultation (from a multicultural perspective);
- multiple intelligences (emotional and multiple types of intelligence);
- academic assessment for racial/ethnic CLD children and youth;
- clinical assessment within a multicultural context (DSM-IV diagnosis in the schools/therapeutic interventions);
- personality and behavioral assessment from a multicultural perspective;
- prejudice reduction;
- gifted racial/ethnic CLD children (assessment and interventions);
- acculturation/cultural identity/racial/ethnic identity development;
- personality and behavioral assessment;
- writing psychological reports for racial/ethnic CLD children and youth.

The chapters in this book present reviews of and practical suggestions for best practices in these major competency domains. As discussed above, professional associations in school psychology have placed accountability on the shoulders of the practicing professional to develop multicultural competency skills.

Ethical and Professional Accountability

Whatever the present multicultural limitations are in the field of school psychology, much has been achieved. School psychologists now have explicit accountability responsibilities in this domain. Ethical and professional responsibilities cover various areas of professional self-scrutiny in order to promote suitable treatment for racial/ethnic CLD populations. As discussed earlier, Rogers et al. (1999) summarized the recommendations made by the American Psychological Association's (APA) Division 16 Taskforce on Cross-Cultural School Psychology Competencies, and the specifications instituted by APA's Division 17 for multicultural counseling mastery for psychologists (2000) in an excellent article that compiled these principles for school psychologists to review. Moreover, D'Andrea et al. (2001) also describe the National Institute for Multicultural Competence (NIMC) actions in this domain. The ethical standards are briefly reviewed below.

1. *Conduct*—Psychologists should adhere to the highest ethical standards, and be aware of any changes in them that may occur. This means keeping abreast of the latest standards of one's profession.

2. *Conflict of interest*—If a conflict of interest should arise between a client, or client group, and the psychologist's institution, the psychologist must assert and satisfy the needs of the client first. This is vital for the school psychologist, who will no doubt have to advocate for the child against the decisions or implied advice of administrators and educators and even the "system."

3. *Confidentiality*—Psychologists must carefully balance disclosure of sensitive or confidential information obtained about clients to other parties against potential gain or harm to the client.

4. *Short-cutting*—Psychologists should never undertake to assist in any case without adequate training, materials, or interpreters, if required. If a particular case is too difficult for the psychologist, then assistance should be sought.

5. *Bias*—As mentioned previously, a personal awareness of one's own cultural biases is crucial for healthy interpersonal interactions. If a bias seems to be in danger of becoming a potential obstacle to a particular case, the psychologist is obliged to refer the client to a more appropriate psychologist.

6. *Upholding the law*—the acquisition of knowledge of pertinent immigration laws, civil rights legislation, and other legal issues that might concern a client is a must. Psychologists must support those conditions that are intended to protect clients.

7. *Commitment*—Psychologists must promise to acquire cultural expertise and culture-focused practice, in addition to learning new techniques that might provide the means to enhanced practice in the profession.

8. *Research*—Needless to say, psychologists conducting research must strictly adhere to ethical standards. Most particularly, an awareness of past Eurocentric-oriented research in the field should help in future research designs since past investigations have proved harmful to certain ethnic groups.

Introduction to Cultural Identity and Acculturation

The first step in attaining multicultural competencies is to have an understanding of some of the construct terminology utilized, as well as certain issues discussed in the literature when discussing racial/ethnic CLD populations. This section presents an overview of these main areas.

To begin with, definitions of cultural identity, acculturation, and other culture-centered descriptions are required to increase multicultural awareness and knowledge. The following definitions provide a basis for this acquisition.

Culture

According to the current APA Guidelines (2003), there has been substantial debate and overlap in the use of terms to signify race, culture, and ethnicity (Helms & Talleyrand, 1997; Phinney, 1996.

The Guidelines state that *culture* is defined as:

the belief systems and value orientations that influence customs, norms, practices, and social institutions, including psychological processes (language, caretaking practices, media, educational systems) and organizations (media, educational systems. . .). Inherent in this definition is the acknowledgment that all individuals are cultural beings and have a cultural, ethnic, and racial heritage. Culture has been described as the embodiment of a worldview through learned and transmitted beliefs, values, and practices, including religious and spiritual traditions. It also encompasses a way of living informed by the historical, economic, ecological, and political forces on a group. These definitions suggest that culture is fluid and dynamic and that there are both cultural universal phenomena and culturally specific or relative constructs.

Rudiments of culture are food, language, and music; beliefs about good and evil; perceptions of time and space; natural and supernatural phenomena; and beliefs about the fundamental nature of humans (Marshall, 2002).

Cultural Identity

Also called *ethnic identity*, cultural identity is very concisely defined by Bernal and Knight (1993) as "how one sees oneself within the context of one's ethnic group." The following provides further descriptions of cultural/ethnic identity:

> Cultural or ethnic identity refers to the degree to which the individual is committed to cultural views and practices, and the outcome of integrating these views into the overall sense of self. (Aponte & Barnes, 1995, cited in Suzuki, Ponterotto, & Meller, 2001, p. 52)

Two types of ethnic identity have been suggested: external and internal. External identity is that part of discernible behaviors which is social or cultural in nature. Internal cultural identity is more in depth, pertaining to cognitive, moral, and emotional characteristics (Isajaw, 1990, cited in Gopaul-McNicol & Brice-Baker, 1998, p. 47).

Ethnicity

This term is included because it is important to differentiate it from culture; however, it does not have an agreed upon definition and is mainly identified as "the acceptance of the group mores and practices of one's culture of origin and the concomitant sense of belonging." Furthermore, one can have varied ethnicities that function with disparate significance at various points in time (APA Guidelines, 2003).

Racial/Ethnic Identity Developmental Models

Basically, the concept of cultural/ethnic identity has been studied through various racial/ethnic identity developmental models that focus on the empirical study of the development of one's racial identity. This developmental growth has been observed to occur in stages in which the individual evolves into different racial self-concepts that range from self-denial to self-acceptance of race and ethnicity. The most renowned ethnicity model—and the one that continues to be investigated for modifications and interpretation revisions— is the Black Racial Identity Development Model (Cross, Parham, & Helms,

1991; Cross, 1971, 1995); others are the Asian American Identity Development Model (Atkinson, Morton, & Sue, 1998; Kim, 1981; Lee, 1991); and the Latino(a)/Hispanic American Identity Development Model (Ruiz, 1990).

Researchers and practitioners of multicultural counseling suggest that the "culturally skilled psychologist . . . has knowledge of models of minority and majority identity, and understands how these models relate to the counseling relationship and counseling process in diverse cultures." (Sue et al., 1998, p. 78). Moreover, they suggest that culturally skilled psychologists adapt interpersonal relationship techniques, intervention plans, and any deliberations regarding referrals to the specific stage of identity development of the client—not forgetting their own level of cultural identity development (see Sue et al., 1998). Chapter 12 discusses these models and the central issues important for school psychology practice.

Acculturation

In 1967, Graves described the phenomenon of acculturation as changes in behaviors and values adopted by the immigrating individual in order to facilitate accommodation to the host culture (country of immigration). According to Kim and Abreu (2001), acculturation involves knowledge and cultural identity that also extends over to ethnic identity.

Interestingly, Kim, Atkinson, and Yang (1999) found that the acculturation process diverges significantly from one ethnic group to another. For example, within consecutive generations of Asian Americans, no significant differences were found regarding "values enculturation." Utilizing the Asian Values Scale (AVS), Kim, Yang, Atkinson, Wolfe, and Hong (2001) found that Filipino Americans were less prone to the Asian value dimension of the scale than were the Chinese, Japanese, or Korean Americans. Such disparities tend to support what researchers such as Sue and Sue (1999) strongly stress: the need to focus on within-group ethnic differences when providing clinical services. In certain situations, a school psychologist may not have complete awareness of the distinct subtle differences that can occur within ethnic groups. However, sensitivity to these issues is an important part of cultural competency.

Acculturation Stressors

Acculturation stressors are difficulties encountered by immigrant students or entire families when the process of acculturation causes stress in various areas of assimilation to the host culture. These stressors can range from second language acquisition difficulties to socioeconomic and environmental problems, fear of not assimilating into the host country, educational background and outlook, and school and learning problems; they can also cause mental health problems (i.e., emotional distress, anxiety, lack of motivation, and withdrawal) (see Canino & Spurlock, 2000).

It is important to note that there are numerous acculturation scales for specific ethnic groups that aid in estimating the level or degree of acculturation an individual has attained. When conducting evaluations or engaged in counseling services for newly arrived immigrants and/or immigrants of longer standing—depending on the particular case and need—it is recommended that school psychologists utilize acculturation scales to establish the level of acculturation of their client. Some of the academic or behavioral problems that may give rise to school-based evaluations and counseling services are a result of acculturation stressors (see Chapter 10 on acculturation).

Obviously, multicultural skills will not be perfected unless students or practitioners are conscious of their own cultural awareness, biases, and knowledge. With this in mind, researchers have insisted on self-evaluation for the practitioner.

Self-Assessment of Multicultural Awareness, Knowledge, and Skills

Multicultural self-assessment is vital to the healthy cultural identity of any mental health professional. There is copious literature (Canino & Spurlock, 2000; Gopaul-McNicol & Brice-Baker, 1998; Ponterotto & Potere, 2003; Sue et al., 1982) providing access to such measures. Rodriquez (2000) stresses that the assessor is the most important "instrument" in the evaluation process and states several reasons for this need—one of them being that assessors must be aware of their cultural competencies, strengths, and weaknesses in addition to having knowledge of their level of ease in the use of various "expressions" that are dissimilar from their individual forms of expression (Rodriquez, 2000, cited in Canino & Spurlock, 2000, p. 85). In brief, all mental health professionals are encouraged to self-assess their own cultural awareness, knowledge, and skills (Gopaul-McNicol & Brice-Baker, 1998; Ponterotto, Rieger, Barrett, & Sparks, 1994; Sue et al., 1998). In fact, from an ethical perspective, multicultural self-assessment is a personal evaluative process that every mental health practitioner should abide by as an introspective journey to self-improvement and awareness.

Instruments to Assess Cross-Cultural Competencies

Gopaul-McNicol & Brice-Baker (1998) recommend "A Comprehensive Instrument to Assess Cross-Cultural Competencies" as a self-assessment instrument. This instrument is based on the research of experts in the field and incorporates a review of a variety of competency self-assessment instruments (D'Andrea, Daniels, & Heck, 1991; Gopaul-McNicol, 1997; Ponterotto et al., 1994). In addition, the final report of the Cultural Competency Workgroup (Grantham, 1996), along with recommendations from the National Council of School Psychologists were also consulted. The latter is largely responsible for the recommendation of professional core competency domains for school psychologists. The instrument is reproduced in Figure 1.1.

Moreover, NASP has developed a *Cultural Diversity and Cultural Competency Self-assessment Checklist* for personnel providing services and support to children and their families. The checklist is intended to deepen the awareness of personnel on the significance of cultural competence and can be downloaded online.

There are numerous instruments/scales to consider for self-assessment. The main advice is to be aware of one's multicultural status in order to promote self-introspection in addition to a healthy attitude toward change.

In summary, it is strongly recommended that practicing school psychologists and school psychologists-in-training self-administer the scale in Figure 1.1 or any other of their choosing.

Instructions: The following cross-cultural competency instrument is designed to provide students/trainers with information to determine their effectiveness as cross-cultural mental health workers. It is not a test, and no grade will be given. Please rate the competencies using the three-point scale. Feel free to elaborate as necessary.

	Important	Not applicable	Unimportant
Theoretical Perspectives Cross-culturally skilled psychologists should have knowledge about:			
1. Different or deficit theories	1	2	3
2. The degree to which major theoretical paradigms in psychology emphasize a Eurocentric ideology	1	2	3

Figure 1.1 *(Continued)*

	Important	Not applicable	Unimportant
Therapist's Own Values Cross-culturally skilled psychologists should have knowledge about:			
1. Own worldview, assumptions, values, beliefs, and priorities, and own cultural heritage	1	2	3
2. How their own cultural background and experiences, attitudes, values, and biases influence delivery of psychological services	1	2	3
3. Limits of their own competencies, including the limits of their own language competencies if working with bilingual clients	1	2	3
Cross-Cultural Awareness Cross-culturally skilled psychologists should have knowledge about:			
1. The specific cultural groups they work with	1	2	3
2. The cultural context, belief system, heritage, history of oppression of the client	1	2	3
Cross-Cultural Ethics Cross-culturally skilled psychologists should have knowledge about:			
1. Ethical issues when working with interpreters (e.g., confidentiality)	1	2	3
2. Laws and regulations that apply to culturally diverse families	1	2	3
Assessment Cross-culturally skilled psychologists should have knowledge about:			
1. Sources of test bias	1	2	3
2. Nonbiased assessment and the process of adapting available instruments to assess culturally diverse families	1	2	3
3. Judging the appropriateness of instruments selected on the basis of linguistic, psychometric, and cultural criteria	1	2	3
4. Adapting measures created for nonminority children for use with culturally diverse families	1	2	3

Figure 1.1 *(Continued)*

	Important	Not applicable	Unimportant
Report Writing Cross-culturally skilled psychologists should have knowledge about:			
1. The importance of integrating cultural background information and language background of the family and child	1	2	3
2. Reporting deviations from standardization during administration of standardized tests	1	2	3
Counseling Cross-culturally skilled psychologists should have knowledge about:			
1. The importance of perceiving the problem within the client's cultural and social context	1	2	3
2. Incorporating knowledge about the stresses of being a minority into the counseling approach	1	2	3
3. Designing and delivering culturally appropriate prevention and counseling strategies	1	2	3
Race Issues Cross-culturally skilled psychologists should have knowledge about:			
1. The interrelationship between the client's racial identity development and the effect on the client's coping behaviors	1	2	3
Language Cross-culturally skilled psychologists should have knowledge about:			
1. The influence of second language acquisition on children's performances	1	2	3
Working With Interpreters Cross-culturally skilled psychologists should have knowledge about:			
1. The problems involved in translating test items from one language to another	1	2	3
2. The effects of translation on validity, reliability, and test interpretation during assessment	1	2	3
3. The competencies needed by interpreters, translation techniques, professional conduct, relevant knowledge	1	2	3

Figure 1.1 *(Continued)*

	Important	Not applicable	Unimportant
Consultation Cross-culturally skilled psychologists should have knowledge about:			
1. Actively learning about other cultures through inservice training, continuing education, working with individuals from other cultures	1	2	3
2. Seeking consultation and supervision from other professionals skilled in delivering services to culturally diverse clients	1	2	3
3. Consultation theory and how it can be applied to culturally diverse populations	1	2	3
Research Cross-culturally skilled psychologists should have knowledge about:			
1. The ethical implications of conducting research with culturally diverse populations			
2. Creating research projects that are ethically valid	1	2	3

Figure 1.1   Self-Assessment of Cross-Cultural Competencies

SOURCE: Gopaul-McNicol, S. & Brice-Baker, J. (1998). *Cross-cultural practice: Assessment, treatment, and training.* New York: John Wiley & Sons Reprinted with permission of John Wiley & Sons, Inc.

NOTE: See Quintana, Troyano, and Taylor (2001); and Ponterotto et al.'s (2001) meta-review of similar instruments used in cultural identity and information on self-assessment measures and practices.

References

American Psychiatric Association. (1994). *Diagnostic and statistical manual of mental disorders* (4th ed.). Washington, DC: Author.

American Psychological Association. (2003). *Guidelines on multicultural education: Training, research, practice, and organizational change for psychologists.* Washington, DC: Author.

Aponte, H., & Van Deusen, J. (1981). Structural family therapy. In A. Gurman, & D. Kniskeren (Eds.), *Handbook of family therapy* (pp. 27–37). New York: Brunner/Mazel.

Aponte, J. F., & Barnes, J. M. (1995). Impact of acculturation and moderator variables on the intervention and treatment of ethnic groups. In J. F. Aponte, R. Y. Rivers, & J. Wohl (Eds.), *Psychological interventions and cultural diversity* (pp. 19–39). Needham Heights, MA: Allyn & Bacon.

Artiles, A. J., Trent, S. C., Hoffman-Kipp, P., & Lopez-Torres, L. (2000). From individual acquisition to cultural-historical practices in multicultural teacher education. *Remedial and Special Education, 21*(2), 79–89.

Atkinson, D. R., Bui, U., & Mori, S. (2001). Multiculturally sensitive empirically supported treatments—an oxymoron? In J. G. Ponterotto, J. M. Casas, L. A. Suzuki, & C. M. Alexander (Eds.), *Handbook of multicultural counseling* (2nd ed.; pp. 542–574). Thousand Oaks, CA: Sage.

Atkinson, D. R., Morton, G., & Sue, D. W. (Eds.). (1998). *Counseling American minorities* (5th ed.). Boston: McGraw Hill.

Banks, J. A. (2002). *An introduction to multicultural education* (3rd ed.). Boston, MA: Allyn & Bacon.

Banks, J. A., & McGee-Banks, C. A. (1995). *Handbook of research on multicultural education.* New York: Macmillan.

Barona, A., Santos de Barona, A., Flores, A. A., & Gutierrez, M. H. (1990). Critical issues in training school psychologists to serve minority school children. In A. Barona & E. Garcia (Eds.), *Children at risk: Poverty, minority status and other issues in educational equity* (pp. 187–200). Washington, DC: National Association of School Psychologists.

Behring, S. T., Cabello, B., Kushida, D., & Murguia, A. (2000). Cultural modifications to current school-based consultation approaches reported by culturally diverse beginning consultants. *School Psychology Review, 29*(3), 354–365.

Bernal, M. E., & Knight, G. P. (1993). (Eds.). Ethnic identity: Formation and transmission among Hispanics and other minorities. Albany, NY: State University of New York Press.

Bernal, M. E., & Padilla, A. M. (1982). Status of minority curricula and training in clinical psychology. *American Psychologist, 37*, 780–787.

Canino, I. A. & Spurlock, J. (2000). *Culturally diverse children and adolescents: Assessment, diagnosis, and treatment* (2nd ed.). New York: Guilford Press.

Carter, R. T. (Ed.) (2005). *Handbook of racial-cultural psychology and counseling: Theory and research.* New York: John Wiley & Sons.

Cross, W. E. (1971). The Negro-to-black conversion experience: Toward a psychology of black liberation. *Black World, 20*, 13–27.

Cross, W. E. (1995). The psychology of nigrescence: Revisiting the Cross model. In J. Ponterotto, J. M. Casas, L. A. Suzuki, & C. M. Alexander (Eds.), *Handbook of multicultural counseling* (pp. 93–122). Thousand Oaks, CA: Sage.

Cross, W. E. Jr., Parham, T. A., & Helms, J. E. (1991). The stages of black identity development: Nigrescence models. In R. L. Jones (Ed.), *Black psychology* (3rd ed.) (pp. 319–338). Berkeley, CA: Cobb & Henry.

Cummins, J. (1984). *Bilingualism and special education: Issues in assessment and pedagogy.* San Diego, CA: College Hill Press.

Curtis, M. J., Hunley, S. A., Walker, K. J., & Baker, A. C. (1999). Demographic characteristics and professional practices in school psychology. *School Psychology Review, 28*, 104–116.

D'Andrea, M. J., Arrendondo, P., Ivey, M. B., Ivey, A. E., Locke, D. C., O'Bryant, B., Parham, T., & Sue, D. W. (2001). Fostering organizational changes to realize the revolutionary potential of the multicultural movement: An updated case study. In J. G. Ponterotto, J. M. Casas, L. A. Suzuki, & C. M. Alexander (Eds.), *Handbook of multicultural counseling*. Thousand Oaks, CA: Sage.

D'Andrea, M., Daniels, J., & Heck, R. (1991). The multicultural awareness-knowledge-skills survey (MAKSS). *Journal of Counseling and Development, 70,* 149–150.

Doyle, A. B. (1998). Are empirically validated treatments valid for culturally diverse populations? In K. S. Dobson & K. D. Craig (Eds.), *Empirically supported therapies: Best practice in professional psychology* (pp. 93–103). Thousand Oaks, CA: Sage.

Frisby, C. L. (1999). Straight talk about cognitive assessment and diversity. *School Psychology Quarterly, 14,* 195–207.

Gay, M. A. (2000). *Culturally responsive teaching: Theory, research, and practice.* New York: Teachers College Press.

Gollnick, D. M., & Chinn, P. C. (2006). *Multicultural education in a pluralistic society* (7th ed.). Englewood Cliffs, NJ: Merrill Prentice Hall.

Gopaul-McNicol, S. (1997). *A multicultural/multimodal/multisystems approach to working with culturally different families.* Westport, CT: Praeger.

Gopaul-McNicol, S., & Brice-Baker, J. (1998). *Cross-cultural practice: Assessment, treatment, and training.* New York: John Wiley & Sons.

Grantham, R. (1996). *Final report of the cultural competency work group.* New York: State Office of Mental Health Strategic Plan.

Graves, T. (1967). Acculturation, access and alcohol in a tri-ethnic community. *American Anthropologist, 69,* 306–321.

Helms, J. E. (1994). How multiculturalism obscures racial factors in the therapy process: Comments on Ridely et al. (1994), Sodowsky, et al. (1994), Ottavi et al. (1994), & Thompson et al. (1994). *Journal of Counseling Psychology, 41,* 162–165.

Helms, J. E., & Talleyrand, R. M. (1997). Race is not ethnicity. *American Psychologist, 52,* 1246–1247.

Henning-Stout, M., & Meyers, J. (2000). Consultation and human diversity: First things first. *School Psychology Review, 29*(3), 419–425.

Ibrahim, F. A., Roysircar-Sodowsky, G., & Ohnishi, H. (2001). *Worldview: Recent developments and needed directions.* In J. G. Ponterotto, J. M. Casas, L. A. Suzuki, & C. M. Alexander (Eds.), *Handbook of multicultural counseling* (2nd ed.) (pp. 425–456). Thousand Oaks, CA: Sage.

Ingraham, C. L. (2000). Consultation through a multicultural lens: Multicultural and cross-cultural consultation in schools. *School Psychology Review, 29*(3), 320–344.

Ingraham, C. L., & Meyers, J. (2000). Introduction to multicultural and cross-cultural consultation in schools: Cultural diversity issues in school consultation. *School Psychology Review, 29,* 315–319.

Isajaw, W. W. (1990). Ethnic identity retention. In R. Breton, W. W. Isajaw, W. E. Kalbach, & J. G. Reitz (Eds.), *Ethnic identity and equality* (pp. 34–91). Toronto: University of Toronto Press.

Kim, B. S. K., & Abreu, J. M. (2001). Acculturation measurement: Theory, current instruments, and future directions. In J. G. Ponterotto, J. M. Casas, L. A. Suzuki, & C. M. Alexander (Eds.), *Handbook of multicultural counseling* (2nd ed.). (pp. 394–424), Thousand Oaks, CA: Sage.

Kim, B. S. K., & Atkinson, D. R. (2002). Asian American client adherence to Asian cultural values, counselor expression of cultural values, counselor ethnicity, and career counseling process. *Journal of Counseling Psychology, 49,* 3–13.

Kim, B. S. K., Atkinson, D. R., & Yang, P. H. (1999). The Asian values scale (AVS): Development, factor analysis, validation, and reliability. *Journal of Counseling Psychology, 46,* 342–352.

Kim, B. S. K., Yang, P. H., Atkinson, D. R., Wolfe, M. M., & Hong, S. (2001). Cultural value similarities and differences among Asian American ethnic groups. *Cultural Diversity and Ethnic Minority Psychology, 7,* 343–361.

Kim, J. (1981). The process of Asian American identity development: A study of Japanese American women's perceptions of their struggle to achieve personal identities as Americans of Asian ancestry. *Dissertation Abstracts International, 42,* 1551A (University Microfilm No. 81-18080).

Ladson-Billings, G. (2001). *Crossing over to Cananan: The journey of new teachers in diverse classrooms.* San Francisco: Jossey-Bass.

Lee, F. Y. (1991). *The relationship of ethnic identity to social support, self-esteem, psychological distress, and help-seeking behavior among Asian American college students.* Unpublished doctoral dissertation, University of Illinois, Urbana-Champaign.

Marshall, P. L. (2002). *Cultural diversity in our schools.* Belmont, CA: Wadsworth/Thomson.

Martens, B. K. (1993). A case against magical thinking in school-based intervention. *Journal of Educational and Psychological Consultation, 4,* 185–189.

Martines, D. (2003). Suggestions for training cross-cultural consultant school psychologists. *Trainer's Forum, 23,* 5–13.

Merrell, K. W., Ervin, R. A., & Gimpel, G. A. (2006). *School psychology for the 21st century.* New York: Guilford Press.

Midgett, T. E., & Meggert, S. S. (1991). Multicultural counseling instruction: A challenge for faculties in the 21st century. *Journal of Counseling and Development, 70,* 136–141.

Nieto, S. (1999). *The light in their eyes: Creating multicultural learning communities.* New York: Teachers College Press.

Paabo, S. (2001). The human genome and our view of ourselves. In U. S. Department of Health and Human Services, *Mental Health: Culture, Race, and Ethnicity* (p. 7). Supplement to *Mental Health: A Report of the Surgeon General.* Rockville, MD: U.S. Department of Health and Human Services.

Pedersen, P. (1985). *Handbook of cross-cultural counseling and therapy.* Westport, CT: Greenwood Press.

Pederson, P. (1987). *Handbook of cross cultural counseling and therapy* (2nd ed.). Westport, CT: Greenwood Press.

Pedersen, P. (1991). Multiculturalism as a generic approach to counseling. *Journal of Counseling and Development, 70*(1), 6–12.

Pedersen, P. (1992). Multiculturalism as a fourth force in counseling. *Journal of Counseling and Development, 70,* 6–12.

Phinney, J. S. (1996). When we talk about American ethnic groups, what do we mean? *American Psychologist, 51,* 918–927.

Plummer, D. L. (1998). Approaching diversity training in the year 2000. *Consulting Psychology Journal: Practice and Research, 50*(3), 181–189.

Ponterotto, J. G. & Casas, J. M. (1991). *Handbook of racial/ethnic minority counseling research*. Springfield, IL: Thomas.

Ponterotto, J. G., Casas, J. M., Suzuki, L. S. & Alexander, C. M. (Eds.) (1995). *Handbook of multicultural counselling*. Thousand Oaks, CA: Sage.

Ponterotto, J. G., Casas, J. M., Suzuki, L. A., & Alexander, C. M. (2001). (Eds.). Handbook of multicultural counseling (2nd ed.). Thousand Oaks, CA: Sage.

Ponterotto, J. G., & Potere, J. C. (2003). The Multicultural Counseling Knowledge and Awareness Scale (MCKAS): Validity, reliability, and user guidelines. In D. B. Pope-Davis, H. L. K. Coleman, W. M. Lie, & R. Toporek (Eds.), *Handbook of multicultural competencies* (pp. 137–153). Thousand Oaks, CA: Sage.

Ponterotto, J. G., Rieger, B. P., Barrett, A., & Sparks, R. (1994). Assessing multicultural counseling competence: A review of instrumentation. *Journal of Counseling and Development, 72*, 316–322.

Quintana, S. M., & Atkinson, D. R. (2002). A multicultural perspective on principles of empirically supported interventions. *The Counseling Psychologist, 30*(2), 281–291.

Quintana, S. M., Troyano, N., & Taylor, G. (2001). Cultural validity and inherent challenges in quantitative methods for multicultural research. In J. Ponterotto, J. M. Casas, L. S. Suzuki, & C. M. Alexander (Eds.), *Handbook of multicultural counseling* (pp. 604–630). Thousand Oaks, CA: Sage.

Ramirez, M. III. (1991). *Psychotherapy and counseling with minorities: A cognitive approach to individual and cultural differences*. New York: Pergamon.

Ramos-Sanchez, L., Atkinson, D., & Fraga, E. (1999). Mexican Americans' bilingual ability, counselor bilingualism cues, counselor ethnicity, and perceived counselor credibility. *Journal of Counseling Psychology, 46*(1), 125–131.

Reynolds, A. (1995). Challenges and strategies for teaching multicultural counseling courses. In J. Ponterotto, J. M. Casas, L. S. Suzuki, & C. M. Alexander (Eds.), *Handbook of multicultural counseling* (pp. 312–330). Thousand Oaks, CA: Sage.

Rodriguez, C. (2000). Standards of culturally competent assessment. In I. A. Canino & J. Spurlock (Eds.), *Culturally diverse children and adolescents: Assessment, diagnosis, and treatment* (2nd ed.; p. 85). New York: Guilford Press.

Rogers, M. R. (2000). Examining the cultural context of consultation. *School Psychology Review, 29*(3), 414–419.

Rogers, M., Close Conoley, J., Ponterotto, J. G., & Wiese, M. J. (1992). Multicultural training in school psychology: A national survey. *School Psychology Review, 21*(4), 603–616.

Rogers, M. R., Ingraham, C. L., Bursztyn, A., Cajigas-Segredo, N., Esquivel, G., Hess, R., Nahari, S. G., & Lopez, E. C. (1999). Providing psychological services to racially, ethnically, culturally, and linguistically diverse individuals in the schools: Recommendations for practice. *School Psychology International, 20*, 243–264.

Rogers, M. R., & Lopez, E. C. (2002). Identifying critical cross-cultural school psychology competencies. *Journal of School Psychology, 2*, 115–141.

Rosenfield, S., & Gravois, T. A. (1998). Working with teams in the school. In C. R. Reynolds & T. B. Gutkin (Eds.), *Handbook of school psychology* (3rd ed.; pp. 598–637). New York: John Wiley & Sons.

Ruiz, A. S. (1990). Ethnic identity: Crisis and resolution. *Journal of Multicultural Counseling and Development, 18*, 29–40.

Sedlacek, W. E. (1994). Issues in advancing diversity through assessment. *Journal of Counseling and Development, 72*, 549–553.

Sheridan, S. M. (2000). Considerations of multiculturalism and diversity in behavioral consultation with parents and teachers. *School Psychology Review, 29*(3), 344–354.

Sheridan, S. M., & Gutkin, T. B. (2000). The ecology of school psychology: Examining and changing our paradigm for the 21st century. *School Psychology Review, 29*, 485-502.

Sodowsky, G. R., & Maestas, M. V. (2000). Acculturation, ethnic identity, and acculturative stress: Evidence and measurement. In R. Dana (Ed.), *Handbook of cross-cultural and multicultural personality assessment* (pp. 131–172). Mahwah, NJ: Lawrence Erlbaum.

Sue, D. (1981). *Counseling the culturally different: Theory and practice.* New York: John Wiley & Sons.

Sue, D. W., Arredondo, P., & McDavis, R. J. (1992). Multicultural counseling competencies and standards: A call to the profession. *Journal of Multicultural Counseling and Development, 20*, 64–88.

Sue, D. W., Bernier, J. E., Durran, A., Feinberg, L., Pedersen, P., Smith, E. J., & Vasquez-Nuttall, E. (1982). Position paper: Cross-cultural counseling competencies. *The Counseling Psychologist, 10*, 45–52.

Sue, D. W., Bingham, R. P., Porche-Burke, L., & Vazquez, M. (1999). The diversification of psychology: A multicultural revolution. *American Psychologist, 12*, 1061–1069.

Sue, D. W., Carter, R. T., Casas, J. M., Fouad, N. A., Ivey, A. E., Jensen, M., LaFromboise, T. D., Manese, J., Ponterotto, J. G., & Vasquez-Nuttall, E. (1998). *Multicultural counseling competencies: Individual and organizational development.* Thousand Oaks, CA: Sage.

Sue, D. W., & Sue, D. (1999). *Counseling the culturally different: Theory and practice* (3rd ed.). New York: John Wiley & Sons.

Sue, S. (1998). In search of cultural competence in psychotherapy and counseling. *American Psychologist, 54*, 1070–1077.

Sue, S. (1999). Science, ethnicity, and bias: Where have we gone wrong? *American Psychologist, 54*, 1070–1077.

Sternberg, R. J., & Grigorenko, E. L. (2001). Ability testing across cultures. In L. A. Suzuki, J. G. Ponterotto, & P. J. Meller (Eds.), *Handbook of multicultural assessment: Clinical, psychological, and educational applications* (pp. 335–358). San Francisco: Jossey-Bass.

Suzuki, L. A., Ponterotto, J. G., & Meller, P. J. (Eds.) (2001). *Handbook of multicultural assessment: Clinical, psychological, and educational applications*. San Francisco: Jossey-Bass.

Suzuki, L. A., Short, E. L., Pieterse, A., & Kugler, J. (2001). Multicultural issues and the assessment of aptitude. In L. A. Suzuki, J. G. Ponterotto, & P. J. Meller (Eds.), *Handbook of multicultural assessment: Clinical, psychological, and educational applications* (pp. 359–382). San Francisco: Jossey-Bass.

U. S. Department of Health and Human Services. (2001). *Mental Health: Culture, Race, and Ethnicity*. Supplement to *Mental Health: A Report of the Surgeon General*. Rockville, MD: U.S. Department of Health and Human Services.

Annotated Bibliography

Marshall, P. L. (2002). *Cultural diversity in our schools*. Belmont, CA: Wadsworth/Thomson. *This text provides an informative review of all aspects of cultural diversity in schools.*

Frisby, C. L., & Reynolds, C. R. (Eds.). *Comprehensive handbook of multicultural school psychology*. Hoboken, NJ: Wiley & Sons. *This handbook covers various multicultural issues in school psychology research.*

Esquivel, G. B., Lopez, E. C., & Nahara, S. (2007). *Handbook of multicultural school psychology: An interdisciplinary perspective*. Mahwah, NJ: Lawrence Erlbaum. *A thorough text reviewing both research and practice-based applications in multicultural school psychology.*

Merrell, K. W., Ervin, R., & Gimpel, G. A. (2006). *School psychology for the 21st century: Foundations and practices*. New York: Guilford Press. *This text provides up-to-date coverage of major concerns and issues in the future of school psychology practice.*

Websites

www.nasponline.org
www.nasponline.org/culturalcompetence/checklist.html

PART II

Multicultural Assessment

2

Multicultural Assessment

What Is Multicultural Assessment?

School psychologists-in-training are often told that the most important course they will take in their training is cognitive assessment. The reason given is that, in most districts, at least 90 percent of their professional practice will be dedicated to psychological evaluations (Braden, 1997; Fagan & Wise, 1994). Certainly, all graduate schools list a cognitive assessment course as a core requirement for graduation and professional credentialing. In contrast, a multicultural assessment course is not incorporated even as an elective course, much less as a core requirement. Ideally, to address cognitive assessment within the confines of multiculturalism, a course on cognitive assessment should be taught by a bilingual/bicultural school psychologist. This trainer would have the appropriate qualifications for teaching multicultural assessment because of the dual language background and bicultural experience. A counterpoint for this recommendation has been that most trainers usually include a "multicultural component" in their assessment training, thereby eliminating the need for a bilingual/multicultural professional. As noted in the previous chapter, this is generally not the case because each university trainer can decide what should be included in the course requirements. Depending on the trainer's viewpoint, a multicultural focus may or may not be incorporated. Regrettably, the latter is usually the case (Dana, 2001; Gopaul-McNicol & Brice-Baker, 1998).

A further dilemma is that school psychologists are servicing school districts with high percentages of ethnically and linguistically diverse students. Failure to possess the required competencies for conducting multicultural evaluations will increase the rate of misdiagnosis and misclassification (Gopaul-McNicol

& Brice-Baker, 1998). Hopefully most school psychologists now have had some minor—if not major—exposure to multicultural psychology that will lead them to make further inquiries when conducting cultural and linguistic evaluations. And one can assume (albeit optimistically) that they will adhere to the NASP and APA standards which require professionals to keep abreast of their occupational responsibilities regarding multicultural competency (see American Educational Research Association (AERA), American Psychological Association (APA), National Association of School Psychologists (NASP), and the National Council on Measurement in Education (NCME) (1999) Standards for Educational and Psychological Testing).

Consequently, multicultural competency in the evaluative area and in all other areas of professional practice demands that the practitioner adhere to culture-centered ethical standards; practice self-examination on cultural competency; know how to conduct a thorough background/historical search on the client; religiously keep abreast of the most current culture-fair assessment measures; and implement alternative methods of assessment. In addition to these competencies, practitioners must have the knowledge and skills necessary for implementing culturally appropriate interventions and recommendations (see Canino & Spurlock, 2000; Helms-Lorenz & Tilburg, 1995; Ochoa, 2003; Suzuki, Ponterotto, & Meller, 2001, Ch. 21; van de Vijver, 2002). In addition to appropriate multicultural training in professional school psychology, the concept of multicultural assessment practice has been summarized in the literature as encompassing several areas of knowledge and skills in multicultural issues pertaining to: clinical interviewing and assessment of individuals from diverse backgrounds; maintaining culturally centered ethics in testing; expertise in cultural identity and acculturation; appropriate selection of assessment instruments; and knowledge of diagnosing individuals from diverse cultures (i.e., the importance of understanding symptomatology in cultural context) (see Dana, 2001; Suzuki, Ponterotto, & Meller, 2001, Ch. 10).

This chapter is designed to address these competencies by providing practical guidance for multicultural assessment. The goal is to provide informative reviews of essential issues pertaining to best assessment practices for school psychologists servicing children from all cultures and racial/ethnicities in the United States. Where practical, checklists and other practice-focused information are included.

Overview of Multicultural Assessment Practice

The first advice given to the culturally sensitive practitioner is to be aware of the cultural limitations involved in assessment practices. These limitations range from the intake interview to the utilization of psychometric instruments, diagnostic methods, and the use of employment and personality assessment instruments (Constantino & Malgady, 1999; Helms, 2002; Ridley, Li, & Hill, 1998; Ivey & Ivey, 1998; Sue, 1998). Much has been said about what should be considered culturally appropriate professional competence in assessment (Armour-Thomas, 1992; Braden, 1997; Scott, 1994). In fact, it has been surmised that there are no empirically and theoretically informed approaches to multicultural assessment (Malgady, 1996; Ridley et al., 1998).

Recently, Ridley and colleagues (1998) assembled various recommendations on how to assess culturally diverse clients into the Multicultural Assessment Procedure (MAP). MAP was developed to provide guidance for the practitioner regarding the varied pertinent issues in multicultural assessment practice. Although it was compiled for counseling psychologists, its contents are equally significant for and adoptable by school psychologists.

A Brief Synopsis of Multicultural Assessment Practice

MAP is relevant for the school psychologist because its core emphasis is on stressing the importance of considering culture in assessment. Lack of awareness of cultural differences between ethnic groups and/or between the practitioner and the client may bring about the possibility of practitioner "judgmental error." Errors can occur in two ways. The first error involves the label of pathology where no pathology is present (such as assuming an abnormality when in fact the client's situation and cultural norms render a less severe conclusion). The second error, on the other hand, may actually find the practitioner failing to identify a true pathology due to a perceived normalcy based on cultural norms and the client's situation (such as mistakenly judging recurrent hallucinations as culturally appropriate or failing to see the need for mental health services for African American juveniles). It is important to realize that assessment involves attention to objective and subjective features of the process (i.e., cultural judgments about normalcy often masquerade as scientific objectivity in diagnostic manuals and epidemiological instruments). In short, MAP suggests that subjectivity is a clinical strength in diagnosis since it brings humanness to the results of objective measures that often cannot standardize the human experience. In an effort to avoid errors in judgment and in order to aid the practitioner to conduct appropriate assessments, MAP offers a reconceptualization of cultural assessment practice. MAP identifies nine crucial micro-decisions to be made during the multicultural assessment process:

1. Are the salient data I have readily identified enough to make a competent assessment conclusion?

2. What additional data-gathering methods should I use?

3. How do I respond to the data?

4. Which data are cultural and which are idiosyncratic?

5. How do base rates apply to cultural data?

6. Which stressors are dispositional and which are environmental?

7. Which data are clinically significant and which are insignificant?

8. What is my working hypothesis?

9. What is my conclusive assessment decision? This includes (a) What is the nature of psychopathology, if any? and (b) How do non-pathological but clinically significant data fit into the assessment conclusion?

MAP provides a procedural phased process which responds to these questions and provides systematic guidelines to follow throughout a multicultural assessment. The first three phases of MAP emphasize cultural sensitivity in multicultural assessment by the identification, interpretation, and incorporation of cultural data. Phase four discusses sound assessment decisions.

The four phases of MAP are:

1. *Identify cultural data.* MAP advocates the use of the clinical interview for cultural information gathering apart from the available questionnaires, personality inventories, and intelligence measures. Directly asking clients about their culture is a good way to begin the interview and to get a cultural history. Reviewing salient overt or covert cultural data, such as data about self and life circumstances (overt) and less routinely identifiable data such as unresolved and unexpressed conflicts, implicit cultural values and assumptions, and repressed memories (covert) is a crucial component in identifying cultural information. Additionally, the use of the Person-In-Culture Interview (PICI) (Berg-Cross & Chinen, 1995) is another way of obtaining cultural information. The PICI consists of 24 open-ended items designed to be sensitive to cultural issues without stereotyping particular individuals.

2. *Interpret cultural data.* This involves the interpretation of the collected cultural data which will aid in establishing a working hypothesis regarding the client's psychological presentation. MAP recommends that practitioners attend to all assessment data and not ignore any of the data. There should be a systematic deliberation of cultural data for diagnostic decision-making. Suggestions for accomplishing this are:

- separating data that are cultural from the idiosyncratic data (i.e., adopting an idiographic perspective where the client's personal meanings are recognized and not solely perceived as part of a particular cultural group);
- applying base-rate information to cultural data (i.e., the use of caution with statistical norms or data that are derived from epidemiological research).

Caution is essential in applying cultural normative base rate information to idiosyncratic data; and

- differentiating dispositional stressors from environmental stressors (i.e., looking at which stressors are dispositional and which are environmental).

MAP stresses that practitioners should differentiate between stressors and realize that some reported symptoms are due to within-the-client origins and others to outside-the-client circumstances. They should then attempt to make a distinction about which symptoms fall into which category as well as determining which are clinically significant or insignificant. To help in this assessment of data, some questions to explore are: Which data are cultural and which are idiosyncratic? What areas is the client most resistant to exploring? What adaptive strategies has the client attempted? What possible dispositional and environmental stressors have not been considered? Finally, practitioners should work in partnership with their clients in order to obtain their viewpoint on the data. Once cultural data are interpreted, practitioners should ask themselves this question: What is my working hypothesis?

MAP suggests the following guidelines to help construct this hypothesis:

- Determine the psychological consequences of a behavior for individuals.
- Determine whether cultural values/belief systems contribute to impairment in the context in which they now live.
- Determine whether the client's cultural behaviors represent extremes, even for a member of their culture.
- Ascertain the client's interpretations of the psychological presentations (i.e., the client's psychological presentation versus the practitioner's perspective of their presentation).

This can be done by requesting clarification and inviting the client to ask for clarification, as well as by asking clients for their interpretation of their own psychological presentation. It is recommended that practitioners be cautious about their own possible distortions of the psychological presentation of their clients, as these can occur easily through one's cultural biases and assumptions. Practitioners are advised to continually self-examine their cultural awareness and search for occasions to confront their worldviews through reflective thinking.

3. *Incorporate cultural data.* This phase addresses the nature of hypothesis testing in assessment. Some ways to refine and test the working hypothesis are:

(a) Rule out medical explanations.

(b) Use psychological testing to support or refute the hypothesis (emphasis is placed on using psychological testing to test the hypothesis, not to generate it) and to follow the Standards for Educational and Psychological (APA) for multicultural assessment guidelines.

(c) Be aware of bias in some psychometric measures and use standardized measures in culturally appropriate ways.

(d) Use non-standardized measures.

(e) Compare data and hypotheses with DSM-IV criteria (i.e., practitioners should be aware of the problems that exist within the DSM-IV with regard to multicultural assessment).

Suggested questions are: What is my conclusive assessment decision? What is the nature of psychopathology, if any? How do non-pathological but clinically significant data fit the assessment conclusion?

4. *Arrive at a sound assessment decision.* Practitioners should review their assessment activities to determine whether they have used de-biasing strategies to minimize the risk of committing clinical judgment errors. MAP discusses three possible problematic judgmental behaviors:

(a) availability—based on the saliency of clinical information;

(b) anchoring—based on focusing on the first data acquired in an assessment and overlooking or downplaying information collected later in the appraisal process; and

(c) representativeness—which is connected to dependence on the existing cognitive schemata that may lead practitioners to assume relationships between client features and diagnostic categories that may not exist.

Specific to assessment, MAP recommends that the findings of psychometric measures should be viewed from a cultural perspective. Furthermore, cultural data collected and analysis should complement standardized evaluations (see Ridley, Li, & Hill, 1998).

In addition to MAP, school psychologists are advised to examine the National Association of School Psychologists' (NASP) multicultural competency standards (www.nasponline.org), as well as the Recommendations for Providing Psychological Services to Racially, Ethnically, Culturally, and Linguistically Diverse Individuals in the Schools by Rogers et al. (1999). By adhering to the above guidelines presented in MAP as well as the recommendations made by NASP, school psychologists will be able conduct culturally fair assessments for CLD children and youth.

Overview of Multicultural Assessment Practice

For practical purposes, the following overview has been compiled from an appraisal of various research/practitioner literature and is presented here as a summarized aid for multicultural assessment practice.

In the schools, a request for an assessment usually follows a series of steps. A review of the traditional stages of assessment as described by Anderson (1988) provides a prescriptive evaluation process:

1. problem identification;

2. obtaining parental permission;

3. gathering assessment data which includes information-based testing;

4. drawing conclusions on the data and formulating recommendations;

5. development of an individual education plan (IEP) by a team; and

6. follow-up.

Although the above process does not emphasize cultural issues, all of the stages are usually followed when conducting a psycho-educational evaluation. For example, when considering stage three, information-based testing, one must understand that multicultural assessment does not start solely with the knowledge of which instrument to use in an evaluation. There are several factors to consider before selecting instruments. Several of these are described below in sequential order.

Determining Ethnicity

CLD children and adolescents are characterized as students who are racially, ethnically, culturally, and linguistically diverse. Prior to proceeding with the evaluative process, knowledge of the various ethnic groups is important for ethnic identification of a student-client. The major diverse groups noted in the literature are: African American, Hispanic (e.g., Mexican American, Latino, Puerto Rican), Pacific Islander (e.g., Samoan, Hawaiian), Native American (e.g., Sioux, Cherokee), Asian American (e.g., Chinese, Japanese, Vietnamese, Cambodian, Korean), biracial, non-English language background and bilingual individuals (see Rogers et al., 1999). Individuals from these groups are notably heterogeneous within their racial, ethnic, or linguistic group. Similarly, Caucasians of European-American descent are also heterogeneous and dissimilar. Correspondingly, Rogers et al. (1999) point out that many of the cultural competencies recommended for psychological practice are also acceptable for Caucasians of European-American descent. Knowledge of various ethnic groups' historical and political oppression, religion, language, educational outlook, and family disciplinary norms is an essential component of a school psychologist's competence.

School psychologists are warned not to be intimidated by the numerous cases added to their caseload each month to the point that they will fail to perform a thorough background search for each referred student. Whether engaged in an initial (first-time) evaluation or a re-evaluation, a review of a student's past history must be completed regardless of the caseload and the ticking compliance clock that may encumber school psychologists in performing culturally appropriate assessments.

Prior to determining what steps to take, the student's cultural ethnicity should be established. This can be accomplished through a clinical interview with the student and the parents. Parents should be included in the cultural identity evaluative process, with the aim of finding out how culture is passed on to the child and how important culture and cultural identity are to the parents (Isajiw, 1990; Gopaul-McNicol & Brice-Baker, 1998). The Family/Student Cultural Ethnicity Identification Checklist in the box is compiled from practitioner/researcher recommendations (Gopaul-McNicol & Brice-Baker, 1998; Canino & Spurlock, 2000; Suzuki, Ponterotto, & Meller, 2001) and the author's own clinical experience in this area.

Family/Student Cultural Ethnicity Identification Checklist

1. Obtain information on birthplace of student and family members.

2. To what ethnic group(s) do the students' parents belong? Grandparents? Extended family members?

3. With what ethnic group does the student most identify (i.e., family ethnic group, majority group, bicultural, or other)? This may be determined by administering a cultural identity scale or by a clinical interview.

4. Is the student a first-, second-, or third-generation immigrant?

5. How long has the student been living in this community? (If recently arrived, how long has the student lived in the United States?) What was the reason for the immigration?

6. What is the level of acculturation of family members, extended family members, and significant others? (See Chapter 5 on Acculturation.)

7. What language is spoken at home?

8. If bilingual, should language proficiency be determined with a screening instrument, or would an informal/alternative measure be more appropriate?

9. With what ethnic groups does the student socialize? Is there diversity in the student's choice of peer relationships? This is significant because identity factors are often at work in the socialization process.

10. Are there any historical/political events associated with the student's ethnic group? Knowledge of the latter will aid in understanding the student's belief system and values.

11. Is religion practiced? Which family members participate in the religious/spiritual practices? How important is religion in the family's activities/practices?

Checking for cultural identity may bring out other relevant factors in the student's history, such as generational pattern of immigration, economic difficulties, and any historical incidences and/or experiences that may have influenced the student's identity formation (Cross, 1991; Parham, White, & Ajamu, 1999). Ponterotto, Gretchen, and Chauhan (2001) describe cultural identity assessment as a consideration of the individual as both a unique entity and a member of a family and cultural group. They propose a six-step counseling framework that can be adopted for school psychologists to implement in a cultural identity evaluation. The suggested steps are:

1. *The client's level of psychological mindedness* can be understood by examining the client's "framework for understanding and interpreting the presenting problems." In addition, understanding the client's framework will aid in assessing whether the perception of the identified problems is from a "Western psychological perspective or from a more culturally indigenous framework" (p. 85).

2. *The family's level of psychological mindedness* needs to be understood. Basically, this is the same as the first step—that is, to understand the "family's interpretation of psychological concerns and the helping process"

(p. 85). However, be aware that the individual being assessed and the family may have different views of the psychological problems. Accordingly, an awareness of the family's perspective should be communicated to the client.

3. *The client's and family's attitudes toward helping and counseling* should be ascertained. For this step, it is recommended that the practitioner attend to both the client and the family on the issues that may arise due to receiving help out of the family realm. Confidentiality should be stressed for optimal client comfort. An appreciation of the client's conflicts relating to having to divulge personal family matters should be considered by the practitioner in the therapy process.

4. *Assessing the client's level of acculturation* involves examining the client's level of acculturation to Western psychological practices, since this will determine the trust or mistrust of the counseling process (see Chapter 5).

5. *The family's level of acculturation* may not be similar to the client's. Once again, an appreciation of the client's possible conflicting differences in acculturation levels with family members should be considered by the practitioner.

6. *The family's attitude towards acculturation* can be assessed by looking at "the family's attitude toward both the larger family and the individual's acculturation attitudes" (p. 86). Sometimes low family acculturation and high client acculturation will result in the family desiring the client member to remain at this level. Alternatively, a low acculturation family may want the client member to reach a higher level in the mainstream society. (For further review of cultural identity procedures, see Ponterotto, Gretchen, & Chauhan, 2001.)

Incorporating these guidelines into the clinical interview with the student, parents, and extended family members will aid in gathering important background information in addition to obtaining a family outlook on various acculturation issues (see Chapter 10 for a more thorough review of acculturation).

Decision-Making Guidelines

In addition to establishing the cultural and ethnic identity of the student, it is prudent to consider what steps to take for decision-making. Liu and Clay (2002) have provided the counseling profession with a five-step model for decision-making guidelines when working with culturally diverse children and adolescents. Some of these guided procedures are presented in the Checklist for Decision-Making Guidelines box in a modified form to suit the school psychology profession. Others are suggested as supplementary aids.

Checklist for Decision-Making Guidelines

1. Is the referral a true identification of the problem? Or is the referral question a sign that an individual is of the opinion that the child is not performing satisfactorily academically?

2. Is the referral question due to lack of skill for achievement in the dominant culture? This information is essential for a culturally sensitive appraisal of the referral.

3. Often what is perceived as "skill" in one culture is different from another culture, including what is perceived as "achievement" (Dana, 1993).

4. Are there any other cultural aspects of the case that are relevant to the referral? What cultural competencies are necessary for this case? (e.g., awareness, knowledge, skills?) Does the examiner have the required level of cultural competency and information necessary for competent treatment and diagnostic decisions? If not, should the examiner seek further assistance from a multicultural competent practitioner?

5. *When*, *how much*, and *how* should cultural issues be incorporated in this case?

6. Were all the potential treatments/services examined for availability and understanding of the possible cultural assumptions of each?

7. How can the treatment/intervention/evaluation be implemented using all possible cultural strengths?

8. Have the student's parents, teachers, and significant others been involved in the culture-based decisions made?

9. What are the student's observed social strengths and weaknesses?

10. What are the student's observed academic strengths and weaknesses? Are there any culturally sensitive instruments or scales that can measure any of the noted strengths/weaknesses?

11. Have informal/alternative methods of assessment been considered or adopted? Observational measures? Curriculum based assessment or performance-based data collection?

12. Are there any ethical dilemmas that may arise as a result of the referral or intended evaluation or interventions selected (e.g., overall recommendations made to the school-based support team and parents)?

Analysis of the response to these questions will guide the school psychologist to make sound culturally sensitive decisions and the formalization of interventions suited to the particular student being referred.

Probably the most important factor to consider in multicultural assessment is the selection of appropriate instruments for a CLD student evaluation. There has been, and continues to be, a lengthy debate regarding culture-biased tests and testing practices, and their discriminatory repercussions on diverse racial/ethnic groups (see Armour-Thomas, 1992; Canino & Spurlock, 2000; Hamayan & Damico, 1991; Padilla, 2001; Kamphaus, 2001; Sternberg & Grigorenko, 2001). The section that follows discusses some of these deliberations, details a number of the more regularly used instruments in the schools, looks at obstacles that may arise, and provides practical suggestions for overcoming them. Additionally, some commonly asked questions are posed. Some are answerable, others not—bearing in mind that inquiry itself is often the response.

Deciding on What Instruments to Use

One basic fact on which all researchers and practitioners will agree is that no single instrument can be successful across the board (Canino & Spurlock, 2000; Kamphaus, 2001; Lidz, 2001; Padilla, 2001; Sternberg & Grigorenko, 2001; Helms, 1992; Herrnstein & Murray, 1994; Reynolds & Kamphaus, 2003; Suzuki, Ponterotto, & Meller, 2001). However, some instruments have been developed and validated for specific ethnic groups. Canino and Spurlock (2000) explain that there are numerous instruments that have been "re-standardized" to include a better representative sample of CLD children and adolescents. Moreover, test developers are certainly more conscious of cultural loadings and adequate ethnic sample representations than ever before. Additionally, test developers have attempted to improve cultural fairness and to establish cultural validity. This effort has aided in reducing culturally loaded pictorial stimuli as well as content areas. How should a school psychologist assess which instrument to use for a multicultural evaluation? Several generally asked questions arise regarding this selective process (see box).

Questions for Selection of Culturally Appropriate Instruments

1. Based on the particular case, what type of instrument is necessary? Is the instrument for: intelligence testing; behavioral; emotional; adaptive living behaviors; communication style and/or language proficiency; attention span; hyperactivity; socialization; vocation/career planning; giftedness and creativity; or other?

2. In contemplation of appropriate testing procedures, were the Standards for Educational and Psychological Testing (American Educational Research Association, American Psychological Association, and National Council on Measurement in Education, 1999) reviewed?

3. Was the test manual reviewed? What does the test manual indicate with regard to the standardization sample? What are the ethnic groups represented? What of the content validity and internal reliability of the intended instrument (Prediger, 1993)?

4. How are test items, administration methods, and style of examinee responses expected in the particular test (e.g., verbal responses, written or timed or bonus timed tasks) (Armour-Thomas & Gopaul-McNicol, 1997a, 1997b, 1998; Gopaul-McNicol & Armour-Thomas, 2002; Gopaul-McNicol & Brice-Baker, 1998; Lidz, 2001)?

5. Was an evaluation of the students' cultural learning style considered? Was a learning style inventory administered? Were test items examined for item equivalency assessment? (*Note*: Both these procedures help to determine whether a student's learning style corresponds with the selected instrument's method of tapping into the specific skills examined and whether test items can be re-matched to the child's culture; see Griggs & Dunn, 1989 for learning styles; Armour-Thomas & Gopaul-McNicol, 1998 for item equivalencies).

Several other cultural questions come to mind when considering an appropriate instrument: How approving is the student's family of the intended testing? How is the student reacting to the proposed testing request? Is the student used to tests in general? Or is collaborative/cooperative learning a more appropriate outcome measure for his/her culture? Moreover, given the controversial issues involved in the assessment of minorities and their overrepresentation in special education classes, Suzuki, Short, Pieterse, and Kugler (2001) have compiled steps to take in a culturally sensitive assessment. These practitioner/researchers agree with the literature recommendations and suggest obtaining adequate background information in addition to determining the appropriateness of cognitive testing (i.e., if referred for an emotional issue, a cognitive measure may not be needed). Additionally, if cognitive testing is required, the examiner (e.g., the school psychologist) should consider the best measure available and, if the student is an immigrant, the level of English language skills should be determined in the event that an interpreter is needed. The school psychologist should also take into account the utilization of non-verbal measures or other measures that may be available in the student's native language (Salvia, Ysseldyke, & Bolt, 2007; Suzuki et al., 2001).

Lastly, on a practical note, are the instruments/scales selected for a particular evaluation available in the school district being serviced? In examining the procedures followed by school psychologists on the East Coast for instrument selection in various school districts with high concentrations of diverse ethnic students, I have found that school psychologists are often coerced by school administrators into using unsuitable instruments for testing intelligence and/or emotional behaviors because their district has a limited supply of appropriate instruments for testing racial/ethnic CLD populations. Indisputably, it is unethical to administer an instrument to a student if that instrument is invalidated because of cultural bias. If the district cannot provide the appropriate instrument, one should find another way to conduct the evaluation—or request purchase of the chosen instrument. In most cases, the particular ethnic student undergoing an evaluation will not be the only student of that same ethnic heritage in the district. This will perhaps convince the administrators to purchase the required instrument(s). School psychologists must be firm in the decision not to test without proper instruments and not to be intimidated by administrators. Legally and ethically, the best instrument should be utilized or, in the event that a proper instrument is unavailable in a school district or that a reliable and valid instrument is non-existent, then an alternative assessment should be conducted. In many cases, both a quantitative and an alternative method of assessment are practiced (Gopaul-McNicol & Brice-Baker, 1998).

Cognitive Tests

It is important to recognize when it comes to psychological assessment that numerous instruments and scales have been developed for specific reasons (e.g., intelligence testing; behavioral; emotional; adaptive living; communication style and/or language proficiency; attention span; hyperactivity; socialization; vocation/career planning; giftedness, and creativity). Unquestionably, the instrument most utilized in school psychology practice is the intelligence test. And, as noted earlier, the majority of the children referred for learning problems come from culturally/ethnically and linguistically diverse backgrounds which are dissimilar to many of the standardized samples used for the available tests. Such differences render these tests invalid (Armour-Thomas, 1992), thus the emphasis on informal/alternative assessment methods for CLD children and youth. The dubious reliability and validity of intelligence tests for CLD populations have triggered ethical and political reforms.

Nonetheless, as one of the leading experts on the Wechsler Scales of Intelligence rightly expresses, "If there is one thing that we have learned from the past, it is that IQ tests are resilient. They have faced challenges of every sort throughout their checkered past, and they have withstood these challenges"

(Kaufman, 2000, p. 13). Kaufman (2000) continues to explain that many of the current intelligence tests have been constructed based on theory, and that there are currently an "abundance of well-developed and well-standardized instruments for assessing the intelligence of children, adolescents, and adults" (p. 11). As reviewed by Kaufman, IQ test developers began to incorporate theories of intelligence in test construction in the 1980s. The first theory-based instruments were: the Kaufman Assessment Battery for Children (K-ABC; Kaufman & Kaufman, 1983); the Stanford-Binet-IV (Thorndike, Hagen, & Sattler, 1986); and the Woodcock-Johnson Tests of Cognitive Ability (WJ-R) (Woodcock & Johnson, 1989; Woodcock, & Mather, 1989). In the 1990s, intelligence tests continued to incorporate theoretical constructs in their scoring measures—for example, the Kaufman Adolescent and Adult Intelligence Test (KAIT) (Kaufman & Kaufman, 1993) and the Kaufman Cognitive Assessment System (CAS) (Naglieri & Das, 1997).

Currently, tests continue to employ several theories of intelligence in their construction. For example, the K-ABC scales are based on psychobiological cerebral specialization theory (Sperry, 1974; Luria, 1966) and neuropsychological theory. Horn and Cattell's 1967 theory of fluid-crystallized dichotomy was adopted to help distinguish between intelligence and achievement. Kaufman clarifies that the renowned Wechsler scales of intelligence (Wechsler Intelligence Test for Children III & Wechsler Intelligence Test for Adults) were not founded on theory but have been influential in the expansion of theory and assisted in the interpretation of varied theoretical perspectives (i.e., Verbal-IQ and Performance-IQ differences to left and right cerebral hemispheres; Kaufman, 1990, Chs. 9–11). Furthermore, the WISC-III (1991) was revised specifically to reduce content bias. To date, this instrument has received endorsement for use with a number of CLD populations (Suzuki, Vraniak, & Kugler, 1996).

At present, the newer versions of the Wechsler scales (WAIS-III and WISC-IV) have adopted research-based theories and include tasks in verbal and non-verbal domains directly related to theory. Future intelligence instruments, Kaufman informs us, will very likely emerge as computerized IQ tests, and this too will lead to many controversial issues—though hopefully not to the abandonment of the psychologist–client practice of administration or to the disappearance of the lengthy 60-year clinical orientation of the Wechsler tradition (for a thorough review on IQ tests and their future, see Braden, 1997; Kaufman, 2000).

Culture and Intelligence

From a multicultural perspective, Sternberg and Grigorenko (2001) discuss two points of view from the literature regarding cognitive ability testing. One view is that "cognitive ability tests are transportable from one culture to another;" the other is that they are not transportable across cultures, therefore rendering the concepts of abilities non-universal (pp. 335–36). Seemingly, Western ideas about intelligence are not the same as other cultures, and the abilities that are needed to adapt in one particular culture may be dissimilar to the abilities that are needed to adapt in another (Sternberg & Grigorenko, 2001). This view is certainly important for school psychologists and for intelligence testing in general, since the tests that are currently available have been developed on Western concepts of intelligence. In short, intelligence may be based on the culture and the culture's perspective of intelligence. And the abilities that are necessary in one culture are not necessarily those perceived by another culture to be the ones that should be tested (Sternberg & Grigorenko, 2001). In this regard, it appears that school psychologists should take into consideration the fact that immigrant and bicultural children from diverse backgrounds, and their parents, will perceive the concept of intelligence and/or abilities according to their culture's unique perspective, and that certain testing procedures and/or tests will seem unnecessary or futile.

With all this said, school psychologists currently choose to use the Wechsler Intelligence Scales more often than other intelligence measures. Indeed, every school psychologist is trained on the Wechsler Scales (Wilson & Reschly, 1996) and they spend the majority of their professional practice using them (Reschly & Wilson, 1995). With the disproportionate numbers of immigrant and minority students being placed into special education programs and the discrimination-based controversy that has developed over the unfair use of IQ tests that got them there (Armour-Thomas, 1992; Armour-Thomas & Gopaul-McNicol, 1997a; 1997b; Gopaul-McNicol, Black, & Clark-Castro, 1997; Gopaul-McNicol & Brice-Baker, 1998; Helms, 1992), probably the best remedy for unfair testing practice is to follow the advice of the many multicultural experts in the field—that is, to consistently adopt alternative qualitative modes of assessment in addition to quantitative measures.

A Bio-Cultural Model of Assessment

A particular method that addresses such twofold methods of assessment is the Bio-Cultural Model advocated by Armour-Thomas and Gopaul-McNicol (1998). This model is especially geared to fair testing practices for CLD children and youth, without completely discrediting the use of standardized measures. Basically, the Bio-Cultural Model is an "ecologically sensitive assessment system that allows for greater heterogeneity in the expression of intelligence" (Gopaul-McNicol & Brice-Baker, 1998, p. 21). The model emphasizes the use of quantitative and qualitative approaches. The idea is that qualitative approaches ought to complement the quantitative psychometric measures of intelligence.

The foundation of the model's structure is that there is no sole psychometric instrument in existence that can tap into the "three interrelated and dynamic dimension of intelligence: biological cognitive processes, cultural coded experiences, and cultural contexts" (Gopaul-McNicol & Brice-Baker, 1998, p. 21). Consequently, all instruments utilized in an assessment that require scoring and give results based on the scoring should be accompanied by non-psychometric ecological methods (see Armour-Thomas & Gopaul-McNicol, 1998).

The Bio-Cultural Model follows a four-tier bio-ecological assessment. Each tier focuses on certain aspects of the evaluation with an ecologically sensitive approach. The first tier adheres wholly to psychometric assessment measures. The second tier assesses the child's potential and/or estimated intellectual performance by using special strategies. This is done by: allowing suspended time for finishing tasks; using contextual methods for vocabulary; permitting the use of paper and pencil; and following a test–teach–retest approach. The third tier involves an ecological taxonomy of intellectual assessment by evaluating: family and community supports; acculturation levels; teacher input via questionnaires; school observations in the classroom, gym, and playground; home; and place of worship. All of these methods focus on the child's ecology in relation to the home, school, and community. The psychologist examines all tasks the child is able to do in all of these surroundings. Tier four comprises four areas of assessment: musical intelligence; bodily/kinesthetic intelligence; interpersonal intelligence; and intrapersonal intelligence. Armour-Thomas and Gopaul-McNicol (1998) explain that the evaluation of other intelligences is important for CLD children since IQ tests do not demonstrate all the intelligences of a child. This approach to a culturally sensitive assessment provides a "safe" method for sound cultural and ethical practice (refer to the case study on the bio-cultural model at the end of this chapter).

Nonverbal Tests

Nonverbal instruments are beneficial for multicultural assessment practice but they too have undergone scrutiny. Although nonverbal measures have been perceived favorably since they do not have cultural loadings, Canino and Spurlock (2000) stress that such measures "require analytical reasoning abilities that are more fully developed through formal education. Children with less exposure to symbolic manipulation in play, and immigrant children with fewer years of formal education than their age-mates, may be at a disadvantage in assessment with these measures" (p. 94). Conversely, it has been recommended that psychologists use non-verbal measures rather than interpreters (the latter technique is considered unethical—American Psychological Association, 1992) if a standardized instrument is unavailable in the language of the examinee.

An additional perspective found in the literature regarding nonverbal measures is the concept of language. Nonverbal tests are not solely perceived as different and culturally fairer for tapping into the intellectual process; they are also regarded as language-free tests to be administered when a measure is unavailable in the examinee's language (see Bracken & McCallum, 2001). In summary, it is the practitioner's decision to administer the instrument that will provide the best observation of the examinee's strengths and weaknesses.

There are several nonverbal tests that may be helpful for assessing CLD children and adolescents:

1. Raven's Progressive Matrices (Raven, Raven, & Court, 1998)

2. The Standard Progressive Matrices (Raven, Court, & Raven, 1947a)

3. The Coloured Progressive Matrices (Raven, Court, & Raven, 1947b), developed for ages 5 to 11. The matrices are excellent researched tests that are used worldwide.

4. The Test of Non-verbal Intelligence, Third Edition (TONI-3), recently renormed (Brown, Sherbenou, & Johnson, 1997). Like the Raven's Matrices, it excludes language usage, thus reducing cultural bias.

5. The Leiter International Scale-Revised (Roid & Miller, 1997), designed for ages 2 to 20, is another nonverbal test of reasoning ability.

6. The Universal Nonverbal Intelligence Test (UNIT) (Bracken & McCallum, 1998) is suitable for ages 5 to 17 and 11 months.

Nonverbal tests are ineffective for obtaining a global intellectual measure. Harris, Reynolds, and Koegel (1996) explain that nonverbal tests are useful for children with language disorders or for whom no other standardized measure exists in the child's particular language. However, the Leiter International Scale-Revised (Roid & Miller, 1997) and the Universal Nonverbal Intelligence Test (UNIT) (Bracken & McCallum, 1998) are the only two nonverbal comprehensive tests of intelligence. Unlike the matrices that measure a rather constricted aspect of intelligence via progressive matrices, a comprehensive nonverbal test taps into multiple aspects of intelligence.

The matrix-type tests most commonly utilized in schools for testing CLD children and youth are:

1. *Comprehensive Test of Nonverbal Intelligence* (C-TONI) (Hammill, Pearson, & Wiederholt, 1996).

2. *Test of Nonverbal Intelligence-Third Edition* (TONI-3) (Brown, Sherbenou, & Johnson, 1997).

3. *Matrix Analogies Test* (MAT) (Naglieri, 1985).

4. *The Naglieri Nonverbal Ability Test* (N-NAT) (Naglieri, 1996), which can be used for group measures.

5. *The General Ability Measure for Adults* (GAMA), (Naglieri & Bardos, 1997), which can be used for group measures.

Bracken and McCallum (2001) have pointed out that nonverbal tests are cost-effective and easy to administer. However, they caution that nonverbal tests furnish screening batteries that consist of a limited amount of subtests and require verbal directions. Alternatively, the authors suggest that the Leiter International Scale-Revised (Roid & Miller, 1997) and the Universal Nonverbal Intelligence Test (UNIT) (Bracken & McCallum, 1998) are best utilized for high-stakes decisions because they are more appropriate. The term "high stakes" is used in the literature to identify the motive for the administration, in addition to the type of test(s) used, that ultimately leads to an important placement decision (e.g., educational placement and/or vocational choice options). Both the Leiter International Scale-Revised and UNIT can be administered by using pantomime instead of language.

Alternative Methods of Assessment

When discussing nonverbal tests and informal methods of assessment, one might easily assume that psychometric tests are inappropriate for CLD children. Consequently, it is necessary to point out that all psychometric tests are *not* unapproachable for the school psychologists servicing CLD youth. Much depends on the individual, the background, and the referral question. If a psychometric test exists which can be administered to a particular CLD child without seriously biasing the outcomes, then the practitioner should follow through. However, other methods should be included in the multicultural assessment process as a means of obtaining additional "qualitative" data.

A primary tenet of the culture-fair assessment process is the prerequisite that tests should be chosen which are not ethnically or culturally biased. In short, any method of assessment that is not psychometrically oriented might be considered a non-biased approach to evaluating a CLD child's strengths and weaknesses. However, Canino and Spurlock (2000), in their review of alternative forms of assessment, caution that it can be arduous to conduct more extensive cultural assessments on account of the tremendous influx of immigrant children in the schools, all coming with their own special needs. The authors stress that clinicians should focus on finding the *right* kind of assessment for *each* individual. Another important factor to consider is that the interpretation of the results of any assessment must take into consideration the type of instrument utilized versus the child's culture and learning style.

Canino and Spurlock (2000) also discuss the notion of *cultural equivalency*. This abstraction assumes that there must be equality of assessment methods/measures for all cultures. However, a child in a particular culture is not always confined to all aspects of that culture. For example, children raised in rural versus urban areas will automatically have had varying experiences, thus causing each to respond differently to certain test items even if they belong to the same ethnic group and the test has been designed specifically for that group. It has been this author's experience that a pure *individual approach* is the key to success in any culturally unbiased evaluation. The use of measures should correspond to the individual's cultural and educational experiences and learning style. In this respect, the weighty pressure placed on the school psychologist to make accurate placement decisions can be alleviated if the assessment is individually designed. While this may very well be considered a more difficult approach to assessment, it certainly is not. What actually are in question here are the school psychologists' intentional involvement and adherence to ethical standards. They should self-examine a number of important personal questions (see box) when determining the extent of their involvement in the assessment.

School Psychologist Involvement Questions

1. What are my culturally unbiased assessment responsibilities? How ethical am I in my review of assessment choices? Do I spurn taking the extra time to appraise an unfamiliar test manual?

2. Do I recognize that the most dangerous element in any *ethical* assessment is the concept of time and how much of it I plan to use?

3. Should I not follow what I have learned to do in a multicultural assessment, regardless of time pressures or barrages?

4. Are my ethical standards in conflict with the need to finish the assessment with the time constraints imposed in my school? Of the multidisciplinary team?

5. Is taking an extra few hours to do a complete background history with family and extended family members, and screen for past educational, emotional, and cultural experiences, actually going to *impede* the completion of my professional duties? My caseload responsibilities?

6. How important is the outcome of this assessment to *me*?

7. Am I using *all* of my skills in this assessment? How ethical am I?

If the school psychologist is genuinely committed to conducting a culture-fair evaluation, the above questions will help guide the process with unbiased results, adequate diagnosis, and sound placement decisions and interventions.

Portfolio Assessment

Another type of alternative assessment is portfolio assessment. Portfolio assessment has received considerable attention and is presently utilized in many school districts throughout the nation (Losardo & Notari-Syverson, 2001). In describing effective instructional and assessment practices, Ysseldyke and Elliott (1998) explain that portfolios are used in *performance-based assessments*. This practice provides educators and school psychologists with the opportunity to "measure and tailor instruction to help students meet learning outcomes." Contrary to psychometric measures, portfolio outcomes are not compared to other children; they are individually based and reviewed. On many occasions, a school psychologist may choose to ask a teacher to permit a CLD student to prepare a portfolio of their class work as an alternate mode of assessment (Dettmer, Thurston, & Dyck, 2002). Portfolios can comprise:

- written essays on topics of interest to the student;
- a group experiment and/or activity assignment;
- a written explanation of the manner selected to solve a math problem, with evidence of this provided;
- progress charts;
- completed learning packets;
- artwork;
- a student-made book;
- lists of mastered vocabulary or spelling words;
- research reports;
- creative writing samples;
- an autobiography;
- classroom tests and records of scores;
- teacher observational notes;
- audio- or videotapes, photographs, drawings;
- a student's self-monitoring of a progress chart;
- the student's selection of his/her finest accomplishment;
- a list of descriptions of good deeds and helpful behavior—the latter is especially helpful for social skills training;
- a list of social affiliations, clubs, activities, engagement in team projects—the last of these aids in assessing social skills, leadership qualities and/or style of social interactions.

Since portfolios usually take a certain amount of time to compile, if the school psychologist's aim is to use such a method of assessment, it is wise to determine in advance how long it will take to accumulate sufficient data prior to the ensuing psycho-educational evaluation. The school psychologist can then evaluate the child's progress, mode of learning, reading, math, and writing abilities over the prescribed time scheduled. This will aid to determine whether the child is learning the curriculum, what strengths and weaknesses are demonstrated, and what may be done to ameliorate the difficulties noted. Losardo and Notari-Syverson (2001) supply examples of rating scales and charts which are useful for monitoring the child's portfolio progress (see Figure 2.1 for the Portfolio Assessment Progress Rating Scale and Figure 2.2 for the Child Self-Evaluation Form).

In some cases, a teacher may have adopted portfolio assessment at the start of a semester, in which case the evaluation can become a collaborative teacher–psychologist review of strengths and weaknesses. What is advantageous about this for the school psychologist is that portfolios are a link to assessing skills across different environments (e.g., classroom, home, community activities) and the materials reviewed can be shared and compared. Portfolios are especially helpful for the follow-up stage of assessment. Multidisciplinary team members (e.g., educational consultants, teachers, social workers, and school psychologists) can review a child's portfolio progress at an appointed time to determine how the child is functioning with the agreed-upon curriculum modifications (e.g., IEP or school–home academic contract). For these reasons, it is wise for school psychologists to familiarize themselves with teachers' evaluative methods in their schools. Knowing when and how portfolios are implemented will help school psychologists with data collection during the assessment process.

Portfolio assessment practices are also associated with Howard Gardner's theory of multiple intelligences (which includes demonstration of comprehension) by having the student use the material to be measured in a significant *contextual* manner (Gardner, 1993). For example, a social studies student may be asked to explain current events and make rational predictions based on learned social studies principles. Multiple intelligence theory has had an impressive impact on the assessment of CLD children and youth. Chapter 3 focuses on this theory and its implications for school psychology practice. Another area mentioned in the literature on school psychology practice is qualitative methods in assessment. The next section will address this recommendation.

Qualitative Methods in Assessment

Qualitative research has received considerable recognition in education and in psychology over the last three decades. Several researchers (Strauss &

Portfolio Assessment: Progress Rating Scale

Child's name: _Robbie_ Reviewers: _OLAC, LK_ Date: _6/5/00_

Date	Behavior/objective	Criteria	Evaluation and comments					
			0	1	2	3	4	5
	Two-word utterances	10 different utterances to express agent-action, action-object, agent-object						
2/1/00					Some two-word utterances, but mostly following peer/adult model.			
6/1/00								Consistently uses two-word utterances in school and at home (English and Spanish).

Scoring system:

0 = No Change
1 = Some improvement
2 = Significant improvement but still needs help
3 = Significant improvement
4 = Meets Criteria with help
5 = Meets Criteria independently

Figure 2.1   Portfolio Progress Rating Scale for an Individual Child

SOURCE: *Portfolio Assessment: Child Self-Evaluation* from *Alternative Approaches to Assessing Young Children* (2001) by A. Losardo and A. Notari-Syverson. Baltimore. Reprinted by permission of Paul H. Brookes Publishing Co., Inc.

Portfolio Assessment: Child Self-Evaluation

Child name: _Tim_ _____   Date: _4/26/00_ _____

What I liked best and why:

I liked when we played restaurant with Amy. She's my best friend. I was the cook. I was cooking pizza and new potatoes.

What I liked the least and why:

Telling a story, That's a lot of words and sentences too tell someone.

What I learned:

That's my picture of Ablyoyo. I learned a lot about Africa.

What was difficult and why:

It was hard to draw the caterpillar and the butterfly. I got the colors mixed up. I colored the butterfly green.

What I want to learn to do better and how:

I want to write my name. You can show me, then I can copy.

Figure 2.2   Self-Evaluation Form for an Individual Child

SOURCE: *Portfolio Assessment: Child Self-Evaluation from Alternative Approaches to Assessing Young Children* (2001) by A. Losardo and A. Notari-Syverson. Baltimore. Reprinted by permission of Paul H. Brookes Publishing Co., Inc.

Corbin, 1990; Bogdan & Biklen, 1992; Glesne & Peshin, 2000; Hatch, 2002) have contributed extensive guidelines for conducting qualitative research studies. School psychologists are advised to review the recommended texts by these leading researchers in order to establish an informational core foundation for qualitative research procedures. However, a brief review and suggestions for qualitative assessment methods follow. Qualitative research is not new to school psychology, since school psychologists make extensive use of qualitative techniques within the assessment process when they incorporate naturalistic approaches in their evaluations. Nonbiased and/or alternative assessment methods may be perceived as a form of qualitative approach to non-quantifiable observations and measures.

A brief review of qualitative research methodology indicates that the focus is on attempting to recall reality as seen through the eyes of the participant, through procedures that are inductive, generative, constructive, and subjective. Qualitative research involves understanding and investigating what individuals are doing, and interpreting what is happening by following patterns and/or themes of the participants' subjective perspectives. Suzuki, Prendes-Lintel, Wertlieb, and Stallings (1999) highlight that qualitative methodology in research promotes the evaluation of multicultural environments and culturally diverse populations. These authors discuss the importance of identifying emerging cultural topics and reviewing these for their meaning, a factor that is of immeasurable importance in the practice of school psychology.

There are three major components of qualitative methodology: (a) data that can come from various sources, interviews, and observations; (b) the use of different analytic or interpretive procedures that are employed to arrive at findings (i.e., techniques for conceptualizing data); and (c) written and verbal reports. Through the use of such reports, the investigator can examine verbatim interviews and extricate patterns, themes, and form categories which aid in the development of the basic knowledge emerging in the investigation. Based on this review, the employment of qualitative methods presents an opportunity to discover and interpret discrete cultural issues of which school psychologists should be aware when assessing CLD students (Kopala & Suzuki, 1999). Furthermore, valuable data can be collected by the school psychologist to assist in CLD research.

Qualitative assessment procedures often involve the use of a case study, which will incorporate multiple sources of information that reveal various themes found in the story of the individual. Case studies can be utilized as either an informational source to be considered during an assessment or a report on a completed assessment case (Polkinghorne & Gribbons, 1999). Case studies can help school-based support teams reach appropriate decisions since they contribute a more sympathetic understanding of an individual's situational and historical background, and also include any particular events that may enhance the evaluation process.

It is important to remember that not all psychological evaluations require psychometric testing. Other sources of information, such as case studies, are needed to improve decision-making outcomes. Since the traditional quantitative approach to assessment has had dire consequences for minority students and others, multicultural school psychologists should pursue the less biased qualitative approach to assessment.

Given that a substantial part of a problem-solving approach to assessment is the referral and the initiation of the assessment process, a *qualitative-minded* school psychologist should undertake several steps in the process of collecting data for such an assessment. The steps described below have been adopted from Polkinghorne and Gribbons (1999).

1. *Referral.* Qualitative inquiries are necessary for analyzing the referral question. These can include interviews—specifically with teachers—that query the behaviors and characteristics of the student who has been referred.

A suggested question is: "What was perceived by the teacher as problematic and why?" (The "*why*" is especially important.) The teacher's role in the referral and the teacher's beliefs about education are important factors to explore. Interviews with other teachers involved with the child are also beneficial. Interviewing is deemed especially productive since it allows teachers to self-express and divulge important information pertaining to the referred student. From the interviews, the school psychologist can extract themes and patterns of themes that will help the psychologist to understand the reason for the referral. Moreover, the interplay of various themes and/or contradictory thematic patterns from different teachers can lead to a better understanding of what types of behaviors and/or academic difficulties lead to referrals in a particular school.

2. *Choosing assessment information.* Information should be collected regarding the student's academic problem. The data should be reviewed in several ways—the inquiry, the student, and the classroom. An optimal qualitative assessment should not overlook cultural and institutional factors pertaining to the student's accomplishments (Ogbu, 1992).

3. *Characteristics of the student.* The characteristics of the student traditionally include intelligence testing and/or obtaining some measure of intellectual abilities. With respect to CLD children and youth, it is important to distinguish between the more traditional IQ tests and their accompanying theories and the less traditional measures of intellectual abilities (Gardner, 1983; Sternberg, 1985). Each type of measure used will render a quite different view of the child's cognitive profile. The analysis of the child's characteristics can be accomplished through various non-traditional measures. For example, dynamic assessment assesses the child's potential for learning (Feurstein, Rand, & Hoffman, 1979). Likewise, there are measures of behaviors for particular settings (Anderson, 1988; Cervantes, 1988).

In their review of qualitative assessment, Polkinghorne and Gribbons (1999) discuss an important measure that has gained considerable attention over the last three decades for its "non-biased" endeavor: the System of Multicultural Pluralistic Assessment (SOMPA) (Mercer & Lewis, 1978; Morrison, 1988). The SOMPA is a measurable method of assessment that focuses on multidimensional ways of looking at a child. Developed to address the overrepresentation of classified minority students in special education, Mercer's (1979) instrument adjusted IQ scores based on social and cultural differences, provides various domains to assess for assistance with placement decisions, and utilizes the Spanish language and relevant materials for assessing Latino children and their families.

Although Polkinghorne and Gribbons (1999) include the SOMPA in their review of qualitative assessment, Kamphaus (2001) explains its lack of usage due to difficulties with the predictive validity of the Estimated Learning Potential (ELP) score, a score derived through a corrective factor that adjusts the WISC-R full-scale IQs according to the child's culture (Anglo, Latino, African American) (see Kamphaus, 2001, Ch. 6 for a description and discussion of the SOMPA).

Suggestions for Overcoming Bias in Qualitative Methods

Although qualitative methods are favorably recommended for servicing CLD students, they are not without bias. Moreover, qualitative methods use reliability and validity to ascertain whether the information/observation is accurate. However, the search for reliability and validity is not the same as it is in quantitative research. In the qualitative process, the responsibility for establishing reliability and validity rests on the examiner/researcher's own analysis. Thus the process is endangered by human bias. There are several factors to consider when engaged in the collection of informational or observational data.

Initially, there must be trustworthiness on the part of the examiner/researcher. Trustworthiness is described as "how one approaches, analyzes, interprets, and reports data" (Merrick, 1999, p. 31). In this respect, the primary emphasis is placed on the examiner/researcher being aware of their engagement in the construction of knowledge or information. In so doing, there should be an acknowledgment of the *reflexive* aspect of the qualitative process. Reflexivity therefore positions the examiner/researcher (i.e., school psychologist) as a scientific observer of the environment, context, and culture being studied and represented. In the evaluation of the qualitative process, the examiner/researcher must also aim toward accurate *representation* of the subject studied. The key is to be cognizant of the fact that the manner in which the obtained data are presented is closely connected to the examiner/researcher. Professionals using qualitative methods need to be aware that the way they present their findings (whether in written form or verbally) will have much to do with who they are and what they say (Merrick, 1999). The crucial point to remember is that the representation of the findings is put together by the examiner/researcher and that issues of reliability, validity, trustworthiness, and reflexivity are interconnected with what one knows and how it will be represented (Fine, 1992; Lather, 1991, cited in Merrick, 1999).

Other factors to consider for determining possible bias refer to the examiner/researcher's detachment versus involvement with the student/participant.

Closeness, identification with the student, and emotional involvement will result in bias and mar objectivity on the part of the observer. Self-analysis of emotions is crucial during the qualitative process. Sciarra (1999) suggests asking the following questions: "What is this strong emotional reaction I am experiencing telling me about the world of the participant(s)? About my world? About the differences between their world and my world?" It is important to note that strong emotions can cause over-rapport while luke-warm emotions can lead to under-rapport.

In sum, whatever the issues in evaluative measures, school psychologists have the option of using both psychometric and qualitative assessment bat-teries to determine a child's learning potential. What is important to note is that qualitative methods can go beyond the measurable results to help deci-sion-making teams analyze individual thematic interpretations as well as structural descriptions concerning CLD children and their families.

What to Look for in Classroom Observations

Classroom observations can provide additional educational insight into the child's learning style and the teacher's instructional methods (Rosenfield, 1987). School psychologists can use *systematic observational systems* in order to gather information on the acquisition of knowledge during a class lesson (see Chapter 6 for a review of systematic observational systems in curriculum-based assessments). The advantage of classroom observations in addition to the use of observational systems is that school psychologists can actively be present in the interactive teaching and learning environment, hence observing at first hand the academic problem and any defective learn-ing style versus teaching style. This process enhances the assessment, as it reveals important information not observable within a single testing session.

Aside from the systematic observational systems available, a classroom observation should check for environmental and academic factors that may affect a student's classroom behavior. The Classroom Observation Checklist in the box reviews these important areas.

Classroom Observation Checklist

1. *Class demographics.* What ethnic groups are represented in the class?

2. *Class environment.* Are there posters and artwork representing various ethnic groups? Are copies of student work only posted because of high grades?

3. *Seating arrangement.* What is the seating arrangement of the students? Who are the students in front, back, and side of the student being observed?

4. *Class atmosphere.* What is the atmosphere of the class? Competitive? Collective?

5. *Student comfort.* Does the student appear comfortable and at ease in the class?

6. *Student involvement.* Is the student's engagement active and motivated?

7. *Student understanding.* Does the student appear to understand the verbal instructions of the teacher? Does the student participate in class discussion, answer questions, read aloud, engage in class work? Could the student's learning style clash with the teaching method?

8. *Teacher's teaching methods.* What are the teacher's instructional methods? Collective, individual, lecture? Use of visual aids? Does the teacher use different approaches to explain the same concept? Is the teacher culturally aware and sensitive to the ethnic class composition?

9. *Student challenge.* Does the student appear challenged by or at ease with the class work?

10. *Documenting changes in student behaviors.* Identify and define specific, concrete behaviors to be observed, and document the frequency, interval, and duration (see Dettmer et al., 2002).

Talking with the child immediately after the class lesson to review the child's notebook and ask questions regarding the material just learned is very helpful. It may be found that, whether due to poor attention span, apathy, distress and frustration, or simply inability to comprehend, a student will not have learned the required material even if the teacher has adopted the appropriate specific learning style methods of instruction. The school psychologist has an ideal opportunity to screen for this during this recommended interview as well as during a classroom observation. Both techniques can be used to corroborate results (see Functional Assessment of Academic Behaviors (FAAB), Ysseldyke & Christensen, 2002).

Dynamic Assessment

Dynamic assessment is another alternative method that encompasses qualitative methods. This is a fairly new approach to assessment that evaluates a child's learning potential. It was originally developed for culturally diverse children. This mode of assessment is in direct opposition to assessing the construct of intelligence on an intelligence test. It strongly counter-attacks the concept of intelligence testing being used on the low-functioning student populations. As a result of the long debate emphasizing the need for culture-free, non-biased testing, dynamic assessment emerged, offering a non-psychometric method of both evaluating a disadvantaged child's potential for learning when the child manifests low performance, and seeking the reasons behind the low performance. Proponents for the assessment of learning potential (Lidz, 1987, 2001; Feuerstein, Falik, & Feuerstein, 1998) explain that:

> dynamic assessment offers an active and modifying approach that does not accept solely the manifested problem but attempts to define the extent of the change that can most likely take place and the interventions that can be implemented by which the needed changes can be reached.

The goal is to modify the cognitive style of the child. The theoretical assumption is that the child possesses characteristics of immutability very much like those proposed by Sternberg and Gardner. In addition, the child is perceived as having the prerequisites for structural change—of having the necessary dynamics for change. This implies that all children can learn, adjust, and adopt required skills when: (a) asked to complete a task—providing a baseline for the child's performance; (b) shown how to complete the task if it was not completed accurately; and (c) asked to re-do the task—a test–teach–retest approach to evaluation and learning. Lastly, a comparison is made of the initial task performance and the performance results subsequent to the teaching intervention.

Losardo and Notari-Syverson (2001) clarify dynamic assessment as:

> An assessment approach that determines the child's potential for learning and responsivity to instruction by comparing what the child does independently and what the child is able to do with additional support and assistance. This corresponds to the child's zone of proximal development (ZPD).

The ZPD is adopted from Vygostsky's (1978) concept that distinguishes the difference between what a child can actually accomplish independently and what the child can accomplish with the direction of an adult. Research has shown that such dynamic methods are inclined to be more predictive of future performance than psychometric measures (Gonzalez, Brusca-Vega, & Yawkey, 1997; Lidz, 1987; Lidz & Elliott, 2000; Vygotsky, 1978). This dynamic approach to assessment, or teaching-based assessment method, is encouraging for the school psychologist working in multiethnic communities where low IQ scores are usually perceived as a stable function of the child. This is an evaluative sphere in which the school psychologist can advocate for the child's true potential as well as assist with culturally unbiased interventions.

Measures for assessing learning potential were studied at the Research Institute for Educational Problems. Among many of the recognized measures are: the Learning Potential Assessment Device (LPAD) (Feuerstein, 1979); Koh's Learning Potential Test (KLPT) (Budoff & Corman, 1974); and the Raven Learning Potential Procedure (Budoff & Corman, 1973).

Meyers (1991) has stressed the need for training school psychologists as *dynamic assessors*, since such assessments require expertise in techniques necessary to differentiate the link between assessment and intervention, within assessment and the environment, and the assessment of the learning process. Adjusting to a new concept of assessing children and departing from the traditional measures and techniques learned in graduate programs might prove to be challenging for the school psychologist. However, as Meyers (1991) points out, there is a need for training institutions to adopt dynamic assessment as an integral part of school psychology training.

Dynamic assessment is an ideal mechanism for the multicultural school psychologist. A noted shortcoming is the longer timeframe involved in such an evaluation. This factor frequently discourages practitioners from substituting psychometric "static" testing for the more time-consuming techniques of dynamic assessment. However, if one were to assess carefully the unequivocal harmful repercussions of a poorly conducted and consequently biased assessment, the additional time needed to accede to dynamic assessment standards is certainly worthwhile. Dynamic assessment is discussed further in Chapter 9.

Response to Instruction/Intervention (RTI)

The main intention of assessment is to plan appropriate interventions and to monitor the progress of the intervention. Although standardized tests are helpful, they do not measure progress achieved through instruction. Salvia, Ysseldyke, and Bolt (2007) explain that, "They [the tests] are time consuming, are insensitive to small but important changes, are expensive, are not suitable for repeated administrations, and fail to match a student's curriculum and instruction" (p. 629). The insistence in the field (from the No Child Left Behind Act) that schools put into practice *evidence-based instruction* has led to alternative ways to check students' progress by monitoring a specific instructional program to determine whether it is effective for the student(s). Schools are judged by the state Departments of Education based on the results of the school's instructional program and students' progress. This has led to the development of response to instruction (RTI) models.

The terms "response to instruction (RTI)" and "response to intervention" have been used interchangeably; however, there is a difference between the two. Salvia et al. (2007) clarify that *response to instruction* refers to the students' response to core instruction and/or response to everyday instruction that occurs for all students. The main goal of this type of RTI is to measure student progress continuously, periodically, annually, or at some other rate of recurrence so as to catch any deviance and/or skill development.

In contrast, *response to intervention* occurs when considerable programming modifications are made, either for groups—large or small—or for an individual in order to reach a *particular instructional outcome* or state standard. In this case, however, the responses are measured for effectiveness.

Salvia et al. (2007) describe three levels of RTI instruction—core instruction (for all students); enhanced instruction (for some students); and intensive instruction (for a few students)—that are similar to Horner, Sugai, and Horner's (2000) model of RTI. For example, a student manifesting severe academic difficulties will receive intensive instruction in the area of difficulty and be monitored daily or weekly for progress. The process of monitoring a continuing progress is termed *progress monitoring* or *data-driven decision-making*. The following are suggestions for implementing progress monitoring/data-driven decision-making:

- Collect and analyze data to ascertain student progress toward mastery of specific skills or general outcomes.
- Use the data collected to make instructional decisions.
- Progress monitoring/data-driven decision making; this can include daily or weekly measurement, or time intervals ranging from minute to minute to annual.
- It is important to note that progress monitoring and data-driven decision-making require both collection of data and use (see www.studentprogress.org) (Salvia et al., 2007).

Frequently, a student's academic deficits will determine how often measurement should take place: the greater the deficit, the more frequently monitoring of progress should be to assure instruction is efficacious.

Models of RTI

School psychologists should be familiar with RTI and the various RTI models. Since RTI is in part preventive for children who are at risk of failure, most RTI models help educators and school psychologists make pre-referral classroom decisions by assessing the student's response to the educator's classroom instruction. The Iowa Problem-Solving Model (Vaughn & Fuchs,

2003, cited in Salvia et al., 2007) identifies children at risk of failure so as to implement alternative interventions. Students are then monitored to determine their response to the implemented intervention (this is measuring response to intervention). To determine whether an invention is efficacious, the RTI process involves comparing a student's rate of learning during the implemented intervention to his/her rate of learning from the regular classroom instruction. With RTI models, students are sometimes referred to child study teams for comprehensive evaluations if they fail to demonstrate progress after a certain amount of time (Salvia et al., 2007).

Through the vehicle of consultation, school psychologists have an exceptional opportunity to collaborate with educators, parents, and other professionals connected with RTI approaches. For example, according to Salvia and Ysseldyke's review of RTI assessment models, the Iowa Problem-Solving Model had its beginnings in the earlier behavioral consultation model (Bergan, 1977; Tharp & Wetzel, 1969, cited in Salvia et al., 2007). The stages implemented in behavioral consultation are used for problem-solving methods similar to this RTI model (see Chapter 8 for a description of behavioral consultation stages).

Preschool Assessment

At present, federal mandates require that assessments and interventions be provided to early childhood populations who are at risk of developmental delays and emotional/behavioral problems. The Individuals with Disabilities Education Act (IDEA), Part B, requires that interventions for children ages 3 to 5 be provided to children with disabilities. Public Law 102-119 has added the category of developmental delays for children aged 3 to 5 years. This latter category includes children with physical, cognitive, communication, social, emotional, or adaptive development. Additionally, Public Law 99-457, reauthorized in 1997 as PL 105-17, provides states with the required funding for intervention services to children from birth in addition to a family plan. Furthermore, the 1997 reauthorization of the Individuals with Disabilities Education Act has legally mandated families to be involved in the assessment and intervention process.

As a consequence of these mandates, the role of the school psychologist has expanded, leading to a need for appropriate training in preschool assessment and interventions (Li, Walton, & Nuttall, 1999; Meller, Ohr, & Marcus, 2001). Training in this domain is different from the traditional school-age assessments since preschool assessment has different purposes. Preschool assessment involves developing expertise in: (a) obtaining specific background information; (b) identification of children in need of further clinical information; (c) diagnosing and determining eligibility for services; (d) planning individual education plans (IEPs); and (e) valid monitoring progress in addition to *treatment integrity* (Appl, 2000; Wolery, 1996). Treatment integrity refers to the IEP goals and objectives that are part of the intervention/treatment plan. Termed differently, the *fidelity of the treatment* must be evaluated.

Additionally, school psychologists must develop cultural competencies for working closely with CLD families. This is especially important since preschool assessment *must* involve parents. Regrettably, professional training at the university level has been scarce and inadequate (Wilson & Reschly, 1996). At present, it appears that school psychologists interested in early intervention practice must attend workshops and institutes that offer preschool assessment training or search for universities that include this preparation in their programs. Although there is much literature to review regarding preschool assessment practices (Appl, 2000; Gredler, 2000; Li et al., 1999; Meller, Ohr, & Marcus, 2001; Nagle, 2000; Saye, 2003), an attempt to summarize some of the fundamental steps to take in such an assessment was reviewed by Appl (2000) as best practice for preschool assessment. An outline of the authors' recommendations is reviewed below:

1. *Identifying children in need of further evaluation.* This process is mandated by IDEA's Child Find and requires systematically locating, identifying, and evaluating children in need of special education services. Parents are informed about their child's development, screening, diagnosis, intervention options, and procedures for referrals. *Data collection* is the initial assessment step to take if a child has been identified with delays or with a disability. The identification process will result in a *screening* or *survey* of the child's abilities to conclude if there is a need for further evaluation. Screening should involve vision, hearing, general development, health, and environmental factors. School psychologists should ensure that the chosen screening instrument includes items that are relevant, culturally sensitive, and appealing to the young child.

The need for reservation in instrument selection also applies to preschool psychometric measures. There is much controversy noted in the literature regarding the need for caution in the use of screening and evaluative instruments; therefore, alternative approaches are suggested to supplement the results obtained from such testing.

2. *Diagnosing and determining eligibility.* This occurs when the screening results indicate a need for concern and a referral for further assessment to

determine any delays or disabilities as well as the child's special education eligibility status. Diagnosis usually includes the use of norm-referenced tests. Practitioners are urged to include multiple sources of information regarding the child's development (e.g., alternative approaches). IDEA states that diagnostic decisions cannot be made on the basis of only one measure.

3. *Planning individual programs.* Both the child's family and the professionals (school psychologist, social worker, educational consultant, speech and language pathologist, physical therapist, occupational therapist, and others) involved in the child's assessment will work together to develop an individual educational plan (IEP). The IEP should include goals and objectives pertaining to the child's strength and weaknesses, as well as specific instructional recommendations, and interventions should be noted. Program and placement decisions should always include the least restrictive environment (LRE). Moreover, parents should agree to the IEP stipulations.

4. *Monitoring progress.* The progress of the child must be monitored. Monitoring is accomplished by data-collection methods such as narrative descriptions, anecdotal records, direct observation procedures, and parental information. Alternative approaches such as portfolio assessment and dynamic assessment are also suggested for monitoring the child's progress.

Knowledge of the above steps when engaged in preschool evaluations is important since this systematic process will ensure that the school psychologist has not by-passed important recommendations for adequate assessment and recommendations.

An important part of preschool assessment is to determine which instrument to use for estimating the intellectual abilities of the infant or toddler. A list of the commonly used intelligence tests is provided below (see Reynolds & Kamphaus, 2003, for test characteristics and psychometrics).

1. Differential Ability Scales (DAS) (Elliott, 1990). Individually administered test of intelligence and achievement for ages 2 years and 6 months to 17 years and 11 months.

2. Wechsler Preschool and Primary Scale of Intelligence—Third Edition (WPPSI-III) (Wechsler, 2002). Individually administered test of intelligence for ages 2 years and 6 months through to 7 years and 3 months.

3. Woodcock-Johnson III Tests of Cognitive Abilities—Third Edition (WJ-III COG) (Woodcock, McGrew, & Mather, 2001). This is an individual assessment battery useful for ages 2 through 90.

4. Stanford-Binet Intelligence Scale–Fifth Edition (SB5) (Roid, 2003). A newly revised individually administered assessment of intelligence and cognitive abilities for ages 2 to 85+.

5. Bracken Basic Concept Scale (BBCS-R)–Revised (Bracken, 1998). An individually administered test used to assess the development of basic concepts (colors, sizes, numbers, and time) for children aged 2 years and 6 months through to 7 years and 11 months. It is useful for cognitive screening and can be used prior to a cognitive assessment but is not the customary intelligence test.

6. The Battelle Development Inventory (BDI) (Newborg, Stock, Wnek, Guidubaldi, & Svinicki, 1984). Individually administered battery of tests that evaluate primary developmental skills in children from birth to age 8. The BDI is not an intelligence test; however, it provides a cognitive measure in addition to adaptive and developmental measures.

As always, knowledge of the instrument's psychometric properties and ethnic breakdown in the standardization sample is vital prior to determining whether the instrument is adequate for particular racial/ethnic CLD children. Meller et al. (2001) provide tables illustrating current instruments for evaluating infants and toddlers as well as for preschool-aged children (see Suzuki, Ponterotto et al., 2001, pp. 478–481, 484–488).

In their review of formal assessment measures, Li and colleagues (1999) include instruments with a standardization sample that included culturally and linguistically diverse (CLD) preschoolers and which have special translations or adaptations with norms in numerous languages other than English. However, Li et al. (1999) caution that, although most of the tests they reviewed included minority populations in their standardized populations in relation to the national census, the tests may still have small numbers of some particular ethnic groups, and the inclusion of minority groups does not establish that the test is unbiased for these groups. Their review includes the following tests:

1. *Batería Woodcock-Muñoz: Pruebas de Habilidad Cognitiva–Revisada* (1996). This instrument is a similar Spanish version of the Woodcock-Johnson test (Woodcock & Johnson, 1989). This is one of the few cognitive batteries available in Spanish for preschoolers. The Batería Woodcock-Muñoz was submitted to a thorough translation/adaptation procedure to make the instrument suitable across different Spanish-speaking groups.

2. *The Bayley Scales of Infant Development–Second Edition* (Bayley, 1993) was included in this review because the 1988 norms represent majority and minority populations. To date, the reliability and validity data with diverse preschoolers have not been established. (*Note:* There is a newer

version, the *Bayley Scales of Infant and Toddler Development–Third Edition* (Bayley, 2005), which is a more comprehensive multi-scale of five subtests used to identify deficits in very young children across five major developmental domains: cognitive, language, motor, adaptive behavior, and social-emotional. This test is used to measure the child's strengths and abilities, and identify the child's competences. With a parent-oriented approach, the parent/caregiver participates in aspects of the administration, and the examiner can assess the infant or young child as he or she is doing something the child enjoys with someone he/she trusts.

3. *The Kaufman Assessment Battery for Children (K-ABC)* (Kaufman & Kaufman, 1983) was included in Li et al.'s (1999) review as a culturally sensitive instrument, and because most cognitive subtests can be administered in Spanish (translations are in the manual and were incorporated in the standardization sample). In addition, this test includes norms for different socioeconomic groups and African Americans. However, there is a newer version, the Kaufman Assessment Battery for Children (K-ABC II) (2003). The test publishers describe the new KABC-II as having a broader theoretical base, making it the instrument of choice for all cognitive assessment applications. Like the original K-ABC, the second edition more fairly assesses children of different backgrounds and with diverse problems, with small score differences between ethnic groups. Described as a test of exceptional cultural fairness, KABC-II subtests are designed to minimize verbal instructions and responses. This gives in-depth data with less "filtering" due to language. Also, test items contain little cultural content, so children of diverse backgrounds are assessed more fairly. Examiners can be confident of obtaining a true picture of a child's abilities—even when language difficulties or cultural differences might affect test scores.

An exceptional alternative to the new K-ABC is the inclusion of a dual theoretical model, which gives the examiner options to choose the Cattell-Horn-Carroll model for children from a mainstream cultural and language background. Or if crystallized ability may not be a fair indicator of the child's cognitive ability, the examiner may choose the Luria model, which excludes verbal ability. The examiner administers the same subtests on four or five ability scales, then interprets the results based on the chosen model. Either approach provides a global score that is highly valid and that shows small differences between ethnic groups in comparison with other comprehensive ability batteries. In addition, a nonverbal option allows the examiner to assess a child whose verbal skills are significantly limited.

4. *The Leiter International Scale–Revised* (LIS-R, 1996). This test may be a major addition to tests available for diverse preschoolers. Its standard

scores were normed on the 1994 census and include African Americans, Latin Americans, Asian Americans, and other minority populations.

Li et al. (1999) also reviewed early screening instruments:

1. *The Brigance Early Preschool Screen* (ages 2 years to 2 years and 6 months) measures gross motor, fine motor, social skills, self-help skills, cognitive skills, pre-academic, expressive, receptive language articulation, and behavioral/ self-control. It has directions in Spanish (Brigance, 1995).

2. *The Denver Developmental Screening Test-R* (ages 2 weeks to 6 years) screens for personal-social, fine-motor, language, and gross motor abilities. The test includes Spanish forms (Frankenburg, Dodds, & Faucal, 1990).

3. *Denver Developmental Indicator for Assessment of Learning-Revised* measures motor, concepts, and language (American Guidance Series, 1991).

4. *Preschool Screening System* (ages 2 years and 6 months to 6 years and 6 months) measures body awareness, visual-motor perception, language, and general information. It includes a parent questionnaire and translations into Spanish, Chinese, French, Vietnamese, Portuguese, Samoan, Laotian, Cambodian, Cape Verdean, Ilocano, Tagalog and Eskimo; none has had specific validity and reliability established (Hainsworth & Hainsworth, 1980) (see Li et al., 1999).

It is important to note that early screening for possible disabilities is a task that demands accuracy, since a valid estimate of weaknesses and/or disabilities should ultimately lead to early intervention planning for optimal developmental growth. For further readings in early identification of culturally and linguistically diverse children (aged 0 to 5 years), see the revised minibibliography prepared by Shaw, Goode, Ringwalt, and Ayankoya (2005).

Alternative Approaches to Preschool Assessment

Since it is mandated that a preschooler's family be included in the assessment process, several family-oriented assessment methods have been developed. Given the high concentration of racial/ethnic CLD student populations, emphasis must be placed on the cultural context of a child's environment. Alternative approaches ought to take into account cultural contextual information for a family-oriented preschool assessment. The Family-Oriented, Culturally Sensitive Assessment (FOCUS) (Meller, Ohr, & Marcus, 2001) is a fairly new model for assessing infants, toddlers, and preschool children that specifically incorporates the cultural context of the child's development. Meller et al. (2001) describe the FOCUS approach as having five assessment parts:

1. All professionals who are involved in assessing children from diverse cultural backgrounds must be adequately trained during their graduate studies, or via continuing professional development.

2. FOCUS assessment must involve comprehensive evaluation of family characteristics, resources, competencies, and needs.

3. A FOCUS assessment must assess all areas of developmental competency. This assessment should include both formal and informal techniques, across settings and over time.

4. FOCUS is an ongoing assessment of both the child and the family during the development and implementation of the (family) intervention plan.

5. FOCUS assessment always considers program evaluation and developmental change due to intervention (Meller, Ohr, & Marcus, 2001, p. 467).

The FOCUS approach involves several steps, objectives, and methods to utilize for completing these parts. These include developing a profile of the family's strengths and weaknesses vis-à-vis the sociocultural environment and a profile of the child's strengths and weaknesses, choosing culturally appropriate modes of assessment, multidisciplinary and parental agreement of adequate interventions, and continuous updating of the child's and family's profile of skills and needs.

Once again, school psychologists are encouraged to acquire the necessary multicultural competencies for delivering services to racial/ethnic and culturally diverse families. This should include knowledge of the culture of the child being evaluated and knowledge of the language. Recommendations have suggested that a "culture-language mediator" be employed when the practitioner is unable to comply with this requisite (Barrera & Kramer, 1997). Employing a mediator will help the school psychologist make the necessary observations of the child and family within a sociocultural context. Rogers-Adkinson, Ochoa, and Delgado (2003) compiled a useful review that assists teachers in understanding the special needs of families from diverse cultural backgrounds who have children with significant developmental delays. The authors note that the way the role of enculturation will affect family expectations and participation in special education is crucial. Knowledge of the various cultural viewpoints regarding developmental disabilities is a must for both educators and for the school psychologist (see Rogers-Adkinson et al., 2003).

Additionally, screening instruments should be norm-referenced and their standardized sample should include the child's ethnic group so as to compare the child's individual scores with a representative sample. The instruments' validity is especially important since it is within this domain that the predictive value is obtained. A reliable instrument should therefore have positive predictive value (see Glascoe, 1991; Taylor, Willits, & Lieberman, 1990). Another alternative process used in assessment of preschoolers is Judgment-Based Assessment (JBA). JBA is focused on obtaining the perceptions of parents, caregivers, and professionals concerning the child in his/her environment (Bagnato & Neisworth, 1994; see also Fleischer, Belgredan, Bagnato, & Ogonosky, 1990 for JBA).

Transdisciplinary Play-Based Assessment Methods

One more promising mode of non-psychometric assessment is the Transdisciplinary Play-Based Assessment (TPBA) model (Linder, 1993). This model uses a *cross-disciplinary* and *simultaneous* assessment method. It involves a team of professionals from different professions observing the child concurrently within motor, cognition, language, and adaptive behavior domains. Rating scales and criterion-referenced developmental checklists are used (see Linder, 1993), although play-based early childhood activities are used to assess the child's developmental strengths and weaknesses. A checklist is used that taps into the necessary skills needed for the play activities. This model has received empirical validation (Myers, McBride, & Peterson, 1996). A survey of school psychologists adopting TPBA practices revealed that play-based assessment was used 44 percent of the time, in combination with or in place of psychometric measures (Bagnato & Neisworth, 1994).

It is important to recall that psychometric measures used in preschool assessment do not include parental input, whereas TPBAs do. TPBA is in direct response to the previously cited mandates for the appropriate assessment of infants and preschoolers. Moreover, standardized assessment methods for early childhood evaluations have been queried because of their lack of predictive validity in determining future functioning as well as their incapacity to provide interventions (Bagnato & Neisworth, 1994). Conversely, many of the norm-referenced preschool measures are considered to have good predictive validity (Meller et al., 2001).

Standardized assessment practices have also been criticized because testing participation takes place under controlled conditions, adheres to consistency and uses only specific directions. With regard to young children, these standardized procedures are contrary to the nature of the young child. Instead, TPBA assessment activities are more relaxed and responsive to the child's nature.

Other benefits of TBPA are helpfulness in planning intervention programs, flexibility in allowing for modifications, and openness to making adaptations for children with disabilities. Particular advantages are its ease of use with children who have language difficulties and its flexibility in testing. These aspects may reduce assessment bias for the less verbal children who come from dissimilar cultural or linguistic backgrounds. Lastly, TPBA was originally developed for children with a range of disabilities. Therefore, the school psychologist conducting culturally sensitive preschool assessment with TPBA must bear in mind that the Observational Guidelines in TPBA primarily indicate the expected functioning/behaviors of English-speaking children from mainstream culture. Cultural issues are not addressed, even though there are cultural play behavior differences. TPBA is a fairly new approach to assessing preschoolers and its validity for CLD preschoolers is not yet known. School psychologists should ensure that each of the Observational Guidelines items are culturally suitable and that they measure the preschooler's behaviors from a cultural perspective since developmental expectations of preschoolers deviate significantly across cultures (Li et al., 1999; Meller et al., 2001; Nagle, 2000; Paget, 1999; Reynolds & Kamphaus, 2003).

Bilingual Preschoolers

As with older children, school psychologists must establish language proficiency of preschoolers as part of the assessment procedure. Several scales have been developed for the bilingual Spanish/English child. The preschool school psychologist should review bilingual issues in early childhood assessment practice (see Hamayan & Damico, 1991). A few possible measures of language skills for CLD preschoolers reviewed by Li and colleagues (1999) are:

1. *The Del Rio Language Screening Test*–English and Spanish (ages 3 years and 6 months to 11 years) (Toronto, Leverman, Hanna, Rosenzweig, & Maldonado, 1975) measures receptive vocabulary, sentence repetition for length and complexity, oral commands, and story comprehension in both languages, and can be used to measure bilingual proficiency and language development.

2. *The Expressive One-Word Picture Vocabulary Test–Revised*–Spanish Version (ages 2 years and 6 months to 10 years) measures expressive vocabulary by showing a picture and asking the child to name it (Gardner, 1990).

3. *The Illinois Test of Psycholinguistic Abilities*–Spanish Version, Japanese Version (ages 2 years and 6 months to 10 years) measures language in expressive and receptive modes and in three phases: input, meaning, and output (Paraskevopoulos & Kirk).

4. *The Peabody Picture Vocabulary Test–Test de Vocabulario de Imagenes* (ages 2 years to adult) measures receptive vocabulary by asking children to listen to a word and then choose the matching picture from a group of four (Dunn, Padilla, Lugo, & Dunn, 1986).

5. *The Preschool Language Scale–III Spanish Version* (ages birth to 3 years) measures auditory and expressive communication (Zimmerman, Steiner, & Pond, 1993).

Dynamic Assessments of Preschoolers

Dynamic assessment methods are also beneficial for preschoolers. Some recently developed tools are:

1. *The Children's Analogical Thinking Modifiability Test* (CATM) (Tzuriel & Klein, 1987) uses activities that involve thinking in analogies with blocks of three shapes, three colors, and two sizes.

2. *The Frame Test of Cognitive Modifiability Test* (FTCM) (Tzuriel & Klein, 1985) uses frames to observe and teach serial and patterning skills.

3. *The Children's Inferential Thinking Modifiability* (CITM) (uses a game of placing objects correctly into houses, which requires inferential thinking (see Li et al., 1999, Ch. 16).

These tools tap into developing cognitive skills in children aged 3 to 5 and are available from the School of Education in Ramat Gan, Israel (see Li et al., 1999, Ch. 16).

Other methods of assessing with the dynamic approach include the use of the House-Tree-Person test with a test-teach-test method when evaluating older preschoolers. In addition, learning styles can be deduced by observing the preschooler solving problems with toys. Dynamic assessment is equally successful in aiding the practitioner to create educational interventions. However, caution is advised with CLD children since this method's cultural impartiality may not be totally free of bias and there is concern regarding intertester reliability (Li et al., 1999). School psychologists are advised not to consider conducting a preschool assessment without appropriate training, either at the university level or from professional development workshops. Clinical supervision is also recommended.

Common Pitfalls in Assessment

School psychologists may encounter certain potential drawbacks. An important observation is the test translation methods that are sometimes employed in the schools by bilingual school psychologists. Some school-based bilingual psychologists working in multiethnic communities have resorted to personally translating the cognitive measures they use for evaluations. More specifically, each practicing bilingual school psychologist uses a personally translated version of the test.

I have attended numerous educational planning conferences (EPC) organized at the Committee of Special Education Review level and read countless psychological reports for monolingual Spanish CLD students that were tested in New York City with the Wechsler Scales and Stanford Binet Scales—all with different "idiosyncratic" translations of the subtest contents. Unable to find appropriate alternative measures for testing CLD children and English language learners (ELL), and very often having to shorten the time needed to conduct informal dynamic or curriculum-based assessments, these bilingual practitioners found themselves creating in Spanish what they perceived were "culturally appropriate" translations for the particular ethnic child being assessed.

On several occasions, Spanish-speaking children from the Dominican Republic, Puerto Rico, Honduras, and Uruguay were evaluated and placed in special education programs based on the results of these personally translated cognitive instruments.

This practice is habitual on the East Coast and probably is occurring in other parts of the United States as well. There are several reasons why self-imposed test translations are inappropriate. First, all cultures may not necessarily utilize the same semantics, and there may be differences between meanings of words, symbols or idioms, thus causing errors in self-imposed translations when the translator/examiner is from a different culture. Secondly, a self-translated test automatically breaks away from the standardized methods of the instrument. There are cutting-edge translations of some tests; however, it is impossible to translate different tests into the over two hundred languages spoken in the United States. This is the main reason why non-verbal tests have been developed.

Another factor that may have contributed to this personalized translation of intelligence tests is that there is a shortage of bilingual school psychologists (Bracken & McCallum, 2001). In consequence of this long-standing scarcity, along with the heavily referred cases of CLD children to school-based support teams, bilingual school psychologists may have been pressed into translating cognitive tests since other measures were nonexistent and they did not have the "time" to conduct more thorough qualitative assessments.

Within student populations which have had the opportunity to study math, numerical digits are not unknown stimuli, and in this area a careful translation of the original cognitive instrument could be used to test short-term memory across cultures—for example, Digit Span on the Wechsler

Scales with an item difficulty increase in digits forward and backward can be anticipated to be universal. However, translating the unique ability of word knowledge, in the form of defining vocabulary words in different languages, may not produce similar results in the instruments in different languages. Words in the target language may be comparatively simple, difficult, uncommon, or even nonexistent (van de Vijver, 2002). Undoubtedly, the proper translation of a cognitive measure involves "having both skills in designing adequate psychological measures and a thorough knowledge of the two languages and cultures involved" (van de Vijver, 2002). Even if the translator has the desired requirements, this is not a process that can be undertaken by a school-based psychologist at the last minute.

School administrators who find themselves intimidating bilingual school psychologists into "quick-fix" evaluations and/or translations in order to meet the compliance time allotted per case are inclined to defend their stance by responding that, due to a lack of bilingual school psychologists, CLD children will not be assessed in a timely manner if assessments are lengthy and time-consuming. And, of course, racial/ethnic CLD children manifesting academic problems that may be due to learning disabilities or emotional problems cannot be serviced properly without a psychological evaluation and recommendation (see Chapter 4 on learning disabilities). But is this truly the case? Anyone taking a guided tour of the New York City school districts to interview monolingual and bilingual school psychologists on this issue would find a resounding consensus on this time debate. As a practitioner, I have taken the tour. It appears that monolingual school psychologists have vented equal concerns about the heavy caseloads and the intimidation they experience to comply with "quick-fix" psychological evaluations. Bilingual school psychologists echo the same coercion experiences. Therefore, is it truly a lack of bilingual school psychologists that is causing this pressure to test speedily? Not if monolingual school psychologists are also pressured into similar quick-fix assessments. Correspondingly, the push for speedy assessments has impaired the mental health field as a result of cutbacks in reimbursement for assessment services (Suzuki, Ponterotto, & Meller, 2001). Perhaps too many children are being referred, or there is a phenomenon of too many racial/ethnic CLD children with too many academic or emotional problems. Maybe this is part of the case for the time debate. However, if it is, why is not the expertise of both monolingual and bilingual school psychologists utilized in the schools more often for consultation and counseling assistance to help resolve some of the referral problems? Certainly, this would alleviate the number of referrals if these were unwarranted? Or perhaps it would help teachers and students resolve the presenting problems?

Perhaps it is not just time that is needed. Certainly appropriate educational funding is an issue. One question that comes to mind concerns the importance of our children and our schools. If adequate funds were allocated to schools in order to hire additional mental health personnel and to increase resources, conceivably school psychologists—whether monolingual or bilingual—would have more time to conduct culturally sound assessments, and to provide consultation services to teachers, parents, and other school staff members. Although informal assessment has been encouraged in the schools (Lidz, 2001; Suzuki, Ponterotto, & Meller, 2001), the alleged supported informal assessment practices are still under the pressure of the ticking clock, thereby creating similar problems for practitioners.

Certainly, there are other issues not here mentioned that impede school psychologists and other school personnel from having the time to provide appropriate services to the many children who require supplementary assistance and supervision. Without doubt, there are many disappointed school psychologists—monolingual and bilingual—who would voice the same views expressed here. They are tired of having to battle with the administrators and the periodic funding "cuts" that impede ethically appropriate professional services. Is there a way out of this professional quandary? Indeed, there are several proactive suggestions.

The 2003 multicultural guidelines of the American Psychological Association (APA) (Guidelines on multicultural education, 2003) encourage all psychologists from every specialty domain to be change agents and policy planners. The recommended practice focus is on organizational change and policy development, and the responsibility of the psychologist is to lead the change and to influence policy. The guidelines further state that:

> Psychologists are often called upon to provide expert testimony to legislative bodies, boards of directors, and the courts on issues that involve ethnic/racial minority individuals and groups. Though it may appear that we are speaking from our informed voices as psychologists, psychologists' participation in these venues reflects the potential for policy development and structural organizational change. (p. 395)

This proactive suggestion is accompanied by the recommendations for psychologists to become familiar with leadership literature as "this offers constructs and descriptions of roles relevant to psychologists in policy planning. In effect, policy development is a change management process, one that can be informed by the vision, research, and experiences of psychologists" (p. 395).

The guidelines of the National Association of School Psychologists (NASP, 2000) also provide counsel on the professional conduct of school psychologists that basically underscores the need for "school psychologists to act as advo-cates for their students/clients" and "at the very least, school psychologists will do no harm" (NASP, 2000, pp.13, 654). This document states that school psychologists are under a professional obligation to speak out for the needs and rights of their students—most importantly, to protest even when it may be difficult to do so.

With this said, it appears that since schools are organizations with specific policies, school psychologists can be proactive in guiding changes that are needed for best practices in assessment. In situations demanding school psy-chologists to conduct "quick-fix" assessments or to "speed up" an informal assessment, school psychologists can become leaders in the promotion of culturally sensitive assessment practice by voicing loudly the policy changes that ought to be made at the district or school levels, and by participating in sociopolitical debates and/or legislative activities that focus on educational funding and school reforms. And their voices will be heard! One has only to review the influence of research on psychological/educational test construc-tion, empirically guided educational and behavioral interventions, and the various legislative actions that have improved the status of psychology in the schools over the years to see that being a change agent and/or advocate does produce the required changes.

On the other hand, unethical and undesirable practices can be intercepted by a single individual acting as a change agent. The true-life vignette in the box illustrates how a bilingual school psychologist on the East Coast was able to act as a change agent in his district.

Becoming a Change Agent

Ricardo, a bilingual Spanish/English school psychologist, was scheduled to serve on the Committee for Special Education (CSE) for a three-year term. Unfortunately, during his first year at the CSE he encountered several unethical practices. First, he was informed that it was "common practice" at the CSE to "test" four to five cases a week. Second, he was told that Fridays were allocated to six CSE reviews on bilingual cases. These expec-tations would leave him with only four days to conduct psychological assessments, notwithstanding the time he needed to write the psychological reports.

He observed that his monolingual and bilingual school psychologist colleagues were all complying with this compulsory schedule. Compliance to this schedule was accom-plished by "quick fix" assessments that eliminated classroom observations; prevented parental and teacher interviews; and in some case utilized inappropriate instruments. Additionally, confidential files or documentation of referral information were often unavailable. Ricardo was astounded at the results of these hurried assessments. He read poorly written psychological reports that failed to provide important culturally centered background information or describe students' abilities based on cultural variables. Although alarmed, Ricardo was determined not to be intimidated. A perusal of his bilingual-case weekly schedule revealed that he had to assess two recently arrived students from Honduras, and re-evaluate two Dominican and African-American students.

Following ethically sound psychological assessment procedures, Ricardo was unable to complete the four cases on his schedule. He was satisfied with the two initial assessments he had completed on the Honduras students. The EPC review of their cases resulted in appropriate recommendations. He overheard two of his colleagues remarking that he had "done a real professional job."

Regrettably, after three weeks at the CSE, he was called "upstairs" to the district manager's office. There he was informed that he was "taking too long" to complete his caseload and was submitted to a review of the "time" spent on his previous assessments. Ricardo remained professional at all times. He clearly explained the steps needed to conduct ethically and culturally sensitive assessments, remarking, "I cannot place a time limit on an assessment; each is individual and different." Although continually reprimanded, Ricardo did not budge. His colleagues began to look up to him. They voiced their own distress at the pressures endured. When presented with similar case schedules, they began to follow Ricardo's lead and conducted more appropriate assessments. Eventually, several were being called "upstairs" and each repeated Ricardo's now well-known response.

At a meeting ordered by the district manager, Ricardo and his colleagues presented their concerns regarding unethical assessments. Ricardo suggested that one day a week be allotted to report writing and that the rigid time expectations for assessments be reduced. He also proposed a new filing system to help organize confidential files, and offered to spend his lunch hour getting the system started. Several of his colleagues agreed to join him in this endeavor. Within two weeks, the CSE was operating on the newly suggested schedule. Stressors related to time pressures were noticeably alleviated. Having gained respect from his administrators and colleagues, Ricardo was asked to help supervise the caseload schedule. Assessments and educational planning conferences were markedly improved. Ricardo was regarded as a hero and a change agent!

This factual example that changes can occur places the onus on the school psychologist. It is an excellent motivator for the many practitioners who experience the same pressures. Moreover, it echoes back the recommendations made by NASP indicating that school psychologists should act as advocates/change agents and endeavor to protest, even when it may be difficult to do so.

Special Cases

This chapter has attempted to review practical recommendations for conducting assessments of racial/ethnic CLD children and youth. While much was covered, there are special cases which require more exact attentiveness. In an effort to alert the practitioner to such cases, the following succinct review is presented.

Bilingualism and English Language Learners

Students without English language skills, as well as those acquiring English language literacy skills have been described in the literature as English language learners (ELL). Currently, there is a large population of students who speak a language other than English. The number of ELL students in the United States is estimated to be between 2 and 6 million (Chavez & Amselle, 1997/98; Menken & Look, 2000; Moran & Hakuta, 1995). In some school districts, more than a hundred different languages are spoken. Languages spoken among the ELL student population include: Spanish, Vietnamese, Hmong, Cantonese, Cambodian, Korean, Laotian, Navajo, Tagalog, Russian, Haitian Creole, Arabic, Portuguese, Japanese, Armenian, Mandarin, Farsi, Hindi, and Polish (Faltis & Hudelson, 1998; Gonzalez et al., 1997, p. 5). Some 74 percent of all ELL students are Spanish speaking. The next largest group comprises Vietnamese speakers, with 3.9 percent population in the schools (Chavez & Amselle, 1997). Of all the languages spoken, Spanish is one of the most dominant in the United States and will continue to be the most dominant language besides English (Gonzalez et al., 1997).

In summary, more than half of the 50 million people in the United States speak Spanish (Cofresi & Gorman, 2004). Monolingual school psychologists should not shy away from acquiring cultural competencies for servicing ELL students. As mentioned, acquiring second language skills is recommended to attain multicultural competency in the assessment and intervention process. In any case, the majority of the students assessed or serviced will be ELL or bilingual students, leaving the practitioner little option but to acquire specific skills.

A school psychologist assessing bilingual or ELL children should review the testing instruments to be used for all areas of assessment (e.g., personality, behavior, cognitive, or language instruments). First, language proficiency must be determined. This can be accomplished by determining whether a bilingual student's languages are both uniformly developed (*proficient bilingual*). Unequally developed language skills will result in a *subordinate bilingual*. Second, for Spanish-English ELL students, Cofresi and Gorman (2004) suggest checking problems such as: the integration of English words into Spanish phrases; the use of English-based speech patterns; word pronunciations in both languages; and word order confusion. Additional suggestions and considerations are discussed in Chapter 11.

Separated Families and Adopted Ethnic Minority Students

Another important factor that school psychologists must take into account when assessing CLD children is that many may come from separated families. Children of divorced or separated families often have difficulties in the academic, emotional, and behavioral domains of functioning. Separation from the family system can involve placement in foster care. Some children are placed in foster homes due to parental abuse and neglect. Fifty-six percent of African American children are placed in foster homes, while 44 percent are serviced in their own homes. Conversely, 28 percent of white children are placed in foster homes and 72 percent receive services in their homes (Petit & Curtis, 1997) while Hispanic children are underrepresented. See Table 2.1 for a breakdown of children in foster care by race and ethnicity.

School psychologists are urged to assess the emotional/behavioral and academic status of children from separated families. Quite often, during the background information phase of assessment, practitioners may tend to accept family separation as common and not unusual (since many minority

Table 2.1   Children in Foster Care by Race/Ethnicity, 2000

Racial/Ethnic Identity	Percentage of Population	Percentage of All Children in Foster Care
White	68.8	47.8
Black or African American	14.8	35.3
American Indian or Alaska Native	1.1	3.1
Asian alone	3.4	1.1
Native Hawaiian/other Pacific Islander	0.2	0.3
Non-Hispanic other race	7.7	7.4
Two or more races	4.1	5.1

SOURCE: U.S. Census Bureau, Census 2000, Summary File 3.

NOTE: Total number of children under age 18 in the United States in 2000 = 71,843,425; total number of children living in foster care in the United States in 2000 = 291,507.

children do not come from intact families), thereby neglecting to search further for possible emotional or educational repercussions from the separation.

With regard to adoption of minority children, African American children are less likely to find adoptive parents than white children. The Multiethnic Placement Act of 1994 was authorized as a result of children in need of adoption. An objective of this federal legislation is to "recruit more foster and adoptive parents who reflect the racial and ethnic diversity of the children . . . who need foster and adoptive homes" (Huang & Arganza, 2003, p. 426). Adoption can affect a child's psychological health and identity development. In addition, researchers have questioned the emotional and identity growth of the transracial adopted child (Bagley, 1993; Brooks & Barth, 1999). Their findings suggest that the reasons for placement, gender, and age at adoption were more likely to have an impact than the adoption type (e.g., transracial versus in-racial). However, African American transracially adopted males tended to experience more problems than females.

Clearly, inquiring about the reasons for adoption can be beneficial. In a qualitative study conducted in three high schools on the East Coast, Martines (2005) found that several recently arrived Latino adolescent immigrants had officially been adopted by extended family members such as aunts and uncles, grandparents or close family friends. These adoption practices of families from Puerto Rico and the Dominican Republic were practiced in an attempt to provide educational and employment opportunities for these adolescents since the biological parents were unable to immigrate to the United States. Several of these youths were observed by their teachers to manifest emotional/behavioral problems. They experienced difficulties adjusting to a new family, culture, and a different educational system. Indeed, the majority had barely attended school in their homeland. Teachers remarked that some of these youths became involved in unlawful activities because they believed that "if they couldn't do well in school they had to find a quicker way to make money for their families back home or for their own independent needs." Indeed, recent reports on Latino and Latina youth incarcerations revealed that many were for drug offenses (Villarruel & Walker, 2002). Certainly there are distinct reasons for adoption; however, for adopted minority youths leaving their mother country, it appears that the effects of adoption may cause acculturation stress as well as discord with adopted parents if they had to separate from their biological parents at a later age. School psychologists should carefully study the reasons for adoption so as to better understand the CLD child's perceptive on the new family system, as well as to check for any possible conflicts between the family's view on education and the student's own ambitions.

Another important area of inquiry which should not be overlooked is the possibility of child neglect and abuse. Many professionals believe that practitioners servicing children who have been abused need to have expertise in the various cultural issues that are connected to the assessment and interventions of maltreatment (Winton & Mara, 2001; see Chapter 4 in this book).

In conclusion, it is now common knowledge that school psychologists are ethically responsible for developing expertise in multicultural assessment practice. This chapter compiled critical factors and assessment practices necessary for racial/ethnic CLD children and youth. Obviously, the mounting work of researchers on multicultural assessment will require practitioners to continuously keep abreast of best practices in this specialized domain of their profession. However, it is hoped that practitioners and researchers will collaborate by uniting and combining empirical and clinical practice techniques for the furtherance of best multicultural practices in school psychology assessment.

Bio-Cultural Case Study

In their explanation of the Bio-Cultural Model, Armour-Thomas & Gopaul-McNicol (1997a) present a cultural case study that includes a bio-cultural psychological assessment report. Their exemplary report is reproduced in Table 2.2 as an illustration of an ecologically sensitive assessment.

Presenting Problem and Client Description

Stephanie, a 12-year-old girl in sixth grade who was originally from Guyana, was referred for an initial evaluation by her teacher due to continued delays in all academic areas. The classroom teacher's records reflect that Stephanie was functioning at a third-grade level in math and a second-grade level in reading. The teacher felt that a special education program was needed to address Stephanie's academic delays.

The social history revealed that Stephanie lives with her mother, father, and grandmother. Her mother first came to the United States in the summer of 1994 and left her family in their homeland. The rest of the family, including Stephanie, followed two years later. All family members present themselves

CASE STUDY SOURCE: Armour-Thomas, E., & Gopaul McNicol, S. (1997a). A bio-ecological approach to intellectual assessment. *Cultural Diversity and Mental Health*, 3(2), 25–39. Reprinted with permission.

Table 2.2   Results of the Core Tests Administered

Assessment	Range
Wechsler Intelligence Scale for Children III	
Psychometric Assessment	
Verbal Scale IQ	Moderate Retardation
Performance Scale IQ	Moderate Retardation
Full-Scale IQ	Moderate Retardation
Psychometric Potential Assessment	
Verbal Scale IQ	Deficient
Performance Scale IQ	Deficient
Full-Scale IQ	Deficient
Vineland Adaptive Behavior Scales–Parent Edition	
Communication	Low
Social	Moderately Low
Daily Living Scales	Moderately Low
Other Intelligences	
Musical Intelligence: Clarinet	Advanced
Bodily/Kinesthetic: Dance	Advanced
Ecological Assessment	
Family/Community Support Assessment	Adequate

SOURCE: Armour-Thomas, E., & Gopaul McNicol, S. (1997a). A bio-ecological approach to intellectual assessment. *Cultural Diversity and Mental Health, 3*(2), 25–39. Reprinted with permission.

as a cohesive unit with strong extended family ties and good family support systems. According to Stephanie's parents, all developmental milestones were attained at age-expectant levels. However, there were reports of delays in reading upon her arrival in the United States. Her grandmother said that, while "Stephanie was not a star in reading in Guyana, she was certainly able to read enough to get by. She is definitely not stupid as they are trying to say in school."

Behavioral Observations

Stephanie, a pleasant, warm, friendly girl, presented herself in a cooperative, compliant manner throughout all phases of the evaluation. In general, her response time was slow and she approached the testing in a cautious, reflective manner. When she clearly did not know the answer, she became noticeably embarrassed: she would lower her head, frown, and look away from the examiner. Anxiety was also noted: she would bite her nails and crack her knuckles. Confidence was clearly lacking on all of the psychometric verbal and nonverbal subtests. In contrast, Stephanie demonstrated more confidence when asked to perform similar tasks in her natural environment. Furthermore, the anxiety noted when presented with the psychometric tests was not evident in her ecology. Stephanie presented herself in a calm, relaxed, self-assured manner while she was doing the grocery shopping and other activities. The result revealed a positive increment in her overall performance when tested at home and in the community.

Psychometric Assessment

On the Wechsler Intelligence Scale for Children III (WISC-III), Stephanie obtained a full-scale IQ score that placed her in the moderate range of retardation in both the verbal and nonverbal areas (see Table 2.2 above for test results). Individual subtests reveal moderate retardation in all areas assessed. Thus, on psychometric tests, Stephanie showed severe cognitive delays compared with her age peers nationwide.

Psychometric Potential Assessment

Of note is that, even when Stephanie was tested to her potential on the IQ test—for instance, when she was not placed under time pressure, when item equivalencies as well as the test-teach-retest techniques were implemented, and when the vocabulary words were contextually determined (that is, when asked to say the words in a surrounding context), or when time was suspended—deficiency in all areas was still evident. It was only when Stephanie was offered the opportunity to use paper and pencil that her cognitive functioning showed some significant gains. For instance, she clearly knew two-digit addition, subtraction, and multiplication, but had difficulty with one-digit division. Thus, by allowing Stephanie to use paper and pencil instead of relying on mental computations only, the examiner was able to determine that Stephanie had mastered some arithmetic skills but was unable to perform them without the aid of paper and pencil. In real-life situations, one is usually allowed the opportunity to work with pencil and paper, thus one can expect that Stephanie will be able to do basic calculations to function adequately well in her day-to-day duties.

Ecological Assessment

At home, in school, on the playground, and in the community, Stephanie is described as "bright, capable, and confident" by her family and friends. According to her mother, Stephanie prepares light lunches, helps with grocery shopping, and cares for her ailing grandmother when her mother is at work. In general, she performs all basic household and community chores commensurate with her age peers.

Moreover, in observing Stephanie on the community playground, it was clearly evident that she was able to perform several of the tasks found on the IQ tests. For instance, while she was unable to put the puzzles and blocks together on the Wechsler scales, she was adept at fixing a fan. Her mother explained that she fixes the appliances that malfunction at home. While assessing her ecologically, the examiner observed her as she dismantled the fan and reassembled it without difficulty. Evidently, this activity involves the same visual-motor coordination skills as putting puzzles together. The fact that Stephanie was unable to reintegrate the pieces of puzzles on the IQ test, but assembled smaller, more complex parts of a fan, suggests that cultural factors must be impeding her ability to perform a similar task on the standardized IQ test. Clearly, she is at least average in her visual-motor integration skills, though this was not evident on the psychometric measure.

Also significant was Stephanie's ability to remember a 13-item grocery list, although she was unable to recall as many as seven numbers on the Digit Span subtest of the Wechsler scales. Equally impressive was her ability to calculate basic addition and subtraction in the grocery store, although she demonstrated no mathematical concepts on the IQ test. Thus, in Stephanie's ecology—that is, in a real-life situation away from the testing environment— she showed good planning ability, good perceptual organization, fair mathematical skills, and good short-term memory. Unfortunately, none of these skills was manifested on the standardized, traditional IQ test or when she was tested to her cognitive potential via the same IQ measure. Evidently, from an ecological perspective, in real-life situations Stephanie's cognitive ability is at least low average.

Other Intelligences Assessment

In spite of Stephanie's deficiencies in the verbal area on the IQ test, she was able to formulate melodic, rhythmic, and harmonic images into elaborate ideas after only one year of learning the clarinet. Furthermore, although she never studied the steelpan, she showed great affinity toward this instrument "after watching her uncle play for only three weeks." Her mother stated that she also has an interest in other musical instruments, such as the guitar and the flute. An interview with her music teacher revealed that Stephanie plays the clarinet with such fluency and composes music so creatively that in the realm of musical intelligence she would be considered superior intellectually.

An interview with Stephanie's gym teacher and the community sports teacher revealed that she was very athletic in most sports. She was said to have a well-developed sense of timing, coordination, and rhythm when these pertained to playing cricket and netball, and is "a star in dancing." Her dance teacher says that she manifested accuracy, grace, speed, power, and great team spirit in all artistic endeavors. Also reported by her instructor was her ability to remain poised under pressure. An observation of her performing one of her dances allowed the examiner the opportunity to observe her bodily intelligence in its purest from, as she demonstrated flexibility and high technical proficiency.

Moreover, in observing her on the netball court, it was obvious that she had a well-developed sense of timing, coordination, and rhythm, which resulted in her being skillful in her gross and fine motor motions. Also of note was the social feedback offered by the sports teacher: "Stephanie is well respected by her peers, who often want her to play a leadership role in most competitions." She is described as "an inspiration to all." Thus, with respect to bodily/kinesthetic intelligence, she seems to be above average to superior.

Intellectually, Stephanie is functioning in the moderate range of retardation on the WISC-III psychometric test and in the mentally deficient range on the psychometric potential assessment. Because Stephanie attended school in her native country on a regular basis, she cannot be said to be educationally deprived. A diagnosis of mental retardation cannot be given either, because only moderately low functioning was noted on the Vineland Adaptive Behavior Scales. To be diagnosed as mentally retarded, low functioning in social adaptation ought to be evident. She was low only on communication, which was comparable to her score on the WISC-III psychometric test. After conducting a family assessment, it is clear that Stephanie functions adequately in her community and is respected by her peers. Thus, in spite of communication delays, there are no overall social adaptive deficiencies to characterize her as mentally retarded. At this juncture, Stephanie's intellectual functioning best fits the diagnosis of Learning Disabled Not Otherwise Specified. This category is for learning disorders that do not meet the criteria for any specific learning disorder and may include problems in all three core areas of reading, mathematics, and written expression.

Given the obvious delays in all academic skill areas and on the psychometric IQ test, one would be inclined to provide Stephanie with intensive instruction in all academic cognitive skill areas on a daily basis in a small, special educational classroom setting. Clearly, she does require the supportive environment of supplemental instruction. However, given her performance when assessed in other settings beyond the IQ testing environment, a less restrictive setting outside of the special education self-contained realm ought to be explored. For instance, Stephanie should be encouraged to pursue music, in particular the clarinet. Likewise, she ought to be encouraged to perfect her athletic skills, given her intellectual prowess in these areas as well. As such, the typical special education self-contained class where there is little emphasis on honing one's career or occupational skills is not recommended.

Stephanie's obvious intelligence in music renders her a prime candidate for a scholarship at a music school. Opportunities for career-related academic skill development, including essential work adjustment skills and direct work experience through daily practice in a music school, are needed for this child to attain her potential and be self-supportive.

Recommendations

The recommendations for Stephanie included a referral to Operation Athlete, an organization in New York City that provides scholarships for gifted athletes. This organization has an afterschool program whose goal is to recruit intelligent athletes who can go on to become professionals in their areas of expertise. Stephanie was recently offered a scholarship for remedial aid in all academic areas. According to school officials, if she remains motivated and shows great effort, other scholarships—even a possible college scholarship (depending on her academic performance)—are guaranteed. Stephanie was also referred to Sesame Flyer, a Caribbean organization that teaches immigrant families to play the steelpan, the guitar, and other musical instruments.

A follow-up on Stephanie's progress one year after the completion of the evaluation revealed a continued superiority in the nonacademic tasks, such as sports, and a slight positive increment in the academic areas. Stephanie was taught to transfer her knowledge from her ecology to the classroom setting by various exercises offered by the examiner, who continued treatment following the evaluation. Teacher and family consultation to assist those who worked more closely with Stephanie was offered on an ongoing basis. The most recent teacher report revealed "significant gains in math, vocabulary, and spelling." Stephanie ought to be monitored closely and assessed every six months to determine whether a less restrictive environment should be provided.

References

American Educational Research Association, American Psychological Association, & National Council on Measurement in Education. (1999). *Standards for educational and psychological testing* (2nd ed.). Washington, DC: American Educational Research Association.

American Psychological Association. (1992). *Ethical principles of psychologists and code of conduct*. Washington, DC: Author.

Anderson, W. A., Jr. (1988). The behavioral assessment of conduct disorders in a black child. In R. L. Jones (Ed.), *Psychoeducational assessment of minority group children: A casebook* (pp. 193–223). Berkeley, CA: Cobb & Henry.

Appl, D. J. (2000). Clarifying the preschool assessment process: Traditional practices and alternative approaches. *Early Childhood Education Journal, 27*(4), pp. 219–225.

Armour-Thomas, E. (1992). Intellectual assessment of children from culturally diverse backgrounds. *School Psychology Review, 21*(4), pp. 552–566.

Armour-Thomas, E., & Gopaul-McNicol, S. (1997a). A bio-ecological approach to intellectual assessment. *Cultural Diversity and Mental Health, 3*(2), 25–39.

Armour-Thomas, E., & Gopaul-McNicol, S. (1997b). Examining the correlates of learning disability: A bio-ecological approach. *Journal of Social Distress and the Homeless, 6*(2), 140–165.

Armour-Thomas, E., & Gopaul-McNicol, S. (1998). *Assessing intelligence: Applying a Bio-Cultural model*. Thousand Oaks, CA: Sage.

Bagley, C. (1993). Transracial adoption in Britain. A follow up study with policy considerations. *Child Welfare, 72,* 285–299.

Bagnato, S.J., & Neisworth, J.T. (1994). A national study of the social and treatment "invalidity" of intelligence testing for early intervention. *School Psychology Quarterly, 9,* 81–102.

Barona, A., & Pfeiffer, I. S. (1992). Effects of test administration and acculturation level on achievement scores. *Journal of Psychological Assessment, 10,* 1224–1232.

Barrera, I., & Kramer, L. (1997). From monologues to skilled dialogues: Teaching the process of crafting culturally competent early childhood environments. In P. J. Winston, J. A. McCollum, & C. Catlett (Eds.), *Reforming personnel preparation in early intervention* (pp. 217–252). Baltimore: Brookes.

Bayley, N. (1993). *Manual: Bayley Scales of Infant Development (2nd ed.)* San Antonio, TX: Psychological Corporation.

Bayley, N. (2005). *Bayley scales of infant and toddler development* (Bayley-III). San Antonio, TX: Harcourt Assessment.

Bergan, J. R. (1977). *Behavioral consultation*. Columbus, Ohio: Merrill.

Berg-Cross, L., & Chinen, R. T. (1995). Multicultural training models and the Person-in-Culture Interview. In J. G. Ponterotto, J. M. Casas, L. A. Suzuki, & C. M. Alexander (Eds.), *Handbook of multicultural counseling* (pp. 333–356). Thousand Oaks, CA: Sage.

Bogdan, R.C., & Biklen, S. K. (1982). *Qualitative research for education: An introduction to theory and methods*. Boston, MA: Allyn & Bacon.

Bracken, B. A. (1998). *Bracken Basic Concept Scale (BBCS-R)–Revised*. San Antonio, TX: Psychological Corporation.

Bracken, B. A., & McCallum, R. S. (1998). *Universal nonverbal intelligence test.* Training video. Itasca, IL: Riverside.

Bracken, B. A., & McCallum, S. (2001). Assessing intelligence in a population that speaks more than two hundred languages: A nonverbal solution. In L. A. Suzuki, J. G. Ponterotto, & P. J. Meller (Eds.), *The handbook of multicultural assessment: Clinical, psychological, and educational applications* (2nd ed.) (pp. 405–431). San Francisco: Jossey-Bass.

Braden, J. P. (1997). The practical impact of intellectual assessment issues. *School Psychology Review*, 26(2), pp. 242–249.

Brigance, A. H. (1995). *Brigance preschool screen.* Billerica, MA: Curriculum Associates.

Brooks D., & Barth, R. P. (1999). Adult transracial and inracial adoptees: Effects of race, gender, adoptive family structure, and placement history on adjustment outcomes. *American Journal of Orthopsychiatry*, 69(1), 87–100.

Brown, L., Sherbenou, R., & Johnson, S. (1997). Test of non-verbal intelligence-3. Austin, TX: Pro-Ed.

Budoff, M., & Corman, L. (1973). *The effectiveness of a group training procedure on the Raven learning potential measure with children of diverse racial and socioeconomic backgrounds.* Cambridge, MA: Research Institute for Educational Problems.

Budoff, M., & Corman, L. (1974). Demographic and psychometric factors elated to improved performance on the Koh's learning potential procedure. *American Journal of Mental Deficiency*, 78, 578–585.

Canino, I. A., & Spurlock, J. (2000). *Culturally diverse children and adolescents: Assessment, diagnosis, and treatment* (2nd ed.). New York: Guilford Press.

Cervantes, H. T. (1988). Nondiscriminatory assessment and informal data gathering: The case of Gonzaldo L. In R. I. Jones (Ed.), *Psychoeducational assessment of minority group children: A casebook* (pp. 239–256). Berkeley, CA: Cobb & Henry.

Chavez, I., & Amselle, J. (1997/98). Bilingual education theory and practice: Its effectiveness and parental opinions. In I. Orozco (Ed.), *Perspectives: Educating diverse populations* (pp. 87–90). Boulder, CO: Coursewise.

Cofresi, N. I., & Gorman, A. A. (2004). Testing and assessment issues with Spanish-speaking bilingual Latinos. *Journal of Counseling and Development*, 82, 99–107.

Constantino, G., & Malgady R. G. (1999). The Tell-Me-a-Story Test: A multicultural offspring of the Thematic Apperception Test. In L. Geiser & M. I. Stein (Eds.), *Evocative images: The Thematic Apperception Test and the art of projection* (pp. 191–206). Washington, DC: American Psychological Association.

Cross, W. E., Jr. (1991). *Shades of black: Diversity in African American identity.* Philadelphia: Temple University Press.

Dana, R. H. (1993). *Multicultural assessment perspectives for professional psychology.* Needham Heights, MA: Allyn & Bacon.

Dana, R. H. (2001). Clinical diagnosis of multicultural populations in the United States. In L. A. Suzuki, J. G. Ponterotto, & P. J. Meller (Eds.), *The handbook of multicultural assessment: Clinical, psychological, and educational applications* (2nd ed.; pp. 101–132). San Francisco: Jossey-Bass.

Dettmer, P., Thurston, L. P., & Dyck, N. (2002). *Consultation, collaboration, and teamwork for students with special needs.* (4th ed.). Boston, MA: Allyn & Bacon.

Dunn, L. M., Padilla, E. R., Lugo, D. E., & Dunn, L. M. (1986). *Examiner's manual for the Test de Vocabulário en Imágenes Peabody (TVIP) Adaptacion Hispanoamericano (Hispanic-American adaptation).* Circle Pines, MN: American Guidance Service.

Elliott, C.D. (1990). *Differential Ability Scales.* San Antonio, TX: Psychological Corporation.

Fagan, T. K., & Wise, P.S. (1994). *School psychology: Past, present, and future.* New York: Longman.

Faltis, C. J., & Hudelson, S. J. (1998). *Bilingual education in elementary and secondary school communities.* Boston: Allyn & Bacon.

Feuerstein, R. (1979). *The dynamic assessment of retarded performers. The Learning Potential Assessment Device, theory, instruments, and techniques.* Baltimore, MD: University Park Press.

Feuerstein, R., Falik, L. H., & Feuerstein, R. (1998). The Learning Potential Assessment Device: An alternative approach to the assessment of learning potential. In R. J. Samuda, R. Feuerstein, A. S. Kaufman, J. Lewis, R. J. Sternberg & Associates (Eds.), *Advances in cross-cultural assessment* (pp. 100–159). Thousand Oaks, CA: Sage.

Feurstein, R., Rand, Y., & Hoffman, M. B. (1979). *The dynamic assessment of retarded performers: The learning potential assessment device, theory, instruments, and techniques.* Glenview, IL: Scott, Foresman.

Fine, M. (1992). *Disruptive voices: The possibilities of feminist research.* Ann Arbor, MI: University of Michigan Press.

Fleischer, K. M., Belgredan, J. H., Bagnato, S. J., & Ogonosky, A. B. (1990). An overview of judgment-based assessment. *Topics in Early Childhood Special Education, 10,* 13–23.

Frankenburg, W. K., Dodds, J. A., & Faucal, A. (1990). *Denver Developmental Screening Test II.* Denver, CO: University of Colorado Press.

Gardner, H. (1983). *Frames of mind: The story of multiple intelligence.* New York: Basic Books.

Gardner, H. (1993). *Frames of mind: The theory of multiple intelligences* (rev. ed.). New York: Basic Books.

Gardner, M. F. (1990). *Expressive One-Word Picture Vocabulary Test—Revised.* Novato, CA: Academic Therapy Publications.

Glascoe, F. P. (1991). Development screening: Rationale, methods, and application. *Infants and Young Children, 4,* 1–10.

Glesne, C., & Peshin, A. (2000). *Becoming qualitative researchers: An introduction.* New York: Longman.

Gonzalez, V., Brusca-Vega, R., & Yawkey, T. (1997). *Assessment and instruction of culturally and linguistically diverse students with or at risk of learning problems. From research to practice.* Boston, MA: Allyn & Bacon.

Gopaul-McNicol, E., & Armour-Thomas, S. (2002). *Assessment and culture: Psychological tests with minority populations.* New York: Academic Press.

Gopaul-McNicol, E., Black, K., & Clark-Castro, S. (1997). Introduction: Intelligence testing with minority children. *Cultural Diversity and Mental Health, 3*(2), 1–4.

Gopaul-McNicol, S., & Brice Baker, J. (1998). *Cross-cultural practice: Assessment, treatment, and training.* New York: John Wiley & Sons.

Gredler, G. R. (2000). Early childhood education—assessment and intervention: What the future holds. *Psychology in the Schools, 37*(1), 73–79.

Griggs, S. A., & Dunn, R. (1989). The learning styles of multicultural groups and counseling implications. *Journal of Counseling and Development, 17*, 146–155.

Guidelines on multicultural education, training, research, practice, and organizational change for psychologists. (2003, May). *American Psychologist,* pp. 377–402.

Gutierrez-Clellen, V., & Pena, E. (2001). Dynamic assessment of diverse children: A tutorial. *Language, Speech, and Hearing Services in Schools, 32*, 212–224.

Hainsworth, P. K., & Hainsworth, M. L. (1980). *Preschool screening system.* Pawtucket, RI: Early Recognition and Intervention Systems.

Hamayan, E. V., & Damico, J. S. (1991). *Limiting bias in the assessment of bilingual students.* Austin, TX: Pro-ed.

Hammill, D.D., Pearson, N.A., & Wiederholt, J. L. (1996). *Comprehensive Test of Nonverbal Intelligence (CTONI).* Austin, TX: Pro-Ed.

Harris, A., Reynolds, M., & Koegel, H. (1996). Nonverbal assessment: Multicultural perspectives. In L. Suzuki, P. Meller, & J. Ponterotto (Eds.), *Handbook of multicultural assessment* (pp. 223–252). San Francisco: Jossey-Bass.

Hatch, J. A. (2002). *Doing qualitative research in education settings.* Albany, NY: State University of New York Press.

Helms, J. E. (1985). Cultural identity in the treatment process. In P. Pedersen (Ed.), *Handbook of cross-cultural counseling and therapy.* Westport, CT: Greenwood Press.

Helms, J. E. (1992). Why is there no study of cultural equivalence in standardized cognitive ability testing? *American Psychologist, 47*, 1083–1101.

Helms, J. E. (2002). A remedy for the black–white test-score disparity. *American Psychologist, 57*, 303–304.

Helms-Lorenz, M., & Tilburg, U. (1995). Cognitive assessment in education in a multicultural society. *European Journal of Psychological Assessment, 11*(3), 158–169.

Herrnstein, R. J., & Murray, C. (1994). *The bell curve: Intelligence and class structure in American life.* New York: Free Press.

Horner, R. H., Sugai, G. H., & Horner, H. F. (2000). A schoolwide approach to student discipline. *School Administrator, 57*(2), 20–23.

Huang, L. N., & Arganza, G. F. (2003). Children of color in systems of care: An imperative for cultural competence. In J. T. Gibbs, & L. N. Huang (Eds.), *Children of color: Psychological interventions with culturally diverse youth* (2nd ed.; p. 426). San Francisco: Jossey-Bass.

Isajiw, W. W. (1990). Ethnic identity retention. In R. Breton, W. W. Isajiw, W. E. Kalbach, & J. G. Reitz (Eds.), *Ethnic identity and equality* (pp. 34–91). Toronto: University of Toronto Press.

Ivey, A., & Ivey, M. (1998). Reframing DSM-IV: Positive strategies from developmental counseling and therapy. *Journal of Counseling and Development, 76*, 334–350.

Kamphaus, R. W. (2001). *Clinical assessment of child and adolescent intelligence* (2nd ed.). Boston, MA: Allyn & Bacon.

Kaufman, A. S. (1990). *Assessing adolescent and adult intelligence.* Boston, MA: Allyn & Bacon.

Kaufman, A. S. (2000). Intelligence tests and school psychology: Predicting the future by studying the past. *Psychology in the Schools, 31*(1), 7–16.

Kaufman, A. S., & Kaufman, N. L. (1983). *Interpretive manual for the Kaufman Assessment Battery for Children.* Circle Pines, MN: American Guidance Service.

Kaufman, A. S., & Kaufman, N. L. (1993). *Manual for the Kaufman Adolescent and Adult Intelligence Test (KAIT).* Circle Pines, MN: American Guidance.

Kaufman, A. S., & Kaufman, N. L. (2004). *Kaufman assessment battery for children– 3rd edition (K-ABC III).* Circle Pines, MN: American Guidance Service.

Kopala, M. & Suzuki, L. A. (Eds.). (1999). *Using qualitative methods in psychology.* Thousand Oaks, CA: Sage.

Li, C., Walton, J. R., & Nuttall, E. V. (1999). Preschool evaluation of culturally and linguistically diverse children. In E. V. Nuttall, I. Romero, & J. Kalesnik (Eds.), *Assessing and screening preschoolers: Psychological and educational dimensions* (pp. 296–317). Boston, MA: Allyn & Bacon.

Lidz, C. S. (Ed.) (1987). *Dynamic assessment: An interactional approach to evaluating learning potential.* New York: Guilford Press.

Lidz, C. (2001). Multicultural issues and dynamic assessment. In L. A. Suzuki, J. G. Ponterotto, & P. J. Meller (Eds.), *The handbook of multicultural assessment: Clinical, psychological, and educational applications* (2nd ed.; pp. 523–540), San Francisco: Jossey-Bass.

Lidz, C. S., & Elliott, J. (Eds.). (2000). *Dynamic assessment: Prevailing models and applications.* Oxford, UK: Elsevier Science.

Linder, T. W. (1993). *Transdisciplinary play-based assessment: A functional approach to working with young children* (rev. ed.). Baltimore, MD: Brookes.

Liu, W. M. & Clay, D. L. (2002). Multicultural counseling competencies: Guidelinesin working with children and adolescents. *Journal of Mental Health Counseling, 24*(2), 177–187.

Lopez, E. (2000). Conducting instructional consultation through interpreters. *School Psychology Review, 29*(3), 378–388.

Losardo, A. & Notari-Syverson, A. (2001). *Alternative approaches to assessing young children.* Baltimore, MD: Brookes.

Luria, A. R. (1966). *Higher cortical functions in man.* New York: Basic Books.

Malgady, R. G. (1996). The question of cultural bias in assessment of diagnosis of ethnic minority clients: Let's reject the null hypothesis. *Professional Psychology: Research and Practice, 27,* 73–77.

Martines, D. (2005). Teachers' perceptions of multicultural issues in psychoeducational settings. *Qualitative Report, 10*(1), 1–20.

Meller, P. J., Ohr, P. S., & Marcus, R. A. (2001). Family-oriented, culturally sensitive (FOCUS) assessment of young children. In L. A. Suzuki, J. G. Ponterotto, & P. J. Meller (Eds.), *The handbook of multicultural assessment: Clinical, psychological, and educational applications* (2nd ed.; pp. 461–496). San Francisco: Jossey-Bass.

Menken, K., & Look, K. (2000). Making chances for linguistically and culturally diverse students. *Education Digest, 65*(8), 14–20.

Mercer, J. R. (1979). In defense of racially and culturally non-discriminatory assessment. *School Psychology Digest, 8*(1), 89–115.

Mercer, J. R., & Lewis, J. (1978). *System of multicultural pluralistic assessment.* New York: Psychological Corporation.

Merrick, E. (1999). An exploration of quality in qualitative research: Are reliability and validity relevant? In M. Kopala, & L.A. Suzuki (Eds.), *Using qualitative methods in psychology* (p. 31). Thousand Oaks, CA: Sage.

Meyers, L. J. (1991). Expanding the psychology of knowledge optimally: The importance of worldview revisited. In R. L. Jones (Ed.), *Black psychology* (pp. 15–28). Berkeley, CA: Cobb and Henry.

Moran, C. E., & Hakuta, K. (1995). Bilingual education: Broadening research perspectives. In J. A. Banks & C. A. McGee Banks (Eds.), *Handbook of research on multicultural education* (pp. 427–444). New York: Macmillan.

Morrison, J. A. (1988). Rudy Garcia: A SOMPA case study. In R. L. Jones (Ed.), *Psychoeducational assessment of minority group children: A casebook.* Berkeley, CA: Cobb and Henry.

Mushi, S. L. P. (2002). Acquisition of multiple languages among children of immigrant families: Parents' role in the home-school language pendulum. *Early Child Development and Care, 172,* 517–530.

Myers, C. L., McBride, S. L., & Peterson, C. A. (1996). Transdisciplinary, playbased assessment in early childhood special education: An examination of social validity. *Topics in Early Childhood Special Education, 16*(1), 102–126.

Nagle, R. J. (2000). Issues in preschool assessment. In B. A. Bracken (Ed.), *The psychoeducational assessment of preschool children* (pp. 19–32). Boston: Allyn & Bacon.

Naglieri, J. A. (1985). *Matrix Analogies Test, Expanded Form.* San Antonio, TX: Psychological Corporation.

Naglieri, J. A. (1996). *Naglieri Nonverbal Ability Test.* San Antonio, TX: Psychological Corporation.

Naglieri, J. A., & Bardos, A. N. (1997). *General Ability Measure for Adults (GAMA).* Minneapolis, MN: NCS Pearson.

Naglieri, J. A., & Das, J. P. (1997). Intelligence revised: The planning, attention, simultaneous, successive (PASS) cognitive processing theory. In R. R. Dillon (Ed.), *Handbook on testing* (pp. 136–163). Westport, CT: Greenwood Press.

National Association of School Psychologists (NASP) (2000). *Professional conduct manual.* Bethesda, MD: NASP.

Neisworth, J. T., & Bagnato, S. J. (1988). Assessment in early childhood special education. In S. L. Odom, & M. B. Karnes (Eds.), *Early intervention for infants and children with handicaps: An empirical base* (pp. 23–49). Baltimore, MD: Brookes.

Newborg, J., Stock, J. R., Wnek, L., Guidabaldi, J., & Svinicki, J. (1984). *Battelle Developmental Inventory Screening Test.* Allen, TX: DLM Teaching Resources.

Ochoa, S. H. (2003). Assessment of culturally and linguistically diverse children. In C. R. Reynolds, & R. W. Kamphaus (Eds.), *Handbook of psychological and educational assessment of children: Intelligence, aptitude, and achievement* (2nd Ed.). New York: Guilford Press.

Ogbu, J. (1992). Understanding cultural diversity and learning. *Educational Research, 21*(8), 5–14.

Padilla, A. M. (2001). Issues in culturally appropriate assessment. In L. A. Suzuki, J. G. Ponterotto, & P. J. Meller (Eds.). *Handbook of multicultural assessment:*

Clinical, psychological, and educational applications (2nd ed.; pp. 5–28). San Francisco: Jossey-Bass.

Paget, K. D. (1999). Ten years later: Trends in the assessment of infants, toddlers, preschoolers, and their families. In C. R. Reynolds and T. R. Gutkin (Eds.), *The handbook of school psychology* (3rd ed.). New York: John Wiley & Sons.

Parham, T. A., White, J. L., & Ajamu, A. (1999). *The psychology of blacks: An African centered perspective* (3rd ed.). Upper Saddle River, NJ: Prentice Hall.

Patton, M.Q. (1990). *Qualitative evaluation and research methods* (2nd ed.). Newbury Park, CA: Sage.

Petit, M., & Curtis, P. (1997). *1997 CWLA stat book: Child abuse and neglect: A look at the states.* Washington, DC: Child Welfare League of America.

Polkinghorne, D. E. & Gribbons, B. C. (1999). Applications of qualitative research strategies to school psychology research problems. In C. R. Reynolds and T. R. Gutkin (Eds.), *The handbook of school psychology* (3rd ed.). New York: John Wiley & Sons.

Ponterotto, J. G., Fuertes, J. N., & Chen, E. C. (2000). Models of multicultural counseling. In S. D. Brown, & R. W. Lent (Eds.), *Handbook of counseling psychology* (3rd ed.; pp. 339–369). New York: John Wiley & Sons.

Ponterotto, J. G., Gretchen, D., & Chauhan, R. V. (2001). Cultural identity and multicultural assessment: Quantitative and qualitative tolls for the clinician. In L. A. Suzuki, J. G. Ponterotto, & P. J. Meller (Eds.), *Handbook of multicultural assessment: Clinical, psychological and educational applications.* San Francisco: Jossey-Bass.

Prediger, D. J. (1993a). Multicultural assessment standards: A compilation for counselors. *Measurement and evaluation in counseling and development, 27*(2), 68–73.

Prediger, D. J. (Ed.). (1993b). *Multicultural assessment standards: A compilation.* Alexandria, VA: Association for Assessment in Counseling.

Quintana, S. M., Troyano, N., & Taylor, G. (2001). Cultural validity and inherent challenges in quantitative methods for multicultural research. In J. Ponterotto, J. M. Casas, L. S. Suzuki, & C. M. Alexander (Eds.), *Handbook of multicultural counseling* (pp. 604–630). Thousand Oaks, CA: Sage.

Raven, J. C., Court, J. H., & Raven, J. (1947a). *Standard progressive matrices.* London: Lewis.

Raven, J. C., Court, J. H., & Raven, J. (1947b). *Coloured standard progressive matrices.* London: Lewis.

Raven, J., Raven, J. C., & Court, J.H. (1998). *Manual for Raven's progressive matrices and vocabulary scales.* Oxford, UK: Oxford University Press.

Reschly, D. J., & Wilson, M. S. (1995). School psychology practitioners and faculty: 1986 to 1991–92 trends in demographics, roles, satisfaction, and system reform. *School Psychology Review, 24*(1), 62–80.

Reynolds, C. R., & Kamphaus, R. W. (Eds.). (2003). *Handbook of psychological and educational assessment of children: Intelligence, aptitude, and achievement* (2nd ed.). New York: Guilford Press.

Ridley, C. R., Li, L., & Hill, C. (1998). Multicultural assessment: reexamination, reconceptualization, and practical application. *Counseling Psychologists, 26*(6), 827–884.

Rogers, M. R., Ingraham, C. L., Bursztyn, A., Cajigas-Segredo, N., Esquivel, G., Hess, R., Nahari, S., & Lopez, E. (1999). Providing psychological services to racially, ethnically, culturally, and linguistically diverse individuals in the schools. *School Psychology International, 20*(3), 243–264.

Rogers-Adkinson, D. L., Ochoa, T. A., & Delgado, B. (2003, Spring). Developing cross-cultural competence: Serving families of children with significant developmental needs. *Focus on Autism and Other Developmental Disabilities, 18*(1), 4–8.

Roid, G. H. (2003). *Stanford-Binet Intelligence Scale–Fifth Edition* (SB5). Itasca, IL: Riverside.

Roid, G. H., & Miller, L. J. (1997). *Leiter International Performance Scale–Revised.* Wood Dale, IL: Stoelting.

Rosenfield, S. A. (1987). *Instructional consultation.* Hillsdale, NJ: Lawrence Erlbaum.

Saenz, T. I., & Huer, B. M. (2003). Testing strategies involving least biased language assessment of bilingual children. *Communication Disorders Quarterly, 24*(40), 184–193.

Salvia, J., Ysseldyke, J. E., & Bolt, S. (2007). *Assessment in special and inclusive education.* Boston: Houghton Mifflin.

Saye, K. B. (2003). Preschool assessment. In C. R. Reynolds & R. W. Kamphaus (Eds.), *Handbook of psychological and educational assessment of children: Intelligence, aptitude, and achievement* (2nd ed.; pp. 187–203). New York: Guilford Press.

Sciarra, D. T. (1999). *Multiculturalism in counseling.* Ithaca, IL: Peacock.

Scott, H. J. (1994). Practitioners and cross-cultural assessment: A practical guide to information and training. *Measurement & Evaluation in Counseling & Development, 27*(2), 103–316.

Shaw, E., Goode, S., Ringwalt, S., & Ayankoya, B. (2005). Minibibliography: Early identification of culturally and linguistically diverse children (aged 0–5). *Communication Disorders Quarterly, 26*(1), 49–54.

Sperry, R. W. (1974). Lateral specialization in the surgically separated hemispheres. In F. O. Schmitt & F. G. Worden (Eds.), *The neurosciences: Third study program.* Cambridge, MA: MIT Press.

Sternberg, R. (1985). *Beyond IQ: A triarchic theory of human intelligence.* New York: Cambridge University Press.

Sternberg, R. J., & Grigorenko, E. L. (2001). Ability testing across cultures. In L. A. Suzuki, J. G. Ponterotto, & P. J. Meller (Eds.). *Handbook of multicultural assessment: Clinical, psychological, and educational applications* (pp. 335–358). San Francisco: Jossey-Bass

Strauss, A., & Corbin, J. (1990). *Basics of qualitative research: Grounded theory procedures and techniques.* New York: Sage.

Sue, S. (1998). In search of cultural competence in psychotherapy and counseling. *American Psychologist, 54*, 1070–1077.

Suzuki, L., Ponterotto, J. G., & Meller, P. (2001). Multicultural assessment: Trends and directions revisited. In L. A. Suzuki, J. G. Ponterotto, & P. J. Meller (Eds.), *Handbook of multicultural assessment: Clinical, psychological and educational applications* (pp. 569–574). San Francisco: Jossey-Bass.

Suzuki, L., Ponterotto, J. G., & Meller, P. J. (Eds.). (2001). *Handbook of multicultural assessment: Clinical, psychological, and educational applications.* San Francisco: Jossey-Bass.

Suzuki, L., Prendes-Lintel, M. Wertlieb, L., & Stallings, A. (1999). Exploring multicultural issues using qualitative methods. In M. Kopala, & L. A. Suzuki (Eds.), *Using qualitative methods in psychology* (pp. 123–133). Thousand Oaks, CA: Sage.

Suzuki, L., Short, E. L., Pieterse, A., & Kugler, J. (2001). Multicultural issues and the assessment of aptitude. In L. A. Suzuki, J. G. Ponterotto, & P. J. Meller (Eds.), *Handbook of multicultural assessment: Clinical, psychological and educational applications* (pp. 359–382). San Francisco: Jossey-Bass.

Suzuki, L., Vraniak, D., & Kugler, J. (1996). Intellectual assessment across cultures. In L. Suzuki, P. Meller, & J. Ponterotto (Eds.), *Handbook of multicultural assessment: Clinical, psychological and educational applications* (pp. 141–177). San Francisco: Jossey-Bass.

Taylor, R. L, Willits, P., & Lieberman, N. (1990). Identification of preschool children with mild handicaps: The importance of cooperative effort. *Childhood Education*, 67(1), 26–31.

Tharp, R. G., & Wetzel, R. J. (1969). *Behavior modification in the natural environment*. New York: Academic Press.

Thorndike, R. L., Hagen, E. P., & Sattler, J. M. (1986). *Technical manual for the Stanford-Binet Intelligence Scale: Fourth Edition*. Chicago: Riverside.

Toronto, A., Leverman, D., Hanna, C., Rosenzweig, P., & Maldonado, A. (1975). *The Del Rio Language Screening Test*. Austin, TX: National Educational Laboratory.

Tzuriel, D., & Klein, P. S. (1985). The assessment of analogical thinking modibiability among regular, special education, and mentally retarded children. *Journal of Abnormal Child Psychology*, (4), 539 -552.

Tzuriel, D., & Klein, P. S. (1987). Assessing the young child: Children's analogical thinking modifiability. In C. S. Lidz (Ed.), *Dynamic assessment: An interactional approach to evaluating learning potential* (pp. 268–287). New York: Guilford.

van de Vijver, F. J. R. (2002). Cross-cultural assessment: Value for money? *Applied Psychology: An international review*, 51(4), 5454–5566.

Vaughn, S., & Fuchs, L. S. (2003). Redefining learning disabilities as inadequate response to instruction: The promise and potential problems. *Learning Disabilities: Research and Practice, 18*(3), 137–146.

Villaruel, F., & Walker, N. E. (2002). *Donde esta la justicia?* Lansing, MI: Michigan State University, Building Blocks for Youth.

Vygotsky, L. S. (1978). *Mind in society: The development of higher psychological processes*. M. Cole, V. John-Steiner, S. Scribner, & E. Souberman, Eds. Cambridge, MA: Harvard University Press.

Wechsler, D. (2002). *Wechsler Preschool and Primary Scale of Intelligence–Third Edition (WPPSI-III)*. San Antonio, TX: Psychological Corporation.

Wilson, M. S., & Reschly, D. J. (1996). Assessment in school psychology training and practice. *School Psychology Review*, 25(1), 9–23.

Winton, M. A., & Mara, B. A. (2001). *Child abuse and neglect: Multidisciplinary approaches*. Needham Heights, MA: Allyn & Bacon.

Wolery, M. (1996). Monitoring child progress. In M. McLean, D. B. Bailey, & M. Wolery (Eds.), *Assessing infants and preschoolers with special needs* (pp. 519–560). Englewood Cliffs, NJ: Merrill.

Woodcock, R. W., McGrew, K. S., & Mather, N. (2001). *Woodcock-Johnson Psycho-Educational Battery, Third Edition (WJ-3)*. Chicago: Riverside.

Woodcock, R. W., & Johnson, M. B. (1989). *Woodcock-Johnson Psycho-Educational Battery–Revised*. Allen, TX: DLM Teaching Resources.

Woodcock, R. W., & Mather, N. (1989). *WJ-R Tests of Achievement: Examiner's manual*. Allen, TX: DLM Teaching Resources.

Ysseldyke, J. E., & Christensen, S. (2002). *Functional assessment of academic behavior: Creating successful learning environments*. Longmont, CO: Sopris West.

Ysseldyke, J. E., & Elliott, J. L. (1998). Effective instructional practices: Implications for assessing instructional environments. In C. Reynolds & T. Gutkin (Eds.), *The handbook of school psychology*. New York: John Wiley & Sons.

Zimmerman, I. L., Steiner, V. G., & Pond, R. E. (1993). *Preschool Language Scale–3: Spanish Edition*. San Antonio, TX: Psychological Corporation.

Annotated Bibliography

Canino, I. A., & Spurlock, J. (2000). *Culturally diverse children and adolescents: Assessment, diagnosis, and treatment* (2nd ed.). New York: Guilford Press. *This text reviews issues in assessment, diagnosis, and treatment and is illustrated with numerous case vignettes.*

Paniagua, F. A. (2005). *Assessing and treating culturally diverse clients: A practical guide*. Thousand Oaks, CA: Sage Publications. *This book briefly summarizes key practical guidelines that all clinicians can apply when assessing, diagnosing, or treating culturally diverse clients. The author accents clinical work with African American, Hispanic, American Indian, and Asian clients.*

Losardo, A., & Notari-Syverson, A. (2001). *Alternative approaches to assessing young children*. Baltimore, MD: Brookes. *This text illustrates six alternative method models—naturalistic, focused, performance, portfolio, dynamic, and curriculum-based language—for culturally, linguistically, and developmentally diverse children.*

Mclean, M. E., Bailey, D. B., & Wolery, M. (Eds.). (2003) *Assessing infants and preschoolers with special needs* (3rd ed). Upper Saddle River, NJ: Prentice Hall. *A good source for assessing preschoolers with disabling conditions.*

Reynolds, C. R., & Kamphaus, R. W. (Eds.). (2003). *Handbook of psychological and educational assessment of children: Intelligence, aptitude, and achievement* (2nd ed.). New York: Guilford Press. *This handbook includes a complete review of the assessment of intelligence and learning styles/strategies, academic skills, and special topics in mental testing.*

Suzuki, L. A., Ponterotto, J. G., & Meller, P. (Eds.). (2001). *The handbook of multicultural assessment: Clinical, psychological, and educational applications* (2nd ed.). San Francisco: Jossey-Bass. *This handbook is a comprehensive text focusing on multicultural assessment and commonly used assessment instruments and their application to diverse populations.*

Recommended Articles

The following articles are important to consider in this area:

Dana, R. H. (2000). An assessment-intervention model for research and practice with multicultural populations. In R. H. Dana (Ed.), *Handbook of cross-cultural and multicultural personality assessment* (pp. 5–16). Mahwah, NJ: Lawrence Erlbaum.

Dana, R. H., Aguilar-Kitibutr, A., Diaz-Vivar, N., & Vetter, H. (2002). A teaching method for multicultural assessment: Psychological report contents and cultural competence. *Journal of Personality Assessment, 79*(2), 207–215.

Lopez, S. R. (2000). Teaching culturally informed psychological assessment. In R. H. Dana (Ed.), *Handbook of cross-cultural and multicultural personality assessment* (pp. 669–687). Mahwah, NJ: Lawrence Erlbaum.

Malgady, R. G. (1996). The question of cultural bias in assessment and diagnosis of ethnic minority clients: Let's reject the null hypothesis. *Professional Psychology: Research and Practice, 27*, 73–77.

van de Vijver, F. J. R. (2002) Cross-cultural assessment: Value for money? *Applied Psychology: An international review, 51*(4), 545–566.

Useful Websites

American Psychological Association (APA): www.apa.org
Association of Assessment in Counseling and Education: http://aac.ncat.edu
National Association of School Psychologists: www.nasponline.org/store

Videos

Portraits of the Children: Culturally Competent Assessment. Video/CD-ROM. Product No. C0603. Available from the National Association of School Psychologists, 4340 East West Highway, Suite 402, Bethesda, MD 20814, Phone: 301 657-0270.

DVD

Applying Response to Intervention (RTI) and Comprehensive Assessment for the Identification of Specific Learning Disabilities. Flanagan, D., Kaufman, N. L., Kaufman, A., & Lichtenberger. (2008). Minneapolis, MN: Pearson. (PearsonAssessments.com)

This DVD helps improve Specific Learning Disability identification process with seven best-practice principles to help

- Integrate data from RTI and comprehensive evaluations
- Use alternative, research-based methods

- Interpret and apply IDEA 2004 and the 2006 regulations
- Develop research-based interventions

The DVD's aim is to sort out important issues across RTI tiers through an in-service training program that includes

- Balanced commentary from 36 acknowledged leaders in the field
- A facilitator's guide and a CD with downloadable training activities
- A glossary of terms, reference list, and other important resources

3

Assessment of Emotional and Multiple Intelligences

Pablo Fernández-Berrocal

Danielle Martines

Natalio Extremera Pacheco

Educators at the secondary and university levels have been encouraged to adopt multicultural education in order to better educate their racial/ethnic and culturally and linguistically diverse (CLD) students (Banks, 2000). The traditional Anglo learner is no longer looked upon as the typical student type. Instead, educators are encouraged to implement various instructional methods for teaching diverse students. Correspondingly, in addition to culturally centered teaching, the search for successful alternative assessment practices has led researchers to inquire about other types of intellectual abilities (Gardner, 1999; Goleman, 1998; Salovey & Mayer, 1990).

Two significant approaches which have received increased recognition are Howard Gardner's (1993) work on multiple intelligences (MI) and Daniel Goleman's (1995) on emotional intelligence (EI). It is now well accepted that when schools attend to students' social and emotional education, behavioral problems decrease and academic achievement increases. There is also an enhanced quality of relationships supporting students (Elias, 1997, cited in Zins, Heron, & Goddard, 1999). Gardner's and Goleman's work can be described as promoting a holistic view of children which advocates an integrated assessment/teaching approach (Mindes, 2007). These are important standpoints because the education and assessment of multiple/emotional intelligences can assist in intervention planning as a way of building upon observed weaknesses. More specifically, teachers and school psychologists can help design plans for assessing multiple and emotional intelligences, and integrating them into the intervention process.

This chapter aims to provide the school psychologist with knowledge of other theories of intelligence. Additionally, for consultative purposes, the chapter covers useful MI and EI educational strategies for practitioners to convey to consultee teachers during the consultation process. From this perspective, the chapter reviews non-traditional views of intelligence with a view toward a more inclusive assessment system for racial/ethnic and CLD children and youth.

Introduction to Emotional Intelligence

For centuries, our society has highly valued a very concrete ideal of the human being: that of the intelligent person. In traditional schools, children were considered to be intelligent when they acquired the classic languages of Latin or Greek, mathematics, algebra, or geometry. More recently, intelligent children have been identified as those who obtain high scores on intelligence tests. The intelligence quotient (IQ) has become the reference point, and this standpoint is based on the positive relationship found between a student's IQ and academic performance. Students who score higher on intelligence tests usually achieve the highest grades in school. It should be noted that, although the commonly used Wechsler scales revisions have provided updated norms and index scores such as Working Memory/Freedom from Distractibility and Processing Speed, the fundamental theories of intelligence and construction of these instruments have remained basically the same for the past five decades in spite of the impressive developments in both theory and measurement—for example, Luria's Planning-Attention-Successive-Sequencing (PASS), Gardner's (1999) independent competencies, Bar-on's (1997, 1998; Bar-On & Parker, 2001) emotional intelligence theory and that of Ciarochi, Chan, and Caputi (2000) (all cited in Groth-Marnat, 2003, p. 140).

This view of the intelligent person has now reached a crisis point for two reasons. First, academic intelligence is not enough to achieve professional success (see Sternberg's [1997] practical commonsense reasoning theory). Lawyers who win more cases, prestigious doctors who service more patients, brilliant professors, successful businesspeople and managers who achieve the best results, were not necessarily the most intelligent in their classes at school. They were not necessarily those teenagers who always raised their hand first when the teacher asked a question, or who stood out for their excellent grades in high school. They were not those adolescents who sat alone during break time, while the other kids had lunch together or played football. However, they were those who knew how to read their own emotions, and how to manage them correctly so that their emotions would work together with their intelligence. They were those who cultivated friendships, who knew the mechanism that motivated people; in short, they were more interested in people than in things. They were those who understood that the largest asset we have is human capital.

Second, intelligence does not guarantee a successful life (Bar-On & Parker, 2001; Ciarrochi, Forgas, & Mayer, 2001). It does not guarantee happiness with significant others, or with one's children, and it does not supply one with more or better friends. People's IQs do not contribute to their emotional equilibrium, nor to their mental health. Emotional and social abilities are responsible for our emotional and mental stability, and for our social and relational adjustment. In this context, society asks itself: Why are emotions so important in everyday life? The answer is not easy, but it has driven us to a more open attitude about other models of human beings.

In this critical moment, the exclusive ideal of the intelligent person does not hold or raise the concept of EI as an alternative to the classic view. This general crisis has reached the schools, showing the limitations of an educational system focused exclusively on intellectual abilities. School psychologists have seen how their students differ, not just in their grades but also in their emotional abilities. These differences in emotions have not gone unnoticed by parents or schoolmates, and they have also been noticed by science. During this decade, science has shown that this range of personal abilities decisively influences a child's psychological adjustment to class, emotional well-being, academic achievements, and future employment (Salovey & Sluyter, 1997). Emotional intelligence theories point out that our ability to perceive, understand, and regulate emotions is crucial for our adjustment to the environment, and contributes substantially to our psychological well-being and personal growth, regardless of cognitive abilities and/or academic performance (Salovey & Mayer, 1990; Mayer & Salovey, 1997).

The concept of EI was first introduced to psychology by Peter Salovey and John Mayer in 1990 (Salovey & Mayer, 1990). Although this is a novel concept, it is easy to find a clear connection with previous research on social intelligence work initiated by Thorndike in the 1920s (Thorndike, 1920), and continued by other prominent psychologists such as Wechsler (1958). Conversely, concepts such as intrapersonal and interpersonal intelligence, developed and explored by Howard Gardner (1983, 1993) are clear antecedents of the concept of EI. These researchers, without minimizing the importance of cognitive aspects of intelligence, recognized the essential value of *noncognitive* components—that is, the affective, personal, and social factors that predict our capacity for adjustment in everyday life. Scientific literature identifies two major models of emotional intelligence: *mixed models* and *ability models*. Mixed models of EI combine personality characteristics such as optimism and self-motivation abilities with emotional abilities (Bar-On, 1997; Goleman, 1995, 1998). Mayer and Salovey's *ability model of emotional intelligence* (Mayer & Salovey, 1997; Mayer, Caruso, & Salovey, 1999) focuses exclusively on the emotional processing of information and studies the abilities related to this processing. This theory defines EI as someone's ability to attend to and perceive emotions appropriately and accurately, their ability to assimilate and understand these emotions properly, and the skills involved in regulating and modifying their own or others' affect. More precisely, these authors define EI as follows: "Emotional intelligence is the ability to perceive emotions, to access and generate emotions so as to assist thought, to understand emotions and emotional knowledge, and to reflectively regulate emotions so as to promote emotional and intellectual growth" (Mayer & Salovey, 1997, p. 10).

The *mental ability model* of EI consists of four major components:

- perceiving emotions;
- using emotions;
- understanding emotions;
- managing emotions (see Table 3.1).

Table 3.1   The Four Branches of Emotional Intelligence

Branch Name	Description of Skills Involved
Perceiving emotions	The ability to perceive emotions in oneself and others as well as in objects, art, stories, music, and other stimuli
Facilitating thought	The ability to generate, use, and feel emotion as necessary to communicate feelings or employ them in other cognitive processes
Understanding emotions	The ability to understand emotional information, to understand how emotions combine and progress through relationship transitions, and to appreciate such emotional meanings
Managing emotions	The ability to be open to feelings, and to modulate them in oneself and others so as to promote personal understanding and growth

These abilities are linked so that, to regulate emotions properly, a good understanding of these emotions is necessary; at the same time, a good understanding of emotions requires the skill to perceive emotions accurately (Martínez-Pons, 1997; Palmer, Gignac, Bates, & Stough, 2003). However, the opposite is not always true. People with a great ability to perceive emotions may lack understanding and regulation of emotions. This ability may be self-used (personal competence or intrapersonal intelligence) or may be used on others (social competence or interpersonal intelligence). In this sense, EI differs from social intelligence and from social abilities since EI comprises self-emotions, private emotions that are important for personal growth and for emotional adjustment. Conversely, intrapersonal and interpersonal dimensions are quite independent and do not necessarily appear together. One can observe people who are very good at understanding and regulating their emotions, and emotionally balanced, but who barely connect with other people. The contrary also happens: some very empathic people who easily understand others' feelings may be very awkward when it comes to managing their own feelings.

Emotional intelligence as an "ability" cannot be understood as a personality trait or as part of a person's *character*. For example, consider a person who, as a characteristic of their personality, is outgoing. It is not possible from this trait to predict that person's intrapersonal or interpersonal degree of EI. However, there is some degree of interaction between EI and personality, as there is between personality and abstract intelligence. Will someone with a low IQ use and develop their emotional intelligence in the same way as a person with a high IQ? In this sense, people with certain personality types will develop their emotional abilities to a greater or lesser extent.

Recent research has shown that the lack of emotional abilities affects students not just in school, but also outside school settings (Ciarrochi, Chan, & Bajgar, 2001; Fernández-Berrocal & Extremera, 2002; Liau, Liau, Teoh, & Liau, 2003; Lopes, Salovey, & Straus, 2003; Trinidad & Johnson, 2002). A review of this research reveals four main areas which demonstrate that a lack of EI facilitates personal conflicts. Those problems within the educational context associated with *low* EI levels are:

1. lack of psychological well-being and adjustment;

2. a decrease in the number and quality of interpersonal relationships;

3. worsening of academic performance;

4. disruptive behaviors and substance abuse.

For the practitioner, knowledge of low EI levels is clinically important but it should not be confused with cultural reactions. The following section presents an overview of the suggested multicultural competencies for the identification of EI.

Emotional Intelligence and Multicultural Competencies

The multicultural competencies of school psychologists imply various aspects, namely (Papadopoulos, Tiki, & Taylor, 1998):

- cultural awareness;
- cultural sensitivity; and
- cultural knowledge.

Theoretical relationships between EI and multicultural competencies have scarcely been studied. However, as Table 3.2 illustrates, some of the abilities needed to reach an optimal level of multicultural competence are related, directly or indirectly, to the two major aspects of EI—*intrapersonal emotional intelligence* and *interpersonal emotional intelligence*—and, more accurately, to the following four aspects:

1. cultural sensitivity;

2. interpersonal and communication skills;

3. respect; and

4. appropriateness.

The significance of EI for developing multicultural competence has been shown in the field of health (medical, nursing work, and health care) (Betancourt, Green, & Carrillo, 2002; Papadopoulos, Tiki, & Taylor, 1998) and its importance is also being emphasized among school psychologists and counselors (Constantine & Gainor, 2001). With respect to school psychologists, possessing a healthy level of EI may be crucial to helping them service students who come from a wide range of cultural backgrounds.

In particular, school psychologists' EI can play an important role in their ability to empathize and to address the mental health concerns of racial/ethnic and CLD children.

Table 3.2   Examples of Multicultural Competencies

- *Preparedness*
  - Self-assessment
  - Linguistic competence
  - Learning skills

- *Willingness*
  - Desire to explore culture of self and others
  - Desire for experience with others

- *Cultural sensitivity*
  - Empathy: willingness to look for and listen to the core message of others

- *Interpersonal and communication skills*

- *Respect*
  - Awareness of self and other limitations

- *Appropriateness*
  - Ability to recognize and respond appropriately to the feelings and practices of a group
  - Rejection of prejudice
  - Awareness of insensitive, inappropriate, and/or discriminatory practices

- *Emotional intelligence*
  - Intrapersonal emotional intelligence
  - Interpersonal emotional intelligence

- *Cultural intelligence*
  - Salient knowledge of culture held with family
  - Understanding of groups sharing family's culture
  - Knowing where family and groups "fit" with region (ethnohistory)

- *Personal interpretation and practices*
  - Stereotyping, ethnocentric thinking
  - Health beliefs, practices, and behaviors
  - Power distribution (self, culture, others)

What Emotional Intelligence Abilities Should a School Psychologist Have?

The relevance of EI for the school psychologists is twofold: On the one hand, the evaluation and improvement of culture-focused emotional intelligence is a matter of growing importance in the educational context. Moreover, school psychologists' emotional competencies must be highly developed. From the socioemotional viewpoint, school psychologists are required to enhance their professional competency profile with two important abilities: *leadership* and *communication*, and these involve EI. This is important since school psychologists must have the ability to lead and communicate with various racial/ethnic and CLD children, individually and in groups. Furthermore, they will need: (a) sound knowledge about their own emotions; (b) the ability to regulate emotional reactions; and (c) interpersonal abilities to help diverse children understand and handle their behavioral, personal, and social problems. These socioemotional competencies are crucial since school psychologists will need to work professionally and efficiently with culturally diverse students to help measure and develop their EI.

It is possible to evaluate a school psychologist's EI level and check whether it fits the ideal profile needed for a professional, using an EI scale such as the Trait Meta-Mood Scale–TMMS (for a detailed description of TMMS, see Appendix 3.2). As delineated in Appendix 3.1, the ideal scores for a school psychologist would be:

- *attention:* between 25 and 36;
- *clarity:* higher than 35;
- *repair:* higher than 35.

However, in order to evaluate interpersonal abilities, the use of an instrument such as the Mayer-Salovey-Caruso Emotional Intelligence Test would be more accurate.

Assessment of Emotional Intelligence in the School Context

Assessing EI in a class setting can result in valuable information for the school practitioner, since this will provide insight into a child's affective and social development. This kind of assessment also implies the need to obtain reliable data to set a starting point for any individual or group intervention. In the educational context, three approaches for assessing EI have been developed, each of which has advantages and disadvantages:

- The *first approach* comprises classic measurement instruments based on questionnaires and self-report measures, completed by the student.
- The *second approach* assembles measures from external observers based on questionnaires that are completed by the students' peers or by the teacher.
- The *third approach* gathers what are called abilities or performance measures of EI. These are emotional tasks that are solved individually by the student.

Classic Instruments for Assessing EI:
Questionnaires, Scales, and Self-Reports

Questionnaires, scales, and self-reports are the most traditional instruments for assessing EI, and the most frequently used in the field of psychology. Through questionnaires, profiles of personality dimensions such as extroversion and neuroticism can be developed. Moreover, emotional aspects such as empathy and self-esteem can be measured in addition to the assessment of more cognitive factors such as constructive thinking and coping strategies. Similarly, scales and questionnaires have been used in the field of EI to assess efficient management of emotions. In most cases, these questionnaires consist of short verbal statements. The student's emotional intelligence is evaluated through estimating the level of various emotional abilities. This is done by means of a Likert scale that provides a selection of responses ranging from (1) strongly disagree to (5) strongly agree. The obtained score is called *perceived or self-reported emotional intelligence*. It indicates students' beliefs and expectations about their abilities to perceive, discriminate, and regulate their emotions. However, as Mayer and Salovey (1997) regard EI as a genuine intelligence, EI cannot be assessed exclusively by means of paper and pencil questionnaires because these methods would be defective. The authors point out that questionnaires may be affected by the respondent's perceptive biases, and also by a tendency to fake an answer to show a more positive impression. In spite of this, the utility of self-report measures in emotional fields is indisputable, mainly to obtain information about intrapersonal abilities and self-reported behaviors from children and youth in educational settings.

As our emotional world is internal, one of the most efficient methods to get to know a student, in spite of its biases, is by asking him about feelings, thoughts, or how certain events occurring in the classroom affect that student. Assessment of EI by means of questionnaires is useful when the school psychologist or educator wants to get an index of a student's emotional adjustment. It is also useful to obtain a profile of the affective deficiencies in certain areas, which may only be evaluated by the introspection of the student. For example, questionnaires are extremely useful in assessing: (a) the ability to discriminate emotions; (b) attention to positive and negative emotions; and (c) the level of regulation of emotions, or the degree of tolerance of frustrations. Figure 3.1 presents an example of the assessment of the level of emotional competence, based on a typical EI scale.

As previously reported, using this approach students self-assess their perceived capacities in several emotional competencies and skills. There are several EI questionnaires with similar structure, but they differ in the

Instructions

Please read each statement and decide whether or not you agree with it.

1	2	3	4	5
Strongly disagree	Somewhat disagree	Neither agree nor disagree	Somewhat agree	Strongly agree

I don't pay much attention to my feelings.	1	2	3	4	5
I don't usually care much about what I'm feeling.	1	2	3	4	5
It is usually a waste of time to think about your emotions.	1	2	3	4	5

Figure 3.1   Example of Emotional Level of Competence Assessment

component of EI that is being evaluated. One such questionnaire is the Trait Meta-Mood Scale (TMMS). The TMMS is one of the most popular questionnaires in the scientific field, and it is also widely used in clinical practice. It can be used from age 12. The scale offers a personal estimate of the reflective aspects of our emotional experiences. The TMMS comprises three crucial dimensions of intrapersonal emotional intelligence:

- *attention:* the degree to which the individual observes and thinks about their feelings (e.g., "I pay a lot of attention to how I feel");
- *clarity:* the understanding of one's emotional states (e.g., "I am usually very clear about my feelings");
- *repair:* the ability to regulate one's feelings (e.g., "When I become upset, I remind myself of all the pleasures in life").

The original version is a 48-item questionnaire, although the use of abridged versions such as the 30-item and 24-item ones is recommended (Salovey, Mayer, Goldman, Turvey, & Palfai, 1995, Spanish adapted version by Fernández-Berrocal, Extremera, & Ramos, 2004). Appendix 3.2 includes English and Spanish versions of the TMMS-24, and the correction criteria for students aged between 12 and 17. For children with reading difficulties, the school psychologist can read the questionnaire to the child. This modified procedure will not affect the results.

Another similar instrument is Schutte et al.'s (1998) Emotional Intelligence Scale. This measurement renders a single score in EI. However, further research has extracted four factors from this scale:

1. emotional perception (e.g., "I find it hard to understand the non-verbal messages of other people");

2. management of emotions in the self (e.g., "I motivate myself by imagining a good outcome to tasks I take on");

3. management of emotions in others (e.g., "I help other people feel better when they are down"); and

4. use of emotions (e.g., "When I feel a change in emotions, I tend to come up with new ideas").

For Spanish respondents, the instrument to use for the assessment of EI is the Bar-On Emotional Quotient Inventory (EQ$_i$) (Bar-On, 1997, Spanish adapted by MHS Inc, Toronto, Canada). However, as the authors state, this instrument is closer to a questionnaire for a broad range of emotional and social abilities, rather than a true questionnaire for EI.

The Bar-On EQ$_i$ consists of 133 items and includes four validity indices and a sophisticated correction factor rendering scores for the following components:

- *intrapersonal* (self-regard, emotional self-awareness, assertiveness, independence, and self-actualization);
- *interpersonal* (empathy, social responsibility, and interpersonal relationships);
- *stress management* (stress tolerance and impulse control);
- *adaptability* (reality testing, flexibility, and problem solving);
- *general mood scale* (optimism and happiness).

Based on the Bar-On EQ inventory, the Bar-On EQ$_i$:YV measures the level of emotional and social functioning in children and adolescents. This questionnaire can be utilized by psychologists, school counselors, and social workers in order to identify a child's strong and weak areas as well as to develop skills. Emotional intelligence assessment can help pinpoint negative and ineffective coping strategies that can contribute to underachievement, dropping out of school, or the development of emotional and behavioral problems.

The Bar-On EQ$_i$:YV consists of 60 items with five subscales that probe the areas of interpersonal and intrapersonal abilities, stress management, adaptability, and general mood. Its multidimensional scales assess the same core elements as the adult version except for the selection and management development features. A Positive Impression scale is included to identify those who may present an exaggerated positive impression, as well as a correction factor to adjust for a positive response bias. The Inconsistency Index identifies inconsistent response styles. The Inventory has a large normative base of approximately 10,000 children and adolescents and includes gender- and age-specific norms. The abbreviated 30-item short form, $EQ_i:YV(S)$, is ideal for screening large groups in situations when time with individual respondents is limited.

For children with reading difficulties, or in other relevant circumstances, the BarOn EQ-Interview may be used and also helps to contrast results. The Bar-On EQ-Interview is based on the same concept as the self-report Bar-On EQ_i. It can be used during the interview process following the administration of an EQ_i self-report. One can use this semi-structured interview in its entirety, or select those sections where one wants to confirm an individual's high or low scores.

The Measurement of EI Based on External Observers

This second method for measurement of EI is based on the following assumption: if EI implies the ability to understand and manage the emotions of people around us, why not ask the closest persons in our lives how we manage our emotions in public and how we cope with everyday life events? This method is considered effective for the assessment of interpersonal EI. That is, it demonstrates the level of EI that others perceive. These instruments are usually called instruments based on external observation or "360 degree assessment." Teachers or classmates are asked for their opinion on how a particular child interacts with other children, how the child resolves troubles in the class, and how the child copes in stressful situations. This type of measurement is complementary to the first approach for assessing EI, since it gives additional information and also abolishes social desirability biases. Some questionnaires, such as the EQ_i by Bar-On (1997, 1998), include an external observation instrument that is complementary to the questionnaire filled out by the child. On other occasions, sociometric techniques called "peer nominations" are used. Here, students and/or teachers evaluate the rest of the class for several emotional adjectives and for usual behaviors. Figure 3.2 presents an example for assessing interpersonal emotional competency using the external observation method.

This type of methodology measures interpersonal aspects, but displays some limitations. First, it is very difficult to be with an individual and/or child for 24 hours a day, so the observer's opinion depends on the way the student/child behaves in the presence of the observer. Therefore, as this assessment is based on another individual's observations, it includes the other individual's perceptive biases. Second, since the observer may not always be where the student/child is, and as behavior varies depending on the context, this methodology gives restricted information limited to one context: the

Instructions

The following set of statements describes ways of being, or people's general behaviors. Please read each statement carefully and grade your partner on each of them.

Please use this scale to indicate the degree to which you agree or disagree with each statement. Mark an X over the appropriate number.

1	2	3	4	5
Strongly disagree	Somewhat disagree	Neither agree nor disagree	Somewhat agree	Strongly agree

Are you capable of understanding people?	1	2	3	4	5
Are you a person to whom personal problems can be told?	1	2	3	4	5
Are you good at managing conflictive or stressful situations?	1	2	3	4	5

Figure 3.2   Example of Interpersonal Emotional Competency Assessment

class. Third, this process hardly gives data about intrapersonal emotional abilities such as emotional conscientiousness, affective attention, or emotional clarity. However, this methodology provides new data not available via other methodologies. Through the external observers' evaluation, valuable information is obtained about how peers perceive the student on a socioemotional level. This method is also very useful for assessing abilities related to interpersonal competencies, such as lack of self-control, impulsivity, and management of the emotions in situations of social conflict—for example, in an altercation between two students. Nevertheless, caution is stressed in some cases. Practitioners are urged to establish rules of confidentiality, and guidelines for evaluators should be enforced so as to avoid potential negative impact on, for example, students who are not well liked.

The Measurement of EI Based on Ability Tasks

This last group of measures was developed to make up for the biases of other approaches. The aim of this group of instruments is to abolish the faking of answers by the respondent when a positive image is desirable. It is also useful to diminish perceptive and situational biases brought about by external observers. This makes tremendous common sense. If we want to assess whether a student/child is good at one skill, the best way to do it is to test the student/child's abilities in this skill.

For example, we are planning a musical in our school. We are looking for the best pianist among our students. The best—and fastest—way to find that person is to give our students a score from Beethoven and ask them to play it as well as they can. In this case, we do not ask our students how good they think they are at playing the piano, or ask their parents how good their children are at playing the piano. The task requires the students to *show* their ability by playing the piano.

In general, ability measures consist of a group of emotional skills, new in both their proceeding and their format, that assess students' styles of solving emotional tasks by comparing the answers with predefined objective score criteria (Mayer et al., 1999; Mayer, 2001). For example, to assess perception of emotions, photographs of faces are presented, and the child is asked to identify the emotion on the face. Is it angry? Sad? Happy? And so on. Similarly, to assess a child's ability to manage emotions, the suitability of the strategies chosen by the child to solve an interpersonal conflict is measured. As is done in the measurement of verbal, spatial, or mathematics intelligence, researchers consider that EI can be measured through several emotional tasks, just as IQ can be measured through the abilities shown in, for example, the Wechsler scales of intelligence.

From this approach, two ability measures are available for assessing EI. These are the Multifactor Emotional Intelligence Scale (MEIS; Mayer et al., 1999), based on Salovey and Mayer's (1990) model of EI, and its updated version, the Mayer-Salovey-Caruso Emotional Intelligence Test (MSCEIT 2.0; Mayer, Salovey, & Caruso, 2002; Mayer et al., 1999; Mayer, Salovey, Caruso, & Sitarenios, 2003). These instruments comprise the four classes, or "branches," of abilities of EI as it is defined by Mayer and Salovey (Mayer & Salovey, 1997):

- *perceiving emotions* (assessed using the Faces task and the Pictures task);
- *using emotions* (assessed using the Sensations task and the Facilitation task);
- *understanding emotions* (assessed using the Blends task and the Changes task);
- *managing emotions* (assessed using the Emotional Management task and the Social Management task).

The MSCEIT is designed to assess EI. There are two versions of this test: the adult version (MSCEIT) and the youth version, Mayer-Salovey-Caruso Emotional Intelligence Test: Youth Version (MSCEIT:YV). The adult version, designed for use with adults aged 17 years or older, consists of 141 items and its administration needs about 45 minutes. The youth version, the MSCEIT:YV, is designed to assess EI among pre-adolescents and adolescents (ages 10–18). This ability-based scale measures how well students perform tasks and solve emotional problems. This scale yields a single overall performance score in addition to the two area scores for Emotional Experience and Emotional Reasoning. Guided by the Four-Branch Model of EI, these area scores are further elaborated to encompass the four central areas of EI, the ability to:

- accurately perceive emotions;
- use emotions to facilitate thinking, problem solving, and creativity;
- understand emotions; and
- manage emotions for personal growth.

The MSCEIT: YV consists of 66 items and its administration time is approximately 30 minutes.

Like the others discussed, this EI assessment approach has several limitations. Just as with other instruments that give concrete situations that must be solved, the tasks are very contextual and cultural. This indicates that the scales must be adapted to the population being measured. Nevertheless, the advantages of this new approach are indubitable, especially combining the scales with previous measures. This type of instrument can obtain indicators of performance of concrete emotional abilities that may be taught and trained later. Moreover, such scales abolish perceptive biases and, because of their format, responses are difficult to fake if students attempt to give a more positive image of themselves. Figure 3.3 presents an example of how to measure EI from this approach—that is, using ability measures. The examples in Figure 3.3 are similar to those used in the MSCEIT. The original items cannot be reproduced due to copyright restrictions.

School Case Example

School psychologists should seriously consider assessing EI since this obviously aids in discovering several aspects of a child's emotional and personality profile. The following case example presents an exemplary step-by-step EI screening/evaluative process for school psychologists to follow when servicing children and youth of diverse cultures and/or racial/ethnic groups.

Suppose a school psychologist would like to detect whether certain racial/ethnic CLD children might be at socioemotional risk. The first step would be to screen children who might be at-risk by administering the TMMS-24. The school psychologist would then choose those racial/ethnic/CLD children who scored below the mean on the TMMS-24 for racial/ethnic/CLD children their age, and would work with several groups (about 100 children). The TMMS-24 profile to look for is racial/ethnic and

Reading Emotions

Instructions

A set of pictures of faces will be shown. Look at them, and then indicate which feelings are expressed on these faces. Indicate the degree to which emotions are expressed in each face, using the emotions listed below.

No disgust	1	2	3	4	5	Extreme disgust
No sadness	1	2	3	4	5	Extreme sadness
No happiness	1	2	3	4	5	Extreme happiness
No fear	1	2	3	4	5	Extreme fear

Using Emotions

Instructions

Next, a set of everyday life situations is shown. Please choose one answer for each item and indicate which emotion or emotions would be useful to solve each situation.

Which mood would be useful when you are trying to solve a difficult problem—as, for example, a math equation?

	Not useful				Useful
Tension	1	2	3	4	5
Sadness	1	2	3	4	5
Joy	1	2	3	4	5

Understanding Emotions

Instructions

Next, several different situations that happen to people are shown. Once you have read the situations, please indicate how these persons may feel.

Albert is tired. He is even stressed when he thinks about all the homework he still has to do and about all the exams he still has to take. When this same day his teacher explains one more essay they have to do which is due at the end of the week, Albert feels . . .

    a. tired.
    b. depressed.
    c. guilty.
    d. frustrated.
    e. anxious.

Figure 3.3 (*Continued*)

Regulating Emotions

Instructions

Next, several situations that happen to different people are shown. Please choose which actions or emotional strategies would be more useful to help people keep their affect.

Kristen has just arrived back from her holiday. She feels relaxed, cheerful, and full of energy. How useful would each of these actions be so that Kristen keeps these emotions?

Action 1: Kristen begins to write a list of all the things she has to do.

1. Very ineffective, 2. Somewhat ineffective, 3. Neutral, 4. Somewhat effective, 5. Very effective

Action 2: Kirsten begins to think about where and when she might go on her next holiday.

1. Very ineffective, 2. Somewhat ineffective, 3. Neutral, 4. Somewhat effective, 5. Very effective

Action 3: Kirsten decides that the best thing to do is to ignore these positive feelings and face reality.

1. Very ineffective, 2. Somewhat ineffective, 3. Neutral, 4. Somewhat effective, 5. Very effective

Action 4: Kirsten calls a friend to tell her about the holiday.

1. Very ineffective, 2. Somewhat ineffective, 3. Neutral, 4. Somewhat effective, 5. Very effective

---

Figure 3.3   Measurement of EI Using Ability Measures

CLD children with a very high or very low score on Attention, and a very low score on each of Clarity and Repair. Table 3.3 shows (in bold) the scores in the TMMS-24 that indicate socioemotional risk. These three factors (Attention, Clarity, and Repair) do not necessarily have to appear together to detect racial/ethnic and CLD children at risk of socioemotional problems. A decisive factor for socioemotional risk is a very low score on Repair (<22).

Once the school psychologist has identified at-risk racial/ethnic/CLD children, a clinical interview, combined with the EQi-YV or with the MSCEIT:YV for each child, is recommended to verify the screening outcomes. These additional instruments will explore the emotional deficits detected and will indicate their importance and their after-effects upon the child's emotional and social life.

Once socioemotional factors have been identified, the practitioner can begin to implement social emotional learning interventions at the classroom level as well as in the home through parental collaboration and teacher-centered consultation (see Elias & Arnold, 2006). The next section addresses social skills training recommendations.

Table 3.3   Indications of Socioemotional Risk

	Scores
Attention	Needs to improve attention: pays little attention **< 21**
	Attention is right 22–33
	Needs to improve attention: pays too much attention **> 34**
Clarity	Needs to improve understanding **< 21**
	Understanding is right 22–33
	Excellent understanding > 34
Repair	Needs to improve repair **< 22**
	Repair is right 23–34
	Excellent repair > 35

Social Skills Training Suggestions

In his more recent book, Daniel Goleman (1995) states that the contribution of EI to personal, scholarly, and professional success is the most important variable. This statement is based on the argument that IQs explain only 20 percent of success in everyday life, and that the remaining percentage—80 percent—could be explained by EI. This view is very optimistic and is well accepted because it has been so widely embraced by the mass media; this has convinced many schools to create very ambitious intervention programs. However, is it possible to improve EI? The answer is yes. Various contrasted studies support the effectiveness of specific EI training programs that have been developed toward specific emotional abilities. In particular, for educational environments, the training program called the Collaborative for the Advancement of Social and Emotional Learning (CASEL—see www.casel.org) has shown very promising results (see Elias, Hunter, & Kress, 2001 and Cohen, 2001 for a specific review).

A representative example is the Social Decision Making and Problem Solving Program (SDM/PS). SDM/PS is a program aimed at the promotion of social and emotional skills from a Mixed Model of EI, which enables children to pursue healthy life choices. The program has been teacher tested and research validated since 1979, and the practice of these skills is easily infused into existing academic curricula. The program works well with general and special education children at the elementary and middle school levels (e.g., Elias & Bruene Butler, 2005).

Recently, Elias and Arnold (2006) reviewed and demonstrated practice programs in action by master teachers who had worked with social and emotional programs which provided empirical and practical support for success. Most of these programs show a wide conception of EI, approaching Mixed Models of EI. The purpose of Elias and Arnold's comprehensive guide is to motivate teachers and professionals with specific examples of activities to be used in the classroom. The programs are presented in developmental ranges from preschool to high school with important applications for both regular and special education curricula.

Similar activities for students are included in different social and emotional literacy programs anchored in Salovey and Mayer's EI model. These programs are also field-tested and provide evidence-based lessons designed to improve emotional and social competence (Brackett & Katulak, in press; Fernández-Berrocal & Ramos, 2004).

For example, the Emotional Literacy in the Middle School (ELMS) program is a multi-year program that incorporates weekly social and emotional learning lessons into presented curricula (see Brackett & Katulak, in press). ELMS provides teachers with six concrete "how to" steps for implementation:

1. introduction of feeling words;

2. designs and personified explanations;

3. academic and real-world associations;

4. personal family association;

5. classroom discussions;

6. creative writing assignments.

In addition, there are student activities which are designed to have students work on the four EI skills: the perception, use, understanding, and management of emotions. A similar program, "Desarrolla tu Inteligencia Emocional" (Increase your Emotional Intelligence), has been developed in Spain for middle and high school students. This program works with six emotional abilities in different relevant aspects of EI. Some examples are shown in Figure 3.4.

	Personal EI	*Interpersonal EI*
Perception of emotions	Reading and expressing my feelings	Reading emotions in others
Understanding emotions	Understanding how it is changing my emotions	Experiencing the emotions of another person within oneself (empathy)
Emotional regulation	Managing personal stressful states	Managing conflictive social situations

Figure 3.4   Examples of Activities From the "Increase Your Emotional Intelligence" Program

EI training can be strengthened through the use of the Salovey and Mayer (1990) model of EI. Presented below is a practice exercise from the "Increase your Emotional Intelligence" program as an example of EI training methodology. The exercise shown in Figure 3.5 pertains to the understanding of emotions (empathy) and can be used at any age. However, in some cases it will be necessary to make some changes to adapt to the ability level of each individual/child. The practice exercise can be self-administered or utilized when working with others.

Is It Possible to Train Both EI and Multiple Intelligences Jointly?

Hatch and Kornhaber (2006) indicate that there are important conceptual differences between EI and multiple intelligences (MI) theories. However, some specific projects from some of the most effective MI schools show that efforts to support cognitive intelligences and to promote EI can go together. These authors illustrate this link between EI and MI with a project developed at Searport Elementary School (Searport) about an archeological dig. The aim of this project was for the class members to create an exhibition of their findings to be placed in the town museum. To attain this goal, the students worked together in groups to collect, select, and organize the materials. During this joint effort, they had to use different cognitive intelligences such as logical-mathematical intelligence, linguistic intelligence, and spatial intelligence. However, they also had to use their intrapersonal and interpersonal intelligences (that is, their EI) to discuss and negotiate with their classmates

---

Practice Exercise
Understanding Emotions: Empathy

Now we present an exercise that you may practice with a friend or a relative. You just need one person to help you in this practice.

- Ask a relative or a close friend to tell you an experience that he or she has lived recently, but in an objective way, describing the facts but not the feelings (e.g., last Wednesday was my birthday, and my mom brought me a present).
- Once the story is finished, try to guess what this person felt in every experience related (e.g., I guess you were surprised, and felt joy, euphoria, love).
- Ask your relative or friend whether you have guessed his/her feelings or not (e.g., you felt very happy and surprised when you opened the door and saw your mom with a beautiful present on her hands).
- In case you have not guessed it, ask him or her to explain the causes of his or her feelings, and the relationship to the exact situation. (e.g., why did you feel disappointed when you opened the present?).
- To clarify what your friend feels and their reasons for their feelings, paraphrase so you make sure you understand the feelings and the situations (e.g., then you felt disappointed because she gave you a tie . . .).

Figure 3.5   Practice Exercise From the "Increase Your Emotional Intelligence" Program

---

regarding the final collection to be exhibited in the museum. Hatch and Kornhaber (2006) propose that, for future intervention programs it would be most helpful for students if schools considered creating programs designed to build on both perspectives (i.e., EI and MI).

The implementation of EI and MI training and these collaborative projects is exciting for school psychology practice since it can provide students of diverse cultures and/or racial/ethnic populations with the opportunity to demonstrate their intelligences (EI and MI) through collaborative group work. Most importantly, such a project(s) can be ideally structured for evaluating individual capacities and contributions through the venue of curriculum-based assessment methods such as portfolio assessment (see Chapter 2).

What's in the Future for EI?

Emotional intelligence research is still in its infancy. It must be stressed that this concept was introduced in scientific literature only 14 years ago. Moreover, instruments for assessing EI have been used for barely six years, and most of them have been used solely for scientific purposes and with adults. Further research should focus on four major aspects:

- developing instruments capable of assessing EI in early ages (from 3 to 12 years of age);
- developing EI assessment instruments that are culturally sensitive;
- taking into consideration the relationship between EI and multicultural aspects, and how each culture expresses and defines socioemotional abilities— for example, can an emotionally correct answer for white students be wrong for African American and/or Latino American students? What are the implications of these cultural differences for training school psychologists' EI when confronted with multicultural groups of students?
- understanding how EI develops and how emotional abilities can be improved.

Attaining improvement in these areas will require researchers, educators, and practitioners to work in partnership for the furtherance of knowledge on the racial/ethnic and cultural differences of EI. At present, there are several culturally focused studies (Fernández-Berrocal, Martines, & Extremera, in press; Fernández-Berrocal, Salovey, Vera, Extremera, & Ramos, 2005; Ghorbani, Bring, Watson, Davison, & Mack, 2002; and Martines, Fernández-Berrocal, & Extremera, 2006) which have attempted to distinguish EI across cultures. However, additional research that includes children and adolescents is needed to help answer both measurement and assessment issues. In this regard, several questions need to be answered. First, it is vital to determine the extent to which the operationalization of the various types of intelligence (i.e., EI and MI) is culturally applicable. Furthermore, when assessing the level of intelligences, how should normative references be established? What are the implications for constructing instruments to assess EI for racial and cultural groups?

At the same time, from a clinical perspective, how does a practitioner help an African American student who has had previous experiences with racism and who might behave in a somewhat withdrawn and defensive way in a predominantly white school? In this context, how can various aspects of the student's multiple intelligences (e.g., emotional, interpersonal) be operationalized and assessed? If administered the same EI (or MI) instrument normed predominantly with white students, how can the African American student's score be interpreted? Lastly, what are the implications for training school psychologists' own emotional intelligence when confronted with such behaviors?

Despite the pervasiveness of the Western concept of traditional intelligence, the popularity of EI and other types of intelligences is strikingly broadening the field of education. This movement will perhaps change the educational system to value other types of intelligences beyond the Western ideology that only recognizes traditional IQ intelligence. School psychologists are in an ideal position to advocate for a systems change that would recognize social-emotional and multiple intelligences. Such an adjustment would bring about a positive impact on academic achievement, assessment, and interventions for racially/ethnically and culturally/linguistically diverse children and youth.

Multiple Intelligences

As discussed earlier, in recent years Howard Gardner (1983, 1993) has generated a theory of multiple intelligences aimed at helping educators meet the educational needs of each child through the acknowledgment of the various types of observable intelligences.

Fortunately, there is much support for the assessment of multiple intelligences and for the instructional combination of EI and MI in the classroom setting (Hatch & Kornhaber, 2006). This new approach to intelligence has greatly enhanced the way educators and practitioners view teaching and assessment practice (Elias & Arnold, 2006). In addition, the importance of culture in the development of other intelligences has been acknowledged (Brualdi, 1996). Gardner recognized that our culture had identified intelligence too narrowly and hence suggested a theory of multiple intelligences which stressed that individuals cannot be removed from their usual learning environment, as well as the values of their culture, and be asked to perform isolated tasks not experienced previously—tasks that most likely will not be performed again. Multiple intelligences theory offers the educator and the school psychologist a chance to build an educational milieu that is favorable for each student. Gardner (1999, p. 8) defines eight intelligences*:

1. *logical-mathematical intelligence:* the ability to reason deductively and think logically;

2. *linguistic intelligence:* the ability to use language proficiently;

3. *spatial intelligence:* the ability to create mental images;

4. *musical intelligence:* the facility to be familiar with and compose musical pitches, tones, and rhythms;

5. *bodily-kinesthetic intelligence:* the use of mental abilities to coordinate bodily movements;

6. *intrapersonal intelligence:* the ability to understand one's own feelings, motivation, and intrapersonal feelings;

---

*SOURCE: Gardner, H. (1999). *Intelligences reframed: Multiple intelligences for the twenty-first century.* New York: Basic Books.

7. *interpersonal intelligence:* the ability to understand the intentions of others;

8. *naturalist intelligence:* the ability to discriminate among living things and to be sensitive to the natural world.

Gardner further accentuates the following:

1. All human beings possess all eight intelligences to varying degrees.

2. Each person has a different intellectual composition.

3. We can improve education by addressing the multiple intelligence of our students.

4. These intelligences are located in different areas of the brain and can either work independently or together.

5. These intelligences may define the human species.

When reviewing the above MI framework, it is important to note that all societies value different kinds of intelligence. Although Gardner proposes eight intelligences, he emphasizes that children will develop those which are most valued by their particular culture. Gardner explains that educators need to think more about both the nature of intelligence and the learning opportunities and activities with which they provide students. He further clarifies that culture also plays an important role in the development of intelligences. Educators and school psychologists are learning that intelligence is a much broader concept, and they must not think unidimensionally about ability. The cultural value placed upon the ability to perform certain tasks provides the motivation to become skilled in those areas. Thus, while particular intelligences might be highly evolved in many people of one culture, those same intelligences might not be as developed in individuals of another culture. School psychologists will recognize that this viewpoint is a challenge for educators. Many educators are set in their routine and find it tedious to prepare particular instructions to meet the needs of their students. This is especially difficult for experienced teachers, content with their long-espoused and practiced instructional methods.

Planning multiple intelligence lessons for a class can be difficult at first. However, the more MI instruction is incorporated into lesson planning, the easier it becomes. School psychologists are encouraged to become familiar with MI instructional methods (see annotated bibliography) to facilitate teachers' MI instruction planning. This can be accomplished through both consultee-centered teacher consultation and/or systematic consultation with the aim of helping to create classroom curriculum and systems-level interventions.

The favorability of using MI instruction becomes even more obvious when student data from MI methodology are linked to the assessment of students' various abilities. Given the limitations of psychometric measures in traditional assessments, the inclusion of MI (and EI) information as part of a comprehensive evaluation can be beneficial for diverse culturally/linguistic and racial/ethnic groups. The inclusion of MI and EI skills as part of a child's overall ability profile can be used as part of a special education evaluation. This is an area in which school psychologists are encouraged to enthusiastically seek to achieve competencies. Collaborative efforts with educators are of vital importance to the success of the practitioner whose goal it is to advocate for the recognition of MI and EI abilities.

Incorporating Multiple Intelligences in the Classroom

Through consultation and in-service training (Conoley & Conoley, 1992; Caplan & Caplan, 1993), consultant psychologists have the opportunity to help teachers adopt MI instruction. As mentioned previously, school psychologists are encouraged to become familiar with the varied MI techniques available. The following is an overview of instructional methods utilized for the common eight MIs by subject matter. Knowledge of these methods can be useful to the school-based psychologist engaged in consultation and classroom observations, where a student's multiple intelligences can be observed in various class lessons.

Linguistic Intelligence

Linguistic intelligence is displayed in the demonstration of strengths in the language arts (e.g., speaking, writing, reading, and listening). Students with this type of intelligence have always been successful in traditional classrooms because linguistic intelligence lends itself to traditional teaching. A linguistic learner likes to read, write, tell stories, do crossword puzzles, analyze language usage, convince someone of their point of view, and understand the syntax and meaning of words. Their strengths include memorizing names, places, dates, and trivia. These student learners have highly developed auditory skills and are generally elegant speakers. They think in words rather than in pictures (Vancouver, 2003). Consideration of linguistic intelligence can be used in any subject area.

Some lesson planning ideas for history are playing "What's My Line?" with figures from history, or debating important issues and decisions from the past. For math, try writing a series of story problems for others to solve, or having linguistic students explain a problem to the class as others try to solve it. For science, have students write a humorous story using science vocabulary and formulas, create a diary on "The Life of a Red Blood Cell" (from the cell's perspective), or have a student write all the steps to take to experiment and have other student do the experiment. Maybe conduct a lesson on the digestive system and begin with students reading the text and answering questions (linguistic). Next, students can label the digestive system (spatial), act out the food as it travels (bodily-kinesthetic), play a body parts board game (interpersonal), and finally describe what happens to the food once it enters the body (logical-mathematical). In social studies/geography, a student could read and learn stories, myths, and poetry from other cultures. In gym class, students who are not athletically inclined could write instructions for the use of the different machines used in gym/physical instruction. For language arts, if linguistic intelligence is the student's strength, have them write a sequel or the next episode to a story or a play or movie. Creating crossword puzzles to help recall vocabulary words is also beneficial, as is playing charades to practice vocabulary words or parts of speech in language arts. Acting out a story that is being read is also enriching for word knowledge recall.

Bodily-Kinesthetic Intelligence

Bodily-kinesthetic intelligence is the ability to control body movements and handle objects skillfully. These student-learners express themselves through movement. They learn best by touching, moving, interacting with space, and processing knowledge through bodily sensations. They have a good sense of balance and hand-eye coordination. Through interacting with the space around them, they are able to remember and process information. Individuals who are kinesthetic learners tend to be good at physical activities (sports, dance, acting, and crafts) (Vancouver, 2003).

Bodily-kinesthetic intelligence can be used in any classroom. In history, students can re-enact great scenes from the past or hold a historical day by dressing up in costumes and bringing food from that time period. For math, students can use different body parts to measure different things or go out to the football field and make life-size geometric shapes. During fine arts class, students can create a human sculpture or practice impromptu dramatic mime activities. Physical education class, which usually makes use of kinesthetic learner strength, presents many options.

Interpersonal Intelligence

Interpersonal intelligence is the ability to relate to and understand others. These student-learners try to see things from other individuals' perspectives in order to understand how the other person thinks and feels. They often have an uncanny ability to sense feelings, intentions, and motivations. They are great organizers, although they can resort to manipulations. Generally, they try to maintain peace within group settings and encourage cooperation. These students can use verbal and non-verbal skills to communicate. Interpersonal learners like to have many friends, converse, and join various types of groups. Their strengths include understanding people, leading others, organizing, communicating, manipulating, and mediating conflicts. These learners learn best by sharing, comparing, relating, cooperating, and interviewing. Some lesson ideas for interpersonal learners are:

History—role-play a conversation with a historical figure or do a historical period jigsaw (where each student learns a part and teaches the other student). Have students conduct group problem-solving activities, or have one student describe a step-by-step solution to another student during math class.

Language arts—joint story writing—one student writes a story and passes it onto another student—or read poetry from a different perspective and in different moods.

Science—assign group research projects and use lab teams for experiments.

Fine arts—sketch your partner with different expressions.

Gym—play team-oriented games like capture the flag.

Intrapersonal Intelligence

Intrapersonal intelligence is the ability to self-reflect and be aware of one's inner state of being. These learners try to understand their inner feelings, dreams, relationships with others, and strengths and weaknesses. Intrapersonal learners like to work alone on individualized projects, and pursue their own interests. Strengths include understanding themselves, focusing inward on feelings/dreams, following instincts, pursuing interests/goals, and being original. They learn best by working alone at self-paced instruction and having their own space. Appropriate lessons for these learners are:

History—Get students to write essays such as "If I could be a historical figure, who would I be and why?"

Math—Have students bridge math concepts beyond school into real-life situations.

Language arts—Students can write an essay about themselves.

Science—Have students reflect on pictures of the solar system and their own life on earth.

Fine arts—Students can do a self-portrait from different angles while looking in a mirror.

Gym—Discuss how various types of physical exercise make one feel.

Naturalist Intelligence

Naturalist intelligence was introduced in 1996, and is the newest addition to Gardner's original list of seven intelligences. Naturalist individuals thrive on identifying patterns and classifying things in nature, including birds, plants, and stars. From a cultural perspective, naturalist intelligence is very important in hunter-gatherer societies for classifying and recognizing edible vegetation. However, while this intelligence appears to have been more beneficial in a less industrialized society, this is no longer the case. Environmental issues are seen more and more every year as populations increase and resources become scarce. Other individuals who display naturalist intelligence include farmers, botanists, anthropologists, biologists, and librarians (Rose & Nicholl, 1997, p. 10). Charles Darwin was a naturalist who excelled in science, especially earth science, chemistry, and biology. The following examples demonstrate methods for targeting the naturalist intelligence in curricula that appear less likely to appeal to these student-learners.

History—The curriculum should recognize how natural events have influenced history (such as the Bearing land bridge or winters during the Revolutionary War).

Math—Incorporate mathematical relationships in the natural world. Have students record rainfall over a given time period and compare its relationship to plant growth. Students can track the relationship in a graph.

Language arts—Widely open to literature and poetry. Allow students to select a story for reading or a poem (Lazear, 1999).

Musical Intelligence

Musical intelligence is found in students who are musical thinkers and frequently have songs in their head or create their own songs. These are frequently seen singing, whistling, or humming to themselves while performing an activity. Music has been proven to help in remembering information—the reason for so many catchy jingles in television and radio commercials. Music is also proven to stimulate the emotional center of the brain and long-term memory is strongly linked to emotions (Rose & Nicholl, 1997, p. 8). Unfortunately, musical intelligence is forgotten in middle and high schools. Musical learners benefit from playing quiet background music, especially classical music, when working or studying. Students with superior musical intelligence will appreciate a larger scope of music, with a greater understanding of specific instruments and tones. Any subject can include music for better understanding. For example:

History—Have students listen to music from different parts of the world and think about how these musical cultures have shaped music in the United States.

Math—Have students perform to a particular beat (learning multiplication tables, comparing music notes to variables in algebra). Learning an algebraic equation is similar to learning a line of music in that both notes and variables represent a specific number and degree or tone.

Language arts—Syllables in poetry can be taught as beats of music.

Science—Study vibrations and how sounds are produced; encourage students to think about songs that mention the topic being studied; or explore the sounds involved within a topic (e.g., heartbeat) (Lazear, 1999).

Logical-Mathematical Intelligence

Logical-mathematical intelligence is commonly emphasized in schools. Although much time is devoted to teaching arithmetic, many schools fail to teach the underlying logic (Battista, 1999, p. 6). Logic is more dependent upon understanding, problem solving, and critical thinking. Students with logical-mathematical intelligence are proficient with numbers, math, science, and systems. Computer programmers, accountants, engineers, and scientists are strong in the area of logical-mathematical intelligence. This intelligence includes the ability to reason in a logical and systematic manner, which supports the fact that detectives are proficient this area. Student-learners tend to question and analyze what they are learning rather than diving into a curriculum (Rose & Nicholl, 1997). Primary logical-mathematical thinkers are seen playing chess or challenging themselves with brainteasers and puzzles during leisure time. Examples of renowned individuals with logical-mathematical ability are Jean Piaget and Albert Einstein. Math and logic should be integrated into every subject. History lessons can use timelines and charts to create a better understanding of a particular era. Time periods should also be compared with one another to find similarities and reasons why history does or does not repeat itself. Comparing and contrasting is an effective way to incorporate the logical-mathematical intelligence in any subject.

Language arts uses this intelligence when critical thinking questions are asked, such as: "What will happen next in the story?" Math and science should concentrate on problem-solving abilities rather than simply teaching arithmetic. The new study of forensic science is an excellent example of the logical-mathematical intelligence that can be used to investigate famous crimes and murders in literature or history.

Visual-Spatial Intelligence

Visual-spatial intelligence is observed in artists, architects, photographers, and strategic planners. This particular intelligence is the ability to visualize and imagine things in the mind. Visual-spatial ability individuals tend to have a keen sense of direction and are skilled navigators. They benefit from learning maps, charts, graphs, and Venn diagrams. Furthermore, they communicate better through images, especially with complicated topics. Spatial learners can also be seen building models, playing chess, and doodling throughout their notebooks. Examples of famous visual-spatial learners are Picasso and Christopher Columbus. Some classroom techniques include using graphic organizers for younger grades (good for beginning readers to understand the components of a story) and the use of flow charts for extensive directions and if–then statements.

For math, *base-ten blocks* help students learn place values of numbers, as well as creating an understanding of carrying and borrowing in arithmetic. In language arts, Pictionary is an effective method for learning new vocabulary words in history, language arts, and science. Spatial processing takes place in the right hemisphere of the brain. Damage to the right hemisphere will lead to impairment in the ability to find one's way, to recognize faces or scenes, or to notice fine detail. A student with poor visual-spatial intelligence does not necessarily suffer from brain trauma, but rather relies upon other intelligences more heavily. When the deficiency is trauma related, learners will compensate with linguistic intelligence from the brain's left hemisphere and reason aloud, but with little success (Dewey, 1993).

In total, there are eight intelligences, and teachers must write a lesson plan for each class period. How can teachers incorporate as many intelligences as possible in one single lesson plan? While the presentation of information from teacher to student is limited to linguistic understanding, intrapersonal inferences, and visual-spatial, the teacher can alter the form of student performance and assessment. The most efficient technique gives students the option to learn through their most prevalent intelligences. If students are able to choose whether they should write, speak, draw, or perform a response, four intelligences are instantly added to the lesson. While it is difficult to include all the intelligences within one lesson, educators should strive to optimize the alternatives as much as possible. Like students, teachers have their own teaching styles. The difference is that a student cannot change their optimal mode in order to learn. Therefore, it is every educator's responsibility to respond to different learning intelligences within every classroom and, as child advocates, it is the responsibility of school psychologists to encourage teachers to use MI curricula and to keep abreast of culturally sensitive MI instructional methods as potential intervention options when servicing teachers and students within the vehicle of consultation.

School psychologists must recognize that educators who have embraced the theory of MI must first analyze which intelligences they are strong in and how this influences their teaching. Fortunately, many educators have embraced the MI theory (i.e., Lazear, 1999). According to Armstrong (2000), teachers must have an experiential understanding of the theory and have personalized its content. Otherwise, they are unlikely to be committed to using it with any of their students. As discussed elsewhere in this book, teachers may often have only a limited understanding of cultures other than their own. Montgomery (2001) provides a self-assessment for teachers to help them examine their assumptions and biases in a thoughtful and productive way.

Educators must realize that all children have the ability to develop all their intelligences to a level of competency, and the school psychologist can help the educator understand this as well as aid in developing MI instructional classroom lesson plans. It is important to note that at least two or three particular intelligences are usually well developed in an individual. As a general rule, effective MI instruction must comprise efforts to teach students interpersonal and intrapersonal skills in addition to developing their abilities to understand and express their emotions properly in various school and daily activities that involve other intelligences as well (Hatch & Kornhaber, 2006, cited in Elias & Arnold, 2006). The most effective schools that have implemented MI methodology are those in which teachers use techniques that focus on such objectives. These MI instructional efforts have been incorporated in the Schools Using Multiple Intelligences Theory (SUMIT) project. This project identified 41 schools that utilized successful applications of MI instructional methodology and sought to create resources that would support educators' efforts to apply MI appropriately (Kornhaber, Fierros, & Veenema, 2004, cited in Elias & Arnold, 2006). Results of the SUMIT project helped to establish six "compass points" for using MI adequately. These are:

- a culture that is marked by care and respect for others;
- hard work and joy in learning;

- collaboration among adults;
- readiness built by understanding and exploring MI before implementing it;
- student choices in assessment and curriculum that are both meaningful to them and within the larger culture;
- the use of MI as a tool to develop high-quality work rather than as an end in itself;
- a significant role for the arts in the life of the school (Kornhaber et al., 2004, cited in Elias & Arnold, 2006, p. 39).

One of the many refreshing viewpoints about SUMIT is that it recognizes the need to involve students' choices in assessment and curriculum. This is of particular interest for school psychology practice since it can allow practitioners to help students select culturally fair and meaningful evaluative methods for class assignments. For racial/ethnic and culturally linguistically diverse children and youth, class tests or formal assessment measures that involve responding to multiple-choice responses or Likert-type choices are often not appropriate based on their educational experiences.

Building on these perspectives, some MI methodology strategies for determining a student's intelligence profile are:

- collecting students' work;
- checking grades over a long period;
- reading the kindergarten teacher's report;
- talking with parents (e.g., listing the home activities the child enjoys, hobbies, music playing, drawings, games, reading, sports, jokes);
- asking the students themselves;
- assessing through specially varied activities that use the different intelligences;
- simple observation in class, gym, at play or during sports.

Observing students in student-initiated activities is also recommended. For example, the linguistic child will talk out of turn, while the highly spatial child will be doodling and daydreaming. How does the child engage in free time? What does the child choose to do when allowed to do so? (See Armstrong [2000] for a checklist to use in organizing students' MI.)

It is important that the teacher explain to the class that all students are intelligent, and not just in one way but in eight different ways. The teacher can explain the theory to the students by simplifying the terms for each of the intelligences. For example, instead of using the words "bodily-kinesthetic," the words "body smart," "sports smart," or "hand smart" might be used. Ask questions such as: "How many of you enjoy working in groups at least part of the time?" The response to this question will provide insight into the preferred intelligence.

Once assessed, the educator's responsibility becomes challenging since the next step is to *activate* the different intelligences of the student(s). It is recommended that students be given two or three activities which help them consciously begin to use their particular intelligences (Nicholson-Nelson, 1998). Students can be encouraged to self-assess their strengths or weaknesses in each of the eight intelligences. By activating a wide assortment of intelligences, all students are engaged in the learning process and when teachers create instructional activities that use what students already know and value in their culture, learning becomes meaningful and lasting. Correspondingly, Green (1999) explains that isolated pieces of information unrelated to what makes sense to the student are resisted by the brain and little learning takes place.

Assessment of Multiple Intelligences

Canino and Spurlock (2000) stress a culturally sensitive assessment of MI. Tests that use paper and pencil are not portable for MI since they only measure two intelligences (linguistic and logical-mathematical). Use of these measures would only tap into two intelligences and ignore the other six types. Lazear (1999) advocates authentic assessment methods for assessing MI. Authentic assessment involves the student in completing tasks and procedures that are created to tap into the student's problem solving for real-world solutions. Assessments are varied and usually employ such methods as portfolios, audiotapes, written reports, teacher-made tests, checklists, videos, rubrics, parent feedback, and self-evaluation. Project-based assessments are also employed. For example, observe a student teach another student about the digestive system. This type of evaluation is exciting because it is often student directed.

Teachers who have adopted MI theory and employed teaching techniques to assess their students often perceive all of their students as gifted, thus reducing the disparity among white and minority student achievement (Campbell & Campbell, 1999). Moreover, students mirror the expectations of their teachers. School psychologists may need to encourage teachers to adopt such assessment methods, especially if they are consulting with veteran consultee-teachers who are set in their ways regarding traditional instructional methods and standardized testing procedures. Quite often, teachers have painstakingly constructed classroom tests and quizzes for testing the particular subject(s) they teach and are reluctant to give them up for what they perceive to be more time-consuming options. MI offers the educator an opportunity to develop an educational environment that is optimal for each student. Moving beyond the limited view of intelligence testing, the use of better measuring methods, along with the recognition that culture is an important variable for motivation to learn, should assist both the teacher and the school psychologist in evaluating a student's strengths. One attempt to develop a valid and reliable instrument that can tap into MIs is the Multiple Intelligence Developmental Assessment Scales (MIDAS, 1999–2008). As an interest inventory, the MIDAS describes the individual's dispositions and follows Howard Gardner's theory of MI.

How well schools do with MI instructional implications and assessment depends on how educators are prepared to create multiple learning environments for meeting the varying experiences, needs, and interest of all racial/ethnic and CLD children. School psychologists are encouraged to use the Bio-Cultural Model of assessment recommended by Gopaul-McNicol (1998) since it incorporates other intelligences as part of a complete psychoeducational assessment (see Chapter 2). Furthermore, consideration of the adoption of EI and MI methods as a natural part of the assessment process would increase the overall authenticity of the evaluative results, recommendations, and interventions—especially for racial/ethnic and culturally/linguistic diverse student populations.

References

Armstrong, T. (2000). *Multiple intelligences in the classroom*. Alexandria, VA: ASCD.

Banks, S. P. (2000). *Multicultural public relations: A social interpretive approach*. Thousand Oaks, CA: Sage.

Bar-On, R. (1997). *Bar-On Emotional Quotient Inventory: User's manual*. Toronto: Multi-Health Systems.

Bar-On, R. (1998). *Bar-On Emotional Quotient Inventory (EQ-itm): Technical manual*. Toronto, CA: Multi-Health Systems.

Bar-On, R., & Parker, J. (2001). *The handbook of emotional intelligence: Theory, development, and application at home, school, and in the workplace*. San Francisco: Jossey-Bass.

Battista, M. T. (1999). The mathematical miseducation of America's youth: Ignoring research and scientific study in education. *Phi Delta Kappan, 80*(6), 13. Retrieved May 30, 2003, from www.pdkintl.org/kappann/kbat9902.htm

Betancourt, J, Green, A., & Carrillo, J. (2002). *Cultural competence in health care: Emerging frameworks and practical approaches*. Field Report, Commonwealth Fund, www.cmwf.org

Brackett, M. A., & Katulak, N. (in press). The emotionally intelligent classroom: Skill-based training for teachers and students. In J. Ciarrochi, & J. D. Mayer (Eds.), *Improving emotional intelligence: A practitioner's guide*. New York: Psychology Press/Taylor & Francis.

Brualdi, A.C. (1996). Multiple intelligences: Gardner's theory. *ERIC Digest* (ERIC Document Reproduction Service, Ed. No. 410 226). Bloomington, IN: ERIC Clearinghouse on Reading and Communication Skills.

Campbell, L., & Campbell, B. (1999). *Multiple intelligences and student achievement: Success stories from six schools.* Alexandria, VA: Association for Supervision and Curriculum Development.

Canino, I. A., & Spurlock, J. (2000). *Culturally diverse children and adolescents: Assessment, diagnosis, and treatment.* New York: Guilford Press.

Caplan, G., & Caplan, R. (1993). *Mental health consultation and collaboration.* San Francisco: Jossey-Bass.

Ciarrochi, J., Chan, A. Y. C., & Bajgar, J. (2001). Measuring emotional intelligence in adolescents. *Personality and Individual Differences, 7,* 1105–1119.

Ciarrochi, J., Forgas, J. P., & Mayer, J. D. (Eds.) (2001). *Emotional intelligence in everyday life: A scientific inquiry.* New York: Psychology Press.

Cohen, J. (2001). (Ed.). *Caring classrooms/intelligent school: The social emotional education of young children.* New York: Teachers College Press.

Conoley, J. C., & Conoley, W. (1992). *School consultation: Practice and training* (2nd ed.). Boston: Allyn & Bacon.

Constantine, M. G., & Gainor, K. A. (2001). Emotional intelligence and empathy: Their relation to multicultural counseling knowledge and awareness. *Professional School Counseling, 5*(2), 131–137.

Dewey, D. (1993). Error analysis of limb and orofacial praxis in children with developmental motor deficits. *Brain and Cognition, 23,* 203–221.

Elias, M.J. (1997). Reinterpreting dissemination of prevention programs as widespread implementation with effectiveness and fidelity. In R. P. Weissberg, T. P. Gullotta, R. L. Hamptom, B. A. Ryan, & G. R. Adams (Eds.), *Establishing preventive services* (pp. 253–289). Thousand Oaks, CA: Sage.

Elias, M. J., & Arnold, H. (Eds.). (2006). *The educator's guide to emotional intelligence and academic achievement,* Thousand Oaks, California: Corwin Press.

Elias, M. J., & Bruene Butler, L. (2005). *Social decision making/social problem solving for middle school students: Skills and activities for academic, social and emotional success.* Champaign, IL: Research Press.

Elias, M. J., Hunter, L., & Kress, J. S. (2001). *Emotional intelligence and education.* In J. Ciarrochi, J. P. Forgas, and J. Mayer (Eds.), *Emotional intelligence in everyday life: A scientific inquiry* (pp. 133–149). Philadelphia: Psychology Press.

Extremera, N., & Fernández-Berrocal, P. (2002). Relation of perceived emotional intelligence and health-related quality of life in middle-aged women. *Psychological Report, 91,* 47–59.

Fernández-Berrocal, P., Alcaide, R., Domínguez, E., Fernández-McNally, C., Ramos, N. S., & Ravira, M. (1998). Adaptación al castellano de la escala rasgo de metaconocimiento sobre estados emocionales de Salovey et al.: datos preliminares. Malaga, Spain: Libro de Actas del V Congreso de Evaluación Psicológica.

Fernández-Berrocal, P., Alcaide, R., Extremera, N., & Pizarro, D. A. (2006). The role of emotional intelligence in anxiety and depression among adolescents. *Individual Differences Research, 4*, 16–27.

Fernández-Berrocal, P., & Extremera, N. (2002). La inteligencia emocional como una habilidad esencial en la escuela. *Revista Iberoamericana de Educación, 29*, 1–6.

Fernández-Berrocal, P., Extremera, N., & Ramos, N. (2004). Validity and reliability of the Spanish modified version of the Trait Meta-Mood Scale. *Psychological Reports, 94*, 751–755.

Fernández-Berrocal, P., Martines, D., & Extremera, N. (in press). *Ethnic and gender differences in emotional intelligence.*

Fernández-Berrocal, P., & Ramos, N. (2004). *Desarrolla tu Inteligencia Emocional.* Barcelona: Kairós.

Fernández-Berrocal, P., Salovey, P., Vera, A., Extremera, N., & Ramos, N. (2005). Cultural influences on the relation between perceived emotional intelligence and depression. *International Review of Social Psychology, 18*, 91–107.

Gardner, H. (1983). *Multiple intelligences: The theory in practice.* New York: Basic Books.

Gardner, H. (1993). *Frames of mind: The theory of multiple intelligences* (rev. ed.). New York: Basic Books.

Gardner, H. (1999). *Intelligences reframed: Multiple intelligences for the twenty-first century.* New York: Basic Books.

Ghorbani, N., Bing, M., Watson, P., Davison, H., & Mack, D. (2002). Self-reported emotional intelligence: Construct similarity and functional dissimilarity of higher-order processing in Iran and the United States. *International Journal of Psychology, 37*, 297–308.

Gohm, C. L., & Clore, G. L. (2002). Four latent traits of emotional experience and their involvement in well-being, coping and attributional style. *Cognition and Emotion, 16*, 495–518.

Goldman, S. L., Kraemer, D. T., & Salovey, P. (1996). Beliefs about mood moderate the relationship of stress to illness and symptom reporting. *Journal of Psychosomatic Research, 41*, 115–128.

Goleman, D. (1995). *Emotional intelligence.* New York: Bantam.

Goleman, D. (1998). *Working with emotional intelligence.* New York: Bantam.

Gopaul-McNicol, S. (1998). Caribbean families: Social and emotional problems. *Journal of Social Distress and the Homeless, 7*, 55–73.

Green, F. E. (1999). Brain and learning research: Implications for meeting the needs of diverse learners. *Education, 19*(4), 681–686.

Groth-Marnat, G. (2003). *Handbook of psychological assessment* (4th ed.). Hoboken, NJ: John Wiley & Sons.

Hatch, T., & Kornhaber, M. L. (2006). Multiple intelligences and emotional intelligences. In M. J. Elias & H. Arnold (Eds.), *The educator's guide to emotional intelligence and academic achievement: Social-emotional learning in the classroom* (pp. 35–42). Thousand Oaks, CA: Corwin Press.

Kornhaber, M., Fierros, E., & Veenema, S. (2004). *Multiple intelligences: Best ideas from research and practice.* Boston: Pearson.

Lazear, D. (1999). *Eight ways of teaching: The artistry of teaching with multiple intelligences.* Arlington Heights, IL: Skylight.

Liau, A. K., Liau, A. W. L., Teoh, G. B. S., & Liau, M. T. L. (2003). The case for emotional literacy: The influence of emotional intelligence on problem behaviours in Malaysian secondary school students. *Journal of Moral Education, 32*(1), 51–66.

Lopes, P. N., Salovey, P., & Straus, R. (2003). Emotional intelligence, personality and the perceived quality of social relationships. *Personality and Individual Differences, 35*(3), 641–658.

Martines, D., Fernández-Berrocal, P., & Extremera, N. (2006). Ethnic group differences in perceived emotional intelligence within the United States and Mexico. *Ansiedad y estrés, 12*(2–3), 317–327.

Martínez-Pons, M. (1997). The relation of emotional intelligence with selected areas of personal functioning. *Imagination, Cognition and Personality, 17,* 3–13.

Mayer, J. D. (2001). A field guide to emotional intelligence. In J. Ciarrochi, J. P. Forgas, & J. D. Mayer (Eds.), *Emotional intelligence in everyday life* (pp. 5–24). Philadelphia, PA: Taylor & Francis.

Mayer, J. D., Caruso, D., & Salovey, P. (1999). Emotional intelligence meets traditional standards for an intelligence. *Intelligence, 27,* 267–298.

Mayer, J. D., & Salovey, P. (1997). What is emotional intelligence? In P. Salovey & D. Sluyter (Eds.), *Emotional development and emotional intelligence: Implications for educators* (pp. 3–31). New York: Basic Books.

Mayer, J. D., Salovey, P., & Caruso, D. R. (2002). *Mayer–Salovey–Caruso Emotional Intelligence Test (MSCEIT) Item Booklet.* Toronto, ON: MHS.

Mayer, J. D., Salovey, P., Caruso, D. R., & Sitarenios, G. (2003). Measuring and modeling emotional intelligence with the MSCEIT V 2.0. *Emotion, 3,* 97–105.

Mindes, G. (2003). *Assessing young children* (2nd ed.). Upper Saddle River, NJ: Merrill-Prentice Hall.

Mindes, G. (2007). *Assessing young children* (3rd ed.). Upper Saddle River, NJ: Pearson Merrill Prentice Hall.

Montgomery, W. (2001). Creating culturally responsive, inclusive classrooms. *Teaching Exceptional Children, 33*(4), 4–10.

Multiple Intelligence Developmental Assessment Scales (MIDAS). (1999-2008). Multiple Intelligence Research and Consulting Inc., MIResearch.org

Nicholson-Nelson, K. (1998). *Developing students' multiple intelligences.* New York: Scholastic.

Palmer, B., Gignac, G., Bates, T., & Stough, C. (2003). Examining the structure of the Trait Meta-Mood Scale. *Australian Journal of Psychology, 55,* 154–159.

Papadopoulos, I., Tiki, M., & Taylor G. (1998). *Transcultural care: A guide for healthcare professionals.* Salisbury, UK: Mark Allen.

Phuntsog, N. (2001). Culturally responsive teaching: What do selected United States elementary school teachers think? *Intercultural Education, 12*(1), 51–64.

Rose, C., & Nicholl, M. (1997). *Accelerated learning for the 21st century: The six step plan to unlock your master-mind.* New York: Delacorte Press.

Salovey, P., & Mayer, J. D. (1990). Emotional intelligence. *Imagination, Cognition, and Personality, 9,* 185–211.

Salovey, P., Mayer, J. D., Goldman, S. L., Turvey, C., & Palfai, T. P. (1995). Emotional attention, clarity, and repair: Exploring emotional intelligence using the Trait Meta-Mood Scale. In J. W. Pennebaker (Ed.), *Emotion, disclosure, & health* (pp. 125-151). Washington: American Psychological Association.

Salovey, P., & Sluyter, D. (1997). *Emotional development and emotional intelligence: Implications for educators*. New York: Basic Books.

Salovey, P., Stroud, L., Woolery, A., & Epel, E. (2002). Perceived emotional intelligence, stress reactivity and symptom reports: Further explorations using the Trait Meta-Mood Scale. *Psychology and Health, 17*, 611–627.

Salovey, P., Woolery, A., & Mayer, J. D. (2001). Emotional intelligence: Conceptualization and measurement. In G. J. O. Fletcher & M. S. Clark (Eds.), *Blackwell handbook of social psychology: Interpersonal processes* (pp. 279–307). Malden, MA: Blackwell.

Schutte, N. S., MaIouff, J. M., Hall, L. E., Haggerty, D. J., Cooper, J. T., Golden, C. J., & Dornheim, L. (1998). Development and validation of a measure of emotional intelligence. *Personality and Individual Differences, 25*, 167–177.

Sternberg, R. J. (1997). *Successful intelligence: How practical and creative intelligence determine success in life*. New York: Plume.

Thorndike, E.L. (1920). Intelligence and its use. *Harper's Magazine, 140*, 227–235.

Trinidad, D. R., & Johnson, C. A. (2002). The association between emotional intelligence and early adolescent tobacco and alcohol use. *Personality and Individual Differences, 32*(1), 95–105.

Vancouver, R. (2003). Learning styles and multiple intelligences. Retrieved May 27, 2003, from www/ldpride.net/learningstyles.MI.htm

Wechsler, D. (1958). *The measurement and appraisal of adult intelligence*. Baltimore, MD: Williams & Wilkins.

Zins, J. E., Heron, T. E., & Goddard, Y. I. (1999). Secondary prevention: Applications through intervention assistance programs and inclusive education. In C.R. Reynolds & T. R. Gutkin (Eds.), *The handbook of school psychology* (pp. 800–821). Hoboken, NJ: John Wiley & Sons.

Suggested Readings

Emotional Intelligence

Bar-On, R., & Parker, J. (2001). *The handbook of emotional intelligence: Theory, development, and application at home, school, and in the workplace*. San Francisco: Jossey-Bass.

Ciarrochi, J., Forgas, J., & Mayer, J. (2001). *Emotional intelligence in everyday life: A scientific inquiry*. New York: Psychology Press.

Salovey, P., & Sluyter, D. (1997). *Emotional development and emotional intelligence: Implications for educators*. New York: Basic Books.

Salovey, P., Brackett, M. A., & Mayer, J. D. (2004). *Emotional intelligence: Key readings on the Mayer and Salovey Model*. New York: Dude.

CASEL, see www.casel.org.

Elias, M. J., & Arnold, H. (2006). *The educator's guide to emotional intelligence and academic achievement: Social-emotional learning in the classroom.* Thousand Oaks, CA: Corwin Press.

Multiple Intelligences

Gardner, H. (1993). *Frames of mind: The theory of multiple intelligences* (rev. ed.). New York: Basic Books.

Gardner, H. (1999). *Intelligences reframed: Multiple intelligences for the twenty-first century.* New York: Basic Books.

Nicholson-Nelson, K. (1998). *Developing students' multiple intelligences.* New York: Scholastic.

Hoerr, T. (2004). How MI informs teaching at New City school. *Teachers College Record, 106*(1), 40–48.

Annotated Bibliography

Emotional Intelligence

Salovey, P., & Sluyter, D. J. (1997). *Emotional development and emotional intelligence: Implications for Educators.* New York: Basic Books. *This book is essential for the study of emotions and EI in schools. It is an edited volume. The first chapter is on emotional intelligence (see Mayer & Salovey, 1997 below). The remaining chapters cover other topics—some closely related to emotional intelligence, others related to emotions more generally. It is an excellent volume, bringing together a number of theoreticians and applied psychologists who are all working on topics of interest to educators.*

Mayer, J. D., & Salovey, P. (1997). What is emotional intelligence? In P. Salovey & D. Sluyter (Eds.), *Emotional development and emotional intelligence: Implications for educators* (pp. 3–31). New York: Basic Books. *Chapter 1 in this book presents the Mayer and Salovey revised model of emotional intelligence, on which their current tests and research are based. Their original 1990 model of emotional intelligence was enlarged, clarified, and better organized. The paper was written for non-psychologists to read.*

Salovey, P., Brackett, M. A., & Mayer, J. D. (2004). *Emotional intelligence: Key readings on the Mayer and Salovey Model.* New York: Dude. *A selection of the most relevant papers on the Mayer and Salovey model of emotional intelligence.*

To obtain the instruments EQ$_i$ by Bar-On and MSCEIT by Salovey, contact Multi-Health Systems Inc. (www.mhs.com), at MHS Inc, 908 Niagara Falls Blvd., North Tonawanda, NY, 14120-2060 (phone: 1-800-456-3003; fax: 416-492-3343 or 888-540-4484; e-mail: customerservice@mhs.com).

Useful Web Sites

For additional information on the topic of emotional intelligence, see the following Web sites.

Collaborative for the Advancement of Social and Emotional Learning (CASEL: www.casel.org) is an international collaborative of educators, scientists, policy makers, foundations, and concerned citizens promoting social and emotional education and development in schools.

The EQ Directory (www.eq.org) is the internet's directory of EQ/EI/emotional intelligence sites, resources, and organizations.

Dr. David Caruso is the author of the Emotional IQ site (www.emotionaliq.com), which is the homepage for the MSCEIT™ assessment. It describes the assessment in detail and lists research with the MSCEIT™ ability test.

EMONET (www.uq.edu.au/emonet) was established in January 1997. Its purpose is to facilitate scholarly discussion of all matters relating to the study of emotion in organizational settings. EMONET is a restricted list. All subscription requests must first go to Neal Ashkanasy for authorization.

Six Seconds (www.6seconds.org) is a non-profit organization supporting the development of EQ in schools, homes, and communities. The site has many articles, resources, and free information as well as an online store. The organization publishes the Self-Science curriculum as well as other materials for schools and families, provides teacher, parent, and trainer training, and runs educational programs for children.

Appendix 3.1: TMMS-24 for School Psychologists

The correction and securing of the score for each of the factors is as follows: sum items 1 to 8 to obtain the score on factor Attention; sum items 9 to 16 to obtain the score on factor Clarity; and, sum items from 17 to 24 to obtain the score on factor Repair. Then look for the scores in Table 3.4. The table shows the cut-point for adults with university education and ideal scores for the school psychologist.

Remember that the veracity and the reliance on the score obtained depend on how honest one is in answering the questions.

Table 3.4   TMMS-24 Scores for School Psychologists

	Scores
Attention	Needs to improve his/her attention: pays little attention < 24
Ideal scores for the school psychologist	Attention is right 25–36
	Needs to improve his/her attention: pays too much attention > 37
Clarity	Needs to improve his/her understanding < 22
	Understanding is right 23–34
Ideal scores for the school psychologist	Excellent understanding > 35
Repair	Needs to improve his/her regulation < 23
	Regulation is right 24–34
Ideal scores for the school psychologist	Excellent regulation > 35

Appendix 3.2: TMMS-24 for children (12–17 years of age)

TMMS-24

The Trait Meta-Mood Scale (Salovey, Mayer, Goldman, Turvey, & Palfai, 1995) is basically a measure of perceived emotional intelligence; that is, individuals" beliefs about their own emotional intelligence. In particular, the Trait Meta-Mood Scale is a self-report measure designed to assess individuals' beliefs about their own emotional abilities. This scale addresses three key aspects of perceived emotional intelligence:

Attention conveys the degree to which individuals tend to observe and think about their feelings and moods (21 items—e.g., "I pay a lot of attention to how I feel" and "I don't think it's worth paying attention to your emotions or moods").

Clarity evaluates the understanding of one's emotional states (15 items—e.g., "I am usually very clear about my feelings" and "I can't make sense out of my feelings").

Repair refers to the individuals' beliefs about ability to regulate their feelings (12 items—e.g., "Although I am sometimes sad, I have a mostly optimistic outlook" and "When I become upset, I remind myself of all the pleasures in life").

Specifically, the Trait Meta-Mood Scale is a 48-item Likert-type scale in which participants are required to rate the extent to which they agreed with each item on a five-point scale ranging from strongly disagree (1) to strongly agree (5). The scale appears to have adequate psychometric characteristics. For example, Salovey et al. (1995) reported finding adequate internal consistency (Attention, α = .86; Clarity, α = .87; and Repair, α = .82), and good convergent and discriminant validity for the different subscales of the Trait Meta-Mood Scale. In a sample of 86 undergraduates Salovey et al. (1995) found that Attention was associated with private and public self-consciousness (r = .42 and .36, respectively), Clarity was negatively associated with ambivalence over emotional expression and depression (r = − .25 and −.27, respectively), and Repair was negatively associated with depression (r = −.37) and positively associated with optimism and beliefs about negative mood regulation (r = .57 and .53, respectively).

Various studies have analyzed the relation between the Trait Meta-Mood Scale and emotional adjustment variables such as depression, anxiety, and overall physical and mental health. The findings of these studies showed that people with lower scores in Attention and higher scores in Clarity and Repair tended to have better emotional adjustment (Salovey et al., 1995; Gohm & Clore, 2002). For instance, individuals who perceived themselves as skilled at Clarity and Repair reported fewer illnesses (Goldman, Kraemer, & Salovey, 1996), lower levels of depression and social anxiety, and greater self-esteem and interpersonal satisfaction (Salovey, Stroud, Woolery, & Epel, 2002), lower scores in anxiety and depression among adolescents (Fernández-Berrocal, Alcaide, Extremera, & Pizarro, 2006), and higher scores on health-related quality of life in middle-aged women (Extremera & Fernández-Berrocal, 2002).

The Spanish modified version of the Trait Meta-Mood Scale was translated and back-translated by two authors, one of whom did not know the original English text. The final translation was fixed by consensus. The results of factor analysis in previous research (Fernández-Berrocal et al., 1998) were then used to help identify poor items. In this research, the original 48 items were subjected to a principal components analysis with a varimax rotation. Results showed a three-factor solution with Attention, Clarity, and Repair as dimensions, in agreement with Salovey et al.'s (1995) findings in the English version. The eigenvalues for these three factors were 6.54, 4.46, and 2.86, respectively, together accounting for 58.8 percent of the variance. Items with loadings $\leq.40$ were then removed, thereby reducing the total number of items from 48 to 24.

The final version of the Trait Meta-Mood Scale asks participants to rate the extent to which they agreed with each item on a five-point Likert-type scale ranging from strongly disagree (1) to strongly agree (5). The final Spanish version consists of three subscales, as in the original, each measuring different aspects of perceived emotional intelligence: Attention (eight items which correspond to items 7, 8, 13, 14, 35, 38, 41, and 46 of the English version), Clarity (eight items, which correspond to items 9, 12, 19, 26, 37, 42, 45, and 48 of the English version), and Repair (eight items, which correspond to items 2, 3, 6, 10, 16, 17, 40, and 43 of the English version).

The internal consistency of the subscales was high as in previous studies of the reliability of the English version (all Cronbach alphas above .85). The Pearson product-moment procedure was used to estimate test-retest correlations. The test–retest correlations after four weeks were satisfactory: Attention $(r = .60)$, Clarity $(r = .70)$, and Repair $(r = .83)$ $(n = 75)$.

The intercorrelations between the Spanish modified version of the Trait Meta-Mood Scale subscales and several criterion variables are shown in Table 3.5. The correlations were in the expected direction. The Repair scale was positively correlated with Clarity but not with Attention. Attention was positively associated with the Beck Depression Inventory and the Ruminative Responses Scale. Clarity and Repair showed similar correlations. Both were negatively associated with the Beck Depression Inventory and positively correlated with the Satisfaction With Life Scale. In addition, the Repair scale was negatively correlated with the Ruminative Responses Scale.

In summary, the Spanish modified version of the Trait Meta-Mood Scale had appropriate reliability and the relations with criterion variables were similar to those found with the English version. The Spanish modified version of the Trait Meta-Mood Scale gives us an adequate instrument with which to examine the influence of culture on Emotional Intelligence in Spanish-speaking populations (Fernández-Berrocal, Salovey, Vera, Extremera, & Ramos, 2005).

Assessment

The correction and securing of the score for each of the factors is as follows: sum items 1 to 8 to obtain the score on factor Attention; sum items 9 to 16 to obtain the score on factor Clarity; and, sum items from 17 to 24 to obtain the score on factor Repair. Then look for the scores in Table 3.6. The table shows the cut-point for boys and girls between 12 and 17 years of age.

Table 3.5   Means and Standard Deviations of Scales, Cronbach's Alphas of Subscales of the Spanish Modified Version of Trait Meta-Mood Scale, and Pearson Correlations With Criterion Variables ($N = 292$)

Scale	M	SD	1	2	3
Attention	3.24	.84	.90		
Clarity	3.24	.83	.18*	.90	
Repair	3.30	.80	.07	.35**	.86
BDI	7.00	6.54	.20**	−.24**	−.33**
SWLS	5.02	1.13	−.04	.37**	.41**
Rumination	22.85	5.95	.37**	−.06	−.20**

* $p < .01$; ** $p < .001$.

NOTE: BDI = Beck Depression Inventory; SWLS = Satisfaction With Life Scale; Rumination = Ruminative Responses Scale.

Remember that the veracity and the reliance on the score obtained depend on how honest one is answering the questions.

Table 3.6   TMMS-24 Cut-Points for Children Aged 12–17 Years

	Scores
Attention	Needs to improve attention: pays little attention < 21
	Attention is right 22–33
	Needs to improve attention: pays too much attention > 34
Clarity	Needs to improve understanding < 21
	Understanding is right 22–33
	Excellent understanding > 34
Repair	Needs to improve regulation < 22
	Regulation is right 23–34
	Excellent regulation > 35

Trait Meta-Mood Scale (TMMS)–24 Spanish Version

Instructions

A continuación encontrará algunas afirmaciones sobre sus emociones y sentimientos. Lea atentamente cada frase y indique por favor el grado de acuerdo o desacuerdo con respecto a las mismas. Señale con una "X" la respuesta que más se aproxime a sus preferencias.

No hay respuestas correctas o incorrectas, ni buenas o malas.

No emplee mucho tiempo en cada respuesta.

1	2	3	4	5
Nada de Acuerdo	Algo de Acuerdo	Bastante de acuerdo	Muy de Acuerdo	Totalmente de acuerdo

1.	Presto mucha atención a los sentimientos.	1	2	3	4	5
2.	Normalmente me preocupo mucho por lo que siento.	1	2	3	4	5
3.	Normalmente dedico tiempo a pensar en mis emociones.	1	2	3	4	5
4.	Pienso que merece la pena prestar atención a mis emociones y estado de ánimo.	1	2	3	4	5
5.	Dejo que mis sentimientos afecten a mis pensamientos.	1	2	3	4	5
6.	Pienso en mi estado de ánimo constantemente.	1	2	3	4	5
7.	A menudo pienso en mis sentimientos.	1	2	3	4	5
8.	Presto mucha atención a cómo me siento.	1	2	3	4	5
9.	Tengo claros mis sentimientos.	1	2	3	4	5
10.	Frecuentemente puedo definir mis sentimientos.	1	2	3	4	5
11.	Casi siempre sé cómo me siento.	1	2	3	4	5
12.	Normalmente conozco mis sentimientos sobre las personas.	1	2	3	4	5
13.	A menudo me doy cuenta de mis sentimientos en diferentes situaciones.	1	2	3	4	5
14.	Siempre puedo decir cómo me siento.	1	2	3	4	5
15.	A veces puedo decir cuáles son mis emociones.	1	2	3	4	5
16.	Puedo llegar a comprender mis sentimientos.	1	2	3	4	5

Figure 3.6 *(Continued)*

17.	Aunque a veces me siento triste, suelo tener una visión optimista.	1	2	3	4	5
18.	Aunque me sienta mal, procuro pensar en cosas agradables.	1	2	3	4	5
19.	Cuando estoy triste, pienso en todos los placeres de la vida.	1	2	3	4	5
20.	Intento tener pensamientos positivos aunque me sienta mal.	1	2	3	4	5
21.	Si doy demasiadas vueltas a las cosas, complicándolas, trato de calmarme.	1	2	3	4	5
22.	Me preocupo por tener un buen estado de ánimo.	1	2	3	4	5
23.	Tengo mucha energía cuando me siento feliz.	1	2	3	4	5
24.	Cuando estoy enfadado intento cambiar mi estado de ánimo.	1	2	3	4	5

SOURCE: This material originally appeared in Salovey, P., Mayer, J. D., Goldman, S., Turvey, C., & Palfai, T. (1995). Emotional attention, clarity, and repair: Exploring emotional intelligence using the Trait Meta-Mood Scale. In J. W. Pennebaker (Ed.) *Emotion, disclosure, and health* (pp. 125–154). Washington, DC: American Psychological Association. Translated and adapted with permission of the publisher and the author. The American Psychological Association is not responsible for the accuracy of this translation.

Trait Meta-Mood Scale (TMMS)

Please read each statement and decide whether or not you agree with it.

1	2	3	4	5
Strongly disagree	Somewhat disagree	Neither agree nor disagree	Somewhat agree	Strongly agree

1.	I don't pay much attention to my feelings.	1	2	3	4	5
2.	I don't usually care much about what I'm feeling.	1	2	3	4	5
3.	It is usually a waste of time to think about your emotions.	1	2	3	4	5

Figure 3.6 *(Continued)*

4.	I don't think it's worth paying attention to your emotions or moods.	1	2	3	4	5
5.	I don't let my feelings interfere with what I am thinking.	1	2	3	4	5
6.	I think about my mood constantly.	1	2	3	4	5
7.	I often think about my feelings.	1	2	3	4	5
8.	I pay a lot of attention to how I feel.	1	2	3	4	5
9.	I am usually very clear about my feelings.	1	2	3	4	5
10.	I am rarely confused about how I feel.	1	2	3	4	5
11.	I almost always know exactly how I am feeling.	1	2	3	4	5
12.	I usually know my feelings about a matter.	1	2	3	4	5
13.	I am often aware of my feelings on a matter.	1	2	3	4	5
14.	I can never tell how I feel.	1	2	3	4	5
15.	Sometimes I can't tell what my feelings are.	1	2	3	4	5
16.	I can't make sense out of my feelings.	1	2	3	4	5
17.	Although I am sometimes sad, I have a mostly optimistic outlook.	1	2	3	4	5
18.	No matter how badly I feel, I try to think about pleasant things.	1	2	3	4	5
19.	When I become upset I remind myself of all the pleasures in life.	1	2	3	4	5
20.	I try to think good thoughts no matter how badly I feel.	1	2	3	4	5
21.	If I find myself getting mad, I try to calm myself down.	1	2	3	4	5
22.	I never worry about being in too good a mood.	1	2	3	4	5
23.	I don't have much energy when I am happy.	1	2	3	4	5
24.	When I'm angry, I usually let myself feel that way.	1	2	3	4	5

Figure 3.6   The Trait Meta-Mood Scale (TMMS) in Spanish and English

SOURCE: *Emotion, Disclosure, and Health*, pp 152–154, Copyright © 1995 by the American Psychological Association. Adapted with permission. Salovey, P., Mayer, J. D., Goldman, S., Turvey, C, & Palfai, T. (1995). Emotional attention, clarity, and repair: Exploring emotional intelligence using the Trait Meta-Mood Scale. In J. W. Pennebaker (Ed.) *Emotion, disclosure, and health* (pp. 125–154). Washington, DC: American Psychological Association.

4

Academic Assessment

When Is Academic Assessment Needed?

Academic assessment is not as contentious a topic as cognitive assessment. It has been inferred that achievement testing has more "face validity" than cognitive measures because educational tests measure an individual's existing performance on basic academic skills such as reading, mathematics, and writing (Merrell, Ervin, & Gimpel, 2006). School psychologists are not trained in standardized norm-referenced measures of achievement. Presumably, they have learned about some of the more commonly used educational psychometric instruments from class discussions or readings; however, the administration, scoring, and interpretation of such measures is not a part of their formal training. Nonetheless, knowledge and skills of educational assessment are crucial in order to authenticate any corroboration or discrepancy found between the level of intellectual functioning and achievement profile of the assessed child or youth. This comparison is essential for clinical classification and school-based decision-making placements. Conversely, in various states and school districts, school psychologists are solely responsible for psychological assessments and are not involved in educational diagnosis. Instead, educational evaluator/ consultants or resource room special education teachers are entrusted with this responsibility (Merrell et al., 2006). Obviously, from the standpoint of best practices, school psychologists ought to be involved in comprehensive academic assessment and/or academic screening for estimating at-risk children's academic standing. A thorough comprehensive educational assessment assists in the establishment of adequate educational diagnosis for children with learning problems and for placement recommendations and interventions.

Academic assessment does not solely require knowledge and skills in various educational tests. It requires knowledge of the neuropsychological processes related to language and the mechanics of reading. Academic assessment also includes having knowledge of the acquisition process of second language development and of the standards and accommodations adhered to for English Language Learners (ELL) in the United States. Children with academic problems manifest reading, writing, and mathematical deficits that are commonly assessed through educational and psychological testing in conjunction with a keen review of any neuropsychological processes that may provide further information about a specific learning disorder.

The profession of school psychology has a growing need for highly trained clinical experts. Not only is it necessary for practitioners to engage in educational and psychological diagnosis in schools, but knowledge of psychiatric illness and neuropsychological functioning is a vital requisite for practitioners. For instance, school clinical neuropsychology is evolving as a specialty in school psychology. Hynd and Reynolds (2005) recognize that school psychology practice has long been involved in the neurobiological basis of childhood learning disabilities as well as attention deficit/hyperactivity disorder (ADHD). With the changing demands on school-based practices, Hynd and Reynolds foresee the training of clinical school neuropsychology as a specialty in school psychology (2005, pp. 3–13). Moreover, these authors anticipate that the larger profession of applied psychology will encourage sixth-year certification or continuing education programs in school psychology for the purposes of further training in the neurobiological bases of behavior. Indeed, school psychology practice increasingly is becoming more biomedical oriented. Interestingly, in New Mexico, Georgia, and Louisiana, applied doctoral level psychologists are trained and licensed to prescribe medication (Hynd & Reynolds, 2005).

With the advent of these important changes and the progressively more demanding degree of skills required, practicing school psychologists need to recognize (regardless of their previous training and experience) that involvement in the processes of assessment, diagnosis/classifications, placement, and interventions is more complex than is currently perceived in the educational milieu. Consequently, academic assessment is obligatory whenever academic or behavioral problems are observed. Behavioral or emotional problems often accompany external manifestations of learning problems. Establishing the level of a child's academic functioning is the first step in determining how much the child has learned in comparison to the basic learning goals of education, which are reading, writing, and mathematics. Still, as previously stated, it is not just about determining reading and math grade levels but involves further scrutiny into the neuropsychological processes and learning style of the child or youth.

For whatever type of assessment, the assessor must always adhere to culture fair evaluations for racial/ethnic and culturally and linguistically diverse student populations. As mentioned throughout this text, the four major ethnic groups in the United States—African Americans, Asian Americans, Hispanic-Latino Americans, and Native Americans—are among the main minority groups with the greatest length of residence in the U.S. which have the greatest variations. Each of these groups derives its variations from its immigration history, socioeconomic status (SES), language, acculturation level, and values (Gibbs & Huang, 2003). The assessment of achievement can therefore be complicated, given the unique and diverse educational and experiential experiences of these children and youth.

This chapter will review recent recommendations for best practices in academic assessment with a continued focus on racial/ethnic and culturally and linguistically diverse (CLD) student populations. Accordingly, practical suggestions are included for bilingual and English language learning assessment (see Chapter 11 for language-based competencies in assessment).

Culture-Fair Academic Assessment

Prior to discussing cultural fairness in educational assessment, a clear definition of academic assessment is necessary. Payne (2003) defines academic assessment as: "Appraising the totality of the student, his or her environment, and his or her accomplishments is the objective of educational assessment" (p. 6). Payne stresses that such assessment must include the entirety of the educational setting as well as the incorporation of measurement and evaluation. This implies that assessment is not merely a series of standardized educational tests given to reach a student's grade level on the various subjects taught from a school curriculum. The examiner must also focus on the nature of the learner, what is to be learned (or should have been learned), and how it was learned (Payne, 2003). There are several "transactions" going on in the classroom between the teacher and the student, instructional materials utilized, instructional methodology, and student-to-student interaction that encompass the entire educational process (Stake, 1967, cited in Payne, 2003, p. 6).

An assessment will only be complete if it incorporates an overall examination of the types of adequate educational tests available for culturally and linguistically and racial/ethnic students in addition to a thorough evaluation of language development processes (first- and second-language proficiency levels) and any observed deficits in neuropsychological processes that may require further examination. Furthermore, classroom interaction and peer socialization of immigrant students (or students in general) should be evaluated to conclude whether behavioral and/or emotional problems may present an impediment to learning.

Culture-fair academic assessment practice includes alternative types of assessments in addition to standardized tests of achievement since standardized educational tests lack validity and should not be used with certain cultural and racial/ethnic groups. There are many types of alternative assessment techniques (portfolio assessment, curriculum-based assessment, dynamic assessment) that can be utilized in the classroom setting by educators and school psychologists. Educators and practitioners are encouraged to teach and evaluate a variety of tasks performed by the learner which at a certain time are assessed to gauge what was learned. This allows an observation of a student's learning style. It has been demonstrated that matching a student's learning style within the assessment method is beneficial. The philosophy followed for this method of assessment is based on the principle that students should be assessed in the same way they were taught (hence the avoidance of multiple-choice questions which may degrade the vulnerable examinee from demonstrating authentic acquired knowledge) (Lu & Suen, 1995).

Culture-fair academic assessment simply means trying different innovative qualitative methods which are judged more appropriate for evaluating a student's current academic performance instead of just using a standardized measure. Accordingly, alternative assessment of achievement is necessary because African Americans, Latino Americans, and English Language Learners (ELL) have been found to not do as well as Anglo students on formal measures (Garcia & Pearson, 1994). Using multiple methods of assessment for culturally diverse students is part of school psychology culture-fair assessment practice. Linguistic diversity is another important area to consider when considering an academic achievement evaluation. The following section reviews academic assessment for English Language Learners (ELL).

English Language Learners and Academic Assessment

Gottlieb (2006) discusses the lack of validity of standardized tests of academic achievement for ELLs and claims this fault originates at the inception of the test development process. More specifically, Gottlieb provides a list of several key weaknesses inherent in standardized tests of academic achievement for ELLs that lead him to question the instrument validity for this population:

- Universal design does not guide test development.
- The developmental nature of the second language acquisition process is not taken into account in item construction.

- Language complexity and density confound students' ability to express conceptual understanding.
- Access to meaning or understanding is dependent on print.
- Bias and content review panels have not focused on linguistic or cultural influences on the items.
- Pilot testing and field testing do not include ample representation of English language learners across various language proficiency levels.
- Modifications or accommodations for English language learners and those with disabilities are not piloted, field tested, or empirically examined.
- English language learners being schooled in their native language do not have comparable, parallel standards-based native language tests to demonstrate their achievement (p. 156).

It is important to review the above list of problems with standardized tests when preparing to select an appropriate instrument for ELLs who are undergoing an evaluation. It is doubly important to use caution in the interpretation of the results of standardized tests and academic performance. In particular, if a student is being measured in English, test selection should be based on the student's level of English proficiency. Some tests of academic achievement include suggested accommodations for ELLs. Practitioners or educators administering these tests should assure that the tests have been well researched on these student populations and that the accommodations suggested are similar to the accommodations allowed ELLs in general education settings (Gottlieb, 2006). Some common accommodations highlighted by Gottlieb are:

- extended testing time;
- small-group administration;
- individual administration;
- oral reading of questions in English (except the reading test);
- use of bilingual lists and dictionaries (Rivera, Stansfield, Scialdone, & Sharkey, 2000).

Accommodations help to enhance the student's participation during the administration and in turn aid in their performance (Butler & Stevens, 1997). Gottlieb suggests alternative assessment of academic achievement for ELL children with cognitive deficits. However, this must be stipulated in their Individualized Educational Plan (IEP). It is important to recognize the needs of ELLs who may also have language and learning problems.

School psychologists need to be aware of their state's policy regarding the types of accommodations permitted during the administration of tests of academic achievement as well as for alternative assessment standards for children with special needs. Furthermore, the No Child Left Behind Act of 2001 stipulates that, in all states, English language proficiency tests be given annually to ELLs from grades K through 12. These tests must follow English language proficiency standards and are used to mark ELLs' language development in English as their second language (see Chapter 11 for English language proficiency levels). Additionally, school psychologists will need to have knowledge of language proficiency standards and second language development in the areas of listening, speaking, and writing. Embedded in the standards for ELL proficiency are the language proficiency levels that determine the ELL's progress. Gottlieb delineates five standards in *PreK–12 ESL Standards*, recently revised by the international association, Teachers of English Speakers of Other Languages (TESOL) (2006). The standards are delineated in the box.

The TESOL English Language Proficiency Standards (2006)

Standard 1: English language learners communicate for social, intercultural, and instructional purposes within the school setting.

Standard 2: English language learners communicate information, ideas, and concepts necessary for academic success in the area of language arts.

Standard 3: English language learners communicate information, ideas, and concepts necessary for academic success in the area of mathematics.

Standard 4: English language learners communicate information, ideas, and concepts necessary for academic success in the area of science.

Standard 5: English language learners communicate information, ideas, and concepts necessary for success in social studies.

SOURCE: Gottlieb (2006), p. 33.

If they have knowledge of ELL standards and proficiency levels, school psychologists can share and collaborate with educators in determining the progressive levels of an ELL student's second language proficiency, and gain further insight into adequate academic assessment practice. Being armed with information about the ELL language acquisition process and the progressive proficiency levels enables the practitioner to communicate with educators by referring to the terminology and methodology of ELL instructional planning, thus adding further collaborative skills for the school psychologist during assessment and consultation.

Curriculum-Based Assessment and English Language Learners

Shapiro, Angello, and Eckert (2004) note that, although Curriculum Based Assessment (CBA) has increasingly become a standard tool of school psychology and assessment practice, nearly half of the school psychologists surveyed by them do not typically use CBA as part of their assessment process. This is regrettable. Unfortunately, minority students may suffer by the sole administration of standardized educational tests in an academic assessment if their racial/ethnic group is not included in the standardization sample. From the standpoint of bilingual and English as a second language (ESL) learners, students are being asked to use the English language in an increasingly complex classroom environment. This is often difficult for ELL students. Additionally, standardized testing is heavily reliant on a knowledge of English and, while more advanced ELL students might cope, the majority of ELLs struggle because this process requires language function, communicative competence, and whole language (Barootchi & Keshavaraz, 2002). Given this information, it is clear that alternative forms of assessment are essential. Educational profiles for ELL students should be based on objectives unique to the needs of those students. Instruments that can help these evaluations range from structured systematic observational systems developed solely for this purpose to prescriptive selection of materials taken directly from a local school. According to Shapiro and Elliott (1999), CBA methodology is characterized by three features:

1. Assessment is linked to the local curriculum and instruction.

2. Educational success is evaluated by student's progress across key indicators taken from the local curriculum.

3. The primary purpose is to determine student's instructional needs (p. 383).

CBA is a general label representing a family of methods that: (a) differ in their relationship to decision making; (b) have underlying assumptions regarding the link between assessment data and instruction; (c) check for test format and type of student response required; and (d) focus on material for monitoring student progress and level of technical adequacy (Shinn, Rosenfield, & Knutson, 1989). When reviewing the invaluable merits of CBA, and its subsets of curriculum-based measurement and portfolio assessment, it is helpful to be acquainted with the instructional consultation model, which first advocated CBA methods of assessment (Rosenfield, 1987). In this model, the consultant (the school psychologist) and the teacher must decide on a child's instructional level based on the child's ability to learn a new skill and determine the variables that influence learning. The consultative plan entails investigating for a possible "instructional mismatch" between the learner's capabilities and the curriculum. Interventions primarily focus on ways to modify instruction and curriculum materials to better accommodate the student (Rosenfield, 1987). From this standpoint, instructional consultation allows consultants to identify problematic academic areas conjointly with teachers in an effort to alleviate the problem before the child is referred for special education evaluation services. Given the over-representation of CLD and racial/ethnic minority students in special education, CBA is an important step toward alleviating this problem (Samuda, 1998; Samuda et al., 1998).

Burns (2002) advocates CBA as a comprehensive system of assessment and highlights the mismatch between the curriculum and the student's skills by referring to Gickling's CBA model (Gickling & Havertape, 1981; Kovaleski, Tucker, & Duffy, 1995). Gickling suggests that students who are appropriately challenged by academic work (the "instructional level") perform optimally, and other researchers have since confirmed this premise (Roberts & Shapiro, 1996; Shapiro, 1992). Burns (2002) presents three case studies to prove his point. One refers to a third-grade male student who was referred to a special education teacher because of reading difficulties. An evaluation revealed low average intelligence and achievement. Because of this congruence, the student was not recommended for special education placement. Rather, baseline reading assessments were undertaken, compared with "average" students, and Curriculum Based Measurements (CBM) were conducted weekly following the determination of an "aim line," and implementation of an intervention method. Within a short time, the student was performing as well as his peers.

There is impressive literature to further suggest that teachers and school psychologists have very different interpretations of evaluation and assessment procedures (Noell, Gansle, & Allison 1999). The way teacher attitudes affect the consultation process is key to understanding the implementation of the specific instructional interventions and how they are accepted in the classroom, and in the success of CBA methods of assessment (see Gonzales, et al., 2004). The literature further denotes that racial/ethnic and CLD children are susceptible to biased assessment techniques when particular standardized instruments of evaluation are employed (Suzuki, Ponterotto, & Meller, 2002). Standardized tests typically rely on an assumption of prior experience and background that may or may not apply to learners from culturally diverse backgrounds and/or different racial/ethnic groups. In particular, research findings have shown that, because of varying cultural backgrounds, approximately five million students are inappropriately tested each year by standardized assessment instruments, including standarized achievement tests (Torres, 1991). As a result of mandated testing, it has been estimated that, on average, each student in the U.S. public school system takes between three and eight district- or state-mandated standardized tests each year (Haney, Madaus, & Lyons, 1993).

Tests may be considered biased if they project only predominant values and knowledge and do not consider the full range of linguistic and cultural experiences of people in the United States. Thus, even though normative test information is very helpful, we need to know what the instrument assesses when used with social groups for which it was not standardized (Sommers, 1989). Payne (2003) provides an informative list of sources for obtaining information about standardized measures prior to selecting a test for assessment purposes. Relevant questions about tests can be found in:

- the Mental Measurements Yearbook (originated by Dr. Oscar K. Buros);
- test reviews in professional journals;
- test manuals and specimen sets;
- textbooks and reference books on testing;
- bibliographies of tests and testing literature;
- educational and psychological abstract indexes;
- publishers' test catalogs; and
- test critiques (e.g., Keyser & Sweetland, 1988).

Other sources are *Test in Print*, the *Directory of Selected National Testing Programs*, and Educational Testing Service Test Collection catalogs. The *Mental Measurement Yearbook* (MMY) is the most popular English-speaking source providing recent comprehensive bibliographies, test reviews, and book reviews. The goal of this yearbook is to enlarge the prospective consumer and publisher's a critical outlook toward tests and testing as well as to increase the quality of published tests. The yearbook also provides extensive bibliographies of verified references on the construction, utilization, and validity of specific tests (Payne, 2003). The MMY has an easily accessible computer-searchable database.

Obtaining information about tests from some of these suggested sources assists the practitioner in searching for the best test to use when assessing a particular racial/ethnic and/or culturally and linguistically diverse student.

CBA in the Bilingual Environment

Recent research has validated the use of CBA in assessing the reading progress of ELLs. Assessment of second language learners by school psychologists using

CBA measures is increasing. However, the majority of school psychologists continue to use traditional measures (McCloskey & Schicke Athanasiou, 2000). In particular, Curriculum Based Measurement (CBM), a subset of CBA, and portfolio assessment have been recommended for use by child study teams in order to follow a second language learner's rate of progress and achievement levels (Baker & Good, 1995; Chamberlain & Medinas-Landurand, 1991). Practitioners visiting the classroom are encouraged to also take note that the implementation of CBA (through the use of CBM) necessitates checking for validity in comparison to the use of other reading measures when attempting to evaluate second language learners' progress (Baker & Good, 1995).

Curriculum-Based Measurement

Broadly defined, CBM is a systematic procedure for monitoring students' progress in an academic area and making instructional decisions (Deno, 1985; Deno & Fuchs, 1987; Shinn, 1989). Basically, CBM is the pragmatic assessment of academic performance using measures precisely linked to the subject material taught in the classroom. It has been researched extensively in elementary schools and is reported to gauge successively the growth of students' reading, spelling, writing, and mathematics. In examining the validity of CBM, Fewster and Macmillan (2002) discovered that CBM scores are able to reliably predict student performance and differentiate between various proficiency levels. Research further demonstrates high correlations with standardized norm-referenced tests, discriminates between special eduction students and those who are ineligible for special education, and incorporates interpretation based on data from local norms (Shapiro & Elliott, 1999; Shinn, 1998; Shinn, Collins, & Gallagher, 1998). In addition, research shows that CBM data can be utilized to monitor the effectiveness of ongoing interventions (Burns, MacQuarrie, & Campbell, 1999).

CBM measures are usually obtained through direct observational procedures, and are standardized. Scores are obtained by counting the quantity of adequate or inadequate responses over a fixed period of time. Deno (2003) states that the purpose of CBM is to help educators conduct formative evaluations and describes the formative evaluation model as systematic in setting goals, monitoring growth, changing programs, and evaluating the changes. Data collected during a CBM on basic academic skills can be used for several purposes (e.g., for screening, prereferral evaluation, placement decisions, or formative evaluation). The systematic approach of CBM requires the assessor (e.g., the school psychologist) to work closely with the teacher with the aims of (a) setting proper goals for the student, (b) closely monitoring the child's progress or lack of it in the current educational program, and (c) modifying and evaluating the effects of any change(s). As always, alternative effective methods that require a more favorably individualized approach are more time-consuming and therefore are not viewed as practical when implemented by assessors and teachers in school districts with high caseloads and insufficient practitioners and educators on their professional staff. Nevertheless, research on the achievement results regarding the utilization of this approach indicates that students of teachers who employ systematic formative evaluation with CBMs have greater achievement rates (Fuchs, Deno, & Mirkin, 1984). However, Bentz and Pavri (2000) caution the use of CBM methods with bilingual students. They point out that the relationship between reading fluency and reading proficiency is not well understood because of the sequence of skills acquisition for students learning to read English as a second language. They argue that bilingual students learning to read and understand text in English use a variety of different skills (e.g., in translations) that may influence the construct validity of CBM reading as a measure of reading proficiency (see Martines & Rodriguez-Srednicki, 2007).

Standardized measures commonly used in the assessment of achievement are the Woodcock Johnson III Tests of Achievement (Woodcock, McGrew, & Mather, 2001), the Batería Woodcock-Muñoz-Revisada: Pruebas de Aprovechamiento (Woodcock & Munoz-Sandoval, 1995), a similar Spanish version of the Woodcock Johnson Psychoeducational-Revised; and the Aprenda: La Prueba de Logros en Español, Segunda Edicion (Psychological Corporation, 1997), which measures the achievement of Spanish-speaking students in the academic domains of reading, language arts, and mathematics (Hess & Rhodes, 2005, Ch. 28). There are few options available to the clinician if the student's first language is not Spanish. This is why CBM is widely used as a method of assessment with bilingual and ELL students.

For school psychologists, it is important to not lose sight of their profession's ethical standards which promote advocacy and culturally fair assessment practices for children of all racial/ethnic and culturally/linguistically diverse groups. Practitioners are responsible for adopting alternative methods to facilitate culturally fair assessments—despite time constraints.

Structured Systematic Observational Systems

It is vital to investigate the methods of instruction used prior to an evaluation, as well as relevant environmental factors, when discussing procedures to assess academic progress and/or difficulties for minority children. Such a practice greatly contributes to the prevention and reduction of academic problems. In this context, one valuable characteristic of CBA assessment is the utilization of various behavioral-observational and structured systematic observation systems to ascertain the instructional level of the student, the environmental and behavioral factors contributing to adequate and/or inadequate learning (Greenwood, Carta, Kamps, Terry, & Delquadri, 1994; Ysseldyke & Christensen, 1993; Saudargas, 1992), and the assessment of bilingual special education (ESCRIBE; Arreaga-Mayer, Tapia, & Carta, 1993). One noteworthy improvement that facilitates teacher and consultant/school psychologist data collection during the evaluative process is computer technology, which consists of software packages designed for use with portable computers to assess educational and parenting applications (Barton & Johnson, 1990), social interaction between peers, and student-teacher interactions (Atwater, Carta, & Schwartz, 1989).

One such useful system is the Functional Assessment of Academic Behavior: Creating Successful Learning Environments (FAAB; Ysseldyke & Christensen, 2002, cited in Martines & Rodriguez-Srednicki, 2007). The FAAB allows the school psychologist to observe and record systematically the class content and students' level of understanding, and to accumulate data on environmental factors and instructional deficiencies, if any. Immediately after a classroom observation, the school psychologist interviews the observed student to determine whether the student has understood the lesson taught. The FAAB further permits school psychologists to review various factors (e.g., home versus school environment, learning style) and does not focus on deficiencies but rather on what can be done to optimize the learning experience of the learner. Moreover, the FAAB can be particularly helpful for ELLs because a multiculturally focused school psychologist can observe the student's learning style, determine previous (cultural) educational experiences, and collaboratively suggest culturally sensitive instructional methods to the student's teacher, leading to more appropriate and culturally sensitive instruction and interventions.

Another noteworthy system is the Code for Instructional Structure and Student Academic Response (CISSAR; Stanley & Greenwood, 1981, cited in Martines & Rodriguez-Srednicki, 2007), which assesses the effectiveness of school-based instruction and interventions. Martines and Rodriguez-Srednicki (2007) summarize the CISSAR contents as comprising five categories of teacher-oriented factors—activity, task, teaching structure, teaching position, and teaching behavior—and three categories of observable student responses, to academic responding, task management, and competing behavior. Activities can include observation of reading, mathematics, spelling, language, social studies, and science. The teacher behavior module also notes whether the instructor was approving or disapproving, and lists other modes of teacher feedback to students. CISSAR is used with computer software to assist data graphing and collection, and reveals a variety of information—for example, augmentations in academic responding such as reading (aloud or silently) and writing and/or other areas under scrutiny (academic responding data are associated with instruction and peer tutoring that ultimately lead to increases in academic outcomes). The CISSAR gauges the student's academic performance from a systemic approach, not in isolation. The system takes into consideration all areas of the environment: teacher, classroom, method of instruction, and student academic responses.

The use of technology-based approaches has assisted the use of such systems. For instance, the Ecobehavioral Assessment Systems Software (EBASS) is a computer-assisted, standard classroom observational system and consists of three instruments largely used for special education research. The EBASS was originally designed for exceptional children (see Greenwood, Carta, Kamps, Terry, & Delquadri, 1994, cited in Martines & Rodriguez-Srednicki, 2007). The Ecobehavioral System for Complex Analyses of Preschool Environments (ESCAPE) (Carta, Greenwood, & Atwater, 1985) is a system designed for preschoolers aged 3–5 years (cited in Martines & Rodriguez-Srednicki, 2007). (For a thorough review of best practices in the assessment of infants and preschools, see McLean, Wolery, & Baily, 2004.)

Additionally, ELLs have benefited from the computer-assisted Class Wide Peer Tutoring Learning Management System (CSPT-LMS) (Greenwood, 2001), developed to improve the literacy of impoverished CLD children and ELLs in urban elementary schools. It is an "intraclass, same-age, reciprocal peer tutoring" system that allows ELL students to "experience one-on-one pupil-tutor dyads during sessions; relatively immediate error correction; fast-pacing multiple opportunities to respond; both teacher and learner roles; written and oral learner response formats; inclusion; and social and academic goals addressed during the same instructional time" (Greenwood, 2001). CSPT-LMS also adopted the use of school-based consultation, and this enhanced the implementation of the CWPT program in addition to student outcomes.

Martines and Rodriguez-Srednicki (2007) advise caution prior to selecting the proper instrument to use with ELL or bilingual children since computer-assisted observational assessment has not been empirically validated for ELLs and bilinguals. The authors stipulate that, due to cultural differences, ELLs and bilingual students "could engage in behaviors different from the norm. The school psychologist must apply a culturally responsive [filter] when conducting the observations and when interpreting the culturally diverse students' behaviors" (see also National Association of School Psychologists, 2003). Given this advice, it is important to consider that such systems may also be biased for various racial/ethnic minority groups as well. As always, it is critical to thoroughly review the research and evaluate what the findings indicate regarding different racial/ethnic groups on the use of a particular measure prior to an actual administration.

Structured systematic observational systems are, however, considered a major asset for practitioners in recording student's academic and behavioral outcomes (see Greenwood, Carta, Kamps, Terry, & Delquadri, 1994). Moreover, structured observational systems can help contribute to the evaluation of academic and/or behavioral performance as part of a multidimensional assessment for CLD and racial/ethnic children (see Chapter 6 for structured behavioral observational systems).

English Language Learners and the Cognitive Academic Language Learning Approach (CALLA)

In a fair academic assessment of achievement, it is important to have knowledge of instructional models and strategies which are used for second language learners. Knowledge of reputable English as a Second Language (ESL) instructional methods can help practitioners determine whether or how an ESL student is exposed to second language acquisition. This section reviews an inspiring ESL model of instruction that has gained considerable attention and has been shown to have several advantages for school psychology practice.

The Cognitive Academic Language Learning Approach (CALLA), developed by Chamot and O'Malley in the mid-1980s, is an empirically validated instructional model designed for students learning English as a second language. Chamot and O'Malley (1996) base their theoretical premise on the research findings of Cummins (1994) and Collier (1989), who found that ELL immigrant students in Canada and the United States learned Basic Interpersonal Communication Skills (BICS) within two years, and Cognitive Academic Skills (CALPS) within five to seven years. The latter is particularly significant since this slower process will inevitably affect the academic progress of ELL learners.

Collier, in the United States, also found that the age at which a child immigrated was significant. ELL learners immigrating at age 12 or older apparently tended to do worse. A noteworthy aspect of these findings is that, while ELL students progress at a slower pace in learning suitable English for cognitive academic success, their native English-speaking peers are accelerating in the more complex academic subjects. Cummins and Collier have continually advocated bilingual education services for ELL learners. Their viewpoint emphasizes that concepts and skills already developed in the native language can be transferred to English once similar modes of expression are learned in the second language. Research has demonstrated that such a transfer will not occur automatically (Grabe, 1991; McLaughlin, 1990; McLeod & McLaughlin, 1986).

A further feature of the CALLA model is the effort made to modify the 1980s ESL curriculum, which incorporated the same linguistic characteristics for English as those taught for foreign language courses, stressing the vocabulary and grammar required for conversation. Researchers such as Mohan (1986); DeAvila and Ducan (1984); and Genesee (1987) advocated the incorporation of language and content for ESL instruction since vocabulary explicit to the subject content in ESL classes heightened ELL learners' knowledge. An additional foundation for CALLA was the research conducted on the cognitive processes (Pressley and Associates, 1990) and learning strategies of successful native-English speakers. The research demonstrates that successful ELL learners are those who have the capacity to incorporate appropriately taught "learning strategies interventions" by means of content-based language instruction. CALLA is affected by research on cognitive theory and application to second language acquisition (see Anderson, 1976; Gagne, 1985; Shuell, 1986; Weinstein & Mayer, 1986), and adopts the assumption that learning will occur through active cognitive and "dynamic mental processes" during the actual course of classroom learning.

In summary, CALLA evolved with the researched fundamentals that "most students can profit from instruction in learning strategies; many students lack academic language skills that would enable them to use English as a tool for learning; adding academic content to ESL curriculum prepares students for grade-level content classrooms and lastly, is sustained by cognitive theory and continual use in classrooms" (Chamot & O'Malley, 1994). Given the impressive CALLA success, school psychologists are urged not only to have knowledge of the CALLA strategies for ELLs but to also advocate for its use in educational settings. This feat can be accomplished during consultee-centered consultation or when presenting at staff workshops and conferences.

Description of the CALLA Instructional Approach

The CALLA model has expanded since its inception and is currently implemented in several ESL and bilingual education programs "to grade-level content classrooms" in the United States, Canada, Spain, and several other countries. Its designers state that their approach targets language minority students at advanced beginning and intermediate levels of English language proficiency.

Thus it targets: (a) ELLs with basic communication skills in English for those who have not yet developed adequate grade level cognitive academic language skills; (b) ELLs who have developed cognitive academic language skills in their native language and a certain proficiency in English, but who need assistance in transferring these skills to the second language; and (c) bilingual English-proficient students who have not evolved their academic skills in any of the two languages: English and their native language. In the CALLA approach, ELL learners are first gradually introduced to content areas that will eventually encompass their curriculum (such as science), in which hands-on experience can be combined with "contextual support" for academic language advancement. Second, academic language skills such as listening, speaking, reading, and writing are incorporated into the daily class content lessons, especially specific word knowledge and grammar of the particular subject's content.

One unique component of CALLA is the instructional techniques/strategies that require cognitive demanding processes for mentally recalling the steps necessary for deciphering and controlling the demanded task(s) of the class lesson. More specifically, ELL learners establish a repertoire of specific strategies that are suitable for the content materials and the language task of the class lesson. In other words, the curriculum determines the specific strategies/interventions to adopt. CALLA is based on three learning strategies—metacognitive, cognitive, and social/affective—chosen and integrated for class instruction with regard to the particular content and language task.

Metacognitive Strategies

Metacognitive strategies are mental processes that are learned for the purpose of enabling ELL students to plan, monitor, and evaluate their own learning activities. An example of a well thought-out metacognitive strategy would be planning for a learning activity by encouraging oneself to focus on the learning task while disregarding disturbances or by concentrating on special vital words, phrases, or kinds of information that are essential to the learning activity and adopted by the ELL prior to the lesson. When the lesson is concluded, ELL learners can deduce by "self-evaluation" whether they have succeeded in reaching their targeted learning goals.

Cognitive Strategies

Cognitive strategies are techniques linked to specific individual tasks that involve both language and content. Examples would be an "elaboration of prior knowledge" wherein ELLs can recollect what they have already learned about the lesson's content, or "linguistic transfer" in which ELLs can identify certain resemblances between their native language and English. Once a comparison is made between native-language and second language resemblances, the ELL student can easily transfer such linguistic skills to the language being used. In this view, ELL students are consciously in charge of their own selected instructional guidelines by applying special learning strategies to help achieve success in a class lesson.

Social/Affective Strategies

Social/affective strategies are considered exceptionally important because they require asking questions, cooperating, and clarifying concepts. An example of a social/affective strategy is self-talk, in which the ELL student is encouraged to use positive statements to boost motivation and success. Additionally, ELL students are encouraged to interact with others in cooperative learning activities and to ask questions when needed. The social/affective aspect of second language learning is viewed as the most rewarding and vital for success.

It is compulsory for educators employing CALLA programs to select methods of assessment as well as the necessary tools that "match" the educational skills being taught and measured in the school curricula. CALLA encourages educators to adopt these assessment methods to meet the instructional needs of ELL students. Following these recommendations is consistent with the CBA practices described above; these practices also link assessment and intervention by using assessment tools and content directly connected to the curriculum (Martines & Rodriguez-Srednicki, 2007).

Mathematics in the CALLA Model

The basic skills taught in our educational settings are mathematics, reading, and writing. In the CALLA model, Chamot and O'Malley (1994) emphasize that mathematics has its own terminology, employing such words as *addend, quotient, altogether, round, table, square root,* and *least common denominator.* ELL students also need to learn such specialized terms as *greater than, six times as high as, eight times as much,* and *divided by.* Familiarity with the jargon of mathematics is imperative to success since ELL students need extra linguistic processing time to decipher word problems if they are not knowledgeable about mathematical linguistics. Cultural background is also essential in discussing mathematic instruction and testing. CALLA lists two types of cultural differences that can be detrimental to ELL students: first, certain math symbols are different or are used differently; and second, disparities exist between studying and learning problem-solving steps. Moreover, the kind of mathematics instruction ELL students received in their native countries will affect the cognitive strategies used for problem solving.

Guidelines for teaching mathematics are inherent to the CALLA model and include linking word problems and solutions, sustaining mentally active students, verbalizing the steps to problem solving, and incorporating learning strategies and problem-solving steps.

Assessment of Math Achievement

The CALLA approach suggests portfolio assessment for the assessment of ELL students' math abilities. This includes worksheets with sample math problems, homework outlining problem-solving methods in writing, written homework assignments with students' work problems, performance measures illustrating the construct of a product wherein mathematics was used, learning logs in which students keep a record of their weekly progress and evaluation, and a weekly progress report written by students describing their problem-solving methods.

Assessing student advancement using CALLA requires a selection of different kinds of alternative assessment, the purpose of which is to determine explicit instructional methods (see Chamot & O'Malley, 1994, Ch. 6). Such methods are considered exemplary in monitoring a student's progress since they are authentic, demonstrating genuine classroom content tasks and illustrating information about academic language, and varied, observing student performance from various standpoints instead of depending upon only one evaluation method and/or measure.

When designing an alternative assessment instrument, Chamot and O'Malley (1994) suggest adequate teacher preparation in construction, administration, scoring, and interpretation. The next section describes these preparatory needs.

Construction

Construction involves considering the rationale for the assessment and selection of appropriate instruments. For example, an instrument that is used for assessing problem-solving math word problems would be different from one used for assessing communication skills and/or science laboratory work.

Administration

Administration involves adequately preparing test administration conditions: suitable preparation for individual or group administration; clear instructions; and time for practice of a similar task prior to testing—most especially for ELL students who might not be familiar with U.S. tests or test items, such as multiple-choice questions. Equally important is sufficient preparation of ELL students for activities that involve actual demonstration of performance, higher-order thinking skills, and cooperation.

Scoring

Alternative assessment requires that scoring procedures be resolved through the use of a rubric. Simply explained, a rubric is similar to a Likert-type scale with scores based on 1, 2, and 3 or higher and in order of effectiveness. Thus 3 would represent the highest score on a scale of 1 to 3. The rubric is prepared by the instructor and should represent a fair breakdown of abilities and skills to be measured. The concept of rubric development in alternative assessment is considered a holistic approach to scoring.

Interpretation

Interpretation in alternative assessment is based on the standards that have been used on the scoring rubric. For example, on a rubric scale of 1 to 3, a 2 might indicate progress with further need for improvement. It is recommended that a criterion score be selected for a student's advancement to the next grade. A criterion score is a minimum score requirement for grade level advancement that includes a total of previous alternative assessments used to measure the same subject and/or academic topic (see Chamot & O'Malley, 1994, Ch. 6).

Another form of alternative assessment is the employment of performance measures that evaluate students on speaking, writing, or problem-solving. In this type of assessment, ELL students are required to utilize knowledge and skills to generate a project by working individually, in dyads, or in groups. The project might involve such activities as responding to open-ended questions, an art piece, a written assignment, an experiment, or an oral presentation. Teachers evaluate the student's project by checklists, scales, and observational procedures. When assessing ELL and CLD students—as in all types of alternative assessment—it is important to emphasize that performance measures are nonstandardized methods of evaluating a student's specific skills and aptitudes on what they have been taught and what they have learned.

Further examples of alternative assessment are text retelling, cloze testing, holistic and analytic scoring of writing samples, teacher rating scales, student self-rating scales, and assessment of higher-order thinking skills. A review of each of these evaluative approaches is beyond the scope of this chapter; hence, the reader is referred to Chamot and O'Malley (1994, Ch. 6) for further information on each of these methods.

In conclusion, CALLA demonstrates beneficial methods of cognitive learning instructional approaches for ELL students and includes valuable nonbiased approaches to testing ELL and CLD students (including ELL students with learning disabilities) by means of alternative types of assessment. Furthermore, the CALLA mathematic techniques/evaluations described above are also used for literature and composition (including reading strategies), science, and social studies. School psychologists are responsible for the instructional and academic success of children and youth, and should be well versed in these methods when engaging in consultation services. More specifically, school psychologists must advocate culturally fair instruction and testing, and therefore should seek to augment the knowledge and skills of their consultee-teachers in non-biased assessment and instruction.

Assessment of Reading Achievement

Tests that are administered to large numbers of students, including statewide and national assessments, are moving away from norm-referenced multiple choice tests to assessments that require students to actively engage in constructing and examining the meaning of reading selections (Education World Trust, 2003). Reading is now regarded as a dynamic process through which readers construct meaning by applying their knowledge and reasoning to the text (Winograd, Paris, & Bridge, 1991). Reading specialists have argued that this conceptualization of reading is not compatible with traditional reading achievement tests (Haney & Madaus, 1989; Wolf, Bixley, Glenn, & Gardner, 1991).

The new "authentic" tests require students to perform real tasks that produce desirable results in a realistic and natural context (Wiggins, 1992). For example, if one wished to assess a student's ability to read an expository article in order to gain new information, it would not seem sensible to ask the student to read artificial paragraphs and answer multiple-choice questions. Rather, it would make more sense to have the student read an actual article without time constraints and then tell or write about what he or she had learned. Similarly, in writing it makes more sense to allow the student time to write a draft, reflect on the work, and revise.

Many state testing programs are developing assessments of reading and writing that are more authentic (Mitchell, 1992; O'Neil, 1992). The National Assessment of Educational Progress (NAEP), the agency authorized by Congress to assess the educational progress of students throughout the nation, collects achievement data from nationally representative samples of students in the fourth, eighth and twelfth grades. The NAEP assessments are determined from: (1) longer passages that were originally written for students to read for information or enjoyment; (2) the students' ability to read a variety of types of text for a variety of different purposes; and (3) asking students to respond to open-ended questions that allow for a variety of interpretations and a range of acceptable responses.

Two types of reading skills practice are *error analysis* and *informal reading inventories* (IRIs). Informal reading inventories are published nonstandard assessment measures which consist of narrative or expository reading passages that students read and answer comprehension and factual questions pertaining to what was read. The reading passages are presented with increasing difficulty from preprimer through sixth grade levels or above (e.g., Bader, 1998; Burns & Roe, 2001; Johns & Lenski, 2005; Leslie & Caldwell, 2006).

Informal reading inventories are designed to assist the teacher in the observation and the identification of students' reading strategies, levels of reading, the strengths and needs of the student, and reading materials that might be appropriate for their development. The assessor can audio record the IRI administration to check for coding and analysis of reading skills such as oral reading errors and processing strategies used with contextual cues in addition to the auto-correction techniques of the reader. One of the most commonly used IRIs is that of Burns and Roe (Burns, Roe, & Ross, 1999). Studies have indicated the utility of IRI assessment of reading (Blachowicz, 1999; Clay, 2002; Neal & Kelly, 1999).

IRIs are helpful in bilingual reading assessments when adapted to bilingual or multicultural classroom settings. Bilingual IRIs are limited in availability (e.g., Spanish–English versions). However, they can be modified methodically to other languages when an assessment of reading is needed for a particular language (Coelho, 1998). Although there is little research to validate IRI use for ELLs and bilinguals, they are useful as part of an all-inclusive portfolio assessment.

Error analysis is most commonly associated with CBA. In this context, a teacher analyzes students' errors, and from this standpoint attempts to identify missing skills. Once deficiencies are identified, teachers can rectify the situation by modifying their instruction. However, Peverly and Kitzen (1998) stress that error analysis must include determining the causes of errors, otherwise the data will not be helpful. For second language learners and bilinguals, reading is affected by word knowledge in English and a fundamental comprehension of a story's organization and sense (Genesee et al., 2005). Studies seem to indicate that children and youth learning a second language lack several basic skills: (a) auditory discrimination of phonemes, (b) phonemic rules, (c) extensive vocabulary, and (d) effective sentence processing skills (Chiappe & Siegel, 1999; Verhoeven, 1990). Research further suggests that in cross-language transfer children transfer their first language skills (e.g., phonological and comprehension skills and strategies) to second language reading (e.g., transfer of phonology, vocabulary knowledge, and reading comprehension; Durgunoglu, Naagy, & Hancin-Bhatt, 1993; Ordoñez, Carlo, Snow, & McLaughlin, 2002; Royer & Carlo, 1991).

School psychologists are advised to have an understanding of these cross-transfer skills, since this can help determine whether reading errors manifested by bilingual and ELL children are a function of the transfer of their knowledge base from their first language to their second language. For example, a child may be decoding words in the second language (e.g., English) by using phonic sounds of their first language. Knowledge of these practices can be particularly helpful when attempting to evaluate reading skills, in determining whether a reading problem is the result of a reading disability, and in differentiating second language learning from a reading disability (see www.readingrockets.org for current information and research on reading, cited in Lerner, 2006, p. 374).

Portfolio Assessment

Another important approach in academic assessment is the use of portfolio assessment. (Portfolio assessment is discussed in Chapter 2 of this book.) Here, we incorporate this assessment method as regards literacy assessment. Portfolio assessment is a focused collection of a student's work over a period of time, which represents different types of academic tasks and assignments taken from the curriculum. As an alternative assessment method, portfolio assessment can be used by educators, in conjunction with practitioners, for determining racial/ethnic and culturally and linguistically diverse students' academic strengths and weaknesses. Students are allowed to set their goals, discuss their academic strengths and weaknesses, choose their work samples, and in due course explain the work's value. What is beneficial about this approach is that students are permitted to claim ownership of their learning within the environment as well as become actively involved in the process as they monitor their progress, and determine what they need for further academic development.

Portfolio assessment practice is a naturalistic approach because it is practiced directly in the classroom setting between the teacher and the student. As a result, the academic progress of the learner is connected to success in the classroom. It is important to note that portfolio assessment is not intended as a replacement for formal measures, but should be used in conjunction with formalized educational measures. Linking qualitative and quantitative data and methods helps to build a better understanding of the students' achievement (Barootchi & Keshavarz, 2002). Once again, this approach is very individualized and time consuming. Nevertheless, it should not be rejected because of time constraints.

Literacy portfolios are used for reading achievement assessments. A literacy portfolio is a systematic collection of diverse student products and teacher observations collected to indicate the student's progress over a period of time—the student products and the teacher observations are related specifically to instructional goals (Lamme & Hysmith, 1991). Teacher observations can include notes and completed checklists; student products can include reading logs, written summaries of reading material, self-reflective journal entries, and taped recounting of stories (Valencia & Pearson, 1990). Through reading logs, the portfolio can indicate the extent to which the student is developing positive attitudes toward reading. Likewise, by summarizing and interpreting passages designed for various grade levels, the portfolio can indicate the student's progress in comprehension.

Portfolio assessment for gauging literacy has been standardized in published vehicles, such as *The Learning Record* (Barr, Craig, Fisette, & Syverson, 1998), a three-part system that guides the collection of data relating to the student's literacy throughout the course of the academic year.

Part A, "Documenting Prior Experience," is completed early in the year. It contains data on the student's language background, parents' or caregivers' descriptions of the student as a learner, and the students' own descriptions of their accomplishments and goals.

Part B, "Documenting Student Learning," takes place throughout the year. Teachers and students use standardized data-collection forms to record evidence about what and how the student is learning. These data are tied to content standards and performance criteria congruent with those set by the district and the state. Near the end of the third quarter, the teacher prepares a summary of the student's achievements accumulated in the data collection forms. In addition, the teacher uses criterion-referenced Learning Record Reading and Writing Scales to rate the student in each area. For ELLs, the teacher also rates the student on a criterion-referenced English language learning scale.

Part C, "Reflecting on the Year's Work," takes place at the end of the year. Parents and students review the record of achievement described in Parts A and B, and add comments to complete the picture. The teacher updates the record and recommends the next steps to be taken.

The principles on which this method of portfolio assessment is based include: (1) thoughtfulness over rote learning; (2) performance capabilities rather than deficits; (3) fostering individual development within a framework of grade level expectations; and (4) stressing bilinguality and the value of understanding cultures beyond one's own. The use of the learning record encourages teachers to observe and record the behaviors of students as they apply new knowledge and/or strategies that are relevant to their prior and current experience.

Proponents of portfolio assessment stress that they: (a) discourage comparison with others and are more self-motivating for self-competition; (b) encourage one-on-one feedback with teacher and student; and (c) make available actual records of academic achievement. However, in spite of these advantages, they have been criticized because it is difficult to keep them organized for the entire school year, much less keep track of them for an eight-year period during the elementary grades (Van Ornum, Dunlap, & Shore, 2008). Siegle (2002) proposes the use of electronic portfolios stored on floppy disks, zip disks, CD-ROMs and school district servers (cited in Van Ornum et al., 2008). Other storage methods are audio files and video clips. The storage capacity of CD-ROMs makes them attractive, in addition to the fact that many of today's students are familiar or adept at storing music and pictures on CD-ROMs. Siegle offers the following tips on the construction of electronic portfolios:

- Involve students in the division of labor.
- Start students when they are young.
- Spread portfolio elections over time.
- Back up information when using digital images.
- Download to disk, and keep visual files small (Siegle, 2002).

Knowledge of portfolio assessments and the varied methods of data collection will increase the school psychologist's knowledge of childhood developmental learning processes and add a qualitative approach to academic testing and interventions.

Dynamic Assessment

Besides CBA, CBM, and portfolio assessments, dynamic assessment is another effective alternative assessment approach advantageous for evaluating culturally different racial/ethnic students. (Dynamic assessment is also discussed in Chapter 2 of this text.) The Russian psychologist Lev Vygotsky is the architect of this educational approach. Vygotsky's model of cognitive development stresses that children's learning potential is contained in what he calls the Zone of Proximal Development (ZPD). As described in Chapter 2, the ZPD is a sociocultural approach that provides the learner with a facilitator (usually the teacher and/or another helping adult) to demonstrate and explain the learning of new tasks. Dynamic assessment adopts this principle (test–teach–retest) by pretesting the child in the selected academic subject, teaching specific tasks through teacher demonstration, and then retesting. The tasks taught are similar to the tasks on the pretest as well as those on the posttest. As with CBM, the child's progress can be monitored by comparing scores on the pretest with the posttest to determine the child's transfer of skills. Elliott (2003) stresses that "instruction and feedback are built into the testing process and are differentiated on the basis of an individual's performance" (pp. 16–17). Thus instructional assistance is contingent upon the student's performance and modifiability. It is important to note that a child's current level of performance in a given area relative to the performance of that child's peers is not always a reflection of the child's true abilities. This is because a child's limited test performance may reflect dissimilar learning experiences and/or lack of educational experiences. It has been observed that children from CLD backgrounds may demonstrate lower scores on tests; however, their scores may not be a sign of their genuine abilities or learning potential (Gutierrez-Clellen & Pena, 2001).

There are various leading dynamic assessment approaches which have been designed in different languages throughout the world. Elliott (2003) refers to several leading dynamic approaches. Below is a replication of Elliott's description of these approaches.

A well-known approach is the Learning Potential Assessment Device, which was designed for low-achieving children. This device provides an unstandardized approach which permits the instructor to use any mediation deemed necessary for maximizing a student's academic performance. This type of method is especially helpful for low-achieving children (see Feuerstein, Feuerstein, & Gross, 1997).

Another method is the Graduated Prompts Approach, designed for children with learning difficulties. The key processes examined are inductive reasoning problems involving abstract or curriculum-related tasks. The type of assistance provided is a series of prompts or hints each time the student makes an error. The output seeks the student's efficiency of learning as determined by reference to the number of hints required and success on various transfer tasks (see Campione & Brown, 1984).

The Application of Cognitive Functions Scale (ACFS) was developed for children aged 3–5 and older children with learning disabilities. The key processes examined are the cognitive processes and learning strategies associated with typical early childhood learning activities. The scale provides a semi-standardized system of administration which yields both qualitative and quantitative information. The aim of the scale is to provide evidence of the child's development of cognitive functions related to typical demands of the preschool curricula and the child's ability to benefit from intervention (see Lidz, 2003).

For infants and toddlers, the Dynamic Assessment of Infants' and Toddlers' Abilities (DAITA) examines cognitive actions. The support provided is seen as a clinical approach in which scores reflect whether mediation is required to achieve a given criterion. The DAITA provides qualitative information about a child's current functioning and future potential with a strong emphasis on informing intervention (see Kahn, 2000). Most importantly, Elliott (2003) concludes his review by suggesting that there is a need for a change in the present model of assessment (classification, prediction, and selection), which aims to develop improved tools to better conduct assessments, to dynamic approaches that, when utilized, can help practitioners and teachers to collaborate in devising classroom-based educational interventions.

For ELLs, dynamic assessment methods are useful in assessing language base abilities. Children with typical language ability should demonstrate improvement on posttests, thus providing critical information for differential diagnosis between ELLs with a learning disability and those without a disability. Dynamic assessment is also recommended as a supplemental method to use with CLD children and youth in differentiating language differences and disorders, and to minimize misdiagnosis (Gutierrez-Clellen & Pena, 2001). Gutierrez-Clellen and Pena (2001) describe two case studies that demonstrate how a distinct test-teach-retest approach can be used effectively to differentiate language differences from disorders in CLD children across various language areas such as vocabulary, narrative, synonyms, and antonyms. Unlike regular test-teach-retest strategies, the dynamic assessment intervention phase recommended does not use the actual test items or materials, but instead provides "sufficient flexibility to address children's individual differences in performance by varying the activities in order to facilitate learning" (Gutierrez-Clellen & Pena, 2001, p. 221).

Learning Disabilities

School psychologists will encounter numerous children from various racial/ethnic and culturally and linguistically diverse backgrounds with learning disabilities. Approximately 15 percent of children in the United States have a learning disability (LD), with the most common type being a reading disorder (Sattler, 2001). The prevalence of children affected by a diagnosis of reading disorder is estimated at approximately 5–10 percent, and as much as 17.5 percent of the general population (Shaywitz, 1998). Consequently, involvement in the diagnosis of specific learning disabilities and placement decisions is an ordinary occurrence for the school psychologist.

This section briefly reviews current views on learning disabilities and applied diagnostic practices for accurate assessment approaches. Given the extent of this topic, the reader is advised to check the annotated bibliography at the end of this chapter for suggested readings.

Lerner (2006) reviews various definitions of an LD, from the federal definition to other significant definitions disseminated by different professional organizations for children and adults with learning disabilities. The federal definition (which is used widely) first appeared in Public Law 94-142 (PL-94-142), the Education for all Handicapped Children Act (1975). In later revisions, the same definition was incorporated into the 1990 PL-101-476

Individuals with Disabilities Education Act (IDEA), the PL-105-17 Individuals With Disabilities Education Act of 1997 (IDEA-1997), and most currently the PL-108-446 Individuals with Disabilities Education Improvement Act (IDEA-2004). The federal law definition serves as a foundational base for most state definitions and is employed in numerous schools. It states:

> The term "specific learning disability" means a disorder in one or more of the basic psychological processes involved in understanding or in using language, spoken or written, which disorder may manifest itself in imperfect ability to listen, think, speak, read, write, spell, or to do mathematical calculations. Such term includes such conditions as perceptual disabilities, brain injury, minimal brain dysfunction, dyslexia, and developmental aphasia. Such term does not include a learning problem that is primarily the result of visual, hearing, or motor disabilities; of mental retardation; of emotional disturbance; or of environmental, cultural, or economic disadvantage. (Lerner, 2006, p. 7)

There is a further definition in the federal law, known as an operational definition for children with learning disabilities (U.S. Office of Education, 1977), which provides directives for children with specific learning disabilities. The directives are reproduced below (as cited in Lerner, 2006):

- There is a specific learning disability if the student does not achieve at the proper age and ability levels in one or more specific areas when provided with appropriate learning experiences
- And, if the student has a severe discrepancy between achievement and intellectual ability in one or more of these seven areas: oral expression, listening comprehension, written expression, basic reading skills, reading comprehension, mathematics calculations, and mathematics reasoning. (p. 7)

A summary taken from Lerner (2006) of the basic concepts of the federal law definition includes the following guidelines for LD identification:

- An individual has a disorder in one or more of the basic psychological processes (e.g., mental abilities such as memory, auditory perception, visual perception, oral language, and thinking).
- An individual has difficulty in learning, specifically, speaking, listening, writing, reading (word recognition skills and comprehension), and mathematics (calculation and reasoning).
- If the problem is not primarily due to other causes, such as visual or hearing impairments; motor disabilities; mental retardation; emotional disturbance; or economic, environmental, or cultural disadvantage.
- To determine eligibility, the school may consider whether a severe discrepancy exists between the student's apparent ability for learning and his or her low level of achievement. (p. 7)

In another approach to determining a child's eligibility for LD services, the IDEA-2004 (PL-108-446) presents a new stipulation that schools are not required to take into consideration whether there is a severe discrepancy between achievement and intellectual ability or oral expression, listening comprehension, written expression, basic reading skill, reading comprehension, mathematics calculations, or mathematics reasoning (Lerner, 2006). Furthermore, IDEA-2004 stipulates that a school may utilize a prereferral process that uses the scientific, research-based intervention Response to Intervention (RTI) (see Chapter 2 for a review of RTIs) to determine whether a student can be evaluated for an LD, thus permitting two approaches for determining eligibility for LD services.

There are other significant definitions of LD detailed by several professional LD organizations that have influenced the definition of learning disabilities. One of the most recognized is from the National Joint Committee on Learning Disabilities (NJCLD). NJCLD is an organization of representatives from several professional organizations and disciplines engaged with LDs. This definition is important because it draws from the various disciplines that practice LD diagnosis. The main points explained by Lerner (2006) for both of these definitions are delineated in the box.

NJCLD Definition

1. Learning disabilities are a heterogeneous group of disorders. Individuals with LDs exhibit many kinds of behaviors and characteristics.

2. Learning disabilities result in significant difficulties in the acquisition and use of listening, speaking, reading, writing, reasoning, and/or mathematical skills.

3. The problem is intrinsic to the individual. LDs are due to factors within the person rather than to external factors, such as environment or the educational system.

4. The problem is presumed to be related to a central nervous system dysfunction. There is a biological basis to the problem.

5. LDs may occur along with other disabilities or conditions. Individuals can have several problems at the same time, such as LDs and emotional disorders.

SOURCE: Lerner (2006, p. 8).

To date, no consensus has been reached on the definition of an LD (Silver & Hagin, 2002). However, many LD definitions have common elements, with all agreeing that LDs have:

- central nervous system dysfunction;
- psychological processing deficits;
- difficulty in academic and learning tasks;
- discrepancy between potential and achievement; and
- exclusion of other causes (Lerner, 2006).

An important element common to LD definitions is that of discrepancy and achievement—specifically, the difference between the student's learning potential and what the student has actually learned. This is part of the federal law operational definition of LDs. A detailed explanation of each of these common elements in the LD definitions is beyond the scope of this text (see Lerner, 2006 for a complete explanation); however, it is important for school psychologists to know that there is abundant research which questions the validity of identifying students with LDs through a discrepancy between ability and achievement (Fletcher et al., 2004; Lyon, Alexander, & Yaffe, 1997; Vellutino, Scanlon, & Lyon, 2000). The major concern is that the IQ-achievement discrepancy criterion is solely affirmed on failure. This has been termed the "wait and fail" model, which obliges students to fall behind the predicted level of performance in order to be eligible for special services. Unfortunately, such a practice delays services until the third grade and further, thus preventing the student from progressing, as well as leading to low self-esteem and loss of interest and/or motivation for learning and schooling. RTIs are therefore considered usable as a prereferral process for students at risk for LDs.

Prior to conducting an assessment of academic achievement, the evaluative process usually begins with a referral to the Child Study Team, at which point school psychologists become involved in data collection within academic learning achievements. For an evaluation to be effective, the practitioner must assess cognitive functioning quantitatively and qualitatively, and examine the degree to which academic achievement is not commensurate with the estimated cognitive abilities.

In practice, the definition of an LD on the basis of an IQ-achievement discrepancy can be helpful since it helps highlight that a student who has difficulties in reading, writing, and mathematics many not necessarily be low-functioning cognitively (Berninger, Hart, Abbott, & Karovsky, 1992). Discrepancy formulas have been accepted in various forms by numerous school districts, yet these formulas have been criticized because of their theoretical and statistical assumptions and the ensuing discontent with current measures of intelligence and achievement (Silver & Hagin, 2002).

The use of an IQ-achievement discrepancy formula implies that the IQ scores obtained are "indices of learning potential, that IQ represents some innate, biological derived factor that sets the upper limit on ability attainment"

(Spearman, 1923). These practitioner/researchers stress that the intelligence quotient is a summary of several aspects of intellectual functioning, and does not measure some of the necessary skills connected to reading proficiency. And there is no question about how important reading is for academic learning (Francis, Epsy, Rourke, & Fletcher, 1991).

An academic assessment automatically includes an evaluation of reading, written language, and mathematics. Analysis of formal and informal measures will reveal whether there is a specific learning disability in reading, writing, and/or mathematics. Developmental reading disabilities are most prevalent in educational settings (Lerner, 1989). School psychologists are often not trained in the diagnosis of reading disabilities, as school psychology training programs usually include a reading disability course as an elective. This is lamentable since a large number of students are diagnosed and classified with developmental reading disabilities. Developing expertise in reading disabilities requires practitioners to further their knowledge and skills in this area through professional development courses as well as additional graduate training.

An important reading disorder (see annotated bibliography for additional readings in this important area of diagnosis) is dyslexia. Dyslexia is considered a very serious learning disability. Individuals (children and adults) with this disorder have difficulties recognizing letters and words, and in the interpretation of printed material. Individuals with dyslexia are intellectually capable and can have good spatial and mathematical skills (there are many famous people who have struggled with dyslexia). Here too we find that there are a number of different definitions of dyslexia. However, there is wide accord on several common elements (Hynd, 1992; Shaywitz, 2003, cited in Lerner, 2006, p. 376):

- Dyslexia has a biological basis and is caused by a disruption in the neural circuits in the brain.
- Dyslexia problems persist into adolescence and adulthood.
- Dyslexia has perceptual, cognitive, and language dimensions.
- Some individuals with dyslexia excel in other areas of life.

A professional organization known as the Orton Dyslexia Society declared in 1994 that dyslexia (a domain of learning disabilities) manifests a proximal processing defect of phonological processing, a defect which is crucial to the definition of learning disability. Furthermore, the Orton Society rejected the discrepancy formula for the identification of LDs as the fundamental part of the definition of LD because there is some evidence that the processing defect in reading disabilities involves phonological processing. Dyslexia experts explain that there are neuropsychological processing deficits, mainly in the language functions, and that there is a family and genetic basis to this disability (Silver & Hagin, 2002). While each individual will manifest unique processing deficits, there is a unifying deficit exhibited in "immaturity in development of language function considered in its broadest sense but most frequently in the ability to make accurate sound/symbol associations (phonemic-phonological processing), sequencing the sounds to make words, retaining the sounds in short-term memory, storing the sounds in long-term memory, understanding the meaning of the sequenced sounds, and finally expressing them in oral or in written form" (Silver & Hagin, 2002, p. 297).

Lerner (2006) reports that research currently provides evidence that dyslexia is caused by an abnormality in brain structure, a difference in brain function, and genetic factors (Gilger & Wise, 2003; Kibby & Hynd, 2001; Shaywitz & Shaywitz, 2003; Shaywitz et al., 1998; Fletcher, Foorman, Shaywitz, & Shaywitz, 1999; Zeffrino & Eden, 2000, cited in Lerner, 2006, p. 376) (see the medical aspects of learning disabilities in Lerner, 2006, Ch. 9). School psychologists are encouraged to become familiar with the elements of reading and reading assessment. This is an essential knowledge base for academic assessment of all children and adolescents. Additionally, teachers must provide reading instruction to dyslexic children. In view of this, school psychologists will automatically be linked to the teacher-child assessment process in prereferrals and referrals (see the National Reading Panel Web site—www.nationalreadingpanel.org—for more information about research findings on evidence-based assessment of reading and its implications for reading instruction; cited in Lerner, 2006). The following section reproduces several important components of reading as described by Lerner (2006). The National Reading Panel (2000) selected several elements of reading necessary for reading effectiveness. These include:

- phonemic awareness;
- phonics;
- fluency;
- vocabulary;
- text comprehension.

A knowledge base of each of these elements is important for academic learning and for assessment of achievement in reading.

Phonemic awareness is the ability to notice, think about, and work with the individual sounds in spoken words. Early on—before learning to read or write—children must learn to decipher words by their sounds. These are speech sounds known as phonemes. Syllables and rhymes are also included as part of phonemic awareness. Also included is word recognition which simply means the ability to recognize words.

Phonics is a critical skill necessary for word recognition. This involves learning the association of letters and sounds and applying that knowledge to recognize words and reading. Phonics is the relationship between printed letters (know as *graphemes*) and the sounds (*phonemes*) in language. The task for the child is to be able to *decode* printed material and translate the printed material into sounds. The latter is referred to as the symbol–sound relationship and is a process known as *breaking the code*. Breaking the code is essential for recognizing words quickly and effortlessly. Children with reading disabilities require direct instruction in phonics and decoding to assist the learning process.

Fluency is defined as the ability to read connected text quickly, without difficulty, and automatically (Hook & Jones, 2004; Meyer, 2002; National Reading Panel, 2000). The reader must develop fluency in order to make a bridge from word recognition to reading comprehension.

Vocabulary is word knowledge, and is obviously essential in reading and in reading comprehension. The reader must know the word and be able to apply it to the context of what is being read (e.g., sentences and/or paragraphs, or a story).

Text comprehension is the use of all of the above elements of reading in combination so as to make sense of what is being read. Reading comprehension skills must be developed by the use of appropriate instruction. Many students with reading disabilities experience great difficulty with reading comprehension, even when they have mastered word recognition skills.

Assessment of the mastery of these elements can be accomplished by both formal and informal methods. Semrud-Clikeman, Goldenring Fine, and Harder (2005) state that all models of reading disorder assume a core of phonological deficits. However, there is controversy as to whether "contributions from other cognitive domains are salient. At issue is whether there are identifiable subtypes within the broad definition of reading disability (RD)" (p. 408). In addition to the elements of reading listed above, Semrud-Clikeman and colleagues (2005) emphasize the importance of the role of memory and learning in conjunction with executive functions. The brain's frontal lobe controls executive functioning, including independent judgment and problem solving, abstraction and generalization, and inhibitory control of thoughts, emotions, and behavior (Connor et al., 2001). Semrud-Clikeman and colleagues (2005) explain that the role of the executive functions, particularly short term memory and learning strategies, is pertinent in the assessment of a reading disability. Executive functions are commonly agreed to mean higher-order cognitive processes that "allow for the perception, integration, and response to environmental stimuli toward a purposeful goal" (Baron, 2004). Consequently, attention, working memory, fluency, planning, and organization are all executive functions involved in reading and writing. Given this complex unconscious process, it is important for school psychologists to screen for possible deficits in these neuropsychological signs with the aim of recommending an assessment of executive functions (neuropsychological examination by a school neuropsychologist) to better describe and treat children and youth with LDs (see Semrud-Clikeman et al., 2005 for a review of neuropsychological services to learners with learning disabilities; see also the list of learning disabilities Web sites in Chapter 2).

Informal measures for the assessment of reading include observation of children as they read aloud, the use of IRIs, and portfolio assessment. Specifically, portfolio assessment in this domain includes collecting samples of the student's writing during the academic year as well as the use of a reflective log on the part of the teacher which records the student's reaction to books read with the aim of demonstrating growth in reading comprehension (Lerner, 2006). The IOTA Informal Word-Reading Test is recommended as an informal test for word-reading skills (Monroe, 1932).

Formal reading tests are classified as survey tests, diagnostic tests, or comprehensive batteries. Survey tests are group tests that provide an overall reading achievement level (e.g., the measure of word recognition and reading comprehension). Diagnostic tests are individually administered. They provide detailed information on the student's reading strengths and weaknesses. Comprehensive batteries include components that gauge several academic areas, including reading.

Some commonly utilized survey tests are the Metropolitan Achievement Tests (Grades K–12) and Wide-Range Achievement Test-3 (WRAT-3) (ages 5 to adult). Diagnostic tests are: the Diagnostic Assessment of Reading With Trail Teaching Strategies (DARTTS) (Grades 1–12, adult); the Stanford Diagnostic Reading Test (4th ed.) (Grades 1–12); and the Woodcock Reading Memory Test–Revised (ages 5 to adult). Lastly, comprehensive batteries to select are: the Brigance Comprehensions Inventory of Basic Skills–Revised (Grades K–9); the Kaufman Test of Educational Achievement (K-TEA) (Grades 1–12); the Peabody Individual Achievement Test–Revised (PIAT-R); and the Woodcock Johnson Tests of Achievement III (preschool to adult) (cited in Lerner, 2006).

This chapter concludes with assessment objectives for culturally and linguistically diverse students and youth. Gonzalez, Brusca-Vega, and Yawkey (1997) discuss how to separate mild disabilities from cultural and linguistic differences, and recommend alternative assessment practices such as portfolio assessment and observation (e.g., keeping anecdotal records, use of rating scales, and checklists). This is important for practitioners, since they must adhere to the most culturally sensitive assessment practices. The next section outlines several noteworthy assessment objectives recommended by Gonzalez et al. (1997).

The first major objective in any evaluative process is screening for academic problem(s). Screening helps to differentiate whether a child will or will not need a follow-up assessment. Screening can be accomplished through the use of screening measurements such as standardized tests, developmental problem-solving tasks, interviews and a home language survey (derived from different evaluation methods). Gonzalez and colleagues (1997) caution the use of standardized tests with culturally/linguistically diverse students since their norms may not represent all the linguistic and cultural groups. There is a danger of proceeding with an assessment if such a measure is used to interpret the culturally/linguistically diverse student by making the incorrect assumption that the results indicate a need for further assessment simply because the student is learning English as a second language or because the student may have been "socialized in a bicultural environment" (p. 99).

Once the screening procedure is accomplished, three other major assessment objectives need to be implemented. These are the identification and diagnosis of at-risk students (this is a major responsibility of school psychologists), program development, and program evaluation.

However, Gonzalez et al. (1997) emphasize that current assessment practices in the U.S. school system make it difficult for culturally/linguistically diverse students since they are at risk for misdiagnosis of LD. Below are three categories of at-risk factors that can be used when diagnosing students (presented by Gonzalez et al., 1997, p. 99):

1. internal conditions present at birth due to genetic disorders that can be medically diagnosed at the neurological level, causing developmental disabilities;

2. internal conditions present at birth (known as sleeper effects—for example, premature birth or susceptibility to environmental agents), that put students at high risk for developing handicaps or disabilities;

3. extreme conditions present in the physical and sociocultural environment (e.g., improper nutrition during a sensitive developmental period or a dysfunctional family) that can prevent internal potentials from developing fully due to a lack of opportunity.

The objective of assessment and program development is to make a placement decision and create an Individualized Educational Plan (IEP). In creating an IEP, it is advised that internal and external factors be assessed. Internal factors may include a student's competence and potentials (i.e., the skills the student has mastered as measured by traditional assessment methods). Learning potential can be measured through the use of qualitative approaches. External factors should include a description of the characteristics of the student's sociocultural environment (e.g., school, home, community, and neighborhood). Family strengths and needs are also important external factors. The inclusion of current family functioning is important too, as well as the identification of linguistic and cultural differences from the mainstream school culture.

Program evaluation (or curriculum evaluation) is recommended for reconsidering placement decisions, in addition to any possible impact observed that may be based on the educational program and the student's progress. To evaluate a program, educators and practitioners should evaluate the student's accomplishments as stated in the IEP goals (see Gonzalez, et al. 1997, Ch. 4).

In summary, this chapter reviewed core issues in academic assessment with the intention of providing an outline for best practices in this domain, and to stimulate school psychologists to continuously seek, through their professional development, appropriate and culturally fair academic assessment practices.

References

Anderson, J. R. (1976). *Language, memory, and thought.* Hillsdale, NJ: Lawrence Erlbaum.

Arreaga-Mayer, C., Tapia, Y., & Carta, J. J. (1993). *Ecobehavioral system for the complex recording of Interactional Bilingual Environments (ESCRIBE): Observer's manual.* Kansas City: Juniper Gardens Children's Project, University of Kansas.

Atwater, J. B., Carta, J. J., & Schwartz, I. S. (1989). *Assessment code/checklist for the evaluation of survival skills: ACCESS.* Kansas City: Juniper Gardens Children's Project, Bureau of Child Research, University of Kansas.

Bader, L. A. (1998). *Reading and Language Inventory [and] Reader's Passages to Accompany Reading and Language Inventory* (3rd ed.). Des Moines, IA: Merrill/Prentice Hall.

Baker, S. K. & Good, R. (1995). Curriculum-based measurement of English reading with bilingual Hispanic students: A validation study with second grade students. *School Psychology Review, 24,* 561–578.

Baron, I. (2004). *Neuropsychological evaluation of the child.* New York: Oxford University Press.

Barr, M. B., Craig, D. A., Fisette, D., & Syverson, M. A. (1998). Assessing literacy with the learning record: A handbook for teachers, grades K–6. Portsmouth, NH: Heinemann.

Barr, M., Craig, D., Syverson, M., & Fisette, D. (1999). *Assessing literacy with the Learning Record: A handbook for teachers, grades K–6* (2nd ed.). Portsmouth, NH: Heinemann.

Barton, L. E., & Johnson, H. A. (1990). Observational technology: An update. In S. R. Schroeder (Ed.), *Ecobehavioral analysis and developmental disabilities: The twenty-first century* (pp. 201–227). New York: Springer-Verlag.

Barootchi, N., & Keshavarz, M. H. (2002). Assessment of achievement through portfolios and teacher-made tests. *Educational Research, 44*(3), 279–288.

Berninger, V.W., Hart, T., Abbott, R., & Karovsky, P. (1992). Defining reading and writing disabilities with and without IQ: A flexible, developmental perspective. *Learning Disability Quarterly, 15*, 103–118.

Bentz, J., & Pavri, S. (2000). Curriculum-based measurement in assessing bilingual students: a promising new direction. *Diagnostique, 25*(3), 229–248.

Blachowicz, C. L. Z. (1999). Vocabulary in dynamic reading assessment: Two case studies. *Journal of Reading Psychology, 20*, 213–236.

Burns, M. K. (2002). Comprehensive system of assessment to intervetnion using curriculum-based asssessments. *Intervention in School and Clinic, 38*, 8–13.

Burns, M. K. (2004). Using curriculum-based assessment in the consultative process: A useful innovation or an educational fad. *Journal of Educational and Psychological Consultation, 14*, 63–78.

Burns, M. K., MacQuarrie, L. I., & Campbell, D. T. (1999). The difference between instructional assessment (curriculum based assessment) and achievement measurements: A focus on purpose and result. *Communiqué, 27*, 18–19.

Burns, P. C., & Roe, B. D. (2001). *Informal Reading Inventory: Preprimer to twelfth grade*. Wilmington, MA: Houghton Mifflin.

Burns, P. C, Roe, B. D., & Ross, E. P. (1999). *Technology for literacy learning: A primer*. Wilmington, MA: Houghton Mifflin.

Butler, F., & Stevens, R. (1997). *Accommodation strategies for English language learners on large-scale assessments: Student characteristics and other considerations*. Los Angeles: National Center for Research on Evaluation, Standards, and Student Testing, University of California.

Campione, J. C., & Brown, A. L. (1984). Learning ability and transfer propensity as sources of individual differences in intelligence. In P. H. Brooks, R. Sperber, & C. McCauley (Eds.), *Learning and cognition in the mentally retarded* (pp. 265–293). Hillsdale, NJ: Lawrence Erlbaum.

Carta, J. J., Greenwood, C. R., & Atwater, J. (1985). *Ecobehavioral System for Complex Assessment of Preschool Environments (ESCAPE)*. Kansas City, KS: Juniper Gardens Children's Project, Bureau of Child Research, University of Kansas.

Chamot, A. U., & O'Malley, J. M. (1994). *The CALLA handbook: Implementing the cognitive academic language learning approach*. Reading, MA: Addison-Wesley.

Chamot, A. U., & O'Malley, J. M. (1996). The cognitive academic language learning approach: A model for linguistically diverse classrooms. *Elementary School Journal, 96*, 259–273.

Chamberlain, P., & Medinas-Landurand, P. (1991). Practical consideratins for the assessment of limited English proficient students with special needs. In E. V. Hamayan & J. S. Damico (Eds.), *Limiting bias in the assessment of bilingual students* (pp. 111–156). Austin, TX: Pro-Ed.

Chiappe, P., & Siegel, L. (1999). Phonological awareness and reading acquisition in English- and Punjabi-speaking Canadian children. *Journal of Educational Psychology, 91*(1), 20–28.

Clay, M. M. (2002). *An observation survey of early literacy achievement.* Portsmouth, NH: Heinemann.

Coelho, E. (1998). *Teaching and learning in multicultural schools: An integrated approach.* Clevedon, UK: Multilingual Matters.

Collier, V. P. (1989). How long? A synthesis of research on academic achievement in a second language. *TESOL Quarterly, 13*, 171–182.

Connor, K., Dettmer, J., Dise-Lewis, J. E., Murphy, M., Santistevan, B., & Seckinger, B. (2001). *Brain injury: A manual for educators.* Denver, CO: Colorado Department of Education State Library and Adult Education Office.

Cummins, J. (1994). The acquisition of English as a second language. In K. Spangenberg-Urbschat, & R. Pritchard (Eds.), *Kids come in all languages: Reading instruction for ESL students* (pp. 36–62). Newark, DE: International Reading Association.

DeAvila, E. A., & Ducan, S. E. (1984). *Finding out/descubrimiento. Training manual.* San Rafael, CA: Linguametrics Group.

Deno, S. L. (1985). Curriculum-based measurement: The emerging alternative. *Exceptional Children, 52*, 219–232.

Deno, S. L. (2003). Developments in curriculum-based measurement. *Journal of Special Education, 37*, 184–192.

Deno, S. L., & Fuchs, L. S. (1987). Developing curriculum-based measurement systems for databased special education problem solving. *Focus on Exceptional Children, 19*(8), 1–16.

Durgunoglu, A. Y., Nagy, W. E., & Hancin-Bhatt, B. J. (1993). Cross-language transfer of phonological awareness. *Journal of Educational Psychology, 85*, 453–465.

Education World (2003). Are high-stakes tests punishing some students? Retrieved September 28, 2007, from www.education-world.com/a_issues/issues093.shtml

Elliott, J. (2003). Dynamic assessment in educational settings: Realising potential. *Educational Review, 55*(1), 15–32.

Feuerstein, R., Feuerstein, R., & Gross, S. 1997. Learning potential assessment device, in D. P. Flanagan, J. L. Genshaft, & P. L. Harrison (Eds.), *Contemporary intellectual assessment: Theories, tests, and issues.* New York: Guilford Press.

Fewster, S., & Macmillan, P. (2002). School based evidence for the validity of Curriculum Based Assessment measurement of reading and writing. *Remedial & Special Education, 23*, 149.

Fletcher, J. M., Coulter, W. A., Reschly, D. J., & Vaughn, S. (2004). Alternative approaches to the definition and identification of learning disabilities: Some questions and answers. *Annals of Dyslexia, 54*, 304–331.

Fletcher, J. M., Foorman, B. R., Shaywitz, S. E., & Shaywitz, B. A. (1999). Conceptual and methodological issues in dyslexia research: A lesson for developmental disorders. In H. Tager-Flusberg (Ed.), *Neurodevelopmental disorders* (pp. 271–306). Cambridge, MA: MIT Press.

Francis, D. J., Epsy, K. A., Rourke, B. P, & Fletcher, J. M. (1991). Validity of intelligence test scores in the definition of learning disability: A critical analysis. In B. P. Byron (Ed.), *Neuropsychological validation of learning disability subtypes* (pp. 15–44). New York: Guilford Press.

Fuchs, L. S., & Deno, S. L. (1994). Must instructionally useful performance assessment be based on the curriculum? *Exceptional Children, 61*(1), 15–24.

Fuchs, L., Deno, S., & Mirkin, P. (1984). Effects of frequent curriculum-based measurement and evaluation on pedagogy, student achievement, and student awareness of learning. *American Educational Research Journal, 21*, 449–460.

Gagne, E. D. (1985). *The cognitive psychology of school learning*. Boston: Little, Brown.

Garcia, G., & Pearson, P. (1994) Assessment and diversity. *Review of research in education, 20*, 337–391.

Genesee, F. (1987). *Learning through two languages: Studies of immersion and bilingual education*. Rowley, MA: Newbury House.

Genesee, F., Lindholm-Leary, K., Saunders, W., & Christian, D. (2005). English language learners in US schools: An overview of research findings. *Journal of Education for Students Placed at Risk, 10*(4), 363–386.

Gibbs, J. T., & Huang, L. N. (2003). *Children of color: Psychological interventions with culturally diverse youth* (2nd ed.). Somerset, NJ: Jossey-Bass.

Gickling, E. E., & Havertape, J. (1981). *Curriculum-based assessment (CBA)*. Minneapolis, MN: National School Psychology Inservice Training Network.

Gilger, J. W., & Wise, S. E. (2004). Genetic correlates of language and literacy impairments. In C. A. Stone, E. R. Silliman, B. J. Ehren, & K. Apel (Eds.), *Handbook of language and literacy: Development and disorders* (pp. 25–48). New York: Guilford Press.

Gonzalez, J. E., Nelson, J. R., Gutkin, T. B., Saunders, A., Galloway, A., & Shwery, C. S. (2004). Rational Emotive Therapy with children and adolescents: A meta-analysis. *Journal of Emotional & Behavioral Disorders, 12*(4), 222–246.

Gonzalez, V., Brusca-Vega, R., & Yawkey, T. (1997). *Assessment and instruction of culturally and linguistically diverse students: With or at-risk of learning problems*. Needham Heights, MA: Allyn & Bacon.

Gottlieb, M. (2006). *Assessing English language learners: Bridges from language proficiency to academic achievement*. Thousand Oaks, CA: Corwin Press.

Grabe, W. (1991). Current development in second language reading research. *TESOL Quarterly, 25*, 375–406.

Greenwood, C. R. (2001). Class wide peer tutoring learning management system. *Remedial & Special Education, 22*, 34–48.

Greenwood, C. R., Carta, J. J., Kamps, D., Terry, B., & Delquadri, J. (1994). Development and validation of standard classroom observation systems for school practitioners: Ecobehavioral assessment systems software (EBASS). (Special technology-based assessment within special education). *Exceptional Children, 61*, 197–211.

Gutierrez-Clellen, V. F., & Pena, E. (2001). Dynamic assessment of diverse children: A Tutorial. *Language, Speech, and, Hearing Services in Schools, 32*, 212–224

Haney, W., & Madaus, G. (1989). Searching for alternatives to standardized tests: Whys, whats, and whatever. *Phi Delta Kappan, 70*, 683–687.

Haney, W., Madaus, G., & Lyons, R. (1993). *The fractured marketplace for standardized testing*. Boston, MA: Kluwer Academic.

Hess, R. S., & Rhodes, R. L. (2005). Providing neuropsychological services to linguistically diverse learners. In R. C. D'Amato, E. Fletcher-Janzen, & C. R. Reynolds (Eds.), *Handbook of School Neuropsychology* (pp. 403–424). Hoboken, NJ: John Wiley & Sons.

Hook, P. E., & Jones, S.D. (2002). The importance of automaticity and fluency for efficient reading comprehension. *Perspectives, 28*(1), 9–14.

Hynd, G. W. (1992). Neurological aspects of dyslexia: Comment on the balance model. *Journal of Learning Disabilities, 25*, 110–112, 123.

Hynd, G. W., & Reynolds, C. R. (2005). School neuropsychology: The evaluation of a specialty in school psychology. In R. C. D'Amato, E. Fletcher-Janzen, & C. R. Reynolds (Eds.), *Handbook of School Neuropsychology* (pp. 3–14). Hoboken, NJ: John Wiley & Sons.

Johns, J. L., & Lenski, S. D. (2005). *Improving reading: Strategies and resources* (4th ed.). Dubuque, IA: Kendall/Hunt.

Kahn, R. (2000). Dynamic assessment of infants and toddlers. In C. S. Lidz, & J. G. Elliott (Eds.), *Dynamic assessment: Prevailing models and applications* (pp. 229–262). Amsterdam: JAI/Elsevier Science.

Keyser, D. J. & Sweetland, R. C. (Eds.). (1988). *Test critiques* (Vol. III). Austin, TX: Pro-Ed.

Kibby, M. Y., & Hynd, G. W. (2001). Neurobiological basis of learning disabilities. In D. P. Hallahan, & B. K. Keogh (Eds.), *Research and global perspectives in learning disabilities* (pp. 25–42). Hillsdale, NJ: Lawrence Erlbaum.

Kovaleski, J. F., Tucker, J. A., & Duffy, D. J. (1995). School reform through instructional support: The Pennsylvania Initiative (Part I). *Communiqué, 23*(8), insert.

Lamme, L. L., & Hysmith, C. (1991). One school's adventure into portfolio assessment. *Language Arts, 68*, 629–640.

Lerner, J. W. (1989). Educational interventions in learning disabilities. *Journal of the American Academy of Child and Adolescent Psychiatry, 28*, 326–331.

Lerner, J., with Kline, F. (2006). *Learning disabilities and related disorders: Characteristics and teaching strategies*. Boston: Houghton Mifflin.

Leslie, L., & Caldwell, J. (2006). *The Qualitative Reading Inventory IV (QRI-IV)*. Boston: Pearson.

Lezak, M. D. (1995). *Neuropsychological assessment* (3rd ed.). New York: Oxford University Press.

Lidz, C. S. (2003). *Early childhood assessment*. Hoboken, NJ: John Wiley & Sons.

Lu, C., & Suen, H. K. (1995). Assessment approaches and cognitive styles. *Journal of educational measurements, 32*(1), 1–17.

Lyon, G. R., Alexander, D., & Yaffe, S. (1997). Progress and promise in research in learning disabilities. *Learning disabilities: A multidisciplinary journal, 8*, 1–6.

Martines, D., & Rodriguez-Srednicki (2007). Academic assessment. In G. B. Esquivel, E. C. Lopez, & S. Nahara, S. (Eds.), *Handbook of multicultural school psychology: An interdisciplinary perspective.* Mahwah, NJ: Lawrence Erlbaum.

McCloskey, D., & Schicke Athanasiou, M. (2000). Assessment and intervention practices with second-language learners among practicing school psychologists. *Psychology in the Schools, 37*(3), 209–225.

McLaughlin, B. (1990). Restructuring. *Applied Linguistics, 11*, 113–128.

McLean, M., Bailey, D. B., & Wolery, M. (2004). *Assessing infants and preschoolers with special needs* (3rd ed.). Upper Saddle River, NJ: Pearson Merrill Prentice Hall.

McLeod, B., & McLaughlin, B. (1986). Restructuring or automatization? Reading in a second language. *Language Learning, 36*, 109–126.

Merrell, K. W., Ervin, R. A., & Gimpel, G. A. (2006). School psychology for the 21st century: Foundations and practices. *British Journal of Educational Psychology, 77*(3), 746–747.

Meyer, M. (2002). Repeated reading: An old standard is revisited and renovated. *Perspectives: International Dyslexia Association, 28*(1), 15–18.

Mitchell, R. (1992). *Testing for learning: How new approaches to evaluation can improve American schools.* New York: The Free Press.

Mohan, B.A. (1986). *Language and content.* Reading, MA: Addison-Wesley.

Monroe, M. (1932). *Children who cannot read.* Chicago: University of Chicago Press.

National Association of School Psychologists. (2003). Portraits of children: Culturally competent assessment. Video and CD-ROM training package. ASPIRE/IDEA.

National Reading Panel (2000). National Reading Panel report on fluency. In J. Lerner & F. Kline (Eds.), *Learning disabilities and related disorders: Characteristics and teaching strategies.* Boston: Houghton Mifflin.

Neal, J., & Kelly, P. (1999). The success of Reading Recovery for English language learners and Descubriendo la Lectura for bilingual students in California. *Literacy Teaching and Learning: An International Journal of Early reading and Writing, 4*(2), 81–108.

Noell, G. H., Gansle, K. A., & Allison, R. (1999). Do you see what I see? Teachers' and school psychologists' evaluations of naturally occurring consultation cases. *Journal of Educational and Psychological Consultation, 10*, 107–128.

O'Neil, J. (1992). Putting performance assessment to the test. *Educational Leadership, 49*, 14-19.

Ordoñez, C., Carlo, M., Show, C., & McLaughlin, B. (2002). Depth and breadth of vocabulary in two languages: Which vocabulary skills transfer? *Journal of educational psychology, 94*, 719–728.

Payne, D. A. (2003). *Applied educational assessment* (2nd ed.). Belmont, CA: Wadsworth Thomson.

Peverly, S. T., & Kitzen, K. R. (1998). Curriculum-based assessment of reading skills: Consideration and caveats for school psychologists. *Psychology in the Schools, 35*, 29–47.

Pressley, M. and Associates (1990). *Cognitive strategy instruction that really improves children's academic performance*. Cambridge, MA: Brookline.

Psychological Corporation (1997). *Spanish-language Aprenda Achievement Test*. New York: Psychological Corporation.

Rivera, C., Stansfield, C., Scialdone, L., & Sharkey, M. (2000). *An analysis of state policies for the inclusion and accommodation of English language learners in state assessment programs during 1998–1999*. Arlington, VA: George Washington University, Center for Equity and Excellence in Education.

Roberts, M. L., & Shapiro, E. S. (1996). Effects of instructional ratios on students' reading performance in a regular education program. *Journal of School Psychology, 34*, 73–91.

Rosenfield, S. (1987). *Instructional consultation*. Mahwah, NJ: Lawrence Erlbaum.

Royer, J. M., & Carlo, M. S. (1991). Transfer of comprehension skills from native to second language. *Journal of Reading, 1*(6), 450–455.

Samuda, R. J. (1998). *Psychological testing of American minorities: Issues and consequences* (2nd ed.). Thousand Oaks, CA: Sage.

Samuda, R. J., Feurstein, R., Kaufman, A. S., Lewis, J. E., Sternberg, R. J., & Associates. (1998). *Advances in cross-cultural assessment*. Thousand Oaks, CA: Sage.

Sattler, J. M. (2001). *Assessment of children: Cognitive applications* (4th ed.). San Diego, CA: Jerome M. Sattler.

Saudargas, R. A. (1992). *State-event classroom observation system (SECOS)*. Knoxville, TN: Department of Psychology, University of Tennessee.

Semrud-Clikeman, M., Goldenring Fine, J., & Harder, L. (2005). Providing neuropsychological services to students with learning disabilities. In R. C. D'Amato, E. Fletcher-Janzen, & C. R. Reynolds (Eds.), *Handbook of School Neuropsychology* (pp. 403–424). Hoboken, NJ: John Wiley & Sons.

Shapiro, E. S. (1990). An integrated model for curriculum-based assessment. *School Psychology Review, 19*, 331–350.

Shapiro, E. S. (1992). Use of Gickling's model of curriculum-based assessment to improve reading in elementary age students. *School Psychology Review, 21*, 168–176.

Shapiro, E. S., Angello, L. M., & Eckert T. L. (2004). Has curriculum-based assessment become a staple of school psychology practice? An update and extension of knowledge, use, and attitudes from 1990 to 2000. *School Psychology Review, 33*, 249–257.

Shapiro, E. S., & Elliott, S. N. (1999). Curriculum-based assessment and other performance-based assessment strategies. In C. R. Reynolds, & T. B. Gutkin (Eds.), *The handbook of school psychology* (3rd ed.; pp. 383–408). New York: John Wiley & Sons.

Shaywitz, S. E. (1998). Dyslexia. *The New England Journal of Medicine, 338*, 307–312.

Shaywitz, S. E., & Shaywitz, B. A. (2003). Neurobiological indices of dyslexia. In H. L. Swanson, K. R. Harris, & S. Graham (Eds.), *Handbook of learning disabilities* (pp. 514–531). New York: Guilford Press.

Shaywitz, S. E., Shaywitz, B. A., Pugh, K. R., Fulbright, R. K., Constable, R. T., Mencl, W. E., et al. (1998). Functional disruption in the organization of the brain for reading in dyslexia. *Proceedings of the National Academy of Sciences USA, 95*, 2636–2641.

Shinn, M. R. (1989). *Curriculum-based measurement: Assessing special children*. New York: Guilford Press.

Shinn, M. (Ed.). (1998). Curriculum-based measurement: Assessing special children. In M. R. Shinn (Ed.), *Advanced applications of curriculum-based measurement*. New York: Guilford Press.

Shinn, M., Collins, V. L., & Gallagher, S. (1998). Curriculum-based measurement and its use in a problem-solving model with students from minority backgrounds. In M. R. Shinn (Ed.), *Advanced applications of curriculum-based measurement* (pp. 143–174). New York: Guilford Press.

Shinn, M. R., Rosenfield, S., & Knutson, N. (1989). Curriculum-based assessment: A comparison of models. *School Psychology Review, 18*, 299–316.

Shuell, T. J. (1986). Cognitive conceptions of learning. *Review of Educational Research, 56*, 411–436.

Siegle, D. (2002). Creating a living portfolio: Documenting student growth with electronic portfolios. *Gifted Child Today Magazine, 25*(3), 60–65.

Silver, A., & Hagin, R. (2002). *Disorders of learning in childhood* (2nd ed.). New York: John Wiley & Sons.

Sommers, R. K. (1989). Language assessment: Issues in the use and interpretation of tests and measures. *School Psychology Review, 18*, 452–462.

Spearman, C. (1923). *Nature of 'intelligence' and principles of cognition*. London: Macmillan.

Stake, R. E. (1967). Toward a technology for the evaluation of educational programs. In R. W. Tyler, R. M. Gagné, & M. Scriven (Eds.), *Perspectives of curriculum evaluation* (pp. 1–18). Chicago: Rand McNally.

Stanley, S. O., & Greenwood, C. R. (1981). *Code for instructional structure and student academic response: CISSAR*. Kansas City: Juniper Gardens Children's Project, Bureau of Child Research, University of Kansas.

Suzuki, L., Ponterotto, J., & Meller, J. P. (Eds.) (2002*). The Handbook of Multicultural Assessment*. San Francisco: Jossey-Bass.

Torres, J. (1991). Equity in education and the language minority student. *Forum, 14*, 1–3.

U.S. Department of Education (2005). Biennial evaluation report to Congress on the implementation of Title III, Part A of the ESEA: Executive Summary, i–vi. Retrieved July 14, 2005, from www.ed.gov/about/offices/list/oela/index.html?src=oc

U.S. Office of Education. (1977). Assistance to states for education of handicapped children: Procedures for evaluating specific learning disabilities. *(Federal Register, 42:65085–65085)*.

Valencia, S. W., & Pearson, P. D. (1990). Alternative assessment: Separating the wheat from the chaff. *Reading Teacher, 43*, 60–61.

Van Ornum, B., Dunlap, L. L., & Shore, M. (2008*). Psychological testing across the lifespan*. Upper Saddle River, NJ: Pearson Prentice Hall.

Vellutino, F. R., Scanlon, D. M., & Lyon, G. R. (2000). Differentiating between difficult-to-remediate and readily remediated poor readers: More evidence against the IQ–achievement discrepancy definition of reading disability. *Journal of Learning Disabilities, 33*, 223–238.

Verhoeven, L. T. (1990). Acquisition of reading in a second language. *Reading research quarterly, 25,* 90–114.

Weinstein, C. E., & Mayer, R. E. (1986). The teaching of learning strategies. In M. C. Wittrock (Ed.), *Handbook of Research on Teaching* (3rd ed.; pp. 315–27). New York: Macmillan.

Wiggins, G. (1992). Creating tests worth taking. *Educational Leadership, 49,* 26–33.

Winograd, P., Paris, S., & Bridge, C. (1991). Improving the assessment of literacy. *The Reading Teacher, 45,* 108–116.

Wolf, D., Bixley, J., Glenn, J., & Gardner, H. (1991). To use their minds well: Investigating new forms of student assessments. In G. Grand (Ed.), *Review of Research in Education (Vol. 17)* (pp. 31–74). Washington, DC: AERA.

Woodcock, R. W., McGrew, K. S., & Mather, N. (2001). *Woodcock-Johnson-III Tests of Achievement.* Itasca, IL: Riverside Publishing.

Woodcock, R. W. & Muñoz-Sandoval, A. F. (1995). *Woodcock Language Proficiency Battery-Revised: Spanish Form.* Itasca, IL: Riverside Publishing.

Ysseldyke, J. E., & Christensen, S. (1993*). TIES-III: The instructional environment system III.* Longmont, CO: Sopris West.

Ysseldyke, J. E., & Christenson, S. (2002*). Functional assessment of academic behavior: Creating successful learning environments.* Longmont, CO: Sopris West.

Zeffrino, T., & Eden, G. (2000). The neural basis of developmental dyslexia. *Annals of Dyslexia, 50,* 3–30.

Annotated Bibliography

D'Amato, R. C., Fletcher-Janzen, E., & Reynolds, C. R. (Eds.). (2005). *Handbook of School Neuropsychology* (pp. 403–424). Hoboken, NJ: John Wiley & Sons. *A comprehensive review of this new field for the school practitioner.*

Gottlieb, M. (2006). *Assessing English language learners: Bridges from language proficiency to academic achievement.* Thousand Oaks, CA: Corwin Press. *This text provides a wide-range of important information for the practitioner assessing and servicing ELLs.*

Lachat, M. (2004). *Standards-based instruction and assessment for English language learners.* Thousand Oaks, CA: Corwin Press. *A comprehensive text that encompasses standard-based instructional approaches and assessment practices for ELLs.*

Lerner, J., with Kline, F. (2006). *Learning disabilities and related disorders: Characteristics and teaching strategies.* Boston, MA: Houghton Mifflin. *An excellent source covering all aspects of learning disabilities—from assessment to interventions.*

McLean, M., Wolery, M., & Bailey, D. B. Jr. (2004). *Assessing infants and preschoolers with speical needs* (3rd ed). Upper Saddle River, NJ: Merrill Prentice Hall. *This text is a must for practitioners assessing infants and preschoolers. The text reviews various assessment methods.*

Silver, A., & Hagin, R. (2002). *Disorders of learning in childhood* (2nd ed.). New York: John Wiley & Sons. *This second edition is a must for the school psychologist. The text is a comprehensive handbook on learning disorders in childhood. The authors cover the legal implications of special education placement as well as providing thorough diagnostic guidelines, which include their decades of research and work with learning-disordered children and youth.*

Useful Websites

Learning Disabilities Online: www.ldonline.org/ldresources
Federation for Children with Special Needs: http://fcsn.org/index.php
Learning Disabilities Worldwide: www.ldam.org/
National Dissemination Center for Children with Disabilities: www.nichcy.org
National Down Syndrome Society: www.ndss.org
Parent Educational Advocacy Training Center: www.peatc.org
Disability Rights Education and Defense Fund: www.dredf.org
National Association for the Education of African American Children with Learning Disabilities: www.charityadvantage.com/aacld/News.asp
Learning Disabilities Association of California: www.ldaca.org

5

Clinical Assessment in a Multicultural Context

When Is a Clinical Assessment Indicated?

The broad perception of school psychology practice is that school psychologists are clinicians responsible for servicing children and youth experiencing academic and behavioral problems associated within school settings. This view usually infers that school settings are not places where the diagnosis and treatment of mental disorders occur. Mental disorders are perceived as psychopathologies that are assessed and treated by psychiatrists outside the school. This is partly correct. Many children and youth manifesting psychopathologies are assessed and treated in mental health clinics. However, these same children attend school daily, thus manifesting their pathologies in the classroom. And many children have suffered mental disorders for years but are not diagnosed or treated until their case reaches the school psychologist.

Child and adolescent mental health needs have become a chronic problem throughout the United States and in educational institutions. Studies from the 1960s to the present have shown that there is a significant prevalence of children with emotional, behavioral, or developmental problems. A 1994 study of incidence rates revealed that between 17 and 22 percent of children and youth under the age of 18 had some kind of significant impairment. Even more remarkable is the fact that this represented between 11 and 14 million of the 64 million youth in the United States (Kazdin & Johnson, 1994). Another study observed that children and adolescents with disorders were not identified by educational, mental health, and social services, leaving them

undiagnosed and therefore, untreated (Doll, 1996). More recent studies estimated that one in five children have a "diagnosable disorder" with one in 10
having a disorder that considerably influences their functioning within the
home, at school, or within the community (Hynd et al., 2005; Tolan &
Dodge, 2005). It is evident that children and adolescents are not being serviced adequately despite close to four decades of research investigations that
have documented the need for more adequate identification and treatment
(Thompson Prout & Brown, 2007).

From this chronic crisis arises the question: What clinical professional is
usually the first to diagnose a psychopathology? Since it is obvious that there
is an increasing emergence of psychiatric disorders in schools, traditional
educational and psychological assessments within schools are no longer the
only responsibility of school psychologists. Currently, school psychologists
are advised to have a thorough knowledge of the American Psychiatric
Association's (APA) *Diagnostic and Statistical Manual of Mental Disorders,*
4th edition (DSM-IV) (APA, 2004). House (2002) explains that this comprehensive diagnostic system has become a tool by which diagnostic deter-
minations are made by school psychologists facing increasing demands.
House refers to a review of epidemiological studies which revealed that, in
an average school of 1,000 students, 180 to 220 students can be expected
to suffer from diagnosable psychiatric disorders (Doll, 1996, cited in
House, 2002). School psychologists are often the first practitioners to diagnose mental disorders in children and adolescents prior to any psychiatric
intervention.

When children and adolescents exhibit symptoms associated with anxiety
and mood problems, addictive behaviors, eating disorders, gender identity
problems, inappropriate behaviors, and learning and cognitive difficulties,
school psychologists are often the first to compile a set of data concerning
the problems and patterns observed by parents and teachers in the child or
student. Observational data, anecdotal reports, and behavioral rating scales
often disclose DSM-IV symptoms that can be diagnosed as:

- Anxiety Disorders (e.g., Separation Anxiety Disorder);
- Panic Disorder and Agoraphobia;
- Social Phobia;
- Obsessive-Compulsive Disorder;
- Post-Traumatic Stress Disorder;
- Major Depressive Disorder;
- Dysthymic Disorder;
- Bipolar Disorder;
- Autistic Spectrum Disorder (including Asperger's Syndrome);
- Attention Deficit Hyperactivity Disorder;

- Eating Disorders (including Anorexia Nervosa or Bulimia);
- Body Dysmorphic Disorder;
- Gender Identity Disorder;
- Conduct Disorder;
- Oppositional Defiant Disorder;
- Learning Disabilities;
- Mental Retardation; and
- Substance Use Disorders.

All of these disorders may require a DSM-IV psychiatric diagnosis and classification at the school level by a school psychologist when no other clinical interventions have occurred. This chapter therefore provides a brief overview of the role of the school psychologist in clinically applied DSM-IV diagnoses and the multicultural factors affecting diagnosis for children and youth. The chapter is not intended for DSM-IV training but to serve as a means of clarification regarding the important issues involved in psychiatric diagnosis in the schools (see House, 2002 for a review of DSM-IV in the schools).

What Is the Role of the School Psychologist?

Becoming involved in clinical diagnostic assessment is only one part of the emerging responsibilities of school psychologists. As mentioned in Chapter 4, the role of the school psychologist is evolving, and one result of the changing demands of school-based practices is that school clinical neuropsychology is becoming an increasingly important specialty in school psychology (Hynd & Reynolds, 2005). Since the publication of the DSM-IV in 1994, changes in the delivery of mental health services have impacted school psychology practice, with an increasing number of formal medical psychiatric diagnoses (House, 2002). One reason for the growing numbers of clinical psychiatric diagnoses in the schools is the need for appropriate DSM-IV classification corresponding to ICD-9CM numerical codes for insurance review and reimbursement in order to obtain school funding (Groth-Marnat, 2003; Power & DuPaul, 1996).

Involvement in a formal mental health assessment changes the traditional assessment approach used by school psychologists. It also challenges the school-based practitioner to be well trained in DSM-IV diagnosis criteria (see House, 2002 for a review of the DSM-IV axes). In fact, school psychologists are advised to consider expanding their professional role by seeking training and supervision in making psychiatric classifications. They are also encouraged to review legal regulations relevant to this domain of practice in conjunction with an attorney who is an expert in mental health practice.

In essence, school psychologists need to further their professional knowledge and skills in psychiatric diagnosis by proactively engaging in educational workshops, reading and learning, supervised practice, and regular participation in professional consultations. School psychologists have already demonstrated their knowledge and skills in psychoeducational and personality assessment of children and adolescents. Their expertise in these areas of assessment is an added professional capability that will enhance their competence in psychiatric classification (House, 2002).

Although the DSM-IV and the DSM-IV-TR (a publication of a text revision to the DSM-IV) are commonly utilized for psychiatric diagnoses, it is also important for school psychologists to have knowledge of other assessment systems, such as *The Classification of Child and Adolescent Mental Diagnoses in Primary Care: Diagnostic and Statistical Manual for Primary Care* (DSM-PC; Wolraich, Felice, & Drotar, 1996), the *International Classification of Impairments, Disabilities, and Handicaps* (ICDH), and the current revision of the *International Classification of Functioning and Disability* (ICDH2-B-2) (World Health Organization, 1999). An important difference between the DSM-IV and the ICDH2-B-2 is that the DSM-IV classifies diagnoses while the ICDH2-B-2 is used to classify functional characteristics. For a review of these systems, the reader is referred to Simeonsson and Scarborough (2001).

Data collected during an assessment can be used to support the diagnosis of a child or adolescent and help to select placements or to decide eligibility for special education services. Clinical data can be used to determine whether a child meets the criteria for mental retardation, autism, or internalized or externalized emotional problems which can then lead to select placement and special services for the child (Simeonsson & McMillen, 2001). It is also important to recognize that the term "diagnosis" can be interpreted differently in different situations, and the decisions which result from a diagnosis can be just as varied. Accordingly, school psychologists can find themselves making a diagnosis *informally*—that is, without actually recording the diagnosis in a formal professional record, or simply as a means to facilitate conversation with other professionals about the referred child/ student. Alternatively, school psychologists may make a *formal* diagnosis by officially recording it. Thus school psychologists often have a choice about whether to make a formal or informal diagnosis. However, they will need to be knowledgeable about policies concerning formal and informal diagnosis. It is important for best practice that the school psychologist keeps abreast of state regulations and district policies regarding mental health diagnosis in relation to educational settings. Particular states stipulate the regulation or license of professional mental health diagnosis, and some state school psychology associations have developed recommendations for third-party reimbursement when issues of diagnosis are involved (see Elliott, 1993). Economic issues are also increasingly influencing educational systems to consider psychiatric classification as part of the school psychologist's role, since the many mental health problems of children and adolescents require DSM-IV classification in order to obtain third-party sources of funding for psychological/educational services.

Although there are commonalities between the DSM-IV and IDEA systems, it is important to recognize that there are significant disparities. Both are classification and categorical systems and both indicate primary allocation of resources such as specific services, treatment interventions, medications, and placement decisions. However, the main differences indicate that both are different taxonomies of behavior, thus rendering it difficult for the professional to make an exact conversion from one system to the other. Most professionals agree that DSM-IV coverage is greater in psychiatric scope of symptomatic behaviors than the intended range of IDEA classification criteria. Nearly always, DSM-IV symptoms, severity, course, effects, and prognosis will be pertinent to IDEA eligibility for classification and services. However, some children with a DSM-IV diagnosis may not be eligible for IDEA services. In contrast, children eligible for IDEA may not have a DSM-IV disorder (House, 2002). In addition to all these considerations, school psychologists are advised to have a solid grasp of the issues involved in psychiatric diagnosis even if legalities prohibit school psychologists from making formal diagnoses. When only an informal diagnosis is permissible, the psychological report can and should include descriptions of observed symptoms and mention of any supporting data or documentation for a potential official diagnosis. By making a point of listing the signs and symptoms supporting a probable psychiatric diagnosis, the school psychologist can provide input that will allow a future review of a diagnosis.

House (2002) discusses several distinct factors that are involved in DSM-IV classification:

1. The DSM-IV is a categorical classification system that requires the practitioner to select a category(s) that best reflects a child's current functioning.

2. The purposes of a DSM-IV classification are: (a) to assign treatment; (b) to serve as a tool for communication with other professionals; (c) to provide statistical record keeping for use in program planning, outcome research, and for other application purposes; and (d) to ultimately lead to appropriate interventions.

3. Use of the DSM-IV for classification depends solely on the professional's clinical judgment, and this in turn results in a classification.

4. Special concern is advised regarding the use of categorical diagnostic classifications with children and youth. (pp. 10–11)

Practitioners are alerted to the significant concerns in the use of diagnostic classifications with children (see Blashfield & Fuller, 1996; Kirk & Kutchins, 1992; Kutchins & Kirk, 1995; Waldman, Lilienfeld, & Lahey, 1995). A review of these concerns is beyond the intent of this book. However, it is important to stress that DSM-IV classifications of childhood behavior problems at the school level is unavoidable. Conversely, it should not be assumed that the diagnostic process is the same as that of the general psychological evaluation normally generated in school settings. Because diagnostic categories for childhood disorders are increasing in number, the school psychologist's role is to take into account the challenges of clinical judgment in the use of such a diagnostic system with children and adolescents (Kronenberger & Meyer, 2001). Some of the developmental features that must be thought out carefully when attempting psychiatric diagnosis of children and adolescents are discussed by House (2002) and are listed below.

- Children and adolescents hardly ever refer themselves for treatment.
- Most children and youth are referred for treatment by their caretakers.
- Things children and youth worry or have anxiety about are not the same as those assumed by their caretakers.
- Children and adolescents tend to be more influenced by their environment than adults, and their problems are therefore more situationally specific.
- Many aspects of children's and youth's adjustment, functioning, and problems are evolving and changing more rapidly than for most adults.
- The evolving and changing aspects of children's and youth's functioning is problematic for categorical classification systems since these systems assume that classified persons will remain relatively steady unless intentionally altered.
- Special attention must be given to the evaluation of situational characteristics and variables before reaching a diagnostic decision for a child or youth.
- Language and cognitive differences between children and adults must be considered (pp. 12–13)

In addition to these differences in the psychiatric diagnosis of children and youth, consideration must be given to the possible inaccuracy or falsehood of verbal self-reports with children and youth. Most probably, preschoolers and early primary grades will not be able to report feelings of depression although they may report physical concerns. For this reason, self-report methods tend to be more valid when used with parents in conjunction with interviews, behavior rating scales, naturalistic observations, and conventional psychological testing. These differences have important implications for the use of the DSM-IV in the assessment of children and adolescents (House, 2002). Clinicians are advised to use structured interviews as a means of gathering information because they may be less biased, while unstructured interviews may result in interviewer perceptual bias (Groth-Marnat, 2003).

Much has been learned in child clinical psychopathology that obligates school psychologists to learn new methods of psychiatric assessment and diagnosis. The important thing is to not avoid the challenge but instead to move forward in expertise and advocacy so as to better service multicultural children and adolescents.

Multicultural Factors Affecting Diagnosis

One of the most important advancements in the assessment and psychiatric diagnosis of mental disorders has been the awareness of culture-bound syndromes. The DSM-IV includes an appendix that provides an outline for cultural formulation of a case in addition to a glossary of commonly talked about culture-bound syndromes in anthropology and cultural psychiatry (House, 2002; Paniagua, 2005). Additionally, the *DSM-IV Casebook* (Spitzer, Gibbon, Skodol, Williams, & First, 1994, cited in House, 2002) reviews various international cases presented to augment awareness of cultural phenomena in the manifestation of emotional and behavioral problems. Moreover, several researchers and applied psychologists have studied ethnic group differences and the impact of the use of the DSM-IV classifications on diverse populations (Bartholomew, 1995; Cervantes & Arrollo, 1994; Novins et al., 1997; Stein, 1993).

Culture-bound syndromes are defined in the DSM-IV (1994) as specific distressing experiences linked to certain societies and/or culturally localized areas. Each culture has its own name for the sign or syndrome (e.g., *attaque de nervios, koro, mal puesto, susto*) (Paniagua, 2005). However, current clinical instruments do not include criteria for assessing culture-bound syndromes. Consequently, practitioners are advised to develop their own system and to be "aware that the symptoms associated with a given mental disorder may be related to a particular cultural context without being part of a culture bound syndrome *per se*" (Paniagua, 2005, p. 140). Cultural variations are another important factor to consider when conducting a clinical assessment. One example of a cultural variation is the high rate of anorexia nervosa observed in the United States. Practitioners should be on the alert for these distinctive indicators of mental illness (Paniagua, 2005). It is important to note that, although the DSM-IV recommends that clinicians consider culture-bound syndromes and cultural variables, they are not obliged to review these in order to assign a psychiatric diagnosis (Paniagua, 2000). Clinicians who intend to adhere to the DSM-IV recommendations are reminded that certain clinical instruments such as the Minnesota Multiphasic Personality Inventory

(MMPI), the Child Behavior Checklist, and the Zung Depression Scale, as well as the DSM-IV, do not necessitate an evaluation of cultural variables that may result in identifying culture-bound syndromes or disorders linked to distinctive cultural contexts (Paniagua, 2005).

The appearance of the DSM-IV-TR in 2000 furthered the quest for culture-bound syndromes and cultural fairness in diagnosis. In essence, the DSM-IV-TR is a DSM-IV revision that was published in order to include modifications on more current information concerning psychopathologies. These alterations have not affected DSM-IV criteria; however, syndromes and their linked characteristics, cultural and gender features, course, and familial pattern have been updated based on current research findings. Clinicians using the DSM-IV-TR should be aware that, while these alterations may not affect a primary diagnosis, they could influence the secondary diagnosis (House, 2002). Thus clinicians will need to note whether any textual modifications that were made pertaining to associated symptoms create the need to further assess for what might possibly be a secondary diagnosis. What this means is that, once the clinician has arrived at a DSM-IV-TR primary diagnosis, any observed additional symptoms may be part of the initial primary diagnosis or may simply be distinct symptoms that will require a secondary diagnosis. Of further importance for school psychology practice is that IDEA 1997 and the DSM-IV comprehensive system are linked to the behavioral problems of children and adolescents (House, 2002). Hence school psychologists have sufficient support for initiating a psychiatric assessment and diagnosis.

Another important source for clinical assessment is Cuellar and Paniagua's (2000) outstandingly informative handbook of multicultural mental health, which reviews culture-bound syndromes, cultural variations, and the assessment and treatment of Asian Americans, Latinos, American Indians and Alaska Natives, and African Americans.

Fortunately, guidelines have been compiled to guide practitioners in minimizing bias during clinical assessment and diagnosis of individuals from multicultural groups when using current psychometric instruments (Bulhan, 1985; Jenkins & Ramsey, 1991; Wilkinson & Spurlock, 1986, cited in Paniagua, 2005). Several of the guidelines are replicated below and can be viewed as part of school psychology best practice when assessing multicultural student populations (i.e., culturally/linguistically, racial/ethnic children and youth).

1. The practitioner should examine his/her own biases and prejudices before engaging in the evaluation of clients who do not share the practitioner's race and ethnicity.

2. The practitioner should be aware of the potential effects of racism.

3. The practitioner should include an evaluation of socioeconomic variables.

4. The practitioner should try to reduce the sociocultural gap between the client and the person conducting the assessment.

5. The practitioner should ask culturally appropriate questions.

6. The practitioner should include an evaluation of culture-related syndromes and distinguish them from cultural variations.

7. The practitioner should consult with paraprofessionals and folk healers within the client's particular cultural group.

8. The practitioner should use the mental health status examination in a cultural context.

9. The practitioner should try to use the least biased assessment strategies first, and then consider using more biased strategies under special circumstances.

10. The practitioner should use Dana's (1993) assessment model as an overall approach to minimizing bias. (Paniagua, 2005, p. 127)

The use of Dana's (1993) model of assessment is recommended for reducing bias in the assessment of multicultural clients (Paniagua, 2005). In this model, clinicians are advised to adhere to the following five steps:

1. *Conduct an assessment of acculturation.* This should be done prior to the official assessment procedures (see Chapter 10).

2. *Provide a culture-specific service delivery style.* This service can be accomplished by observing culturally appropriate interpersonal etiquette.

3. *Use the client's native language (or preferred language).* Clinicians should always ask the client which is their preferred mode of communication.

4. *Select assessment measures that are appropriate for the client's cultural orientation and preferences.* Clinicians should use culture-specific instruments and base their assessment on a process that is adapted to the client's level of acculturation so as to understand the client in their cultural context (this is known as the *emic perspective*).

5. *Use culture-specific strategy when informing the client about the findings derived from the assessment process.* For example, a practitioner should give the results of psychometric tests such as the MMPI to a Hispanic adolescent's parents by stating, "I understand that in the Hispanic culture, many people believe that they can be affected by evil spirits. Perhaps the findings from this test (MMPI) suggest that your son is expressing this cultural belief rather than that he is really mentally ill." (pp. 149–152)

In practice, the "multicultural" school psychologist executing a DSM-IV or DSM-IV-TR diagnostic decision is obliged to review the possible impact of culture-bound syndromes and cultural variables to ensure accuracy of diagnosis. When appropriate, the psychologist should explain these to teachers and other school personnel. Although it is important to ascertain that cultural fairness has been considered carefully, an overemphasis on these variables may impede the identification of symptoms that are associated to serious psychiatric disorders, resulting in misdiagnosis (Paniagua, 2000). Consideration should also be given to what is developmentally expected at various age levels in children and adolescents if accurate diagnosis and interventions are to be effective. A crucial factor is that an observed undesirable behavior in early childhood may be age-appropriate. Distinguishing between normal and deviant behaviors can be difficult and could result in misdiagnosis (Erk, 2004). School psychologists are encouraged to expand their knowledge and skills in DSM-IV psychiatric diagnosis and to extend their advocacy for psychiatric follow-up beyond the school setting to the community at large.

References

American Psychiatric Association (APA). (2004). *Diagnostic and statistical manual of mental disorders* (4th ed.) (DSM-IV). Washington, DC: APA.

Bartholomew, R. E. (1995). Culture-bound syndromes as fakery. *Skeptical Inquirer, 19,* 36–41.

Blashfield, R. K., & Fuller, A. K. (1996). Predicting the *DSM-V. Journal of Nervous and Mental Disease, 186,* 244–246.

Bulhan, H. A. (1985). *Frantz Fanon and the psychology of oppression.* New York: Plenum.

Cervantes, R. C., & Arrollo, W. (1994). DSM-IV: Implications for Hispanic children and adolescents. *Hispanic Journal of Behavioral Sciences, 16*(1), 8–27.

Cuellar, I., & Paniagua, F. A. (Eds.). (2000). *Handbook of multicultural mental health.* San Diego, CA: Academic Press.

Dana, R. H. (1993). *Multicultural assessment perspectives for professional psychology.* Boston: Allyn & Bacon.

Doll, B. (1996). Children without friends: Implications for practice and policy. *School Psychology Review, 25,* 165–183.

Elliott, J. E. (1993). What have we learned from action research in school-based evaluation? *Educational Action Research, 1*(1), 175–186.

Erk, R. R. (2004). *Counseling treatment for children and adolescents with DSM-IV-TR disorders.* Upper Saddle River, NJ: Pearson Prentice Hall.

Groth-Marnat, G. (2003). *Handbook of psychological assessment* (4th ed.). Hoboken, NJ: John Wiley & Sons.

House, A. E. (2002). *DSM-IV diagnosis in the schools.* New York: Guilford Press.

Hynd, G. W., & Reynolds, C. R. (2005). School neuropsychology: The evaluation of a specialty in school psychology. In R. C. D'Amato, E. Fletcher-Janzen, & C. R. Reynolds (Eds.), *Handbook of School Neuropsychology* (pp. 403–424). Hoboken, NJ: John Wiley & Sons.

Hynd, L., Stroul, B., Friedman, R., Mrazek, P., Friesen, B., Pires, S., et al. (2005). Transforming mental health care for children and their families. *American Psychologist, 60*, 615–627.

Jenkins, J. O., & Ramsey, G. A. (1991). Minorities. In M. Hersen, A. E. Kazdin, & A. S. Bellack (Eds.), *The clinical psychology handbook* (pp. 724–740). New York: Pergamon.

Kazdin, A. E., & Johnson, B. (1994). Advances in psychotherapy for children and adolescents: Interrelations of adjustment, development, and intervention. *Journal of School Psychology, 32*, 217–246.

Kirk, S. & Kutchins, H. (1992). *The selling of DSM*. Hawthorne, NY: Aldine de Gruyter.

Kronenberger, W. G., & Meyer, R. G. (2001). *The child clinician's handbook* (2nd ed.). Needham Heights, MA: Allyn & Bacon.

Kutchins, H., & Kirk, S. (1995). Should DSM be the basis for teaching social work practice? No. *Journal of Social Work Education, 31*(2), 148–168.

Novins, D. K., Bechtold, D. W., Sack, W. H., Thompson, M. D., Carter, D. R., & Manson, S. M. (1997). The DSM-IV outline for cultural formulation: A critical demonstration with American Indian children. *Journal of the American Academy of Child and Adolescent Psychiatry, 36*, 1244–1251.

Paniagua, F. A. (2000). Culture-bound syndromes, cultural variations, and psychopathology. In I. Cuellar & F. A. Paniagua, *Handbook of multicultural mental health* (pp. 139–169). San Diego, CA: Academic Press.

Paniagua, F. A. (2005). *Assessing and treating culturally diverse clients: A practical guide* (3rd ed.). Thousand Oaks, CA: Sage.

Power, T. J., & DuPaul, G. J. (1997). Attention Deficit Hyperactivity Disorder: The reemergence of subtypes. In D. L. Smallwood (Ed.), *Attention disorders in children: Resources for school psychologists* (pp. 51–60). Bethesda, MD: National Association of School Psychologists.

Simeonsson, R. J., & McMillen, J. S. (2001). Clinical assessment in planning and evaluating intervention. In R. J. Simeonsson, & S. L. Rosenthal (Eds.), *Psychological and developmental assessment: Children with disabilities and chronic conditions* (pp. 32–50). New York: Guilford Press.

Simeonsson, R. J., & Rosenthal, S. L. (2001). *Psychological and developmental assessment: Children with disabilities and chronic conditions*. New York: Guilford Press.

Simeonsson, R. J., & Scarborough, S. L. (2001). Issues in clinical assessment. In R. J. Simeonsson, & S. L. Rosenthal, *Psychological and developmental assessment: Children with disabilities and chronic conditions* (pp. 17–31). New York: Guilford Press.

Spitzer, R. L., Gibbon, M., Skodol, A. E., Williams, J. B. W., & First, M. B. (Eds.). (1994). *DSM–IV casebook: A learning companion to the Diagnostic and Statistical Manual of Mental Disorders (4th edition)*. Washington, DC: American Psychiatric Press.

Stein, D. J. (1993). Cross-cultural psychiatry and the DSM-IV. *Comprehensive Psychiatry, 34*, 322–329.

Thompson Prout, H., & Brown, D. T. (2007). *Counseling and psychotherapy with children and adolescents: Theory and practice for school and clinical settings*. Hoboken, NJ: John Wiley & Sons.

Tolan, P. H. & Dodge, K. A. (2005). Children's mental health as a primary care and concern: A system for comprehensive support and service. *American psychologist, 60*(6), 601–614.

Waldman, I., Lilienfeld, S., & Lahey, B. (1995). Toward construct validity in the childhood disruptive behavior disorders: Classification and diagnosis in DSM-IV and beyond. *Advances in Clinical Child Psychology, 17*, 323–363.

Wilkinson, C. B., & Spurlock, J. (1986). The mental health of black Americans: Psychiatric diagnosis and treatment. In C. B. Wilkerson (Ed.), *Ethnic psychiatry* (pp. 13–59). New York: Plenum.

Wolraich, M., Felice, M. E., & Drotar, D. (Eds.). (1996). *The classification of child and adolescent mental diagnoses in primary care: Diagnostic and statistical manual for primary care* (DSM-PC). Elk Grove Village, Ill: American Academy of Pediatrics.

World Health Organization (WHO). (1999). *International classification of impariments, activities, and participation: A manual of dimensions of disablement and functioning.* Geneva: Author.

Recommended Readings

Cuellar, I., & Paniagua, F. A. (Eds.). (2000). *Handbook of multicultural mental health: Assessment and treatment of diverse populations.* San Diego, CA: Academic Press.

Elliott, C., Pruett, S., Vaal, J., Agner, J., Harvey, M., Boyd, L., et al. (1993). *Best practices for third-party reimbursement.* Bloomingdale, IL: Illinois School Psychologists Association (ISPA).

House, A. E. (2002). *DSM-IV diagnosis in the schools.* New York: Guilford Press.

Kronenberger, W. G. (1996). *The child clinician's handbook.* Needham Heights, MA: Allyn & Bacon.

Paniagua, F. A. (2003). *Assessing and treating culturally diverse clients: A practical guide* (3rd ed). Thousand Oaks, CA: Sage.

Suzuki, L. A., Alexander, C. M., & Lin, Pei-Ying (2006). Psychopathology in the schools: Multicultural factors that impact assessment and intervention. *Psychology in the Schools, 43*(4), 429–438

NASP Publications

To order, go directly to the NASP Center, email center@naspweb.org

Exemplary Mental Health Programs: School Psychologists as Mental Health Providers (3rd ed.) (2002). *This text responds to growing demand by policy makers and school administrators for research-based programs that make a sustained and proven contribution to children's healthy learning and development. This latest edition offers 105 of the most effective school-based mental health programs in 38 states.*

Thomas, A., & Grimes, J. (Eds.). (2002). *Best Practices in School Psychology IV* (BPIV). *The BPIV serves as a primary reference on the core body of knowledge regarding children's healthy learning and development. It reflects on changes in: theory, research, and practice; expectations and roles within schools; needs and diversity of students, families, and educators; collaboration; assessment and intervention strategies; laws, funding, and public policy; mental health and education systems; and training and professional standards.*

6

Personality and
Behavioral Assessment

When Are Personality/Behavioral
Assessments Needed?

Aside from evaluating a child's cognitive functioning, perceptual-motor development, and academic achievement, a complete psychological assessment typically involves an accumulation of information pertaining to behavioral, emotional, or social characteristics of the child with the aim of arriving at a clinical diagnosis. This type of assessment produces valid and reliable information pertaining to a child's problems. However, the information and measures used to achieve appropriate clinical results depend on the reason for the evaluation. School psychology assessment practices indicate that in the evaluation of children referred for social, behavioral, and emotional problems, practitioners are consistent in their use of structured interviews, direct observations, behavioral rating scales, and checklists as part of the methods of assessment (Shapiro & Heick, 2004). Moreover, in a recent survey study, results indicated practitioners agreed that the use of behavioral assessment had increased in their school practice; they also observed that behavioral assessment was valuable in connecting assessment to interventions.

Since the 1990s, school psychology assessment practices have demonstrated the integration of behavioral assessment as part of typical clinical practice (with the use of methodologies such as structured interviews, direct observation, and checklist/rating scales) in evaluating social/emotional and behavioral problems (Shapiro & Heick, 2004). It is now evident that assessment in the social/behavioral/emotional domains at the school level is consistent with those customary in child clinical psychology (Mash & Terdal, 1997).

The chapter summarizes some of the more important domains of personality and behavioral assessment. Various reliable multicultural and cross-cultural sources were selected (Arredondo et al., 1996; Constantino & Malgady, 2000; Dana, 2000; Flanagan, & Di Giuseppe, 1999; Kratochwill, Sheridan, Carlson, & Lasecki, 1998; Moon & Cundick, 1983; Paniagua, 2005; Sattler & Hoge, 2006; Sue, Arrendondo, & McDavis, 1992; Watson & Steege, 2006) in an attempt to equip the school practitioner with a sense of informed choice when conducting personality and behavioral assessments. Leading authorities on behavioral/personality assessment, Sattler and Hoge (2006), Panaguia (2005) and Dana (2000) are frequently cited, as these researchers have compiled current information on the most useful techniques to use in personality and social/clinical behavioral assessment in addition to cross-cultural research implications. To a degree, this chapter is more content focused than practice-based because of the numerous diagnostic recommendations in cross-cultural personality and behavioral assessment research. Therefore, diagnostic practical guidance and resources for interventions and techniques are described for further study.

In practice, school psychologists are habitually responsible for servicing children with behavioral and emotional problems; such services usually take place through either a prereferral or direct referral process. A collection of teacher anecdotes describing the inappropriate behavior(s) of the child or youth is reviewed at the prereferral stage, out of which school-based and/or family interventions are recommended and initiated. School psychologists are involved in this process, and are frequently asked to assist in making recommendations for appropriate interventions. If interventions implemented to decrease the undesirable behaviors are unsuccessful, an official referral for an assessment is activated with the Individualized Educational Plan (IEP) Team. At this stage of the process, school psychologists begin to review and collect data on the referred child's background through such sources as parents (or other family members and/or significant others in the child's environment), other informants, school/medical records, and reports on any previous evaluations.

Although a psychological assessment routinely involves assessing the social and emotional functioning of a child, it is not until background information and the required scheduled interviews with the child and family and teachers have been completed that decisions can be made about the type of behavioral (and personality) assessment deemed necessary and what formal and informal measures should be administered. Assessment methods can encompass norm-referenced tests, semistructured interviews, observations, and other informal methods. Obviously, the school psychologist will decide whether further areas need to be probed or assessed, such as intelligence, memory, achievement, visual and auditory skills, motor skills, oral language, and adaptive behavior, even if a routine evaluation usually includes these domains (Sattler & Hoge, 2006).

There are three distinct types of psychological assessment, although they are not always clearly distinguished. The first is the cognitive and ability evaluation that heavily relies on correct and incorrect responses which are numerically scored (e.g., intelligence and neuropsychological tests and aptitude and achievement tests). The second is objective personality assessment, which relies on test items that center on external behavior or internal emotional behavior. The responses on these measures are not scored on a correct or incorrect scoring system, but rather on how the responses indicate the presence or absence of specific positive qualities (e.g., appropriate social skills, autonomy, persistence) or negative ones (e.g., depression, aggression, and anxiety). Lastly, there is a clinical assessment, which greatly depends on the collection of more "open-ended" information attained through parent reports of the child's developmental history, extended family and teacher interviews, and the use of unstructured observational techniques (Sattler & Hoge, 2006).

Projective measures and apperception tests are commonly used in clinical assessment (e.g., Thematic Apperception Test, Tell-Me-a-Story [TEMAS], House-Tree-Person [HTP]). These measures are not scored. The responses obtained are viewed as "descriptive evidence" by the practitioner and are reviewed with other formal assessment data. Sattler and Hoge (2006) state that there are certain procedures that follow the classification of responses; however, "the psychometric properties of the scores cannot be evaluated because the statistical procedures do not yield conventional scaled scores" (p. 5). To evaluate the accuracy of classification, practitioners must compare rates of correct classification with rates of incorrect classification. There are five theoretical perspectives to consider when conducting personality and behavioral assessment:

- the developmental perspective;
- the normative-developmental perspective;
- the cognitive-behavioral perspective;
- the family-systems perspective; and
- the eclectic perspective.

These theoretical viewpoints help guide the personality and behavioral assessment process. Sattler and Hoge review each of these perspectives. Excerpts of the main points of their review are presented in the next section.

The developmental perspective views the interaction of genetic and environmental influences as following a distinct and non-haphazard course. This interaction causes specific developmental results, such as learning to walk and talk, the development of an interrelated coordination of movements, and complex cognitive thinking skills. Obviously, there are intraindividual and interindividual differences that will affect the developmental process (e.g., differences in the rate and timing of development). Different abilities within and across individuals, such as physical, cognitive, social skills, and language and speech, develop at different rates. Sattler and Hoge (2006) explain that, from this perspective, "development focuses both on individual differences in the rate or sequence of development and on general changes common to most individuals at a given age or stage" (p. 7). Moreover, this perspective views biological, physiological, and social factors as continually interacting and influencing children's development. Consequently, environmental deprivation (e.g., a disparity between the needs of the child and a lack of favorable environmental conditions) may lead to maladaptive behaviors. The developmental perspective adopts the principle that growth is both qualitative and quantitative.

Lerner (2002) describes qualitative growth as involving "differences in what exists, in what sort of phenomenon is present," whereas quantitative growth refers to "differences in how much or how many of something exists" (p. 109). Obtaining background data regarding a child's development is critical during the initial part of the evaluative process.

In the normative-developmental perspective, changes in the child's cognitions, affect, and behavior are evaluated compared with a reference group (same age and gender group). This perspective looks at demographic variables like grade level, gender, ethnicity, and socioeconomic status as well as developmental variables such as language, motor skills, social skills, and self-help skills, counting the influence of development on present and future development. Obtaining normative data provides the school psychologist with information on how a child's development compares with that of the average child. Established norms are essential for determining treatment plans and for assessing the clinical meaning of changes incurred from implemented interventions.

Another important factor of this perspective is that the normative data collected guide the clinician in selecting those behaviors in the child that are in need of change (e.g., determining whether the child has attained specific age-appropriate skills). Normative data are also helpful for comparing information about the child obtained from parents and teachers to determine whether the child's behavior is consistent across settings (i.e., the home and school and community). This type of data also assists researchers to form homogeneous groups and to compare samples across studies.

The cognitive-behavioral perspective emphasizes the importance of cognitions on behavior. Cognitions (which are a child's thoughts and mode of processing information) are viewed as having a central influence on emotion and behavior. This perspective analyzes how values, beliefs, perceived self-confidence, problem-solving strategies, and goals affect the development of maladaptive behaviors.

A strong emphasis is placed on individual and environmental influences, which in turn may influence a child's thoughts, feelings, and behaviors. This perspective stresses the empirical validation of the assessment and intervention procedure. This is done by quantitatively recording targeted behaviors with measurements such as frequency counts, duration time, and intensity level, and keeping a record of the times of occurrence (i.e., behavior modification). Recording this information is usually part of a behavioral observation and/or intervention plan that can be the combined responsibility of the child's teacher and parents, as well as the school psychologist. It is important to note that, from this perspective, changes in cognitions can propel changes in behaviors. According to this standpoint, cognitions and behaviors are modifiable. Such changes are usually induced through the use of cognitive-behavioral treatment interventions. This approach, termed *functional behavioral analysis*, follows the principle that antecedents lead to behavior, which in turn leads to consequences of behavior(s). Functional behavior analysis is the observation of a particular behavior as it occurs in a specific setting (see section below).

The family-systems perspective focuses on the structure (i.e., characteristics of each member) and dynamics of the family. This standpoint postulates several central points pertaining to family systems:

- The parts of a family must be interrelated.
- One part of the family cannot be understood in isolation from the rest of the family.
- Family functioning cannot fully be understood simply by understanding each part.
- Changes in one part of the family will affect the other parts.
- The family's structure and organization are important factors determining the behavior of family members.
- Interactions among family members shape the behavior of the family members (Epstein, Bishop, & Baldwin, 1981).

Knowledge of the above factors can help school psychologists to better understand the various dynamics of different families. A healthy family system is crucial for infant and child development. It is the family which provides infant and child with the nurturance necessary for growth in such areas as cognitive functioning (i.e., enriched environmental stimuli), culture (i.e., family cultural beliefs, values, morals, and traditions), and sense of self-worth (i.e., positive feedback and praise). There is much literature on family systems and family therapy which can help practitioners treating various family situations (see annotated bibliography). It is advisable for school psychologists to increase their knowledge and skills in this important domain of child development. An excellent way for the school psychologist to obtain expertise on different family types (whether monolingual or bilingual) is to engage in direct contact with the child's family and to learn about their cultural norms, traditions, religion, and beliefs and values by asking questions about these areas of interest. The more "up-front" contact with diverse cultures a practitioner has, the more they will become a multicultural expert.

The eclectic perspective emphasizes the same elements as the other four perspectives combined. An eclectic viewpoint stresses that:

- Individual, family, and environmental influences are crucial for a child's development.
- Children are shaped by their environments and by their genetic constitutions.
- What can be observed in children may not always reflect their potentials.
- Children also shape their environments. (Sattler & Hoge, 2006)

These factors help practitioners to recognize the importance not only of the client child in a behavioral/personality assessment but to also concentrate on other domains such as family, environmental influences, genetics, the true potential of the child, and the power of children in shaping their surroundings. This perspective is also helpful in the interpretation of behavioral problems, and focuses on several methods for collecting data about the child, such as:

- conducting a medical and social history;
- considering genetic factors affecting development;
- checking for interactions of environmental and biological factors;
- considering the child's behavior with his/her reference group;
- looking at the frequency, intensity, and duration of the identified behavioral problem;
- evaluating cognitions and affect and how these relate to a child's development (including personality, temperament, intelligence, language, motor and social skills, emotions, and interpersonal skills; Sattler & Hoge, 2006, p. 10).

In addition to these crucial factors, school psychologists are required to:

- identify the problem behavior and to note how motivated parents are in their desire to see a change in the specified behavior;
- find appropriate measures for assessing the observed behavior (i.e., standardized tests, checklists, interviews, systematic observations, and self-monitoring techniques), noting family structure/dynamics/communication patterns, roles,

emotional responses, and the capability of the family to satisfy the needs of its members (Sattler & Hoge, 2006, p. 10).

Sattler and Hoge (2006) conclude their review of the theoretical perspectives by summarizing several propositions based on these viewpoints. The propositions are based on the developmental, normative-developmental, cognitive-behavioral, and family-systems perspectives, and are divided into normal and deviant functioning which serve as the basics for the assessment of children (Bornstein & Lamb, 1999; Campbell, 1989; Achenbach & Edelbrock, 1984; Luiselli, 1989; Mash & Wolfe, 2002; Masten & Braswell, 1991; Millon, 1987; Turk & Kerns, 1985).

Tables 6.1 and 6.2 show several of Sattler and Hoge's (2006) foundations for the assessment of normal and deviant functioning. The tables can be used as quick reference for identifying important factual knowledge and concerns during the assessment process.

The information in Table 6.1 can serve to mark off those areas that may need to be clinically observed or further investigated. For example, a practitioner may wish to check a child's sense of self and his/her capacity for interpersonal relationships. Since interpersonal relationships are normally based on a child's parent–child relationship, the practitioner would endeavor to examine the normality of the child's functioning in this domain. Simultaneously, the above determinants help to make a distinction for normal development in cognitive, behavioral, and family systems of children and youth.

Table 6.2 provides the practitioner with detailed delineations of deviant functioning. Knowledge of deviant functioning is important for assessment purposes. By checking those areas that appear to be associated with the observed deviances, school psychologists can determine which assessment instruments to use, as well as what recommendations to make for appropriate culturally sensitive interventions.

Because school psychologists are responsible for making diagnostic and classification recommendations, it is important for them to have an awareness and knowledge of the potential bias in diagnostic criteria. With the spread of multiculturalism in education and psychology, it is no longer news to clinicians that the diagnostic criteria utilized in the United States are prone to bias, since the established criteria originated on middle-class European American values and principles of appropriate behaviors that may not reflect those of other diverse cultural groups. What is perceived as acceptable behavior in one culture may not necessarily reflect similar views in another culture. As a result, psychologists and psychiatrists have the difficult task of identifying whether a behavior manifested by a culturally and linguistically racial/ethnic child is deviant or pathological (see Cuellar & Paniagua, 2000; House, 1999; Sattler & Hoge, 2006). Due to these cultural variations in the

Table 6.1   Normal Functioning

- Children change and evolve rapidly, experiencing changes that are both qualitative and quantitative.
- Children possess relatively enduring biological dispensations which give a consistent coloration and direction to their experiences.
- Children's temperaments, early experiences, learning histories, and cultural backgrounds simultaneously interact to affect the development and nature of their emerging psychological structures, abilities, and functions.
- Children develop relatively stable behaviors, cognitions, and affects that stem partially from generalized learning and partially from similarities among related situations.
- Children's cognitions can be major determinants of emotion and behavior.
- Children gradually replace reflexive, sensory-bound, and concrete behavior with more conceptual, symbolic, and cognitively mediated behavior.
- Children may develop abilities which are not fully expressed in their behavior at a particular stage of development but which may be expressed at a later stage of development.
- Children's behavior is influenced by their chronological age and their developmental status (including physical maturation).
- Children's motives and emotions become more refined, advanced, and controlled over the course of their development.
- Children engage in behaviors and seek situations that are rewarding.
- Behavior that is appropriate at one age may be inappropriate at another age.
- Children's development can better be understood by reference to normative data.
- Children's environments during their formative years are usually highly structured (except possibly in highly dysfunctional families) and closely monitored by parents and other caregivers. Children's interactions with others in their environments contribute to shaping their behavior, and in turn children also shape their environments.
- Children's sense of self and capacity for interpersonal relationships develop, in part, from the parent–child relationship.
- Families which function well overall may continue to function adequately during stressful periods. For example, well-functioning families cope with stress successfully, protect their members, adjust to role changes within the family, and continue to carry out their functions. Supportive intervention may nevertheless be beneficial for these families.

SOURCE: U.S. Department of Commerce, Census Bureau, Current Population Survey, October 2001: http://nces.ed.gov/pubs2005/dropout2001/tables/table_3.asp

assessment and diagnosis of pathological conditions, clinicians are in danger of overdiagnosis, underdiagnosis, and misdiagnosis (see Chapter 5). It is also important to underscore that whatever behavioral and personality measures are used to help identify problem behaviors or pathologies, biases are inevitable—whether in standardization, methodology, or contents (i.e., items, questions, tasks) of the instrument or scale utilized. For these reasons, school

Table 6.2   Deviant Functioning

- Children's problems are influenced by complex interactions of biological, psychological, and environmental factors.
- Children's maladaptive behavior may be related to their cognitions (e.g., emotional problems may be caused by distortions or deficiencies in thinking).
- The most serious long-term consequences tend to be associated with problems that occur early, express themselves in several forms, are pervasive across settings, and persist throughout children's development.
- Children with similar psychological disorders may have different behavioral symptoms, and children with different psychological disorders may have similar behavioral symptoms.
- Children's referrals for assessment and treatment are influenced by their parents' perceptions and interpretations of behavior, and by their parents' psychological and emotional status.
- Children may have transient problems (such as fears and worries, nightmares, bedwetting, and tantrums) characteristic of a particular developmental period; these problems, if atypical for the child's developmental period, may serve as a warning signal for the development of more serious problems, and therefore must be handled skillfully. Because some problems disappear or abate with maturity, premature labeling should be avoided.
- Children may have developmental problems that reflect: (a) an exaggeration or distortion of age-appropriate behaviors (e.g., attachment problems in infancy); (b) difficult transitions from one developmental period to the next (e.g., noncompliance in toddlers and preschoolers); (c) age-related but maladaptive reactions to environmental, particularly familial, stress (e.g., school difficulties among older children associated with moving or with a parent's loss of a job).
- Families which function poorly may make their members more susceptible to stress. For example, a family may induce in its members maladaptive behavior, illness, or persistent problems that are likely to require treatment, or a family may be unable to protect its members from maladaptive reactions.
- Children must receive interventions appropriate to their developmental level.

SOURCE: U.S. Department of Commerce, Census Bureau, Current Population Survey, October 2001: http://nces.ed.gov/pubs2005/dropout2001/tables/table_3.asp

practitioners are warned that even the most current accessible behavior scales and personality tests need to be scrutinized carefully when using them to pool information for diagnosis and/or classification.

Personality and Behavioral Assessment

An important step to take in a personality and behavioral assessment is to determine what instruments to use in assessing particular problem behavior(s) or emotional factors leading to "reported" inappropriate behavior(s). As mentioned throughout this text, practitioners must take into consideration a child's racial/ethnic identity development, culture and language, educational experiences, and, if applicable, acculturation level (Knauss, 2001). All of these factors are routinely connected to the type of assessment selected by the examiner. To reach such a decision, there should be a culture-focused pre-assessment period, whereby the school psychologist reviews cultural background information with the aim of determining what steps to take (e.g., define/operationalize the behaviors/emotional problem, decide who to interview, determine how to evaluate possible bias in interviewing techniques, identify possible bias in diagnostic criteria and/or bias in normative data).

The prospective multicultural psychologist is advised not only to learn about culture but also to consider the role of language of the children (and parents) they serve so as to better evaluate emotional and behavioral problems of diverse groups (e.g., Hispanic/Latino Americans, Asian Americans, African Americans, Native Americans). These competencies are very important when conducting interviews for assessment purposes (see Paniagua, 2005; Sattler & Hoge, 2006, Ch. 4). Additionally, practitioners must be on guard concerning their clinical interpretation of an examinee's self-reporting during an interview. The reliability and validity of information obtained from parents, teachers, and children could be misinterpreted due to malingering. Malingering is described as an interviewee's purposeful distortion or misrepresentation of psychological symptoms and/or attempts to distort a self-report, or sheer dishonesty. Most psychological or physical disorders are at risk of malingering on the part of the interviewee (Rogers, 1988). An attempt should be made to evaluate any possible malingering. Questions to pose are: Does the child have the capacity to deceive? (If under age 6, lying or deceiving is difficult to do successfully at this age.) Is the interviewee a persistent liar? Are there any grave psychological symptoms that could seriously distort any of the responses? When possible, it is best to verify the self-report by an independent observer (Cummins, 1988). These factors are important for collecting personal data that will ultimately pool together the clinician's own interpretation of the child or adolescent's personality.

Personality Assessment

When deciding appropriate interventions for children with special needs, evaluating behavioral, social, and emotional domains of functioning will help to determinate whether environmental stressors (such as acculturative stress) or a specific pathology may be causing the observed symptoms. Nearly 20 percent of children and youth in the United States manifest symptoms of psychological disorder in a given year, although most symptoms are unidentified and many psychological disorders remain untreated (U.S. Department of Health and Human Services, 1999, cited in Sattler & Hoge, 2006). There are numerous measures of behaviors and social/emotional functioning for children and adolescents (i.e., objective and projective measures of personality).

The following section presents synthesized reviews and recommendations taken from widespread sources on personality measures considered relevant for identifying children with special needs, along with cross-cultural implications (Aronow, Altman Weiss, & Reznikoff, 2001; Bellak, 1993; Costantino, Malgady, & Rogler, 1988; Dana, 2000; Machover, 1949; Paniagua, 2005; Sattler & Hoge, 2006).

Objective measures provide scores that can be quantified and normed, and that can assist in developing an examinee's profile. In contrast, projective measures comprise vague stimuli (e.g., inkblots, pictures of people or situations) on which examinees project aspects of their personality by recounting what they see and/or perceive. Some projective measures provide quantifiable scores and the scoring results and their interpretation requires clinical expertise (Avila-Espada, 2000; Ephraim, 2000; Sattler & Hoge, 2006). A distinct point to emphasize is that personality measures, which tap into psychopathological conditions, may use different diagnostic systems such as the DSM-IV-TR or empirically constructed measures that probe normal personality traits. Sattler and Hoge (2006) point out that results from personality tests, behavioral rating and checklist measures, and/or observational methods may not correspond to, or be consistent with, each other. Additionally, such tests and scales are commonly used to sample behaviors that have been ongoing for a certain period of time. Conversely, observational systems observe behaviors occurring at the present time.

Personality tests are mainly self-report measures that require the respondent to reply to a series of set questions. A drawback of such measures is the psychometric concerns of validity and reliability. Validity of test scores may be affected by the respondent's reading and/or understanding of the questions/items; consequently, checking the reading level of the respondent is important or questions/items may be misread, thus reducing the reliability of the questions/items. Another validity issue is the possibility of response bias; this usually occurs because a particular response is fixed to a presented item. One type of response bias can be the respondent's intentional faking of a bad or good response. There are several types of response bias that can be reasons for faking:

1. *acquiescence responses*—the tendency to agree with each item, despite the content;

2. *deviance responses*—the tendency to respond in a deviant/adverse or unusual manner;

3. *social desirability response*—the tendency to answer items in what the respondent perceives is the socially acceptable or appropriate way, even if the respondent thinks or believes differently (Sattler & Hoge, 2006, p. 271).

Researchers have analyzed responses to particular items in an effort to study the response equivalence on empirical measures across cultures on personality and psychopathology measures. A more recent approach to test validations in cross-cultural/multicultural assessments is item response theory (IRT). There are three types of IRT models, and each conceptualizes a response pattern in which there is an assumed relationship between the person's responses and the personality trait, or attribute of interest (Allen & Walsh, 2000). Test developers attempt to control for response bias by using a grouping of positive, negative, and neutrally worded items for detecting biased responses. Interpretation guidelines for self-report personality measures that may lead to biased responses are:

- Does the respondent have a pattern of answering all items with either "yes" or "no" or "disagree"?
- Did the respondent always reply yes to either positive or negative items (i.e., faking good or faking bad responses)?
- Did the respondent reply in a constant pattern of alternative "yes" and "no" responses?
- Was the respondent uncaring or careless in completing the test/scale? (Sattler & Hoge, 2006, p. 271)

Results of personality tests should be reviewed and scrutinized carefully to determine whether responses accurately reflect the respondent's feelings or beliefs. School psychologists will need to consider carefully which test to use by appraising the set of questions/items posed as well as the psychometric properties of the measure being considered for administration (i.e., cultural and ethnic variables that may affect the validity and reliability of the measure). This is of crucial importance since inaccuracies in the assessment and diagnosis of mental disorders can result in overdiagnosis, underdiagnosis, and misdiagnosis. Researchers have tried to control bias in the assessment of multicultural groups by developing culturally appropriate norms and by translations of instruments into languages for diverse groups (Paniagua, 2005). Currently, most researchers and practitioners would agree that there are still culturally biased tests (Anastasi, 1988; Dana, 1993). The validity criteria for culture-free tests is summarized by Flaherty et al. (1988; see box).

Validity Criteria for Culture-Free Tests

1. *Content equivalence*—questions whether the main items are relevant for the cultures being tested.

2. *Semantic equivalence*—checks to see whether the meaning of each item is the same for all cultures being tested.

3. *Technical equivalence*—questions whether the method of assessment is comparable across cultures.

4. *Criterion equivalence*—questions whether the interpretation of variables remains the same when compared with the norms for all cultures.

5. *Conceptual equivalence*—checks to see whether the test measures the same theoretical construct across cultures.

SOURCE: Flaherty et al. (1988)

There is currently no instrument that accomplishes all of the above (Escobar, 1993). Does this mean that school psychologists and/or clinical practitioners should totally disregard the use of an instrument if the above criteria are not met? Paniagua (2005) explains that researchers and clinicians are in agreement that practitioners should continue to use the tests that are available even if they are biased because: (a) they provide a shared language in their evaluation and diagnosis of psychiatric disorders; and (b) clinicians need to use existing tests in their practice for reimbursement and institutional purposes (Yamamoto, 1986; Dana, 1993, 2000). Practitioners are advised that, although an instrument utilized for multicultural groups may contain some bias, they must learn how to best utilize the information gleaned when using it with individuals from diverse cultural backgrounds (Pedersen, 1993; Yamamoto, 1986).

Personality Measures

School psychologists are trained to conduct personality assessments by using a common battery of projective techniques. Proponents of projective techniques affirm that projective techniques have a number of strengths, even though researchers have debated their validity. Overall, Sattler and Hoge (2006) emphasize that projective measures:

- allow exposure of personality states and processes;
- help reveal suppressed and repressed conditions;
- help avoid less deliberate faking because the stimuli presented are ambiguous and the tests' purposes are vague;
- are less structured and provide opportunity for rapport with a child; and
- permit clinicians to use their knowledge and experience to an analysis of a child's personality dynamics (p. 291).

In addition to psychometric measures, supporters of projective techniques argue that these methods of personality assessment can provide information not usually observed on normative measures. Consequently, they are generally utilized by mental health practitioners as sources for theorizing on a particular problem(s) under investigation. Table 6.3 illustrates frequently employed projective measures with an appraisal of their appropriateness for ethnic groups. The Thematic Apperception Test (TAT), the Rorschach, and the House-Tree-Person (HTP) are the most commonly used techniques in schools. These measures are part of the norm in school psychology training programs. The use of projective techniques requires expert clinical training in interpretative skills. Because of their delicate clinical nature, as well as the sensitivity of the interpretation outcome, a thorough review of each of these personality instruments in this chapter is impracticable. Accordingly, the reader is referred to Aronow et al. (2001) for a practical guide to the TAT and to Dana's (2000) outstandingly edited *Handbook of Cross-Cultural and Multicultural Personality Assessment*, which includes such personality measures as the TAT and TEMAS, the Rorschach Comprehensive System, the Holtzman Inkblot Test, and the Minnesota Multiphasic Personality Inventory II (MMPI-II). Most importantly, Dana's handbook includes several chapters that examine cross-culturally relevant research and practice concerning these instruments. The seminal work of Hammer (1980) for the clinical application of projective drawings should not be overlooked, nor should the work of Cubillos (2000) and Sattler and Hoge (2006)—all of which includes a detailed review of projective techniques. In addition, see the section on test developers at the end of this chapter.

The important point to emphasize (somewhat redundantly) is that culture effects some behavior, or a set of behaviors. However, at the same time, culture undergoes continual change; therefore, assessment instruments and approaches also need to adapt to change (see Greenfield, 1997). School practitioners have a responsibility to keep abreast of cross-cultural research on

Table 6.3 Personality Assessment Instruments

Technique	Age Groups (Years)	Ethnic Groups	Description
a. Rorschach inkblot test	5 and up	Can be used in a wide range of ethnic groups. Research has found that perceptions of Rorschach drawings vary across cultures (Moon & Cundick, 1983).	Projective test of personality in which the client's interpretations of ten standard abstract inkblots are analyzed.
b. Draw-a-Person (DAP)	6–17	Can be used in a wide range of ethnic groups. Some cultural influences may appear in the drawing of the human figure (Machover, 1949).	The child is asked to produce three drawings—man, woman, and self. The drawings are scored for content, size, and placement.
c. Thematic Apperception Test (TAT)	10 and up	Modified versions include stimuli cards for use with African American populations, and Indian populations.	Picture interpretation technique which uses a standard series of 31 ambiguous and provocative pictures about which the client must tell a story.
d. Tell-Me-a-Story (TEMAS)	5–18	Two parallel forms: one for minority children, the other for nonminority children. The minority version uses cultural themes and symbols, urban settings, and ethnic minority figures. Norms for whites, blacks, Puerto Ricans, and other Hispanics.	Multicultural thematic apperception test designed for use with minority and non-minority children and adolescents with a set of stimulus cards. Used to identify strengths and deficits in cognitive, affective, intrapersonal, and interpersonal functioning.
e. House-Tree-Person (HTP)	3 and up	Ideal way to assess individuals who are culturally diverse because task consists of drawing pictures.	The subject produces drawings of a house, a tree, and a person and is given the opportunity to describe, define, and interpret these drawings.
f. Children's Apperception Test (CAT)	3–10	The choice of animal characters was based on having figures that are ambiguous with regard to age, sex, and cultural attributes (Bellak, 1993). Cultural differences may arise in interpretation of the cards.	The examiner shows the child cards consisting of animals and/or humans in various situations, identities, and settings, and encourages the child to tell a story about the characters. Each story is carefully analyzed to reveal the child's underlying desires, conflicts, attitudes, and response patterns.

SOURCE: Adapted from Volpe et al. (2005), Leff and Lakin (2005), Reynolds and Kamphaus (2004).

projective measures. Holding on to a narrow view of a given instrument they may be accustomed to using (e.g., the commonly used projective measures) may result in misuse and increase the chances of a misdiagnosis. The inclusion of a cross-cultural research review on a particular projective measure prior to usage is recommended because of the rapidity of research in this area, mainly due to the continuing cultural diversity in the United States. Ephraim (2000) points out that, "when assessment instruments are transported across cultures, researchers and clinicians tend to ignore indigenous perspectives that are intrinsic to the particular sociocultural system" (Marsella & Kameoka, 1989). For instance, one must consider that there are always tendencies to find equally important similarities and differences when using an instrument such as the Rorschach across cultures (Kleinman, 1988). This can be applied to any other instrument for that matter!

Besides projective techniques, school psychologists are encouraged to utilize personality tests that are mainly self-report scales and incorporate a paper and pencil administration format (or computerized response formats). Such tests are frequently utilized for identifying pathological states (and/or normal personality traits). Sattler and Hoge (2006) provide a commentary of five personality tests (pp. 270–276):

1. *Adolescent Psychopathology Scale* (APS; Reynolds, 1998);

2. *Adolescent Psychopathology Scale–Short Form* (APS-SF; Reynolds, 2000);

3. *Millon Adolescent Clinical Inventory* (MACI; Millon, 1993);

4. *Minnesota Multiphasic Personality Inventory–Adolescent* (MMPI-A; Butcher et al., 1992)

5. *Personality Inventory for Youth* (PIY; Lachar & Gruber, 1995).

To familiarize the reader with the common features of self-report scales, the next section summarizes Sattler and Hoge's description of these measures. Knowledge of these frequently used scales can increase the examiner's flexibility of selection when attempting to reach a decision on which measures to choose for administration.

The Adolescent Psychopathology Scale (APS) consists of 346 items and the Adolescent Psychopathology Scale–Short Form (APS-SF) has 115 items. Both are related self-report comprehensive measures. The APS taps into 25 DSM-IV-TR disorders and other social and emotional problems. The APS-SF taps into 12 clinical disorders. The APS was developed for adolescents aged 12 to 19 and measures psychopathology, personality, and psychosocial problems. Self-administration time is approximately 45–60 minutes. In contrast, the companion APS-SF administration time is 20 minutes and this is used when a briefer measure is needed. It too is developed for adolescents aged 12–19 years. A third grade reading level is required.

A number of the clinical disorders tapped into for these scales include domains such as: Attention-Deficit/Hyperactivity Disorder, Conduct Disorder, Oppositional Defiant Disorder, Substance Disorder, Anorexia Nervosa/Bulimia Nervosa; Obsessive Compulsive Disorder; Social Phobia; Posttraumatic Stress Disorder; Major Depression; and Schizophrenia. Some of the personality disorders are: Borderline Personality Disorder; Avoidant Personality Disorder; and Paranoid Personality Disorder. Psychosocial problems included are self-concept, anger, suicide, aggression, introversion, and interpersonal problems (pp. 272–273).

The Millon Adolescent Clinical Inventory (MACI) is a 160-item self-report scale designed for measuring adolescent personality characteristics and clinical syndromes in adolescents aged 13–19. The MACI requires a sixth grade reading level and a self-administration time of approximately 30 minutes. The MACI is based on Millon's (1987, 1993) theory of personality, which theorizes that "normal and abnormal personality styles are derived by combining three polarities: pleasure-pain; active-passive; and self-other" (p. 273). Some of the domains tapped into are personality patterns such as introversive, inhibited, submissive, dramatizing, egotistic, unruly, forceful, conforming, oppositional, and borderline tendency. Several of the clinical syndromes are eating dysfunctions, substance abuse proneness, delinquency predisposition, impulsive propensity, anxious feelings, depressive affect, and suicidal tendency (see Sattler & Hoge, 2006, pp. 273–274).

Another long-standing personality measure that is frequently used is the Minnesota Multiphasic Personality Inventory–Adolescent (MMPI-A). The MMPI-A is designed for ages 14–18 years, requires a seventh grade reading level (although many items require a higher reading level), and takes approximately 45–60 minutes to complete. The MMPI-A attempts to detect hypochondriasis, depression, hysteria, psychopathic deviance, masculinity-femininity, paranoia, schizophrenia, hypomania, and social introversion (Sattler & Hoge, 2006, pp. 274–275; see also Dana, 2000 for a review of the MMPI).

The Personality Inventory for Youth (PIY) is a 270-item self-report scale that measures psychopathology. The PIY can be used for children and adolescents in the fourth to twelfth grades and requires a third grade reading level. Self-administration time is approximately 60 minutes. Some of the scales on the PIY are: cognitive impairment; impulsivity and distractibility; delinquency; family dysfunction; reality distortion; somatic concern; psychological discomfort; social withdrawal; and social skills deficits (Sattler & Hoge, 2006, pp. 275–276).

As always, clinical practitioners need to review the validity and reliability of each scale they plan to administer in order to judge how best to interpret results. It is a basic measure to check for required reading levels, the possibility of response bias, and faking good and bad responses. At all times, it is crucial to be mindful of potential cultural instrument bias by researching for updated cultural reviews of the instrument under consideration.

Behavioral Assessment

School psychologists are urged to keep in mind that assessment of behavior is predominantly idiographic and individualized, and for this reason self-reporting can lack validity or reliability (Kratochwill, Sheridan, Carlson, & Lasecki, 1998). Steps for behavioral assessment suggested by Kratochwill et al. are identical to the six stages of behavioral consultation (problem identification, problem analysis, treatment implementation, treatment evaluation, generalization, and follow-up). The authors emphasize that assessment procedures for the study of behaviors should be used to design specific interventions that are followed through various phases; thus the use of consultation stages fits well into this framework. In the behavioral consultation model, a consultee-teacher collaborates with the consultant (i.e., the school psychologist) on a child/student's problem behavior. The process follows several consultation stages that do not usually conclude until the target behavior has decreased or become extinct.

Problem identification—The primary focus in this stage is to define the extent and type of the problem. Assessment during this stage can include the DSM-IV; multiaxial, empirically based assessment; and/or assessment of target behaviors. At this point, it is recommended that the school psychologist (in consultation with the teacher) determine whether the identified referral problem is the sole area to assess or whether there is any other interconnected behavior that should be addressed.

Problem analysis—During this stage, the specified target behavior discussed in the problem identification stage is analyzed with the aim of observing the behavior (direct observation) in order to establish a baseline level of the target behavior and to determine what may be contributing to the maintenance of the behavior. This may be achieved through functional analysis strategies that can be used by the school psychologists (discussed below).

Treatment implementation—Based on the information obtained, a mutually agreed upon treatment plan is generated between the school psychologist and consultee-teacher. The plan should consist of a monitoring system that will ensure that the treatment/intervention is being implemented as agreed upon.

Treatment evaluation—Direct observational systems should be used at this stage to evaluate the effectiveness of the treatment/intervention.

Generalization—This phase refers to the transfer of behavior change across behaviors, since improvement in the target behavior may have crossed over into other areas of functioning. School psychologists are encouraged to assess this crossover of behavior as it may be clinically important.

Follow-up—This last stage is crucial since it follows up the effects of the treatment/ intervention plan activated for the client/student. What is important here is to evaluate whatever generalizations of behavior have been observed in addition to any maintenance of behavior over time. Self-reports are usually utilized for this purpose, as well as validation obtained from others (e.g., teachers, parents). School psychologists can make use of the feedback obtained from the prescribed treatment plan and consider using the same plan in similar situations in the future (this is known as generalization) (see Kratochwill et al., 1998).

In general, there are several behavioral methods of assessment:

- behavioral interviews;
- self-reports, checklists, rating scales;
- self-monitoring;
- analogue measures;
- direct observation procedures.

Kratochwill and colleagues discuss each of these methods. Their review is summarized below.

Behavioral interviews are popular methods for collecting insightful clinical data, although little research has been conducted on such methods (Ciminero & Drabman, 1977; Gresham & Davis, 1988; Hay, Hay, Angle, & Nelson, 1979; Golfred & Lineham, 1977). A major behavioral system for interviewing clients/students and consultees (i.e., teachers) is the behavioral consultation model (Bergan & Kratochwill, 1990, cited in Kratochwill et al., 1998). This model provides a systematic format to operationalize the verbal interactions during the interviewing process. It helps consultee-teachers and parents to collaborate with the consultant school psychologist to identify problems, and to initiate the implementation of treatment intervention plans. It is up to the consultant school psychologist to ask significantly useful questions and make statements in a strategically formulated format so that clinical information will be obtained in a structured and well-organized manner. Although the reliability of interviewing procedures is still in question, certain systematic interviewing systems have been developed with adequate interrater reliability (see below).

Self-report inventories provide clinically relevant behavior information directly from clients/students, parents, and teachers. There are numerous self-report measures that can be used to help the assessment process. They are useful for gathering data on various important functions such as motor responses, physiological activity, and cognitions. Self-reports also help obtain information on the child's/student's subjective and affective experiences (e.g., How do you feel about your teacher? Are you afraid of failing?).

Teachers and parents are usually the respondents on behavior checklists and rating scales, which help provide information on their observations of the child's/student's behavior(s). Information gleaned from these scales can add additional information of clinical interest regarding the identified behavior. The rating is obtained subsequent to the actual behavior under clinical observation. Rating scales and checklists are not without limitations. Kratochwill and colleagues (1998) delineate some of the problems:

- Ratings are merely summaries of observations of the frequency of specific behaviors and are not completely objective accounts.
- Ratings are affected by the environment as well as the rater's standard of performance.
- Ratings of behaviors should be obtained from multiple sources but the ratings may agree moderately. (p. 356)

Self-monitoring is used as an intervention and is the responsibility of the child/student. In this type of assessment, the student is responsible for observing and recording the identified behavior. Self-monitoring can be used during the assessment process or as part of a treatment/intervention plan to collect baseline data and/or to check on the progress of the treatment (see Gardner & Cole, 1988; Haynes, 1978; Mahoney, 1977; Ciminero, Nelson, & Lipinski, 1977). There are several factors that can affect self-monitoring accuracy (see box).

Factors Affecting Self-Monitoring Accuracy

- Training is crucial: the child must be trained on how to self-monitor.
- Monitoring must be systematic, such as the use of a record form.
- Timing is important: the child must be trained to check off when a behavior occurred immediately after its occurrence rather than at the end of the day.
- Only one behavior should be monitored at a time.
- To increase the accuracy of the recording, some external criterion which is contingent on positive reinforcement should be established that will ensure the process is done adequately.

This is an especially useful method, as it allows the child to develop responsibility for behaviors. However, the child or youth must demonstrate sufficient maturity and willingness to participate. The method requires continual follow-up on the part of educators or the clinician.

Analogue assessment is a procedure that requires children/students to "respond to stimuli that simulate those found in the environment" (Kratochwill et al., 1998, p. 358). The most commonly used analogue assessment comprises intellectual and psychoeducational tests. These are paper-and-pencil, audiotape, videotape, enactment, and role-play analogues. For example, paper and pencil analogues may require parents or teachers to respond to multiple-choice questions pertaining to various options for implementing a behavior management plan. Audiotape analogue involves the auditory presentation of specific items. Responses are usually in verbal or physical form.

In enactment analogue, the child/student is required to participate in a clinically contrived situation with relevant persons (e.g., teachers, peers) or objects that are typically present in the environment. From this interactive process, much information can be gathered to confirm or refute a behavioral hypothesis. The limitation of this assessment technique is that the enacted situation may not completely duplicate the natural environment.

Role-play is also used in analogue assessment. This strategy requires the school psychologist or counselor to ask the child or adolescent to role-play a particular scenario that may be educational (e.g., for a shy child, how to ask a question in class; for an adolescent, how to interact in a job interview).

Direct observation assessment is a very popular naturalistic observational system of behavior that is commonly used in behavior therapy practice. This strategy requires the recording of behavioral incidents within the natural environment at the time the behavior occurs. This method has two requirements: a trained unbiased observer/coder, and descriptions of the behavior that do not require any inferences on the part of the observer to code the behavioral/incident occurrence (Kratochwill et al., 1998, p. 362). School psychologists conduct direct observations in the classroom, and can also involve parents or teachers in recording the occurrence of a child's behavior, frequency, and duration during a specific amount of time.

Because behavioral problems necessitate thorough evaluation, following the prescribed consultative stages brings about a systematic structure to the assessment and intervention process. School psychologists and counselors can also collaborate by offering counseling services through individual and group sessions to children and youth with behavioral problems. Counseling can become a part of the consultative process when both professionals engaged in collaborative consultation assess a behavioral symptom(s) to require early intervention and determine to work together to offer this service. However, practitioners and counselors need to be exceptionally sensitive to the numerous racial/ethnic, cultural, and linguistic variations among children and youth requiring behavioral or emotional interventions through counseling. Sue et al.'s (1992) highly influential article on multicultural counseling competencies and standards, as well as Arredondo et al.'s (1996) operationalization of multicultural counseling competencies can help the school psychologist and counselor develop appropriate competencies in this important area (see suggested articles at the end of this chapter).

Another systematic approach for addressing challenging behaviors that has obligated school psychologists since the passage of Public Law 105-17 is functional behavioral assessment (FBA).

Functional Behavioral Assessment

As a result of amendments to the Individuals with Disabilities Education Act (IDEA) in 1997, federal law mandates the use of functional behavioral assessments (FBA) and positive support plans for children and youth who are exhibiting inappropriate behaviors in schools. The study of behavior and how to change undesirable manifestations of behavior is not new to psychology. Behaviorists tell us that behavior is not isolated but occurs as a response to various complex variables interacting together—such as environmental, biological, and instructional factors that affect the individual. The study of this complex interaction is known as *applied behavior analysis*. FBAs have not emerged with the legislation of the IDEA amendment, but have been considered best practice for some time. However, this is a fairly new challenge for school psychology practice (Drasgow & Yell, 2001; Gresham, Watson, & Skinner, 2001).

Currently, school psychologists may adopt an applied analytic approach in order to satisfy IDEA mandates for conducting FBA. By working collaboratively with the Individualized Education Plan (IEP) Team, professionals and family members develop a behavioral intervention plan and determine whether there is a need for positive behavioral strategies and supports. The IEP team—of which the school psychologist is a member—has ten days to develop a functional behavioral assessment plan. Practitioners adopting an applied behavioral standpoint are in an ideal position to fulfill the mandates of IDEA for conducting FBAs in addition to designing and implementing positive behavioral support plans for students manifesting challenging behaviors (Gresham et. al., 2001; McConnell Patton, & Polloway, 2000).

FBA is defined as "a collection of methods for gathering information about antecedents, behaviors, and consequences in order to determine the reason (function) of behavior" (Gresham et. al., 2001, p. 3). FBA attempts to discover the relationship between the individual and those variables that interact to trigger, reinforce, and maintain the target behavior. The study of a specifically inappropriate behavior begins by gathering objective information. It is important to make sure that any collected anecdotes or descriptions of the behavior are accurate. For this reason, it is recommended that more than one report of the unwanted behavior is gathered in order to corroborate the authenticity of the problem behavior. Also, it is advisable to collect more than one report of the behavioral incident through the use of more than one method (Watson & Steege, 2003). Overall, FBA is a detective-like effort that involves several evaluative steps.

The following section presents a brief overview of FBA assessment procedures delineated by Watson and Steege (2003). There are three forms of FBA:

1. indirect functional behavioral assessment;

2. direct descriptive functional behavioral assessment; and

3. functional behavioral analysis.

Indirect functional assessment comprises various methods that include reviewing records, behavior rating scales, social skills ratings, adaptive behavior assessments, informal interviews, and semi-structured interviews. The purpose of the indirect FBA approach is to identify and explain the behavior and to formulate a hypothesized functional relationship with regard to the antecedent, the individual, and consequent variables that are linked to the targeted interfering behavior. This FBA approach is usually the first step in the evaluation of the intrusive behavior(s). It is strongly recommended that the evaluation not stop here because of the biased information that can occur during interviews (Watson & Steege, 2003, p. 13).

At this point, what should continue in the FBA process is a direct descriptive functional behavioral assessment, which involves compiling observational information of the behavioral incidents/events in addition to any variables forming, relating to, or contained in the context of the child's/student's environment. What this means is that the school psychologist should engage in direct observations of the target behavior(s) and note any causal conditions (e.g., and/or relationships) within the child's daily environment. The next step is to use the data collected to formulate interventions to decrease the undesirable behavior.

Whereas indirect FBA and direct descriptive FBA provide valuable information for identifying and developing interventions, they are known to be "only suggestive of functional relationships because they do not systematically isolate and manipulate environmental variables" (McComas & Mace, 2000 cited in Watson & Steege, 2003, p. 13). Functional behavioral analysis helps to confirm the hypothesized functional relationships by conducting a more meticulous assessment. Functional behavioral analysis is defined as an assessment method in which, "environmental events are systematically manipulated and examined within single-subject experimental designs variables" (McComas & Mace, 2000). Following this FBA procedure involves the observation of the behavior and the variables associated with the direct manipulation of its antecedent and consequences. The intention is to discover the motivating function of the behavior (McComas & Mace, 2000, cited in Watson & Steege, 2003).

As members of the IEP Team, school psychologists will find themselves facing a continual obligation to conduct FBAs on children and adolescents who exhibit "identified inappropriate behaviors." An important point to emphasize is that during the course of an FBA, the multicultural school psychologist should not overlook the possibility of cultural differences in behaviors. For example, what may be perceived as inappropriate behavior in our Western culture may not be considered so in another. The observation of hyperactive behaviors in a classroom setting as inappropriate can sometimes result in confounding information or uncorroborated responses when interviewing parents and family members whose culture allows certain "typical" hyperactive behaviors in the home or within the family's social milieu.

The DSM-IV is a clinical classification system that provides a topographical, not a functional, description of behavior. With regard to behaviors, it is important to distinguish that the DSM-IV asks "What?" (topography) rather than a "What for?" (function) with regard to behavior (Scotti, Morris, McNeil, & Hawkins, 1996). From this standpoint, the DSM-IV provides a structural or descriptive account of behavior but does not provide information regarding any identifiable environmental variables leading to the behavior. For example, Gresham and colleagues (2001), referring to the DSM-IV, explain that a diagnosis of Conduct Disorder requires the occurrence of three of 15 symptoms (behaviors) such as bullying, fights, lying, and so on, but a description of the particular behaviors does not provide sufficient information regarding the function served by the behavior(s). Devoid of an awareness of the function served by the behavior, treatment/intervention planning is not viable (p. 3).

The concern for fairness and objectivity in the assessment of minority group children has been stressed emphatically. Anderson (1988) presents a case study that prompted a behavioral psychologist to conduct a behavioral assessment on a black child manifesting behavioral problems. The diagnosis of Conduct Disorder in a black child may be fraught with bias, as is often suspected in the assessment of minority children. The controversy is initiated when a decision needs to be made regarding the type of intervention to use in order to resolve the identified problems. However, Anderson argues that behavioral assessments are inclined to be less biased than psychological assessments because of the use of objective and, "non-inferential empirically derived procedures" (p. 217). This does not imply that behavioral assessments are without bias. However, studies have shown that behavioral assessment approaches can be beneficial for black children (Anderson, 1988, p. 218). For racial/ethnic, culturally, and linguistically diverse children, who are often assessed with standardized tests designed for non-minority children and treated with interventions that may not always be culturally sensitive, behavioral assessments can be customized if the practitioner is aware of cultural bias in assessment. Further research in this area is needed. However, the assumption bodes well for racial/ethnic/culturally diverse children and youth.

FBAs are usually written up in report format or on special one-page FBA forms that are provided for speedy overviews. Watson and Steege (2003) advise against these "quick" approaches. Instead, they stress the importance of writing a complete FBA report. Figure 6.1 presents a modified version of Watson and Steege's (2003) example of a functional behavioral assessment report. Headings are in bold type for clarity of format.

School psychologists can perfect their knowledge of FBAs and develop skills in the observation and recording of behavior by referring to Watson and Steege's (2006) FBA practitioner's guidebook (see annotated bibliography). Developing expertise in FBA is of utmost importance for implementing structured behavioral interventions for children and youth from diverse backgrounds. Research on the effectiveness and efficiency of FBA behavior intervention support planning is scanty and insufficient to provide educators and practitioners with data on its complete adequacy. Consequently, school psychologists (and others involved in the FBA process) need to work collaboratively so as to assist in applying different strategies that will result in desired outcomes (Johnston & O'Neill, 2001). It is advisable for practitioners to keep a record of culturally sensitive designed FBAs that have demonstrated effective (or ineffective) behavioral changes for the diverse students they have serviced. Additionally, practitioners are encouraged to keep clinical progress notes (on CD) as these can later be used for research purposes.

Behavioral Observational Systems

(with Katherine Warner)

As mentioned previously, one of the most commonly used methods of assessing behavior is direct observation (Shapiro & Kratchowill, 2000).

Functional Behavioral Assessment Report

Student Information

Name, date of birth, grade, school district, evaluation dates, and report date.

Reason for Referral

Student/child was referred by _____ for a functional behavioral assessment for behaviors that interfere with his/her academic progress.

Assessment Procedures

Indirect FBA

Direct descriptive FBA

Identification, Description, and Current Levels of Occurrence of Interfering Behaviors

    Examples of behavioral descriptions are:
        Stereotypic Behaviors
        Self-Injurious Behaviors
        Tantrum Behaviors

Identification of Antecedent, Individual, and Consequence Variables

    The following antecedent variables appear to serve as triggers:

1. Examples are: unstructured time, verbal prompting, classroom timer, etc.
2. Language-based instructional activities contribute to the appearance of _____ [list behavior here] _____.
3. Physically prompting _____ [student name] _____ to stop _____ [name of behavior] _____ behaviors contributes to the occurrence of _____ behaviors.

    The following individual variables were identified as factors that appear to contribute to the occurrence of interfering behaviors:

1. Social skills deficits
2. Expressive and receptive communication skill delays
3. Delays in independent and cooperative leisure skills

    The following variables were identified as *consequences* of interfering behaviors (i.e., variables that follow the occurrence of interfering behaviors):

1. Here list the consequences of the interfering behaviors (i.e., no play or computer time).
2. Withdrawal of staff physically prompting typically occurs following _____ and _____ behaviors.

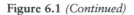

Figure 6.1 *(Continued)*

Hypothesized Functions of Interfering Behaviors

Here the practitioner lists the names of the identified behaviors and provides an explanation for their occurrence.

Example: Stereotypic behaviors appear to be motivated by automatic positive reinforcement.

Impressions and Considerations for the Team

The team usually comprises members of the disciplinary team that met to discuss the student, such as the school psychologist, counselor, teacher, and parents.

This last section of the report is comparable to that of the psychoeducational report in that it provides important information regarding the results of the FBA assessment and discusses the hypothesized reasons for the interfering behaviors along with a structured outline of suggested interventions. Watson and Steege provide the following example:

The results of FBA of interfering behaviors indicate that these behaviors appear to have multiple functions. Accordingly, interventions addressing these behaviors need to take into consideration the respective triggers, internal/individual variables, and consequences for each target behavior.

A positive behavioral support (PBS) plan needs to be developed that takes into account the results of the FBA. The PBS plan might include the following strategies as a way of preventing the occurrence of interfering behaviors and of increasing appropriate and prosocial behaviors:

- [List here in bullet form the strategies decided]
-
-

Ongoing data using the _____ [name of procedure to be used]_____ _____ is suggested as a method of documenting current level of occurrence of behaviors. It is recommended that the _____ be expanded from its present use of documenting only interfering behaviors to include the documentation of appropriate behaviors (e.g., active participation, initiation of social interactions with peers).

Ongoing behavioral consultation to include: (1) ongoing FBA of interfering behaviors; and (2) design, implementation, and evaluation of positive behavioral support interventions is suggested.

Courtney Bracey, Ph.D.
School Psychologist

Figure 6.1   Functional Behavioral Assessment Report

SOURCE: Adapted from Watson and Steege (2003, pp. 161–163).

Direct observation is a systematic measurement procedure in which the observer identifies and assesses an individual's behavior (Nock & Kurtz, 2005). Attention is given to antecedents and consequences that maintain the behavior. A systematic observation commonly includes the use of behavioral observational systems to identify the frequency, duration, and intensity of a targeted behavior. The target behavior is determined prior to the inception of the observation (Thompson, Quenemoen, Thurlow, & Ysseldyke, 2001). Although standardized behavioral rating scales and checklist measures usually assess inappropriate behaviors, some also evaluate constructive behavioral competencies. An advantage of the competency approach to systematic observation is that it is a direct measure of actual skills. From this standpoint, systematic behavioral observation is beneficial for students who experience high levels of anxiety in formal testing situations, and allows the observer to record data while the assessment is occurring (Hosp & Hosp, 2001). This avoids the limitations of reporting after an assessment has already occurred. Several recommendations are made by Hosp and Hosp (2001) for effective behavioral observations:

- Use a team approach to specify the behavior.
- Make sure the behavior is described in clear, observable and measurable terms.
- Plan the details of the observation session prior to scheduling the session.
- Observe the behavior over multiple days, times, settings, and during different activities.
- Observe the behavior of other students for comparison purposes. (Hosp & Hosp, 2001, pp. 343–344)

Although behavioral observational systems are widely recommended, no standard procedure exists for assessing student problem behavior. School psychologists and other professionals responsible for behavioral assessment in schools are expected to select the method of assessment. One possible reason for this is the disparity in training and resources among educational settings. Because resources vary from school to school, the same observational systems may not consistently be available (Nock & Kurtz, 2005).

One benefit of having many observational systems to choose from is that clinicians are able to consider a child's culture. Obviously, culture can influence various aspects of children's lives that affect behaviors. Thus the culture of a child can influence a behavioral assessment. A culturally focused school psychologist will be able to identify behaviors that are influenced by a child's culture and recognize the behavioral differences among cultures and ethnicities. According to Castillo, Quintana, and Zamarripa (2000), a child's culture can influence "the child's values, beliefs, and attitudes that affect behaviors the way disorders are expressed and beliefs about mental health the ways children and families do (or do not) seek help how children and families accept and respond to treatment" (Gibbs & Huang, 1998).

Hosp and Hosp (2001) assert that African American and Caucasian students exhibit certain behaviors according to their culture and ethnicity. In a study that examined behavioral differences between African American and Caucasian students, the authors identified commonalities among the behaviors displayed by African American and Caucasian students. They termed these behavioral commonalities the African American Behavioral Style (AABS) and the Caucasian Behavioral Style (CBS). The AABS demonstrates a preference for seeking comfort in other people, being active, understanding social cues, and an interactive communication style.

In contrast, the CBS is associated with a preference for seeking help from objects rather than people, exhibiting passive behaviors, and a "turn-taking" communication style. Evidently, African American and Caucasian students have unique behavioral styles. Hence the observer must be careful to not misinterpret behavior(s). Hosp and Hosp (2001) provide an example of a student acting in the AABS who may shout out while the teacher is speaking. The student may view the classroom as a social setting in which he or she is able to interact with others. However, the teacher will most likely view "shouting out" as a disruptive or problematic behavior.

There is insufficient research on which observational systems are best for culturally diverse students. Further research must be conducted to enable observers to fully recognize cultural differences and their effects on observations (Castillo et al., 2000). Given this disparity, practitioners must thoroughly examine behavioral observational systems before selecting one for use.

Volpe, DiPerna, Hintze, and Shapiro (2005) reviewed several systems for direct observational assessment of student classroom behavior. Similarly, Leff and Lakin (2005) evaluated school-based observational systems which can be used in multiple settings. Several of the observational systems reviewed by these researchers are summarized in this section. Practical suggestions are also provided for analyzing and organizing data. Table 6.4 illustrates the behavioral observational systems described below.

One of the more simplistic behavioral observational systems is the Child Behavior Checklist–Direct Observation Form (CBCL-DOF; Achenbach & Edelbrock, 1986). It is part of the Achenbach System of Empirically-Based Assessment (ASEBA—Achenbach & Rescorla, 2001). The DOF is just one part of the CBCL, and is intended to be interpreted with its other components. These include parent, teacher, and child self-reports. The DOF is intended for use with children aged 5 to 14 (Achenbach, 2007). The coding system uses a four-point Likert scale to assess 97 items concerning student problem behaviors and on-task behaviors in group settings. The scale's

Table 6.4   Behavioral Observational Systems

Behavioral Observational Systems	Length of Observation	Behavior Categories
Direct Observation Form (DOF)	10	Problem behaviors and on-task behaviors in group settings (classroom, playground, lunchroom)
The Behavioral Observation of Students in School (BOSS)	15	On- and off-task academic behavior; active and passive engaged time
Behavior Assessment System for Children— 2nd Edition (BASC-2)	NA	Primary scales (anxiety, depression, hyperactivity, etc.); Content scales (anger control, bullying, resiliency, etc.); Composite scales (adaptive skills, internalizing problems, school problems, etc.)
Student Observation System (SOS)	15 minutes	Adaptive and maladaptive behaviors in elementary classroom
Academic Engaged Time Code (AET-SSBD)	15 minutes	Time spent engaged in academic work (completing worksheets, writing, listening to teacher)
Teacher's Report Form (TRF)	NA	Internalizing scales (withdrawn/depressed, thought problems); Externalizing scales (rule-breaking behavior, aggressive behavior); DSM-oriented scales (somatic problems, oppositional defiant problems)
Interpersonal Process Code (IPC)	10-minute sessions	Peer and family interactions across school and home settings
State-Event Classroom Observation System (SECOS)	20 minutes	Evaluate the effectiveness of classroom interventions; state behaviors (out of seat, looking around) and event behaviors (raising hand, calling out)
Attention-Deficit Hyperactivity Disorder School Observation Code (ADHD-SOC)	15 minutes	Evaluate interventions for ADHD, ODD, and CD; targeted behaviors include verbal, symbolic, and object aggression, interference, motor movement, and off-task
The Classroom Observation Code (COC)	32 minutes	Diagnostic assessment and evaluating interventions for ADHD; 12 behavior categories including noncompliance, off-task, out of chair, solicitation of teacher, and physical aggression

SOURCE: Volpe et al. (2005); Leff & Lakin (2005); Reynolds & Kamphaus (2004).

behavior categories include aggression, hyperactive, nervous-obsessive, and on-task. The length of a typical observation is approximately 10 minutes and the developers recommend performing three to six observations. The DOF is easy to learn and use, and provides an extensive evaluation of externalizing and internalizing student behaviors.

Another classroom-based observational system is the Behavioral Observation of Students in School (BOSS; Shapiro, 2004). The BOSS is used to observe academic behaviors of children in grades from pre-K through 12. On- and off-task behavior is measured by observing active versus passive engaged time. The observational sessions are divided into five intervals, four of which are used to measure behavior of the child while the fifth is used to code a preselected peer whose data are used to make comparisons. Examples of active engaged time are reading aloud and completing worksheets. Passive engaged time includes activities such as listening quietly as someone speaks or watching a demonstration. Momentary time sampling is used to measure both active and passive engaged time. A partial interval method is used to score off-task behavior. The BOSS takes between 10 and 15 hours of training.

The Behavior Assessment System for Children–2nd edition (BASC-2; Reynolds & Kamphaus, 2004) is another widely used system of behavioral assessment. The BASC-2 is intended for use with individuals aged from 2 through 25. Using an integrative approach, this system employs multiple informants to assess child or adolescent behavior. Adaptive and problem behaviors are measured using Teacher Rating Scales, Parent Rating Scales, a Self-Report of Personality, a structured developmental history, and a behavioral observation system. The Teacher and Parent Rating Scales are available for three age ranges: preschool (2 through 5 years), child (6 through 11 years), and adolescent (12 through 21 years). The Self Report of Personality excludes the preschool age range. This scale is available for three different age ranges: child (8 through 11 years), adolescent (12 through 21 years), and young adult (18 through 25 years, in an educational program following high school). The Teacher Rating Scale, Parent Rating Scale, and Self-Report of Personality all contain primary scales, content scales, and composite scales. See Table 6.4 for examples of the behaviors evaluated with these scales.

One component of the BASC-2 is the Student Observation System (SOS; Reynolds & Kamphaus, 2004). The SOS is a system used to assess adaptive and maladaptive behaviors in the classroom. It can be used with other components of the BASC-2, or on its own. Observational sessions of the SOS last approximately 30 minutes and occur over a period of three to four days. Each observational session is divided into 30-second intervals.

The observer records student and teacher behavior for 27 seconds. Student adaptive and maladaptive behavior is recorded in the last three seconds of the observation. Adaptive behaviors include response to teacher, peer interaction, work on school subjects, and transition movement. Inappropriate movement, inattention, inappropriate vocalization, somatization, repetitive motor movement, aggression, self-injurious behavior, inappropriate sexual behavior, and bowel or bladder problems compose the maladaptive behaviors.

Another widely used observational system for classroom behavior is the Academic Engaged Time Code (AET of SSBD; Walker & Severson, 1990). The AET is part of the Systematic Screening for Behavior Disorders and measures the amount of time during which the student is engaged in academic work compared with the overall time of the observation session. Examples of academic engaged time are completing a worksheet and listening to the teacher. The AET developers suggest finding the average of two observations in order to obtain a more stable academic engaged time score. Adequate training in the AET consists of as little as four to six hours (Walker & Severson, 1990).

An additional source of information concerning a child's behavior in the classroom is the teacher. The Teacher's Report Form (TRF; Achenbach & Rescorla, 2001, cited in Sattler & Hoge, 2006) is available for teachers of children aged 6 to 18 years. Scales include: internalizing scales (anxious/ depressed, somatic complaints, social problems, attention problems); externalizing scales (rule-breaking behavior, aggressive behavior); and DSM-oriented scales (affective problems, anxiety problems, attention-deficit/hyperactivity problems, conduct problems).

When conducting behavioral observations, school psychologists may need to observe behaviors across both school and home settings, since behaviors change depending on the setting or the situation. Furthermore, observing behaviors across settings is important to determine the consistency of the behavior.

The Interpersonal Process Code (IPC; Rusby, Estes, & Dishion, 1991) is one such system that is used to assess student behavior across multiple settings. The IPC uses a hand-held electronic event recorder to assess peer and family interactions across school and home settings. Using the IPC, three dimensions—*Activity*, *Content*, and *Affect Valence*—are coded concurrently to measure the frequency of each behavior. The Activity code refers to the actual setting in which the behavior takes place, with examples including classroom, playground, and home. The Content code involves the interactional behaviors and includes 14 behavioral codes such as cooperative behavior and negative physical behavior. The Affect code considers the emotional and nonverbal displays that are determined by the child's facial expressions, body language, and tone of voice. Examples of the affect code include happy, distressed, sad, and caring.

On occasion, school psychologists may need to evaluate the effectiveness of classroom interventions (National Association of School Psychologists, 2000). The State-Event Classroom Observation System (SECOS; Saudargas, 1997) was developed for this purpose. The SECOS is used for students from first grade through high school to measure state and event behaviors simultaneously. *State behaviors* (which have significant duration) include out of seat, school work, looking around, social interaction with another child, social interaction with the teacher, and other activity. *Event behaviors* begin and end quickly and include raising hand, calling out to teacher, approaching child, other child approaches, and teacher approaches. Training for the SECOS takes approximately 13 to 15 hours.

Several behavior rating scales and behavioral observational systems are intended for assessing childhood disorders. Attention-Deficit Hyperactivity Disorder (ADHD) is one of the most widely recognized childhood disorders (Merrell, 2000). Behavior rating scales have been developed to assess ADHD. Although most of these scales have been normed on large samples, the normative groups used to develop the scales often do not represent culturally diverse populations (Barkley, 1990). Naturally, any scale not culturally representative of a student's culture should not be considered for assessment use.

There are several important issues that may influence the assessment of ADHD across diverse cultural backgrounds. Marsella and Kameoka (1989, cited in Reid, 1995) provide several factors to review when examining an assessment system:

- *linguistic equivalence*: the extent to which the content and grammar of the scale have similar meanings across cultures;
- *conceptual equivalence*: the similarities of the behaviors that are thought to constitute ADHD;
- *scale equivalence*: an understanding of how the scale should be used; a common interpretation of the scale's metric descriptors;
- *normative equivalence*: the extent to which comparisons can be made with a norm group; standards developed for one culture must be appropriate for another.

Reid (1995) emphasizes that the diagnosis or presence of ADHD should on no account be determined by a single assessment instrument. One instrument that is widely used for the assessment of ADHD is the Attention-Deficit Hyperactivity Disorder School Observation Code (ADHD-SOC; Gadow, Sprafkin, & Nolan, 1996). The ADHD-SOC is primarily useful to evaluate the effects of medications and interventions for children diagnosed with Attention-Deficit Hyperactivity Disorder, Oppositional Defiant Disorder, and Conduct Disorder. The ADHD-SOC assesses social and antisocial behaviors of elementary school children across various settings within the school (e.g., classroom, lunchroom, and playground). A partial-interval method is used to measure the presence or absence of particular behaviors during 15-second intervals for a period of 15 minutes. Interference, motor movement, verbal aggression, symbolic aggression, object aggression, and off-task behaviors are the primary behaviors targeted. Adequate training in the ADHD-SOC takes approximately 20–25 hours.

Another system used in the assessment of ADHD is the Classroom Observation Code (COC; Abikoff & Gittelman, 1985). The COC can also be used to evaluate interventions that have already been implemented. A total of 12 behavior categories are assessed. Some of these categories include interference, minor motor movement, physical aggression, and solicitation of teacher. Two procedures are used to measure behavior during the observation session: the partial interval and the whole interval. During the partial interval procedure, discrete behaviors are scored in 15-second intervals. A whole interval method is used for coding off-task, noncompliance, and out-of-chair behavior. Observational sessions last approximately 32 minutes. The child is observed for 16 minutes and a preselected peer is observed for the other 16 minutes for comparison purposes. Training for the COC takes approximately 50 hours.

When a behavioral observation is completed, the observer is advised to speak with the teacher to determine whether the observation is representative of the child's typical behavior (Nock & Kurtz, 2005). Upon clarifying the typicality of the observed behavior, a report should be written up shortly after the observation. This will ensure that valuable observational information is not forgotten.

Direct Behavioral Observational Report Writing

There are several guidelines to follow for preparing a direct behavioral observational report. Presented below is a summary provided by Nock and Kurtz (2005) on how to report data, make recommendations, and conduct follow-up observations.

Reporting the Data

First, the observer should support all surveyed interpretations with evidence. Evidence usually includes the frequency, duration, antecedents, and consequences of a specific behavior. Second, the data can be presented in a table or integrated into the body of the report. Some of the major questions guiding the school observation report are:

Descriptive information:

- What is the child's name, date of birth, parents' names, and contact information?
- Who is the referring clinician?

Reason for observation:

- What are the primary referral questions?
- What are the specific target behaviors?

Teacher interview:

- What academic difficulties are reported by the teacher?
- What problem behaviors are reported by the teacher?
- What are the suspected triggers of the problem behaviors?

Classroom environment:

- What is the number of students and staff in the classroom?
- Are there distracting stimuli, background noises, or outside-class interruptions?
- Are the class rules and consequences posted in a visible location?
- Are the rules reinforced?

Child observation:

- What classes, lessons, or tasks occurred during the observation period?
- What evaluation procedures were used and are they described?
- What were the results of the observation?
- Describe the severity, frequency, and duration of target behaviors.
- Describe the antecedents and consequences of the observed behaviors.

Recommendations:

- Based on the results, what should the teachers and school personnel do to effectively modify the child's behavior? What can the parents do?
- What implications do the results have for the therapist treating the child?

Making Recommendations

The recommendation should directly relate to the referral question. They should be specific and based on the obtained data. A brief statement describing the observed data and main conclusions must be included when making a recommendation.

Follow-Up Observations

Follow-up observations are useful in evaluating interventions that were implemented *after* the first observation. During this process, additional behavior problems can be identified. It is wise to have a new observer conduct the follow-up session, as this may reduce any reactivity on the part of the observed student. A second observer will also decrease any biases related to having a single observer. Unfortunately, a possible drawback to the use of a second observer is the likelihood of an "inter-observer" discrepancy if a change in behavior is recorded. Despite the fact that a change in behavior may truly exist—or that there may be an inconsistency in the identification of behaviors between observers—follow-up observations are beneficial because they allow professionals to provide students with ongoing support.

In conclusion, it should not be overlooked that professionals (school psychologist, counselors, social workers) will at all times benefit by collecting information from teachers and parents, as these persons can provide valuable information about child behavior. Appropriate culturally competent assessment of personality and behaviors is a powerful thrust into all areas of a child or adolescent's life at the home and school levels. Although cognitive and educational assessment is essential to arrive at a desirable outcome, looking for and understanding cultural factors, and differences in the observed "undesirable" behavior, is the more crucial clinical expertise needed for fair assessments and successful interventions. After all, it is a psychologically healthy personality that produces all important aspects of an individual's life (i.e., academic achievement, interpersonal relationships/ socialization, vocation). Also related to personality is the research finding that there is a significant relationship between acculturation and personality (see Cuellar & Paniagua, 2000). The possibility of acculturative stress should not go by unassessed (see Chapter 10).

This chapter focused on varied methods of and instruments for evaluation, along with suggested primary sources of culturally packed information as an attempt to aid the school practitioner develop an awareness of the choices available. It is hoped that the reviews presented will decrease errors in diagnosis and increase the reliability of accurate personality and behavioral assessment. Let us not close this page and fail to follow up on the information provided.

References

Abikoff, H. & Gittelman, R. (1985). The normalizing effects of methylphenidate on the classroom behavior of ADHD children. *Journal of Abnormal Child Psychology, 13*(1), 33–44.

Achenbach, T. (2007). "Direct Observation Form for Ages 5–14 (DOF)." Achenbach System of Empirically Based Assessment. 2007. Accessed March 9, 2007 from www.aseba.org/products/dof.html.

Achenbach, T. M., & Edelbrock, C. S. (1984). Psychopathology of childhood. *Annual Review of Psychology, 35*, 227–256.

Achenbach, T. M., & Edelbrock, C. (1986). *Manual for the TRF and teacher version of the Child Behavior Profile.* Burlington, VT: Department of Psychiatry, University of Vermont.

Achenbach, T. M., & Rescorla, L. A. (2001). *Manual for the ASEBA school-age forms and profiles.* Burlington, VT: University of Vermont, Research Center for Children, Youths, and Families.

Allen, J., & Walsh, J. A. (2000). A construct-based approach to equivalence: Methodologies for cross-cultural/multicultural personality assessment. In R. H. Dana (Ed.), *Handbook of cross-cultural and multicultural personality assessment* (pp. 63–85). Mahwah, NJ: Lawrence Erlbaum.

Anastasi, A. (1988). *Psychological testing.* New York: Macmillan.

Anderson, W. H. (1988). The behavioral assessment of conduct disorder in a black child. In R. L. Jones (Ed.), *Psychoeducational assessment of minority group children: A casebook* (pp. 192–219). Berkeley, CA: Cobb Henry.

Aronow, E., Altman Weiss, K., & Reznikoff, M. (2001). *A practical guide to the Thematic Apperception Test: The TAT in clinical practice.* New York: Psychology Press.

Arredondo, P., Toporek, R., Brown, S. P., Jones, J., Locke, D. C., Sanchez, J., & Stadler, H. (1996). Operationalization of the multicultural competencies. *Journal of Multicultural Counseling and Development, 24*(1), 42–78.

Avila-Espada, A. (2000). Objective scoring for the TAT. In R. H. Dana (Ed.), *Handbook of cross-cultural and multicultural personality assessment* (pp. 465–480). Mahwah, NJ: Lawrence Erlbaum.

Barkley, R. A. (1990). *Attention Deficit Hyperactivity Disorder: A handbook for diagnosis and treatment.* New York: Guilford Press.

Bellak, L. (1993). *The Thematic Apperception Test, the Children's Apperception Test, and the Senior Apperception Technique in clinical use.* Upper Saddle River, NJ: Prentice Hall.

Bergan, J. R., & Kratochwill, T. R. (1990). *Behavioral consultation and therapy*. New York: Plenum.

Bornstein, M. H. & Lamb, M. E. (Eds.). (1999). *Developmental psychology: An advanced textbook* (4th ed.). Mahwah, NJ: Lawrence Erlbaum.

Butcher, J. N., Williams, C. L., Graham, J. R., Archer, R. P., Tellegen, A., Ben-Porath, Y. S., & Kaemmer, B. (1992). *MMPI-A (Minnesota Multiphasic Personality Inventory-Adolescent): Manual for administration, scoring, and interpretation*. Minneapolis, MN: University of Minnesota Press.

Campbell, S.B. (1989). Developmental perspectives. In T. H. Ollendick, & M. Hersen (Eds.), *Handbook of child psychopathology* (pp. 5–28). New York: Plenum.

Castillo, E. M., Quintana, S. M., & Zamarripa, M. X. (2000). Cultural and linguistic issues. In E. S. Shapiro, & T. R. Kratochwill (Eds.), *Conducting school-based assessments of child and adolescent behavior* (pp. 274–308). New York: Guilford Press.

Ciminero, A. R., & Drabman, R. S. (1977). Current developments in the behavioral assessment of children. In B. B. Lahey, & A. E. Kazdin (Eds.), *Advances in clinical child psychology: Vol. 1* (pp. 47–82). New York: Plenum.

Ciminero, A. R., Nelson, R., & Lipinski, D. P. (1977). Self-monitoring procedures. In *Handbook of behavioral assessment* (pp. 195–229). New York: Wiley.

Constantino, G., & Malgady, R. G. (2000). Multicultural and cross-cultural utility of TEMAS (Tell-Me-A-Story) Test. In R. H. Dana (Ed.), *Handbook of cross-cultural and multicultural personality assessment* (pp. 481–513). Mahwah, NJ: Lawrence Erlbaum.

Costantino, G., Malgady, R., & Rogler, L. (1988). *TEMAS (Tell-Me-A-Story)*. Los Angeles, CA: Western Psychological Services.

Cubillos, J. H. (2000). *TEMAS: Spanish for the global community*. Boston, MA: H. H. Heinle & Heinle Thomson Learning.

Cuellar, I., & Paniagua, F. (Eds.). (2000). *Handbook of multicultural mental health*. New York: Academic Press.

Cummins, R. A. (1988). *The neurologically impaired child: Doman-Delacato techniques reappraisal*. London: Croom Helm.

Dana, R. H. (1993). *Multicultural assessment perspectives for professional psychology*. Boston: Allyn & Bacon.

Dana, R. H. (2000). *Handbook of cross-cultural and multicultural personality assessment*. Mahwah, NJ: Lawrence Erlbaum.

Drasgow, E. & Yell, M. L. (2001). Functional behavioral assessments: legal requirements and challenges. *The School Psychology Review, 30*(2), 239–251.

Ephraim, D. (2000a). Culturally relevant research and practice with the Rorschach Comprehensive System. In R. H. Dana (Ed.), *Handbook of cross-cultural and multicultural personality assessment* (pp. 303–328). Mahwah, NJ: Lawrence Erlbaum.

Ephraim, D. (2000b). A psychocultural approach to TAT scoring and interpretation. R. H. Dana (Ed.), *Handbook of cross-cultural and multicultural personality assessment* (pp. 427–446). Mahwah, NJ: Lawrence Erlbaum.

Epstein, N. B., Bishop, D. S., & Baldwin, L. M. (1982). McMaster model of family functioning: A view of the normal family. In F. Walsh (Ed.), *Normal family processes* (pp. 115–141). New York: Guilford Press.

Escobar, J. E. (1993). Psychiatric epidemiology. In A. C. Gaw (Ed.), *Culture, ethnicity, and mental illness* (pp. 43–73). Washington, DC: American Psychiatric Press.

Flaherty, J. A., Gaviria, F. M., Pathak, D., Mitchell, T., Wintrob, R., Richiman, J. A., et al. (1988). Developing instruments for cross-cultural psychiatric research. *Journal of Nervous and Mental Disorders, 176*, 257–263.

Flanagan, R., & Di Giuseppe, R. (1999). Critical review of the TEMAS: A step within the development of thematic apperception instruments. *Psychology in the Schools, 36*(1), 21–30.

Gadow, K. D., Sprafkin, J., & Nolan, E. E. (1996). *ADHD School Observation Code.* Stony Brook, NY: Checkmate Plus

Gardner, W. I., & Cole, C. (1988). *Self monitoring.* In E. S. Shapiro, & T. R. Kratochwill (eds.), *Behavioral assessment in the schools* (pp. 206–246). New York: Guilford Press.

Gibbs, J., & Huang, L. N. (1998). *Children of color: Psychological interventions with culturally diverse youth* (2nd ed.). San Francisco: Jossey-Bass.

Goldfred, M. R., & Lineham, M. M. (1977). Basic issues in behavioral assessment. In A. R. Ciminero, K. S. Calhoun, & H. E. Adams (Eds.), *Handbook of behavioral assessment* (pp. 15–46). New York: John Wiley & Sons.

Greenfield, P. M. (1997). Culture as process: Empirical methods for cultural psychology. In J. W. Berry, Y. H. Poortinga, & J. Pandey (Eds.), *Handbook of cross-cultural psychology: Theory and method* (2nd ed). Boston: Allyn & Bacon.

Gresham, F. M., & Davis, C. J. (1988). Behavioral interviews with teachers and parents. In E. S. Shapiro, & T. R. Kratochwill (Eds.), *Behavioral assessment in schools: Conceptual foundations and practical applications* (pp. 455–493). New York: Guilford Press.

Gresham, F. M., Watson, T. S., & Skinner, C. H. (2001). Functional behavioral assessment: Principles, procedures, and future directions. *School Psychology Review, 30*(2), 156–172.

Hammer, E. F. (1980). *The clinical application of projective drawings* (6th ed.). Springfield, IL: Charles C Thomas.

Hay, W. M., Hay, L. R., Angle, H. V., & Nelson, R. O. (1979). The reliability of problem identification in the behavioral interview. *Behavioral Assessment, 1*, 107–118.

Haynes, S. N. (1978). *Principles of behavioral assessment.* New York: Garnerd Press.

Hosp, J. L., & Hosp, M. K. (2001). Behavior differences between African American and Caucasian students: Issues for assessment and intervention. *Education and Treatment of Children, 24*(3), 336–350.

House, A. E. (1999). *DSM-IV diagnosis in the schools.* New York: Guilford Press.

Johnston, S. S., & O'Neill, R. (2001). Searching for effectiveness and efficiency in conducting functional assessments: A review and proposed process for teachers and other practitioners. *Focus on Autism and Other Developmental Disabilities, 16*(4), 205–214.

Kleinman, A. (1988). *Rethinking psychiatry: From cultural category to personal experience*. New York: Free Press.

Knauss, L. K. (2001). Ethical issues in psychological assessment in school settings. *Journal of Personality Assessment, 77*(2), 231–241.

Kratochwill, T. R., Sheridan, S. M., Carlson, J., & Lasecki, K. L. (1998). Advances in behavioral assessment. In C. R. Reynolds & T. B. Gutkin (Eds.), *The handbook of school psychology* (3rd ed.; pp. 350–383). New York: John Wiley & Sons.

Lachar, D., & Gruber, C. (1995). *Personality inventory for youth*. Los Angeles, CA: Western Psychological Services.

Leff, S. S., & Lakin, R. (2005). Playgound-based observational systems: A review and implications for practitioners and researchers. *School Psychology Review, 34*(4), 475–489.

Lerner, R. M. (2002). *Concepts and theories of human development* (3rd ed). Mahwah, NJ: Lawrence Erlbaum.

Luiselli, J. K. (1989). Behavioral assessment and treatment of pediatric feeding disorders in developmental disabilities. In M. Hershen, & R. Eisler (Eds.), *Progress in behavior modification, Vol. 24*. Thousand Oaks, CA: Sage.

Machover, K. (1949). *Personality projection in the drawing of the human figure*. Springfield, IL: Charles C Thomas.

Mahoney, M. J. (1977). Reflections on the cognitive-learning trend in psychotherapy. *American Psychologist, 32*, 5–13.

Marsella, A. J., & Kameoka, V. A. (1989). Ethnocultural issues in the assessment of psychopathology. In S. Wetzler (Ed.), *Measuring mental illness: Psychometric assessment for clinicians* (pp. 231–256). Washington, DC: American Psychiatric Association.

Mash, E. J., & Terdal, L. G. (1997). *Behavioral assessment of childhood disorders*. New York: Guilford Press.

Mash, E. J., & Wolfe, D. A. (Eds.) (2002). *Abnormal child psychology* (2nd ed.). Belmont, CA: Wadsworth.

Masten, A. S., & Braswell, L. (1991). Developmental psychopathology: An integrative framework. In P. R. Martin (Ed.), *Handbook of behavior therapy and psychological science: An integrative approach* (pp. 35–56). New York: Pergamon Press.

McComas, J. J., & Mace, C. E. (2000). Theory and practice in conducting functional analysis. In E. S. Shapiro, & T. R. Kratochwill (Eds.), *Behavioral assessment in the schools* (2nd ed.; pp. 78–103). New York: Guilford Press.

McConnell, K., Patton, J. R., & Polloway, E. A. (2000). *Behavioral intervention planning: Completing a Functional Behavioral Assessment and developing a Behavioral Intervention Plan* (rev. ed.). Austin, TX: Pro-Ed.

Merrell, K. W. (2000). Informant report: Rating scale measures. In E. S. Shapiro, & T. R. Kratochwill (Eds.), *Conducting school-based assessments of child and adolescent behavior* (pp. 203–234). New York: Guilford Press.

Millon, T. (1987). *Millon Clinical Multiaxial Inventory–II*. Minneapolis, MN: National Computer Systems.

Millon, T. (1993). *Millon Adolescent Clinical Inventory manual*. Minneapolis, MN: National Computer Systems.

Moon, T., & Cundick, B. P. (1983). Shifts and constancies in Rorschach responses as a function of culture and language. *Journal of Personality Assessment, 47*, 345–349.

National Association of School Psychologists. (2000). *Professional conduct manual: Principles for professional ethics, guidelines for the provision of school psychological services*. Bethesda, MD: NASP.

Nock, M. K., & Kurtz, S. M. S. (2005). Direct behavioral observation in school settings: Bringing science to practice. *Cognitive and Behavioral Practice, 12*, 359–370.

Paniagua, F. (2005). *Assessing and treating culturally diverse clients: A practical guide*. Thousand Oaks, CA: Sage.

Pedersen, S. (1993), *Family, dependence and the origins of the welfare state*. New York: Cambridge University Press.

Reid, R. (1995). Assessment of ADHD with culturally different groups: The use of behavioral rating scales. *School Psychology Review, 24*(4), 537–561.

Reynolds, W. M. (1998). *Adolescent Psychopathology Scale*. Odessa, FL: Psychological Assessment Resources.

Reynolds, W. M. (2000). *Adolescent Psychopathology Scale, Short Form: Professional manual*. Odessa, FL: Psychological Assessment Resources.

Reynolds, C. R., & Kamphaus, R. W. (2004). *Behavior assessment system for children* (2nd ed.). Circle Pines, MN: American Guidance System Publishing.

Rogers, R. (Ed.). (1988). *Clinical assessment of malingering and deception*. New York: Guilford Press.

Rusby, J. C., Estes, A., & Dishion, T. (1991). *The interpersonal process code (IPC)*. Eugene, OR: Oregon Social Learning Center.

Sattler, J. M., & Hoge, R. D. (2006). *Assessment of children: Behavioral, social, and clinical foundations* (5th ed.). San Diego, CA: Jerome M. Sattler.

Saudargas, R. A. (1997). *State-Event Classroom Observation System (SECOS)*. Knoxville, TN: University of Tennessee.

Scotti, J. R., Morris, T. L., McNeil, C.M., & Hawkins, R.P. (1996). DSM-IV and disorders of childhood and adolescence: Can structural criteria be functional? *Journal of Consulting and Clinical Psychology, 64*, 1177–1191.

Shapiro, E. S. (2004). *Academic skills problems: Direct assessment and intervention*. New York: Guilford Press.

Shapiro, E. S., & Heick, P. F. (2004). School psychologist assessment practices in the evaluation of students referred for social/behavioral/emotional problems. *Psychology in the Schools, 41*(5), 551–561.

Shapiro, E. S., & Kratochwill, T. R. (Eds.). (2000). *Behavioral assessment in the schools* (2nd ed.). New York: Guilford Press.

Sue, D. W., Arredondo, P., & McDavis, R. J. (1992). Multicultural counseling competencies and standards: A call to the profession. *Journal of Counseling and Development, 70*, 477–486.

Thompson, S. J., Quenemoen, R. F., Thurlow, M. L, & Ysseldyke, J. E. (2001). *Alternate assessments for students with disabilities*. Thousand Oaks, CA: Corwin Press.

Turk, D. C., & Kerns, R. D. (1985). *Health, illness, and families: A life-span perspective.* New York: John Wiley & Sons.

Volpe, R. J., DiPerna, J. C., Hintze, J. M., & Shapiro, E. S. (2005). Observing students in classroom settings: A review of seven coding schemes. *School Psychology Review, 34*(4), 454–474.

Walker, H. M., & Severson, H. H. (1990). *Systematic screening for behavior disorders: Observer training manual.* Longmont, CO: Sopris West.

Watson, T. S., & Steege, M. W. (2003). *Conducting school-based functional behavioral assessments: A practitioner's guide.* New York: Guilford Press.

Yamamoto, J. (1986). Therapy for Asian Americans and Pacific Islanders. In C. B. Wilkinson (Ed.), *Ethnic psychiatry* (pp. 89–141). New York: Plenum Medical.

Annotated Bibliography

Dana, R. H. (Ed.). (2000). *Handbook of cross-cultural and multicultural personality assessment.* Mahwah, NJ: Lawrence Erlbaum. *This excellent handbook offers the first comprehensive view of consistent approach to cultural competence in assessment—a necessary precursor to effective intervention. A good reference for those whose practice or research involves individuals with different ethnic and racial identities.*

Shapiro, E. S., & Kratochwill, T. R. (2000). *Behavioral assessment in schools: Theory, research, and clinical foundations* (2nd ed). New York: Guilford Press. *This text is a comprehensive review of behavioral assessment procedures in the schools. A good reference for practitioners conducting behavioral assessments.*

Watson, T. S., & Steege, M. W. (2003). *Conducting school-based functional behavioral assessments: A practitioner's guide.* New York: Guilford Press. *This guidebook takes school practitioners step by step through the procedures for conducting Functional Behavioral Assessments (FBA) and shows how to use FBAs to plan effective interventions.*

NASP Publications

To order on the internet: www.nasponline.org/store; phone: 301-657-0270.

Bear, G. G., Minke, K. M., & Thomas, A. (1997). *Children's Needs II: Development, Problems and Alternatives. This text comprises 86 chapters that provide a quick yet thorough reference for a wide spectrum of child development topics. In addressing those factors that contribute to both healthy and atypical development, each chapter includes suggested interventions that are grounded in research and theory, as well as suggestions for further reading. Parent/child resources are also available.*

Canter, A. S., & Carroll, S. A. (Eds.) (1998). *Helping Children at Home and School: Handouts From Your School Psychologist. These handouts can be distributed to parents and educators. They provide relevant, easy-to-use information on a wide range of learning and developmental issues, such as ADHD, Reading, Anger, Anxiety, Depression, Chronic Illness, Homework, Self-Esteem, Suicide, Substance Abuse, Discipline, Retention/Promotion. Also available in Bilingual Spanish/English:* Ayudando a los ninos en el hogar y en la escuela: Hojas informativas de su psicologo escolar *(2001).*

Shinn, M. R., Walker, M. H., & Stoner, G. (Eds.). (2002). *Interventions for Academic and Behavior Problems II: Preventive and Remedial Approaches. This offers the latest in evidence-based measures that have been proven to create safer, more effective schools. Thirty-eight updated and expanded chapters offer the latest knowledge on issues such as violence, prevention, intervention and assessment strategies for social-emotional functioning, reading and academic achievement, and system-level strategies and policies.*

Recommended Articles

The following articles are important to consider in this area:

Arrendondo, P., Toporek, R., Brown, S. P., Jones, J., Locke, D. C., Sanchez, J., & Stadler, H. (1996). Operationalization of the multicultural counseling competencies. *Journal of Multicultural Counseling and Development, 24,* 42–78.

Paunonen, S., Haddock, G., Forsterling, F., & Keinonen, M. (2003). Broad versus narrow personality measures and the prediction of behavior across cultures. *European Journal of Personality, 17,* 413–433.

Sue, D. W., Arredondo, P., & McDavis, R. J. (1992). Multicultural counseling competencies and standards: A call to the profession. *Journal of Multicultural Counseling and Development, 20,* 64–88.

Suzuki, L. A., Alexander, C.M., & Lin, Pei-Ying (2006). Psychopathology in the schools: Multicultural factors that impact assessment and intervention. *Psychology in the Schools, 43*(4), 429–438.

Useful Websites

Books related to functional assessment: www.psych-books.com
Psychology and assessment: www.questia.com/library/psychology
Information on Learning Disability: www.ldonline.org

Functional Academic Assessments

Sopris West Educational Services: www.sopriswest.com

Psychology Research on Assessments

American Institutes for Research: www.air.org/assessment
Multimodal Functional Behavioral Assessment: www.mfba.net

Projective Techniques Developers

Bellak, L., & Bellak, S. S. (1948). *The CAT.* Larchmont, NY: CPS.

Buck, J. N. (1966). *The House-Tree-Person Technique: A Revised Manual.* Beverly Hills, CA: Western Psychological Services.

Costantino, G., Malgady, R.G., & Rogler, L. H. (1988). *Technical manual: TEMAS thematic apperception test.* Los Angeles: Western Psychological Services.

Goodenough, F. L. (1926). *Measurement of intelligence by drawings.* Yonkers: World Book Co.

Hathaway, S. R., & McKinley, J. C. (1943). *The Minnesota Multiphasic Personality Inventory.* Minneapolis: University of Minnesota.

Murray, H. A. (1943). *The Thematic Apperception Test: Plates and manual.* Cambridge, MA: Harvard University Press.

Rorschach, H. (1921). *Psychodiagnostik.* Bern, Switzerland: Bircher.35

7

Writing Psychological and Educational Reports for Culturally and Linguistically Diverse Students

Sara Nahari

Danielle Martines

Much has been discussed in the literature regarding culturally sensitive assessment procedures for culturally and linguistically diverse (CLD) children and youth (Gopaul-McNicol & Brice-Baker, 1998; Padilla, 2001; Ponterotto, Gretchen, & Chauhan, 2001; Sattler, 2001) but very little has been dedicated to addressing the components of a solidly grounded, culturally fair psycho-educational report. As a result, school psychologists in training, and even those in practice, most likely have not developed the necessary skills for culturally and linguistically fair report writing. However, if the guidelines in the literature for conducting multicultural assessment (Ortiz & Flanagan, 2002; Padilla, 2001; Ridley et al., 2001; Prediger, 1993; Sternberg & Grigorenko, 2001; Suzuki, Short, Pieterse, & Kugler, 2001) are followed, it can reasonably be assumed that psycho-educational report writing for CLD children—from a variety of racial, cultural, ethnic, experiential, and linguistic backgrounds—should incorporate the same guiding principles. This assumption is made clearer when assessment and report writing are viewed as interconnected. From this standpoint, objectives and goals for culturally and linguistically sensitive report writing should be addressed in best practice.

A review of the literature on report writing reveals that no specific guidelines have been proposed for constructing culturally competent reports. Drawing from this lack of criteria, this chapter provides school psychologists with a framework that addresses the competencies and ethics required for writing culturally sensitive psycho-educational reports for CLD children and youth from diverse racial/ethnic backgrounds.

What Is a Psychological and Educational Report?

A psychological and educational report (often termed a psycho-educational report) is an organized, comprehensive, and integrated written account of the results obtained from a psychological/educational assessment. Traditionally, the criteria followed are to write such a report plainly and succinctly, describing personal student history, the results of quantitative measures, clinical deductions, and specific recommendations. There are several purposes for a psychological report; for the school psychologist, the primary reasons are to explain the results of the assessment, to provide recommendations for interventions, and to stress the need for special services when applicable.

Objectives of the Report

The objectives currently available for best practices define several purposes of a psychological report (Sattler, 2001):

1. To provide accurate assessment-related aspects to the referral source and other concerned parties—for example, developmental, medical, intellectual, and educational history, as well as current interpersonal skills, intellectual and cognitive abilities, motor skills, and personality.

2. To serve as a source of clinical hypotheses, appropriate interventions, and information for program evaluation and research.

3. To furnish meaningful baseline information for evaluating (a) the examinee's progress after the interventions have been implemented, or (b) changes that occur as a result of time alone.

4. To serve as a legal document. (p. 677)

In addition, the purpose of the report is to provide parents, teachers, the student, and (when appropriate) health care professionals with the information gleaned from the overall outcomes of the evaluative process. Hence the completion of the report is the final product of the school psychologist's investigation of the student's current social, emotional, and cognitive functioning. Moreover, since the psycho-educational report constitutes a legal document, it should be a well-written and clinically informative professional testimony of the abilities of the student, because such documents can be subpoenaed in court, whether or not the school psychologist believes the material has the basis of a privileged communication (Tallent, 1998, p. 66). In short, the report is a blueprint that addresses the needs of the student as deduced from the assessment. It is also a conduit for providing information on the current status of the educational and emotional well-being of the student. Most importantly, the report should ensure that the student's cultural ethnic group and values have been respected. Based on this point of view, a psycho-educational report prepared for a CLD student should adhere to the various cultural and language factors that influenced and impacted the assessment.

Professional and Legal Mandates Relevant to Writing Reports

Rogers et al. (1999), representing the APA's Division 16 Task Force on Cross-Cultural School Psychology Competencies, suggest that school psychologists be well informed about local, state, and federal regulations, but be aware particularly of major court cases, both historical and ongoing, that involve CLD children and their families. For example, *Diana v. California State Board of Education* provides the legal underpinnings for school psychologists to examine children in the native (dominant non-English) language. The authors also highlight the need for fluency with regard to: (a) immigration and naturalization laws; (b) civil rights, as they pertain to educational services; and (c) bilingual and ESL program legislation—in particular, the implementation of such laws in different states, and their relative effectiveness. School psychologists are also encouraged to enter the debate regarding public educational policies, and advocate for such policies when they determine they will have a beneficial outcome for their racial/ethnic CLD students. In the *Professional Conduct Manual* prepared by the National Association of School Psychologists (NASP) (2000), culturally diverse populations Practice Guideline 5 highlights the following:

> School psychologists have the sensitivity, knowledge, and skills to work with individuals and groups with a diverse range of strengths and needs from a variety of racial, cultural, ethnic, experiential, and linguistic backgrounds.

Practice Guideline 5.4 further elaborates:

> School psychologists incorporate their understanding of the influence of culture, background, and individual learning characteristics when designing and implementing interventions to achieve learning and behavioral outcomes.

These guidelines are certainly helpful, but unfortunately they are not specific enough in many instances. Concerning such guidelines in general, Lopez (1997) comments:

> Practitioners are left to implement those guidelines and mandates at a time when the fields of education and psychology are confronted with many questions regarding test bias, lack of assessment resources (e.g., shortage of instrument validity validated with a variety of language groups), and a questionable knowledge base as to how to assess children LEP [Limited English Proficient] and bilingual backgrounds.

In other words, she suggests that, worthwhile as much of this content is, lack of sufficient specific knowledge on the part of the school psychologist could be a considerable handicap.

Ethical Standards

Both the American Psychological Association (APA) and the National Association of School Psychologists have compiled codes of ethics for psychologists to follow when providing services in schools or in independent practice.

The NASP (2000) *Professional Conduct Manual* defines ethical standards for report writing in a list provided for the Professional Practices-General Principles, Assessment and Interventions (Section IV: Professional Practices—General Principles; D: Reporting Data and Conference Results, Point 3, p. 28). This particular principle addresses psychological report writing, and reads as follows:

> School psychologists prepare written reports in such form and style that the recipient of the report will be able to assist the child or other clients. Reports should emphasize recommendations and interpretations; unedited computer-generated reports, pre-printed "check-off" or "fill-in-the-blank" reports, and reports that present only test scores or global statements regarding eligibility for special education without specific recommendations for intervention are seldom useful. Reports should include an appraisal of the degree of confidence that could be assigned to the information.

An additional principle cautions school psychologists to "review all of their written documents for accuracy, signing them only when correct." The ethical principles take account of important aspects of the report, but do not provide in-depth information on how to structure a report, or what to include in it.

As mentioned previously, the literature reveals that specific ethical guidelines for writing culturally competent reports have not been proposed. However, it has been assumed that practitioners who practice ethically appropriate multicultural assessments are both interested in the theoretical and practical considerations in ethics, and put their ethical knowledge into practice (Ridley, Hill, & Li, 1998). As defined in this context, ethics involve acquiring ethical competence and practicing professional responsibility by acting upon the recommended ethics. In this respect, it can be assumed that ethical report writing should abide by the same ethical competence and responsibility. Consequently, report writing has to be interconnected once again to assessment practice in an attempt to review ethical codes and laws. In addition, NASP's standards recommend the following five areas of sound psychological assessment that should be adhered to, so as to ensure that ethical and legal concerns have been respected (Jacob-Timm & Hartshorne, 1998).

Assessment should be:

- *multifaceted*—it should ensure the use of multiple methods of assessment to avoid a single test score being used as the sole basis for decision-making;
- *comprehensive*—assessments should cover all areas of the child's difficulties (e.g., health, vision, hearing, social/emotional functioning, intellectual abilities, educational achievement, communication skills, and motor abilities);
- *fair*—the selection of assessment instruments and procedures takes into consideration age, gender, native language, socioeconomic status, disabilities, and cultural and ethnic background. More specifically, for the child with a disability, appropriate assessment procedures must be selected in order to ensure that cognitive ability, educational achievement, and adaptive behavior are fairly evaluated. Additionally, students with limited English proficiency (LEP) should undergo a language proficiency and dominance screening; the latter will aid in the selection of instruments, as well as the interpretation of outcomes. Furthermore, ethical codes and special education laws also mandate that nonbiased assessment methods be adopted for culturally and racially diverse children;
- *valid*—the validity of the test utilized should be assured by following the Standards for Educational and Psychological Testing (AERA, APA, & NCME, 1999). A summary of the standards indicates that school psychologists are ethically responsible for evaluating the technical standards (validity, reliability, standardization norms) of the tests they use, so as to guarantee that they are valid for their intended purposes;
- *useful*—appropriate assessment instruments should be selected that provide the strengths and weaknesses of the assessed child and aid in formulating an assigned

diagnosis. Accordingly, the results of an assessment are shared with parents and educators through a written report and in conferences. Furthermore, parents have a legal right to obtain a copy of their child's psychological report (Public Law 94-142). School psychologists should make certain that reports include recommendations and interventions, and do not solely describe test scores.

It is apparent that all of the above-mentioned ethical standards for fair assessment practice are applicable to psychological report writing, because the two are so obviously intertwined.

Tallent (1998, p. 62) discusses ethical and legal responsibilities and issues of confidentiality in report writing, in particular framing the need for writing that is understandable and serviceable for care providers. A landmark decision reached by a U.S. district court in Alabama in the case of *Wyatt v. Aderholt* in 1974 found that "evidence established that the hospitals [involved in the case] failed to meet the conditions of individualized treatment programs." Patient records were determined to be "wholly inadequate," and both inaccessible and incomprehensible to the aide-level staff whose primary responsibility was the care of the patients. Tallent (1998) submits that individualized case-focused reports are of far more benefit than those written in more general terms. He also argues that psychologists should be mindful when writing reports that, historically, the courts do not share the same code of ethics or guidelines that psychologists do, especially when an individual's rights are at stake.

In general, the scarcity of research conducted on writing reports addressing issues related to CLD populations is substantial.

Practice Implications of Writing Psycho-Educational Reports for CLD Students

It is important to recognize that there are several important variations involved in conducting an appropriate assessment for a CLD child or youth. Among these differences are the gathering of cultural and experiential background, determining language dominance in addition to second-language acquisition, acculturation stages and/or stressors, educational levels, and other important community/school/home factors. This additional essential information obtained from the assessment is vital to the report. Failure to accomplish this results in a more traditional report prepared for a monolingual English-dominant U.S. mainstream student, which will be distinctly unhelpful for the CLD student.

Several additional objectives are needed to provide school psychologists with the appropriate framework for CLD report writing. To carry out this aim, the following culture-specific objectives are presented.

Prior to discussing the objectives of a culturally focused psycho-educational report, the format of a traditional psychological report should be examined. Sattler (2001) describes the typical sections of a report as follows:

1. Identifying Information

2. Assessment Instruments

3. Reason for Referral

4. Background Information

5. Observations During the Assessment

6. Assessment Results and Clinical Impressions

7. Recommendations

8. Summary

9. Signature (p. 678).

The traditional sections that address the objectives of a report continue to be appropriate; however, a review of the literature regarding multicultural assessment competencies revealed additional objectives necessary for inclusion in order to ensure a culturally fair report. Several supplementary objectives are suggested below.

1. Adhere to the recommendations for conducting a multicultural assessment (Armour-Thomas & Gopaul-McNicol, 1998; Gopaul-McNicol & Brice-Baker, 1998; Ortiz, 2002; Rogers et al., 1999; Ridley et al., 1998).

2. Report all results in a culturally sensitive manner.

3. View the report as an instrument to plan instruction and provide guidance with regard to the academic strengths and weaknesses of the CLD student.

4. Consider the impact of social and cultural issues, language, and environmental/political factors (Rogers et al., 1999).

5. Include background information that covers cultural information pertaining to ethnic and racial/biracial identity, religious/traditional beliefs, social class, health care practices, immigration and/or acculturation stages of the student and parents, and disciplinary norms of the family (Gopaul-McNicol & Brice-Baker, 1998).

6. Acknowledge the weight of learning a second language and adjustment to a second culture on the social/emotional and intellectual development of the CLD student (Rogers et al., 1999).

7. Report language proficiency and, for English Language Learners (ELL), provide a description of the current progress in the acquisition of a second language (Meller, Ohr, & Marcus, 2001; Ortiz, 2002; Rogers et al., 1999).

8. A good report should address cultural and linguistic information (Rogers et al., 1999) and, when appropriate, the results of some screening measure or other qualitative method used to assess the CLD student's language dominance and/or bilingualism (e.g., The Bilingual Verbal Ability Test (BVAT) (Munoz-Sandoval et al., 1998), which is used for students who are less dominant in the native language, and the Woodcock language proficiency assessment).

9. Address the quantitative results of the evaluation, and endeavor to assess the outcomes in an unbiased manner, as well as describe any deviations/modifications adopted during the testing (Ortiz, 2002; Rogers et al., 1999). If a standardized test was used that has not been normed for the CLD student, the results should be explained in a descriptive and qualitative manner (Rogers et al., 1999).

10. Use appropriate comparison groups when discussing the assessed CLD student (Rogers et al., 1999).

11. Incorporate in the interpretation of tests section of the report a *psychometric estimate* of the cognitive results. This section describes the child's potential and provides an estimate of intellectual functioning when certain biases in testing practices are removed or modified (Gopaul-McNicol & Brice-Baker, 1998; Ortiz, 2002).

12. Include qualitative outcomes obtained from *other assessments*. Other assessments imply the integration of alternative methods of assessment that consist of the evaluation of *other intelligences* in the areas of musical, bodily kinesthetic, interpersonal, and intrapersonal abilities, and other domains of functioning (Suzuki et al., 2001). A description of the latter covers those areas of functioning that are not commonly included in a psycho-educational report, causing important areas of functioning of the CLD child to be overlooked. Performance-based assessment, functional assessment, dynamic assessment, and/or developmental assessment techniques can also be regarded as part of qualitative, alternative methods of assessment (Rogers et al., 1999).

13. Include a section that addresses the results of the *learning ecology* assessment which involves the following steps: (a) review of educational records; (b) observation of the student during class instruction, as well as an examination of the content of the instruction; (c) suitability of the curriculum; (d) evaluation of the fit between the student and the curriculum with consideration of the student's needs; (e) deductions made from parent and teacher interviews; and (f) review of medical records (Ortiz, 2002).

14. Ensure that the clinical impressions of the report truly reflect the CLD child's personality and behaviors according to his/her culture and ethnicity.

15. Describe the results of an *ecological* assessment. In this section, the goal is to provide information concerning the CLD child's functioning within her/his family and community (Gopaul-McNicol & Brice-Baker, 1998).

16. Describe the limitations of using interpreters for interviewing or testing purposes in conjunction with a detailed explanation of the interpreters' training and credentials (Hamayan & Damico, 1991; Figueroa, Sandoval, & Merino, 1984).

17. Acknowledge the use of a translated test and to explain that the psychometric structure of the original non-translated instrument and the translated version of the instrument are not comparable (Rogers et al., 1999; Tallent, 1998, p. 250) (see Appendix 7.2 for Checklist of Objectives).

The Relationship Between Assessment and Report Writing

In essence, the main reason for the psycho-educational report is to clearly explain all the procedures/results observed in the assessment and to make appropriate recommendations. Consequently, there is a direct linear relationship between a multicultural assessment and the writing up of the psychological report. Each section of the report follows the steps the school psychologist has taken to ensure a complete evaluation and, just as the assessment practices for CLD children and youth conform to a culturally sensitive approach, so must the report follow the same method. Specifically, the of data obtained during the assessment are *transferred* to written form, although Tallent (1998) stresses that raw data as such must be subject to logical analysis (p. 73)—what he considers "adequate interpretation of such material." Accordingly, the same culturally centered manner that was followed throughout the evaluation should be narrated with identical sensitivity and accuracy. Thus the report is a final written representation of the assessment procedure and its outcome. It is the most important part of the assessment process, because it is a legal document that records all domains of a student's functioning in tandem with recommendations.

Implications of Quantitative and Qualitative Assessments and Report Writing

Quantitative assessment typically refers to psychometric testing. Ordinarily, the psychological report includes a very detailed explanation of the results of the psychometric tests administered (e.g., intelligence tests, personality assessment scales and/or inventories, behavioral scales, educational tests). However, over the years there have been serious allegations made regarding standardized measures, predominantly intelligence tests. Intelligence tests have been described as culturally biased and as failing to accurately demonstrate the true achievements and potential of CLD racial/ethnic children. Consequently, various types of authentic and alternative qualitative (non-psychometric) assessments have been implemented for estimating CLD (and/or racial/ethnic) children's abilities (e.g., dynamic assessment, portfolio assessment, curriculum-based measurement, naturalistic observations, other intelligences assessment). Hence it has been recommended that school psychologists incorporate both quantitative and qualitative methods for evaluating culturally diverse children (Armour-Thomas & Gopaul-McNicol, 1998; Ortiz, 2002).

Armour-Thomas and Gopaul-McNicol (1998) have developed a four-tier Bio-Cultural Model of assessment that advocates the integration of quantitative and qualitative measures in assessment. The four tiers are: psychometric; psychometric potential; ecological assessment; and an evaluation of other intelligences. These researchers/practitioners propose conducting culturally fair *bio-ecological* assessments, and suggest incorporating the results under the following sections of the psychological report:

1. *Psychometric Assessment*—Although results are quantitative, they should be described in a qualitative manner, indicating the "child's strengths and weaknesses in the constructs measured by each subtest" (p. 22).

2. *Psychometric Potential Assessment*—This section describes the following practices in the assessment of potential: (a) suspending time tasks; (b) contextualizing vocabulary appraisal; (c) paper and pencil tasks; and (d) test–teach–retest strategies employed. The section evaluates the child's potential and/or estimated intellectual abilities; if the child manifests an improvement, the report should include the noted increase.

3. *Ecological Assessment*—This section reports the psychologist's evaluation of the CLD child's family/community supports, stage of acculturation, and teacher interview/questionnaire results.

4. *Other Intelligences*—This section includes commonly found intelligences among CLD racial/ethnic children and youth, such as musical, bodily/kinesthetic, interpersonal, intrapersonal, and naturalistic intelligences. These should be assessed, because intelligence tests do not reflect the other intelligences of CLD children (Gardner, 1999; Gopaul-McNicol & Brice-Baker, 1998; Lopez, 1997).

In the same vein, Ortiz (2002) advocates using a similar framework for nondiscriminatory assessment that suggests taking into consideration cultural and linguistic factors, a reduction of bias in testing practices, and utilizing authentic and alternative assessments.

In summary, a complete report ought to reflect both quantitative and qualitative results obtained in the assessment process; this practice is in keeping with the recommendations made for conducting multicultural assessments (Gopaul-McNicol & Brice-Baker, 1998; Lidz, 2001; Ortiz, 2002; Ponterotto, Gretchen, & Chauhan, 2001; Suzuki et al., 2001; Sternberg & Grigorenko, 2001).

Language and Culture

When conducting a culturally sensitive assessment, school psychologists are advised to assess language within the context of culture. Briefly explained, this implies that language is more than a manner of communicating; it is cultural and is used to socialize children into linguistic and cultural communities/regions. This leads to the development of patterns that aid in differentiating one community (or region) from another (e.g., dialectical differences). Moreover, many CLD children are bilingual (they have the ability to use two languages) or in the process of second language acquisition (English Language Learners, or ELL) (Hakuta, 1986; Cummins, 1984). The interaction between language and culture is a multifaceted process that is vital to the socialization of children into satisfactory cultural patterns—children learn the syntax of their native language and what words mean in varying contexts. Thus, within their own communities, children develop specific language skills; however these skills can differ significantly from school demands (Wolfram, Adger, & Christian, 1999). For this reason, children and adolescents with limited English proficiency or without English language skills should be evaluated cautiously within their cultural milieu.

In the assessment process, it is recommended that a language screening take place either through the use of language scales or informal measures when evaluating language in the CLD child and their parents (Ortiz, 2002; Sattler, 2001). Consequently, as already stated, an objective of a culturally sensitive report is to reserve a specific section dedicated to a description of language screening results, language dominance of the student, and second language acquisition progress within the context of culture.

The report should integrate the following relevant cultural and linguistic information obtained from the assessment:

- the results of an examination of the experiential effects of biculturalism and/or bilingualism during childhood development and their influence on school learning;
- the assessment of native and home language;
- the acculturation stages of both parents and student;

- the parents' fluency in native and English languages;
- the parents' level of literacy in native and English languages;
- the education and socioeconomic status of the parents (Ortiz, 2002).

Accordingly, the interconnectedness between language and culture should not be overlooked in the assessment of culturally/linguistically diverse children (Cummins, 1984; Gopaul-McNicol & Brice-Baker, 1998; Hamayan & Damico, 1991; Meller et al., 2001; Ortiz, 2002; Sattler, 2001). It should also be borne in mind that the school psychologist's role in writing the report is not only to assess, but to problem-solve, guide, and recommend potential interventions and solutions to the interested parties. In this regard, the report writer should concisely summarize the determined cultural and linguistic issues found, and their ramifications, without resorting to jargon or more abstract concepts. When interested parties understand the language capabilities of the CLD student, and the student's cultural specifics, they will be more motivated to work with the school psychologist in problem solving.

The use of interpreters in psycho-educational assessment is a variable that must not be ignored since it will affect the results of the assessment as well as the way the report is written. Therefore, it is essential to record the use of an interpreter during the evaluation. The section below examines the use of interpreters during assessment and the implications of this type of assessment on report writing.

Working With Interpreters and Implications for Report Writing

The National Association of School Psychologists (NASP) briefly identifies competency guidelines for working with interpreters:

Domain V. Working With Interpreters

1. Knowledge of recommended systemic practices, including guidelines from professional organizations and national and state policies, and plans for hiring, training, and managing interpreters.

2. Knowledge of recommended practices for interpreters translating for parent conferences, including using school personnel and community members as interpreters (never children or family members).

These guidelines address systemic practices and suggest that school psychologists be aware of the recommendations for using interpreters. The guidelines do not, however, provide detailed recommendations with regard to training or to assessment procedures. Several attempts to further clarify these non-exclusions are found in the literature (Gopaul-McNicol, & Brice-Baker, 1998; Lopez, 2000; Sattler, 2001).

However, in consequence of the scarcity of bilingual school psychologists, the assessment of culturally/linguistically diverse children often requires the use of an interpreter, and any use of an interpreter for interviews and testing should be detailed in the report.

Cross-Cultural Competencies Relevant to Report Writing

The notion of multicultural assessment practice has been summarized in the literature as encompassing several areas of competencies, such as knowledge and skills in cross-cultural issues concerning: (a) clinical interviewing and assessment of individuals from diverse backgrounds; (b) maintaining culturally centered ethics in testing; (c) expertise in cultural identity and acculturation; (d) appropriate selection of assessment instruments; and (e) knowledge of diagnosing individuals from diverse cultures. Correspondingly, knowledge and skills for selecting culturally appropriate interventions and recommendations are also part of cross-cultural practice (Suzuki et al., 2001), and report writing should adhere to the same competencies recommended for cross-cultural assessment practice because the two are directly related.

However, since the field is lacking in specific cross-cultural competencies for report writing, the best way to distinguish the competencies that are relevant to report writing is to review the specific domain of culturally competent practice in assessment advocated by the National Association of School Psychologists (NASP), and observe how it might be connected to psychological report writing.

Standard III. Psychoeducational Assessment:

1. Knowledge of and skills in assessing CLD students, including consideration of variables such as environment, social issues, language development, second language acquisition, acculturation, educational history, quality of educational program, SES and racism.

2. Understanding that normed tests may not be a valid measure for English Language Learners (ELLs) due to inappropriateness of norms, scores reflecting English proficiency, product as opposed to process orientation, fairness of content, and differences in educational background, acculturation, and economic situation; need to be familiar with second language acquisition stages; cultural variables that influence the results of an assessment; use of translators.

Note that many of the considerations stated have a bearing on a culturally/linguistically diverse student's assessment, and therefore should be discussed in the report. Enumeration and a discussion of the interplay of these factors by the school psychologist will suggest possible strategies, interventions, and insights into solving the specific problems first raised by the referring person, which can be communicated to all interested parties.

Rogers et al. (1999) outline several guidelines for cross-cultural competencies that are relevant (Domain 3):

1. Psychologists acknowledge that assessment is a comprehensive process that includes gathering information that considers the impact of socio-cultural, environmental, political, experiential, and language based factors; might include standardized testing; and is baseless unless culturally appropriate and effective interventions are designed and implemented.

2. Psychologists should seek culture-specific confirmatory data, and only compare appropriate comparison group members.

3. Psychologists should be able to differentiate a language disorder from second language acquisition developmental stages.

4. Psychologists should be able to comprehend the verbal ability of the CLD student with reference to the group or familial dynamics of the relevant culture.

5. Psychologists should have the knowledge to select particular standardized instruments, and suggest alternatives when standardized tests normed on non-CLD populations are likely to provide erroneous results when administered to a CLD student; deviations from standard assessment tools to improve assessment of a CLD student should specifically be noted in the report.

6. Psychologists should not assume that the psychometric properties of original and translated versions of a test are comparable in the case of translated tests.

Guide for a Psycho-Educational Report for CLD Students

Addressing the issues mentioned above, Lopez, Elizalde-Utnick and Nahari (2000) developed a psycho-educational report model that integrates language and cultural issues for culturally/linguistically diverse students. This model of report recommends the inclusion of language proficiency data, as well as the procedures and tools used to collect this data, and should document the language proficiency of the student. The authors suggest that it is necessary to pinpoint the strengths and weaknesses of the student in both languages, and to ensure that it includes relevant interpretations such as the implications of the language proficiency data obtained for future assessment, placement, and intervention activities.

Furthermore, cultural implications such as the varied responses to acculturation that may be exhibited by the student should be incorporated into the report and considered within the learning and assessment context. Finally, the report should clarify whether differences in school behavior are due to cultural differences and whether cultural differences account for much of the discrepancy between achievement and ability seen in culturally/ linguistically diverse students (Lopez et al., 2000).

See the box for a sample of this model, with an emphasis on the language and cultural data that need to be integrated within each section of a report written for a CLD student.

Introductory Information

This section should mention Languages Spoken at Home and Languages Used During the Evaluation (see item in italics below).

Name: _____   Date of Testing: _____

School: _____   Date of Birth: _____

Grade: _____   Chronological Age: _____

Evaluator: _____

Languages Spoken at Home: _____

Languages Used During the Evaluation: _____

Evaluation Procedures and Tools

This section includes analysis of all formal as well as informal tools and procedures used to assess CLDs. Examples of informal tools are observations, interviews, and language samples. Informal procedures include type of language samples collected and brief summary of procedures used, use of interpreters and procedures used with interpreters. Included in this section is a description of any modifications of test procedures (i.e., testing of limits) or adaptations of test instruments.

Reason for Referral

Describe the reason(s) for the referral and the referral source (e.g., parent, teacher). If the referral reason is related to language development or second language acquisition issues, provide a description of the referral problem.

(Continued)

(Continued)

Background Information Related to Language Proficiency and Acculturation

In addition to the usual information, this segment of the report should address background on both native language (L1) and second language (L2), cultural and acculturation information. Answers to questions such as time and reasons for emigration, present contact with the native culture, and cultural factors that impact behavior and achievement will help to explore the possible ramifications of cultural background and acculturations stages on behaviors and on the results of the assessment.

The background information should address both L1 and L2. This section incorporates the history of development for L1 and L2 and documents possible language delays, as well as usage of language at home and with different people (i.e., parents, other family members in home, peers, and teachers). In addition, it should include type of language instruction received and duration, and where this occurred.

The assessor needs to answer questions about areas such as how well developed the student's expressive and receptive language skills are (Payan, 1989), how well developed the student's reading and writing skills are in each language, and in what language(s) the instruction is provided (i.e., primarily in English or native language). The assessor should also review the student's adjustment to the mainstream and to the school culture, and assess how much the student interacts with mainstream peers. This information may be obtained from school records, observations, and interviews (i.e., parent, teacher, and student).

Behavioral Observations

This section includes the observations made by the examiner during the assessment and other observations conducted in a variety of settings (e.g., classroom, home, testing situation, playground), and while the student is interacting with a variety of people (e.g., parents, siblings, peers, teachers). For observations of the child interacting in the classroom, describe the context in which the observation was made (i.e., lesson, individual work, lecture, group activity), the content of the instruction (i.e., topic of instruction, sequence of instruction, presentation style, language(s) used for instruction), and the interactions with teacher(s) and peers. Does the student exhibit linguistic non-fluencies, revisions, delayed responses, use of nonspecific terms, inappropriate responses, poor topic maintenance, or need for repetition? Are these due to the second language acquisition process, language loss, or a language disorder? What is the degree of code switching and under what circumstances does code switching occur? Is there borrowing, and under what circumstances does borrowing occur? (Sattler, 2001).

Test Results and Procedures

This section includes the results of all formal as well as informal tools and procedures used to assess CLDs. Examples of informal tools are observation, interviews, and language samples. Formal tools include the Munoz Language Survey, Language Assessment

Battery (LAB), Language Assessment Scale (LAS), the Universal Non-verbal Intelligence Test (UNIT), the Bateria III–Aprovechamiento (Achievement) and the Bateria III–Cognitiva (Cognitive). There should also be a brief summary of procedures used, use of interpreters, and procedures used with interpreters. Describe any modifications of test procedures (i.e., testing of limits) or adaptations of test instruments (i.e., changes in task or content to reflect linguistically or culturally appropriate stimuli) (Kayser, 1989).

Summary and Recommendations

Discuss the effect of the language proficiency and sociocultural data to make decisions regarding languages for further assessment, future evaluations, program placements, and language and other instructional strategies. Appendix 7.1 contains a sample report that describes the findings of an assessment of a CLD student.

Implications for Future Research and Practice

Obviously, the majority of existing procedures of report writing are designed for the monolingual population. As stated previously, very little is found in the literature that addresses report writing for CLD populations and very few sources are available for practitioners. Culturally and linguistically relevant approaches to report writing need to be explored and documented, with the objective of defining a permanent model that looks for the student's optimal capabilities and is capable of differentiating between those difficulties due to intrinsic disorders of exceptional students and the cultural and linguistic differences of CLD students.

The racial/ethnic, linguistic, and cultural composition of the population serviced by school practitioners challenges both researchers and practitioners, and compels them to reexamine the existing approaches to psycho-educational assessment practices as well as a view toward establishing a different approach to report writing. These changes include an overall reconceptualization of the psycho-educational assessment and report-writing process for racial/ethnic and CLD students. Under this reconceptualization, in this chapter we reviewed the issues that should be addressed: (a) the inclusion of socioeconomic, cultural, environmental, political, experiential, and language-based factors; (b) the need to incorporate linguistic information, including second-language acquisition, and issues of language proficiency; (c) the limitations of standardized instruments; and (d) the use of translated versions, their cultural and linguistic pitfalls, and questionable validity, amongst others.

Psychologists can utilize the techniques and strategies described in this chapter to develop meaningful information and clinical judgments in their report writing. Most importantly, cultural sensitivity and the ability to collaborate with others, such as bilingual personnel, the family, and the teacher, are essential requirements to keep in mind when reporting the results of an assessment.

References

American Educational Research Association (AERA), American Psychological Association (APA), & National Council on Measurement in Education (NCME). (1999). *Standards for educational and psychological testing* (2nd ed.). Washington, DC: American Educational Research Association.

Armour-Thomas, E., & Gopaul-McNicol, S. (1998). *Assessing intelligence: Applying a Bio-Cultural model*. Thousand Oaks, CA: Sage.

Cummins, J. (1984). *Bilingualism and special education: Issues in assessment and pedagogy*. San Diego, CA: College-Hill Press.

Figueroa, A. F., Sandoval, J., & Merino, B. (1984). School psychology and limited English proficient children: New competencies. *Journal of School Psychology, 22,* 133–143.

Flanagan, D. P., Andrews, T. J., & Genshaft, J. L. (1997). The functional utility of intelligence tests with special education populations. In D. P. Flanagan, J. L. Genshaft, & P. L. Harrison (Eds.), *Contemporary intellectual assessment: Theories, tests, and issues* (pp. 503–516). New York: Guilford Press.

Gardner, H. (1999). *Intelligences reframed: Multiple intelligences for the twenty-first century*. New York: Basic Books.

Gopaul-McNicol, S., & Brice-Baker, J. (1998). *Cross-cultural practice: Assessment, treatment, and training*. New York: John Wiley & Sons.

Hakuta, K. (1986). *Mirror of language: The debate on bilingualism*. New York: Basic Books.

Hamayan, E. V., & Damico, J. S. (Eds.) (1991). *Limiting bias in the assessment of bilingual students*. Austin, TX: Pro-Ed.

Jacob-Timm, S., & Hartshorne, T. S. (1998). *Ethics and law for school psychologists* (3rd ed.). New York: Wiley.

Kayser, H. (1989). Speech and language assessment of Spanish–English speaking children. *Language, speech, & hearing services in schools, 20,* 226–244.

Lidz, C. (2001). Multicultural issues and dynamic assessment. In L. A. Suzuki, J. G. Ponterotto, & P. J. Meller (Eds.), *The handbook of multicultural assessment: Clinical, psychological, and educational applications* (2nd ed.; pp. 523–540). San Francisco: Jossey-Bass.

Lopez, E. C. (1997). The cognitive assessment of limited English proficient and bilingual children. In D. P. Flanagan, J. L. Genshaft, & P. L. Harrison (Eds.), *Contemporary intellectual assessment: Theories, tests, and issues* (pp. 503–516). New York: Guilford Press.

Lopez, E. C. (2000). Conducting instructional consultation through interpreters. *School Psychology Review, 29,* 378–388.

Lopez, E. C., Elizalde-Utnick, G. & Nahari, S. (2000). *Training Module V: Reporting the results of the language proficiency assessment data*. Available from the Bilingual Psychological and Educational Assessment Support Center at the School Psychology Programs of Brooklyn College/CUNY, Queens College/CUNY, and the New York State Education Department, Office of Vocational and Educational Services for Individuals with Disabilities (VESID).

Meller, P. J., Ohr, P. S., & Marcus, R. A. (2001). Family-oriented, culturally sensitive (FOCUS) assessment of young children. In L. A. Suzuki, J. G. Ponterotto, & P. J. Meller (Eds.) (2nd ed.). *The handbook of multicultural assessment: Clinical, psychological, and educational applications* (pp. 461–496) San Francisco: Jossey-Bass.

Muñoz-Sandoval, A. F., Cummins, J., Alvarado, C. G., & Ruef, M. L. (1998). *Bilingual verbal ability tests: Comprehensive manual*. Itasca, IL: Riverside Publishing.

National Association of School Psychologists (NASP) (2000). *Professional Conduct Manual*. Retrieved December 13, 2004, from www.nasponline.org/pdf/ProfessionalCond.pdf

Ortiz, S. O. (2002). Best practices in nondiscriminatory assessment. In A. Thomas & J. Grimes (Eds.), *Best practices in school psychology IV* (pp. 1321–1336). Washington, DC: National Association of School Psychologists.

Ortiz, S. O., & Flanagan, D.P. (2002). Best practices in working with culturally diverse children and families. In A. Thomas, & J. Grimes (Eds.), *Best practices in school psychology: IV* (pp. 337–352). Bethesda, MD: National Association of School Psychologists.

Padilla, A. M. (2001). Issues in culturally appropriate assessment. In L. A. Suzuki, J. G. Ponterotto, & P. J. Meller (Eds.), *Handbook of multicultural assessment: Clinical, psychological, and educational applications* (2nd ed.; pp. 5–28). San Francisco: Jossey-Bass.

Payan, R. M. (1989). Language assessment for the bilingual exceptional child. In L. M. Baca, & H. T. Cervantes (Eds.). *The bilingual special education interface* (pp. 125–152). New York: Merrill.

Ponterotto, J. G., Gretchen, D., & Chauhan, R. V. (2001). Cultural identity and multicultural assessment: Quantitative and qualitative tolls for the clinician. In L. A. Suzuki, J. G. Ponterotto, & P.J. Meller, (Eds.). *Handbook of multicultural assessment: Clinical, psychological and educational applications*(2nd ed.). San Francisco: Jossey-Bass.

Prediger, D. J. (1993). Multicultural assessment standards: A compilation for counselors. *Measurement and Evaluation in Counseling and Development*, 27(2), 68–73.

Ridley, C. R., Baker, D. M., & Hill, C. L. (2001). Critical issues concerning cultural competence. *The Counseling Psychologist*, 29(6), 822–832.

Ridley, C. R., Hill, C., & Li, L. (1998). Revisiting and refining the multicultural assessment procedure. *The Counseling Psychologist*, 6, 939–947.

Rogers, M. R., Ingraham, C. L., Bursztyn, A., Cajigas-Segredo, N., Esquivel, G., Hess, R. S., Lopez, E. C. & Nahari, S. G. (1999). Best practices in providing psychological services to racially, ethnically, culturally, and linguistically diverse individuals in the schools. *School Psychology International*, 20, 243–264.

Sattler, J. (2001). *Assessment of children: Cognitive applications* (4th ed.). San Diego, CA: Jerome M. Sattler.

Sternberg, R. J., & Grigorenko, E. L. (2001). Ability testing across cultures. In
L. A. Suzuki, J. G. Ponterotto, & P. J. Meller (Eds.). *Handbook of multicultural
assessment: Clinical, psychological, and educational applications* (2nd ed.)
(pp. 335–358). San Francisco: Jossey-Bass.

Suzuki, L.A., Ponterotto, J.G., & Meller, P.J. (Eds.) (2001). *Handbook of multicultural assessment: Clinical, psychological, and educational applications*. San
Francisco: Jossey-Bass.

Suzuki, L. A., Short, E. L., Pieterse, A., & Kugler, J. (2001). Multicultural issues and
the assessment of aptitude. In L. A. Suzuki, J. G. Ponterotto, & P. J. Meller (Eds.),
*Handbook of multicultural assessment: Clinical, psychological and educational
applications* (pp. 359–382). San Francisco: Jossey-Bass.

Tallent, N. (1998). *Psychological report writing* (4th ed.). Upper Saddle River, NJ:
Prentice Hall.

Wolfram, W., Adger, C., & Christian, D. (1999). *Dialects in schools and communities*. Mahwah, NJ: Lawrence Erlbaum.

Cases

Diana v. California State Board of Education. (1970). No. C-70, RFT, Dist. Ct. No. Cal.
Wyatt v. Aderholt. (1974). 503 F 2d 1 305 (5th Cir).

Appendix 7.2: Ana's Case

Name: Ana   *Date of Testing:* xx/xx/xxxx
School: Island Park   *Date of Birth:* 03/13/1993
Grade: 4   *Chronological Age:* 10.3
Evaluator: XXXX XXXXXXXXX
Languages Spoken at Home: Spanish and English
Languages Used During the Evaluation: Spanish and English

Background Information

Ana is an only child. Her parents moved to the United States as teenagers. Mr. A. is from
Ecuador and Mrs. A. is from Peru. Both parents attended high school in the United States.
Mr. A. went on to graduate school from college and is presently employed. Mrs. A. left
high school in the eleventh grade to attend vocational training in cosmetology. She is
presently employed at a department store.

Ana lives at home with her parents and paternal grandfather. Until three years ago,
the grandmother and aunt also lived in the house. When the grandparents divorced, however, the grandmother and aunt moved out of the house. Although Ana continues to see
her grandmother, she expressed a desire for her to move back into the house. Ana's
maternal grandmother lives in Puerto Rico. Ana does not see her very often; however,
they do speak frequently on the phone. She lived with her maternal grandmother in
Puerto Rico for a period of two months when she was 3 years old. Her parents were in

the United States during that time. Mr. A. did not elaborate on the reason for Ana's temporary residence with the grandmother.

Ana's linguistic background is Spanish and English, which varies with different family members. English is the dominant language spoken in the home. Her parents communicate with her in English, yet in Spanish with the paternal grandfather. Ana speaks both English and Spanish to her paternal grandfather. In fact, she said her grandfather is teaching her Spanish. Ana speaks to her maternal grandparents on the telephone in Spanish. Communication with the extended family is bilingual, the adults speaking Spanish and the children speaking English. At times, Ana will communicate with her cousins in Spanish.

According to the Social History, Ana was a full-term baby, born of an uncomplicated pregnancy and delivery. Developmental milestones were attained within age expectancy limits. Ana never sustained any major accident or illness. All medical records, including annual vision and hearing screening, are normal.

Ana entered the District as a kindergartner. The kindergarten screening placed her at risk and she was referred for an academic evaluation. Results of Ana's monolingual English evaluation indicated a possible learning disability and she was referred to the Committee on Special Education. The evaluation, conducted *exclusively in English*, found her cognitive functioning to be in the average range with academic achievement significantly below potential. Ana was classified as learning disabled and placed in a first grade special education class. She has remained in self-contained special education classes and is currently a fourth grader in a fourth and fifth grade special class. She does not receive any related services.

A review of Ana's cumulative record indicated Spanish and English were noted as the home languages on her kindergarten enrollment form, yet the screening was administered only in English. No recommendation for an ESL evaluation was made. Her attendance record indicates a high number of absences, particularly in kindergarten, with 32 days off. On her previous Social History, taken in first grade, Ana's parents described her as not liking school and often difficult to get out in the morning. This is further evidenced by her usually high rate of lateness, continuing up to last year with 16 instances in third grade.

Mr. A. expressed concerns about Ana's communication skills in English and sees her struggling to express her thoughts. He describes Ana as English dominant with limited ability to speak Spanish. Mr. A. did say, however, that she understands more than she can speak. In fact, he laughed and said she often understands things she is not supposed to hear. He did not express any strong desire for Ana to speak Spanish. He sees Ana experiencing difficulty with school. Mr. A. would like Ana to be a college graduate, but his primary concern is for her to be happy.

Assessment Results and Discussion

Classroom Observation: Small Group Science Lesson

Ana was observed during a fourth grade science lesson on the way plants reproduce. The student-teacher ratio was 8:1. The teacher began the lesson by introducing the

(Continued)

(Continued)

vocabulary words in isolation. Ana experienced difficulty pronouncing the words, particularly multisyllabic words such as fertilization. She appeared anxious when the teacher went around the room asking the students to individually say the vocabulary words. The students then began to take turns reading the text aloud. Ana followed along in the text as other students were reading. She read aloud when called upon by the teacher in a slow, hesitant manner, often stumbling over words. When she was unable to decode a word, she would often make an initial consonant guess, sometimes supplying a word that was irrelevant or not contextually correct. When the teacher supplied her with the correct word, Ana would not repeat it. Instead, she skipped the word and continued reading. Although actively engaged in the lesson, Ana did not volunteer to answer questions. When called upon she would respond; however, her answers were frequently incorrect. She appeared to be experiencing difficulty with the concepts of the lesson.

Classroom Observation: Independent Reading Work

On a separate occasion, Ana was observed working independently on reading comprehension questions. She appeared very distracted and had to be refocused to the task several times by the teacher. Ana frequently engaged in conversation with a nearby classmate.

Behavioral Observations During Assessment

Ana is tall and sturdy looking, appearing somewhat older than her actual age. Throughout the evaluation, she was pleasant, outgoing, and cooperative. Ana readily engaged in conversation, not only responding to questions, but also offering much spontaneous conversation. While she presented as social and mature, her responses were often unrelated and difficult to follow.

Ana worked with effort on all tasks presented to her. Directions often had to be repeated before they were understood. She began each task with energy and enthusiasm, yet when items became difficult she typically gave up. Ana freely offered her opinion about difficult items with facial expressions, sighs, and comments such as, "That's a tricky one!" She appeared unconcerned about her failures and readily moved on to the next item, often shrugging her shoulders and stating. "That's the best I can do" or "That's all I know."

Acculturation

Results of the Acculturation Quick Screen identify Ana as In Transition, which coincides with her level of proficiency in English. Linguistically Ana has not developed total fluency in the mainstream language, inhibiting her ability to become more acculturated. Culturally, Ana considers herself Spanish and seems very proud of her ethnic background. She expressed strong desire to learn to read and write in Spanish. Although part of a minority in the Island Park School District, Ana views her diversity as something special. She did not hesitate to engage in a conversation in Spanish with two Spanish-speaking boys in her class and enjoyed the attention it provided.

Informal Language Samples

Informal language samples obtained in both Spanish and English provide further evidence of Ana's English dominance and proficiency.

Tell-a-Story

Ana was able to tell a sequential story in English with a clear beginning and end. Her story contained simple sentences that were grammatically correct, demonstrating understanding of past, present, and future verb tenses. Her Spanish story was not as clear, containing many run-on sentences that were sometimes difficult to follow. She demonstrated numerous errors in syntax, particularly verb tense and subject-verb agreement. She frequently borrowed words from English and specific vocabulary or conjunctions to connect sentences. Her Spanish story contained an element of warmth and personal meaning with numerous adjectives adding emphasis. Ana was very comfortable communicating in Spanish. Unconcerned about lacking vocabulary, she smoothly inserted borrowed English words into her story and went on to her next thought. Difficulty with topic maintenance was evident in both languages.

Woodcock-Muñoz Language Proficiency Survey–R

Results of the language proficiency testing reveal that Ana is dominant and more proficient in English than Spanish. Although Ana does exhibit Basic Interpersonal Communication Skills (BICS) in Spanish, her Broad Spanish Ability Tests at level 1 were of negligible proficiency, with an age equivalent of 3 years and 10 months. Broad Spanish Ability encompasses oral language, pre-reading, and writing abilities. Ana does not demonstrate any Cognitive Academic Language Proficiency (CALP) skills in Spanish.

On Broad English Ability, Ana demonstrated Level 3, or limited English proficiency. The age equivalent of her English CALP skills is 7 years and 7 months. Within her Broad English Ability, Ana demonstrated level 3–4, limited to fluent Oral Language Ability that measures vocabulary and verbal reasoning. Her Reading and Writing Ability fell to level 2–3, very limited English. While demonstrating limited receptive and expressive language skills in Spanish, her English skills are not yet at a level of fluency. Therefore, Ana's English language proficiency will have an impact on her academic success. At level 3, Ana will experience difficulty with the language demands of academic learning tasks that are context-reduced and cognitively demanding.

Wechsler Intelligence Scale for Children (WISC-III)

Ana was administered all subtests of the WISC-III in English and the verbal subtests, with the exception of Digit Span, in Spanish. She does not know the numbers 1 to 10 in Spanish; therefore Digit Span could not be administered. Due to cultural and linguistic diversity, norms are inappropriate for comparison. Therefore Ana's test results will be

(Continued)

(Continued)

discussed qualitatively. Ana's verbal and performance scores revealed inter- and intra-test scatter, with relative strength in nonverbal abilities.

Verbal Scale Index. More specifically, subtest analysis of the Verbal scale indicates that Ana benefits from open-ended questions in which she can provide lengthy responses. She was not as successful on verbal tasks which required more specific single word responses. Ana displayed adequate general knowledge. Item analysis, however, showed variability in responses. Ana often missed easy items, yet was able to correctly answer more difficult ones. For example, she was unable to state how many days in a week, but correctly named the month that has an extra day during leap year. It appears that retrieval from long-term memory is inconsistent.

Ana demonstrated good skills in placing objects and events together in a meaningful group. However, she required extra time and various attempts to be successful or provide the best answer. For the most part, Ana grouped items in a functional or concrete manner, focusing on superficial rather than essential likenesses. On occasion she was able to expand a concrete response into a broader more complex classification. Given the stimulus horse and cow, Ana responded, "both have tails," "both have four legs," and finally, "they are animals." Noted difficulty with retrieval was again apparent as Ana actively searched for the best and most accurate response. She visibly reacted with facial expression and sighs of relief, almost as if to say, "I finally got it!" when she completed the search process.

An evaluation of Ana's arithmetic skills revealed difficulty with basic addition and subtraction facts. She continues to rely on concrete manipulatives. When no pictorial representation was provided, she counted on her fingers. In addition, she had difficulty understanding word problems as well as remembering numerical information presented auditorily. Ana frequently asked for repetition of the numbers and would repeat the question to herself before answering. On items where Ana put in an effort, she appeared to be using this strategy to allow herself time to process the information. On items perceived to be too difficult, she would immediately guess. Interestingly, in testing limits she did not benefit by extended time or use of paper and pencil. Presented with verbal word problems, Ana was unable to manipulate the numbers and conceptualize the operation necessary for a solution. Ana's difficulty manipulating auditory numerical information was evidenced in her relative weakness in retaining and sequencing numbers. She was significantly stronger when she had to repeat digits exactly as they were presented. In contrast, she had great difficulty repeating digits in a backwards direction. Apparently, manipulating and retaining auditory information is Ana's relative weakness.

Ana's word knowledge seems to be adequately developed, yet her response time was lengthy with numerous pauses and fillers such as "mmm. . . ." She repeated the stimulus word several times before responding and occasionally forgot the word midway through a response. Her definitions typically described actions related to personal experiences.

Ana demonstrated a relative strength in social judgment. Her experiences with numerous adults ranging from her parents to grandparents to aunts and uncles have helped her develop a good understanding of social conventions.

Performance Scale. Ana demonstrated well-developed nonverbal reasoning skills. Her ability to determine the missing part of a picture and sequence pictures correctly to tell a story are relative strengths. However, she again demonstrated difficulty with word retrieval when identifying the missing part of a picture. She frequently pointed to the correct location and described the object, but was unable to label it. Her ability to put puzzle pieces together to form common objects is a relative weakness. Ana's concentration, attention, and temporal sequencing skills are stronger with nonverbal than verbal stimuli. She approached problems in a deliberate, careful manner and did not appear concerned about time limits, often giving up on a difficult task before time ran out. When she was asked to move a pencil through a maze without an overall plan, she frequently got stuck. If an alternative route was not immediately evident, she would stop at that point.

Summary and Recommendations

Ana is an English-dominant youngster with adequate cognitive functioning. Performance skills are somewhat better developed that her verbal skills. Particular strengths lie in her visual alertness and social judgment, manifested in both verbal and nonverbal tests. While overall verbal abilities appear to be adequately developed, informal assessment and behavioral observations indicate language delay which seems to interfere with academic functioning.

Although English-dominant, Ana is a culturally and linguistically diverse youngster. Her bilingual home environment has helped her to develop receptive and expressive skills in Spanish for interpersonal communication. Academic training, while exclusively in English, has not enabled her to develop sufficient cognitive proficiency for success.

Aside from the naturally occurring process of acquiring a second language Ana exhibits language deficits in both Spanish and English. She exhibits difficulties with syntax, semantics, morphology and pragmatics, both receptively and expressively. Most notable are her difficulties with word retrieval and verbal conceptualization. Although she gets to the point, she has to go through a lengthy and complicated process. Language delays interfere with her ability to learn. She is unable to build concepts and make generalizations independently.

Ana has difficulty remaining on task when working independently. Her attention and concentration seem to improve when she is interacting with others. She views school as a cooperative rather than competitive environment. Her very social personality, learning style, and need for auditory feedback lend themselves well to cooperative learning.

Ana's language input needs to be simplified and context-embedded to improve comprehension. Care should be taken to introduce new learning in concrete terms, making association with her personal experiences. Ana would benefit from language instructional techniques which build on personal experiences to enrich her language as well as strengthen reading and writing skills. Task analysis of concepts is essential to assist Ana with organizing and categorizing information. She would further benefit from instruction in learning and problem-solving strategies. Ana is limited in the tools available

(Continued)

(Continued)

to assist her with learning and retaining information. She needs direct instruction on looking for clue words in arithmetic word problems to identify the correct operation. Additionally, she needs to develop a variety of strategies such as visual imagery and grouping to increase her flexibility in solving problems and learning new information. She needs to strengthen her ability to reflect on and discuss her performance. Portfolio Assessment would be beneficial in developing her ability to devise a plan for dealing with tasks, monitor progress, and evaluate the outcome.

In view of the findings, the following recommendations are offered:

1. speech and language evaluation;

2. continued placement in special education small-class setting;

3. English language enrichment;

4. mainstream in one subject (to be determined by the classroom teacher).

—Dra. Rafaela Delgado Flores Bilingual Psychologist

Appendix 7.2   Checklist of Objectives for a Multicultural Psycho-educational Report

The report includes:	Yes	No
A review of educational records observation of the student during class instruction		
An examination of the content of the instruction		
Evaluation of the fit between the student and the curriculum with consideration of the student's needs		
Deductions made from parent and teacher interviews		
Review of medical records		
Relevant background information that covers cultural information pertaining to:		
ethnic and racial/biracial identity, religious/ traditional beliefs		
social class, health care practices, immigration		
acculturation stages of the student and parents		
disciplinary norms of the family		
A plan for instruction		
Guidance with regard to the academic strengths and weaknesses of the CLD student		
A psychometric estimate of the cognitive results, describing the child's potential		
An estimate of intellectual functioning, if certain biases in testing practices were removed or modified		
Consideration of the impact of social and cultural issues, language, and environmental/political factors		
A note that the appropriate comparison groups were used when discussing the assessed CLD student		

(Continued)

Appendix 7.2 (Continued)

The report includes:	Yes	No
Consideration of the impact of learning a second language and adjustment to a second culture on the social/emotional and intellectual development of the CLD student		
Clinical impressions that truly reflect the CLD child's personality and behaviors according to his/her culture and ethnicity		
The results of some screening measure or other qualitative method used to assess the CLD student's language dominance and/or bilingualism (e.g., The Bilingual Verbal Ability Test or the Woodcock-Muñoz language survey)		
A note as to whether a translator was used during the assessment		
A description of the limitations of using interpreters for interviewing or testing purposes in conjunction with a detailed explanation of the interpreter's training and credentials		
An explanation that the psychometric structure of the original non-translated instrument and the translated version of the instrument are not comparable		
Data on language proficiency		
Details of whether ELL describes current progress in the acquisition of a second language		
A note that the standardized test used is not normed for the CLD student, and therefore results are presented in a descriptive and qualitative manner		
Results reported in a culturally sensitive manner		
Clear adherence to the recommendations for conducting a multicultural assessment		

PART III

Consultations and Interventions

8

Consultations and Interventions Involving Teachers

The Role of the Teacher in Interventions and Consultations

Multicultural consultation competency includes the facility to consult successfully with teachers of various ethnic backgrounds. School psychologists must recognize the need to develop a "multifaceted cultural consultation expertise" since they will be faced with the challenging tasks of working with client-teachers of culturally diverse backgrounds (Ingraham & Meyers, 2000; Jackson & Hayes, 1993; Nastasi, Varjas, Bernstein, & Jayasena, 2000). As with parents and students, the cultural status of client-teachers must be considered (Ingraham & Meyers, 2000). Consequently, school psychologists must be very observant of the differences between themselves and the client-teachers regarding ethnicity, background, cultural values (belief systems, religious affiliation, lifestyle orientation), attitudes, customs, education, and language. This method of "consultant self-awareness" and "client-teacher ethnic match awareness" is known as cultural saliency (Jackson & Hayes, 1993). Another important factor to consider is the multicultural perspective of the teacher. Checking for client-teachers' cultural awareness, knowledge, and skills will aid in rapport building as well as intervention planning. Accordingly, school psychologists should follow a multicultural consultation approach when servicing multi-ethnic communities.

The aim of this chapter is to highlight multicultural consultation as an important component in the quality of consultation services in the schools.

The chapter first presents an overview of consultation and some of the general skills necessary for effective consultation. Pivotal issues in consultation (i.e., teacher resistance, change) will be reviewed. A special section addresses multicultural evaluation of teachers and training programs, and makes some useful suggestions for trainers (Martines, 2003).

A Multicultural Approach to Consultation

During their training, school psychologists are educated on several models of consultation even though training programs offer only one course in consultation. The founding model is the Mental Health Consultation Model developed by Gerald Caplan (see Caplan, 1970; Caplan & Caplan, 1999). Other prominent models are the Instructional Consultation Model (Rosenfield, 1987) and the Behavioral Consultation Model (Bergan & Tombari, 1976; Fuchs, Fuchs, & Bahr, 1990). Progressively, the collaborative emphasis of most consultation models has led to an education-based Collaborative School Consultation model (see Dettmar, Dyck, & Thurston, 2002; Pryzwansky, 1974; Sheridan, Welch, & Orme, 1996) that has generic principles for building collaborative relationships between client-teachers and consultants (see West & Idol, 1987). Today, collaborative consultation is considered beneficial for direct service to teachers of students with special needs (Dettmar et al., 2002). Dettmar et al. (2002) offer the following description:

> Collaborative school consultation is interaction in which school personnel and families confer, consult, and collaborate as a team to identify learning and behavioral needs, and to plan, implement, evaluate, and revise as needed the educational programs that are expected to serve those needs.

Since this model incorporates a problem-solving approach, as well as adopting a family-focused home–school collaboration, it is of special importance to the school psychologist servicing racial/ethnic, culturally, and linguistically diverse (CLD) children and parents. Whatever model of consultation school psychologists choose to adopt, the collaborative approach to consultation is perhaps the most appealing since it advocates servicing teachers and parents as well as other school personnel. Dettmer et al. (2002) provide the consultant with tips for structuring collaborative school consultation:

- Be knowledgeable about the history and outcomes of school reform movements.
- Keep up to date on educational issues and concerns.
- Be aware of education legislation and litigation.
- Be on the alert for new methods or revisions of existing methods through which consultation and collaboration can occur in your school context.

- Create specific ways that teachers can get your help.
- Read current research on school consultation and collaboration and highlight references to these processes in other professional material you read (e.g., Journal of Educational and Psychological Consultation).
- Visit programs where models different from those in your school(s) are being used.
- Find sessions at professional conferences that feature different models and methods, and attend them to broaden your knowledge about educational systems.

Multicultural consultant school psychologists should not only adhere to Dettmer and colleagues' (2002) recommendations on collaborative school consultation but attain what has been termed "cultural competence" (Davis, 1997, p. 13). This term defines the "ability to understand the unique perspective of people from other cultures, assimilate cultural knowledge about an individual or group, and develop specific policies and practices to increase the quality of the consultation provided" (Brown, Pryzwansky, & Schulte, 2006, p. 13). As the authors stress, culturally competent consultant school psychologists should: (a) be sensitive to the communication style of the consultee; (b) learn the cultural values of the consultee; and (c) adapt the consultation session/interview and problem-solving process to the above variables (Altarriba & Bauer, 1998, p. 13). Acquiring cultural knowledge of the various modes of communication is beneficial for interacting with CLD children and their parents. Hanna, Bemak, and Chung (1999) stress the recognition of different modes of communication between ethnic groups. Awareness and understanding of various meanings in different communication systems are both crucial to healthy interactions.

Verbal styles and traditional values vary among cultural groups. Knowledge of the differences between cultural groups is important in order to achieve multicultural competency within the consultation process. Table 8.1 represents verbal styles among cultural groups. Table 8.2 summarizes the traditional values of cultural groups that have not acculturated.

Brown et al. reviewed cultural group values to provide consultant knowledge when consulting with CLD consultee teachers and parents. The following paraphrases their review.

Some cultural values place significant importance on self-control, time orientation, social relationships, relationships related to nature, and have different ways of dealing with problems. For example, Eurocentric values incline individuals to value the person rather than the group, to support the person when difficulties arise, to be only somewhat concerned about self-disclosure of thoughts or feelings (therefore, more open to sharing personal information), and to be future oriented. Numerous African Americans have adopted Eurocentric values; however, they have a "collateral social value"

Table 8.1 Stylistic Differences in Verbal Communication Styles Among U.S. Cultural Groups

Group	Self-Disclosure	Loudness	Rapidity	Interruptions	Pauses	Directness
European American	Acceptable; content oriented	Moderate	Moderate	Acceptable	Yes; may make uncomfortable	Direct; task oriented
American Indian	Unacceptable; loss of control	Soft	Slow; controlled	Unacceptable	Yes; comfortable	Indirect
Hispanic	Acceptable	Moderate	Varies	Unacceptable	Comfortable	Indirect
African American	Acceptable; expressive	Moderate initially	Moderate	Acceptable	Yes; may make uncomfortable	Indirect initially
Asian American	Unacceptable; sign of weakness	Soft	Slow	Unacceptable	Yes; comfortable	Indirect

SOURCE: From Srebalus, David J. & Duane Brown, *A Guide to the Helping Professions*, 1e. Published by Allyn and Bacon, Boston, MA. Copyright © 2001 by Pearson Education. Reprinted with permission of the publisher.

Table 8.2   Nonverbal Communication Styles Among U.S. Cultural Groups

	Preferred Style in Helping	*Implications*
European Americans		
Eye contact	Maintain eye contact during conversations at least three-quarters of the time.	Eye contact is a sign of respect; lack of eye contact may be interpreted as dishonesty.
Interpersonal space	Prefer 36–42 inches of interaction space.	Closer interaction space may be seen as an invasion of personal space; farther away may be equated to withdrawal.
Nods, facial expressions	Smiles and head nods indicate interest.	Failure to smile or nod head seen as sign of disinterest.
Handshake	Firm	"Weak fish" handshake may be interpreted as lack of enthusiasm or a weak personality.
American Indians		
Eye contact	Indirect	Direct eye contact may be viewed as disrespectful.
Interpersonal space	Respectful distance initially; later much closer distances are okay.	Initially, close interpersonal distances may be viewed as invasion of personal space.
Nods, facial expressions	Few smiles and head nods	Until client knows helper, smiles and head nods may be seen as a lack of self-control or foolishness.
Handshake	Soft and pliable	Firm handshake may be viewed as aggression.
African American		
Eye contact	May look away when helper is speaking; can show disrespect in same manner	Lack of eye contact is seen as disrespectful
Interpersonal space	36–42 inches preferred	More tolerant of closer distances then European Americans.
Nods, facial expressions	Expressive; nods and facial expressions common.	Prefer helper to smile and exhibit warmth
Handshake	Firm; males may use brother's handshake.	May misinterpret weak handshake as lack of enthusiasm.

(Continued)

Table 8.2 (Continued)

	Preferred Style in Helping	Implications
Hispanics		
Eye contact	Indirect eye contact, at least initially	Uncomfortable with eye contact; seen as sign of intimacy.
Interpersonal space	24–36 inches with no barriers	Larger distances and barriers may be interpreted as aloofness
Nods, facial expressions	Initially reserved; smiles and head nods may occur frequently later.	Lack of smiles may be seen as lack of interest or enthusiasm.
Handshake	Firm for males; soft and pliable for unacculturated females	For males, weak handshake may be viewed as lack of enthusiasm.
Asian Americans		
Eye contact	Indirect	Direct eye contact may be seen as aggression or sign of unwanted affection.
Interpersonal space	Prefer respectful distance, 36–42 inches okay.	May interpret closer interactions as aggression or unwanted affection.
Nods, facial expressions	Few smiles, head nods may be used to signal respect.	Smiles from client may convey negative feelings such as embarrassment.
Handshake	Soft and pliable	Firm handshake may be viewed as aggression.

SOURCE: From Srebalus, David J. & Duane Brown *A Guide to the Helping Professions*, 1e. Published by Allyn and Bacon, Boston, MA. Copyright © 2001 by Pearson Education. Reprinted with permission of the publisher.

instead of independence and are more inclined to provide support collaterally. They also tend to be oriented to the present rather than the future. In contrast, numerous American Indians who are not acculturated are unwilling to self-disclose thoughts or feelings and tend to follow group norms instead of placing emphasis on self-promotion. Their orientation to time is not connected to calendars or clocks but to natural occurrences that are in accordance with the usual course of nature. American Indians believe that people do not have to bring about impulsive actions. Taking action mostly occurs on behalf of others rather than for the individual. Asian Americans, on the other hand, tend to value self-control and are not apt to self-disclose thoughts or feelings. Social relationships are seen as hierarchical and problems are solved by action.

Respecting traditions and learning from the past is of primordial importance for the future (Brown et al., 2006).

Srebalus and Brown (2001) describe Hispanic/Latino Americans as tending to be more inclined to be active, both verbally and non-verbally, as a helping relationship progresses. They tend to live "in the moment" and are less future oriented. Decision-making may be more dependent upon family because of their group orientation in social relationships (for cultural diversity and helping, refer to Srebalus & Brown, 2001, pp. 44–70).

For effective multicultural consultation, knowledge of a consultee's worldview, cultural communication style, values, traditions, and religious beliefs serves to establish unconditional rapport and hopefully result in applicable intervention planning. Learning about cultural differences is recommended not only for better rapport building with parents and students, but also with consultee-teachers seeking consultative services.

The Teacher's Role in Consultation

The role of the teacher in consultation is just as complex as those of parents and students. A positive consideration is that, once the teacher has decided to voluntarily participate in consultation, the process is expected to have better outcomes. Furthermore, teachers in consultation are responsible for implementing the suggested interventions.

On a personal level, teachers may have several motives for seeking consultation services, and each affects the teacher's role in consultation. The following reflects on some of these reasons.

- Teachers come to consultation because they are experiencing some level of frustration and/or professional difficulty in dealing with a particular student and/or students.
- Teachers are stagnated at a particular impasse and recognize the need to collaborate with another expert in order to augment their professional skills.
- Teachers need an expert colleague to "vent with" in order to feel some common understanding of their problem.
- Teachers expect to find relief from *their* difficulties through the development of an intervention plan with the aid of the school psychologist (often perceived as the expert).
- A teacher may have been asked by an administrator to seek consultation services because of difficulties with a student, an entire class, or a personal professional problem (in this case, the consultation process is not voluntary).

Furthermore, a teacher may find it difficult to develop specific instructional goals or other needed interventions with a CLD student. The latter will usually require more time and, most importantly, more distinct skills. If these impediments are not resolved through multicultural consultation, there is a serious risk that the teacher, as well as the child, will experience frustration, disappointment, and feelings of failure. These experiences may result in the child retreating from class tasks, which in turn may lead the teacher to reject any new—and possibly future—endeavors to participate on the part of the child. In the ensuing period, labeling may take place, either of the child directly or in relation to the ethnic group with which the child is affiliated. In such cases, the teacher will indulge in what is described as "stereotyped thinking" pertaining to different ethnic groups, thus setting up a negative mental schema for similar cases in the future.

Of particular concern is the possibility that a teacher may personally identify with a student's problem and/or identify with a peculiarly undesirable characteristic of the student, parent, or other circumstance. This is an unconscious personal identification comparable to the "theme interference" obstructions described by Caplan and Caplan (1999) where themes and/or irrational perceptions on the part of the client-teacher may need to be addressed to prevent further misunderstandings and unpleasant repercussions. Usually certain of these irrational themes can be corrected by evolvement of multicultural awareness, open-mindedness of cultural diversity, and multicultural education training (Maital, 2000).

With regard to teacher multicultural training, consultant school psychologists are ethically responsible for picking up in cases where staff development and graduate education programs disappoint. It is not only multicultural pedagogical competencies that teachers have to augment, but their cultural awareness and knowledge of the various stressors experienced by CLD students. Since it is recommended that school consultant psychologists assess the acculturation levels of client students and their families (Brown et al., 2001), they should make sure that consultee-teachers are aware of the various cultural variables involved (first and second language use, observance of rituals/traditions, and religious beliefs—see Chapter 10 on acculturation). Observed acculturation stressors include prejudice, educational disadvantages, ethnic identity conflicts, and other difficult situations that may cause severe psychological harm to students (and decline in academic progress) and their parents.

Since consultant school psychologists must offer their professional services to teachers, children, parents, and administrators, they need to consider helping one of the most important individuals (the teacher) in reaching optimal competency. Therefore, the teacher's role in consultation can and should be examined and guided by the consultant school psychologist. Since it can be presupposed that roles change in different situations and environments, an examination of a specific teacher's role in consultation will aid in the establishment of a collaborative relationship. If the teacher role is examined in a dyad relationship, there is a better chance of establishing collaboration.

To determine a client-teacher's particular role, the consultant school psychologist should do the following:

- Examine the client-teacher's reason for seeking consultation (is it due to any of the above-mentioned reasons? Are there other factors that compel this initiative? Are personal factors involved?).
- Carefully assess the types of characteristics the client-teacher manifests in the consultation dyad (passive/aggressive, assertive, angry, meek, receptive, dominant, leadership).
- Determine the client-teacher's level of flexibility (appraise this by scrutinizing the versatility of any previous interventions implemented by the teacher, acceptance/ rejections of suggestions, self-description of teaching philosophy, utilization of resources/materials, creativity in the use of instructional methods, or a classroom observation to assess classroom management techniques/classroom environment). *Note*: Flexibility is an important characteristic that is associated with the capacity to *change*, which is desired in consultation for various reasons (see the section on resistance below).
- Early on in the consultation process, strive to determine the level of the client-teacher's awareness, knowledge, and skills within cross-cultural domains (when applicable, use cultural awareness scales).
- Attempt to ascertain the consultative support the client-teacher will need (for example, if the client-teacher is lacking in self-confidence, then consultative support may be needed in instructional methodology, classroom management, collegiality-building, assertiveness training, and culturally sensitive communication techniques).

Caplan and Caplan's (1999) mental health consultation model provides four prescriptive types of consultee client setbacks:

1. lack of knowledge regarding the problem and its circumstances;

2. lack of skills to solve the problem effectively;

3. lack of self-confidence to deal with the problem; and

4. lack of professional objectivity in identifying with the student.

Whatever the area of support needed, the consultant's goal should be to assist the client-teacher in developing a healthy educator role. This is especially important for new teachers. A strong supportive relationship with new teachers can be very productive in developing teacher competencies.

Notwithstanding these issues, when discussing roles it is always important to contemplate that a teacher may see their role as being strong and resilient, and may not wish to "give in" to the urgency for assistance from an "expert" colleague. In this regard, the appropriate role of the teacher, as an educator and client, may be hindered by pride or lack of flexibility. This is an avenue where resistance is a dominant barrier that disables not only the teacher's professional growth but the students' growth as well (see the section on resistance). In order to further comprehend the role of a teacher in consultation, a review of teacher types is necessary.

Teacher Types

There is relatively little literature that details different teacher types. Most of the literature dichotomizes effective versus ineffective teachers. Fallahi (2003) attempted to classify four types of teachers as viewed through the consultation dyad. These are: (a) effective teachers; (b) ineffective teachers; (c) new teachers; and (d) resistant teachers.

Effective teachers are described as experienced and motivated; they have a positive attitude about their students and positively enjoy teaching. Consequently, they are respected by their students, peers, and school administrators. One of the most noteworthy attributes of these teachers is that they are not likely to complain about the lack of appropriate materials but use their resourcefulness to resolve this deficit. Such teachers are usually flexible with their culturally diverse students; they will not feel uncomfortable or grumble at an intervention plan that suggests a curriculum modification for a particular student or group of students. Likewise, they may be more informed about multicultural education and will not resist adaptations of this nature. These teachers are ideal candidates for consultation. In addition, they are good role models for their peers (an excellent match/pairing for the new teacher).

In contrast, the *ineffective teacher* is unquestionably discontented. This dissatisfaction may be due to disappointment with the school to which they have been assigned, the system's organizational flaws, a lack of materials/ resources, or their students. These teachers tend to blame their students or the "system" for their resentment. It may be estimated that some of the difficulties are due to lack of knowledge or skills for effective teaching. Moreover, as a result of a shortage of teachers, some non-certified teachers may not have acquired sufficient knowledge and skills, and have therefore entered the educational system with a defensive attitude born out of fear of failure. This particular group of teachers is more likely to cause complications and be unbending in cultural adaptations for students. Their lack of motivation— caused by their discontent—will often make them uncooperative toward change and/or interventions suggested in any manner, most especially in consultation where the consultant may be perceived as a "know it all" (possibly resistant to the power and expertise of the consultant).

New teachers recently certified or en route are usually assumed to be enthusiastic. These teachers are generally good candidates for consultation as they tend to be cooperative and are eager to be good educators. The consultant school psychologist is advised to "watch out" for these new teachers and check on their specific needs. As a promoter of the child advocacy policy, the consultant can guide the novice teacher into the "right path" of cross-cultural justice, knowledge, and skills by their role modeling and consultative services. The term "new" may also be applied to a teacher assigned and/or transferred to a different school. In this sense, they are new to the school. Depending on their outlook, experienced teachers in difficulty may or may not seek consultation services. On occasion, it may be assumed that experienced teachers in a new school will not wish to express difficulties out of pride. These are the teachers that consultant school psychologists should seek out.

Resistant teachers should not be labeled as "troublesome" because they are resistant to change. The literature is plentiful on the concept of change and the extreme complexity that most individuals experience in a "change-required situation" (Dettmer et al., 2002). In actuality, most teachers will be resistant to change at one time or another. Fallahi (2003) describes resistant teachers as mostly experienced and settled in the system for decades. They have witnessed the numerous well-meaning initiatives that have failed or harmed the schools in various ways and have accepted their "lot," finding little room for further attempts on change. In short, they are comfortable as things are, and unwilling to use their energy on interventions that require innovative alterations. Most have good relationships with their students and make pleasant clients. They will listen to advice, accept suggestions, but ultimately resist any intervention/implementation plan attempts.

An important variable that can significantly affect the consultant–consultee relationship is the sociocultural background of the consultee-teacher. This variable may influence the outcome of the consultation process (see Gibbs, 1980) since both the consultant and the consultee-teacher most likely will come from different racial/ethnic backgrounds. Interestingly, Brown and colleagues (2001) describe a study conducted by Duncan and Pryzwansky (1993) in which no significant preferences were noted for either a same- or opposite race-consultant; however, the authors stress that the teachers in this study had attained the highest stage of racial identity development, which implies that these consultees were at ease with their racial identity. Thus the efficacy of the interactive process in consultation may depend on the comfort level of the consultee-teacher's (and consultant's) ethnic identity.

Improving consultant-consultee teacher relations is an important part of overcoming resistance in consultation. A review of cultural modifications in consultation by Behring, Cabello, Kushida, and Murguia (2000) suggests taking time for relationship building with parent consultees. Latino and Asian Americans tend to need extended time for relationship building with families and students. Furthermore, additional time was reported as being needed for relationship building with African American and Latino consultants, even with cultural similarities between consultee parents and students.

Soo-Hoo (1998) emphasizes the importance of understanding the consultee's frame of reference. This implies understanding the consultee's problem within a sociopolitical context, bearing in mind that culture involves the cultural influences that help establish the value system of the consultee and how culture is instrumental in the way he or she will define family and the roles played in the family. Most notably, culture influences how and what we think (Soo-Hoo, 1998). Thus the duty of the consultant school psychologist is to attain sufficient understanding of the consultee's frame of reference by being a good listener (and, in some cases, observer) of the consultee's presenting problem(s). This cultural strategy may be applied when servicing CLD children and their families.

Reframing is defined as taking a set of facts and developing a different explanation based on those very same facts. Through this process, the actual meaning of the facts will change. Reframing therefore changes the person's views, thus leading them to arrive at a new and different significance. This new view will in turn change the person's responses and behaviors. Consequently, for consultant school psychologists the objective is to assist the consultee-teacher to adopt new worldviews, to see themselves and the presenting problem from a new perspective. Reframing is a highly recommended technique in multicultural consultation (Soo-Hoo, 1998). For whatever reason, culturally sensitive consultant school psychologists are advised to accept resistance as a professional challenge and to single out all possible cultural variables that may be causing the refusal to comply.

Teacher Resistance in Consultation

Resistance is said to occur when one is asked to change or participate in a change. The reasons for client resistances are that:

- the client-teacher is more confident;
- the client-teacher resents any change in the balance of power and status; or
- the client-teacher does not accept the expert power of the consultant school psychologist and is employing their right to refuse a consultant's suggestions (Brown et al., 2001; Kratochwill & Pittman, 2002).

Consultant school psychologists need to recognize the fear involved in change when it is present.

Martines (2002) asked a cohort of consultant school psychologists practicing in New York City and New Jersey schools to describe techniques they found useful for alleviating resistance in consultation. Their suggestions were:

- Define clearly the consultant and client role early on in the problem identification consultation session.
- Ask the client what they expect from the consultation service. Be "up front" about resistance to change that might occur during the consultation process.
- Describe some of the possible pitfalls of resistance in consultation to the consultee-teacher (e.g., on the part of the resistant client, or of the CLD children and families participating in home–school collaborative consultation).
- Be aware of the nature of resistive areas—for example, privacy, ethnic norms, values, time management, multicultural teaching methods, necessary changes in classroom discipline or curriculum modifications, and home-based disciplinary methods—and share these with the consultee-teacher.

Finally, it is important to accept the consultee-teacher's culture and racial/ethnic background unconditionally. By demonstrating true respect for a consultee-teacher, practitioners will ultimately overcome any cultural and/or racial/ethnic differences.

To further understand the complexities of *resistive reactions* on the part of the client-teacher, knowledge of the concept of power in consultation is required. The consultant school psychologist should be knowledgeable about the various *power bases* discussed in the literature (see Raven, 1992; Erchul, Raven, & Ray, 2001). The following is a brief review of some of the different power bases described by Erchul and Martens (2002).

Coercive power is based on the client-teacher's perception that they can be reprimanded by the consultant if they do not comply.

Reward power is based on the client-teacher's perception that the consultant has the power to provide a reward for compliance.

Legitimate power is based on the client-teacher's obligation to accept the consultant's influence attempt because the client-teacher believes the consultant has a legitimate right to influence—perhaps because of the consultant's professional role or position.

Expert power is based on the client-teacher's perception that the consultant possesses knowledge or expertise in a specific area of interest to the consultee-teacher.

Referent power is the consultant's potential to influence the client-teacher based on the client-teacher's identification with the consultant and/or desire for such identification.

Correspondingly, Erchul and colleagues (2001) queried which of the power bases might be helpful when dealing with resistant teachers. Referent power appears to be the only one that might be beneficial. Apparently, referent power that evolves from similarities in background and interests appears to render better results. Kratochwill and Pittman (2002) have advocated the use of alternative consultation when dealing with inflexible teachers. The authors suggest using the student as an agent of change to help overcome the resistance noted in the client-teacher. There are few strategies in the literature for dealing with the various power bases; however, knowledge of their interactive presence provides the school consultant psychologist with the protective armor needed for combat in resistant type consultation interactions. Again, it is stressed that resistance is not to be viewed negatively (Brown et al., 2001).

Resistance can be encountered within the social system, in the student's family, in the consultant psychologist, or in the consultee-teacher. The origins of resistance are often multifarious and complicated (O'Keefe & Medway, 1997).

Rhone (2001) conducted a teaching seminar on multicultural education for preservice teachers and asked her students to list reasons why pedagogues tend to resist training in multicultural education. Some of the themes obtained can be adopted for the identification of resistance in consultation practice within a multicultural prospective.

Determinants that can assist with the identification of resistance are:

- fear of the unknown;
- fear of losing one's culture;
- fear of losing one's American identity;
- the view that multicultural education is irrelevant;
- the view that multicultural education is too time consuming to implement;
- the idea that multicultural education is not their job to implement;
- limited understanding of multicultural education;
- issues of prejudice, racism, and sexism which have not been understood fully;
- a lack of understanding of the concept that all people in the United States can assimilate.

Rhone's (2001) information was for preservice teachers; however, it is very similar to that of the literature on practicing teachers (Banks & McGee-Banks, 2001). Furthermore, the areas listed coincide with the cultural issues/concerns that consultant school psychologists may encounter when dealing with resistant teachers, most especially when intervening for multicultural instructional methodology.

Martines (2005) found the following patterns of resistance with consultee-teachers who voluntarily participated in a consultee-centered consultation investigation:

- unwillingness on the part of the consultee-teacher to discuss prejudicial issues observed in their classrooms (e.g., bullying, gender identity conflicts, sexual harassment);
- denial of bicultural identity (second- and third-generation teachers tended to ignore their bicultural identity and identified themselves as "American");
- resistance to suggestions for multicultural interventions (consultee-teachers either stated that they already knew all about culturally sensitive interventions or stated that the problem discussed was not really dependent on a cultural intervention);
- tight schedules which prevented multicultural emphasis/focus on implementation of interventions;
- lack of self-introspection relating to their own racial/ethnic prejudice when discussing their diverse students' race/ethnicity. This appeared to lead to resistance when culturally sensitive interventions were suggested.

Determining the reason for the observed resistance(s) will help re-route suggested intervention plans and/or any other implied modifications under discussion.

A skilled multicultural consultant school psychologist should regularly watch for possible cultural and racial/ethnic issues in resistance that may affect the interactive process of consultation. It is also of special importance that racist or non-multicultural inept teachers should not be seen as problematic. Creating consultative collaboration implies that multicultural consultant school psychologists should help such teachers understand multiculturalism and its attached required competencies. Helping teachers create multicultural classrooms will reduce inappropriate student behaviors, increase multi-ethnic group class performance, and generate collegial relationships between all students.

Tips for Dealing With Resistance

Is all this really helpful in reducing resistance? As mentioned above, if the resistance theme is demystified, it may become easier to make adjustments, or help suggest variations for an intervention plan with the purpose of alleviating the resistance. Since the resistance may not be manifested immediately in the consultation process, adopting a progress note approach after each session to record possible statements, concerns and/or behaviors made by the consultee-teacher may be helpful.

Keeping a written form that records possible resistant statements/actions, and that is reviewed periodically between sessions, will help to identify the source of the resistance. Very often, verbalizations are not noticed immediately in the rush of a consultation session, and a consultant's eagerness to help may hinder the observant eye needed for recalling possible impediments. The quick jotting down after a session of a client's statements/actions during the session will aid in recalling and in qualitatively "piecing together the themes" noted, thus unveiling the problematic obstacles (see Figure 8.1 for a Consultation Resistance Form). Furthermore, if verbalizations are not noticed, specific mannerisms/actions should be recorded. Signs to look out for are:

- body language (culturally appropriate types);
- silence (or not verbally expressive);
- changing the subject;
- always agreeing;
- being in a hurry;
- being too busy;
- hesitance and uncertainty;
- blaming others;
- getting involved in other projects;
- missing consultation appointments, arriving late (although this could be cultural, as some cultures have a different time concept) or leaving early.

All of these can also be recorded in the Consultation Resistance Form (see Figure 8.1) as a sort of handy storage/retrieval information system to help the consultant better recall and reevaluate the resistance. The recorded data will require a good deal of professional objectivity, as there is always the danger that one may be blinded by one's *own* resistance.

Reflective questions to pose might be:

1. "Is this a client's resistant issue or my own?"

2. "Could I be the one that is being inflexible to the possible difficulties of this plan?" "How attached am I to this plan?" "Is this the only plan available?"

3. "Do I like (or dislike) this client?" "Why do I like/dislike this client?" The latter question will force the consultant to face any personal counter-transference issues they may be experiencing.

Additional Factors to Consider With Resistance

Brown and colleagues (2001) remind consultants that certain consultee-teacher resistance may originate from psychological deficiencies. Resistance stemming from psychological conflicts cannot be addressed in consultation, as it is not the role of the consultant to provide psychological services of this

Consultation Resistance Record

Name of Client: _____ Date: _____

Consultation Session/Stage _____

Complete only those sections that apply.

1. Ambiguity. Are there any factors that might indicate that the client is confused about his/her reason for seeking consultation? Is the client seeking consultation or therapy for her/his personal problem(s)?

   _____

   _____

   _____

2. Overwork. Does the client have too many responsibilities? Time concerns?

   _____

   _____

   _____

3. Complexity of intervention. How complex and difficult is the proposed intervention plan?

   _____

   _____

   _____

4. Tradition/habit. Are any traditional methods being changed? Are any changes in behavior, tasks, or functioning required of the client?

   _____

   _____

   _____

5. Psychic costs. Is the client's time or "psychic energy" low? Does the client appear tired and overburdened mentally and/or physically?

   _____

   _____

   _____

Figure 8.1 *(Continued)*

6. Upsetting the power or status balance. Is any loss of power or status involved?

7. Insensitivity to cultural differences, sexual orientation, and gender. Is any insensitivity to culture, sexual orientation, or gender involved in this case?

8. Relevance of attitudes to behaviors. What is the client's attitude about this case or student? Are there any racial or SES concerns?

9. Social factors. Is the client experiencing any social pressures as a result of this case? Because of the suggested changes?

10. Control issues. Are there any control issues on the part of the client? Any control issues on the part of the consultation dyad?

Figure 8.1   Consultation Resistance Form

SOURCE: From Brown, Duane, Water B. Pryzwansky & Ann C. Schulte. *Psychological consultation: Introduction to Theory and Practice*, 5e. Published by Allyn & Bacon, Boston, MA. Copyright © 2001 by Pearson Education. Reprinted with permission of the publisher.

kind. Caplan and Caplan's (1999) mental health consultation model provides suggestions for "characterological" disorders that are helpful (see Caplan & Caplan, 1999). The authors summarize four sources of resistance to intervention implementation:

1. a practical discernment that the plan may not really work;

2. lack of sufficient information/resources to implement the plan;

3. lack of skills to implement the plan;

4. lack of objectivity.

However, situations will arise in which it will be difficult to judge psychological conflicts versus "normal" resistance to change. A particular example (cited by Brown et al., 2001) suggests that, when bias or lack of self-confidence have been treated by the consultant through the sharing of objective data and/or information that contradicts the problem(s) and the client continues with the same difficulties, then the consultant is clearly faced with client psychological problems.

When conducting consultee-teacher interviews, there are several factors of which the consultant needs to be wary that may increase resistance. Brown et al. (2001) cite several reasons that can increase resistance. These are:

1. *Ambiguity*—This occurs when the client-teacher is confused and is really seeking counseling and/or therapy from the consultant. This arises from the misconception of what consultation is and can be avoided early on by the consultant's careful description of their role as well as the role of the client-teacher.

2. *Overwork*—Consultees come to consultation with an already heavy burden of responsibilities. In this case, resistance may be due to the lack of time and overload. A consultant should be sensitive to this and suggest intervention plans that are not too time consuming.

3. *Complexity of intervention*—The more complex and difficult it is, the less appeal the intervention plan will have, and the more resistance there will be.

4. *Tradition/habit*—Individuals and groups become attached to various traditional ways of functioning because they are comfortable with them. Trying to change a pattern of behavior, task, or method will be difficult for the consultant. It is best to remember that changes in ingrained methods will

cause fear and ambiguity. The consultant should be prepared to have additional time, patience, and adequate resources (i.e., information and data, demonstrations of the actual "successful" intervention) to present to the client in an attempt to quell the fear/ambiguity about the desired change.

5. *Psychic costs*—This simply means that when time and "psychic energy" are low, it will cost more to implement change.

6. *Upsetting the power or status balance*—Any loss of power or status will cause a client to experience resistance.

7. *Insensitivity to cultural differences, sexual orientation, and gender*—This type of insensitivity applies to both the consultant and the client. Consultants should be on the "lookout" for any such forms of intolerance, both in themselves and in others. An effective method for controlling intolerance is education on the topic and/or issue. This involves providing information and data or, in the case of prejudice, engaging in an activity with a culturally different educator and taking note of the differences that are workable as well as commendable. As a rule of thumb, when any of the above appear to be legitimate then the suggested intervention is appropriate. However, if it is deemed to be coming from personal concern, then the resistance is unwarranted and should be treated accordingly.

8. *Relevance of attitudes to behaviors*—Consultees may not see the relevance of their existing attitude with regard to a preferred behavior. O'Keefe and Medway (1997) provide a model scenario for this type of resistance. For example, a client-teacher that expresses a positive attitude about total racial and ethnic integration will have to be reminded of this attitude when children from ethnic or low SES groups are referred for special education evaluations or services. In this respect, the consultant will have to remind the client of their attitudes and how these are connected to their behaviors.

9. *Social factors*—In another situation, a client may have a positive attitude but experience blockage due to social pressures. For example, the majority of the faculty may not support the inception of a bilingual tutoring program that the consultee believes is essential for her linguistically diverse students. She may resist an intervention plan because of the social pressure of the school. The consultant will have to convince the client to overlook these social demands and go ahead with the intervention for the welfare of her student(s). The consultant school psychologist may also give a presentation to the faculty that focuses on the benefits of bilingual education for linguistically diverse students (see Caplan & Caplan, 1999; O'Keefe & Medway, 1997).

Control Issues in Resistance

Another important factor to consider when faced with resistance is the issue of control. It may be difficult to differentiate between the need to control a situation as opposed to a refusal to move forward with an intervention because of a dislike of the intervention—as opposed to a need to control the situation from one's perspective only. When faced with control-type obstacles, it may be best to retreat and wait, or to try to mediate for an acceptable solution.

Moreover, self-efficacy has been connected with control. Bandura (1982) explains that individuals with high self-efficacy:

> set themselves challenging goals and maintain strong commitment to them. They maintain a task-diagnostic focus that guides effective performance. They heighten and sustain their effort in the face of failure. They attribute failure to insufficient effort or deficient knowledge and skills that are acquirable. They quickly recover their sense of efficacy after failures or setbacks. They approach threatening situations with assurance that they can exercise *control* over them. (italics added) (pp. 144–145).

Consequently, any noticeable assertion of control should be evaluated by the consultant. This will require a good deal of professional objectivity, as there is always the danger that one is blinded to one's own control issues. Self-examination questions are: "Is this a control issue?" "Is it a client control issue or my own?" "How can I best resist this control?" How can I derail the control noted in the sessions?"

In summary, consultant school psychologists may need to resort to a sort of "prescreening" evaluation of teacher types, possible resistance conflicts, fear of change, control issues, and degree of self-efficacy in order to render effective consultation services. It is best to conduct this prescreening evaluation during the early stages of consultation, although some issues of resistance and/or control may not surface until the later stages. An astute appraisal in these areas, as well as adequate data-based evaluation strategies, will aid in formulating a more effective intervention plan. Further review of the literature reveals the subsequent prescriptive evaluative strategies:

1. *Identifying resistance*—The consultant must identify the cause of resistance in order to defeat it.
   - What are the attitudes of the client?
   - Is the client overwhelmed with schedule pressures?
   - Is the client unmotivated? What are the possible causes of this?
   - Is the client hoping to "dump" the problem on the consultant?
   - Is the client seeking consultation voluntarily?
   - Is the client experiencing any social pressure?

Knowledge of the organizational system of the school and its teachers will aid with this goal. Spending time in the faculty room or school cafeteria, learning the dynamics/leadership of the school, will clarify the school's organizational system. The consultant should develop an understanding of the client-teacher's situation and attitudes. This will assist in identifying any possible resistance (Graham, Taylor, & Hudley, 1998).

2. *Understanding the circumstances*—Consultants should use *accessible reasoning* to obtain an understanding of the client-teacher's situation. Accessible reasoning is a process that enables the consultant to attempt to make clear to clients *their thinking* regarding the information divulged to the consultant during a consultation session. Specifically, the consultant *rephrases* what the client has stated, and also shares ideas on the situation. This strategy will give a client the time to add supplementary facts and study the consultant's thinking, thereby allowing the consultant to acquire an enhanced understanding of the situation. The consultant needs to allow the client sufficient time to "vent" openly about the situation. Additionally, the use of open-ended instead of closed-ended questions is recommended for obtaining a better understanding of the problem presented (closed-ended questions require "yes" or "no" answers—open-ended questions extract more information). Open-ended questions and accessible reasoning should be used in combination (Monsen & Frederickson, 2002).

3. *Cultural mismatch and resistance*—Racial mismatch is not an uncommon phenomenon. Numerous scholars have ascertained that racial mismatch is a difficulty, especially between a client of color and a Caucasian consultant, since the client of color may experience difficulties when attempting to establish a trusting relationship (Rogers, 1998). People of color need to have something in common with the Caucasian consultant. For example, when this does not occur, African Americans are more likely to terminate counseling prematurely (Rogers, 1998). In consultee-centered consultations, the same phenomenon may occur. A consultee-teacher who is experiencing discomfort confiding in a consultant school psychology (and vice versa for the consultant) of a different racial/ethnic group than their own may terminate the consultation process.

However, it is almost impossible to match every consultant and client by race. Ingraham (2000) notes that 95 percent of school psychologists are white, and almost all of them are working in culturally diverse schools. At the same time, students are becoming increasingly diverse. The number of public school teachers representing diverse racial/ethnic groups and cultures is also growing (Rogers, 1998). In order to abate racial/ethnic resistance within the consultation process (or the counseling process), consultant school psychologists should engage in culturally sensitive communications and demonstrate culturally competent interpersonal skills. Also, the focus should not solely be on developing racial/ethnic group knowledge but on recognizing the heterogeneity within ethnic groups. These heterogeneous differences must be noted so that the consultant can treat the client as an individual with their own values and beliefs. Moreover, Goldstein (1998) advises consultants to recognize the heterogeneity within bicultural communities. A "common thread" should be found between the consultant and the client. However, consultants should not overemphasize culture to the point where it obstructs their objectivity and thus impairs the resolution of the problems originally presented in consultation.

Cultural differences may lead to "mismatched" goals/expectations, and quite possibly encumber interventions for students (Sheridan, 2000). Statements for initiating a common thread are:

"As two professionals working in the schools, we. . . ."

"We have similar viewpoints on this. . . ."

"We have the same ideas about this problem. . . ."

"I see you have experienced the same . . . as I have."

4. *Persuasive messages*—These may be used to help overcome resistance. However, these messages must "match the underlying bases of the attitude to be effective" (O'Keefe & Medway, 1997). Consultants should:

- deliver clear messages—be specific, define clearly but avoid using terminology with which the client is unfamiliar;
- impart information, but make sure it is information that is needed—do not assume that knowledge is lacking, as it may offend the client to be given information already learned;
- provide examples to clarify an issue or present information;
- handle objections without defensiveness—address the dissatisfaction and give specific reasons for the differences in opinion or viewpoints;
- avoid making suggestions/interventions that may cause resistance;
- give examples to prove a point or to provide information on a particular intervention. Consultants can explain in statistical terms by citing percentages, means, and other significant information. Or a consultant can describe a particular case in which the suggested intervention was effective. The latter is considered more effective than statistical data (O'Keefe & Medway, 1997).

5. *Two-sided messages*—When faced with resistance, the two-sided message approach can be effective. This approach deliberates both supporting and opposing arguments. A refutational two-sided message is one that bashes or weakens the opposing argument. This type of message approach should be used with careful consideration lest it harm the client–consultant relationship (O'Keefe & Medway, 1997).

Finally, O'Keefe and Medway (1997) warn consultants not to assume that all resistance is detrimental to the client. Consultants need to thoughtfully consider the client's objections. Their resistance to a proposed plan of action might be legitimate. Consultants must realize that the client has more experience with the student and often knows what strategies will work better with a particular student. With experience, consultants will be able to tell when it is legitimate and when it needs to be overcome. In the end, it is important to recognize that teachers also come from culturally diverse backgrounds, and knowledge of their culture is essential for good consultative practice.

Consultation Evaluation

Accountability and a Data-Based Approach to Consultation

Evaluating the effectiveness of consultation through the use of objective process and outcome assessment measures is now a crucial practice component of the consultative service (for review, see Barlow, Hayes, & Nelson, 1984; Brown et al., 2001; Lambert, 1993). Accountability-based approaches are sensible, and part of the consultant's ethical responsibility. Accordingly, consultant school psychologists are encouraged to employ an *evaluation procedure* during each consultation case. Accountability and evaluation procedures in consultation are emphasized as an ongoing adjunct to the continuing development of the consultant's skills. Additionally, a client's evaluative data may be used for the study of the consultation process and of the particular models utilized.

Suggestions for Data-Based Evaluations

First and foremost, an attempt should be made to use the appropriate type of systematic data-based approach (e.g., special scales and/or forms). In the event that a research question might be answered and/or further investigated as a result of the consultation process analysis, outcome measures utilized should be culturally sensitive.

Brown et al. (2001) suggest determining the reason for the evaluation. Is it for the professional growth of the consultant psychologist? To process and debrief solely with the client-teacher? For data collection to be used later for research? The nature of the outcome measures (e.g., evaluation forms and/or scales) will be determined by the reason for the evaluation. Evaluation data can also be useful for sharing (anonymously) successes and failures—the latter process aids in the assimilation of knowledge and skills for similar future cases.

One recommended evaluation outcome measure, Goal Attainment Scaling (GAS) (see Kiresuk, Smith, & Cardillo, 1994), is a goal-oriented evaluation. GAS is both an outcome measure and a monitoring tool that aids both the consultant school psychologist and the client-teacher to set expected goals, detail implementations adopted, and collect information concerning the goal attained. It is important that the consultant school psychologist learn to adhere to some type of evaluation outcome which looks not only at the progress of the offered consultation service, but at the personal professional growth (Zins, 1981). The GAS is also helpful for future intervention planning (see Kiresuk et al., 1994).

Moreover, the National Association of School Psychologists (NASP) has embraced standards that require the evaluation of the consultation process. It is recommended that consultants develop their evaluation of consultation objectives form. In exploring this kind of evaluative approach, a consultant (and/or trainer) could adopt the list of training objectives presented by Conoley and Conoley (1992) and add qualifiers to address multicultural issues where appropriate. Thus an objective such as "develop the ability to enter into and terminate smoothly individual consultative relationships" would be expanded to taking into account the ethnicity factors of the client. In evaluating the objectives, the consultant and the client should decide jointly whether each target was met.

Evaluating Consultation Training

Since not all practitioners have received comprehensive consultation training, utilizing Conoley and Conoley's (1992) educators' learning objectives can be of tremendous help to the practicing school psychologist, as well as to the student. The objectives help direct the practitioner/student to the appropriate consultative skills needed in order to assess the consultative process. Conoley and Conoley (1992) suggest that educators assess these objectives as part of a continuing evaluation of consultation education.

Learning/evaluative objectives are*:

1. Increase skills in conceptualizing school (and other) cultures and processes of change likely to match the cultural regularities.

2. Develop a repertoire of interventions with clients to increase their effectiveness with clients and each other.

*SOURCE: From Conoley, Jane Close & Collie W. Conoley. *School Consultation: Practice and Training*, 2e. Published by Allyn and Bacon, Boston, MA. Copyright © 1992 by Pearson Education. Reprinted with permission of the publisher.

3. Develop skills in evaluation of service delivery programs.

4. Develop knowledge of consultation models.

5. Develop the ability to use theory to guide case conceptualization and intervention according to the presenting situation.

6. Develop the ability to synthesize a personal model of consultation intervention.

7. Develop skills in formulating problems in ways that facilitate resolution.

8. Develop expertise in listening and feedback skills.

9. Develop the ability to enter into and terminate smoothly individual consultative relationships.

10. Develop the ability to design and deliver in-service training to clients.

11. Develop expertise in design and implementation of preventive mental health strategies.

12. Develop the ability to diagnose organizational variables, and design, implement, and evaluate appropriate interventions.

13. Develop awareness of personal impact in the consultative relationship, including important ethical dimensions.

14. Apply a wide variety of assessment and intervention skills, especially behavioral analyses and interventions.

School psychologists can examine these objectives and decide whether they have mastered them or have applied them to their current consultation case. Additionally, school psychologists can use a simple Consultation Analysis Record (CAR) form (see Figure 8.2). The CAR should detail: (a) the consultation stage; (b) the consultant's reflective reactions during consultation with culturally diverse teachers, students, and parents; (c) observations of the client-teacher's multicultural awareness, knowledge, and skills; and (d) any possible resistance surfacing within each session. Keeping an adequate CAR is important for growth, objectivity, structure, or recall of events/statements. Information collected can be used for future cases and/or research purposes. Other methods of accountability/evaluation are discussed below in the suggestions for university training.

Client-Teacher Evaluation

Ingraham (2000) identifies eight areas that a consultant school psychologist can review to help the client-teacher learn and develop over a period of

Consultation Analysis Record

Problem Identification Interview

Client Name: _____ Age: _____ Gender: _____

Ethnicity: _____ Religion: _____ Practicing? Yes No

Teaching Experience: _____ Grade Teaching: _____

Subjects:

_____

_____

_____

_____

Problem Identified (academic, behavioral, emotional):

_____

_____

_____

_____

Previous at-risk interventions attempted by client-teacher (instructional, behavioral, emotional, student contracts, family contacts):

_____

_____

_____

_____

Type of consultation (direct/indirect):

_____

_____

_____

_____

Describe type of resistance suspected:

_____

_____

_____

_____

Actions agreed upon:

_____

_____

_____

_____

Figure 8.2 *(Continued)*

Session time: _____

Analysis of Interview

Type of intervention agreed upon:

_____
_____
_____
_____

Intervention plan details:

_____
_____
_____
_____

Implementation

Teacher training required:

_____
_____
_____
_____

Monitoring procedures:

_____
_____
_____
_____

Possible plan revisions:

_____
_____
_____
_____

Figure 8.2 *(Continued)*

Session time: _____

(*Note:* this stage may consist of more than one session. If so, record total time spent.)

Evaluation

Outcome:

_____
_____
_____
_____

Modifications required:

_____
_____
_____
_____

Consultee satisfaction/dissatisfaction, based on consultee self-report satisfaction scale and/or interview:

_____
_____
_____
_____

List mistakes and successes for the next time:

_____
_____
_____
_____

Figure 8.2   Consultation Analysis Record

time. These areas can also be adopted as evaluative measures for checking teacher multicultural perspective during consultation. They are:

1. *Knowledge*—of interventions in both cultural and non-cultural context.

2. *Skill*—with culturally needed modifications of teaching methods; individualism versus collectivism; and acknowledgment of diverse views of achievement.

3. *Objectivity*—being too closely aligned to a student or too detached for motives of racism, bias, prejudice, or over-identification.

4. *Perception through stereotyping*—the teacher's perceptions cloud judgments through stereotyping a student.

5. *Overemphasis of culture*—a teacher forgets the individual student and is overly concerned about multiculturalism.

6. *The color-blind approach*—overemphasizing individuality to the detriment of cultural identity—certain students may be offended in spite of a teacher's good intentions.

7. *The fear of being called a racist*—teachers experience a loss of objectivity as they deal with internal conflict and approach-avoidance behavior in responding to the system.

8. *Confidence*—a teacher's self awareness of lack of knowledge or skills, especially when combined with authority conflicts, dependency, anger, or hostility, can lead to problems.

Two notable results—intervention paralysis and reactive dominance—can be particularly tricky, but can be resolved with a consultant's help. There are multicultural competency rating scales available for assessing a teacher's cultural viewpoint. One such scale that has been used often is the Teacher Multicultural Attitude Survey (TMAS) (Ponterotto, Baluch, Greig, & Rivera, 1998). The TMAS is a 20-item Likert scale that taps into teachers' cultural awareness. It is easy to administer and has acceptable validity and reliability.

Multicultural Assessment of Teachers and Training Programs

Although substantiation is unavailable to support the claim that school psychology programs are falling short in the area of training multicultural competent school psychologists, it is certain that the counseling profession has been much more attentive in this area than school psychology (Atkinson, Morton, & Sue, 1998). Various counseling competency guidelines and scales, as well as empirically based treatments, are available. However, there is little literature on the training of cross-culturally skilled consultant school psychologists. Then again, lack of empirical evidence of practice-based outcomes in school psychology is not rare. Ringeisen, Henderson, and Hoagwood (2003) have addressed the gap between what researchers have investigated and what practitioners have actually put into practice. One of the key points is that the field of school psychology must provide the practitioner with empirically based interventions for actual practice. Correspondingly, DuPaul and Stoner (2003) state that "school-specific contextual factors at various levels are critically important in designing and implementing interventions that are empirically supported on the one hand and also are feasible and acceptable to the consumers on the other hand" (p. 178).

Similarly, it appears that university trainers should adopt culture-centered training consultation methods. However, few consultative training suggestions to date have been empirically tested. So far, the literature has not addressed the need to bridge the gap between research and practice (DuPaul, & Stoner, 2003; Martines, 2003). and for this reason the following segment has been added to this chapter. This section's aim is to provide culturally focused training suggestions for consultation trainers in the hope that they will integrate multicultural contents and techniques as part of their consultation curriculum. Additionally, the section is directed to practitioners who may need to update their multicultural consultation skills.

Suggestions for Trainers

Why the Need for Multiculturally Competent Consultant School Psychologists?

As mentioned previously, there is abundant literature emphasizing the need for the cross-cultural training of psychotherapists and counselors (Gopaul-McNicol & Brice-Baker, 1998; Sue, Arrendondo, & McDavis, 1992) and for multicultural teacher education (Artiles, Trent, Hoffman-Kipp, & López-Torres, 2000; Banks, 2002). Moreover, several researchers have highlighted the need for cross-cultural considerations during the consultation process (Henning-Stout & Meyers, 2000; Ingraham & Meyers, 2000; Sheridan, 2000).

Although it is inevitable that newly minted consultant school psychologists working in schools, agencies, clinics, and hospitals will be asked to provide consultation services to educators, parents, administrators, and even medical professionals, the implementation of cross-cultural competency training associated with the consultation process remains problematic at the university level. Indeed, the literature regarding this subject is scarce.

Historically, training in consultation at the graduate school level has mainly focused on the acquisition of skills in the various four-stage models of school-based consultation, with a brief practicum experience; trainers have not attempted to address the development of competencies for working with culturally diverse teachers, students, and families (Caplan & Caplan, 1999; Conoley & Conoley, 1992; Erchul & Martens, 2002; Rosenfield, 1987). Therefore, while school psychologists-in-training are apt to be proficient in consultation methods and techniques that accentuate suitable communication, interventions, and interactive skills, they are likely to be indifferent with regard to cultural issues.

Nonetheless, it is this lack of awareness and knowledge of cultural issues that frequently limits the consultant school-psychologist's role of providing effective consultation services to client-teachers and parents. The situation is further exacerbated by the fact that, in spite of having had two decades of counselor-educators advocating multicultural training at the university level, only one or two courses are offered at most universities, if at all (Banks & McGee-Banks, 1995; Gopaul-McNicol & Brice-Baker, 1998; Rosenfield & Gravois, 1998). Consequently, a graduate student taking a consultation course is unlikely to have prior multicultural knowledge, much less appropriate skills. If this deficit is not addressed during the course, the consultation training and practicum experience will focus mainly on developing interpersonal communication and intervention skills, leaving the student ill-equipped to work with cross-culturally diverse client-teachers and culturally and linguistically diverse (CLD) children and families.

As a result, it has been proposed that trainers of prospective consultant school psychologists incorporate sufficient multicultural elements to increase students' cultural sensitivity as well as culture-specific knowledge and skills within the confines of consultation (Behring, Cabello, Kushida, & Murguia, 2000; Ingraham & Meyers, 2000; Rogers, 2000). This section summarizes various pedagogic-training strategies for implementing a generic, multicultural, consultation graduate curriculum, and focuses on a select set of objectives, discussing new material that will assist trainers in developing their syllabi.

What Should the Multiculturally Competent Consultant School Psychologist Know?

As already mentioned, the literature abounds with propositions for developing multicultural counseling competencies (Liu & Clay, 2002; Pedersen, 1985; Soo-Hoo, 1998; Sue et al., 1992; Weinrach & Thomas, 2002). Mainly, these competencies have been described as characteristics that a counselor and/or therapist should possess to better service culturally diverse populations. Specifically, Sue and colleagues (1992) identified the competencies as:

(a) an awareness of one's own assumptions, values, and biases; (b) an understanding of the worldview of the culturally different client; and (c) the capability to develop appropriate intervention strategies and techniques. Implicit in these characteristics is cognizance of various cultural beliefs, attitudes, knowledge, and skills. These competencies have been widely acknowledged and accepted by the Association for Multicultural Counseling and Development (AMCD) and can be adopted as guidelines in other domains of psychology, such as in human service consultation.

In the same vein, several professionals have advocated the adoption of a multicultural approach to consultation (Henning-Stout & Meyers, 2000; Ingraham, 2000; Jackson & Hayes, 1993; Sheridan, 2000). While numerous culturally sensitive knowledge-based enhancements have been suggested, little has been delineated by way of an actual instructional package that will aid the university trainer in educating multicultural school consultant psychologists. More recently, Gopaul-McNicol and Brice-Baker (1998) have contributed notable pedagogical suggestions for effective cross-cultural therapeutic practice and espouse Sue and Sue's (1981) training goals of cross-cultural competency for psychologists. It is important to note that, while Sue and Sue's (1981) competencies for psychologists were not specifically established for consultant school psychologists, they are nonetheless appropriate for practicing effective culturally sensitive consultation since they outline the core foundations of cross-cultural therapeutic practice. While psychological therapeutic practice is not a logical sequitur of consultation *per se*, the latter is viewed as a form of corrective/remedial and preventive practice that incorporates core psychological foundations for serving students, parents, and client-teachers. Furthermore, adequate interpersonal skills for consultation most likely cannot be attained without cultural knowledge of individual and group differences that build more effective cross-cultural therapeutic competencies.

Sue and Sue's (1981) proposed training goals form the basis of the remaining outline of this section, and suggestions for teachers of school consultant psychologists in training have been added. It is advised that these goals be included as part of the course objectives for a consultation syllabus since they have been endorsed as core competencies for the practice of psychology and, accordingly, should also be included as part of the school consultant psychologist's repertoire.

Attitudinal Competencies

Psychologist is Knowledgeable About Personal Ethnic Heritage

At the outset, students should be given a written assignment that includes a personal and/or family autobiography describing their ethnic groups' beliefs, values, norms, religion, and cultural rituals. The assignment may be embellished by having students present their family autobiographies, followed by group discussion. What is important, and more advantageous, is that students' awareness of their ethnic heritage be raised and shared with their classmates so as to obtain exposure to diverse cultural experiences and perspectives.

Psychologist Is Aware of Personal Biases

A definition of "biases" should initiate a class discussion prior to the following prescribed assignment (see Ponterotto & Pedersen, 1993 for bias definitions). Students should be asked to briefly write up and/or verbally recount recollections of a personal "bias" experience. The importance of this assignment is to bring to consciousness the experienced bias as well as to help the student develop introspective skills within this area. This assignment should be accompanied by a group discussion so students are able to listen to the experiences of others. It is necessary that students understand that biases are a natural occurrence and that admitting to them is the first step toward healthier self-introspection and the reduction of bias.

Psychologist Has Developed a Level of Comfort With Ethnic Differences

Students should be given assignments that place them in direct and indirect contact with different ethnic groups. For example, designate a consultation practicum requirement that specifies providing consultation services to culturally diverse teachers, students, and their families—then have students break up into small groups to work on a project that requires researching the beliefs, values, norms, religion, and cultural rituals of various ethnic groups. Following the assimilation of this information, allocate students to informal group presentations on the denoted ethnic groups and/or apportion Web-based assignments with other culturally different consultant school psychologists and/or teachers in various school districts, cities, and states.

Especially beneficial are Web-based assignments that direct students to contact a culturally diverse consultant psychologist and/or teacher in an urban or rural district heavily populated with different ethnic groups, for the purposes of establishing a Web-mail partnership. Consultant psychologist students can be asked to share information with their Web-mail partners on demographics, school culture, and various intervention consultation services (for example, conjoint behavioral consultation or home-bound consultation) that are practiced at different districts. Collected experiences can subsequently be shared in class discussions or activities. This particular kind of assignment succeeds well when the trainer has endeavored to establish an internet Web-mail agreement with various school districts that are willing to collaborate in such a partnership manner.

Psychologist Knows When It Is Appropriate to Make a Referral to a Psychologist of the Same Ethnic Background as the Client

For this training goal, advise students to be sensitive to the probability that certain clients will be better serviced with a consultant-psychologist of their own ethnicity (see Midgett & Meggert, 1991). Case studies should be discussed in class that describe cases in which gender issues, racial, educational, or language barriers impeded the consultation process. Ethical issues and standards should also be reviewed for this goal's objective.

Knowledge Competencies

Psychologist Understands the Sociology of Minority Groups

Students should be encouraged to acquire knowledge of the sociology of minority groups. The challenge for the faculty instructor is to help students attain the ability to view society from diverse ethnic perspectives, while preserving the recognition, receptiveness, and value of cultural differences prevalent in our nation. A good start for this competency is to have a brief review of the history of the different ethnic groups that immigrated to America (see Yetman, 1985). Another useful class exercise is to divide the countries of the world into ethnic or cultural groups based upon dominant themes—for example, religion, language, and customs—and determine the various societal factors that predominate in such a culture. Recognizing that attaining full comprehension of the sociology of dozens of ethnic cultures is virtually impossible, students should be assigned a particular ethnic group to study in depth, and afterward engage in role-playing in pairs, with one playing the consultant psychologist, and the other the ethnic group client. (Each pair should swap after 15–20 minutes so that two to three "consultations" can be achieved.) The object of this exercise is to familiarize the prospective student with the multiplicity of minority sociologies, and gauge when one might be out of one's depth in a consultation.

Psychologist Has the Necessary Cultural Knowledge About the Client

It is hoped that consultant school psychologists will not complete their graduate studies without knowledge of diverse ethnic groups. Although a consultation course cannot possibly fill in the missing "multicultural" educational gaps, it is recommended that weekly readings and writing tasks be assigned that will equip the consultant school psychologist-in-training with adequate knowledge of culturally diverse populations. Reading assignments, ethnic-based projects, and group discussions of various ethnic groups practiced throughout the semester should augment students' knowledge of the different ethnic groups.

Students should also have knowledge of the various Racial Ethnic Identity Development Models that delineate the varied psychological experiences and stages of ethnic identity development, and reading assignments given on the basis of perfecting this knowledge base (Helms, 1990; Ponterotto & Pedersen, 1993).

Follow-up class and group participation should be encouraged to focus on the psychological implications of each of these models. Students can be asked to break up into groups and prepare a brief class presentation on a specific Racial Ethnic Identity Development Model—discussions can follow, with other groups describing and comparing their own assigned models of racial ethnic identity. Examples or the elicitation of vignettes regarding some of the psychological implications of racial ethnic development can be conversationally interchanged. In addition, due to the demands of this particular competency, it should be stressed that students are ethically responsible to continually seek information about their current clients' ethnic group beliefs, values, religion, and norms if they have not gained previous knowledge of a particular group.

Psychologist Has Basic Therapeutic/Counseling Skills

For this goal, it should be understood that the term "basic" does not include multicultural components; therefore, it is assumed that consultant school psychologists-in-training have already acquired cross-cultural knowledge and skills in fundamental therapeutic/counseling interventions prior to their consultation training. To ensure this, a brief assessment of the class's prior skills in this area should be conducted at the beginning. Furthermore, it is highly recommended that students be exposed to literature pertaining to culturally sensitive therapeutic/counseling skills (see Ponterotto, Casas, Suzuki, & Alexander, 2001; Sheridan, 2000). Refer to the skills competence sections below for further recommendations.

Psychologist Is Aware of
Institutional Barriers to Minority Clients

In the attainment of this training goal, the following tasks should aid in developing an awareness of institutional barriers to minority clients:

- Appoint students to search newspapers, news magazines, and internet news Websites for news stories describing institutional impediments.
- Conduct class discussions based on collected vignettes and/or case studies of examples of institutional obstacles.
- Review educational laws that might cause such barriers.
- Have students research educational journals to locate examples of institutional barriers in school settings.
- Research online advocacy Websites founded for aiding minority clients facing institutional barriers to minorities.
- Have students share their own experiences or knowledge of such incidents in their schools and/or other institutions.
- Assign readings that will aid students to develop historical knowledge in this area (see Canino & Spurlock, 2000; Gopaul-McNicol & Brice-Baker, 1998; Ponterotto et al., 2001; Reynolds, 1995).

Skill Competencies

Psychologist Is Able to Choose and Implement Appropriate and Effective Interventions With Minority Clients

General considerations. This training goal addresses several components of effective interventions. For the consultant school psychologist, it is understood that the term "effective interventions" encompasses therapeutic counseling interventions (for emotional or behavioral problems) as well as academic interventions since these are the most common school-based intervention exigencies. Moreover, the consultant school psychologist must collaborate with client-teachers, CLD students, and parents when designing intervention and implementation plans in these areas.

Correspondingly, the following are suggested for augmenting both counseling and academic intervention competencies for the consultant-school psychologist.

Counseling interventions. Ideally, students should possess knowledge of the various cross-cultural counseling and therapeutic interventions recommended in the literature. However, if a class evaluation of skill competencies demonstrates inadequate preparation in this area, the latter can be rectified by assigning readings that emphasize a culturally sensitive intervention knowledge-base (see Canino & Spurlock, 2000; Gopaul-McNicol & Brice-Baker, 1998; Ponterotto et al., 2001; Sue, Arredondo, & McDavis, 1992). In addition, students should be encouraged to investigate a particular client-centered consultation case that will require the formulation of a counseling intervention plan for a CLD child.

Academic interventions—Curriculum Based Assessment (CBA). Consultant school psychologists are invariably faced with client-teachers who describe students with learning problems in their classrooms. Along with the knowledge of Instructional Consultation (Rosenfield, 1987), consultant school psychologists-in-training should acquire knowledge and expertise in Curriculum Based Assessment (CBA). CBA is an essential skill for the practice of consultation. It is a method of assessing a child's academic problems within the confines of the actual classroom curriculum, given that norm-referenced tests are not suitable for curriculum intervention decisions (see Rosenfield, 1987).

The process of CBA is facilitated by several evaluative Systematic Observational Systems, such as the Teacher's Instructional Environment System III (TIES) (Ysseldyke & Christensen, 1992; Shapiro & Lentz, 1986) recommended by Rosenthal (1987). Operationally, these instruments are used in conducting CBA. For example, the TIES III instrument may be administered as part of the academic (CBA) assessment of a CLD child with the aim of modifying any cultural biases or inappropriate learning strategies, as well as suggestions for a more culture-specific curriculum. In this regard, knowledge of bilingual issues in assessment should be encouraged and referenced for consultant school psychologists in training (Hamayan & Damico, 1991; Lopez, 2000).

Classroom observations. As part of the consultation training experience, and for the purposes of developing academic interventions, students should be required to conduct a classroom observation with a CLD student. This will aid in the design and implementation of an academic intervention plan. Additionally, classroom observations are also useful for the observation of behavioral problems in the classroom, and are often part of the consultation process (Rosenfield, 1987).

Multicultural behavioral interventions. For consultation cases that require behavioral interventions, consultant school psychologists-in-training should be directed to the appropriate literature for assistance in developing a culturally sensitive behavioral intervention plan (see Canino & Spurlock, 2000; Everston, Emmer, & Worsham, 2000; Gopaul-McNicol & Brice-Baker, 1998; Ingraham, 2000; Ponterotto et al., 2001). Brown et al. (2001) discuss two pertinent behavioral approaches to consultation, one with its foundation grounded in operant learning theory and the other emanating from a cognitive-behavioral learning theory. Consultant school psychologists-in-training, however, must be cautious when adopting such models due to their cultural limitations. The models are rooted in two traditional values of the Eurocentric culture—individual achievement, and future time orientation—and these values can be detrimental for certain cultural groups which place importance on cooperative approaches to achievement (e.g., Asian Americans, Native Americans, Latin Americans).

In this respect, behavioral interventions should be group-oriented (whole classroom) and focus on cooperative activities (e.g., homework support groups, study groups, social training groups, and specific behavior-oriented groups). Time-orientation interventions (such as contracting interventions) may prove to be ineffective with particular groups that do not hold the Eurocentric approach to long- and short-term goals. In the latter respect, consultant-psychologists will need to accommodate the time perspective of their clients (see Brown et al., 2001). Once again, consultant school psychologists-in-training need to be reminded that culturally sensitive behavioral intervention plans must consider the ethnicity of educators, students, and parents, as these individuals ultimately will be invited to participate in the implementation of the intervention plan.

Multicultural consultation practicum. As already mentioned, course requirements should mandate a culturally sensitive school-based consultation practicum (e.g., students should engage in a practicum consultation case with at least one client-teacher and student of an ethnic group other than their own). The consultation practicum should require the consultant school psychologist to follow through on all four stages of the consultation process.

Consultation practicum log. Students should keep a log of their consultation case on a per session basis, describing: (a) the particular consultation stage; (b) their introspective reactions during consultation with culturally different teachers, students, and parents; (c) any observations of multicultural awareness, knowledge, and skills on the part of their clients; and (d) any resistance issues surfacing within the session(s).

Audio-recorded consultation sessions. It is recommended that each session be audio-recorded. The audio-tapes will allow the trainer to monitor and supervise each session and provide feedback when appropriate.

Class discussions should be scheduled for students to either play back parts of their audio-recorded sessions and/or recount their practicum experiences concerning their culturally diverse student clientele.

Inspire students to describe the noted cultural differences between self, teacher, and student. Students should also be encouraged to describe cultural differences which might potentially be conflicting or which might have led to actual conflicts (see Ingraham & Meyers, 2000; Rogers, 2000). Conclude with a debriefing period for students to vent regarding their consultation experiences.

Case notes and/or diary. Monitoring of the consultation process in written form should be emphasized. The collection of consultative information obtained throughout the consultation case should be recorded by the consultant school psychologist, and students should be urged to maintain accurate and adequately described case notes and/or the keeping of a diary of each consultation case (Brown et al., 2001). There are several points to stress for this recommendation:

- It provides a detailed description of the case.
- It aids in the recollection of information discussed.
- It records the progress made in the case.
- It helps the consultant to be objective.
- It provides the consultant with easy access to information concerning the case if there is a need to provide reflections and/or recommendations.
- It provides information helpful to report writing.
- It provides documentation of the consultation type, duration, and overall time period the consultant was engaged in the consultation case.
- It can be used as a study of the consultation process of each particular case and is beneficial for the professional growth of the consultant (see Brown et al., 2001, Ch. 10).

Special Section: Consultation Training Goals and Strategies for Class Sessions

The following is a compilation of instructional goals and strategies for class sessions—useful steps to follow for the facilitation of multicultural consultation training. In addition, these strategies are particularly helpful in addressing critical multicultural issues during the instructional consultation period.

Multicultural Self-Awareness Instrument

At the inception of the course, students should be administered a multicultural self-awareness questionnaire/scale (see Gopaul-McNicol & Brice-Baker, 1998). Hold group discussions during which students can comfortably share their self-reported findings. Emphasize the importance of noting the individual differences in self-awareness as well as one's conscious and unconscious awareness of the differences. It is key that beginning consultants learn the first goal of multicultural competencies: an awareness of one's own biases and/or prejudices (Ponterotto & Pedersen, 1993).

Consultation Models

Several classes will naturally be dedicated to developing students' knowledge of various consultation models. However, an emphasis on cultural modifications for each model is recommended (e.g., mental health, behavioral, instructional, home–school collaboration, collaborative/teamwork, and organizational).

Each of the models can be modified to fit culture-specific needs. For example, when using a mental-health consultation approach, students can be guided to review the cultural factors of the particular client-centered case and to design appropriate culture-specific intervention plans. For all models, a culture-specific intervention plan should include a background check of the discussed student's ethnicity, values, religion, beliefs, parental disciplinary norms, and parents' view of appropriate and inappropriate behaviors.

It has been postulated in the literature that all consultation models can be modified to incorporate a multicultural framework that will enable the multicultural consultant school psychologist to delineate appropriate culturally sensitive interventions (see "The Five Components of the Multicultural School Consultation Framework" in Ingraham & Meyers, 2000). Furthermore, it is important that consultant psychologists-in-training understand that cultural differences in educators, students, and parents will automatically change the course of services of the more generic consultation models since intervention and implementation plans will be affected by these cultural differences. Moreover, educators, students, and parents will ultimately need to participate in the implementation plan. In this respect, culturally sensitive adaptations are essential.

Furthermore, the adoption of a multicultural consultation framework in consultation training is in keeping with the second basic multicultural competency goal of obtaining multicultural knowledge (Sue et al., 1992; Sue, 1992).

Communication Skills

Students should develop cogent communication skills for effective consultation (see Brown et al., 2001, Ch. 3; Dettmer, Thurston, & Dyck, 2002, Ch. 5; Gazda et al., 1999; Rosenfield, 1987; Stone, Patton, & Heen, 1999); however, an emphasis should be placed on culturally sensitive communication skills (see "Communication Skills and Cultural Competency in Skilled Dialogue" in Barrera & Corso, 2002). For example, have students adopt and practice cultural sensitivity by encouraging a self-analysis of their use of *culturally sensitive emitters* and *elicitors* during consultation dialogue (see Brown et al., 2001, Ch. 3). The latter goal can be attained by role-playing activities in which students practice dialogue and enter changes obtained from a cultural consultation transcript. It might be beneficial for culturally sensitive communication skills to be enhanced and practiced during class role-playing activities prior to having students engage in the consultation practicum.

Cross-Cultural Consultation Case Study

Provide students with a consultation case vignette that describes an actual case with a CLD child or adolescent and have the students analyze the cultural dialogues.

Encourage students to build a *Cross-Cultural CD Resource File* to be equipped with: (a) literature references on culturally sensitive school-based behavioral interventions; (b) intervention techniques to address academic performance problems, including various learning styles; and (c) inventories of cross-cultural interventions obtained from the literature suitable for working with CLD children and families. This can be accomplished throughout the semester by having students add to their file all pertinent information obtained from their readings, practicum interventions, scales utilized, class discussions, and so forth. An ideal way to do this is to have students share their CD files. This will augment their resources.

Additionally, it has been recommended in the literature that school psychologists be prepared with a repertoire of empirically based intervention techniques for providing appropriate consultation service. The implication is that consultant school psychologists must research the prospective intervention *prior* to suggesting it to the client-teacher. Therefore, the research literature should be reviewed to determine the efficacy of an intended treatment (Gutkin & Curtis, 1998; Reynolds & Gutkin, 1998). It is good practice to recommend this to beginning consultant school psychologists early on so that they become accustomed to keeping abreast of the latest empirical findings in their profession.

Moreover, developing a consultant's culturally sensitive intervention skills is in keeping with the third basic multicultural competency goal of acquiring multicultural skills (Sue et al., 1992).

Class Presentations

Another avenue for students to obtain multicultural awareness, knowledge, and skills for consultation and staff development training practice is through participation in professional class presentations. Topics for consultation presentations should focus mainly on having the beginning consultant research specific areas that are beneficial for developing consultation cross-cultural competencies. The latter does not solely emphasize erudition in the consultation process, but also the knowledge and skills required of a well-prepared school consultant psychologist in all areas of school-based functioning.

Suggested topics for class presentations include:

- ethnic group differences—a review of the norms, value systems, religion, and customs of various ethnic groups;

- multicultural interventions for classroom management (in elementary and/or high schools);
- techniques and strategies for multicultural instruction;
- effects of diversity on school consultation and collaboration;
- interventions for family-focused home–school consultation;
- techniques to facilitate group consultation;
- ethics of collaborative consultation;
- ethics and legal considerations in consultation;
- the limits of consultation;
- research directions in consultation;
- manipulation in consultation;
- strategies for classroom management;
- planning and organizing multicultural instruction;
- classroom techniques for prejudice prevention;
- the use of interpreters in consultation;
- multicultural considerations for behavioral consultation with parents and teachers;
- conducting culturally sensitive classroom observations;
- advocacy and the role of the consultant;
- reading and math remediation strategies for challenged children;
- culture and resistance to consultation.

It should be noted that developing a Cross-Cultural CD Resource File in this area is beneficial for prospective consultant school psychologists because it means each will possess an active file on diverse topics to resort to when needed in future practice. Students can be encouraged to share CD files of their presentations with classmates.

Curriculum Based Assessment (CBA)

Introduce a culturally sensitive Curriculum Based Assessment (CBA) approach (Rosenfield, 1987). As a training objective, students should be counseled to acquire: (a) knowledge of various "cultural" learning styles; (b) knowledge of multicultural instructional strategies for teaching CLD children; (c) knowledge of different observational systems; and (d) an understanding of the need to authenticate with CLD parents *their* approach to homework, home-study scheduling, and discipline methods (since different cultures have distinct disciplinary and punishment methods).

Culturally Sensitive School-Based Consultation Practicum

As previously mentioned, request a culturally sensitive school-based consultation practicum experience.

Resistance to Consultation and Change

Review and describe issues of resistance in consultation and the fear of change. Encourage students to:

- define consultant and client roles during the problem identification consultation session;
- ask the client what she/he expects from the consultation service;
- be up front about resistance to change that might occur during the consultation process; and
- learn about the pitfalls of resistance in consultation, not only with resistant client-teachers, but also with CLD children and families within the realm of home–school collaborative consultation (this is a new area of research since the implementation of home-bound consultation).

Students should be advised on the nature of resistive area—for example, privacy, ethnic norms, values, time management, and disciplinary methods. If CLD children and families are to participate in home–school consultation interventions, training for consultant school psychologists should include culturally sensitive approaches that will enable their practice to be successful with the least resistance and/or be prepared to overcome some of the resistance interference.

Accountability and Data-Based Approach to Consultation

Improving the consultant's effectiveness through the use of objective assessment measures of the process and outcome of consultation should be stressed to beginning consultant school psychologists-in-training (see Barlow et al., 1984; Brown et al., 2001; Lambert, 1993). In this respect, an accountability orientation is judicious and part of the consultant's ethical responsibility. Therefore, consultant school psychologist students are to be encouraged to employ an evaluation procedure during each consultation case. Accountability and evaluation procedures in consultation should be emphasized as an ongoing adjunct to the continuing development of the consultant's skills. Additionally, a client's evaluative input can be used for the study of the consultation process and of the models utilized. In the latter regard, the training objective can focus on instructing consultant school psychologist students to adhere to data-based evaluations. The instructor is encouraged to become familiar with the various evaluative consultation forms/scales recommended by Brown et al. (2001, Ch. 10).

Steps to Consider for Data-Based Evaluations

First and foremost, try to use the same kind of systematic data-based approach (e.g., special scales and/or forms). In the event that a research question might be answered and/or further investigated as a result of the consultation process analysis, outcome measures used should be the same or they will not be valid in consultation research projects. Brown et al. (2001) suggest determining the reason for the evaluation. Is it for the personal professional growth of the consultant psychologist? To process and debrief solely with the client-teacher? For data collection to be used later for research? The nature of the outcome measures (e.g., evaluation forms and/or scales) will be determined by the reason for the evaluation.

Evaluation data can also be useful for sharing (anonymously) successes and failures—the latter aids in the assimilation of knowledge and skills for similar future cases. As previously mentioned, the GAS is a useful tool to use as an evaluation outcome measure, as well as a monitoring agent that can aid both the consultant psychologist and the client-teacher. Use of the GAS is recommended for data-based evaluations. It is important that the consultant school psychologist learn to adhere to some type of evaluation outcome that looks at not only the progress of the offered consultation service, but at personal professional growth (Zins, 1981).

Reflections on Training

Although certain trainers of school psychologists might feel that their students are already overburdened academically, and question the need for the incorporation of formal multicultural elements into their courses, especially in the area of consultation, it is important to realize that "on-the-job training" will not suffice in this situation. America, more than most countries, is a melting pot—an assorted mixture of dozens of ethnicities, which will only continue to diversify further. While recognizing that school psychologists cannot be minority sociology experts, developing multicultural competencies will go a long way towards ensuring that consultations will go more smoothly with less resistance on the part of the participants, that interventions will be more appropriately chosen, and that cultural factors will not be giant barriers to successful outcomes.

Probably the most significant dynamic that a trainer can impart to his or her students is the professional motivation to further their abilities and to continue learning about multicultural issues in their chosen profession, having given them the framework to do so. Moreover, such trained school psychologists will know when they are out of their depth in a specific situation, and what options are available to them to proceed.

A final point to consider is that the astute researcher may be inclined to ask such questions as: "Is this where we are in the multicultural consultation literature?" "Do we know how to assess our students for bias, racism, cultural insensitivity, or Eurocentrism?" "Can we measure change in their attitudes of skills?" "Do we have evidence that cultural competence makes a difference in outcome for clients or client?" These questions are stimulating and appropriate but the responses are not completely available at this time. We do have culture-sensitive competency screening scales, and we are presently trying to measure change in skills via data-based performance measures in student evaluation. We have evidence of differences in outcomes if we use data-based performance measures. At this point, perhaps it is not too presumptuous to state that the practitioner and/or trainer ought to be as closely and respectfully listened to as the researcher. Not only can practitioners help provide evidence-based outcomes; they can contribute to the reality of what is observed at the school level. What is needed is their cooperation in collecting data-based performance measures as well as their collaboration in multicultural research projects that focus on the consumer-practitioner testing the adoptability of the proposed interventions.

References

Altarriba, J., & Bauer, L. M. (1998). Counseling the Hispanic client: Cuban Americans, Mexican Americans, and Puerto Ricans. *Journal of Counseling and Development, 76*(4), 389–396.

Artiles, A. J., Trent, S. C., Hoffman-Kipp, P., & López-Torres, L. (2000). From individual acquisition to cultural-historical practices in multicultural teacher education. *Remedial and Special Education, 21*(2), 79–89.

Atkinson, D.R., Morten, G., & Sue, D. W. (Eds.). (1998). *Counseling American minorities*. New York: McGraw-Hill.

Au, K. H. (1993). *Literacy instruction in multicultural settings*. Belmont, CA: Wadsworth/Thompson.

Bandura, A. (1982). Self-efficacy mechanism in human agency. *American Psychologists, 37*, 122–147.

Banks, J. A. (1993). Multicultural education: Historical development, dimensions, and practice. In J. A. Banks, & C. A. McGee-Banks (Eds.), *Handbook of research on multicultural education*. New York: Simon & Schuster Macmillan.

Banks, J. A. (2002). *An introduction to multicultural education*. Boston: Allyn & Bacon.

Banks, J. A., & McGee-Banks, C.A. (Eds.). (1995). *Handbook of research on multicultural education*. New York: Simon & Schuster Macmillan.

Barlow, D. H., Hayes, S. C., & Nelson, R. O. (1984). *The scientist-practitioner: Research and accountability in clinical and educational settings*. New York: Pergamon.

Barrera, I. & Corso, R. M. (2002). Cultural competency as skilled dialogue. *Topics in early childhood education*, 22(2), 103–113.

Behring, S. T., Cabello, B., Kushida, D., & Murguia, A. (2000). Cultural modifications to current school-based consultation approaches reported by culturally diverse beginning consultants. *School Psychology Review, 29*(3), 354–365.

Bergan, J. R., & Tombari, M. L. (1976). Consultant skill and efficiency and the implementation and outcomes of consultation. *Journal of School Psychology, 14*, 3–14.

Brown, D. (1997). Implications of cultural values for cross-cultural consultation with families. *Journal of Counseling and Development, 76*(1), 29–36.

Brown, D., Pryzwanski, W. B., & Schulte, A. C. (2001). *Psychological consultation: Introduction to theory and practice* (5th ed.). Boston: Allyn & Bacon.

Brown, D., Pryzwansky, W. B., & Schulte, A. C. (2006). *Psychological consultation and collaboration: Introduction to theory and practice* (6th ed.). Boston: Allyn & Bacon.

Canino, I., & Spurlock, J. (2000). *Culturally diverse children and adolescents. Assessment, diagnosis, and treatment* (2nd ed.). New York: Guilford Press.

Caplan, G. (1970). *The theory and practice of mental health consultation.* New York: Basic Books.

Caplan, G., & Caplan, R. B. (1999 [1993]). *Mental health consultation and collaboration.* Prospect Heights, IL: Waveland Press.

Christenson, S. L., & Close-Conoley, J. (Eds.) (1992). *Home–school collaboration.* Silver Springs, MD: National Association of School Psychologists.

Conoley, J. C., & Conoley, C. W. (1992). *School consultation: Practice and training* (2nd ed.). Boston: Allyn & Bacon.

Davis, K. (1997). *Exploring the intersection between cultural competency and managed behavioral health care policy: Implications for state and county mental health agencies.* Alexandria, VA: National Technical Assistance Center for State Mental Health Planning.

Dettmar, P., Dyck, N. & Thurston, L. P. (1999). *Consultation, collaboration and teamwork for students with special needs.* Boston: Allyn & Bacon.

Duncan, C., & Pryzwansky, W. B. (1993). Effects of race, racial identity development, and orientation style on perceived consultant effectiveness. *Journal of Multicultural Counseling and Development, 21*(2), 88–96.

DuPaul, G. J., & Stoner, G. (2003). *ADHD in the schools: Assessment and intervention strategies* (2nd ed.). New York: Guilford Press.

Erchul, W. P., & Martens, B. R. (2002). *School consultation: Conceptual and empirical bases of practice* (2nd ed.). New York: Plenum.

Erchul, W. P., Raven, B. H., & Ray, A. G. (2001). School psychologists' perceptions of social power bases in teacher consultation. *Journal of Educational and Psychological Consultation, 12*, 1–23.

Everston, C., Emmer, E. T., & Worsham, M. E. (2000). *Classroom management for elementary teachers* (5th ed.). Boston: Allyn & Bacon.

Fallahi, M. (2003). Teach America with care: Reflections on two years working in an urban school. *Electronic Magazine of Multicultural Education* [online], 5(1). Available from www.eastern.edu/publications/emme/2003spring/fallahi.html.

Fuchs, D., Fuchs., L. S., & Bahr, M. W. (1990). Mainstream assistance teams: A scientific basis for the art of consultation. *Exceptional Children, 57,* 128–139.

Gazda, G. M., Asbury, F. R., Balzer, F. J., Childers, W. C., Phelps, R. E., & Walters, R. P. (1999). *Human relations development: A manual for educators.* Boston: Allyn & Bacon.

Gibbs, J. T. (1980). The interpersonal orientation in mental health: Toward a mode of ethnic variations in consultation. *Journal of Community Psychology, 8*(3), 195–207.

Goldstein, B.S.C. (1998). Creating a context for collaborative consultation: Working across bicultural communities. *Journal of Educational and Psychological Consultation, 9*(4), 367–374.

Gopaul-McNicol, S. & Brice-Baker, J. (1998). *Cross-cultural practice: Assessment, treatment, and training.* New York: John Wiley & Sons.

Graham, S., Taylor, A., & Hudley, C. (1998). Exploring achievement values among ethnic minority early adolescents. *Journal of Educational Psychology, 90,* 606–620.

Gutkin, T. B. & Curtis, M. J. (1998). School-based consultation theory and practice: The art and science of indirect service delivery. In C. R. Reynolds & T. B. Gutkin (Eds.), *The handbook of school psychology* (pp. 598–637). New York: John Wiley & Sons.

Hamayan, E. V., & Damico, J. S. (Eds.) (1991). *Limiting bias in the assessment of bilingual students.* Austin, TX: Pro-ed.

Hanna, F. J., Bemak, F., & Chung, R. (1999). Toward a new paradigm for multicultural counseling. *Journal of Counseling and Development, 77,* 125–134.

Helms, J. E. (1990). *Black and white racial identity: Theory, research, and practice.* New York: Greenwood Press.

Henning-Stout, M., & Meyers, J. (2000). Consultation and human diversity: First things first. *School Psychology Review, 29*(3), 419–425.

Ingraham, C. (2000). Consultation through a multicultural lens: Multicultural and cross-cultural consultation in schools. *School Psychology Review, 29*(3), 320–343.

Ingraham, C. L., & Meyers, J. (2000). Introduction to multicultural and cross-cultural consultation in schools: Cultural diversity issues in school consultation. *School Psychology Review, 29*(3), 315–319.

Jackson, D. N., & Hayes, D. (1993). Multicultural issues in consultation. *Journal of Counseling & Development, 72,* 144–147.

Kiresuk, T. J., Smith, A., & Cardillo, J. E. (Eds.) (1994). *Goal attainment scaling: Applications, theory and measurement.* Hillsdale, NJ: Lawrence Erlbaum.

Kratochwill, T. R., & Pittman, P. H. (2002). Expanding problem-solving consultation training: Prospects and frameworks. *Journal of Educational and Psychological Consultation, 13*(1&2), 69–95.

Lambert, N. M. (1993). Historical perspective on school psychology: A scientist practitioner specialization in school psychology. *Journal of School Psychology, 31,* 163–193.

Liu, W. M. & Clay, D. L. (2002). Multicultural counseling competencies: Guidelines in working with children and adolescents. *Journal of Mental Health Counseling, 24*(2), 177–187.

Lopez, E. C. (2000). Conducting instructional consultation through interpreters. *School Psychology Review, 29,* 378–388.

Maital, S. L. (2000). Reciprocal distancing: A systems model of interpersonal processes in cross-cultural consultation. *School Psychology Review, 29*(3), 389–401.

Martines, D. (2002). Suggestions from practicing consultant school psychologists for alleviating resistance in consultation. Unpublished raw data.

Martines, D. (2003). Suggestions for training cross-cultural consultant school psychologists. *Trainers Forum, 23*, 5–13.

Martines, D. (2005). Teachers' perceptions of multicultural issues in psychoeducational settings. *The Qualitative Report, 10*(1), 1–20.

Midgett, T. E., & Meggert, S. S. (1991). Multicultural counseling instruction: A challenge for faculties in the 21st century. *Journal of Counseling and Development, 70*, 136–141.

Monsen, J. J., & Frederickson, N. (2002). Consultant problem understanding as a function of training in interviewing to promote accessible reasoning. *Journal of School Psychology, 40*(3), 197–212.

Nastasi, B. K., Varjas, K., Bernstein,, R., & Jayasena, A. (2000). Conducting participatory culture-specific consultation: A global perspective on multicultural consultation. *School Psychology Review, 29*(3), 401–413.

O'Keefe, D. J. & Medway, F. J. (1997). The application of persuasion research to consultation in school psychology. *Journal of School Psychology, 35*, 173–193.

Pedersen, P. (Ed.). (1985). *Handbook of Cross-Cultural Counseling and Therapy.* Westport, CT: Greenwood Press.

Ponterotto, J. G., Baluch, S., Greig, T., & Rivera, S. (1998). Development and initial score validation of the Teacher Multicultural Attitude Survey (TMAS). *Educational and Psychological Measurement, 58*, 1002–1015.

Ponterotto, J. G., & Casas, J. M. (1991). *Handbook of racial/ethnic minority counseling research.* Springfield, IL: Charles C Thomas.

Ponterotto, J. G., Casas, J. M., Suzuki, L. A., & Alexander, C. M. (2001). *Handbook of multicultural counseling.* Thousand Oaks, CA: Sage.

Ponterotto, J. G., & Pedersen, P. (1993). *Preventing prejudice: A guide for counselors and educators.* Newbury Park, CA: Sage.

Pryzwansky, W. B. (1974). A reconsideration of the consultation model for delivery of school-based psychological services. *Journal of Orthopsychiatry, 44*, 579–583.

Raven, B. H. (1992). A power/interaction model of interpersonal influence: French and Raven thirty years later. *Journal of Social Behavior and Personality, 7*, 217–244.

Reynolds, A. (1995). Challenges and strategies for teaching multicultural counseling courses. In J. Ponterotto, J. M. Casas, L. S. Suzuki, & C. M. Alexander (Eds.), *Handbook of multicultural counseling* (pp. 312–330). Thousand Oaks, CA: Sage.

Reynolds, C. R., & Gutkin, T. B. (Eds.). (1998). *The handbook of school psychology* (4th ed.). New York: John Wiley & Sons.

Rhone, A. E. (2001). *A Study guide to multi-cultural education.* Dubuque, IA: Kendall Hunt.

Ringeisen, H., Henderson, K., & Hoagwood, K. (2003). Context matters: schools and the "Research to Practice Gap" in children's mental health. *School Psychology Review, 32*(2), 153–168.

Rogers, M. R. (1998). The influence of race and consultant verbal behavior on perception of consultant competence and multicultural sensitivity. *School Psychology Quarterly, 13*(4), 265–280.

Rogers, M. R. (2000). Examining the cultural context of consultation. *School Psychology Review, 29*(3), 414–418.

Rosenfield, S. (1987). *Instructional consultation*. Hillsdale, NJ: Lawrence Erlbaum.

Rosenfield, S., & Gravois, T. A. (1998). Working with teams in the school. In C. R. Reynolds, & T. B. Gutkin (Eds.), *Handbook of school psychology* (3rd ed.) (pp. 1025–1040). New York: John Wiley & Sons.

Rosenthal, R. (1987). Pygmalion effects: Existence, magnitude, and social importance. *Educational Researcher, 16,* 37–41.

Sandargas, R. A. (1992). *State-event classroom observation system*. Knoxville, TN: Dept. of Psychology, University of Tennessee.

Shapiro, E. S., & Lentz, F. E. (1986). Behavioral assessment of academic behavior. In T. R. Kratochwill (Ed.), *Advances in School Psychology* (pp. 87–140). Hillsdale, NJ: Lawrence Erlbaum.

Sheridan, S. M. (2000). Considerations of multiculturalism and diversity in behavioral consultation with parents and teachers. *School Psychology Review, 29*(3), 344–353.

Sheridan, S. M., Welch, M., & Orme, S. F. (1996). Is consultation effective? A review of outcome research. *Remedial and Special Education, 17,* 341–354.

Soo-Hoo, T. (1998). Applying frame of reference and reframing techniques to improve school consultation in multicultural settings. *Journal of Educational and Psychological Consultation, 9*(4), 325–345.

Srebalus, D. J., & Brown, D. (2001). *A guide to the helping professions*. Needham Heights, MA: Allyn & Bacon.

Stone, D., Patton, B., & Heen, S. (1999). *Difficult conversations: How to discuss what matters most*. New York: Random House.

Sue, D. W., Arrendondo, P., & McDavis, R. J. (1992). Multicultural counseling competencies and standards: A call to the profession. *Journal of Multicultural Counseling and Development, 20,* 64–88.

Sue D. W., & Sue, D. (1981). *Counseling the culturally different: Theory and practice*. New York: John Wiley & Sons.

Weinrach, S. G., & Thomas, K. R. (2002). A critical analysis of the multicultural counseling competencies: Implications for the practice of mental health counseling. *Journal of Mental Health Counseling, 24*(1), 20–35.

West, J. F., & Idol, L. (1987). School consultation (Part 1): An interdisciplinary perspective on theory, models, and research. *Journal of Learning Disabilities, 20,* 388–408.

Yetman, N. R. (1985). *Majority and minority: The dynamics of race and ethnicity in American life* (4th ed.). Boston: Allyn & Bacon.

Ysseldyke, J. E., & Christenson, S.L. (1993). *The instructional environment scale*. Longmont, CO: Sopris West.

Zins, J. E. (1981). Using data-based evaluation in developing school consultation services. In M. J. Curtis & J. E. Zins (Eds.), *The theory and practice of school consultation* (pp. 261–268). Springfield, IL: Charles C Thomas.

Annotated Bibliography

Brown, D., Pryzwansky, W. B., & Schulte, A. C. (2006). *Psychological consultation and collaboration: Introduction to theory and practice* (6th ed.). Boston, MA: Pearson Allyn & Bacon. *This text highlights the major theoretical approaches and strategies to consultation and collaboration.*

Caplan, G., & Caplan, R. B. (1999). *Mental health consultation and collaboration.* Prospect Heights, IL: Waveland Press. *The authors provide a thorough review of the mental health consultation model as well as a special section on manipulation and collaboration in the schools.*

Conoley, J. C., & Conoley, C. W. (1992). *School consultation: Practice and training* (2nd ed.). Boston, MA: Allyn & Bacon. *This text presents a practical guide to consultation in schools, including the various approaches (such as behavioral and advocacy), implementation issues, skills, obstacles to practice, transcripts, and ethical issues. The text includes a section on training.*

Dettmar, P., Dyck, N. & Thurston, L. P. (1999*). Consultation, collaboration and team work for students with special needs.* Boston, MA: Allyn & Bacon. *A very informative text that provides numerous collaborative interventions/vignettes/ checklists for servicing special education teachers.*

Erchul, W. P., & Martens, B. K. (2002). *School consultation: Conceptual and empirical bases of practice* (2nd ed.). New York: Kluwer Academic/Plenum. *This text offers a systematic approach to school consultation by combining the most useful and/or empirically validated practices for mental health and behavioral consultation (i.e., behavior analysis, social influence, implementation support).*

9

Multicultural Competencies for Parental Training Programs

Sara Nahari

Introduction

Although there is no question about the importance and worth of parental involvement programs, parents of racial/ethnic and culturally and linguistically diverse (CLD) students continue to avoid involvement in the school system. Schools very often assume that lack of participation is due to parental disinterest in the academic achievement of their children, rather than addressing the barriers that cause the lack of participation. According to Santarelli, Koegel, Casas and Koegel (2001), awareness and acceptance of the cultural, linguistic and socioeconomic differences existing amongst CLD parents are the foundation on which to build rapport for a better working relationship. To bridge these barriers, multicultural school psychologists have historically played an important role in providing services to parents. Families stand out as the main partners of schools in this endeavor. As a result of their training, which includes "knowledge of family systems, including family strengths and influences on student development, learning, and behavior, and of methods to involve families in education and service delivery" (NASP, 2006), multicultural school psychologists are equipped to work effectively with families, educators, and others. In their role as facilitators, psychologists help parents and families to understand the variety of services and programs available to children and their families today. Through consultation and direct services, psychologists assist teachers and other school staff to understand the needs of racial/ethnic and CLD parents and create parental involvement programs which address the barriers that keep parents from becoming involved. As a result of this training, they are at an advantage in addressing one of the most critical issues affecting today's schools: how to support high-quality learning by children and how to involve parents in promoting the learning of their children. According to Harrison et al. (2004), "There is increased pressure for schools to be accountable. Building partnerships with parents and families is one way to increase the likelihood of improvement in achievement, attendance, graduation, and other critical outcomes [and] school psychologists have knowledge, skills, and competencies to work across these contexts."

This chapter summarizes the consensus in the field about parental involvement, examines the research on effectiveness of parental involvement, and presents a sample of programs which have been successful in establishing parental involvement for racial/ethnic and CLD parents in their schools. In addition, it will review those additional competencies required by multicultural school psychologists to support programs of parental involvement.

For several decades, family and professional collaboration has been seen as an endorsed practice in the educational and social services fields. Major legislation such as PL94-142 and the Individuals with Disabilities Education Act (IDEA) Amendments of 1998 and 2001 have encouraged the establishment of parental involvement programs. Today the No Child Left Behind (2002) Statutes mandate parental involvement:

> the participation of parents in regular, two way, and meaningful communication involving student academic learning and other school activities, including ensuring—
>
> - that parents play an integral role in assisting their child's learning;
> - that parents are encouraged to be actively involved in their child's education at school;
> - that parents are full partners in their child's education and are included, as appropriate, in decision-making and on advisory committees to assist in the education of their child; and
> - that other activities are carried out, such as those (described in section 1118 of the ESEA (Parental Involvement). [Section 9101(32), ESEA.] p. 3)

One approach to engage parents so that they become part of this integral role is the creation and maintenance of parental involvement programs. Although parental involvement programs have been in existence for many years, schools have not been as successful in reaching one parental segment: culturally and linguistically diverse parents. According to the National Center for Children in Poverty (NCCP), a large number of these families have low incomes and possess lower levels of formal education (NCCP, 2005). Additional data from the U.S. Census Bureau (2005) corroborate that English Language Learners (ELLs) are more likely than either bilingual or English monolingual children to live in families whose income is below 185 percent of the federal poverty threshold. In 2000, 65 percent of Limited English Proficient (LEP) children lived in poor families compared with 51 percent of bilingual children and 32 percent of English monolingual children (U.S. Census Bureau, 2005).

Linked factors that have contributed to the lack of success in promoting parent involvement and accessibility for these parents are language and cultural differences that act as barriers, cultural differences in the intensity of parents' involvement, and the quality of communications between school and parents (Nahari, Cheng, & Falquez, 1999).

Parental Involvement Definitions

While many researchers have focused on defining "parent involvement," the concept remains unclear and there is currently no standard definition. Rather, the term is used loosely and is understood in a number of ways. The No Child Left Behind Act (NCLB) in 2002 for first time established a statutory definition, even though parental involvement has been a component of most of the federal legislation funding. The NCLB (2002) furthermore mandates and authorizes the use of federal funds to support parental involvement:

[State Education Agencies (SEAs)] must encourage an LEA [(local education agencies)] and its schools receiving Title I, Part A funds to offer family literacy services (using Title I, Part A funds) if the LEA or school determines that a substantial number of Title I, Part A students have parents who do not have a secondary school diploma or its recognized equivalent or who have low levels of literacy. [Section 1111(c)(14), ESEA]

Title I, Part A funds can be used to support the full range of family literacy activities, including parenting education and educational services for adults who need improved literacy skills in order to support their children's learning, if the LEA has exhausted all other reasonably available sources of funding for those activities. [Section 1118(e)(7), ESEA]

The U.S. Department of Education, National Center for Education Statistics (Snyder, Tan, & Hoffman, 2005) defines parental involvement in school "as parent reported participation at least once during the school year in attending a general school meeting; attending a scheduled meeting with their child's teacher; attending a school event; or volunteering in the school or serving on a school committee." Jeynes (2005) explains parental involvement programs as school-sponsored initiatives that are designed to require or encourage parental participation in their children's education.

Hoard and Shepard (2005), in a review of the treatment efficacy of 16 parent education studies, make the distinction between parent education and parent training. They define parent training as an intervention for an existing condition, while parent education is defined as an intervention aimed at prevention. In their study, Hoard and Shepard found that, in the different programs they evaluated, as a school-based intervention, parent education showed a wide range of effectiveness (p. 451).

Epstein et al. (1995) describe parental involvement as a typology of several varieties of participatory activities, which include:

- involvement in assisting families with parenting skills and other activities that support child well being at home;
- providing different means of communication that make families aware about school programs, ensuring that parents obtain clear information about student progress;
- involvement of families as volunteers and audiences, making it possible for educators to utilize these volunteers for additional help and support to students and the school;
- supporting families in academic learning activities at home, including homework, goal setting, and other curriculum-related activities;
- incorporating families as part of school decisions, such as governance and improvement teams, and encouraging advocacy through state, school, and parent organizations; and
- establishing links with the community and bringing together resources and services for families, students, and the school with community businesses, agencies, cultural and civic organizations, colleges or universities, and other community groups.

Scribner and Scribner (2001) found that "parent involvement encompasses a multitude of complex phenomena. Differences in the family structure, culture, ethnic background, social class, age and gender represent only a few of the factors affecting interpretations of or generalizations about the nature of parent involvement" (p. 36). This definition points out that, as stated by Jackson and Hayes (1993), schools need to recognize the uniqueness of each family in terms of its ethnic heritage, attitudes, values, norms, customs, socioeconomic status, level of acculturation, language practices, belief systems, religious and lifestyle orientations, family structures, and involvement with extended family members. In addition, Kalyanpur and Harry (1997) suggest the adoption of "a posture of cultural reciprocity" that will allow the establishment of culturally inclusive partnerships and communities. Nonetheless, even with of all these different definitions, researchers continue to perceive parent involvement in terms of parental participation in school-based activities and parents' direct involvement with school (Garcia Coll et al., 2002).

What Do We Know About Parental Involvement?

The evidence that parental involvement activities enhance children's school success is well documented. A report prepared by the U.S. Department of Education Office of the Deputy Secretary (2001) indicates that:

> When third-grade teachers were especially active in outreach to low achievers' parents, students made faster gains in reading over the next 2 years, gaining 4.6 points more than students whose teachers made only an average amount of outreach. In addition, in schools where all third-grade teachers were especially active in outreach to low achievers' parents, students gained an additional 3.7 points by fifth grade. Third-grade classrooms with generally low achievement tended to be the ones in which teachers reported contacting more parents of low achievers. (p. 11)

Recently, in a meta-analysis of 41 studies, Jeynes (2005) examined the relationship between parental involvement and the academic achievement of urban elementary school children. Results indicated a significant relationship between parental involvement overall and academic achievement. Additional evidence is also found in parental involvement programs that help CLD students and their families. Fan and Chen (2001) and Marcon (1999) corroborate these findings on the benefits of parental involvement. In addition, training activities that allow for the development of parental skills and knowledge in working cooperatively with the school for the benefit of their children have demonstrated additional benefits. Indeed, these results place schools under a compelling need to restructure and engage in activities within the school and the community—in particular with parents. However, studies conducted with at-risk students also demonstrated lower average parental involvement among CLD, single, and low-socioeconomic status parents (Griffith, 1997). These findings indicate the need to focus on the cultural and social factors and issues that are most relevant to these diverse groups. Ideally, multicultural school psychologists can use their expertise in consultation and corroborative teamwork as a medium to help bring about this much-needed school and parental involvement.

Parent Training Models

The parent involvement training activities discussed in the following paragraphs involve mainstream parent groups. Among them are several programs that have led to the recognition of what the cultural context of families is made up of: (a) geography and climate; (b) history and origin of a population; (c) employment and religion; and (d) values and goals. This recognition, amongst other factors, has led to the implementation of successful parental involvement programs. The following review of varied parent training models is especially important for school psychologists, since an awareness of the different models will augment their knowledge-base repertoire for providing teacher and parent consultation. In addition, it is hoped that their advocacy will result in the replication of a parent training program in the schools they service.

Consultation Programs Directed at Parental Involvement

The International High School, New York City

A report describes the parental involvement in the International High School (IHS) as housing a diversity of educational backgrounds of the student population at the secondary level. Students' education varies from no previous schooling to some students who are on grade level but do not speak English. The staff developed a program to expand parental involvement by recruiting parents who were interested in learning about the school and to teach them about the dynamics of language development. These parents became experts about the school and its philosophy, and were supporters of the program. Parents at three school sites met and compared notes. Currently, they lead workshops for other parents on such topics as college and high school culture, the college admissions process, and adult ESL classes. Workshops are planned to accommodate parents' schedules and are usually scheduled for Saturdays or evenings. When parents visit the school, they can speak their native languages due to a resource bank of interpreters who can explain the school culture, procedures, and resources to parents. IHS involves parents in instruction and encourages them to act as translators and serve as representatives of the school at district meetings. Parents get stipends to work in classes as aides (U.S. Department of Education, 1996).

Roosevelt Elementary Magnet School, St. Paul, Minnesota

In this school, a team approach is used to serve a diverse community of Latino, Hmong, African American, Native American, and white students. The school's 12-member Action Team for Partnership (ATP) includes the principal, teachers, parents, grandparents, and community partners, who select and organize family involvement activities. The ATP held a "Girls' Night In," which gave third grade girls, mothers, and others a chance to hear women talk about their careers and the educational paths that led them there (Allen, 2005).

Na'Neelzhiin Ji Olta Dual Language Program, Cuba, New Mexico

This program serves a school with a population of 99 percent Navajo and 1 percent non-Navajo students in grades K through 8. The parental involvement includes a Parent Advisory Committee, school–home partnerships, parent orientation, parent–teacher conferences, and parent training. Parent trainings include computer training, a parent institute, engaged learning training, math training, guided reading, and accelerated reading. Parents are bussed to the training to ensure that transportation is not an obstacle to their participation (Herrin, Toledo, & Torres-Carrion, 2003).

Other Programs

Other programs involving psychologists as consultants have also been successful in the development and implementation of parental involvement programs. Koonce and Harper (2005) discuss a parental involvement consultation model that works with African American parents by constructing a positive collaborative relationship with families. This model of parental consultation was based on a triad where the school and the parent-child dyad were the consultees, and the consultant was a member of the Community Social Services Agency (CSSA) and/or the school psychologist. The thrust of the consultation process was aimed at strengthening interpersonal relations, teaching parents to use human relations strategies, and developing general behavioral management skills (Koonce & Harper, 2005).

Alvy (1994) describes a number of parenting training programs which use scaffolding to build parenting skills: Parenting Effectiveness Training (PET); Systematic Training for Effective Parenting (STEP); and Confident Parenting (CP). These programs are aimed at assisting parents "in building enjoyable relationships with their children and fostering a supportive environment that is supportive of the needs and growth of each family member" (p. 76). There have been several revisions to these programs, exploring culture-adapted versions, and using different mediums to teach and deliver the programs. The Center for the Improvement of Child Caring (CICC) created culturally adapted versions of these programs and has developed two culturally adapted versions of the Confident Parenting Program for the Afro-American and

Latino communities: Black Parenting: Strategies for Training; and Los Niños Bien Educados (Alvy, 1994). These two programs blend and integrate cultural themes with the teaching of basic parenting skills. (Further information on these programs is available at the Center for the Improvement of Child Caring at www.ciccparenting.org.)

Nahari, Cheng, and Falquez (1999) targeted parents of severely disabled CLD students. This model uses a collaborative format by which the psychologist assumes the role of "resource-collaborator" as suggested by Tyler, Pargament, and Gatz (1983). In this model, parents and child, as well as the school, are the consultees. The goals of this program were to empower and train parents in how to become active participants in their children's educational and psychological well-being.

Sheridan (2000) offers a conjoint consultation multicultural model that includes families who are multicultural and the school (teachers), with the intent of achieving positive changes in a student-client. Sheridan (2000) found that a trusting consultation, which includes the acknowledgment of diversity, making sure that there is complete understanding when language differences are present, and careful use of interpreters, is extremely important for the success of the consultation process (see Chapter 8 for more on consultation).

Overview of Competencies Needed to Provide Training to CLD Families and How to Increase Parental Involvement at the Home and School Level

Blue-Banning, Summers, Frankland, Nelson, and Beegle (2004), in their study of family-professional partnerships, developed six categories of themes crucial for successful parental involvement programs. These themes are:

1. *Communication*: positive, understandable (particularly for those non-English speakers), and respectful of all members at all levels of the partnership.

2. *Commitment:* The members of the partnership share a sense of allegiance to the child and family, and the desire to accomplish the goals of the program.

3. *Equality:* Participants need to feel a sense that decisions are made by all parties involved, and all members feel the capability of influencing the outcomes.

4. *Skills:* The ability of school partners to provide training to the parents and to students with special needs, and an open mind to learn from the parents as well.

5. *Trust:* The ability of the partners to rely on each other and be sure of the truthfulness of their relationship.

6. *Respect:* Partners respect cultural diversity, respect privacy and the value of the child and the family. (p. 174)

Furthermore, multicultural psychologists involved in the planning of parental involvement programs need to address cultural diversity by adopting a "posture of cultural reciprocity" (Kalyanpur & Harry, 1997).

Consultation and educational literature also discuss the necessary competencies to service multicultural populations. Harris (1998) delineates four salient competencies recommended by consultants to address the needs of multicultural populations:

- understanding one's culture and its relationship to others' cultures;
- use of effective interpersonal and communicative skills;
- understanding the roles of collaborators; and
- using appropriate assessment and instructional strategies (p. 333).

Lynch (1998) suggests the following three major areas of competencies needed to maintain a collaborative partnership between service providers and parents.

1. *Self-awareness:* To understand and appreciate other cultures service providers need to understand their own culture.

2. *Cultural-specific awareness and understanding:* Learning about other cultures through readings, interaction and involvement.

3. *Communication issues, including working with interpreters and translators:* Communication—both verbal and non-verbal—is critical to cross-cultural competency. Making sure that language barriers are broken and both sending and understanding messages are "prerequisites to effective interpersonal interactions" (Lynch, 1998, pp. 47–75)

Multicultural school psychologists need to increase personal awareness of their own cultures and values as the starting point "for developing sensitivity to the diverse linguistic and cultural backgrounds, attitudes, and customs of the children and youth with whom they work and their families" (Sileo, Sileo, & Prater, 1996).

The data obtained by the several studies reviewed above present a very strong argument for the influence of families in academic achievement, as well as in the overall life of children. In addition, the evidence points directly to the benefits of school, community, and family partnerships in the support of learning.

Different research studies (Henderson & Mapp, 2002; Blue-Banning et al., 2004; Jeynes, 2005; Koonce & Harper, 2005; Nahari et al., 1999) note a number of themes common to successful training and parental involvement programs. These comprise some of the benchmarks that should be followed by educators, school psychologists, and other professionals attempting to design and implement training programs for parents. These include:

- determination of what parents expect from schools;
- maintenance of ongoing training programs in which parents and staff are learners;
- acknowledgment by school personnel that sharing power with parents is an opportunity to understand parents' interests and goals for their children;
- home–school collaborative programs directed at CLD families; these need to view parental involvement as a developmental process of actualizing the parent's potential;
- identification and utilization of parents' strengths and expertise for the benefit of their family and themselves—for example, workshops for parents on how to help their children at home;
- consistent teacher outreach to parents. This could include face-to-face meetings, sending materials home, and keeping in touch about progress;
- recognition of, and respect for, class and cultural differences;
- the ability to share responsibility;
- creation of programs that are practical and meaningful to the parents.

In addition to the above themes, additional interventive suggestions are presented below to further assist school practitioners in the design and implementation of training programs for parents.

The principal needs to demonstrate a very strong and clear commitment to family-school collaboration, and this commitment needs to be shared with the school staff and the parents. A second integral component of successful partnerships is the involvement of the staff in training activities that create awareness of the acculturation processes, the stresses of immigration and the burden on immigrant families and children, and finally training for staff on techniques for using parents as volunteers in the classrooms. A third key element is the identification of resources within the community and the establishment of a level of cooperation in which there is respect for each collaborating member. The final key element is the participation of the students during planned training activities for the parents. In this type of interaction, the parents act as models for their children, who can then observe the importance of learning and their parents' interest in school.

In conclusion, both schools and families share a vested interest in the academic success of children, and clearly the participation of the parents in supporting their children's achievements is a necessary step to increase the effectiveness of schools in working with all families, but particularly those of multicultural backgrounds. A psychologist is described by National Association of School Psychologists' (NASP) *Guidelines for the Provision of School Psychological Services* (NASP, 2000a) as a practitioner who is aware of family influences and active in the role of program development to promote home–school partnerships. Therefore, involvement by psychologists in parent education programs, as well as other type of supporting services to increase parenting success, is important.

Practical Suggestions to Establish and Maintain Parental Involvement Programs for Multicultural Parents and Families

Most parents, as mentioned before, want to be involved with the schools, care about the education of their children, and are looking for ways to contribute. Based on the findings discussed earlier, this section will provide a number of practical tips that can be used effectively in the process of reaching out to CLD parents.

1. Create reliable systems of communications (Greenough, 2007), such as:
   - maintaining a bilingual newsletter, where classroom happenings, special events, and projects can be shared with the parents. Articles can be written by the children, teachers or the parents;
   - telephone use to communicate often with parents. Telephone calls can be a valuable tool of communication and should be used to share both positive as well as negative events. These might be brief teacher-recorded messages encouraging parents to help their children learn the basic skills, or short messages with some suggestion for activities at home. These messages can be recorded by teachers in other languages to be made available to those parents who do not speak English;
   - translating communications that the school sends home;
   - giving parents a list of names and phone numbers of bilingual staff in the school and district who they can contact to deal with educational concerns.

2. Implement services that support parent participation by:
   - providing child care or transportation to attend parental involvement meetings;
   - offering workshops on Saturdays or evenings for working parents;
   - polling parents about their interests in different potential areas of training.

   A parent questionnaire can be an effective way to obtain comprehensive information on the target population (see Appendix 9.1 for a sample questionnaire in Spanish and English).

3. Educate parents in the U.S. school system and culture (Calderón & Minaya-Row, 2003) by:

- providing information on school routines, administrative school structure, curricula, and standards;
- establishing teachers' and schools' expectations of parents, such as their involvement in homework, visiting the public library or at times providing tutors for their children;
- understanding parents' rights, No Child Left Behind, and IDEAA;
- making special programs available in the school for gifted children, special education, and so on (Colorín Colorado, 2007).

Appendix 9.2 provides a sample assessment profile that can be used to compile information gathered from the survey for planning future training sessions for the parents. Finally, Appendix 9.3 contains a number of suggested topics for parental training activities. In addition to the training offered on the survey, a number of other topics can be included, such as special education, positive behavioral interventions, planning for college, advocacy and leadership skills, family math, and improvement of reading.

In conclusion, a psychologist is described by the *Guidelines for the Provision of School Psychological Services* (NASP, 2000a) as a practitioner who is aware of family influences and active in the role of program development to promote home–school partnerships. However, both schools and families share a vested interest in the academic success of children, and clearly the participation of parents in supporting their children's achievements is essential. In addition—though not of less importance—is the awareness that little preservice and inservice training is dedicated to preparing staff for the variety of parent and family interactions. Therefore, to increase the odds of success, consultation services should be implemented by school psychologists to help teachers, school administrators, and staff establish welcoming environments that provide strong, healthy lines of communication, respect educational and cultural differences, and are able to collaborate to ensure positive learning situations and academic success for all children.

Additional Resources

Parent Information Regional Centers (PIRCs) provide parents, schools, and organizations working with families with training, information, and technical assistance to understand how children develop and what they need to succeed in school. They work closely with parents, educators, and community organizations to strengthen partnerships so that children can reach high academic standards. The different regional centers can be accessed at www.pirc-info.net.

The National Coalition for Parent Involvement in Education (NCPIE) supports parent and family involvement initiatives at the national level and conducts activities that are directed to increase family involvement. In addition, it provides resources and legislative information to help organizations promote parent and family involvement. It is located at 3929 Old Lee Highway, Suite 91-A, Fairfax, VA 22030-2401; Phone: 703-359-8973; Fax: 703-359-0972; Website: www.ncpie.org.

Sinergia, in New York City, operates two Parent Training Information Centers (PTI), the Metropolitan Parent Center (MPC) and the Long Island Parent Center (LIPC). The MPC provides an array of trainings on site, involving current issues of interest to parents of students with disabilities (whether classified or suspected). These include all special education issues. Simultaneous interpretation (Spanish/English) for most training is available. Assistance is provided to grassroots parent organizations to strengthen and empower parent groups in their local communities.

The National Parent Teachers Association works in cooperation with many national education, health, safety, and child advocacy groups and federal agencies. National PTA collaborates on projects that benefit children and that bring valuable resources to its members. The organization can be reached at National PTA Washington DC Office, 1090 Vermont Ave. NW, Suite 1200, Washington, DC 20005-4905; Phone: (202) 289-6790; Fax: (202) 289-6791; Hotline: (888) 425-5537; Website: www.pta.org.

The Harvard Family Research Project's (HFRP) work strengthens family, school, and community partnerships and early childhood care and education, promotes evaluation and accountability, and offers professional development to those who work directly with children, youth, and families. The audiences for HFRP's work include policy makers, practitioners, philanthropists, and concerned individuals. Contact the project at Harvard Family Research Project, 3 Garden Street, Cambridge, MA 02138. Phone: 617-495-9108; Fax: 617-495-8594; Website: www.gse.harvard.edu.

The School-Family Partnership Lab at Vanderbilt University is dedicated to the scientific investigation of the reciprocal relationships among families, schools, and children. This project offers information on papers and measures developed during the course of its research on the parental involvement process. The Family-School Partnership Lab is part of the Psychology and Human Development Department, Peabody College, Vanderbilt University. More information is available at www.vanderbilt.edu/Peabody/family-school.

References

Allen, R. (2005). New paradigms for parental involvement: Stronger family role in schools seen as key to achievement. *Education Update, 42*(3), 3–5.

Alvy, K. T. (1994). *Parent training today.* Studio City, CA: Center for the Improvement of Child Caring.

Bermúdez, A. B., & Marquéz, J. A. (1996). An examination of a four way collaborative to increase parental involvement in the schools. *The Journal of Educational Issues of Language Minorities Students, Special Issue, 16,* 1–16.

Blue-Banning, M., Summers, J. A., Frankland, H. C., Nelson, L. L., & Beegle, G. (2004). Dimensions of family and professional partnerships: Constructive guidelines for collaboration. *Exceptional Children, 70*(2), 167–184.

Calderon, M. E., & Minaya-Rowe, L. (2003). *Designing and implementing two-way bilingual programs: A step-by-step guide for administrators, teachers, and parents.* Thousand Oaks, CA: Corwin Press.

Careaga, R. (Comp.). (1988). *Parental involvement: A resource for the education of limited English proficient students.* Program Information Guide Series NCBE No. 8. Washington, DC: National Clearing House for English Language Acquisition (NCELA).

Colorín Colorado. (2007). How to reach out to parents of ELLs. Retrieved on June 20, 2007, from www.colorincolorado.org/educators/reachingout/outreach

Epstein, J. L., Swap, S. M., Bright, A., Hidalgo, N. M., & Siu, S. F. (1995). Research on families, schools, and communities: A multicultural perspective. In J. A. Banks, & C. A. Banks (Eds.), *Handbook of multicultural research* (pp. 498–524). New York: Simon and Schuster Macmillan.

Fan, X., & Chen, M. (2001). Parental involvement and students' academic achievement: A meta-analysis. *Educational Psychology Review, 13*(1), 1–22.

Garcia Coll, C. T., Akiba, D., Palacios, N., Bailey, B., Silver, R., DiMartino, L., & Chin, C. (2002). Parental involvement in children's education: Lessons from three immigrant groups. *Parenting: Science and Practice, 2*(3), 303–324

Griffith, J. (1997). Linkages of school structural and socio-environmental characteristics to parental satisfaction with public education and student academic achievement *Journal of Applied Social Psychology, 27*(2), 156–186.

Greenough, R. (2007). A place at the table: Parent involvement activities. *Northwest Education, 12*(3). Retrieved June 20, 2007, from www.nwrel.org/nwedu/index.php

Harris, J. R. (1998). *The nurture assumption.* New York: Free Press.

Harrison, P. L., Cummings, J. A., Dawson, M., Short, R. J., Gorin, S., & Palomares, R. (2004). Responding to the needs of children, families, and schools: The 2002 Multisite Conference on the Future of School Psychology. *School Psychology Review, 33*(1), 12-33.

Henderson, A., & Mapp, K. L. (2002). *A new wave of evidence: The impact of school, family, and community connections on student achievement.* Austin,TX: Southwest Educational Development Laboratory.

Herrin, J., Toledo, K., & Torres-Carrion, T. (2003). Paper presented at the Special Session for Native American and Alaska Native Children in School Grantees. Washington, DC: OELA Summit 2003. Retrieved August 29, 2005 from www.ncela.gwu.edu/oela/summit2003/SummitSummaries.htm.

Hoard, D., & Shepard, K. (2005). Parent education as parent-centered prevention: A review of school-related outcomes. *School Psychology Quarterly, 20*(4). New York: Guilford Press.

Jackson, D. N., & Hayes, H. D. (1993). Multicultural issues in consultation. *Journal of Counseling and Development, 72,* 144–147.

Jeynes, W. H. (2005). A meta-analysis of the relation of parental involvement to urban elementary school student academic achievement. *Urban Education, 40*(3), 237–69.

Kalyanpur, M., & Harry, B. (1997). A posture of reciprocity: A practical approach to collaboration between professionals and parents of culturally diverse backgrounds. *Journal of Child and Family Studies, 6,* 487–509.

Koonce, D. A., & Harper, W. (2005). Engaging African American parents in the schools: A community-based consultation model. *Journal of Educational & Psychological Consultation, 16*(1&2), 55–74.

Lynch, E. (1998). Developing cross-cultural competence. In E. W. Lynch & M. J. Hanson (Eds.), *Developing cross-cultural competence: A guide for working with young children and their families* (2nd ed.; pp. 47–75). Baltimore, MD: Paul H. Brookes.

Marcon, L. A. (1999). Positive relationships between parent school involvement and public school inner-city preschoolers' development and academic performance. *School Psychology Review, 28*(3), 395–412.

Nahari, S. (1999). Conducting cross-cultural consultation with parents of students with severe disabilities. In E. Vazquez-Nutall (Chair), *Cross-cultural consultation themes.* Symposium conducted at the annual meeting of the American Psychological Association, Boston.

Nahari, S., Cheng, S., & Falquez, A. (1999). Enhancing the school involvement of culturally diverse students with severe disabilities. *The School Psychologist,* newsletter of the American Psychological Association, Division 16.

National Association of School Psychologists (NASP). (2000a). *Guidelines for the provision of school psychological services.* Washington, DC: NASP.

National Association of School Psychologists (NASP). (2000b). *Standards for Training and Field Placement Programs in School Psychology Standards for the Credentialing of School Psychologists.* Washington, DC: NASP.

National Center for Children in Poverty (NCCP) (2005). Basic facts about low-income children: Birth to age 18. Retrieved August 29, 2005, from www.nccp.org/pub_lic05.html.

Santarelli, G., Koegel, R. L., Casas, J. M., & Koegel, L. K. (2001). Culturally diverse families participating in behavior therapy parent education programs for children with developmental disabilities. *Journal of Positive Behavior Interventions, 3*(2), 120–126.

Scribner, A. P., & Scribner, J. D. (2001). High-performing schools serving Mexican American students: What they can teach us. *ERIC Digest*. (ERIC Document Reproduction Service No. ED459048).

Sheridan, S. M. (2000). Considerations of multiculturalism and diversity in behavioral consultation with parents and teachers. *School Psychology Review*, 29(3), 344–353.

Sileo, T. W., Sileo, A., & Prater, P. (1996). Parent and professional partnerships in special education: Multicultural considerations. *Intervention in School & Clinic*, 31(3), 145–154.

Snyder, T. D., Tan, A. G., & Hoffman, C. M. (2005). *Digest of education statistics, 2005*. Washington, DC: U.S. Department of Education, National Center for Education Statistics.

Tyler, F. B., Pargament, K. I., & Gatz, M. (1983). The resource collaborator role. *American Psychologist, 38,* 388–397.

U.S. Census Bureau. (2005). *American Community Survey Reports (ACS-02): Income, earnings, and poverty.* Washington, DC: U.S. Government Printing Office. Retrieved on July 7, 2007, from http://factfinder.census.gov/servlet/IPCharIterationServlet?_lang=en&_ts=227962308015

U.S. Department of Education, Office of Bilingual Education and Minority Languages Affairs (OBEMLA). (1996). *Final report: A descriptive study of the ESEA TITLE VII educational services provided for secondary school limited English proficient students.* Retrieved August 30, 2005, from www.ncela.gwu.edu/pubs/devtech/secondary

U.S. Department of Education. (1998). *To assure the free appropriate public education of all children with disabilities: Twentieth annual report to Congress on the Implementation of the Individuals with Disabilities Education Act.* Washington, DC: U.S. Department of Education.

U.S. Department of Education. (2001). *To assure the free appropriate public education of all children with disabilities: Twenty-Third annual report to Congress on the Implementation of the Individuals with Disabilities Education Act.* Washington, DC: U.S. Department of Education.

U.S. Department of Education. (2004). *Title I Part A Non-Regulatory Guidance.* Retrieved August 2, 2005 from www.ed.gov/programs/titleiparta/parentinvguid.pdf.

U.S. Department of Education, Office of the Deputy Secretary, Planning and Evaluation Service. (2001). *The longitudinal evaluation of school change and performance in Title I schools, Volume 1: Executive summary*, Washington, DC: U.S. Department of Education. Retrieved February 2, 2006 from www.ed.gov/offices/OUS/PES/esed/lescp_vol1.pdf.

Appendix 9.1. Parent Survey: Sample Questionnaire

We want to provide the best school program possible to your child. To do that, we need you to be an important part of it. We would like to know more about your family, how you feel about the program, and the kind of information you would like us to provide about the school. With this information, we can improve the way we work with you. You can help us develop the program by answering the following questions.

Parent names	
Address	
Phone	

Children's names		Grade/age	
		Grade/age	
		Grade/age	

A. Basic Information Questions

How long have you lived in the U.S.? _____

What language do you generally speak at home with your children?

_____

With your spouse? _____

Do you have a job? _____

What is the most convenient time for you to visit school or come to a meeting? _____

What level of education have you completed?

Elementary _____ High School _____

College/University _____

In order to participate in school activities, please check what times and days would you prefer (check all that apply)

Monday _____   Tuesday _____   Wednesday _____

Thursday _____   Friday _____   Saturday _____

Mornings _____   Afternoons _____   Evenings _____

To participate in parent activities, which would you prefer? (Check all that apply)

____ on-site babysitting   ____ a neighbor to accompany you

____ transportation   ____ an interpreter

B. Bilingual/ESL Program

1. Do you know what the purpose of the bilingual/ESL program is?

    Yes _____   No _____

2. Do you feel the program is helping your child in:
    - reading?   Yes _____   No _____
    - mathematics?   Yes _____   No _____
    - English?   Yes _____   No _____

3. Have you ever met with your child's teacher?

    Yes _____   No _____

4. Have you ever attended any bilingual/ESL parent meetings?

    Yes _____   No _____

C. Interests

Would you like to participate in a parent-school program to learn more about:

what your child learns in school?	Yes _____	No _____
how to help your child with schoolwork?	Yes _____	No _____
volunteering to help in the classroom?	Yes _____	No _____
school decision-making activity?	Yes _____	No _____
how the American schools are different from your native country's schools?	Yes _____	No _____
community resources services available?	Yes _____	No _____

Would you like to:

visit your child's classes?	Yes _____	No _____
come to school to a meeting to learn more about the program?	Yes _____	No _____
volunteer in the classroom?	Yes _____	No _____
participate on a parent advisory committee?	Yes _____	No _____
talk to other parents about the program?	Yes _____	No _____

Thank you.

Appendix 9.2. Assessment Profile

Parent Name: _____

Child Name: _____

Complete the grid below to ascertain the numbers of interested parents by topic and similarities.

Children's ages	Under 5 ___	5–7 ____	8–11 ____	12–15 ____	15+ ____
Grade levels	pre-K ____	K ____	1–5 ____	6–8 ____	9–12 ____
Length of residence	less than 1 year	1–5 years	6–10 years	more than 10 years	
Language spoken at home	English	Spanish	Haitian-Creole	Chinese	Hmong

Preferred Time for Meeting	Monday	Tuesday	Wednesday	Thursday	Friday	Saturday
Morning						
Afternoon						
Evening						

	Interest Areas			
	General information	Parent as tutor/learner	Community services	Active participation in parent action committee (PAC)
Number of Parents				

Appendix 9.3. Sample Informational Meeting Plans

Goal 1: To orient the parents to the American school system. Parents will become aware of some of the major differences between schools in their native land and the U.S. system. Special emphasis will be on the importance of the role of parent involvement in American schools.

	Objective	*Activities*	*Materials/Resources*
1.	Inform parents about activities in a regular school day	Show parents a slide presentation of several classes participating in a variety of school activities Discuss the objectives of these activities	Slide presentation, samples of student work
2.	Familiarize parents with the similarities and differences between schools in the USA and their native countries	Discuss the differences in structure of program, focus of activities and increased role of parent interacting with school staff	Comparative chart
3.	Orient parents to the idea of closer interaction with school staff	Inform parents of their role in education and how increased interaction with the school helps to develop better programs	Parent handbook, report cards, student folders

Goal 2: To encourage parents to reinforce and extend children's native language skills through activities in the home. Parents will become acquainted with the importance of developing strong native language skills and learn how to provide experiences which promote the development of these skills in the home.

	Objective	*Activities*	*Materials/Resources*
1.	Inform parents of the importance of developing strong native language skills	Invite parents to a meeting at which discussion will focus on benefits of strong native language skill development, both through demonstration lessons of skill transfer and through discussion	Manipulative needed for language lesson, tape recorder, fact sheet
2.	Identify for parents some games, songs, and play activities that are appropriate for children to promote skills development	Invite parents to an open house where they will be able to preview books and records and try out equipment, which can be borrowed and used in the home for further native language skill development	Song sheets, games, books, toys and other manipulatives that can be used in the home
3.	Teach parents how to apply basic principles of learning discussed for home activities such as story-reading/telling	Present a demonstration of simple activities and story-telling techniques that employ basic principles that parents can follow in the home	School library books, pictures, magazines, children's drawings

SOURCE: Adapted from Careaga (1988).

PART IV

Special Topics

10

Acculturation

Almost 20 percent of children in the United States are the offspring of immigrants. Children who are immigrants or American-born progeny of immigrants numbered 13.7 million in 1997 (cited in Drugger, 1998). Many of these children are from Central America, Asia, Russia, and other Eastern European countries. Historically, immigrants have not always been welcomed to the United States, specifically by citizens who give preferentiality to controls on immigration and perceive them to be a threat to the dominant culture and to our society's economic strength (Simcox, 1997). For immigrants seeking to find a new life in our country, this biased and offensive belief often brings about feelings of isolation and acculturation problems. Consequently, children of immigrants are propelled into two worlds, and repeatedly encounter conflicts between their own cultural values and those of the dominant culture. The collision of two cultures often has adverse effects on both children and adolescents. Another important factor to consider is that not all racial/ethnic groups in the United States have recently immigrated. Some have had their roots in American society for decades and/or centuries, and continue to have similar experiences that lead to acculturation stress—especially those who are perceived as "minority" groups.

Researchers have found that transition to the Western culture for Asians can disrupt the family's hierarchical structure, interdependence, and self-identity among young Asians; this is sometimes attributed to drug use (James, Kim, & Moore, 1997). Moreover, Latino American families have been found to view education as the job of the school and consider it rude to intrude on a teacher's judgment (Espinosa, 1995). This can cause an educator or school psychologist to misconstrue a parent's silence or lack of initiative in communicating with school personnel. School psychologists must be aware that not all Latino American families follow the same communication and socialization styles, and that there are differences between as well as within racial/ethnic groups (Haycock & Duany, 1991; James, Kim, & Moore, 1997; Matsumoto, 2000). Lack of cultural knowledge of a child's family will lead to false assumptions that may lead to misclassification and inappropriate treatment interventions. In order to remedy the plight of immigrant children (whether first, second, or third generation), educators and school psychologists must gain an understanding of the immigrant child's culture and the impact of immigration on the family.

Because, in the United States, schools are more culturally diverse than ever, it is highly likely that a school psychologist will encounter children manifesting cultural identity conflicts and acculturative stress. Furthermore, many of these children come from estranged families and from countries in which ethnic violence, genocide, or persecution thrive. If children who have experienced such traumas, or recent migration, are referred for a special education evaluation, the school psychologist must first determine the validity of the referral and proceed by assessing the cultural identity and acculturation levels of the child and family. This is a vital professional competency that cannot be overlooked by the practitioner. Unfortunately, unless university trainers intentionally address cultural identity and acculturation in a school psychology, counseling, and/or assessment course, these important areas of concern are often not part of the practitioner's repertoire of knowledge.

With this apprehension in mind, this chapter reviews acculturation and its relation to cultural identity. Recently recommended guidelines for assessing acculturation and cultural identity are presented. The chapter also includes a brief overview of racial/ethnic identity development although further coverage of these models, and their related assessment scales are reviewed in Chapter 12. In addition, child abuse and neglect, school dropout, and substance abuse (all of which have been linked with minority and immigrant racial/ethnic groups and which can affect the acculturation process) are examined briefly.

Cultural Identity

As highlighted throughout this text, there are numerous racial/ethnic groups which have immigrated to the United States. School psychologists working with various groups of children will find that some of them will be recently arrived first-generation émigrés as well as second- or third-generation immigrants. Therefore, each child will have a special family and educational history and language development. For the recently arrived child, the progression of second language acquisition must be examined, since learning a second language is closely linked to the acculturation process. For the second- and third-generation child, background history will be different, since acculturation and language development will have followed a different path that hopefully has led to absolute acculturation within the U.S. culture, in addition to monolingual or bilingual language development. As previously mentioned, there are differences in the various generations of immigrants. For these reasons, assessing a child's cultural identity will assist in understanding several important variables that may affect the acculturation process.

Since culture consists of the beliefs, customs, accomplishments, language, and history of a group discernible by its members' habitual behaviors (Brislin, 2000; Gopaul-McNicol & Armour-Thomas, 2002; Kim & Abreu, 2001; Matsumoto, 2000; Roysircar-Sodowsky & Maestes, 2000), it is no wonder that cultural identity is vital to an individual's overall psychological well-being. The social and emotional implications of culture affect cognitions, feelings, and ultimately self-esteem. Cultural identity theory does not focus on distinguishing the individual's identity on a continuum between the dominant and non-dominant culture. Instead, the theory views individual attitudes toward the dominant and non-dominant culture as connective, and suggests that particular *clusters* of attitudes toward *both* cultures define cultural identity status at a specific point in time in an individual's development (Helms, 1995). In other words, an individual's *stage* of cultural identity may shift from a particular worldview, causing a better or worse appreciation of either culture or a healthy combination of both (Gushue & Sciarra, 1995).

In the past two decades, numerous cultural identity assessment methods have emerged which have emphasized the use of both quantitative and qualitative tools for practitioners (see Ponterotto, Gretchen, & Chauhan, 2001, pp. 67–99).

Cultural identity is closely associated with ethnic identity and acculturation. Takushi and Uomoto (2001) explain that, "Although cultural and ethnic identity refers to the outcome of integrating the cultural values of both the group of origin and the majority group, acculturation focuses on the process of psychological change in values, beliefs and behaviors when adapting to a new culture" (p. 53). Central to cultural identity is the evaluation of the individual's worldview and level of acculturation. Both of these interrelate with the individual's psychological identity process, which is affected by cultural variables. Thus, when estimating acculturation stress, it is necessary to assess child and parent cultural and racial/ethnic identity. Since racial/ethnic identity formation may include psychological conflicts, acculturation stress most likely will affect cultural and racial/ethnic development (Casas & Pytluk, 1995).

Racial/Ethnic Identity Development Models

In the last several decades, racial/ethnic identity development models have propelled various scales, which have been developed for African Americans, Whites, Native American/Indians, Asian Americans, Latina/Latinos, and Jewish

Americans (Fischer & Moradi, 2001). In addition to developing competency in the various models and scales available, school psychologists should have knowledge of the four major racial/ethnic groups in the United States and their differences. Expertise in this area is essential during the evaluative process, and for determining appropriate assessment methods and counseling interventions for culturally and linguistically diverse and racial/ethnic children (see Pedersen & Carey, 2003; Ponterotto, Casas et al., 2001, for an in-depth review of various racial/ethnic identity models and how various groups differ).

Racial/ethnic identity developmental models have focused on the importance of developing a healthy self-concept and positive intercultural attitudes. The study of racial/ethnic identity models has aided in the understanding of the existence of distinct developmental identity stages and the likelihood of prejudicial encounters with, or beliefs, biases, and attitudes toward, one's own ethnic group or the white majority group. Although the models differ in terms of the number of stages of racial/ethnic identity development, certain generic themes can be taken from all of these models. Compressing stages across different models has elicited four commonly observed themes or stages found to be prevalent in the minority identity models (Ponterotto & Pedersen, 1993). The four stages are:

1. identification;

2. awareness, encounter, and search;

3. identification and immersion; and

4. integration and internalization.

In the first stage, there is identification with the majority culture (i.e., white). The extent of the intensity of this identification can vary; however, there is the risk that an individual may develop a more overt identification with the majority culture, thereby disowning one's own racial or ethnic group. Stage two is highlighted by an evaluation and probing of previously adopted white majority preferences and attitudes. During this stage, minority adolescents begin to question their role as minorities in a racist society and begin to seek their own racial/ethnic identity. Such a search can be spurred even by a single brusque confrontation resulting from a racist experience or by an accumulation of more subtle oppressive experiences. The consequences of this stage include having to confront emotions of confusion and indignation. Furthermore, it has been demonstrated that this stage precipitates an overall diminution in psychological well-being with a concomitant degree of depression and lower degrees of educational independence. Consequently, the incidence of high self-esteem has been noted at this stage as well.

According to Ponterotto and Pedersen (1993), it can be hypothesized that confusion of one's racial group in comparison with other racial groups at this stage is generally prominent. Individuals at this stage may begin to develop a "positive prejudice" toward their own racial/ethnic group and a congruent negative discrimination toward the white majority group. Such individuals can be ambiguous about affiliations with other minority groups. At times, they may feel dwarfed in regard to the white majority group's system and prefer to align themselves with their own racial group. It is quite probable that individuals in this stage are forming racial/ethnic prejudices; however, they may not be so completely developed as to be easily converted into racism and its ensuing behaviors (see Chapter 12 on prejudice reduction).

Stage three depicts individuals who have sought their own racial/ethnic identity (a process beginning at stage two) in the full immersion process of accepting their own racial/ethnic cultural roots. These individuals are more prone to assiduously sanction the norms, values, and customs of their own racial/ethnic group. Concomitantly, they may totally disavow the values and norms associated with the mainstream society system. At this stage, resistance and denial, or both, may be experienced. It is a stage of intense emotionality, often evidenced by anger and rage at the majority group, congruent with a more or less apotheosized view of their own racial/ethnic group. Psychologically, the research findings indicate that this stage tends to bring about symptoms of low self-esteem, an elevated degree of anxiety, and feelings of inferiority. Additionally, this high level of the full immersion of attitudes was found to correlate with a lessening of intimacy, educational independence, and mature interpersonal relationships (Ponterotto & Pedersen, 1993).

In the final stage, individuals begin to reevaluate through introspection and the intense emotions of the previous stage (which resulted in negative prejudices toward the majority group and positive prejudices toward their own racial/ethnic group) and develop a more balanced bicultural identity. This final stage results in the development of a positive racial/ethnic identity blended with an affinity for other cultures. The main characteristic of this final stage is that a bicultural or multicultural identity development is ingrained and fully appreciated by the individual.

From a psychological perspective, individuals at this stage experience higher self-esteem and an overall sound psychological realignment. The major advantage of this enhanced psychological wellness and bicultural identity is that it results in more frequent participation in both cultural and noncultural activities and associations, which aids in the ongoing perpetuation of biculturalism. This "integrated" stage model is applicable to African Americans, Asian Americans, and Mexican Americans.

The major point for school psychologists to consider is the importance of learning about racial/ethnic identity development and its varied psychological repercussions. They must also attempt to reach their level of absolute approval and respect for the entire spectrum of racial/ethnic groups. When assessing cultural identity, it is important to become informed about the different racial/ethnic developmental stages with the aim of determining what stage the vulnerable student has reached and what psychological distress may be associated with it.

Cultural Identity Assessment

It is also important to recognize that a child's cultural socializations are part of their cultural identity formation. In our own Western culture, children tend to relate more to an independent individual cultural identity, whereas in Eastern cultures it is more a group identity formation (Lu, Lim, & Mezzich, 1995). Gopaul-McNicol and Armour-Thomas (2002) have accentuated the importance of cultural identity and Helms' (1985) three-stage model of cultural identity. Similar to the above integrated model, Helms' cultural identity stages are the *pre-counter*—in which individuals are still emerged in the Eurocentric worldview (i.e., the Western culture); the *transitional*—in this stage, individuals reidentify with their native culture; and the *transcendent*—when individuals become even more bicultural and employ the experiences from both cultural groups that most suit their personal circumstances. An analysis of the stages of cultural and racial/ethnic identity will help the school psychologist in the assessment of the personality and emotional functioning of the culturally diverse child. With an emphasis on cultural identity, Gopaul-McNicol and Armour-Thomas (2002) have compiled a list of critical areas they view as important to examine in assessing the personality and emotional functioning of culturally diverse children. Their suggestions are replicated in the box.

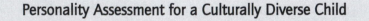

Personality Assessment for a Culturally Diverse Child

1. Migration history:
   - Country of origin
   - Individual, family, and community support
   - Individual and family educational level
   - Individual and family socioeconomic status
   - Reasons for migrating
   - Which family members or close friends were left behind?
   - Any traumatic experiences prior to migration?

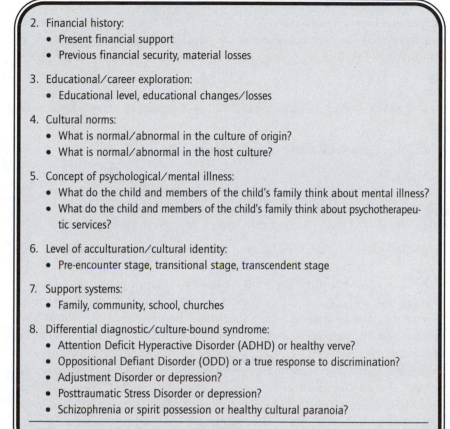

2. Financial history:
   - Present financial support
   - Previous financial security, material losses

3. Educational/career exploration:
   - Educational level, educational changes/losses

4. Cultural norms:
   - What is normal/abnormal in the culture of origin?
   - What is normal/abnormal in the host culture?

5. Concept of psychological/mental illness:
   - What do the child and members of the child's family think about mental illness?
   - What do the child and members of the child's family think about psychotherapeutic services?

6. Level of acculturation/cultural identity:
   - Pre-encounter stage, transitional stage, transcendent stage

7. Support systems:
   - Family, community, school, churches

8. Differential diagnostic/culture-bound syndrome:
   - Attention Deficit Hyperactive Disorder (ADHD) or healthy verve?
   - Oppositional Defiant Disorder (ODD) or a true response to discrimination?
   - Adjustment Disorder or depression?
   - Posttraumatic Stress Disorder or depression?
   - Schizophrenia or spirit possession or healthy cultural paranoia?

SOURCE: Gopaul-McNicol and Armour-Thomas (2002).

This checklist can be used at the inception of a formal or informal assessment. Depending on the child's age, some of the necessary information may have to be requested or obtained from school records, teachers, and parents when appropriate, and always with respect for the privacy and knowledge of the norms of the particular culture of the child being evaluated.

Semistructured Interview Protocols

Although quantitative measures have been constructed for assessing cultural and racial/ethnic identity and acculturative stress, practitioners often prefer to revert to qualitative methods. The semistructured interview is deemed an appropriate procedure to evaluate cultural and racial/ethnic identity and acculturation levels and/or stress (Ponterotto, Gretchen, & Chauhan, 2001; Gopaul-McNicol & Armour-Thomas, 2002; Sciarra, 2001).

There are various *interview protocols* that have been developed specifically for cultural identity assessment. The contents of the protocols were reviewed and integrated into six frameworks for practice (Ponterotto, Gretchen, & Chauhan, 2001). The six frameworks described in Ponterotto et al. (2001) are:

1. DSM-IV Outline for Cultural Formulation (American Psychiatric Association, 1994);

2. Dana's (1998) Cultural Assessment Model;

3. Jacobsen's (1988) Ethnocultural Assessment;

4. Washington's (1994) Wittgensteinian Model;

5. Grieger and Ponterotto's (1995) Applied Assessment Framework; and

6. Berg-Cross and Takushi-Chinen's (1995) Person-in-Culture Interview.

Each of these six models adopts a slightly different perspective on how to interview and counsel the culturally diverse client (i.e., psychodynamic, humanistic, family systems, and existential). Ponterotto et al. (2001) have compressed the strengths of each model's contributions into a *Holistic Idiographic Framework for Practice* (see box) which they recommend using during the initial interview and ongoing counseling sessions with culturally diverse clients (for a thorough review, see APA, 1994; Berg-Cross & Takushi-Chinen, 1995; Dana, 1998; Grieger & Ponterotto, 1995; Jacobsen, 1988; Ponterotto et al., 2001; Washington, 1994). While this framework is intended for adults, it is presented in modified form in the box as a guide for school psychologists to follow when working with culturally diverse families and their children. Several of the sample questions can be used for parents or have been rephrased for the student and in some instances for the teacher.

Holistic Idiographic Framework for Practice

I.

A. Student's Worldview and Perception of the Problem

> *Sample questions to ask:*
> Education, language(s), health problems/illnesses, current medications, SES, religion. (For the younger child, these questions are appropriate for parents or other significant adults in the student's life.)

B. Student's Explanation of the Problem(s)

Sample questions to ask:

What brought the student to seek assessment at this time? (For the school psychologist: Who referred the child for an assessment?)

What is the reason for the referral? (Does the student understand the identified referral problem?)

What factors are contributing to the problem(s), as the student (or the student's family) understands it/them?

What has the student done thus far to deal with the problem(s)? (What have teachers or the parents done?)

What has worked? What has not worked? (What interventions were implemented prior to the referral?)

C. Student's Level of Psychological Mindedness

Sample questions to ask:

Are basic Western psychological constructs within the student's frame of reference? Does the student conceptualize problems from a psychological point of view?

Does the student have the construct of emotional disturbance as part of their interpretative lens? (These questions refer to the student's pattern of thinking or feeling based on their particular ethnic group.)

D. Student's Attitude Toward Helping and Counseling

Sample questions to ask:

How does the student feel about getting help for emotional problems? (Or what are the feelings of the student—or their parents—about a psycho-educational evaluation or accepting school-based counseling services?)

What are the student's current preferences for and past experience with professional and popular sources of care?

What are the student's attitudes about discussing "problems" outside of their family? (Will the student feel comfortable about self-disclosure within an individual or group counseling session?)

E. Cultural Identity of the Student

Sample questions to ask:

Cultural and ethnic reference groups? Culture of origin for maternal and paternal lines? The student's view of his or her cultural adjustment as an individual? The student's view of his or her cultural adjustment as compared to the family's level of adjustment?

Language abilities, use, and preference, including bilingualism or multilingualism? Feelings and emotions associated with speaking the native language? Are there instances in which the native language is preferred? What are they? (These questions aid in determining the student's linguistic acculturation and may also provide information about the second language acquisition process.)

(Continued)

(Continued)

F. Religion

Sample questions to ask:

What is the student's religion?

How important is religion to the student? What are the rules for being a religious person for someone from the student's religion?

What religious beliefs does the student value most?

Have the student describe a significant religious experience he or she has had.

G. Education and Work

Sample questions to ask:

Which experience in school does the student remember and value the most?

What are the student's beliefs about work? (For younger children, the parents' view of work is important in establishing their children's educational goals.)

How will the student obtain the job he or she wants? (For the adolescent, this question is important since they may have different views about vocations to their parents or may wish to obtain part-time employment.)

What benefits will a good job bring the client? (Immigrant adolescents often want to work to help support their families and are not interested in higher education.)

How does the family feel about education versus work? How does the student feel?

H. Peers

Sample questions to ask:

What is the age and gender makeup of the student's peer group?

What are or were the "critical" peer activities the student considered most important during early childhood, elementary school years, and adolescent years?

What activities does the student enjoy doing with friends?

What are the areas of conflict or trouble experienced between the student and friends?

What is the cultural and ethnic makeup of the student's neighborhood?

I. Leisure Activities

Sample questions to ask:

What are the student's favorite music and musicians, dancers, artists, authors, magazines, etc.?

What are the student's hobbies? What does he or she do with free time?

What types of activities, interactions, and thoughts are most and least rewarding to the student?

(These questions can be posed to the student and are important for establishing an understanding of their functioning outside of school and within the community.)

II. Student's Family Background

A. Family Roles

Sample questions to ask:
What is a "typical" day in the student's family?
What is the role of kin networks in providing support to the student?
What are the rules that characterize a good mother? A good father?
What are the rules for being a good son or daughter?
What are the rules for a good marriage?
Who are the role models for family life that have meant the most to the student, and why?

B. Family Values and Norms

Sample questions to ask:
How do the members of the student's family express anger?
How do members of the student's family feel important and increase their self-esteem?
What types of things make family members feel safe?
(While some of these questions may be posed directly to the student being evaluated, parents or extended family members can contribute valuable information in this critical area of cultural standards.)

C. Family's View of Student's Problem

Sample questions to ask:
Why would the student's family want the student to get rid of the problem (or of the school's reason for referral, which implicates that there is a problem)?
In what way do the student's problems create pain in the student's family? (Is the school's referral problem perceived as a painful or detrimental problem for the child/student or family?)
Does the family conceptualize the problems as psychological in nature?
How does the family seek help for "emotional" problems (or for school-related academic problems)?
How do they view help from an "outsider" to the family (such as from the school based school psychologist, guidance counselor, or social worker)?

D. Family Acculturation Status

Sample questions to ask:
Where do family members live?
When did family members immigrate?
Did the family stay together, or are they dispersed?
What are the family's relations like with similar others?

(Continued)

(Continued)

> What are the family's members' attitudes toward acculturation for themselves, and for the children?
>
> (For the school psychologist, these questions are essential as they will aid in determining the acculturation level of the family as well as that of the student).
>
> ### III. Cultural Explanations of the Individual's Presenting Illness (or Student's Presenting Problem that Led to a Referral)
>
> #### A. Appraisal of Acculturative Stress
>
> *Sample questions to ask:*
>
> What are the cultural definitions of behavioral options, beliefs about operating in mainstream system, group efficacy, availability of family, community and social networks? Cultural idioms of distress? Meaning and perceived severity of the student's symptoms in relation to norms of the cultural reference group?
>
> What is the local illness category used to identify the condition? What are the perceived causes or explanatory models used to explain the illness?
>
> (These questions can provide useful information and help the school psychologist to determine acculturative stress or stressors and also are useful for students referred for an evaluation for behavioral problems or depressive symptoms.)

The Holistic Idiographic Framework for practice should be utilized during the initial interview with the student, teachers, and/or parent(s). Parts of it may be set aside for those individuals who the school psychologist deems able to provide the information sought. Some of the questions may also be put aside for the student if she/he is scheduled to receive school counseling by the examiner/school psychologist.

There are several factors that may cause difficulties for the school psychologist engaging in cultural identity and acculturation assessment. Differences in language and status between the school psychologist and the parents and/or child will impede communication and rapport. Moreover, lack of knowledge of the family's cultural norms will make it difficult to determine which behaviors are pathological or normative. This is why it is so important for the school psychologist to have knowledge of the culture of the student undergoing an evaluation.

At the same time, caution must be used when attempting to interview parents and/or the child being assessed. Certain families may see the interview process and its questioning as intrusive as well as threatening to their child. School psychologists are advised to thoroughly explain the reason for the referral and the need for a family consultation as well as the clinical interviewing process. A good way to start this process, which may reduce the intrusive issue, is to share with the family all questions to be posed during the family interview prior to the actual meeting. On occasion—and depending on the reason for the referral—it is also helpful to let parents know what questions will be asked of their child during the clinical interview and to explain the reason(s) why each has to be posed.

The Acculturation Process

Acculturation is linked firmly to cultural identity since the self is expected to adopt and adjust to a new culture and its norms. This adoption/adjustment is bound to create a new or second cultural identity. Acculturation has been defined in various ways. Diller and Moule (2005) identify it as the "taking on of cultural patterns of another group." Takushi and Uomoto (2001) describe acculturation as "the process of psychological change in values, beliefs, and behaviors when adapting to a new culture." In fact, the process of acculturation has been defined repeatedly over the past 60 years (Kim & Abreu, 2001). Cueller, Arnold, and Maldonado (1995) describe acculturation as a process of change that occurs at three different levels of functioning: (a) *behavioral*— various types of behaviors, including language development, customs, foods, music, and dance; (b) *affective*—emotions that have cultural associations, such as important feelings about ethnic identity, the symbols one loves or despises; and (c) *cognitive*—the cognitive aspects of language development, beliefs about different gender roles, illness and attitude toward illness, and underlying values. In addition, acculturation has been recognized as directly involving six dimensions of psychological functioning: language, cognitive styles, personality, identity, attitudes, and acculturative stress. These dimensions undergo changes as the individual moves through the acculturation process and reaches different "levels" of acculturation (i.e., the degree to which the immigrant has adopted the dominant culture's values, beliefs, and customs). The process causes conflicts for individuals, depending on their adaptation strategies (Berry, 1980). Such conflicts, defined as acculturative stress, have been known to cause emotional distress and in certain cases psychopathological disorders, as well as problems with substance abuse (Szapoznik & Kurtines, 1980).

Acculturation stress is often identified in children of refugees who have experienced the trauma of war. Common indicators associated with acculturative stress are deviant behaviors, marginality, and psychosomatic symptoms (Berry, 1980). Collier (2001) explains that certain types of acculturative stress may have side effects that are similar to the indicators of learning disabilities (i.e., anxiety, confusion in locus of control, silence or withdrawal, distractibility, response fatigue). School psychologists are advised to be aware of these indicators, and conscious that there are variations in stress patterns based on the culture's group distinctiveness and psychological characteristics in addition to previous exposure with culturally diverse groups (Berry, 1980). A specific indicator of acculturative stress is the degree of "culture shock" that an individual will experience while attempting to adjust to new circumstances. The degree of culture shock is related to the amount of intensity with which an individual has compared a new situation with that to which was previously enculturated (i.e., enculturation is defined as the process by which individuals learn and adopt the ways and manners of their culture—Matsumoto, 2000).

Research on differences in academic achievement emphasizes the function of the educational system as a significant *enculturation emissary* of any society. Expectantly, school psychologists should be astute in screening for acculturative stressors that will influence instructional programs and placement decisions. In some cases, counseling services and acculturation assistance programs may be more appropriate than special education placement (Collier, 2007).

Today, acculturation is no longer perceived as simply a process of adjusting to a new culture. Researchers have conceptualized the process of acculturation from several perspectives. One such perspective is the unidimensional view of acculturation. This position implies that individuals who are adopting dominant culture patterns concurrently relinquish the traditional ways of their own culture. Moreover, the individual is perceived as trying to acculturate to the dominant culture but instead ends up meandering between two cultures, a *marginal* person enmeshed between two cultures. The dilemma for such an individual takes place when that person is *transformed* too much to return to traditional practices and at the same time is not accepted into the dominant culture because of skin color (Cose, 1993; Lewin, 1948; Stonequist, 1961).

The bidimensional or multidimensional view of acculturation is that one can function healthily in two or more cultures. The bicultural individual can connect to both cultures and select parts of each culture to adopt (i.e., the beliefs, values, and attitudes of others). This can occur consciously or unconsciously. For example, in this viewpoint it is possible for a Latino American adolescent to be committed to family traditions and at the same time interact comfortably within the white dominant culture in relation to school, socialization, and recreation (Cross, 1987; Oetting & Beauvais, 1990; Valentine, 1971). Biculturalism is not always viewed positively, however, because individuals who are well adjusted to the dominant culture norms can also be perceived negatively by their families and friends as rejecting their own culture.

Another view of acculturation implies that there should be an assessment of what *material* has been lost or gained during the process. Marin (1992) differentiates how this material can be lost or gained by identifying three levels of acculturation:

1. the *superficial* level—which entails learning and forgetting facts that are part of a culture's history or tradition;

2. the *intermediate* level—which involves gaining or losing more central aspects of behaviors of an individual's social world (such as language preference and use, ethnicity of spouse, friends, and neighbors, names given to children, and choice of media); and

3. the *significant* level—which involves core values, beliefs, and norms that are necessary to the very cultural paradigm or worldview of the individual.

According to Marin's model, the immigrant generation has been inclined to exchange more superficial cultural material. Their children, in turn, replace more urgent cultural material as they progressively acculturate and so on (Diller & Moule, 2005).

Acculturation is not considered an easy process, especially for children who have been left behind in the country of origin and sent for after several years of separation from their families. Such children face various stressors: first, they are severed from their adopted extended family or caregivers with which they have lived in their native country, sometimes for several years; and second, they are asked to adjust to a new country, home, language, and school. This is why acculturative stress is most identified when a family or child is in transition. School psychologists should consider the causes leading to the transition and plan to seek answers to such issues as:

- the reason for the migration and whether the expectations were reached;
- the accessibility of community and extended family support systems;
- the structure of the family and whether it was obligated to adopt a different structure (such as an extended family structure switching to a nuclear family structure);
- the level to which the new dominant culture is similar to that of the country of origin (the greater the difference between the two, the more considerable the stress); and
- the family's overall elasticity and adaptability (Landau, 1982).

Additionally, school psychologists should have knowledge of the four kinds of outcomes associated with the acculturative process (Berry, 1980; La Fromboise, Coleman, & Gerton, 1993; Diller & Moule, 2005). These are described below.

Assimilation is defined as a process occurring when an individual relinquishes their native cultural identity and willingly acquires a second cultural identity with the aim of having good relationships with the dominant culture (Berry, 1980). Assimilation has also been described as the "coming together of two distinct cultures to create a new and unique third cultural form" (Diller & Moule, 2005).

Separation occurs when an individual retains their own cultural identity and purposely does not seek to obtain a second cultural identity so as to have positive relationships with the dominant culture (Berry, 1980, 1990, 1994).

Integration is reached when an individual desires to hold on to their cultural identity of origin as well as maintain positive relationships with the dominant culture (Berry, 1980, 1990, 1994).

Marginalization is observed when an individual does not retain their cultural identity and has no desire to adjust/adopt a second culture (Berry, 1980, 1990, 1994).

In summary, the acculturation process is considered an ongoing transformation in various domains (e.g., language, cognitive style, personality, identity, attitudes, and acculturative stress). From this point of view, any of the acculturative outcomes aforementioned can be identified through changes in one of many significant areas (e.g., language use, personal identity) (Marin, Organista, & Chun, 2003). With regard to school and achievement, several studies have shown that poor achievement scores of children of color do not necessarily stem from cultural and linguistic differences, nor does the success of children of color occur because they have adopted the dominant culture and its language. Instead, it appears that, globally, students tend to do better when they perceive themselves as "immigrants" in the new culture since this term is considered better than the inferiorly labeled and oppressed group they were associated with in their native country (Ogbu, 1992). In this respect, acculturation or assimilation strongly depends on the family members' own view of themselves in the new culture. Apparently, poor achievement scores appear to be more common where: (a) children start schooling with different cultural expectations; (b) some concepts of the core curriculum are different from their native culture; (c) students are non-English-speaking; and (d) children's learning styles differ from the main teaching style in the classroom (Ogbu, 1992). Reviewing these issues prior to servicing an immigrant child or youth can be a powerful tool for the school psychologist, and will ultimately lead to safer culturally sensitive diagnosis and intervention planning.

School psychologists are encouraged to review the important educational factors that are associated with successful acculturation for racial/ethnic CLD children and youth. These are:

- bilingual and English as a second language (ESL) programs;
- strength in English language skills;

- strength in one or both first and second language skills;
- length of time in school; and
- amount of interaction with mainstream American students (Collier, 2007).

First and second language abilities should be screened since language acquisition is associated with sounder mental health (Szapocznik & Kurtines, 1980).

Assessment of Acculturation

Presumably, for the immigrant child, the acculturation process begins when the child steps into the society of the dominant culture. Perhaps it even begins prior to that, when there is gradual psychological awareness of the anticipated migration through familial planning for relocation. The beginning of acculturation certainly relates to the individual, familial circumstances, and attitudes toward the culture change and adjustment. Given the continued influx of immigrant children to American schools, acculturation it is now recognized as a germane psychosocial process that will continue to markedly affect children and their parents. Consequently, the construction of valid quantitative measures is important for the assessment of acculturation.

Acculturation Measures

Researchers have developed several measures for assessing the acculturation level of various ethnic groups. To date, there are acculturation scales designed for such ethnic groups as Asian Americans, Cuban Americans, Mexican Americans, Puerto Ricans, Hawaiian Americans, and Native Americans. According to Kim and Abreu (2001), few have been developed for African Americans because they are not considered immigrants or part of an ethnic group. However, these researchers explain that, according to Landrine and Klonoff (1994), this pass over is deemed to be the result of traditional psychology's view of this particular group as not part of an ethnic group; it is therefore not regarded as necessary to purview issues of culture and ethnicity (Kim & Abreu, 2001, p. 400). Kim and Abreu point out that there is empirical evidence indicating a "a distant African American minority culture, making the acculturation construct just as applicable to African Americans as it is to other minority groups in the United States" (p. 400). Kim and Abreu further explain that the acculturation construct is also applicable to other minority groups residing in the United States.

Regrettably, a review of available acculturation instruments revealed that a number of scales utilized the unidimensional approach to assess acculturation, failing to adopt the newly recognized bidimensionality and multidimensionality of acculturation. For example, respondents on these scales are required to choose among terms that assess the unidimensional movement of an individual from their native culture to the majority culture (Marin, Organista, & Chun, 2003). Researchers have attempted to correct this problem by designing bidimensional scales; however, the scoring techniques employed have been criticized because a score moving toward the white dominant culture (or majority culture) implies well-being, whereas a score in the other direction would signify a pathology. Furthermore, many of these scales have inadequate reliability and validity (Kim & Abreu, 2001). Fortunately, there are a few new measures of acculturation that have been designed to estimate the many dimensions of acculturation by measuring two or more cultures independently of each other (Cueller et al., 1995; Marin & Gamba, 1996). This approach is more positively viewed as it presumes that individuals can adapt to a new culture and still preserve all or part of their native cultural identity.

Disappointingly, research on acculturation measures has produced very few acculturation scales for children. Two recurrently mentioned in the literature are the Short Acculturation Scale for Hispanic Youth (SASH-Y) (Barona & Miller, 1994) and the 10-item Children's Acculturation Scale (CAS) (Franco, 1983) for Mexican American children. The SASH-Y is viewed as having excellent psychometric features but generates unidimensional scores. It addresses familial and cultural contexts and has been assessed on Latino preteens. The scale was found to be valid and reliable for a young rural population (Serrano & Anderson, 2003). Other recommended scales are: the AHIMSA Acculturation Scale, a new measure of acculturation for adolescents in a multicultural society (Unger, Gallaher, & Shakib, 2002); the African American Acculturation Scale II, a cross-validation and short form (Landrine & Klonoff, 1994); the Bidimensional Acculturation Scale for Hispanics (BAS) (Marin & Gamba, 1996); and the Asian Values Scale (AVS) (Kim, Atkinson, & Yang, 1999).

Another measure of acculturation is the Acculturation Quick Screen (AQS), which was developed to measure the level and rate of acculturation of students to public school culture in the United States and Canada (Collier, 2000). Designed as a tool for school psychologists and general education personnel, the AQS is not specific to any one language or ethnic group, and measures adaptation to academic instructional settings. The AQS is based on research that studied the factors predicting the degree of successful integration for those students who may be experiencing culture shock. Apparently, students acculturate to new environments at different rates. The AQS measures this acculturation rate and guides the strategies that address culture shock. By measuring the rate of acculturation, Collier (2007) stresses that the AQS can be used to (a) separate difference from disability concerns when diverse learners manifest learning and behavior problems; (b) monitor the adaptation progress being made by migrant, immigrant, and refugee students; and (c) as an indicator of system weakness when studying the achievement rate within a school versus the acculturation rate of its racial/ethnic CLD student population. The AQS is also recommended for use as part of the information gathering that is used to make instructional decisions, and can be used to plan specific learning and behavioral interventions for racial/ethnic CLD students.

Ideally, the AQS should be administered four weeks after students have enrolled in the school. This allows the school psychologist to determine the student's language abilities and to review previous school records. This first administration of the AQS should be used as a baseline from which to measure the rate and level of acculturation. Additional administrations of the AQS should be yearly during the same time period, so as to record the rate of adaptation to the school system. Scoring results range from less acculturated to more acculturated on a 48-point scale. The AQS measures five levels of acculturation: (a) significantly less acculturated; (b) less acculturated; (c) in transition; (d) more acculturated; and (e) significantly more acculturated. The average rate of acculturation is between 10 and 12 percent each school year, dependent on the sort of program available to students. A particular advantage of the AQS is that it is most useful for students whose background differs significantly from the mainstream of their public school.

The information needed to complete the AQS is:

- the number of years the student has been in the United States;
- the number of years the student has been in the current school (should be the actual cumulative time in the school);
- the number of years the student has received direct instruction in bilingual or English as a Second Language (ESL) classes (the latter should be the actual cumulative time in this particular instruction);
- the degree of language proficiency in the native language or dialect;
- the student's degree of English proficiency
- the student's degree of bilingual proficiency;
- the student's ethnicity or national origin; and
- the percentage of the population in the student's school speaking the student's language or dialect.

The AQS can be a useful assessment tool for school psychologists (see Collier, 2000). Hopefully, future research will provide practitioners with improved acculturation scales for children. In the interim, since scales for assessing acculturation are limited and those available for adults are judged to be lacking in psychometric soundness, practitioners may have to revert to structured interview(s) for assessing acculturation.

Gathering information from parents and teachers, reviewing school records, and determining length of time the student may have spent in direct instruction in bilingual education or ESL classes is of primary importance for determining acculturation levels. It is particularly important for school clinicians to approach students and families in a respectful, appropriate manner when seeking to evaluate the acculturation of a child or family. This is a sensitive domain of evaluation, and families should be approached in a non-judgmental, non-threatening way. School psychologist need to be clear on their expectations for acculturation (i.e., are they expecting assimilation as appropriate?). As stated in Chapter 1, a culturally competent psychologist should recognize that their own beliefs, attitudes, and values may influence their service to racial/ethnic CLD children and parents.

Other Measures of Acculturation

Because there are so few acculturation scales for children, school psychologists will have to adopt informal methods for assessing acculturation. The first step in the multicultural assessment of a racial/ethnic CLD child or youth is to determine their level of acculturation. Apart from the need to assess the psychosocial and emotional issues that often accompany the acculturation process, determining the acculturation level is important for instrument selection (e.g., cognitive measures, personality scales, language, and educational measures). The degree of the child/adolescent's level of acculturation and second language acquisition will aid in deciding whether an instrument is appropriate. Frequently, practitioners have relied on interviews to assess a family or child's level of acculturation. The recommended evaluative task for the practitioner is to assess the family's adaptation to the second culture. It is important to understand that family members will acculturate differently. In general, children are observed to acculturate more easily because of their ease in second language acquisition and their opportunities to socialize frequently with the new culture through school peers and educators (Sciarra, 2001). Assessing the second language process of family members is important, as this helps the school psychologist know how the child is encouraged in learning a second dominant group language. Sciarra (2001) provides several questions to pose when assessing a diverse family system. These questions and others have been compiled in a checklist (see box).

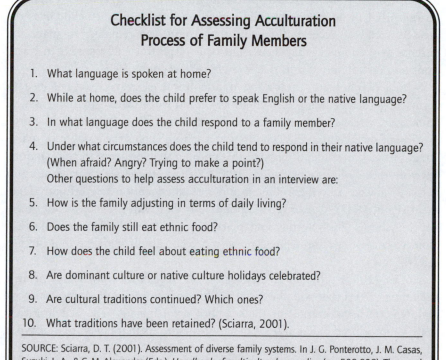

Checklist for Assessing Acculturation Process of Family Members

1. What language is spoken at home?

2. While at home, does the child prefer to speak English or the native language?

3. In what language does the child respond to a family member?

4. Under what circumstances does the child tend to respond in their native language? (When afraid? Angry? Trying to make a point?)
    Other questions to help assess acculturation in an interview are:

5. How is the family adjusting in terms of daily living?

6. Does the family still eat ethnic food?

7. How does the child feel about eating ethnic food?

8. Are dominant culture or native culture holidays celebrated?

9. Are cultural traditions continued? Which ones?

10. What traditions have been retained? (Sciarra, 2001).

SOURCE: Sciarra, D. T. (2001). Assessment of diverse family systems. In J. G. Ponterotto, J. M. Casas, Suzuki, L. A., & C. M. Alexander (Eds.), *Handbook of multicultural counseling* (pp. 506-606). Thousand Oaks, CA: Sage.

Other measures, such as rating scales, or questionnaires, can be used to assess the student's values, language proficiency, culturally specific attitudes, participation in ethnic organizations, and traditional holiday celebrations (Cueller, Arnold, & Maldonando, 1995; Dana, 1993). Cultural identity development models have been applied to families (Gushue, 1993). Qualitatively, practitioners can assess cultural identity by listening to family members and picking up cues that may divulge the particular stage each member has reached. However, practitioners are advised to be aware of the differences in stages of cultural identity between family members. The stages of cultural identity development, in addition to the level of acculturation to the second culture, may cause conflicts among family members who have not acculturated to the dominant culture. This is especially noticed in children who seem to acculturate with more flexibility, and see their parents as rigid and unwilling to adopt the traditions/norms of the dominant culture. Such conflicts can cause serious problems in the parent-child/adolescent relationship. If a child has progressed steadily in acculturation while the parents have remained stagnant, the parents may complain that their child is disrespectful and resistant to traditions and disciplinary norms that were once accepted.

School psychologists practicing multicultural assessment or engaged in counseling racial/ethnic CLD children should be attentive to these issues. Moreover, research indicates that acculturation will be affected by the proportion of racial/ethnic CLD children in a school versus the amount of mainstream American students, because this number will influence the interactions between these two groups (Juffer, 1983). In fact, there is a clear connection between diverse school enrollment and special education referral and placement (Finn, 1982). Collier (2007) points out that with the increase of diversity in schools, the referrals and placements to special education of CLD children and youth are inclined to be more consistent with the mainstream referral rates.

Collier (2007) provides an Acculturation Matrix to aid assessment at a preliminary level that will allow the practitioner to pick out where and how children are acculturating to their school environment. The acculturation matrix reproduced in Figure 10.1 has four quadrants that illustrate four types of possible adaptations to acculturation.

Assimilation Home/heritage replaced by school/new culture and language	**Integration** Home/heritage blended with school/new culture and language
Deculturation Acceptance of neither home/ heritage nor school/new culture/ language of school/new for home/heritage	**Rejection** Intentional rejection of home/ heritage for school/new culture and language *or* intentional rejection

Figure 10.1   Acculturation Matrix

SOURCE: Collier, C. (2007). The assessment of acculturation. In G. B. Esquivel, E. C. Lopez, & S. Nahara, S. (Eds.), *Handbook of multicultural school psychology: An interdisciplinary perspective*. Mahwah, NJ: Lawrence Erlbaum Associates.

Figure 10.1 clearly delineates those areas of concern (assimilation, integration, deculturation, and rejection) that school psychologists should assess. Collier explains that, as a preliminary step, this matrix will assist in gauging the acculturative experience. For example, if assimilation concerns are considered, the practitioner should list all of the noted areas in which a racial/ethnic CLD child or youth has replaced aspects from the mainstream culture for those in their home/heritage (i.e., behaviors, words, clothing, manners, or other characteristic patterns). If integration is suspected, a list should be made of all the ways the student has integrated language, behavior, clothing, food, religion, and other characteristic patterns from the mainstream culture and the racial/ethnic CLD student's home/heritage. Successful integration would mean that the student uses English in school and in other social events as well as continuing to utilize their native language at home. Additionally, traditional attire for religious activities would continue to be respected by the student in addition to combining ethnic foods with the new foods of the new culture.

Assimilation and integration are considered "positive" acculturation experiences while deculturation and rejection are considered detrimental to the acculturation process. Rejection is observed when a student purposely selects to abide by only one model of behavior and language. In this case, the student may rebuff the new culture and language while actually residing in the dominant culture and continually utilizing their native language, foods, and clothing, with no intention of integrating into the dominant culture. An opposite reaction to rejection would be for the student to adopt the dominant culture's language, foods, and so on, and totally reject their own. Collier (2007) explains that very often refugees adopt rejection tactics of solely adhering to the new culture's language, foods, etc. because of their hope of integration into the dominant culture since they do not expect to return to their native country. This, however, can be a temporary situation. Families are important in aiding how their children will integrate and/or reject the new culture. Research indicates that individuals experiencing this type of rejection may also experience psychological repercussions (Padilla, 1980). Suggested interventions for rejection include assisting the family and child/student to overcome possible discomfort with the bilingual and/or bicultural acculturation process. The deculturation concept noted in the matrix is perhaps the most serious, as it involves severing from the native culture as well as the dominant culture. This is marginalization, which indicates that the student is not interested in either culture. It appears that deculturation and/or marginalization can occur if the student and/or their family are severed from their cultural community in addition to not having the opportunity to transition effectively to the new culture. Another effect of deculturation or marginalization may be the lack of appropriate interventions during the rejection period.

When evaluating a racial/ethnic CLD student, the school psychologist should note whether there are deculturation and/or rejection concerns and list these two in the lower quadrants of the matrix in Figure 10.1. Priority should be given to these two concerns, as they may be indicators of learning and behavioral difficulties that will need to be reduced through appropriate interventions (Collier, 2007).

Acculturation in the Classroom

Another area where school psychologists can observe acculturation and assimilation is in the classroom. This naturalistic observation can be beneficial for assessment purposes, counseling interventions, and client-centered consultation practice. Ogbu (1992) describes two types of immigrants and their views of education. The *voluntary immigrant* is likely to view learning English as a second language as a requirement and willingly plays the "school game" because it will ultimately lead to a bigger reward later on. The *involuntary immigrant* tends to view education as "learning the culture and language of White Americans, that is the learning of the cultural language and frames of reference of their 'enemy' or 'oppressors'" (Ogbu, 1992, p. 10). Such a view makes the unwilling immigrant feel that learning is "detrimental to their social identity, sense of security, and self-worth" (Ogbu, 1992, p. 10). Peer groups may negatively impact any resolute academic efforts if academic success is perceived as "acting white." Ogbu's (1992) research with children of color (various racial groups) has led to an enumeration of strategies used by students who have consciously defeated the pressures against achievement. These are illustrated below to bring awareness to the school psychologist of the fundamental reasons why many children do poorly in school, and several can be observed in the classroom setting by the astute practitioner. Pragmatically, these strategies can be examined more comprehensively in clinical interviews and/or counseling sessions with racial/ethnic CLD children and youth.

> *Emulation of white academic behavior or cultural passing* (i.e., adopting "white" academic attitudes and behaviors or trying to behave like middle-class, white students). Some students have stated that, "If it takes acting like white people to do well in school, I'll do that." Such students usually tend to do well academically. However, they are inclined to experience isolation from other black peers, often causing some psychological distress.

> *Accommodation without assimilation.* Students will follow school norms while at school and black norms while at home. Black students who espouse this approach do not experience the same psychological costs as the white emulators.

> *Camouflage* (i.e., disguising true academic attitudes and behaviors). Students use numerous means, such as becoming a jester or class clown, claiming to lack interest in school, or studying in secret to obscure their academic efforts.

Involvement in church activities. Students find an alternative peer group.

Attending a private school where there are few anti-academic norms.

Mentors. Students find adult support for achievement.

Protection. Students secure the help of bullies to protect them from peer pressure in return for helping the bullies with their homework.

Remedial and intervention programs. Students seek out help in areas of academic need.

Encapsulation. Students become encapsulated in peer group logic and activities, not wanting to "do the White man's thing" or school work.*

For the school psychologist, knowledge of strategies used by children of color can be shared with teachers during consultee-centered consultation sessions and workshops, and by forming shared educators' reading groups where such reading materials can be disseminated. Having knowledge of these issues will enable the school psychologist to better observe classroom behaviors and academic motivation.

Similarly, Latino-American children and youths have demonstrated different needs in schools. In view of the fact that the projection of Latino demographics by 2010 suggests that this racial minority group will encompass one third of the U.S. population, educators and practitioners are urged to consider knowing the family and its cultural values prior to making important decisions about instructional methods and educational placement. Latino culture is collective, which implies Latino Americans entrust their children to extended family members as well as to their teachers. They trust that teachers, school personnel—and, of course, school psychologists—will do the best they can for their children. Carrasquillo (1991) provides several shared values among Latinos:

- importance of the family, both nuclear and extended, or *familialismo;*
- emphasis on the worth and dignity of the individual, or *personalismo;*
- valuing the spiritual side of life;
- an acceptance of life as it exists.

Latinos place great importance on family unity and honor. As a collective culture, they focus on the group rather than on the individual.

---

*SOURCE: Ogbu, J. U. (1992). Understanding cultural diversity and learning. *Educational Researcher, 21*(8), 5–14.

Difficulties due to differences in cultural styles and values may affect the education of the Latino child. For Latino families, egocentric concepts such as time are perceived differently. Latinos do not worry about "saving time." Moreover, communication styles are different from one culture to another. Latinos speak in a "circular" style, meaning they tend to elaborate around the main issue, to better explain the concept. English language learners (ELL) are defined as children in the process of learning English. Some Latinos may do poorly in school because they lack proficiency in both languages. Understandably, these children will do poorly on English teacher-made tests since they do not have the skills in their native language (Gopaul-McNicol & Armour-Thomas, 2002) (see Chapter 11).

School psychologists are counseled to review the various issues which may be affecting the Latino/a child's academic progress. Knowledge of these issues will help in the observation of children engaged or disengaged during classroom activities. Knowledge of norms and values of various racial/ethnic children will facilitate classroom observations because this will help the school psychologist to discern whether activities are educationally traditional or non-traditional for the observed culturally and linguistically diverse racial/ethnic child.

Special Cases

The process of acculturation and assimilation can be successful, resulting in bilingualism and biculturalism. However, a number of special cases do exist that complicate acculturation—for example, separation of family members, and emigration from countries in which ethnic violence, genocide, or persecution prevails. At-risk youth problems of which school psychologists should be aware when servicing racial/ethnic CLD children are cited frequently in the literature. These are: children separated from family members; children with disabilities; gifted children; children in poverty and/or chronic health; children of substance-abusing parents; school dropouts; child abuse and neglect (McWhirter et al., 2004). It is important to note that children newly immigrated to the United States can also be at risk of the above-mentioned problems. The following section briefly reviews only a few of these critical impediments in the hope that school psychologists will not overlook them when servicing racial/ethnic CLD children and their parents (see suggested readings and annotated bibliography for further information on at-risk youth).

School Dropouts

Dropping out of high school indicates that a student has left school before graduation. Reasons for racial/ethnic CLD youth dropping out appear to be largely stress related. Immigrant children entering school in a new culture are often exposed to stress, anxiety, and language difficulties. Latino students may have experienced other factors, such as poverty, pregnancy, poor academic achievement, lack of educational motivation, modest aspirations, and single-parent families—obstacles that may impede prolongation of school (Velez & Saenz, 2001). Recent studies have revealed that teachers may have low expectations and stereotypes of the Latino student (e.g., Latinos are lazy, or not inclined to try hard) (Conchas, 2001). Such perceived pessimistic stereotypes may leave Latino students with very little ambition to attend school. English as a second language (ESL) students drop out of school more often than monolingual English students (Fashola & Slavin, 1998). Not surprisingly, students with disabilities are also at risk of not finishing school. Latino dropout rates for the year 2000 were 27 percent of the U.S. school population (Kaufman, Alt, & Chapman, 2001). Part of this rate is due to the high dropout rate among Latino immigrants as opposed to first- and second-generation Latinos. Likewise, blacks (African Americans and other black, non-Hispanic) and Asians/Pacific Islanders experience difficulties that cause notably high dropout rates (see Table 10.1 for a breakdown of dropout rates for 16- through 24-year-olds by race and ethnicity).

As advocacy and prevention agents, school psychologists are advised to promote preventive interventions at the home and school levels. Reviewing the issues which may lead to dropping out of school may help a student stay in school through appropriate interventions. School psychologists should know how to identify potentially at-risk dropouts early in the immigrant acculturation process. There are four types of school dropouts:

1. *Disengaged dropouts*—These students do not like school and, although they may be achieving well, they have few academic aspirations.

2. *Low-achiever dropouts*—In addition to having little commitment to education, these students do not have behavior problems but tend to have poor grades and lack the ability to pass their courses.

3. *Quiet dropouts*—These students have few problems and are generally not obvious because of their active involvement in school; however, they experience poor grades and unobtrusively drop out.

4. *Maladjusted dropouts*—These dropouts manifest severe behavioral problems, no academic commitment, and poor grades; they eventually drop out. (Janosz, et al., 2000)

Table 10.1   Dropout Rates and Number and Distribution of Dropouts of 16- to 24-Year-Olds, by Race/Ethnicity: October 2001

	Dropout Rate (%)	Number of Dropouts (thousands)	Population (thousands)	Percent of Population	Percent of All Dropouts
Total	10.7	3,774	35,195	100.0	100.0
White, non-Hispanic	7.3	1,677	22,903	65.1	44.4
Black, non-Hispanic	10.9	557	5,111	14.5	14.7
Hispanic	27.0	1,442	5,350	15.2	38.2
Asian/Pacific Islander	3.6	53	1,487	4.2	1.4

SOURCE: U.S. Department of Commerce, Census Bureau, Current Population Survey, October 2001, http://nces.ed.gov/pubs2005/dropout2001/tables/table_3.asp.

An important factor contributing to dropout rates is the instructional environment. For example, if a low achiever is treated differently than a high achiever in the classroom, this obvious difference can encourage a low achiever to leave school.

Accordingly, during the acculturation process certain at-risk problems can be observed and perhaps prevented with adequate interventions. School psychologists should check for other factors, such as any family issues that may be contributing to a child or youth's lack of school motivation. Additionally, school psychologists are encouraged to get involved in, and/or initiate, prevention programs at the school level that will identify at-risk children and youth. They can conduct workshops for parents and/or children to help educate them on whatever particular at-risk situations are occurring at the school level (e.g., latchkey children, substance abuse, teenage pregnancy, and at-risk sexual behaviors). School psychologists can also help by their involvement in prevention programs that address personal and success issues of dropouts, review curriculum issues, and look at types and availability of after-school activities. Furthermore, school psychologists can provide comprehensive services such as assessment, sharing information with parents and educators, consultation, counseling, referral placement decisions, and follow-up with the immigrant racial/ethnic CLD child and family (McWhirter et al., 2004). Developing specific interventions that are solution-oriented and applied through counseling services is essential for dropout prevention. Finally, developing a solid counseling plan that includes parents and teachers is vital for solving any potential problems.

Substance Abuse

Substance abuse includes the overuse of alcohol, drugs, and tobacco. According to the National Institute on Drug Abuse, 50 percent of high school seniors regularly use alcohol, with 26 percent engaging in binge drinking (Johnston, O'Malley, & Bachman, 2003). Many children indulge in tobacco use by age 9. Children and youth who engage in such substance abuse are at risk of more serious drug use. Marijuana use now occurs nationwide among all ethnic groups, beginning as early as age 13 in over 10 percent of the population. Moreover, nearly 10 percent of adolescents have used a certain type of cocaine at least once, with Latino and European American students (15 and 10 percent respectively) more likely to engage in this particular abuse than African American students (2 percent) (Johnston et al., 2003). The common stereotype implying that adolescents of color are most inclined to abuse substances is not confirmed by the research. In contrast, African American students are significantly less likely to indulge in alcohol, tobacco, and drugs (Johnston et al., 2003). However, Latino youths as early as the eighth grade have the highest rates all types of substance abuse. Native American Indian adolescents use alcohol, tobacco, and drugs considerably more than other groups. The latter is problematic since it causes fetal alcohol syndrome (Plunkett & Mitchell, 2000). See Table 10.2 for a breakdown of children with substance abuse problems by race/ethnicity.

Table 10.2   Race/Ethnicity of Children Engaging in Substance Abuse

Racial/Ethnic Identity	Percentage of Population	Percentage of All Children in Substance Abuse
White	69.7	61.9
Black or African American	11.6	15.0
American Indian or Alaska Native	0.5	0.7
Asian	3.8	3.3
Native Hawaiian/Other Pacific Islander	0.2	0.3
Hispanic	12.7	16.5

SOURCE: United States Department of Health and Human Services, Substance Abuse and Mental Health Services Administration, Office of Applied Studies, National Survey on Drug Use and Health (2002, 2003, 2004).

NOTE: Total number of children aged 12–17 = 239,098,000; total number of children engaged in substance abuse = 25,105,000.

Another extremely at-risk group comprises adolescents who are gay, lesbian, bisexual, or transgendered (Jordan, 2000). School psychologists must adhere to strict at-risk screenings since these adolescents often experience feelings of hopelessness, suicidal ideations, and depression. Furthermore, they will most probably have experienced bullying and/or been victimized in one manner or other.

Some identifying factors of substance abuse for which the practitioner should screen are presented in the box.

At-Risk Substance Abuse Checklist

1. *Check for environmental factors* (e.g., low socioeconomic status, poverty, adverse school conditions, trauma, immigration, harmful peer influence, poor parental supervision).

2. Determine whether substance abuse is correlated to parents' influence and/or use.

3. *Evaluate the student's self-concept.* Is the student experiencing emotional pain or manifesting an inability to cope?

4. *Are there any high risk-taking behaviors on the part of the student* (e.g., pleasure and sensation seeking, rebelliousness, nontraditionalism, an acute desire for interdependence and autonomy, low impulse control, low interpersonal trust)?

5. *What types of interventions are appropriate* (e.g., psychotherapy, school-based substance abuse support groups, prevention strategies, community treatment programs, assertiveness training, resistance and refusal skills, peer-based programs that emphasize assertiveness and social skills, and student assistant programs)?

6. *Screen for potential risk factors of suicide* (e.g., chemical dependence is a high risk for suicide, as are social isolation, under- and/or overachievement, disruptive or dysfunctional family experiences, family violence, poor communication, loss and separation).

7. *Evaluate intrapersonal and personality characteristics* (e.g., assess self-image, anger, feelings of loneliness, impulsivity, hopelessness/depression, irrational thinking patterns, motivation for suicide).

SOURCE: Comeau, Stewart, & Loba (2001); McWhirter (1998).

In general, the best interventions to recommend are individual and family counseling, group therapy, and recreational, vocational, and educational activities. School psychologists must consider that some immigrant/racial/ethnic CLD youth may experience acculturation stress, which in turn may lead to substance abuse.

Child Abuse and Neglect

Approximately 903,000 children were victims of abuse and neglect during 2001. Half of all victims were white (50.2%), a quarter (25.0%) were African American, and one-sixth (14.5%) were Hispanic. American Indians and Alaska Natives accounted for 2.0 percent of victims, and Asian-Pacific Islanders accounted for 1.3 percent. These percentages have remained stable for the past several years (www.acf.hhs.gov/programs/cb/publications/cm01/Chapterthree .htm#race). School psychologists and educators must be vigilant for the signs of child abuse. It may be difficult to distinguish between physical abuse and corporal punishment. Child abuse is defined as:

> the sustaining of physical injury of a child by any parent or other person who has permanent or temporary care or custody or responsibility for supervision of that child, or by any household or family member, under circumstances that indicate that the child's health or welfare is significantly harmed or at risk of being significantly harmed; or sexual abuse of a child, whether physical injuries are sustained or not. Neglect means the sustaining by a child of significant physical or mental harm or injury from: the absence of the child's parents, guardian, or custodian; the leaving of a child unattended or other failure to give proper care and attention to a child by the child's parents, guardian, or custodian under circumstances that indicate that the child's health or welfare is significantly harmed or placed at risk of significant harm. (Annotated Code of Maryland, "Family Law" S5-701-710)

Childhelp USA has a National Child Abuse Hotline (1-800-4-A-CHILD) that provides extensive information on the treatment and prevention of child abuse. Some of the physical and behavioral indicators of child abuse and neglect listed by Childhelp USA are shown in the box.

Signs and Symptoms of Child Abuse

Please note that the listed indicators in each category may pertain to more than one type of abuse or neglect. For example, "lack of concentration" could be a sign of sexual abuse, as well as of emotional abuse. The most common signs and symptoms are indicated in bold.

Physical Abuse

1. **Unexplained burns, cuts, bruises, or welts in the shape of an object**
2. Bite marks

(Continued)

(Continued)

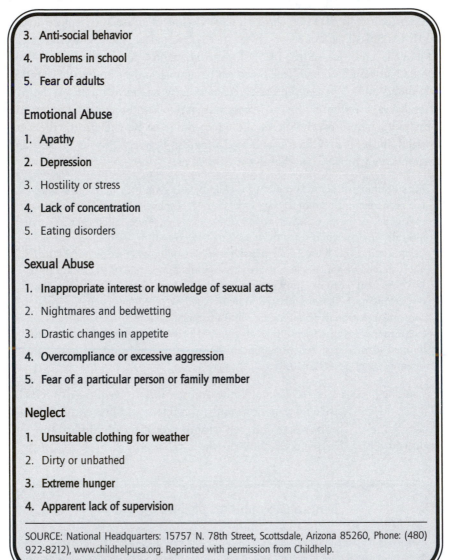

3. Anti-social behavior

4. Problems in school

5. Fear of adults

Emotional Abuse

1. Apathy

2. Depression

3. Hostility or stress

4. Lack of concentration

5. Eating disorders

Sexual Abuse

1. Inappropriate interest or knowledge of sexual acts

2. Nightmares and bedwetting

3. Drastic changes in appetite

4. Overcompliance or excessive aggression

5. Fear of a particular person or family member

Neglect

1. Unsuitable clothing for weather

2. Dirty or unbathed

3. Extreme hunger

4. Apparent lack of supervision

SOURCE: National Headquarters: 15757 N. 78th Street, Scottsdale, Arizona 85260, Phone: (480) 922-8212), www.childhelpusa.org. Reprinted with permission from Childhelp.

For professionals servicing children on federal ground or in federally contracted establishments, there are laws that require health care and educational professionals to give an account and proof of child abuse or neglect. Maryland and Wyoming are the only two states that do not enforce criminal legal responsibility for failing to report signs or evidence of child abuse (Small, Lyons, & Guy, 2002). Practicing professionals are protected from criminal and civil liability for reporting alleged child abuse that may be unsubstantiated. Reporting must be done with good intent and with sound judgment that abuse has actually taken place. To date, there have not been any cases in which psychologists have been deprived of immunity because they failed to report a child abuse case (Small, Lyons, & Guy, 2002). There are several inquiries and practices a school psychologist should consider regarding child abuse and reporting (see box).

Checklist of Inquiries on Child Abuse and Reporting Practices

- Check the laws of the state regarding child abuse reporting. Past abuse in some states is required even if the abuse occurred several years back. Verify time limitations on reporting abuse.
- Know the ethics codes of the American Psychological Association, the National Association of School Psychologists, and the American Counseling Association. These codes define the standard practices and help to avoid legal and ethical dilemmas.
- If engaged in a counseling relationship, inform the child or adolescent at the onset of therapy of the limits to confidentiality and of the duty to report any harmful incidences/behaviors. Establishing this guideline may reduce possible harm to the therapeutic relationship if reporting becomes necessary.
- Be on the lookout for dysfunctional families, substance abuse, interpersonal violence, and parental psychopathology. Such families subject children to stress and possible abuse (McWhirter et al., 2004).
- Be aware that child abuse is not the sole domain of parents. Siblings and extended family members can also be possible offenders.
- Watch for signs of abuse at the school level, such as bruises, burns, welts, abrasions, scars or wounds that could have been caused by cigarette burns or belt buckles. Ask the child about the marks: do not ignore the possibility of abuse. Be alert to explanations of wounds that don't make sense. Coming to school ill kempt and falling asleep in school are other indicators.
- For younger children, watch them at play and note how the child interacts or reacts to doll play, and what the child verbalizes. Is the child enacting an imaginary abusive situation in their play? Is there evidence of playing in a sexual manner that is developmentally more advanced than the child's age? Adolescents often seek to self-disclose in their writings.
- If there is reasonable suspicion of child abuse, school psychologists should trust their professional training and ethical standards. If unsure, consult a supervisor or colleagues and keep a written documentation of meetings and what was decided and why. (Friedman, 2001)

School psychologists serving first-, second- and third-generation immigrant families affected by child maltreatment are advised both to have knowledge of how to assess families for child maltreatment (know how to work with interpreters in child maltreatment cases), and to initiate arranging interventions for prevention and parent education. When school psychologists and educators understand the various acculturation stressors that lead to at-risk problems of immigrant racial/ethnic CLD children, they will better be able to identify the needs of these vulnerable children. Preparing to service a multicultural nation with culturally sensitive expertise will ensure the attainment of such an important mission.

References

American Psychiatric Association (APA) (1994). *Diagnostic and statistical manual of mental disorders* (4th ed.). Washington, DC: APA.

Barona, A., & Miller, J. A. (1994). Short Acculturation Scale for Hispanic Youth (SASH-Y): A preliminary report. *Hispanic Journal of Behavioral Sciences, 16,* 155–162.

Berg-Cross, L., & Takushi-Chinen, R. (1995). Multicultural training models and the person-in-culture interview. In J. G. Ponterotto, J. M. Casas, L. A. Suzuki, & C. M. Alexander (Eds.), *Handbook of multicultural counseling* (pp. 506–606). Thousand Oaks, CA: Sage.

Berry, J. W. (1980). Acculturation as varieties of adaptation. In A. Padilla (Ed.), *Acculturation: Theory, models and some new findings* (pp. 9–26). Boulder, CO: Westview.

Berry, J. W. (1990). Imposed etics, emics, derived etics: Their conceptual and operational status in cross-cultural psychology. In T. N. Headland, K. L. Pike, & M. Harris (Eds.), *Emics and etics: The insider/outsider debate* (pp. 28–47). Thousand Oaks, CA: Sage.

Berry, J. W. (1994). Acculturation and psychological adaptation. In A. M. Bouvry, E. R. Van de Vijver, & P. Schmitz (Eds.), *Journeys into cross-cultural psychology* (pp.129–141). Lisse, Netherlands: Swets & Zeitlinger.

Brislin, R. (2000). *Understanding culture's influence on behavior* (2nd ed.). Belmont, CA: Wadsworth Thompson.

Carrasquillo, A. (1991). *Hispanic children and youth in the United States: A resource guide.* New York: Garland.

Casas, J. M., & Pytluk, S. D. (1995). Hispanic identity development: Implications for research and practice. In J. G. Ponterotto, J. M. Casas, L. A. Suzuki, & C. M. Alexander (Eds), *Handbook of Multicultural Counseling* (pp.155–180). Thousand Oaks, CA: Sage.

Collier, C. (2000). *Acculturation quick screen.* Ferndale, WA: Cross Cultural Developmental Education Services.

Collier, C. (2001). Separating difference and disability. Paper presented at the Annual Meeting of Teachers of English to Speakers of Other Languages. St. Louis, MO, March 1, 2001.

Collier, C. (2007). The assessment of acculturation. In G. B. Esquivel, E. C. Lopez, & S. Nahara, S. (Eds.), *Handbook of multicultural school psychology: An interdisciplinary perspective.* Mahwah, NJ: Lawrence Erlbaum.

Comeau, N., Stewart, S. H., & Loba, P. (2001). The relations of trait anxiety, anxiety sensitivity and sensation seeking to adolescents' motivations for alcohol, cigarette, and marijuana use. *Addictive Behaviors, 26,* 803–825.

Conchas, G. Q. (2001). Structuring failure and success: Understanding the variability in Latino school engagement. *Harvard Educational Review, 71*(3), 579–589.

Cose, E. (1993). *The rage of the privileged class*. New York: Harper Collins.

Cross, T. L. (1987). *The black power imperative: Racial inequality and the politics of nonviolence*. New York: Faulkner.

Cueller, I., Arnold, B., & Maldonado, R. (1995). Acculturation rating scale for Mexican Americans-II: A revision of the original ARSMA scale. *Hispanic Journal of Behavioral Sciences, 17*, 275–304.

Dana, R. H. (1993). *Multicultural assessment perspectives for professional psychology*. Needham Heights, MA: Allyn & Bacon.

Dana, R. H. (1998). *Understanding cultural identity in intervention and assessment*. Thousand Oaks, CA: Sage.

Dana, R. H. (2000). Acculturation, ethnic identity, and acculturative stress: Evidence and measurement. In R. H. Dana (Ed.), *Handbook of cross-cultural and multicultural assessment* (pp. 131–172). Mahwah, NJ: Lawrence Erlbaum.

Diller, J. V., & Moule, J. (2005). *Cultural competence: A primer for educators*. Belmont, CA: Wadsworth Thompson.

Drugger, C. W. (1998). Report: English favored by kids. *San Jose Mercury News*, March 21. Available from www-rcf.usc.edu/~cmmr/SJMerc_March21.htm.

Espinosa, L. M. (1995). *Hispanic parent involvement in early childhood programs*. Washington, DC: US Government Printing Office.

Fashola, O. S., & Slavin, R. E. (1998). Effective dropout prevention and college attendance programs for students placed at risk. *Journal of Education for Students Placed at Risk, 3*(2), 159–183.

Finn, J. D. (1982). Patterns in special education placement as revealed by the OCR survey. In K. A. Heller, W. H. Holtzman, & S. Messick (Eds.), *Placing children in special education: A strategy for equity* (pp. 322–381). Washington, DC: National Academy of Sciences National Academy Press.

Fischer, A. R., & Moradi, B. (2001). Racial and ethnic identity: Recent developments and needed directions. In J. G. Ponterotto, J. M. Casas, L. A., Suzuki, & C. M. Alexander (Eds.), *Handbook of multicultural counseling* (2nd ed., pp. 341–370). Thousand Oaks, CA: Sage.

Franco, J. N. (1983). An acculturation scale for Mexican-American children. *Journal of General Psychology, 108*, 175–181.

Friedman, B. B. (2001). *What teachers need to know about children at risk*. New York: McGraw-Hill.

Gopaul-McNicol, S., & Armour-Thomas, E. (2002). *Assessment and culture: Psychological tests with minority populations* San Diego, CA: Academic Press.

Grieger, I., & Ponterotto, J. G. (1995). A framework for assessment in multicultural counseling. In J.G. Ponterotto, J. M. Casas, L. A. Suzuki, & C. M. Alexander (Eds.), *Handbook of multicultural counseling* (pp. 357–374). Thousand Oaks, CA: Sage.

Gushue, G.V. (1993). Cultural identity development and family assessment: An interaction model. *Counseling Psychologist, 21*, 487–513.

Gushue, G. V., & Sciarra, D.T. (1995). Culture and families. In J. G. Ponterotto, J. M. Casas, L. A. Suzuki, & C. M. Alexander (Eds.), *Handbook of multicultural counseling* (pp. 506–606). Thousand Oaks, CA: Sage.

Haycock, K., & Duany, L. (1991). Developing the potential of Latino students. *Principal, 70*, 25-27.

Helms, J. E. (1985). Cultural identity in the treatment process. In P. Pedersen (Ed.), *Handbook of cross-cultural counseling and therapy.* Westport, CT: Greenwood Press.

Helms, J. E. (1995). An update of Helms' White and People of Color racial identity models. In J. G. Ponterotto, J. M. Casas, L. A. Suzuki, & C. M. Alexander (Eds.), *Handbook of multicultural counseling* (pp. 181–198). Thousand Oaks, CA: Sage.

Jacobsen, F.M. (1988) Ethnocultural assessment. In L. Comas-Diaz & E. E. H. Griffith (Eds.), *Clinical guidelines in cross-cultural mental health* (pp. 135–147). New York: Wiley.

James, W. H., Kim, G. K., & Moore, D. D. (1997). Examining racial and ethnic differences in Asian adolescent drug use: The contributions of culture, background, and lifestyle. *Drugs: Education, Prevention and Policy, 4,* 39–51.

Janosz, M., LeBlanc, M., Boulerice, B., & Tremblay, R. (Eds.) (2000). Predicting different types of school dropouts: A typological approach with two longitudinal samples. *Journal of Educational Psychology, 92*(1), 171–190.

Johnston, L. D., O'Malley, P. M., & Bachman, J. G. (2003). *The Monitoring the Future national survey results on adolescent drug use: Overview of key findings, 2002* (NIH Publication No. 03-5374). Bethesda, MD: National Institute on Drug Abuse.

Jordan, K.M. (2000). Substance abuse among gay, lesbian, bisexual, transgender, and questioning adolescents. *School Psychology, 29,* 201–206.

Juffer, K. A. (1983) Culture shock: A theoretical framework for understanding adaptation. In J. Bransford (Ed.) *BUENO Center for Multicultural Education Monograph Series* (Vol. 4, No. 1). Boulder, CO: University of Colorado.

Kaufman, P., Alt, M. N., & Chapman, C. (2001). *Dropout rates in the United States.* Washington, DC: National Center for Education Statistics. Retrieved August 28, 2007 from http://nces.ed.gov/pubsearch/pubsinfo.asp?pubid+2002114.

Kim, B. K., & Abreu, J. M. (2001). Acculturation measurement: Theory, current instruments, and future directions. In J. G. Ponterotto, J. M. Casas, L. A. Suzuki, & C. M. Alexander (Eds), *Handbook of multicultural counseling* (2nd ed.). Thousand Oaks, CA: Sage.

Kim, B. S. K., Atkinson, D. R., & Yang, P. H. (1999). The Asian Values Scale: Development, factor analysis, validation, and reliability. *Journal of Counseling Psychology, 46,* 342–352.

La Fromboise, T., Coleman, H. L. R., & Gerton, J. (1993). Psychological impact of biculturalism: Evidence and theory. *Psychological Bulletin, 1114,* 395–412.

Landau, J. (1982). Therapy with families in cultural transition. In M. McGoldrick (Ed.), *Ethnicity and family therapy* (pp. 552–572). New York: Guilford Press.

Landrine, H., & Klonoff, E. A. (1994). The African American Acculturation Scale: Development, reliability, and validity. *Journal of Black Psychology, 20,* 104–127.

Landrine, H., & Klonoff, E. A. (1996). The African American Acculturation Scale: Origin and current status. In R. I. Jones (Ed.), *Handbook of tests and measurements for black populations* (vol. 2, pp. 119–138). Hampton, VA: Cobb and Henry.

Lewin, K. (1948). *Researching social conflicts: Selected papers on group dynamics.* New York: Harper & Row.

Lu, F., Lim, R. R., & Mezzich, J. E. (1995). Issues in the assessment and diagnosis of culturally diverse individuals. In J. M. Oldham & M. B. Riba (Eds.), *Review of psychiatry* (Vol. 14). Washington, DC: American Psychiatric Press.

Marin, G. (1992). Issues in the measurement of acculturation among Hispanics. In K. F. Geisinger (Ed.), *Psychological testing of Hispanics* (pp. 235–252). Washington, DC: American Psychological Association.

Marin, G., & Gamba, R. J. (1996). A new measurement of acculturation for Hispanics: The bidimensional acculturation scale for Hispanics. *Hispanic Journal of Behavioral Sciences, 18,* 297–316.

Marin, G., Organista, P. B., & Chun, K. M. (2003). Acculturation research. In G. B. Bernal, J. E. Trimble, & A. K. Burlew (Eds.), *Handbook of racial & ethnic minority psychology* (pp. 208–219). Thousand Oaks, CA: Sage

Matsumoto, D. (2000). *Culture and psychology: People around the world* (2nd ed.). Belmont, CA: Wadsworth Thompson.

McWhirter, P.T. (1998). *Risk factors associated with adolescent alcohol, tobacco, marijuana, solvent inhalant, and cocaine use.* National Institute on Drug Abuse Research Monograph. Pacific Grove, CA: Brooks/Cole.

McWhirter, J. J., McWhirter, B. T., McWhirter, E. H., & McWhirter, R. J. (2004). *At risk youth: A comprehensive response.* Pacific Grove, CA: Brooks/Cole.

Oetting, E. R., & Beauvais, R. (1990). Orthogonal cultural identity theory: The cultural identification in minority adolescents. *International Journal of Addiction, 25,* 655–685.

Ogbu, J.U. (1992). Understanding cultural diversity and learning. *Educational Researcher, 21*(8), 5–14.

Padilla, A. M. (1980). The role of cultural awareness and ethnic loyalty in acculturation. In A. M. Padilla (Ed.), *Acculturation: Theory, models, and some new findings* (pp. 47–84). Boulder, CO: Westview Press.

Pedersen, P. B., & Carey, J. C. (Eds.). (2003). *Multicultural counseling in schools: A practical handbook* (2nd ed.). Needham Heights, MA: Allyn & Bacon.

Plunkett, M., & Mitchell, C.M. (2000). Substance use rates among American Indian adolescents: Regional comparisons with Monitoring the Future high school seniors. *Journal of Drug Issues, 30,* 575–592.

Ponterotto, J. G., Casas, J. M., Suzuki, L. A., & Alexander, C. M. (Eds.). (2001). *Handbook of multicultural counseling* (pp. 506–606). Thousand Oaks, CA: Sage.

Ponterotto, J. G., Gretchen, D., & Chauhan, R. V. (2001). Cultural identity and multicultural assessment: Quantitative and qualitative tools for the clinician. In L. A. Suzuki, J. G. Ponterotto, & P. J. Meller (Eds.), *Handbook of multicultural assessment: Clinical, psychological, and educational applications.* San Francisco: Jossey-Bass.

Ponterotto, J. G., & Pedersen, P. B. (1993). *Preventing prejudice: A guide for counselors and educators.* Thousand Oaks, CA: Sage.

Roysircar-Sodowsky, G., & Maestes, M. V. (2000). Acculturation, ethnic identity, and acculturative stress: Evidence and measurement. In R. H. Dana (Ed.), *Handbook of cross-cultural and multicultural personality assessment* (pp. 131–172). Hillsdale, NJ: Lawrence Erlbaum.

Sciarra, D. T. (2001). Assessment of diverse family systems. In J. G. Ponterotto, J. M. Casas, L. A. Suzuki, & C. M. Alexander (Eds.), *Handbook of multicultural counseling* (pp. 506–606). Thousand Oaks, CA: Sage.

Serrano, E., & Anderson, J. (2003). Assessment of a refined short acculturation scale for Latino preteens in rural Colorado. *Journal of Behavioral Sciences, 25*(2), 240–253.

Simcox, D. (1997). Major predictors of immigration restrictionism. *Population and Environment: A Journal of Interdisciplinary Studies, 19,* 129–143.

Small, M. A., Lyons, P. M., & Guy, L. S. (2002). Liability issues in child abuse and neglect reporting statutes. *Professional Psychology: Research and Practice, 33,* 13–18.

Sodowsky, G. R., & Maestas, M. V. (2000). Acculturation, ethnic identity, and acculturative stress: Evidence and measurement. In R. Dana (Ed.), *Handbook of cross-cultural and multicultural personality assessment* (pp. 131–172). Mahwah, NJ: Lawrence Erlbaum.

Stonequist, E. V. (1961). *The marginal man: A study in personality and culture conflict.* New York: Russell & Russell.

Szapocznik, J., & Kurtines, W. (1980). Acculturation, biculturalism and adjustment among Cuban Americans. In A. Padilla (Ed.), *Acculturation: Theory, models, and some new findings.* American Association for the advancement of Science, Symposium Series, No. 39 (pp. 139–159). Boulder, CO: Westview.

Takushi, R., & Uomoto (2001). The clinical interview from a multicultural perspective. In L. A. Suzuki, J. G. Ponterotto, & P. J. Meller (Eds.), *Handbook of multicultural assessment: Clinical, psychological, and educational applications* (2nd ed.). San Francisco: Jossey-Bass.

Unger, J. B., Gallaher, P., Shakib, S., Ritt-Olson, A., Palmer, P. H., & Johnson, C. A. (2002). The AHIMSA Acculturation Scale: A new measure of acculturation for adolescents in a multicultural society. *Journal of Early Adolescence, 22*(3), 225–251.

Valentine, C. A. (1971). Deficit, difference, and bicultural models of Afro-American behavior. *Harvard Educational Review, 41,*135–157.

Velez, W., & Saenz, R. (2001). Toward a comprehensive model of the school leaving process among Latinos. *School Psychology Quarterly, 16*(4), 445–467.

Washington, E. D. (1994). Three steps to cultural awareness: A Wittgensteinian approach. In P. Pedersen, & J. C. Carey (Eds.), *Multicultural counseling in schools: A practical handbook* (pp. 81–102). Needham Heights, MA: Allyn & Bacon.

Annotated Bibliography

Aronson Fontes, L. (2005). *Child abuse and culture: Working with diverse families.* New York: Guilford Press. *This book provides a framework for culturally competent practice with children and families in child maltreatment cases. Numerous workable strategies and concrete examples are included to help professionals address cultural concerns at each stage of the assessment and intervention process.*

Chun, K. M., Organista, P. B., & Marin, G. (Eds.). (2003). *Acculturation: Advances in theory, measurement, and applied research.* Washington, DC: American Psychological Association. *This text assembles contributions from top scholars in the field of acculturation research. Chapters cover understanding individual and family processes, acculturation, psychosocial adjustment and health, and psychological distress and depression.*

Winton, M. A., & Mara, B. A. (2001). *Child abuse and neglect: Multidisciplinary approaches.* Needham Heights, MA: Allyn & Bacon. *This text provides a thorough review on child abuse and neglect. Chapters cover sexual, physical, and emotional and psychological abuse, cultural diversity issues in counseling, and the process of diagnosing, assessing, and interviewing in child abuse.*

11

The Language Barrier

The Problem of Language in the United States

The increasingly culturally diverse society in the United States has led to an increase in the number of English Language Learners (ELLs) in American schools (Cofresi & Gorman, 2004; Salvia & Ysseldyke, with Bolt, 2007). This student population is escalating and will continue to grow (Kindler, 2002, cited in Rhodes, Ochoa, & Ortiz, 2005; Salvia et al., 2007). Garcia (2002) predicts that at least 25 percent of students ranging from kindergarten to high school will be considered Limited English Proficient (LEP) by the year 2026. These facts should not be alarming, since most of the world's population acquires at least two languages (Piper, 1993).

In spite of this, learning a second language has been controversial in the United States and in other countries (Piper, 1993; Mushi, 2002). The debate about second language learning in the United States reached public visibility through the now famous 1974 Supreme Court case *Lau v. Nichols*. This case involved a young Chinese boy who was being instructed in English only, although he did not understand this language. The court concurred that this limiting instructional method was a civil rights violation of the boy's right to an education. However, the courts did not state how the boy should be educated. Instructional linguistic programs for educators to adopt were not specified. A year later, the U.S. Department of Education's Office of Civil Rights (OCR) put out a more thorough report, *Task-Force Findings Specifying Remedies Available for Eliminating Past Educational Practices Ruled Unlawful Under Lau v. Nichols*, which elaborated the *Lau* case outcome by recommending that elementary schools offer ELL students bilingual education (see Rhodes, Ochoa, & Ortiz, 2005). In its early days, the implementation of bilingual programs for ELL was not research based, and therefore led to district and local situations which depended on qualified personnel, funding, and the number of ELL students. Today, there are five categories of instructional programs (see Hakuta, 2000; Rhodes et al., 2005) and various instructional approaches for ELL students (see Chamot & O'Malley, 1994).

Mushi (2002) points out that, although the number of children learning two languages may be the same as the number of monolingual children, bilingualism *per se* is not well comprehended by educators. Some educators have viewed the problem of *simultaneous second language learning* as confusing to a child, and as causing possible delays in language development. In fact, simultaneous second language learning can be a normal process that leads to proficiency by the time a child reaches the end of the preschool years (Arnberg, 1987). Based on this observation, immigrant children may have difficulties when they are exposed to dominant cultures (such as the host culture) that practice disparate instructional approaches. Currently, the recommended evaluation and instructional approach is to utilize the language that the student normally uses—not the one his or her parents use (see Individuals with Disabilities Education Act 1997). Furthermore, utilizing the student's native language to instruct will not necessarily interfere—as some believe—with English language learning, but rather enhance the connections between the two—in terms of culture, language, and cognition. Stipulations of the No Child Left Behind law (January 2002) made provision for federal funds to be made available for English language instruction. School districts are held accountable by annual appraisal guidelines on the number of ELL students who develop their language skills into English proficiency.

The diversity of language in the United States has been ongoing as a result of the influx of immigration of non-English speaking families. Gollnick and Chinn (2006) mention that most reference books cite four to five thousand languages in the world, with an estimated ten thousand in existence. In Los Angeles, California, there are 324 identified languages, with many having different dialects (see Gollnick & Chinn, 2006, Ch. 7). As a result of this multiplicity, today's children are learning their native language at home, commonly defined as the *first language acquisition* (L1) process, and acquire English as a second language (L2) at school. The ability to speak two languages proficiently is known as *bilingualism*. Learning two languages or more is certainly an added strength for any child. Unfortunately, to the dismay of many parents, children tend to lose L1 in favor of acquiring language proficiency in the dominant language of their new culture, often becoming monolingual. Adding to this decreased proficiency is the loss of ethnic preservation of language (Gollnick & Chinn, 2006).

Naturally, the cultural diversity of students and second language learning has impacted upon psychological assessments and school-based therapeutic interventions, which are primarily monolingual and founded on Euro-American philosophy and standards (Canino & Spurlock, 2000; Cofresi & Gorman, 2004). Rhodes and colleagues (2005) cite a study by Ochoa, Galarza, and Gonzalez (1996) that examined language proficiency assessment practices of school psychologists and found that many school psychologists do not observe appropriate assessment practices. In fact, research indicates that numerous school psychologists have not been properly trained in the assessment practices of culturally and linguistically diverse students. School psychologists in states with a large population of Hispanic children and youth (i.e., Arizona, California, Colorado, Florida, New Jersey, New Mexico, New York, and Texas) reported that they had not been adequately trained in bilingual assessment procedures in their university training programs. However, even without adequate training, school psychologists reported that they had conducted assessments for limited English proficiency (LEP) students (Ochoa, Rivera, & Ford; 997). Ochoa and colleagues (1997) conclude that the validity of test results for LEP students is therefore questionable, and thus raises some frightening implications regarding the eligibility decisions made.

Consequently, school psychologists must receive proper training to acquire expertise in various critical areas necessary for servicing ELL students. This chapter's goal is to provide a review of guidelines compiled from recent literature (Collier, 2001; Salvia et al., 2007; Rhodes et al., 2005; Hakuta, 2000) on recent ELL issues and recommendations that will enhance school psychologists' competencies in this important area.

ELL Misrepresentation in Special Education

Gottlieb (2006) defines ELLs as follows: "Any school-aged child exposed to culture and language, other than English, in daily interaction in his or her home environment is considered a linguistically and culturally diverse student" (p. 3). She cites several interesting demographics:

- As of the 2002–2003 academic year, the five million-plus ELLs in U.S. schools represented approximately 10 percent of the total, from prekindergarten through grade twelve.
- The top five reported languages, along with their percentage of the total, are as follows: Spanish (79.2%), Vietnamese (2%), Hmong (1.6%), Cantonese (1%), and Korean (1%), with an additional 19 languages (Kindler, 2002, cited in Gottlieb, 2006, p. 2).
- Latinos/Hispanics are the largest minority group in the United States, with 38.8 million residents (U.S. Census Bureau, June 2003, cited in Gottlieb, 2006).

- An update by the U.S. Census Bureau (July 2003, cited in Gottlieb, 2006) revealed an ongoing increase in the Latino/Hispanic population of 9.8 percent, with a 9 percent increase in the number of Asians. (Gottlieb, 2006, p. 2)

These statistics increase the need for the appropriate education of ELL children and youth. This issue is particularly a concern for educators and practitioners because of the overrepresentation of minority students in special education. A review of some twenty years of history and data regarding the disproportionate representation of racial/ethnic and culturally and linguistically diverse (CLD) children and youth in special education is beyond the scope of this chapter. However, it is important to summarize certain points. There is sufficient evidence documented in the literature (Oakland & Gallegos, 2005; Rhodes et al., 2005; Salvia et al., 2007) to confirm an overrepresentation of ELL and CLD children and youth in special education who have been classified as mentally retarded, learning disabled, and emotionally disturbed, in addition to an underrepresentation in gifted programs (Donovan & Cross, 2002). Understanding this ethnic overrepresentation in special education has been difficult for researchers, due to limitations in research and the inconsistency among states in the data collected that document the referral process. Furthermore, insufficient research has been conducted on ELL students. Language-based issues did not gain much notice in special education studies with regard to overrepresentation (see Ochoa, 2005). In general, there is little doubt that many second language learners have been misdiagnosed and/or misplaced, and that language may very often have been an essential factor for unsuitable placements.

This observed underachievement gap for ELL students places the responsibility on school psychologists to understand and continually review the Individuals with Disabilities Education Act (IDEA) 1997. Keeping abreast of the IDEA amendments and ensuring that ELLs are not misclassified as a result of limited L2 language is an advocacy responsibility of practitioners and educators. The problem of disproportionality was enacted in the 1997 amendment to the IDEA. States are required to amass data for the U.S. Department of Education to ascertain whether overrepresentation is occurring, and are mandated to correct the problem. This is important for school psychologists servicing ELL populations since it directly addresses advocacy for culturally and linguistically appropriate assessments and placement in adequate bilingual education programs.

Regrettably, there are many cases in which the assessment practices of professionals and eligibility decisions for special education services have led to unwise recommendations that placed second language learners in special education programs because the linguistic needs of the learner could not be met in a general education environment. This unprincipled resolution has often been due to school or local district funding problems that prevented schools from providing specifically needed language-based programs. Unfortunately, this is not likely to affect the classification and placement of ELL students or any other culturally diverse students. However, clinicians often face placement dilemmas trying to obtain an adequate learning environment for assessed ELL students. Apparently, state and federal governments support cultural diversity, but the intent of providing an adequate education for ELLs is ultimately placed on local community school districts whose responsibility it is to fund suitable educational instruction for ELL students in their local schools (Salvia et al., 2007). This is not always established, and ELL children and adolescents are misclassified as having learning problems in order to obtain proper instructional services. In many cases, parents are informed of this dilemma and eventually sign legal documents (Individual Education Plans, or IEP) accepting a misdiagnosis to facilitate proper instruction for their child. In terms of advocacy efforts and students' rights, it is unfortunate that clinicians (educational evaluators and school psychologists) do not attempt to end this falsified practice by raising complaints to the proper authorities (e.g., school administrators regarding IDEA and Section 504 student rights).

It is especially important to recognize that school psychologists will often face ethical dilemmas in their practice that will be at odds with their school and district employers who may encourage certain unethical practices. When under pressure regarding ethical responsibilities, school psychologists must develop strategies to avoid conflicts, while not forgetting their ethical responsibilities to their student-clients. Ways of responding to ethical dilemmas are outlined in Helton et al. (2000; see also NASP, 2000). Advocacy on the part of the school psychologist is of the utmost importance.

Initial Steps to Consider for Best Practice

To ensure that unfair referrals and assessments are not attributed to poor practice, Rhodes et al. (2005) recommend that there are four critical factors with which practitioners should initially be familiar in their school-based practice. First, school psychologists should make a point of having a full understanding of how students are identified as ELL in their respective states in order to be able to review, evaluate, and integrate the identifiable process into their treatment and decision-making procedures.

Second, school psychologists should recognize that the ELL student population will differ significantly in native and English-language abilities such as oral skills, listening, reading, and writing. Determining whether the ELL student is a *simultaneous* instead of a *sequential* language learner is important in order to determine the extent to which the English language has been developed, and to assess whether there is a need for *dual-language* instruction.

Third, it is important to realize that the United States has "language diversity." That is, there are over 400 different languages spoken in the United States. Spanish is the majority language spoken by schoo-age students besides English. School psychologists should be cognizant of the different language groups in their schools, especially the low-incidence language groups that most likely will require special assistance.

Lastly, demographical data indicate that the ELL student population has doubled during the 1990s and, as mentioned above, continues to escalate. With the current student demographics, teachers, school counselors, and school psychologist have experience in teaching, counseling, and assessing ELL students. Proper training for servicing racial/ethnic CLD children and youth is necessary for all of these professions, or the repercussions of inadequate instruction, evaluations, and interventions will be severe—indeed, in many documented cases it already has been (see litigations on *Diana v. California*, 1970 and *Larry P. v. Riles*, 1972, cited in Rhodes et al., 2005, pp. 15–41).

Factors Affecting the Learning of a Second Language

At present, school psychologists must have knowledge of the second language acquisition process since it is estimated that, by the year 2026, approximately 15 million students with limited English proficiency will be enrolled in schools (Gollnick & Chinn, 2006). Lack of knowledge of the L2 process will affect a practitioner's interactions with ELL students as well as the appropriateness of assessments and recommendations. Children learn L1 through continual interaction with parents and extended family members. Early language structure and concepts in L1 can directly be transferred to L2. For this reason, it is important for the child to have a thorough grasp of L1 prior to transferring skills to L2. If L1 is not well developed in the early stages of acquisition, L2 will adversely be affected. Gollnick and Chinn (2006) cite several studies (Cummins, 1984, 1996, 2000; Crawford, 2004; Hakuta, Butler, & Witt, 2000) which have contributed to the understanding of the process of L1 and L2 acquisition. The next section is a summary of these findings.

An early attempt at pinpointing the L2 process was Cummins' (1984) study of conversational language versus cognitive academic language. Cummins (1984, 1996) found that it takes two years for English language learner (ELL) students to acquire what he terms basic interpersonal communicative skills

(BICS). In essence, after two years students have sufficient skills in L2 to carry on a conversation. While this may be perceived as adequate language skills—and can often fool teachers into thinking the student is L2 proficient—these skills are not adequate for academic learning. According to Cummins' research, it takes five to seven years for an ELL student to attain cognitive academic language proficiency (CALPS). It has been proposed that the linguistic acquisition of CALP is "a level of linguistic proficiency that is required for abstract and analytical thinking and expressions with complex meaning" (Crawford, 2004, p. 289, cited in Gollnick & Chinn, 2006). This level of proficiency is needed for writing descriptive journals or oral presentations, and for testing purposes.

Two main reasons have been noted for the longer time period it takes ELL students to acquire L2 CALPS. First, academic language—the language of subject-matter (i.e., math, science)—is very different from BICS and requires more complex syntax and abstract expressions. Furthermore, academic language is what English proficient students are learning in the classroom as they enter school, with basic conversational skills learned at home. However, the ELL student is learning BICS while his classmates are learning higher level academic English (i.e., CALPS) (Cummins, 2000; Hakuta, Butler, & Witt, 2000, cited in Gollnick & Chinn, 2006). Another point to consider is that sociocultural influences may be more important than linguistic factors. Several questions need to be considered: Can power and status relationships between majority and minority groups exert influence on the school performance of these students? Do students belonging to lower-status minority groups have lower academic achievement? Cummins (1996) suggests that these factors do influence minority groups. Given the sociocultural problems associated with learning, it becomes the responsibility of educators to ensure that students learn in L1 until they can attain a competent level of L2 (i.e., CALPS). This is a student right that has led to English as a second language (ESL) and bilingual education programs. Moreover, educators (and school psychologists) should have an understanding of cultural and linguistic differences (Gollnick & Chinn, 2006). Lastly, Mushi (2002) emphasizes that parents, in addition to the home environment, are influential in primary language development as well as the second language acquisition of their child. Concentration on the L2 also influences the educational progress of the child. Furthermore, parents are responsible for creating environments in which linguistic diversity is encouraged. However, Ortiz (1997) advises that parents should not be encouraged to avoid L1 at the expense of the acquisition of L2, and Cummins (1984) stresses that proficiency in L1 is critical for learning English proficiency (Castillo, Quintana, & Zamarripa, 2000). School psychologists should check for parents' attitudes about education and English language acquisition as well as the child's own standpoint.

Language-Based Competencies for Best Practice

Whether the school psychologist is monolingual or bilingual, there are certain competencies each should attain for servicing ELL students. Given that there is a long-standing argument stressing that university training programs have not adequately prepared graduate students for servicing culturally and linguistically diverse populations (Bernal & Castro, 1994; Ochoa, Rivera, & Ford, 1997), school psychologists need to accept the responsibility of self-preparation in this domain as a professional development commitment. As in any profession, competencies for professional practice will not advance unless the practitioner keeps resourcefully abreast of change. In this instance, practitioners must be aware of the linguistic issues and ethical guidelines to be considered prior to servicing racial/ethnic CLD children and youth who are ELLs. The subsequent sections present critical information that will enhance practitioner competencies necessary for servicing bilingual and second language learners.

Initially, school psychologists should examine the following steps to take *prior* to engaging in an ELL student referral for a special education evaluation.

Checklist of Steps to Take Before ELL Assessment

1. Develop a thorough understanding of the legal requirements of federal law, federal regulations, and state requirements before assessing any student for an eligibility determination (i.e., IDEA, ADA, FERPA). Since the IDEA is constantly updated, it is important to keep a current copy of the IDEA and associated final regulations of the statute. See Office of Special Education Programs (OSEP) at the U.S. Department of Education website: www.ed.gov/offices/OSERS/Policy/IDEA.

2. Have knowledge of pertinent *case law* and its resulting foundation for public law (for example, *Brown v. Board of Education*, 1954).

3. Develop a thorough understanding of *informed parental consent*. Parents must be knowledgeable and legally competent, and consent must be voluntary (Bersoff & Hofer, 1990).

4. Goals for adequate professional practice should incorporate individual students' history, skills, and needs by: (a) situation-specific ethical guidelines (e.g., ethical guidelines to follow if an interpreter is required); (b) discipline-specific ethical guidelines (e.g., NASP and APA ethical guidelines); (c) discipline-specific standards (e.g., NASP and APA professional standards); and (d) general professional standards.

SOURCE: Compiled from Rhodes et al. (2005).

It is necessary to have full knowledge of IDEA regulations, since this will aid the practitioner in diagnoses and placement decisions. Furthermore, knowledge of pertinent case laws provides practitioners with a historical background of important cases and this will help for advocacy purposes should the need arise. Finally, in every service rendered to children and youth from different backgrounds, the goals for adequate professional practice from NASP and APA should be incorporated and adhered to.

Accordingly, school psychologists assessing ELL students must have knowledge of the theoretical and political debates involved in second language acquisition and bilingual education (see Rhodes et al., 2005, pp. 42–53, 57–75). Rhodes and colleagues discuss several key factors pertaining to bilingual education and second language acquisition for determining adequate practice. First, how do children successfully acquire a second language? Knowledge of the linguistic research of Cummins (1984) regarding second language acquisition (e.g., BICS and CALPS) and the school-based problems ELL children and youth experience—such as inadequate teaching and the fallacies about bilingualism among educators—assists us to answer this question. Thus it is particularly important for school practitioners to be aware of the history of bilingual education in the United States since many educators believe receiving dual language instruction will delay or impede second language acquisition (e.g., English). This misconception has led parents of ELL students to reject bilingual education services, because they assume that such a program will cause their children delays in learning English. Unfortunately, in some cases parental decisions to decline bilingual services were encouraged by school personnel (Rhodes et al., 2005). For this reason, it is important for school psychologists to ascertain that their decisions as well as those of parents are based on theory and research, not on possible biases.

Second, what is the language-based reason for the ELL student referral? Research has shown that limited English proficiency (LEP) children are referred for special education because of *oral language-related factors* (Ochoa, Robles-Pina, Garcia, & Breunig, 1999; Ortiz & Polyzoi, 1986; Rueda, Cardoza, Mercer, & Carpenter, 1985). Oral-language related factors should carefully be examined by the school psychologist to see whether: (a) the oral language referrals are commonly observed among second language learners; and (b) any detected behavioral problems could have arisen due to limited English skills—and school psychologists must differentiate the similarities in behavioral problems that are observed between LEP students and learning disabled (LD) students (Ochoa et al., 1999; Ortiz & Polyzoi, 1986; Rueda et al., 1985).

Third, what were the educational opportunities of the ELL student? As noted before, background information about the ELL student is essential. School psychologists should make sure that a lack of educational opportunity and LEP are not factors determining academic failure that later meet the criteria for a disability (IDEA, 1997). In determining whether a lack of opportunity is an important factor, the school psychologist should consider the possibility that academic problems may directly be related to inappropriate instruction or the lack of opportunity to obtain suitable instruction. Regarding these recommendations, Rhodes et al. (2005) question, "How can school-based practitioners truly meet the egalitarian intent of these legal provisions if they do not have knowledge about the second-language acquisition process and what types of bilingual education programming result in positive achievement outcomes?" (p. 58). This is an important question that should not be overlooked by school psychologists seeking to improve their competencies.

Fourth, should LEP students be tested in their native language only, or in both languages, or in English only? For cognitive testing, it is imperative that the practitioner recognize that second language acquisition undergoes a stage process that begins with the child acquiring certain early learning informal communication skills that can easily deceive the practitioner into thinking the LEP child has attained full knowledge of the second language (e.g., BICS and CALPS) and can therefore be tested in this language. Moreover, if a child has been removed from a bilingual program, it is important to know why. The removal does not necessarily mean that the child has attained full second language acquisition. Rhodes et al. (2005) emphasize two important points. The authors explain that states have guidelines detailing the criteria an LEP child must meet to be *removed* from a bilingual education program, and school psychologists should make it a point to learn their state's criteria to ascertain that the second language learner has met the criteria. Lastly, school psychologists must keep abreast of the research on the efficacy of certain bilingual education programs, since research has demonstrated that not all programs are alike and, as a result, each will directly affect academic performance. To date, there are five bilingual programs available for bilingual students (bilingual programs are described below).

Factors Affecting L2 Cognitive and Academic Proficiency

In distinguishing the linguistic process of L2 English learners, Salvia et al. (2007) discuss three considerations that can affect the L2 cognitive and academic proficiency process:

1. *Age*—Younger children acquire language faster than older children (e.g., at 12 to 14 years of age, language learning becomes more difficult).

2. *Immersion in English*—The more exposure/immersion to English L2, the faster the acquisition. Hence children will learn quicker if L2 is spoken at

home. If only L1 is spoken at home, L2 acquisition will be slower. This is often a dilemma for parents who want their children to learn English L2 while being fearful that L1 will be forgotten.

3. *Similarity to English*—If the L1 language has similar features to English L2, children will acquire L2 more quickly and with less difficulty.

Some examples of dissimilarities are:

- The speech sounds in English may be different from speech sounds of other languages.
- Orthography may be different. English uses the Latin alphabet; other languages may use other alphabets or diacritical marks (a mark above or below a printed letter that indicates a change in the way it is to be pronounced or stressed).
- The letter-sound correspondences may be different from L1 (e.g., the letter *h* in Spanish is silent but in one Brazilian dialect it is pronounced as the English *r*).
- The grammar may be different. English is mainly *noun* governed; other languages are *verb* directed.
- Word order differs. For example, in Spanish adjectives follow nouns, in English nouns follow adjectives. (Modified from Salvia et al., 2007, p. 177)

These factors that can affect the L2 cognitive and academic proficiency process are essential to consider when reviewing an ELL student's language development history, since this will help to determine how progress or difficulties occur. Additionally, for assessment purposes, it is wise to collect as much information as possible regarding L2 acquisition.

Additional factors to consider include the child's culture and language background, since learning styles will differ from culture to culture. Moreover, children learning English as a second language may manifest difficulties in auditory perception and recognizing sounds or phonemes of the English language (Lerner, 2005). The assessor should not confuse errors in L2 as signs of language disorder or speech disorder. Speech disorders are aberrations in the production of sounds (i.e., articulation difficulties, hoarse voice, fluency/ stuttering). Language disorders are delayed speech, receptive language disorders, and expressive language disorders (see Lerner, 2005, pp. 323–367).

Assessment of L2

Obviously, school psychologists must evaluate L1 and L2 proficiency prior to a psycho-educational assessment. Establishing language proficiency and dominance is an integral part of an assessment. A requirement of the Individuals with Disabilities Education Act (IDEA) is that limited English proficiency (LEP) students' achievement levels and abilities be assessed in an unbiased manner with the appropriate materials and procedures selected and administered with the intent of determining whether a child with LEP has a disability and requires special education services rather than measuring the LEP child's English skills. However, professionals are often inclined to misunderstand language proficiency and language dominance. When conceptualized improperly, this mistake can cause complications in assessment, recommendations, and interventions. Language proficiency and dominance should be viewed distinctly. *Language dominance* indicates that one language is better developed in the habitual domains of oral expression, reading, and writing abilities. However, as Rhodes et al. (2005) state, "patterns of dominance are most often a reflection of history and circumstance, not developmental problems. In addition, dominance indicates only that one language is better developed than the other but reveals nothing about overall proficiency in either language" (p. 148). For instance, if minimal proficiency is demonstrated both in English and the native language, there may very well be language dominance in the native language even where actual language proficiency is low in both. Therefore, language dominance does not necessarily lead to assessment. It is the proficiency level in each language that directs the assessment procedure (Rhodes et al., 2005). *Language proficiency* provides information that determines how efficiently individuals can converse in, read, write, and comprehend the language in comparison with their peers. For example, a child's primary language may be English but this does not mean that the child is English proficient (Oakland & Gallegos, 2005, Ch. 38). It is important to remember that language dominance does not mean the student has the language competence necessary for testing.

More importantly, determining language proficiency is required in order to determine what type of assessment measure to use to produce valid and reliable results. Consequently, an ELL student referred for a psycho-educational evaluation should be screened for language proficiency in both L1 and L2. If not properly screened for the student's current language abilities, practitioners will not be able to determine: (a) whether the student's present educational setting is appropriate; (b) whether the appropriate assessment practices were used to determine achievement and cognitive intellectual abilities; (c) the extent to which L1 and L2 affect or explain test performance on cognitive and achievement instruments; and (d) whether the noted referral problem(s) are due to a genuine disability or part of the common L2 acquisition process (Ochoa, Galarza, & Gonzalez, 1996; Figueroa, 1990; Chamberlain & Medinos-Landurand, 1991; Willig, 1986). It is important to determine language proficiency in L1 and L2 because a disability (such as a learning disability) cannot be diagnosed if a problem is not observed in both languages. As Rhodes et al. (2005) point out, if a child can accurately decode words in

L1 but not in L2, then the child cannot be diagnosed as learning disabled. To identify a true disability, the child must manifest deficits in both languages.

Considerations in the assessment of bilingual or ELL students are presented in a checklist compressed from several research recommendations for further strengthening the assessment process (see box).

Checklist for Bilingual and ELL Assessment

1. If parents have adopted English as the main language in the home, what language was spoken at home when the student was a child?

2. How old was the student before exposure to the second language?

3. Were there previous language testing experiences for the student?

4. How involved are the student's parents in the first and second language acquisition of their child (Mushi, 2002)?

5. Are there any social and cultural concerns?

6. Is there a need for an interpreter or alternative test form that will ensure a more accurate demonstration of the student's abilities (Cofresi & Gorman, 2004)?

7. What alternative methods will be adopted (e.g., interviews, checklists, ethnographic/ qualitative, informal speech analysis, curriculum based assessment (CBA) or dynamic assessment) (Saenz & Huer, 2003)?

8. Are any testing modifications necessary? Would renorming the considered instrument be more appropriate (Saenz & Huer, 2003)?

9. Has the examiner checked for validity and reliability of the testing instruments/scales to be utilized in the language screening? Will the instrument/scale establish proficiency levels for the students' ethnic group representation?

Prior to assessing a bilingual or ELL student, practitioners are advised to review the above questions or steps to take as guidelines for the purpose of accomplishing a linguistically fair assessment.

Gottlieb (2006) provides a Sample Oral Language Use Survey (see Figure 11.1) that is used for assessing language proficiency of English language leaners. The survey is environment focused and is administered by the assessor to the English language learner. The questions posed help the assessor determine *where* the ELL student uses L1 or L2. The survey can be used by school psychologists during an initial interview to establish the ELL's L1 and L2 mode of communication in various domains.

A Sample Oral Language Use Survey

Directions: I am going to ask you which language you use around your home, neighborhood, and school. Tell me if you use your first (or native) language (L1), _____, English (L2), or both languages with the people and places that I name. [As the student responds, mark the designated box.]

	First or Native Language (L1)	Second Language English (L2)	Both Languages (L1 + L2)	Not Applicable
Around your home				
With your parents or guardian				
With your grandparents				
With your brothers and sisters				
With other relatives who live with you				
With your caregivers (if any)				
With your neighbors				
With your friends				
Around your neighborhood				
At the store				
At the clinic or doctor's office				
At church (if applicable)				
Outside, as in a park				
At a restaurant or fast food place				
Around your school				
On the playground or outside				
In the lunchroom				
In the halls				
During free time				

Figure 11.1   Sample Oral Language Use Survey

SOURCE: Adapted from Gottlieb and Hamayan (2007). Reprinted with permission.

Another measure developed by Gottlieb in 1999, a Sample Survey for English Language Learners, is ideal for estimating the ELL's self-reported literacy practices (reproduced in Gottlieb, 2006, p. 18). The questions asked help the assessor determine what kinds of materials the ELL student reads and writes outside the school. The survey is replicated in Figure 11.2 and can be used by school psychologists during an initial interview to estimate the ELL student's reading and writing habits of L1 and L2.

For children and youth with learning disabilities in reading or delays in oral language comprehension, the examiner may have to read the survey questions aloud to the student or repeat questions slowly.

Supplementary Guidelines for Servicing English Language Learners

Mushi (2002) emphasizes that the parents, in addition to the home environment, are influential in the language development and second language acquisition of the child. Concentration on the latter also influences the educational progress of the child. Furthermore, parents are responsible for creating environments in which linguistic diversity is encouraged. The school psychologist should check for parents' attitudes about education and English language acquisition as well as the child's own standpoint.

Another important question for the practitioner to consider is, "In what languages should interventions be recommended?" Gutierrez-Clellen (1996) conducted an extensive review regarding this important question and concluded that:

1. Learning in one language does not necessarily impede language development in another language.

2. Learning involves processes that are interrelated in both languages a child speaks.

3. Language skills can be transferred from L1 to L2 through mediation in the native language.

Consideration of these findings prior to recommending interventions is suggested. Lastly, school psychologists should remember that ELLs come from diverse economic and ethnic backgrounds, and that these differences will also affect the ELL's progress.

In their discussion on the cultural variation within Hispanic American families, Lopez, Lopez, Suarez-Morales, & Gonzalez Castro (2006) explain

A Sample Survey for English Language Learners

Directions: Which kinds of materials do you read and write outside of school? Mark the box to show whether you use your first (or native) language (L1), _____ , English (L2), or both languages when you read or write.

Before or after school. . . .	First or Native Language (L1)	Second Language English (L2)	Both Languages (L1 + L2)	Not Applicable
I read				
Street signs and names				
Maps or directions				
Schedules (e.g., school bus or train)				
Newspapers				
Magazines				
Notes from friends, such as e-mail messages				
Information from the internet				
Brochures/pamphlets				
Short stories				
Poetry				
Books				
I write				
Information on papers or forms				
Lists				
Memos or notes				
E-mail messages				
Letters to family members or for school				
Short stories				
Poetry or songs				

Figure 11.2   Sample Survey for English Language Learners

SOURCE: Gottlieb (2006), p. 18.

that the immigration status is strongly linked to poverty and to lack of educational opportunities, and that this ultimately affects achievement. The school classification of "limited English proficient" is predictive of low academic achievement and school dropout (Rumberger & Larson, 1998; Steinberg, Blinde, & Chan, 1984). Several factors have been delineated regarding educational underachievement in consequence of limited English proficiency:

- being instructed in L2 when an individual has low levels of competence;
- having to rely on L2 for learning and reading;
- L1 being totally ignored in the educational process;
- not having cognitive academic language proficiency in L2; and
- having low-level reading and listening skills (see Collier, 1992).

For a review of cognitive theories of bilingual education (e. g., interpersonal communicative skills and cognitive academic language), Lopez et al. (2006) direct readers to the following website: http://iteachilearn.com/uh/guadarrama/sociopsycho/cogeng.htn.

Formal and Informal Assessment Methods for English Language Learners

The two types of assessment recommended in the literature for evaluating second language learners use formal and informal methods. Rhodes et al. (2005) and Salvia et al. (2007) stress that the appropriate approach recommended by numerous school psychology and special education educators involves both formal and informal techniques (Figueroa, 1990; Maldonado-Colon, 1986; Ochoa, 2003; Ochoa, Galarza, & Gonzalez, 1996; Salvia et al., 2007). Informal methods provide observation of how language is used in real-life situations and in the classroom setting. Moreover, informal language assessments can provide information as to the student's language preference. Teachers and parents should be encouraged to participate in an informal language assessment and asked to indicate the language preference of the child. Sattler (2001) provides structured interview questionnaires for teachers and parents in order to determine student language preference. The questionnaires are reproduced in modified form in Figure 11.3.

Prior to testing, the ELL child should be asked about language preference. However, caution should be used. We have observed that some

Questions for Teacher

1. What language does the child use in the classroom?

2. In what language does the child read?

3. In what language does the child speak with his/her classmate?

4. In what language does the child write?

5. Overall, how competent is the child in English?

6. Overall, how competent is _____ in
   _____ [language]?

Questions for Parent

1. In what language do you speak with your child?

2. In what language does your husband (wife) speak with your child?

3. In what language do you speak with your husband (wife)?

4. In what language does your child speak with you?

5. In what language does your child speak with his/her father (mother)?

6. [If applicable] In what language does your child speak with his/her sisters and brothers?

7. What language does your child prefer to speak at school?

8. In what language are the television programs that your child watches?

9. In what language do you read stories to your child?

10. In what language does your child prefer to be tested?

Figure 11.3   Interview Questions for Teacher and Parent to Determine Child's Language Preference

SOURCE: Sattler, J. 2001. *Assessment of children: Cognitive applications*, 4th edition, 2001. pp. 635–656. Reprinted with permission.

racial/ethnic CLD children or adolescents may select L2 (i.e., English) as a preference for testing for two reasons: either the child/adolescent truly believes they have attained proficiency in L2 when proficiency (CALPS) has not been acquired or, in an attempt to assimilate, the child and/or adolescent identifies with the majority group language by preferring to be tested in L2, even though proficiency has not been acquired. In addition, some students may overrate their English language skills because of shame. The risk of not being accepted by peers or by the examiner because of low English language skills may cause embarrassment and fear of discovery, leading the examinee to the selection of L2 as the language of preference (Harris, Echemendia, Ardila, & Rosselli, 2001).

In addition to questionnaires, other informal methods are: (a) observations of ELLs in classroom and other settings; (b) teacher rating scales (i.e., the SOLOM); (c) storytelling/retelling in L1 and L2 (to assess the ELL's expressive abilities); (d) written or oral cloze/techniques/procedures using the current curriculum being taught; and (e) language samples (examiner has a conversation with the examinee on a topic of interest to the child or examiner observes the child in conversation with a classmate or teacher) (Ochoa & Ortiz, 2006, Ch. 9). Assessing by language samples can be difficult for school psychologists, since a background in linguistics is required for determining structural mistakes (see Hamayan & Damico, 1991, for more information on analyzing language samples).

Distinctive Factors of ELL and Bilingual Assessment

Assessment of bilingual students is closely connected to ELL students, since ELLs in due course will expectantly become bilingual. As mentioned above, bilingualism is described as the ability to use two languages. In most cases, this involves learning a second language (L2) concurrently. Bilingual assessment is defined as an evaluation of a bilingual student, conducted by a bilingual examiner, in a manner in which both the examiner and the examinee can use both languages as often as required during the entire evaluative process. Bilinguals tend to *code switch* from one language to another as the testing procedure necessitates. The opportunity to code switch during testing is important, as it allows the examinee to respond in a manner in which he or she is able to better demonstrate language skills as well as the specific knowledge required from the administered test (Rhodes et al., 2005).

An important fact to keep in mind is that there is consensus on the unavailability of properly trained bilingual practitioners, which in turn demotes authentic bilingual assessment. Properly trained bilingual practitioners should:

- possess expertise in the examinee's culture;
- have acquired training in non-discriminatory assessment in addition to knowledge regarding culture and language differences and how these have an effect on test performance; and
- be fluent in the examinee's language in order to assess performance correctly (Ochoa, Powell, & Robles-Pina, 1996; Ortiz, 2002).

Given this shortage of appropriate practitioners, Rhodes et al. (2005) explain that in all likelihood most of the alleged bilingual assessments conducted are not truly bilingual, even if the examiner speaks the examinee's language fluently and administers tests in the native language of the examinee. If the examiner is not properly trained (as described above), the evaluation cannot be considered bilingual in nature. Consequently, school psychologists who possess bilingual language skills should endeavor to obtain proper training in the competencies recommended.

There are several factors to consider when determining the level of bilingualism. First, is the child adding L2 to a well-developed first language? Second, is the child gradually replacing L1 (Sattler, 2001)? English is usually L2 for Hispanic American children. This second language (English) is used for schoolwork, while L1 continues to be utilized at home and in their communities. L2, however, is infrequently used for reading (Sattler, 2001). As a result of this manner of developing bilingualism, some Hispanic American children and youth fail to master either L1 or L2, and this in turn causes difficulties in learning (Sattler, 2001). School psychologists should observe second language learners in the classroom to determine which language is used most frequently. It is also important to obtain further information from the family about what language is used at home (see Figures 11.1 and 11.2).

Third, Sattler (2001) recommends requesting the child's teacher to complete the SOLOM rating scale (see Sattler, 2001, p. 649). The SOLOM (Student Oral Language Observation Matrix, developed by San Jose Area Bilingual Consortium) is a Likert scale that covers five major domains of language development. The domains are Comprehension, Fluency, Vocabulary, Pronunciation, and Grammar. A total score of 20 points is considered proficient.

Nonverbal Measures

Nonverbal assessment is another kind of evaluative method generally used by practitioners, mostly to estimate intellectual abilities of LEP children.

There are several types of tests for measuring cognitive abilities that have been perceived as being culture-free and unbiased in nature because they are non-verbal and do not assess language skills.

In fact, the tests still involve the use of language for directions in English. Others permit the use of oral or mime for directions. Most importantly, tests of non-verbal intelligence do not relate as closely to school success as those measuring verbal intelligence (Salvia et al., 2007). Some tests of non-verbal intelligence are: the Leiter International Performance Scale (which does not use oral language—Leiter, 1948); the Test of Non-Verbal Intelligence (uses oral and pantomine—Brown, Sherbenou, & Johnson, 1982); the Columbia Mental Maturity Scale (Burgemeister, Blum, & Lorge, 1972); and the Raven's Progressive Matrices (Raven, Court, & Raven 1986).

Rogers (1998) explains that evaluators have assumed non-verbal tests are more suitable for CLD children and youth because they are more culture fair than the traditional cognitive measures available, and do not have the cultural loadings found on many cognitive scales which lower minority student scores. However, Rogers refers to a review by Anastasi (1988) citing several studies indicating that "minority children achieve higher overall scores on the more traditional scales than on the verbal devices" (Rogers, 1998, p. 376). Another important fact mentioned is that "none of the non-verbal scales have been normed on LEP youngsters, which makes using the scale for normative comparisons inappropriate" (p. 376). An example cited is the Leiter International Performance Scale (Leiter, 1948), which has outdated norms and is based on a homogeneous sample of only 289 children. Given these limitations, Rogers advises evaluators to use caution when using non-verbal measures, and suggests that they should not be used as a single estimate of abilities.

Formal Measures

Formal measures are used to evaluate both intellectual and language abilities of LEP students. Although there are several formal measures available to assess bilingual verbal ability, Sattler (2001) states that none has obtained a nationally representative sample of individuals with proficiency in each language of the test. Formal measures, Sattler (2001) explains, have several technical problems with each test. Even when standardized tests are translated into the ELL's native language, the questions on the test often rely heavily on an individual's knowledge of American culture. If interpreters are used, the interpreter must be familiar with the testing procedures and the instrument (Gopaul-McNicol & Armour-Thomas, 2002; Gopaul-McNicol & Brice-Baker; 1998; Sattler, 2001).

Formal tests used for individual administration to assess language proficiency are: the Bilingual Verbal Ability Tests (BVAT) (Muñoz-Sandoval,

Cummins, Alvarado, & Ruef, 1998) (translated into 15 languages); the Language Assessment Scales-Oral (LAS-O) (Duncan & DeAvila, 1990); the Language Assessment Scales-Reading and Writing (LAS-R/W) (Duncan & DeAvila, 1994); and the Woodcock-Muñoz Language Survey (Woodcock & Muñoz-Sandoval, 1993, 2001) (see Sattler, 2001, Ch. 19).

The Woodcock-Muñoz Language Survey (WMLS; Woodcock & Muñoz-Sandoval, 1993), reviewed by Ochoa and Ortiz (2005), follows theoretical concepts of BICS and CALPS and provides specific information about the student's CALP development in English and Spanish L1 and L2. Another particular test discussed by Rhodes et al. (2005) that deserves special mention is the Bilingual Verbal Ability Test (BVAT; Muñoz-Sandoval, Cummins, Alvarado, & Ruef, 1998); this test is important because of its unique attempt to examine the bilingual abilities of bilingual individuals (Rhodes et al., 2005, p. 162). Rhodes and colleagues describe the BVAT as encompassing three tests taken from the Woodcock–Johnson COG (Picture Vocabulary, Oral Vocabulary, and Verbal Analogies). The exceptionality of this test is that it provides a composite score that distinguishes an individual's combined knowledge of both languages, expressed as bilingual verbal ability. An additional special feature is the BVAT's measure of cognitive academic language proficiency (CALPS; Cummins, 1984) in English. An aptitude score is also available that can be used to predict or compare performance on the Woodcock-Johnson–Revised Tests of Achievement (WJ-R ACH; Woodcock & Johnson, 1989). What is important about this new kind of instrument is its new method of combining the verbal abilities of both languages, thus departing from the traditional approach of conceptualizing independent language abilities (Rhodes et al., 2005). As with all psychometric measures, there is still work to be done to perfect this instrument (see Rhodes et al., 2005 for a review of psychometric guidelines).

Translated Tests

Another option is the use of translated tests. However, this also is hesitantly recommended due to various issues. Salvia et al. (2007) discuss these issues in their review of alternative ways to test students with LEP. First, examiners seeking translated tests should be aware that there are several tests available in various languages besides English, many of them in Spanish. However, as Salvia and colleagues point out, while a translated test will help the examinee to understand questions posed and directions given, the actual scored items may be of different complexity in the U.S. culture and the English language. The reason for this is that vocabulary items may differ in difficulty from language to language (e.g., in letter length and syllable count). Content may also differ in item difficulty from one culture to another (e.g., depending of the level of previous educational experiences).

Second, from a psychological perspective, the psychological demands of a test item may not be the same across languages. Depending on the personal experiences and the native language of the examinee, a test item may have separate psychological weight. For instance, identifying a vocabulary word (e.g., a fruit, such as peach or apple) will require a U.S. examinee to recall the biological class as well as the characteristics of what has previously been experienced as an edible fruit, whereas an examinee from another country may never have seen or eaten such a fruit. In the latter case, a correct response to the test item would measure achievement, while for the U.S. student the accurate answer would measure intelligence (Salvia et al., 2007, p.179; Rhodes et al., 2005). To ensure equality for the difficulty of test items, these factors are important for school psychologist to consider when using translated tests. As emphasized previously, knowledge of the culture and educational experiences of the examinee is imperative to attain fairness on assessments.

Selecting Instruments

There are several safety factors to consider prior to selecting formal measures of language proficiency, such as checking for: (a) norming properties; (b) reliability and validity; (c) type of skills assessed; (d) theoretical foundations used to develop the test/scale; and (e) how well the test/scale assesses L1 and L2, BICS and CALPS development, and receptive and expressive language skills (Ochoa & Ortiz, 2005). Furthermore, collecting current testing information (not more than six months old) on the student's language proficiency is vital because of the ongoing language acquisition process. This information is usually obtained through the English as a second language (ESL) or bilingual education programs in the schools. If unavailable, language proficiency levels will have to be established by the evaluator. Monolingual assessors will need to seek the help of bilingual professionals (i.e., bilingual school psychologists, bilingual speech and language pathologists, special education teachers, or trained interpreters—although the latter will have limitations; Ochoa & Ortiz, 2005, Ch. 9).

After formal and/or informal measures have been administered, practitioners can also use a helpful informal five-point scale for classifying the child's degree of language proficiency (see Figure 11.4).

Research on L1 and L2 language assessment has led to the recommendation that assessors/practitioners also address the emotional, cognitive, and academic concerns of ELL students (Castillo, Quintana, & Zamarripa, 2000). Regarding emotional factors, children need to identify their cultural

1. Monolingual speaker of a language other than English (speaks the other language exclusively).

2. Predominantly speaks a language other than English (speaks mostly the other language, but also speaks some English).

3. Bilingual (speaks the other language and English with equal ease).

4. Predominantly speaks English (speaks mostly English, but also speaks some in the other language).

5. Monolingual speaker of English (speaks English exclusively).

Figure 11.4   Five Point Classification Language Proficiency Scale

SOURCE: *Assessment of children: Cognitive applications* (4th ed.) (2001) Jerome Sattler, Chapter 19, pp. 635–656; Assessment of culturally and linguistically diverse children: Background considerations and dynamics. Reprinted with permission of Jerome M. Sattler, Publisher, Inc.

norms and have developed emotional vocabulary in L1 for self-expression. Additionally, bilingualism has been associated with positive cognitive characteristics. Bilingual children and youth tend to: (a) score higher on intelligence and achievement tests on both verbal and nonverbal measures; (b) be more cognitively flexible; and (c) be more creative and have higher degrees of problem-solving capacity (Lambert, 1981, p. 288).

All the considerations mentioned in this section are important for monolingual and bilingual school psychologists, since both will inevitably have to service ELL students from various countries. The following section incorporates language factors in consultation and interventions, and the use of interpreters.

Language Factors in Consultation and Interventions

Much of this chapter has focused on language acquisition and assessment procedures for ELL students. However, there are additional issues regarding ELL students that merit mention here due to changes that are occurring in assessment practices.

First, professionals servicing culturally diverse and LEP students should not overlook what Salvia et al. (2007) term "the evolution of assessment practice" (p. 674). The recent expansion of assessment practices focuses on a more dynamic—preventive-oriented—and intervention approach to evaluations. Assessment is dynamic in the sense that it is continually changing for the improvement of best practices. Professional associations and government mandates are constantly announcing alterations intended for the betterment of assessment practice. Currently, due to legal mandates, schools must report student progress on an annual basis. State-specified educational standards for which tests are developed to go with the standards are now accepted procedure. Additionally, assessors are required to demonstrate students' eligibility for services, identify students' skill levels as well as the preferred skill levels, and develop interventions intended to increase students' present skills to appropriate levels. In addition to assessors having to demonstrate students' eligibility for special services, they must also concentrate on treatment requirements obtained from assessment findings (Salvia et al., 2007).

Second, at present there is increased impetus for early identification and prevention as a means to avoid referrals for assessment. In the current assessment approaches discussed in this chapter, the focus of the evaluative process according to the literature reviewed is to identify deficits or limitations. This practice does not take the identification of the deficit(s) a step further: to implementation and follow-up of interventions with a focus on improving students' life. In the changing assessment practices, assessors (e.g., school psychologists) are required to identify academic problems early on in addition to physical disabilities and behavioral/emotional problems for the purposes of recommending interventions that are expected to bring about the desired outcomes for the student. The entire focus is placed on the intervention and its success. Consequently, assessment practice is now directed at "assessment for instructional planning" (Salvia et al., 2007, p. 675), which implies a linkage of the actual assessment to instruction (e.g., the intervention). When viewed another way, assessment for instructional planning could also be part of an early identification of a particular academic/linguistic/behavioral problem a student may manifest and could be viewed as preventive in that it stops the problem from getting worse in many cases.

Third, Salvia and colleagues describe a problem-solving model presently used (in the Heartland Educational Services Area in Johnston, Iowa) for special education assessments and the decision-making process. As a preventive approach, the model requires the implementation of thorough interventions *before* referrals to special education services are made. In this way, assessors/educators/school psychologists are responsible for following problem solving steps that include "systematic application of effective instruction and collection of data on student performance" (Salvia et al., 2007, p. 677). What this means is that educators/school psychologists must collect data indicating the student's performance in order to make appropriate decisions regarding instructional methodology (e.g., the subject taught and how it is taught). This problem-solving model is briefly reviewed here because it includes consultation with teachers, parents, and school personnel remediation teams.

While promising because of its methodical problem-solving and preventive approach, the model refers to consultation as a discussion to ascertain opinions and/or reach agreement on certain student problems. In fact, consultation is a delicate process. It is described in school psychology literature as a confidential and collaborative relationship between two experts that focuses on solving a particular problem described by the consultee who is seeking expert assistance from the consultant (e.g., teacher and school psychologist) (Caplan & Caplan, 1993). The consultative process requires competent consultants who are both familiar with the issues at hand and trained in communication techniques necessary for effective consulting with teachers/parents/administrators. In other words, trained consultants involved in problem-solving consultations can direct and guide professionals to reach decisions in collaborative and amenable ways. Ideally, school psychologists are well trained in various consultation models that advocate consulting with teachers, parents, and other school personnel. By offering consultation services, school psychologists can help prevent referrals by aiding teachers to: (a) plan culturally sensitive instruction for ELL students as well as interventions; and (b) attend remediation meetings as a consultant, and/or meeting with parents and teachers in a consultative group format (Caplan & Caplan, 1993).

In their review of the academic assessment of bilingual and English language learning students, Martines and Rodriguez-Srednicki (2007) discuss Curriculum Based Assessment (CBA) as an informal venue for the evaluation of ELL students. CBA is a method of assessing a child's academic problems within the confines of the actual classroom curriculum, given that norm-referenced tests are not suitable for curriculum intervention decisions. The use of CBA methods is highly recommended in the Instructional Consultation model developed by Rosenfield (1987), which initially advocated CBA methods for academic assessment. As described by Martines and Rodriguez-Srednicki, in this model the consultant (school psychologist) and the teacher (consultee) collaboratively (and confidentially) consult to reach an agreement on the student's instructional level derived from the student's aptitude in learning a new skill. Additionally, through consultation, both the consultant and consultee work together to determine what variables helped to influence learning. Along with the knowledge of instructional consultation, consultant school psychologists acquire expertise in CBA methods.

Elliott, Shapiro and Mack (1999) explain that curriculum-based criterion-referenced assessments are better than published norm-referenced tests (PNRTs) for a number of reasons:

1. CBAs test students directly on the material that they are expected to learn.

2. The outcomes of CBAs are linked directly to instruction.

3. CBAs have been shown to provide reliable and valid measures of students' performance in reading, spelling, and writing.

4. CBAs are highly sensitive to short- and long-term changes in students' performance.

5. CBAs can be used on both an idiographic basis, for evaluating the progress of individual students and on a nomothetic basis, in accordance with program-based evaluation. (Elliott et al., 1999, p. 385)

Because of CBA's digression from standardized testing and its emphasis on the use of actual materials, or the curriculum adopted by a school system, it is an important addition to the assessment of ELLs, and culturally and linguistically diverse students (Dettmer, Thurston, & Dyck, 2002, cited in Martines & Rodriguez-Srednicki, 2007). In view of this, CBA offers some advantages to teachers of bilingual and ELL students by assisting in the identification of academic strengths and weaknesses, and helping to monitor students' progress both in academic learning and language proficiency. CBA can be implementred in a bilingual fashion for bilingual classrooms as well as in English for ESL or English-only programs. Ochoa et al. (1996) observe that most school psychologists test educational achievement in English— probably because they do not speak Spanish. Even so, CBA assessment is increasing in popularity for all populations, as well as bilinguals (Ochoa et al., 1996; Shapiro, Angello, & Eckert, 2004).

Another important area in which CBA can play a preventive role with ELL and bilingual students is in determining whether these students are receiving adequate opportunities to learn or the necessary content instruction to perform adequately in classroom tasks and tests (Butler & Stevens, 2001, p. 420). When analyzing the results of CBA methods with ELL and bilingual populations, consultee-teachers and the consultant school psychologist will need to take into consideration CLD and ELL students' education curriculum histories, levels of proficiency in L1 and L2, as well as the degree of educational instruction in both languages. Also, does the CBA procedure incorporate content that is culturally appropriate for students being assessed (Bentz & Pavri, 2000)? In collaboration with consultee-teachers, consultant school psychologists can help plan culturally appropriate and referral preventive interventions for ELL and culturally diverse students.

Planning and Executing Interventions

In deciding which type of intervention is appropriate, the chosen intervention must be planned using cultural referents. For the consultant school psychologist, it is understood that the term *effective intervention* encompasses not only academic but emotional or behavioral problems, since these are the most common school-based intervention exigencies. For ELL and culturally diverse students, emotional or behavioral problems may occur due to the L2 acquisition process. Acculturation stressors of ELL students are often part of social adjustment as well as learning a second language in a new school culture which, in turn, can be manifested by emotional and/or behavioral problems.

Cultural norms can—and often are—different from those of the consultant's ethnicity, so great care must be exercised that the intervention does not accidentally or deliberately impose norms that conflict with those of the consultee-teacher, student, and parents. Such norms include parenting, familial hierarchies and interactions, reward and punishment strategies, priorities, and homework evaluation. Successful collaboration in intervention planning requires a number of skills: capable communication between diverse parties; understanding of other points of view; willingness to accommodate; ability to compromise; and receptive leadership. While it is relatively easy for a consultant and consultee-teacher of similar backgrounds and ethnicities to collaborate, care must be taken if both parties are of different cultures and ethnicities, or if consultation necessitates family involvement or school administrators' participation. Very often, interpreters will need to assist the consultant school psychologist and consultee-teacher during various types of consultation and/or CBA or other informal assessment methods. It is the responsibility of the school psychologist to train interpreters prior to offering these services, even though they are part of preventive efforts and not initial referral assessments.

Classroom Observations

As part of consultation services, and for the purpose of observing an ELL students' learning style prior to CBA initiation as well as aiding in developing academic interventions, consultant school psychologists may decide to conduct a *classroom observation* of an ELL student. A classroom observation requires observing the ELL student's learning style and the instructional methodology used in order to ensure that there is an instructional match between the ELL student's academic learning and the teacher's method of teaching. Failure to observe this ideal match results in an "instructional mismatch" (see Rosenfield, 1987), which is often the reason for academic problems. Classroom observations are also useful for the observation of possible ELL student emotional/behavioral problems in the classroom due to difficulties in the L2 process and/or acculturation/assimilation stressors.

CBA methods for ELL students can only be effective if school psychologists are knowledgeable about both different ethnicities and first and second language acquisition processes, and eager to adopt assessment changes (see Martines & Rodriguez-Srednicki, 2007).

Guidelines for the Use of Interpreters

Given the shortage of bilingual school psychologists, as well as the frequent unavailability of practitioners for assessing many low-incidence language students, both monolingual and bilingual school psychologists will encounter situations when an interpreter is needed, whether for interviewing purposes (i.e., parents, extended family members) or for testing purposes. There are several guidelines available for both interviewing and testing with interpreters.

Confidentiality and Code of Ethics for Interpreters

The most important factor to consider when using an interpreter is the issue of confidentiality. An interpreter must be aware of the ethical guidelines regarding confidentiality. Parent and student information must be confidential in accordance with the Family Education Rights and Privacy Act of 1974, the Individuals with Disabilities Education Act Revisions of 1997, and the National Association of School Psychologists' (2000) Principles for Professional Ethics. According to Rhodes et al. (2005), the National Register of Interpreters for the Deaf (RID) 2002 Code of Ethnics provides guidelines for interpreters servicing school settings. School psychologists should have knowledge of these ethical guidelines in order to ensure that interviews, assessments, and recommendations are properly conducted. The guidelines are replicated in Table 11.1, as recommended by Rhodes et al. (2005).

What to Do Before the Interview or Assessment

The first step is to engage an interpreter who is familiar with the child's culture, values, and beliefs. The school psychologist should have the interpreter contact the parents to ask permission if an interpreter is to be used for interviewing and testing. The child's permission is also requested if it has previously been decided that L1 is the child's language preference. The interpreter should: (a) inform the parents that all information is confidential; (b) tell parents that all shared information should be accurate; (c) explain the assessment process and services clearly; and (d) make parents and child comfortable (Sattler, 2001). If parents have attained L2, offer the services of the interpreter anyway, just in case they may have minimal English proficiency.

Table 11.1   Confidentiality Guidelines for Interpreters

Interpreters shall keep all assignment-related information strictly confidential.

- No information regarding any assignment shall be revealed, including the fact that the service is being performed, unless the service is being provided for a general audience and anyone being informed about the service can attend the event.

Interpreters shall render the message faithfully, always conveying the content and spirit of the speaker; using language most readily understood by the persons(s) whom they serve.

- Interpreters are not editors, and must transmit everything that is said in exactly the same way it was intended. This may be especially difficult when the interpreter disagrees with what is being said or has to interpret profane language.

Interpreters should not counsel, advise, or interject personal opinions.

- Interpreters are to refrain from adding anything to the situation, even when they are asked to by other parties involved. They shall remain personally uninvolved because, in doing so, they leave the responsibility of the outcome to those for whom they are facilitating the communication and do not assume this responsibility themselves.

Service providers shall accept assignments using discretion with regard to skill, setting, and the consumers involved.

- Interpreters shall accept assignments for which they are qualified.

Interpreters shall request compensation for services in a professional and judicious manner.

- Interpreters shall be knowledgable about fees that are appropriate to the profession and shall be informed about the current suggested fee schedule of the national interpreter organization.

Interpreters shall function in a manner appropriate to the situation.

- Interpreters shall conduct themselves in such a manner that brings respect to themselves, the consumers, the institution, and the RID organization.

Interpreters shall strive to further knowledge and skills through participation in workshops, professional meetings, interactions with professional colleagues, and reading of current literature in the field.

SOURCE: Adapted from Rhodes, R. L., Ochoa, S. H., & Ortiz, S. O. (2005). *Assessing culturally and linguistically diverse students: A practical guide.* NY: The Guilford Press.

What to Do Prior to Interviewing or Testing

There are several steps for the school psychologist to follow when working with interpreters. The first and most important one is informing the interpreter about confidentiality and the importance of establishing rapport. Several suggestions are presented below in modified form.

Suggestions for Interviewing/Assessment Procedures When Working With an Interpreter

1. *Selection of the interpreter*—The interpreter selected should be thoroughly familiar with the child's language and its linguistic variations and/or dialect, as well as culture.

2. *Briefing the interpreter on the upcoming interview/assessment*—The school psychologist should share certain information with the interpreter prior to interviewing and/or testing. The interpreter should be informed of: (a) the reason for the referral; (b) the goal of the assessment; (c) what is to be discussed; and (d) the need to preserve composure on sensitive topics (i.e., suicide, rape). In addition, the level of competence the interpreter has in both languages needs to be established, as does the attitude of the interpreter with the child and any possible difficulties. It is important to stress the importance of translating the school psychologist's and child's questions/comments precisely, as well as the need for the interpreter to maintain confidentiality and to not add words or delete words or try to interpret what the child is saying. Additionally, the interpreter should not attempt to repeat questions/responses unless asked to do so by the child. Finally, the interpreter should be briefed on the importance of translating test questions or responses accurately, and on following standard procedures (avoiding prompting, commenting on responses, or praising).

SOURCE: Sattler, J. 2001. *Assessment of children: Cognitive applications*, 4th edition, 2001. pp. 635–656. Reprinted with permission.

The school psychologist must stress the importance of maintaining neutrality and of an unbiased non-judgmental outlook on the entire interview or testing situation. In addition, the interpreter should become familiar with technical psychological terms and have practiced in advance the questions and/or directions of the instrument to be used during the assessment. After the assessment, a debriefing session should be arranged with the interpreter (preferably immediately after testing) in order to discuss and review any problems encountered. Lastly, the psychological report should include the name and qualifications of the interpreter, and any reservations about the reliability and validity of the information obtained during the translation.

Possible Pitfalls When Using an Interpreter

Some of the obstacles in the use of an interpreter are:

- There may be some unintentional distortions of information, embellishments, or deletion of information on the part of the interpreter, altering the accuracy of the information obtained.
- Errors in cueing the child may occur during testing if the interpreter is unfamiliar with the instrument to be used during the assessment.
- The child's responses during testing may not be relayed accurately.
- There may be a loss of rapport between the child and the assessor.
- The assessor will not know whether the interpreter is performing accurately. (Sattler, 2001)

The box contains a list of some possible drawbacks to working with interpreters.

Examples of Difficulties When Using an Interpreter

1. *Interpreter fails to divulge symptoms*—In defense or protection of the child and parents, the interpreter may not explain important symptoms. In keeping with the child and family's values and culture, the interpreter may decide not to reveal what may be perceived as private, such as suicidal thoughts, financial problems, or distorted statements that may reveal the mental status of the child.

2. *Mistrust of the interpreter*—The child or family may mistrust the interpreter as a result of the differences in age, sex, level of education, or most importantly because of the child's or parent's trepidations about self-disclosure for fear of being judged or due to breach of confidentiality.

3. *Preaching to the examinees*—This may occur if the interpreter perceives the child and/or parents to be digressing from their cultural norms. The interpreter may "preach" the need to follow traditions.

4. *Lack of equivalent concepts*—This obstacle refers to the lack of an equivalent concept to translate. It is important to bear in mind since translating and/or explaining concepts from one culture to another may be difficult, leading to the loss of important phrases in the translation.

5. *Dialectical and regional differences and mixture of two languages*—There are variations in languages that cannot always be translated into a standard language. Depending on the child's country and/or the variations within that country's language, a word may have several meanings. For example, in the Spanish language—depending on the region—the word *cometa* in Spain means a kite. In Venezuela, the

word *papagayo* also means kite. Similarly, CLD children may use words that are a mixture of two languages, such as *los baggies* for baggy jeans or *lonche* for lunch.

6. *Changes in level of difficulty and alteration of meaning*—As a result of translation, a word may be more difficult in one language than in another (this is especially important on intelligence testing because vocabulary word definitions are asked by level of difficulty). Translations can also change the meaning of words. For seeking background information and for testing purposes, translating a word that reflects a different meaning or feeling may offend the examinee and/or distort the testing response.

SOURCE: Adapted from Sattler (2001).

Because non-verbal communication cues are also in danger of being misinterpreted if the interpreter is not familiar with the child's culture, it is recommended that the clinician use audio- or videotapes to control this slip-up during testing. Having an accurate recording of the testing session will allow the school psychologist to review the session (Figueroa et al., 1984, cited in Gopaul-McNicol & Brice-Baker, 2002). To ensure the use of an interpreter brings about the best outcomes, clinicians are responsible for training interpreters in the goals of the assessment (Harris, Echemendia, Ardila, & Rosselli, 2001). In fact, training should go further than the goals of assessment procedures, since the interpreter will also be needed during all matters relating to interviews with parents and teachers, from testing to recommendations/ interventions made at multidisciplinary meetings. School psychologists are obliged to train interpreters for all sessions of the evaluation. Additionally, school psychologists are advised to develop skills to conduct preservice and inservice programs to train interpreters for psychological service to racial/ ethnic CLD children and youth (Gopaul-McNicol & Brice-Baker, 2002).

After the assessment process is completed, psycho-educational reports are written (in a timely manner), and a preliminary meeting and a final multidisciplinary educational planning conference are held with teachers, parents, student, and (when appropriate) other professionals and/or significant individuals involved in the evaluation. At the educational planning conference, school psychologists will need to make recommendations for adequate instructional placement. Given this important responsibility, it is imperative that school psychologists have complete knowledge of the types of bilingual education programs that exist. Accordingly, in closing this chapter on ELLs and bilingual students, a review of the different kinds of bilingual education programs presently implemented in many U.S. schools is presented below.

A brief examination of the various language profiles of second language learners is also included.

Types of Bilingual Education Programs

Currently, there are five types of bilingual instructional programs for ELL students. Knowledge of how each program is implemented in a school district is important for school psychologists, particularly for assessment and placement recommendations (Gopaul-McNicol & Brice-Baker, 1998). Ochoa (2005) provides a descriptive review of each of the five programs. In essence, the programs can be divided into two categories: bilingual education and ESL. The bilingual education programs provide instruction in both L1 and L2. The ESL programs impart instruction in English only. The programs have multiple names, and may vary in their implementation. A summarized description of each program taken from Ochoa and Ortiz (2005) is presented below.

1. *Transitional/Early-Exit Bilingual Education Program*—This bilingual program is for limited English proficiency students of the same language group, and is set up as a transitional or early exit program that usually lasts for two years. Students are instructed in English and in L1. However, L1 is gradually terminated. This program is known as a *subtractive* bilingual program because it is perceived by many to eliminate the progress of the ELL student's native language since the goal is to immerse the student in L2. Despite this, it does allow the ELL student to acculturate to the school setting.

2. *Maintenance/Late-Exit/Development Bilingual Education Program*— This sort of bilingual program is designed similarly to the transitional program, but allows the ELL to be instructed in *both* L1 and L2 and for four to six years. Thus it is considered an *additive* bilingual program. In additive programs, the amount of instructional time for L1 and L2 can follow ratios of 90:10 and 50:50 in the amount of instructional time that is spent on L1 and L2. A 50:50 ratio program provides equal instructional time in L1 and L2. This program allows the student to become bilingual.

3. *Two-Way/Dual-Language Bilingual Education Program*—The two-way language program is considered additive since the goal is for English-speaking students to become bilingual while ELL students learn English as L2 in the same class. ELLs and English-proficient students are equally allocated. Entry into the two-way program is usually voluntary on the part of the English-proficient student since this placement entails four to six years of bilingual instruction. The ELL student is serviced by instruction in both L1 and L2.

4. *Content-Based ESL/Sheltered English*—The content-based ESL program adopts a strictly English instructional model. Students in the program can be from different language groups. The goal of this program is for ELLs to maintain L1 while learning L2. Another objective is to teach academic subjects in English with the *total physical response* (TPR) method of instruction. In this instructional methodology, physical gestures and visual cues are used to assist the ELL's understanding of the curriculum context. The ratio of daily time spent varies from 50 to 100 percent of the day.

5. *Pullout ESL*—The pullout ESL program is almost identical to the content-based program. The differences are that: (a) the goal is not on academic material but on developing the ELL's language skills; (b) ELL students are "pulled out" of their classes to receive instruction; and (c) students usually spent less than half a day in this program.

It is critical for school psychologists to review the types of programs ELL student have attended, given that research has indicated that different bilingual programs can cause significant and long-lasting difficulties for academic outcomes. For a more thorough review of bilingual education and the L2 process, see Rhodes et al. (2005) and Collier (2007).

Language Profiles of English Language Students

In addition to possessing knowledge of the various bilingual programs, it is also obligatory for school psychologists to obtain expertise in the identification of the different profiles of second language students. In essence, this identification is part of a diagnostic process since language proficiency and the development of both languages in the second language learner is examined to determine what specific language-based profile a student falls under. Establishing profile type assists the practitioner in determining how to progress in both academic and intellectual assessment (Rhodes et al., 2005). Ascertaining a language profile prior to assessment decreases the risk of unfair evaluations, as well as possible improper interpretation of intellectual and academic abilities.

In total, there are nine language profiles described by Rhodes et al. (2005) that cover the frequently observed variations in second language students. Three levels of proficiency (minimal, emergent, and fluent) are used to illustrate L1 and L2 proficiency. In addition to proficiency levels, profiles are established by obtaining the student's WMLS broad CALP scores (ranging from one to five) in Spanish and English. Table 11.2 illustrates the nine language profiles.

Table 11.2   Language Profiles of Second-Language Learners

Language Profile	L1 Proficiency Level	L2 Proficiency Level	Description
Profile 1	Minimal	Minimal	CALP level in native language (L1) and English (L2) are both in the 1–2 range: individual has no significant and dominant language, and proficiency and skills in both languages are extremely limited.
Profile 2	Emergent	Minimal	CALP level in native language is in the 3 range and English is in the 1–2 range: individual is relatively more dominant in native language, and proficiency and skills are developing but limited. English proficiency and skills remain extremely limited.
Profile 3	Fluent	Minimal	CALP level in native language is in the 4–5 range: individual is highly dominant and very proficient in native language. English proficiency and skills remain extremely limited.
Profile 4	Minimal	Emergent	CALP level in native language is in the 1–2 range and English is in the 3 range: individual is relatively more dominant in English, with developing but limited proficiency and skills; native proficiency and skills are extremely limited.
Profile 5	Emergent	Emergent	CALP level in native language is in the 3 range and English is in the 3 range: individual has no significant language dominance and is developing proficiency and skills in both but is still limited in both.
Profile 6	Fluent	Emergent	CALP level in native language is in the 4–5 range and English is in the 3 range: individual is relatively more dominant in native language, with high proficiency and skills. English proficiency and skills are developing but still limited.

Language Profile	L1 Proficiency Level	L2 Proficiency Level	Description
Profile 7	Minimal	Fluent	CALP level in native language is in the 1–2 range and English is in the 4–5 range: individual is highly dominant and very proficient in English; native language proficiency and skills are extremely limited.
Profile 8	Emergent	Fluent	CALP level in native language is in the 3 range and English is in the 4–5 range: individual is dominant and very proficient in English; native language proficiency and skills are developing but limited.
Profile 9	Fluent	Fluent	CALP level in native language and English are both in the 4–5 range: individual has no significant dominant language and is very fluent and very proficient in both.

SOURCE: Adapted from Rhodes, R. L., Ochoa, S. H., & Ortiz, S. O. (2005). *Assessing culturally and linguistically diverse students: A practical guide.* NY: The Guilford Press.

NOTE: For a complete review of second language learner profiles, see Rhodes et al. (2005), pp. 137–152.

By acquiring knowledge of the varied bilingual education programs and the different second language learner profiles, practitioners are able to match a student's language profile to a fitting bilingual education program, and are thus able to make more accurate placement decisions. Moreover, school psychologists should make it a point to develop expertise in the different types of bilingual instructional programs available in the district of the schools they service. In many cases, the appropriate program for a particular ESL need may not be offered in the school that initially referred the ESL student for evaluation. Knowledge of the various bilingual programs implemented in each district school will assist the school psychologist in determining the right placement.

With regard to placement decisions, this author/practitioner has often observed cases in which the ESL student referred for evaluation has acculturated and assimilated sucessfully to their present school culture (including the parents) and is reluctant to be transferred to another school that offers the specific bilingual program needed for academic achievement. This dilemma is not easy to solve since, as is natural with all students, ESL students become attached to their teachers and classmates. Unfortunately, at Educational Planning Conferences (EPC), parents tend to request that their child remain in the initial school of attendance and unwisely opt for a different bilingual program that will *not* accommodate their child's second language profile.

Such a predicament is a situation that school psychologists will often confront since it is likely that a particular school will not offer a preferred bilingual program and a transfer must be recommended. Although a solution is difficult, inviting the student and parents to visit the proposed school and observe classes may help reduce the uneasiness associated with attending a new school. Matching up the referred ESL student with ESL peers in the recommended school prior to the actual transfer may reduce the anxiety experienced when transferring schools. Obviously, it is assumed that a school psychologist would have informed the student and parents thoroughly about the different types of second language profiles, and the appropriate and available bilingual education programs in the various district schools. Lastly, it is imperative that educational misplacements are avoided due to the academic seriousness of their consequences. This should be strongly stressed to ELL parents.

Should School Psychologists Learn Languages?

Although it may be unrealistic to propose, it would be ideal for school psychologists to learn a second language, not only because of the shortage of bilingual psychologists, but most importantly for the advancement of cultural and linguistical best practices in school psychology clinical practice. Interestingly, in the United States high school students are required to learn a second language and given a choice of which language to study, including the commonly offered languages of Spanish, French, Italian, and German. Upon entering college, most students continue taking courses in the same language studied in high school. It is a rather discouraging phenomenon that this emphasis on second language learning has not led to an increase in bilingualism, such as that which exists in European countries. Were this the case, we would have more bilingual professionals. Nevertheless, monolingual examiners can develop other skills that will compensate for the inability to communicate with their examinee. Ridley et al. (1998) encourage practitioners to learn key idioms and phrases particular to the examinee's language as well as becoming well-informed in "different communication styles and dialect variants" (cited in Shapiro & Kratochwill, 2000, p. 296). Practicing school psychologists and those in training should consider these suggestions if they are to better service the numerous refugees and immigrant children who will require school-based clinical expertise in their particular culture and language.

References

Anastasi, A. (1988). *Psychological testing*. New York: Macmillan.

Arnberg, L. (1987). *Raising children bilingually: The preschool years*. Clevedon, UK: Multilingual Matters.

Bentz, J., & Pavri, S. (2000). Curriculum-based measurement in assessing bilingual students: A promising new direction. *Diagnostique, 25*(3), 229–248.

Bernal, M. E., & Castro, F. G. (1994). Are clinical psychologists prepared for service and research with ethnic minorities? *American Psychologist, 49*, 797–805.

Bersoff, D. N., & Hofer, P.T. (1990). The legal regulation of school psychology. In C. R. Reynolds, & T. B. Gutkin (Eds.), *The handbook of school psychology* (2nd ed.) (pp. 937–961). New York: John Wiley & Sons.

Brown, L., Sherbenou, R. J., & Johnson, S. K. (1982). *Test of Nonverbal Intelligence*. Austin, TX: Pro-Ed.

Burgemeister, B. B., Blum, L. H., & Lorge, I. (1972). *Columbia assessment of nonverbal abilities*. New York: Psychological Corporation.

Butler, F. A., & Stevens, R. (2001). Standardized assessment of the content knowledge of English language learners K–12: Current trends and old dilemmas. *Language Testing, 18*(4), 409–427.

Canino, I., & Spurlock, J. (2000*). Culturally diverse children and adolescents. assessment, diagnosis, and treatment* (2nd ed.). New York: Guilford Press.

Caplan, G., & Caplan, R. (1993). *Mental health consultation and collaboration*. San Francisco: Jossey-Bass.

Castillo, E. M., Quintana, S. M., & Zamarripa, M. X. (2000). Cultural and linguistic issues. In E. S. Shapiro, & T. R. Kratochwill (Eds.), *Conducting school-based assessments of child and adolescent behavior*. New York: Guilford Press.

Chamberlain, P., & Medinos-Landurand, P. (1991). Practical considerations for the assessment of LEP students with special needs. In E. V. Hamayan, & J. S. Damico (Eds.), *Limiting bias in the assessment of bilingual students* (pp. 111–156). Austin, TX: Pro-Ed.

Chamot, A. U., & O'Malley, J. M. (1994). *The CALLA handbook: Implementing the cognitive academic language learning approach*. Reading, MA: Addison-Wesley.

Chamot, A. U., & O'Malley, J. M. (1996). The cognitive academic language learning approach: A model for linguistically diverse classrooms. *The Elementary School Journal, 96*, 259–273.

Cofresi, N. I., & Gorman, A. A. (2004). Testing and assessment issues with Spanish-speaking bilingual Latinos. *Journal of Counseling and Development, 82*, 99–107.

Collier, C. (1992). Culture change: Impact on children. *Diversity, 3*(2), 4–6.

Collier, C. (2001). Separating difference and disability. Paper presented at the Annual Meeting of Teachers of English to Speakers of Other Languages. St. Louis, MO, March 1, 2001.

Collier, V. P. (2007). Assessment of acculturation. In G. B. Esquivel, E. C. Lopez, & S. Nahara, S. (Eds.), *Handbook of multicultural school psychology: An interdisciplinary perspective.* Mahwah, NJ: Lawrence Erlbaum.

Crawford, J. (2004). No Child Left Behind: Misguided approach to school accountability for English language learners. Paper presented at the Center on Educational Policy's Forum on Ideas to Improve the NCLB Accountability Provisions for Students with Disabilities and English Language Learners. Retrieved January 16, 2008, from www.cep-dc.org/pubs/Forum14September 2004/Crawford Paper.pdf.

Cummins, J. (1984). *Bilingualism and special education: Issues in assessment and pedagogy.* Clevedon, UK: Multilingual Matters.

Cummins, J. (1996). *Negotiating identities: Education for empowerment in a diverse society.* Ontario, CA: California Association for Bilingual Education.

Cummins, J. (2000). *Language, power, and pedagogy: Bilingual children in the crossfire.* Clevedon, UK: Multilingual Matters.

Cummins, J. (2001). Assessment and intervention with culturally and linguistically diverse learners. In S. R. Hurley & J. V. Tinajero (Eds.), *Literacy assessment of second language learners.* Boston: Allyn & Bacon.

Dettmer, P., Thurston, L. P., & Dyck, N. (2002). *Consultation, collaboration and teamwork for students with special needs.* Needham Heights, MA: Allyn & Bacon.

Donovan, M. S., & Cross, C. T. (2002). *Minority students in special and gifted education.* Washington, DC: National Academy Press.

Duncan, S. E., & De Avila, E. A. (1990). *Language Assessment Scales–Oral.* Monterey, CA: CTB McGraw-Hill.

Duncan, S. E., & De Avila, E. A. (1994). *Language Assessment Scales–Oral (LAS-O)* (2nd ed.) Monterey, CA: CTB/McGraw-Hill.

Elliott, R., Shapiro, D.A., & Mack, C. (1999). *Simplified Personal Questionnaire procedure.* Toledo, OH: University of Toledo, Department of Psychology.

Figueroa, R. A. (1990). Assessment of linguistic minority group children. In C. R. Reynolds & R. W. Kamphaus (Eds.), *Handbook of psychological and educational assessment of children: Intelligence and achievement: Vol. 1* (pp. 671–696). New York: Guilford Press.

Garcia, E. (2002). *Student cultural diversity: Understanding and meeting the challenge* (3rd ed.). Boston: Houghton Mifflin.

Gollnick, D. M., & Chinn, P. C. (2006). *Multicultural education in a pluralistic society* (7th ed.). Englewood Cliffs, NJ: Pearson Prentice Hall.

Gopaul-McNicol, S., & Armour-Thomas, E. (2002). *Assessment and culture: psychological tests with minority populations.* San Diego, CA: Academic Press.

Gopaul-McNicol, S., & Brice-Baker, J. (1998). *Cross-cultural practice: Assessment, treatment, and training.* New York: John Wiley & Sons.

Gopaul-McNicol, S., & Brice-Baker, J. (2002). *Cross-cultural practice: Assessment, treatment, and training.* New York: Wiley & Sons.

Gottlieb, M. (2006). *Assessing English language learners: Bridges from language proficiency to academic achievement.* Thousand Oaks, CA: Corwin Press.

Gottlieb, M., & Hamayan, E. (2007). Assessing oral and written language proficiency: A guide for psychologists and teachers. In A. E. Brice (Ed.), *Multicultural handbook of school psychology: An interdisciplinary perspective* (pp. 245–264). New York: Routledge.

Gutierrez-Clellen, V. F. (1996). Language diversity: Implications for assessment. In K. N. Cole, P. S. Dale, & D. J. Thal (Eds.), *Assessment of communcation and language* (pp. 29-56). Baltimore: Paul H. Brookes.

Hakuta, K. (2000). Improving schools for language minority students: Moving from what we know. Presentation to a Pew Network meeting, January 27.

Hakuta, K., Butler, Y. G., & Witt, D. (2000). *How long does it take English learners to attain proficiency?* Santa Barbara, CA: University of California Linguistic Minority Research Institute, Policy Report 2000–01.

Hamayan, E. V., & Damico, J. (Eds.). (1991). *Limiting bias in the assessment of bilingual students.* Austin, TX: Pro-Ed.

Harris, J. G., Echemendia, R., Ardila, A., & Rosselli, M. (2001). Cross-cultural cognitive neuropsychological assessment. In J. J. Andrews, D. H. Saklofske, & H. L. Janzen (Eds.), *Handbook of psychoeducational assessment: Ability, achievement, and behavior in children* (pp. 391–414). San Diego, CA: Academic Press.

Helton, G. B., Ray, B. A., & Biderman, M. D. (2000). Responses of school psychologists and teachers to administrative pressures to practice unethically: A national survey. *Special services in the schools, 16*(1/2), 111–134.

Huie Hofstetter, C. (2003). Contextual and mathematics accomodation test effects for English-language learners. *Applied Measurement in Education, 16*(2), 159–188.

Jacob, S., & Hartshorne, T.S. (2003). *Ethics and law for school psychologists* (4th ed.). Hoboken, NJ: John Wiley & Sons.

Kindler, A. L. (2002). *Survey of the states' limited English proficient students and available educational programs and services: 1999–2000 summary report.* Washington, DC: National Clearinghouse for English Acquisition and Language Instruction Educational Programs.

Lambert, W. E. (1981). Bilingualism and language acquisition. In H. Winitz (Ed.), *Native language and foreign language acquisition* (pp. 9–22). New York: New York Academy of Sciences.

Leiter, R. G. (1948). *Leiter International Performance Scale.* Chicago, IL: Stoelting.

Lerner, J. (2005). *Learning disabilities and related disorders: Characteristics and teaching strategies* (10th ed.). Boston: Houghton Mifflin.

Lopez, C., Lopez, V., Suarez-Morales, L., & Gonzalez Castro, F. (2006). Cultural variation within Hispanic American families. In C. L. Frisby & C. R. Reynolds (Eds.), *Comprehensive handbook of multicultural school psychology* (pp. 234–264). Hoboken, NJ: John Wiley & Sons.

Maldonado-Colon, E. (1986). The communication disordered Hispanic child. *Monograph of the BUENO Center for Multicultural Education, 1*(4), 59–67.

Martines, D., & Rodriguez-Srednicki, O. (2007). Academic assessment of culturally and linguistically diverse students. In G. B. Esquivel, E. C. Lopez, & S. Nahara, S. (Eds.), *Handbook of multicultural school psychology: An interdisciplinary perspective* (pp. 381–408). Mahwah, NJ: Lawrence Erlbaum.

Muñoz-Sandoval, A. F., Cummins, J., Alvarado, C. G., & Ruef, M. L. (1998). *Bilingual verbal ability tests: Comprehensive manual.* Itasca, IL: Riverside.

Mushi, S. L. (2002). Acquisition of multiple languages among children of immigrant families: Parents' role in the home-school language pendulum. *Early Child Development and Care, 172,* 517–530.

National Association of School Psychologists (2000). *NASP Principles for Professional Ethics.* Retrieved January 17, 2008, from www.nasponline.org/pdf/ProfessionalCond.pdf

Oakland, T., & Gallegos, E. M. (2005). Selected legal issues affecting students from multicultural backgrounds. In C. Frisby & C. R. Reynolds (Eds.), *Comprehensive handbook of multicultural school psychology.* San Francisco: Jossey-Bass.

Ochoa, S. H. (2003). Assessment of culturally and linguistically diverse children. In C. R. Reynolds & R. W. Kamphaus (Eds.), *Handbook of psychological and educational assessment of children: Intelligence and achievement* (2nd ed., pp. 563–583). New York: Guilford Press.

Ochoa, S. H. (2005). Assessment of culturally and linguistically diverse children. In R. L. Rhodes, S. H. Ochoa, & S. O. Ortiz (Eds.), *Assessing culturally and linguistically diverse students: A practical guide* (pp. 15–41). New York: Guilford Press.

Ochoa, S. H., Galarza, A., & Gonzalez, D. (1996). An investigation of school psychologists' assessment practices of language proficiency with bilingual and limited-English-proficient students. *Diagnostique, 21*(4), 17–36.

Ochoa, S. H., & Ortiz, S. O. (2005) Language proficiency assessment: The foundation for psychoeductional assessment of second-language learners. In R. L. Rhodes, S. H. Ochoa, & S. O. Ortiz (Eds.), *Assessing culturally and linguistically diverse students: A practical guide* (pp. 137–152). New York: Guilford Press.

Ochoa, S. H., Powell, M. P., & Robles-Pina, R. (1996). School psychologists' assessment practices with bilingual and limited-English proficient students. *Journal of Psychoeducational Assessment, 14,* 250–275.

Ochoa, S. H., Rivera, B. D., & Ford, L. (1997). An investigation of school psychology training pertaining to bilingual-psycho-educational assessment of primarily Hispanic students: Twenty-five years after *Diana v. California. Journal of School Psychology, 35*(4), 329–349.

Ochoa, S. H., Robles-Pina, R., Garcia, S. B, & Breunig, N. (1999). School psychologists' perspectives on referrals of language minority students. *Multiple Voices of Ethnically Diverse Exceptional Learners, 3*(1), 1–14.

Ortiz, A. A. (1997). Learning disabilities occurring concomitantly with linguistic differences. *Journal of Learning Disabilities, 30*(3), 321–332.

Ortiz, A. A., & Polyzoi, E. (1986). Characteristics of limited English proficiency Hispanic students in programs for the learning disabled: Implications for policy, practice and research-Part I: Report summary (ERIC Reproduction No. ED 267578). Austin, TX: ERIC Clearinghouse.

Ortiz, S. O. (2002). Best practices in nondiscriminatory assessment. In A. Thomas & J. Grimes (Eds.), *Best practices in school psychology IV* (pp. 1321–1336). Washington, DC: National Association of School Psychologists.

Piper, T. (1993). *And then there were two: Children and second language learning.* Markham, ON: Pippin.

Raven, J. C., Court, J. H., & Raven, J. (1986). *Raven's Progressive Matrices and Raven's Coloured Matrices.* London: H.K. Lewis.

Rhodes, R. L., Ochoa, S. H., & Ortiz, S. O. (2005). *Assessing culturally and linguistically diverse students: A practical guide.* New York: Guilford Press.

Ridley, C. R., Li, L. C., & Hill, C. L. (1998). Multicultural assessment: reexamination, reconceptualization, and practical application. *The Counseling Psychologist, 26*(6), 827–910.

Rogers, M. R. (1998). Psychoeducational assessment of culturally and linguistically diverse children and youth. In H. B. Vance (Ed.), *Psychological assessment of children: Best practices for school and clinical settings* (2nd ed., pp. 355–384). New York: John Wiley & Sons.

Rosenfield, S. (1987). *Instructional consultation.* Hillsdale, NJ: Lawrence Erlbaum.

Rueda, R., Cardoza, D., Mercer, J., & Carpenter, L. (1985). An examination of special education decision making with Hispanic first-time referral in large urban school districts: Longitudinal study I report, final report (ERIC Reproduction No. ED312 8100). Austin, TX: ERIC Clearinghouse.

Rumberger, R. W., & Larson, K. A. (1998). Student mobility and the increased risk of high school dropout. *American Journal of Education, 107*, 1–35.

Saenz, T., & Huer, M. (2003). Testing strategies involving least biased language assessment of bilingual children. *Communication Disorders Quarterly, 24*, 184–193.

Salvia, J., & Ysseldyke, J. E., with Bolt, S. (2001). *Assessment in special and inclusive education.* Boston: Houghton Mifflin.

Salvia, J., & Ysseldyke, J. E., with Bolt, S. (2007). *Assessment in special and inclusive education* (10th ed.). New York: Houghton Mifflin.

Sattler, J. (2001). Assessment of culturally and linguistically diverse children: Background considerations and dynamics. In *Assessment of children: Cognitive applications* (4th ed.). San Diego, CA: Jerome M. Sattler.

Shapiro, E. S., Angello, L. M., & Eckert, T. L. (2004). Has curriculum-based assessment become a staple of school psychology practice? An update and extension of knowledge, use, and attitudes from 1990 to 2000. *School Psychology Review, 33*(2), 249–257.

Shapiro, E. S. & Kratochwill, T. R., eds. (2000). *Conducting school-based assessments of child and adolescent behavior.* New York: Guilford Press.

Steinberg, L., Blinde, P. L., & Chan, K. S. (1984). Dropping out among language minority youth. *Review of Educational Research, 54*(1), 113–132.

Willig, A. (1985). A meta-analysis of selected studies on the effectiveness of bilingual education. *Review of Educational Research, 55*(3), 269–317.

Woodcock, R. W., & Johnson, M. B. (1989). *Woodcock-Johnson Psycho-Educational Battery–Revised.* Allen, TX: DLM Teaching Resources.

Woodcock, R., & Muñoz-Sandoval, A. (1993). *Woodcock-Muñoz Language Survey.* Itasca, IL: Riverside.

Woodcock, R., & Muñoz-Sandoval, A. (2001). *Woodcock-Muñoz Language Survey Normative Update, English Form.* Itasca, IL: Riverside.

Annotated Bibliography

Chamot, A. U., & O'Malley, J. M. (1994). *The CALLA handbook: Implementing the cognitive academic language learning approach.* Reading, MA: Addison-Wesley. *This manual is an excellent source of practical instructional techniques for implementing the CALLA method of language learning in all school subjects.*

Gottlieb, M. (2006). *Assessing English Language Learners: Bridges from language proficiency to academic achievement.* Thousand Oaks, CA: Corwin Press. *This recent text reviews important issues ranging from assessment to academic achievement of English language learners.*

Rhodes, R. L., Ochoa, S. H., & Ortiz, S. O. (2005). *Assessing culturally and linguistically diverse students: A practical guide.* New York: Guilford Press. *This is an excellent resource for practitioners which covers all areas of English language learners from legal issues to assessment.*

Recommended Articles

The following articles are important to consider in this area:

Chamot, A. U., & O'Malley, J. M. (1996). The cognitive academic language learning approach: A model for linguistically diverse classrooms. *The Elementary School Journal, 96,* 259–273.

Cummins, J. (2001). Assessment and intervention with culturally and linguistically diverse learners. In S. R. Hurley, & J. V. Tinajero (Eds), *Literacy assessment of second language learners.* Boston: Allyn & Bacon.

Huie Hofstetter, C. (2003). Contextual and mathematics accomodation test effects for English-language learners. *Applied Measurement in Education, 16*(2), 159–188.

Mushi, S. L. (2002). Acquisition of multiple languages among children of immigrant families: Parents' role in the home-school language pendulum. *Early Child Development and Care, 172,* 517–530.

Ochoa, S. H., Rivera, B. D., & Ford, L. (1997). An investigation of school psychology training pertaining to bilingual-psycho-educational assessment of primarily Hispanic students: Twenty-five years after *Diana v. California. Journal of School Psychology, 35*(4), 329–349.

12

Prejudice Reduction

Prejudice continues to be prevalent throughout the world, and is currently a serious concern within educational settings. It can affect educators, school personnel, students, and their parents. Most significantly at the school level, prejudice can be dangerous to the point of violence (i.e., physical altercations, bullying, ethnic gang wars). It is the professional responsibility of school professionals to help children and adolescents learn to understand their cultural biases and to recognize the value of interacting with diverse ethnic groups. School psychologists (and counselors), in concert with educators, can collaborate to develop successful prejudice prevention/reduction programs. Such programs are generally effectively undertaken if school psychologists engage in collaborative relationships with teachers, such as providing consultation services and/or participating in collaborative teamwork in which several educators and other professional staff members work together in a joint effort, each contributing to an identified outcome. Obviously, school psychologists must have an understanding of their own cultural biases and grow as multicultural professionals in order to be effective in training and guiding others in prejudice reduction.

This chapter was included in this guidebook because of the pervasiveness of prejudice in our schools, and because of the need for school psychologists to recognize that student-centered and school-based prejudice prevention/reduction interventions should be included as part of their professional multicultural competency. Many of the points reviewed come from some of the most respected scholars in interethnic relations, thus covering the most recent research findings that can assist practitioners attain best practices in school psychology. The chapter also reviews racial/ethnic identity development models and assessment approaches.

What Is Prejudice?

Throughout the years, there have been countless definitions of prejudice and even considerable debate on how prejudice should be defined. By far the most popular description is Allport's (1954) earlier definition of prejudice as:

> an antipathy [intense dislike] based upon a faulty and inflexible generalization. It may be felt or expressed. It may be directed toward a group as a whole, or toward an individual because he is a member of that group. (p. 9)

Taken from this classically traditional perspective, prejudice is a strong *negative feeling* about an individual, based on generalizations one has about that individual's group. This type of definition identifies an *affective* component to prejudice. One can have negative and positive prejudices toward the *ingroup* or the *outgroup*. The ingroup is the group to which the individual belongs and the outgroup is the alien group, to which misconceptions or stereotypical reactions are linked. Prejudice has also been identified as an *attitude*. As an attitude, prejudice is viewed as having cognitive (e.g., beliefs that release hostility to the outgroup), affective (e.g., emotional, such as anger), and behavioral (e.g., avoidant or hostile) components. Here too, there is ongoing debate as to whether prejudice should be viewed as an attitude. Some researchers assert that an attitude is not the same as affect (Fiske, 1998; Zanna & Rempel, 1988). Affect is defined as including both emotions and evaluations toward other groups (Oskamp, 2000).

In fact, a definition of prejudice will vary based on how it is addressed, especially in prejudice research. Nonetheless, researchers concur on the following points. Prejudice usually:

- occurs between groups;
- involves an evaluation (positive or negative) of a group;
- is a biased perception of a group; and
- is based on the real or imagined characteristics of the group (Devine, 1995; Jones, 1997).

School professionals should develop an awareness of their own conception of this human reaction to others. Moreover, knowledge of the etiology of prejudice (Burkard, Medler, & Boticki, 2001; Jones, 2002; Oskamp, 2000; Nelson, 2002) is necessary for successful prevention and reduction intervention planning.

Causes of Prejudice

Many researchers have theorized that there are multiple causes of prejudice (Duckitt, 1992; Stephan & Stephan, 2000). Oskamp's (2000) review of four possible factors that cause prejudice, proposed by Duckitt (1992), is paraphrased below.

1. *Genetic* and evolutionary predispositions (at this level, short-term or intermediate interventions are relatively nil because of its biological foundation).

2. *Societal*, organizational, and inter-group patterns of contact and norms for intergroup relations (e.g., laws, regulations, and norms of segregation or unequal access, which maintain the power of dominant groups over subordinate ones). This level is considered the most influential ground for inducing changes in interactions with others.

3. *Mechanisms* of social influence that operate in group and interpersonal interactions (e.g., influences from the mass media, the educational system, and the structure and functioning of work organizations). This level of etiology focuses more on heuristic influences such as mass media, the public education system, and organizational work roles.

4. *Personal* differences in susceptibility to prejudiced attitudes and behaviors, and an unacceptability of specific intergroup attitudes. At this level, the personal differences are based on personality factors that would make an individual susceptible to prejudice and/or non-prejudice messages and attitudes.

Intergroup relations are generally affected when norms and personal influences are considered. Psychologists usually focus on group influences and interpersonal interactions to resolve prejudice beliefs, attitudes, and interactive patterns. However, Oskamp (2000) urges the importance of influential societal and organizational laws and regulations by citing the 1954 decisions of the U.S. Supreme Court that outlawed segregation in public schools, and equal opportunity and affirmative action laws which have had national effects on norms, attitudes, and behaviors (Oskamp, 2000, pp. 3–17). When personality factors are perceived to be the causes of prejudice, Duckitt (1992) suggests modification through intensive group or individual psychotherapeutic interventions. Oskamp (2000) concludes that psychologists may develop interventions to reduce prejudice by following different approaches (e.g., laws, regulations, prevalent norms, mass influence processes, group and intergroup influence processes, and psychotherapy to transform personality characteristics). Stephan and Stephan (2000) propose a theoretical approach reviewed by Oskamp (2000) on the causes of prejudice. In essence, the theory adds to Duckitt's by including *fears* and *threats* as other major causes of prejudice. Oskamp (2000) restates Stephan and Stephan's (2000) four main bases of prejudice:

1. realistic threats posed from an outgroup;

2. symbolic threats from an outgroup (e.g., perceived group differences in morals, values, standards, beliefs, and attitudes);

3. intergroup anxiety in interactions with outgroup members (e.g., apprehension about negative experiences such as being embarrassed, rejected, or mocked);

4. negative stereotypes of the outgroup (e.g., negative expectations of particular behaviors that will cause conflict and/or uncomfortable interactions). (Oskamp, 2000, p. 5)

All four bases are intertwined and operate in combination with one another. Prejudice reduction interventions should address all of these for effective results. Additionally, *cognitive or knowledge-based* interventions can lessen feelings of threat whether they are realistic or symbolic. Interactive interventions can lessen negative stereotyping and intergroup anxiety (Oskamp, 2000, p. 6). Researchers have also linked stereotyping to prejudice (Lewin, 1948; Stephan, 1999; Sue & Sue, 2003), and have found ways to measure stereotyping and prejudice. Furthermore, the formation and maintenance of prejudice have also been studied, as well as how to conceptualize the roles of personality, emotion, cognition, and motivation in connection with the nature of stereotyping and prejudice.

Presently, stereotyping is considered a natural consequence of cognition (Fiske, 1998). It is important to recognize that children are exposed at a very young age to stereotyping and prejudices. Initially, they are exposed to their parents' beliefs and values, which in turn may affect the internalizing of stereotypes and prejudices, thus causing negative outgroup perceptions. However, there is contradictory evidence regarding such negative perceptions (Aboud & Doyle, 1996). Apparently, children can develop their own biases from other individuals who may influence them, even if their parents are more tolerant towards outgroup differences.

Furthermore, children receive overt and covert information from the media through movies, television, reading materials, video and computer games, and other types of media experiences. Clearly, it is recognized that the media are often less objective and/or may err in reporting certain incidents of crimes that involve a particular ethnic group—thus influencing the stereotyping and developing attitudes toward specific ethnic groups. Stereotypes are therefore maintained through social cognition. Judgments are reached (whether they are accurate or not) and quick evaluations are made of an individual or group. Consequently, cognitions must change in order to eradicate the induced cognitive stereotype (Nelson, 2002).

Practitioners are alerted to recognize that stereotyping is a "cognitive" process. It is not related to any psychological aberration or the result of deviant characteristics (Nelson, 2002). Frequently, stereotyping has been perceived as part of the mind's normal propensity to *categorize* (a cognitive classification of similar objects in the environment) stimuli from the environment (Duckitt, 1992; Nelson, 2002). Researchers have questioned whether certain individuals are more prone to a prejudiced personality than others. At present, there is no evidence that indicates they are. Current research tends to view prejudice as a cognitive process that adheres to social categorization (Duckitt, 1991). Conversely, in their more recent book on prejudice prevention, Ponterotto, Utsey, and Pedersen (2006) discuss a fairly new construct in psychology, the *multicultural personality*. Research taken from counseling psychology, social psychology, organizational psychology, feminist studies, and African-centered psychology proposes that a multicultural personality disposition may be predictive of psychological wellbeing and assist in intercultural ease (Ponterotto et al., 2006). A recent comprehensive definition of the multicultural personality described by Ponterotto et al. (2006) identifies several characteristics:

- The individual has attributes of emotional stability.
- The individual is confident in their ethnic identity.
- The individual welcomes cultural diversity.
- The individual is eager to learn about new cultures.
- The individual interacts well with culturally diverse people.
- The individual spiritually connects to others.
- The individual is emphatic in various milieus, contemplative and cognitively flexible.
- The individual is able to work with culturally diverse people.
- The individual is a staunch advocate for social justice.

Most impressive is the individual's ability to understand his or her biases, openness to exploring other worldviews, and recognition of the effects of racism and homophobia. This is a new area of research which, when validated, will bring further understanding of personality types. The furtherance in knowledge of the characteristics of a multicultural personality will also assist in the formation of techniques to enhance multicultural personality growth (see Ponterotto et al., 2006 for further clarification of multicultural personality research). An assessment instrument that is deemed psychometrically adequate and recommended by Ponterotto et al. (2006) is the Multicultural Personality Questionnaire (MPQ—Van der Zee & Van Oudenhoven, 2000, 2001).

This 91-item scale measures five factors that tap into multicultural effectiveness: (a) cultural empathy; (b) open-mindedness; (c) social initiative; (d) emotional stability; and (e) flexibility.

Racial/Ethnic Identity Development

A review of prejudice should not overlook racial/ethnic identity development (Cross, 1971, 1991; Helms, 1995; Phinney, 1990; Ponterotto et al., 2006; Stephan, 1999). First and foremost, psychologists should acquire competencies in racial/ethnic identity development due to the increase in ethnic diversity in schools and the anticipated psychological distress that may occur during the developmental process of ethnic self-identification. Moreover, when conducting assessments, school psychologists must inquire about their students' ethnicity and culture, and possible political oppression, and screen for any individual and family war experiences. Most of the following overview of racial/ethnic identity development is taken from the works of Rollins and Riccio (2005), Ponterotto et al. (2006), and Stephan (1999). The term *identity* is defined as:

> a person's ability to maintain a stable, coherent, and integrated sense of self; positive and negative identification with parents and their interests, values, and morals lead to personal identity development. (Erickson, 1968)

Ethnicity or ethnic identity is defined as "one's sense of belonging to an ethnic group and the part of one's thinking, perception, feelings, and behavior that is due to group membership" (Phinney & Rotheram, 1986, p. 13, cited in Sattler & Hoge, 2006). Group identity is closely attached to self-concept because individuals usually value the group to which they belong and tie their self-concept to their group. Ethnic identity is recognized as being closely connected to group identity in that it is important to the self-concept of members of ethnic minority groups (Roberts et al., 1999). An ethnic group has commonalities such as language, physiology, ancestry, culture, and nationality. In contrast, *race* is described as the biological and physiological characteristics that make up a group of individuals. *Culture* is viewed as "a set of people who have shared values, customs, habits, social rules of behavior, interpersonal relationships, and art" (Rollins & Riccio, 2005, p. 555).

There are several factors that influence identity formation. Self-perception has been found to relate to ethnicity and ethnic group status. Positive correlations between ethnicity and self-concept have been observed. Attaining the highest stage of ethnic identity has been found to relieve psychological ordeal and promote a positive self-image (Oyserman, 1993; Phinney, 1992, 1993;

Phinney & Kohatsu, 1997). Ultimately, racial/ethnic identity ultimately directs how an individual will process information about himself within the environment (Markus & Nurisu, 1986) and, depending on the information ingrained about the self, how he will relate to others.

When discussing racial/ethnic identity, it is important to understand that numerous minorities have experienced prejudicial degradation in various areas of social conditions (political, educational, and economic) because of their skin color. The societal racism experiences endured by minorities (people of color) have resulted in an unhealthy impact on their racial/ethnic identity development (Helms, 2003). For several decades, researchers have studied how individuals develop their racial and ethnic identity (both are interconnected) and, as previously mentioned, this has led to the conjecture that ethnic identity development can lead to psychological distress in childhood, adolescence, and adulthood. In fact, some of the psychological symptoms (e.g., confusion, dissonance, stress, guilt, withdrawal, depression, anger, or antisocial behaviors) may continue through life (see Chapter 10 on acculturation). Researchers observe that racial/ethnic identity development occurs in similar developmental stages across the various models. Ponterotto et al. (2006) delineate several stage models, each attributed to a specific racial/ethnic group:

- African American/Nigrescence racial ethnic identity (Cross, 1971, 1991);
- white racial identity (Helms, 1990, 1995);
- biracial/racial ethnic identity (Kich, 1992; Poston, 1990; Root, 1990);
- Hispanic racial identity (Matute-Blanchi, 1986; Ruiz, 1990; Sodowsky, Kwan, & Pannu, 1995) (see Ponterotto et al., 2006 for a review of various racial/ethnic identity models).

Cross's (1971, 1991) racial ethnic identity model initiated the onset of research of other developmental stage models. Ponterotto et al. (2006) explain that the purpose of Cross's model is to describe how individuals react to majority groups. Most of the models that have ensued are general in that they describe how an individual reacts to the majority group or address a specific ethnic group. The authors discuss Helms' (1984, 1995) white racial ethnic development model, since this majority model also includes how a person internalizes feelings about their own ethnic group. It is important to note that racial/ethnic identity development is perceived to be different for minority and majority groups (Ponterotto & Pedersen, 1993). Given the plurality of ethnic group students in educational settings, school psychologists will inevitably encounter students, parents, and educators progressing through different stages of racial/ethnic identity development— sometimes interchangeably (see Chapter 10 for an overview of racial/ethnic models).

The study of racial/ethnic identity is not without limitations. However, although the research on various studies is not always consistent, the findings are persuasive (see Ponterotto et al., 2006; Stephan, 1999 for a review of research findings). Martines (1993–2000) observes having counseled a number of ethnically diverse adolescents who experienced psychological distress concerning their racial/ethnic identity—at times on a conscious or unconscious level. Her observations of symptomatic manifestations are:

1. The individual's self-image is negatively affected regarding acceptance of a (minority) racial/ethnic identity.

2. There is withdrawal, depression, and/or anger during counseling sessions.

3. Withdrawal occurs from the adolescent's own ethnic-group friends.

4. Anxiety and guilt are manifested, caused by a reluctance to accept the family's racial/ethnic identity.

5. Family conflicts take place, resulting from detachment with the adolescent's own racial/ethnic group.

6. There is self-degradation of the adolescent's racial/ethnic background and the need to identify with the dominant ethnic group.

7. Home-based behavioral problems emerge, linked to familial disapproval of the loss of ethnic values and over-identification with the dominant ethnic group.

It is now deemed vital that children and adolescents develop a positive sense of their racial/ethnic identity. This will be difficult to attain if a child or adolescent experiences prejudice regarding their racial/ethnic group. While the developmental process of racial/ethnic identity can be ongoing throughout the lifespan, it can also stagnate at a particular stage; children and youth struggling with identity formation can be at a disadvantage in schools. There is evidence to suggest that children who have more knowledge of ethnic group differences may have a higher propensity for ethnic prejudice. Children aged between 6 and 10 are able to distinguish the physical characteristics associated with race and ethnicity Between the ages of 10 and 14, children reach a level of cognition that allows them to understand how society views different ethnic groups. They begin to recognize differences in prejudicial views and social class. Adolescence introduces a cognitive awareness of social groups, and adolescents have been observed to socialize within their own ethnic group. Apparently, social cognition is analogous to all the stage models of ethnic/racial identity development. It has further been observed that high school students may experience frustration because of their allegiance to their ethnic group while having a desire to also socialize with other ethnic groups—especially since children and adolescents form their identity through social interactions with peer groups. What children observe, and how they are treated, will inevitably impact on their behaviors as well as influence the formation of their identity (Quintana, 1994; Quintana & Vera, 1999; Selman, 1980, cited in Rollins & Ricci, 2005).

In their chapter on culturally and linguistically diverse children, Sattler and Hoge (2006) review several potential impediments children may experience when developing their ethnic identity; knowledge of these is beneficial for the practitioner. The observed obstacles are as follows:

- CLD children and youth may have difficulty developing a sound ethnic identity if they have to choose between the dominant culture's values and their own.
- Identity formation may seriously be impeded by the dominant group's perceived negative stereotypes of a child's ethnic group.
- Negative stereotyping can also cause anxiety and doubt about a CLD child's ethnic group, as well forming a poor self-image (a CLD child may internalize the negative stereotypes held by the dominant cultural group, consequently leading to poor self-esteem and behavioral problems).
- Ethnic identity is encumbered when CLD children's parents and other family members do not openly discuss societal, ethnic, and racial concerns.
- Children of biracial and/or a multiracial heritage may experience a complex ethnic identity formation. This formation complexity usually depends on how parents pass on their cultural heritage and ethnic identity (parents may stress membership in one ethnic group or other, or may not consider any group and/or give attention to race or color).
- Biracial and/or multicultural identity development can detrimentally be affected by the dominant group/culture's manner of accepting and/or rejecting (i.e. discrimination) biracial or multicultural children.
- Identity formation depends on how the CLD child merges their personal racial or cultural identification.

Several additional factual considerations are necessary to understand racial/ethnic identity development in order to ensure optimal practice. The box contains a factual practice-centered list (comprised from various researcher's observations) to review when servicing racial/ethnic CLD children and youth.

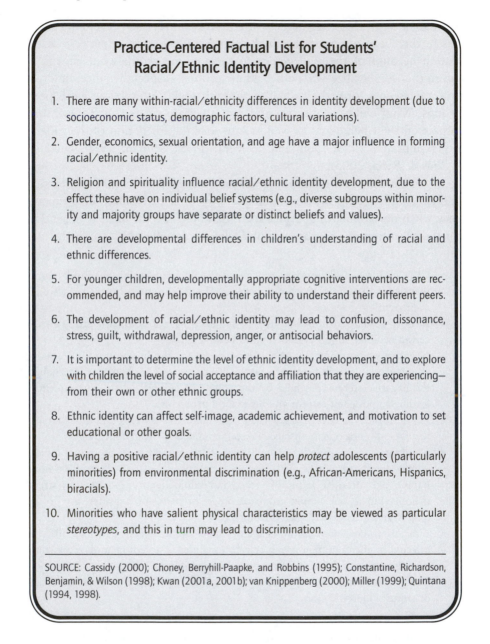

Practice-Centered Factual List for Students' Racial/Ethnic Identity Development

1. There are many within-racial/ethnicity differences in identity development (due to socioeconomic status, demographic factors, cultural variations).

2. Gender, economics, sexual orientation, and age have a major influence in forming racial/ethnic identity.

3. Religion and spirituality influence racial/ethnic identity development, due to the effect these have on individual belief systems (e.g., diverse subgroups within minority and majority groups have separate or distinct beliefs and values).

4. There are developmental differences in children's understanding of racial and ethnic differences.

5. For younger children, developmentally appropriate cognitive interventions are recommended, and may help improve their ability to understand their different peers.

6. The development of racial/ethnic identity may lead to confusion, dissonance, stress, guilt, withdrawal, depression, anger, or antisocial behaviors.

7. It is important to determine the level of ethnic identity development, and to explore with children the level of social acceptance and affiliation that they are experiencing— from their own or other ethnic groups.

8. Ethnic identity can affect self-image, academic achievement, and motivation to set educational or other goals.

9. Having a positive racial/ethnic identity can help *protect* adolescents (particularly minorities) from environmental discrimination (e.g., African-Americans, Hispanics, biracials).

10. Minorities who have salient physical characteristics may be viewed as particular *stereotypes*, and this in turn may lead to discrimination.

SOURCE: Cassidy (2000); Choney, Berryhill-Paapke, and Robbins (1995); Constantine, Richardson, Benjamin, & Wilson (1998); Kwan (2001a, 2001b); van Knippenberg (2000); Miller (1999); Quintana (1994, 1998).

School psychologists are advised to review facts in the box, and commit to an ongoing expansion of their knowledge regarding the experiences ethnic/racial and CLD children may endure during the development of their ethnic identity, not overlooking that racial/ethnic identity development may negatively affect psychological wellbeing. Concerning this developmental process, school psychologists must remember to be aware that their racial/ethnic identity could influence the therapeutic relationship; simultaneously, they are encouraged to explore their own attitudes and beliefs and look at how these may affect the interactive process.

Biracial/Multiracial Identity Development

The rise in the population of biracial and multiracial students has led to recent ethnic identity models. As a new construct, and in comparison with other models of identity development, the study of biracial and multiracial identity development has not been as fruitful as it might, but it is on the rise as an area of empirical investigation. In the last decades, social attitudes toward biracial and/or multiracial individuals have become more acceptable—particularly of interracial relationships and the children born of these unions.

Outlined in the following paragraphs are recaps of Ponterotto et al.'s (2006) evaluation of various models of biracial/multiracial identity development. The authors identify the terms *biracial* as children whose parents have different racial heritage, and *multiracial* as children who have two or more racial heritages. They cite the following models as receiving recognition:

- Poston's Biracial Identity Development Model;
- Jacob's Model of Biracial Identity Development;
- Kich's Three-Stage Model of Japanese–White Biracial Identity Development;
- the Kerwin–Ponterotto Model of Biracial Identity Development;
- Root's Evolving Model of Multiracial Identity (see Ponterotto et al., 2006, pp. 109–119).

Models of biracial/multiracial identity development also theorize multi-stage models. Ponterotto et al. (2006) discuss several models of biracial/multiracial identity development. A particular five-stage model that can be beneficial for school psychologists' augmentation of knowledge in this new domain is Poston's Biracial Identity Development Model, since the model covers various psychological processes of the biracial individual. Ponterotto and colleagues' descriptions of the five stages (2006, p. 111) are briefly restated below.

The first stage is the *personal identity stage*. In this stage, the child's sense of self is not linked to identifying with a racial reference group. The child's personal identity (self-esteem) is related to early childhood family experiences and events that form the child's environment. In stage 2, *choice of group categorization*, there is a feeling of being obliged to identify with a single racial group. Since this stage is rather early on in children's maturation process, it is hypothesized that they may not have acquired the cognitive maturity to form a multiracial identity (Poston, 1990). The third stage, *enmeshment/denial*, involves identifying with one racial group while rejecting the other. Choosing between racial groups can lead to an intense psychological ordeal. Whatever the choice, feelings of guilt and self-contempt are usually experienced. The fourth stage, *appreciation*, brings about an acceptance and appreciation of the entirety of one's racial background, and a desire to discover the previously rejected racial ethnicity. In the final stage, *integration*, the individual accepts both racial identities, and consequently reaches a well-integrated multiracial identity (see Ponterotto et al., 2006).

Lesbian, Gay, Bisexual Identity Development

Another area of research that has illumined the field of identity formation is the lesbian, gay, bisexual (LGB) identity development model(s). Once more, we find that empirical investigations in this area of identity development are sparse. However, given the oppressed state of the gay, lesbian, and bisexual youth in U.S. schools, and the humanitarian needs in this sensitive area, some researchers have made significant progress in investigating lesbian and gay identity formation. Ponterotto et al. (2006) identify the few LGB identity development models currently recognized:

- Cass's Theoretical Model of Homosexuality Identity Formation (Cass, 1979);
- Coleman's Stages of the Coming Out Process (Coleman, 1982);
- Fassinger and colleagues' Inclusive Model of Lesbian and Gay Identity Formation (Fassinger, 1998; Fassinger & Miller, 1997; McCarn & Fassinger, 1996).

LGB identity development models also theorize multi-stages—with the exception of Fassinger's model, which proposes a four-phase model. Cass's (1979) notable model is an earlier model that appears to more closely describe the psychological processes of which school psychologists should be aware when servicing LGB youth. Cass emphasizes a "bilinear dual-process" that perceives the self-concept as developmentally fully meshed with the homosexual identity, and maintains that this dual-process continues in consequence of the individual's experiential connections to a heterosexual dominant society. There is a division between the individual's private and public identity with, justifiably, the public identity probably seen as more secure due to the recognized discrimination and acts of violence committed against homosexuals. The following is a description of Cass's six-stage model rephrased from Ponterotto et al.'s (2006) review.

1. *Identity confusion*—In this early stage (can be adolescent years and earlier), the individual questions their sexual orientation and begins to feel a pull toward same-sex persons. Since this type of querying is new to the self,

a sense of confusion is experienced, bringing about several possible reactions: (a) the experienced same-sex feelings of attraction may be perceived as acceptable; (b) the feelings and thoughts may be self-recognized although they are seen as undesirable, in which case the individual controls such thoughts or feelings; (c) although the same-sex feelings are considered undesirable, there is an attempt to mentally change their view of homosexual behavior. For example, the person engages in homosexual behavior without identifying himself or the behavior as homosexual. If the person's response is to agree to their gay feelings, stage 2 is reached. If acknowledgement of homosexual behavior is not accepted as homosexual in nature, there is danger the person will remain stagnant in stage 1.

2. *Identity comparison*—In this stage, there is personal acknowledgment of homosexual feelings and thoughts. This is, however, perceived negatively, given the idea of being "different" and of the observed societal discrimination; both of these lead to isolation. As in the above stage, the individual faces alternatives in order to move on to the next stage. There can be an acceptance of being different but a continuance of private versus covert public life or, even if there is an acceptance of homosexual behavior, a perception that this particular identity is unwanted, in which case the individual can use self-deception by considering their homosexuality to be a one-time occurrence of a bisexual incident. Such deceptions can cause self-hatred.

3. *Identity tolerance*—This stage brings about the individual's tolerance of their gay or lesbian orientation; however, it is not an acceptance of homosexuality. The process in this stage involves the person seeking out other gay and lesbian persons for the benefit of reducing feelings of alienation. Seeking to socialize with other homosexuals can be advantageous for further integration of identity formation if the experiences are positive. In contrast, if involvement with gay or lesbian person(s) is negative because such person(s) may have a negative self-image, then the effects can prevent the furtherance of identity formation.

4. *Identity acceptance*—In this stage, homosexual identity is fully accepted and acknowledged. Ongoing socialization with gays and lesbian acquaintances assists the person to normalize their same-sex sexuality. A particular strategy that may be utilized at this stage is the person's decision to "pass" as heterosexual in public, even though sexual identity has been internalized.

5. *Identity pride*—In this stage, both private and public gay/lesbian identity is accepted with pride, while heterosexual values are rejected. There may be residual anger for past feelings of isolation.

6. *Identity synthesis*—In this final stage, the gay or lesbian identity is integrated into the self-concept and personality, leading to a complete identity. Previously harbored negativity toward heterosexuals is reduced through increasing involvement with more tolerant heterosexuals.

Knowledge of the Cass model's psychological processes at each stage can guide school psychologists to evaluate their students' emerging LGB orientation as well as assist them in their personal identity pursuit. Moreover, since school psychologists are ethically required to advocate and promote equality for all students, they should encourage collaboration with teachers regarding racial/ethnic identity and LGB psychological issues to begin the process of forming educational workshops and group sessions within a teamwork approach. Additionally, in order to improve intergroup relations, they should encourage teachers to implement intergroup relations programs. An ideal method to use in improving intergroup relations is for educators to be cognizant of the racial/ethnic identity stages of both minority and majority groups that typify their students so as to determine appropriate supportive techniques to use with students at different stages (Stephan, 1999). Imparting educators with this knowledge is a task school psychologists are ideally prepared to undertake in their multicultural practice.

Ponterotto et al. (2006) caution that racial/ethnic identity models have their limitations, and that not all findings have been consistent across studies in combination with the complexity of analyzing the construct of racial identity formation. However, regardless of the limitations, the models have provided valuable psychological benefits that promote well-being. From another perspective, Stephan (1999) questions the authenticity of the sequential stages, and queries whether all children experience them. He points out that the theories can be useful as "descriptions of some of the possible developmental phases that children may experience as they grow and learn about their own group and other groups" (p. 75). An additional point he makes refers to the current view on the difficulties children of "mixed heritage" encounter when establishing their racial and ethnic identity. Stephan argues that this is not the case, and that many students of mixed heritage have flexible ethnic identities and do not appear to have mental health problems (see Johnson & Nagoshi, 1986; Stephan & Stephan, 1991).

The debate over the need for empirical validation of these models should not prevent practitioners from assessing the racial/ethnic identity development of the children and youth they service. Furthermore, the development of identity formation should be reexamined throughout the therapeutic relationship because development is not considered linear and unchanging, but rather tends to be multidimensional and continuing (Rollins & Riccio, 2005).

Religiosity, Lesbian/Gay/Bisexuality, and Racial/Ethnic Identity Development

Religion and its influence on the believers' ethnic and racial identity formation is another issue that requires mention when discussing the various models of racial/ethnic identity development. The brief overview below is included with the aim of recognizing religion as an important part of self-identity development, particularly for the various cultural and ethnic groups whose ancestry is closely attached to religious practice.

Currently, there is no consensus among various scholars on the definition of the term "religion." In her well-reviewed chapter on religiosity in children and youth, Bosacki (2005) explains that, "The fact that we use one word to describe a complex myriad of beliefs, behaviors and experiences leads many researchers to believe that religion is one entity and that we can expect to find the same or similar phenomena anywhere else in the world" (p. 613). The question Bosacki poses next is, "if religion defies definition, then how can it be considered universal?" (Bosacki, 2005, p. 613) Bosacki does not offer a conclusive response, other than a suggestion stated in the literature that considers "all religious phenomena must be manifested in both the culture and the person" (Wax, 1984). For instance, Bosacki explains that psychologists studying religion would propose that people tend to express their religious faith by behavior, belief, and experience. This is usually observed through church attendance, belief in the supernatural, and experiential mystical states (Bosacki, 2005).

Although every school psychologist is trained to not overlook religion and spirituality when collecting background information and/or counseling student-clients, the role of religion is not often emphasized when considering such factos as "psychological adjustment and behavioral outcomes" (Bosacki, 2005, p. 613). However, through the influence of beliefs and morals, religiosity may affect behavior, and this may be manifested via internal and/or external mechanisms (Cochran, Beehgley, & Bock, 1988). Internalizing religious beliefs may take place during self-identity development, which could bring about feelings of shame and guilt if religious norms have been disrespected. Nevertheless, Bosacki states that school psychologists and educators concur that religion can be beneficial to individuals' developmental process as well as in their communities (Lantieri, 2001; Trulear, 2000; Youniss, McLellan, & Yates, 1999). For example, religious children and youth are exposed to several factors that tend to promote healthy development. Religion-related facts or activities that can lead to psychological health, according to Bosacki (2005), are:

- religious involvement (church attendance, participating in religious activities, prayers);
- the importance of culture in shaping religious thoughts and behaviors through religious socialization;

- religious persons carrying on the religious beliefs/legacies of their parents and ancestors;
- participating in activities that provide service to others;
- placing a high value on caring for others;
- personal integrity and honesty;
- religious affiliation countering deviant behaviors among adolescents;
- religious participation and dedication intensifying school attendance and achievement;
- religious participation enhancing self-esteem, and alleviating unwanted behaviors such as delinquency, substance abuse, teen pregnancy, and sexual permissiveness;
- religious affiliation promoting mental health in adolescents in addition to physical health (Bosacki, 2005, pp. 616–620).

The above factors are encouraging, and suggest the need for school psychologists and educators to recognize the positive benefits found in religiosity. Bosacki (2005) emphasizes that school psychologists and teachers can steer students' sense of meaning and emotional wellbeing through programs that focus on directives aimed at students' inner lives. By acknowledging the beneficial connection between education and religiosity, school psychologists and educators can help promote programs that can "go beyond knowledge acquisition and enter the realms of personal meaning and purpose" (Bosacki, 2005, p. 635). Such programs have been implemented without infringing on students' religion or cultural norms. It appears that the research on children and religious practice has revealed a number of positive results. Equally, there seems to be a connection to religious development and racial/ethnic identity development. The inner sense of wellbeing often attained through religious beliefs, involvement, and mystical experiences may be as similarly ingrained as the inner sense of self-identity that is attached to racial/ethnic identification.

In discussing the two, there appears to be a similarity in the development of religious beliefs and racial/ethnic identity formation. Typically, religious beliefs and practices are firmly established over a long-term period from early childhood on, through exposure to parents' religious affiliation and practices. In the same manner, racial/ethnic identity formation is developed through parents' ethnic group affiliation and subsequently through socialization. The two appear to be intertwined, each influencing the other and resulting in conflicts when religious doctrine is in opposition to homosexuality.

Apart from doctrine, are there cultural norms that, when broken by an individual, can incite certain prejudicial acts from family and peers and cause alienation and emotional damage? For instance, prejudice directed at homosexuals has also included the disapproval of parents whose religious doctrines disagree with homosexuality. It is of utmost importance that school professionals understand the delicate ground they tread when attempting to intervene for student-clients manifesting homosexual inclinations. Adolescents who are loyal to their religious beliefs (or to their parents' religious beliefs), and who at the same time are attempting to differentiate their sexual identity, may seek assistance from a school psychologist or school counselor.

Practitioners must be alerted to the fact that, although there are various religions that view homosexuality as naturally and morally wrong, they do not condemn or manifest psychological or spiritual hostilities to the homosexual individual, but instead offer abstinence counseling services through the ministry of non-profit organizations (e.g., Courage & Courage International, Exodus International, Jonah, Evergreen International, One-By-One—website addresses are listed at the end of this chapter) dedicated to educating their religious communities about the prevention, intervention, and curative alternatives to same-sex orientation. Students with same-sex attraction concerns should be made aware of these organizations so that they do not abandon their faith due to feelings of rejection or desertion or misconstrued unresolvable differences. Having to renounce one's religion because of falsely believed hostility or rejection can cause severe psychological trauma and unwarranted feelings of alienation. Moreover, once informed, some student-counselees may opt to contact these organizations to seek resources and professional assistance for their dilemmas.

The point is that counselees with same-sex attractions should be given the opportunity to experience both traditional psychotherapy and/or their own clergy and pastoral counseling or other support systems. This may be particularly significant if the affected individual is manifesting psychologically identified spiritual trauma because of their homosexual inclinations. It is not suggested that school psychologists use their therapeutic power to engage in religious *conversion therapy* (which has been unpopularly called *reparative* or *reorientation* therapy—implying the need to "repair"; see Gronsiorek, 2004; Shido & Schroeder, 2002; Worthington, Savoy, Dillon, & Vernaglia, 2002)—in order to disaffirm lesbian/gay identity; rather, they need to provide additional options and appropriate resources for their clients in an effort to offer complete psychological and spiritual healing.

From a cultural perspective, there are cultural influences on behavior, development, and psychological adjustment, as well as traditional norms/values and religious affiliation. Anti-LGB cultural beliefs on homosexuality can have devastating results on a young person. In clinical practice, Martines (1993–1997) observed that culturally diverse adolescents with homosexual inclinations manifested certain apprehensions within the therapeutic relationship, such as:

- fear of sharing emerging feelings and thoughts regarding same-sex orientation with the therapist;
- feelings of anxiety and guilt concerning the possibility of an LGB identity;
- apprehension pertaining to real or unreal alienation from peers and/or society;
- excessive fear of parents becoming aware of their same-sex inclination;
- psychological distress due to particular religious doctrines that view same-sex orientation as immoral and wrong;
- feelings of abandonment and rejection from place of worship; and
- suicidal thoughts or attempts arising from shame and fear of discovery by parents and peers.

In addition to these observed manifestations, Martines (1993–1997) found that Latino-American youths appeared to be especially distressed in cases when well-meaning teachers or professional staff tried to intervene by informing parents about their son or daughter's same-sex sexual identity conflicts or bullying incidents aimed at adolescents with effeminate behaviors. The case study in the box describes the repercussions of such an occurrence.

Latino-American Case Study of Religious/Gender Identity Conflict

A specific case in which parental involvement proved to be almost fatal for a Latino adolescent youth occurred when an educator who had been supportive of a youth's same-sex orientation dilemma offered to invite his legal guardian grandmother to the school to discuss her grandson's homosexual identity formation. The Latino adolescent initially agreed, but on the appointed day of the meeting the youth became excessively anxious and afraid of the forthcoming "discovery," and jumped out of his math class fourth-floor classroom window right after the schedule bell rang, when students were easing out of the various classrooms. Although seriously injured, he recuperated after several months and returned to a different school the following year. Immediately after the incident, the school psychologist (a member of the school-based crisis intervention team) was asked to interview the youth's math teacher, who confessed he had observed the Latino youth being bullied (regarding his effeminate mannerisms) in his classroom and had not intervened. This teacher was devastated by guilt and remorse that eventually led to noticeable depressive symptoms. After several crisis-counseling sessions, at the advice of the school psychologist the math teacher began psychotherapy at a local community clinic.

A counselor on the crisis intervention team treated the educator who had arranged the meeting with the youth's grandmother for shock. Presumably, this distressing incident occurred due to a lack of cultural knowledge of specific ethnic groups' likely reactions to homosexuality, as well as inappropriate training in adequate methods to use to support students in distress. In this particular case, the Latino youth's cultural manhood expectations, in addition to his family's religious beliefs, were in contradiction to his emerging sexual inclinations. His initial longing to articulate his feelings to his grandmother later turned to fear of discovery and causing familial shame. As a religious youth and devoted grandson, the emotional conflict proved too overwhelming for him, resulting in an attempt to end his life. The math teacher remained in therapy for over a year. It is not known what happened to the youth after his transfer to a different school. (Martines, 1993–1997)

The reasons for including this case in this chapter are threefold:

1. Individuals of same-sex orientation are likely to increase in numbers among the general student population.

2. There are few guidelines for educators on how to support students with same-sex orientation, and most especially how to avoid or help stop the dangers of inappropriate but well-meaning interventions.

3. School psychologists need to be encouraged to form collaborative relations with educators and students by conducting workshops or classroom educative presentations on LGB issues and the ensuing problems of religious beliefs and doctrines that oppose homosexuality. Resources for individuals seeking psychotherapy and/or abstinence counseling services should be disseminated. Active involvement on the part of professionals can prevent tragic incidents.

Practitioners providing therapeutic services to counselees with LGB conflicts will also need to be aware that there are many individuals with strong religious beliefs who will experience severe conflicts between their desire to accept and adhere to their religion's anti-same-sex attraction doctrines and the contrasting LGB affirmation they may receive concerning sexual diversity in psychotherapy. Fischer and DeBord (2007) present a thorough discussion on the dilemma within the field of psychology regarding how to respect a client's religious beliefs and at the same time manifest therapeutic respect for sexual diversity. The authors question the probable ethical dilemma ensuing in psychology practice between respect for the client's LGB orientation in conjunction with the APA's (2002) *Ethical Principles of*

Psychologists and Code of Conduct, in which it is delineated that psychologists are to "minimize bias and prejudice regarding both religion and sexual orientation in our work but does not address potential conflicts arising from the sometimes competing demands to affirm both" (p. 318). Apart from trying to provide appropriate therapy with the most "avoidance of harm" (p. 337) to the client, Fischer and DeBord (2007) point out that the "perceived" conflictual question regarding the affirmation of religious diversity and affirmation of sexual diversity is a problem facing trainers and psychologists-in-training. Apparently, a recurring issue observed by the authors is that trainee-students, because of their own religious beliefs, have demonstrated a desire to decline working with LGB clients. Complete competency on the part of the practitioner or trainee may be defined as having the skills to deal with LGB issues and religious beliefs, regardless of one's own opposing homosexual religious doctrines. It certainly should not be done by referring the "gay" client to a supposed specialist in this area of therapy. Such a referral in itself may be perceived as biased by the client/counselee (Fischer & DeBord, 2007). It should not be overlooked that, during the same period of sexual identity struggles, an adolescent may also be experiencing racial/ethnic identity conflicts. This dual possibility ought to be considered by the practitioner at the inception of the therapeutic process. Having to deal with dual psychological stressors could lead to severe depression or other mental health problems.

All of these ethical dilemmas and training concerns regarding LGB issues are thought-provoking for the evolving multicultural school psychologist. Thus the primary objective of the professional can only be to continually keep abreast of the latest research and supportive outlets in traditional psychology practice, as well as in the non-changing and diversely changing religious doctrines. In the end, a truly dedicated and committed professional will not fail their client.

Racial/Ethnic Identity Assessment

There are many reasons why it is important for school psychologists to assess the racial/ethnic identity of their student-clients. In their review on the implications for practice, Rollins and Riccio (2005) make several points about why school psychologists need to have an awareness and knowledge of racial identity development across groups. First and foremost, this is because of the multiethnic student population in U.S. schools. Second, the authors go on to suggest that, "In the assessment and diagnosis process, school psychologists need to be aware of the appropriate racial, cultural, and political contexts in which the children they serve need to function. This awareness will help school psychologist look at salient physical characteristics to ethnic identity and the person as an individual" (Rollins & Riccio, 2005, p. 567). Moreover, school psychologists are obliged to "understand the cross-cultural dynamics in a therapeutic relationship (Kwan, 2001a, 2001b) and in a community setting such as schools" (Rollins & Riccio, 2005, p. 567). Helping a child or adolescent who is exhibiting behavioral or emotional problems will ultimately lead to counseling sessions and the establishment of a therapeutic relationship. During this confidential process, school psychologists can evaluate how positively or negatively their counselee's racial/ethnic identity formation is progressing. A point to consider when assessing this construct is that the level of racial/ethnic identity is changeable and adjustable, and for this reason the school psychologist may need to periodically assess and reassess their counselee's level of racial/ethnic identity development. Rollins and Riccio (2005) caution about the need to evaluate and eliminate any potentially harmful interethnic concerns that may affect adjustment. The status of a student's identity is thought to connect to the student's goal-setting behavior. Motivation and academic achievement have been found to influence ethnic identity formation, given that the self-concept is so closely attached to motivation and to the setting of prospective goals (e.g., educational growth, behavioral changes) (Cassidy, 2000; van Knippenberg, 2000, cited in Rollins & Riccio, 2005).

Fortunately, the need for assessment has not been overlooked in this area. Researchers have developed psychometric instruments (scales) to measure racial/ethnic identity, not discounting the use of interviews and qualitative methods to further evaluate ethnic developmental processes. In clinical practice, anecdotal accounts have corroborated evidence of a Hispanic racial/ethnic identity developmental process (Ruiz, 1990). Qualitative methods have used focus groups and interviews to investigate the development of racial/ethnic identity. Some of the reviews of self-report measures (Ponterotto et al., 2006; Rollins & Riccio, 2005) used to assess racial/ethnic identity that have gained recognition are:

1. *Black Racial Identity Attitude Scales* (RIAS-B—Helms, 1990). The RIAS-B measures attitudes that follow the stages of racial identity proposed by Cross (1971).

2. *White Racial Identity Attitude Scale* (WRIAS—Helms & Carter, 1990). The WRIAS evaluates attitudes relating to white racial identity. This measure comprises 60 items with a five-point Likert scale.

3. *Multi-Group Ethnic Identity Measure* (MEIM—Phinney, 1992). The MEIM hypothesizes three domains of ethnic identity: affirmation and belonging; ethnic identity achievement; and ethnic behaviors. The MEIM is used to

examine ethnic identity across diverse samples. It is a 14-item measure with a four-point rating scale. It can be administered to high school and college students.

4. *Cross's Racial Identity Scale* (Vandiver et al., 2002). This has been adopted from a revised model of nigrescence for African-Americans.

These measures can only be administered to individuals with good reading skills (see Rollins & Riccio, 2005; Ponterotto et al., 2006). As with all assessment instruments, the psychometric properties (e.g., reliability, validity) should be reviewed to ensure appropriate selection (for guidelines on selecting instruments, see Ponterotto et al., 2006, pp. 261–262).

Assessment of Prejudice

In their commitment to reducing prejudice in children and youth, school psychologists are advised to assess prejudice attitudes. The abundant research on prejudice has led to the development of assessment measures designed to evaluate prejudicial attitudes and racism. Presently, racial prejudice self-report measures focus on cognitive and affective aspects of prejudice. The ensuing review is cited in Ponterotto et al. (2006), and covers some of the various psychometric scales developed to assess prejudice attitudes and racism; they are all considered to have adequate psychometric properties (i.e., reliability and validity).

Psychometric Instruments

- *The Quick Discrimination Index* (QDI) (Ponterotto, Burkard et al., 1995; Utsey & Ponterotto, 1999) is a Likert-type scale that was designed to address cognitive and affective aspects of prejudice. It comprises three factors that measure cognitive attitudes toward racial diversity, interpersonal-affective attitudes regarding racial diversity, and general attitudes toward women's equality. It is practical and applicable to diverse populations, and can be used with adolescents and adult populations.
- *Modern Racism Scale* (McConahay, 1986) measures whites' racial attitudes toward blacks. Includes six- and seven-item versions of unidimensional factors. Appropriate for adolescents and adults.
- *Institutional Racism Scale* (Barbarin & Gilbert, 1981). This scale measures institutional racism (discernable prejudice/racism observed in institutional policies and practices limiting privileges of minority groups), and is appropriate for adolescents and adults. Includes six factors and 72 items that tap into

indices of racism, strategies to reduce racism, extent of strategy use, agency climate, administrative and personal efforts.

* *Motivation to Control Prejudice Reactions* (Dunton & Fazio, 1997) measures motivation to control expressions of prejudice and can be used with adolescents and adults. Includes two factors and 17 items that measure the concern with acting prejudiced and restraint to avoid dispute.

There are several points to consider in the assessment of prejudice. First, the quantitative measures that were developed are aimed at evaluating the level of individual prejudicial attitudes and racism. In other words, it is a method of probing into a person's thinking. Second, most quantitative measures are self-reporting questionnaires that probe into the person's extent of racism or prejudice based on a score. The scoring results, of course, depend on the truthfulness of the respondent. Third, in assessing an individual's level of prejudicial attitudes or racism, it has been observed that racial/ethnic identity development, multicultural personality, and multicultural competence are constructs that correlate with prejudice and multicultural awareness. For instance, the higher the level of racial/ethnic identity, multicultural personality, and multicultural competence, the less prejudiced and more at ease and competent an individual is when interacting with culturally diverse groups (Ponterotto et al., 2006). Lastly, as reviewed by Ponterotto et al. (2006), research indicates that a high score on the measured constructs leads to psychological wellbeing and better quality of life.

Any type of assessment—whether qualitative or quantitative—ultimately leads to interventions. For prejudice, the aim of an evaluation is to reduce or prevent further negativity and bias toward diverse ethnic groups. School psychologists need to analyze the level or kind of prejudice, as well as the racial/ethnic identity stage based on the ethnic reference group (e.g., African American, Latino, Asian-American etc.), and decide on what cultural-specific interventions to adopt, while being careful not to overlook the status of racial/ethnic identity development. It is important to keep in mind the variability within and across ethnic groups. For instance, an intervention that is effective for one young person may not be for another of the same race. Additionally, the level of ethnic identity development can affect the young person's response to counseling and the therapeutic process, as well as the practitioner (Youngman & Sadongei, 1974; Aldarondo, 2001; Atkinson et al., 1983; Ponterotto & Casas, 1987; Sue & Sue, 1999). Lastly, school psychologists are ethically obliged to carefully reflect on the level and status of their racial/ethnic identity, since this may cause certain biases and influence the selection of interventions (Rollins & Riccio, 2005) (for multicultural counseling interventions, see Pedersen & Carey, 2003; Sue & Sue, 1999).

Prejudice Reduction Programs, and Teacher Collaboration and Teamwork Approaches

We have reached a point in history where we have observed centuries of the profound malevolence of prejudice and studied strategic methods to reduce it. It is now the responsibility of those persons whose profession places them in positions where they have the opportunity to influence others in diverse settings (corporate and educational institutions, organizations, community) to facilitate prejudice reduction interventions. Teachers have this responsibility, as do school psychologists. The stoppage of individual oppression leading to the development of negative self-identity and interracial group conflicts in school settings is left to these educators and healers. Their collaboration and teamwork efforts can lead to a world of children and youth who have learned to respect, and if need be defend, different racial groups' humanitarian rights. Ideally, teachers educated in racial/ethnic identity development and in the various methods for reducing prejudice can positively impact their students in many ways. However, educators first need to attain self-awareness and cultural sensitivity, hopefully so as to recognize their uniquely positioned role in prejudice reduction (Ponterotto et al., 2006; Stephan, 1999).

In their preparation, school psychologists receive training in consultation. Models of consultation advocate consultative-type in-service training and collaborative teamwork with teachers (Caplan & Caplan, 1993; Connelly & Connelly, 1992). Consultant school psychologists can conduct multicultural workshops to train teachers, help put into practice intergroup relations interventions, and collaborate with them on prejudice reduction programs (Martines, 2003, 2005) (see Chapter 8 on consultation practice). At every opportunity, through the vehicle of consultation, the consultant school psychologist is encouraged to assist in the implementation of prejudice reduction interventions in collaboration with consultee-teachers, students, and other school personnel. There are several techniques used for improving intergroup relations and prejudice reduction in educational settings, and it is important to have knowledge of these for the furtherance of skills, so as to expand multicultural competencies in this area. Below are restated descriptions of a number of techniques, reviewed by Stephan (1999).

Didactic Programs

Didactic programs are designed to impart information and are usually short term in nature. The goal is to provide students (or teachers) with "brief experiences that will give them insights into stereotyping and prejudice, often using role playing, groups discussions, or simulation games" (Stephan, 1999, p. 59). Stephen distinguishes two types of didactic programs: *narrowly focused* educational programs (which focus on a single aspect of prejudice) and *comprehensive* programs (which center on wide-ranging aspects of prejudice and are integrated into an entire curriculum). The narrowly focused programs provide students with different cultural and ethnic readings. lectures, videos, movies, music, dance, and art (pp. 59-60). Stephan's review covers specific techniques that help to emphasize the similarities between ethnic groups (p. 60):

- emphasizing positive aspects between groups
- acquiring knowledge of the norms, roles, and values of the other group;
- writing essays that describe various improvement opportunities for minority groups;
- having students act out cases of unfair treatment because of prejudice that take place in school settings;
- role-playing being a member of another group;
- having low-prejudiced children discuss their racial attitudes with high-prejudiced children;
- assigning journal keeping to students who relate to intergroup relations.

Stephan (1999) cautions that the problem with these programs is that they are too restricted because they center on a particular ethnic group or convey a specific skill. These single-focus methods fail to impart the complexity of intergroup relations.

Multicultural Education

Multicultural education is a comprehensive didactic program designed to impart students with knowledge of diverse ethnic groups that comprise the current population of the United States. Such a program should have a long-term curriculum commitment that helps students gain awareness of the differences and similarities between groups and their history, and thus improves intergroup relations (Stephan, 1999; Banks, 1997). An important aim is to improve race relations by having students acquire the knowledge, skills, and attitudes required for cross-cultural interactions (Banks, 1997). The multicultural curriculum is carried over into all subjects (social studies, history, language, math, science, music, art). Another important goal of the program is prejudice reduction, which can be achieved through: (a) the acquired cultural and historical knowledge of diverse ethnic groups; (b) increasing the empowerment of minority students; and (c) creating higher achievement in consequence of the acceptance of group differences and the development of a positive ethnic identity created by all the above factors (see Banks, 1994 for a review of multicultural education).

Cooperative Learning Goups

Cooperative learning involves arranging small teams of students from diverse racial/ethnic backgrounds and exposing them to various learning techniques developed to improve intergroup relations in school settings. Studies have shown that students will interact well together in a cooperative environment and form friendships; this technique also reduces ingroup/outgroup bias, increases self-esteem and minority student achievement, and provides students with the chance to obtain information that is contradictory to their stereotypes of different ethnic groups. Research studies have reported favorable effects of cooperative learning (Stephan recommends Johnson & Johnson, 1992a, 1992b for a review of the effects of cooperative learning techniques).

Moral Development Training Programs

Stephan (1999) refers to Davidson and Davidson (1994) and Kohlberg (1969, 1981) for a description of moral development programs based on Kohlberg's theory of moral development. Moral development programs which arrange student dialogues of intergroup perceptual differences, along with dissimilar cultural backgrounds, have been found to increase children and youth's moral reasoning and enhance intergroup associations (Stephen, 1999). Presenting such techniques as moral dilemma exercises regarding historically recorded ethnic groups' oppression, role-playing ethnic dramas, and describing different ethnic norms and noting the between group similarities has helped to increase children's and youth's moral reasoning and social intergroup relations. For a review of studies describing the effectiveness of these techniques, see Stephan (1999, Ch. 4).

Within the educational arena, such series as Teaching Tolerance (Southern Poverty Law Center) and programs of multicultural education (Banks, 1997) in school settings are examples of *informational interventions*. School programs that include interactive interventions are cooperative learning and intergroup dialogue programs in college and/or community settings (Johnson, Johnson, & Holubec, 1994; Gurin, Penig, Lopez, & Nagda, 1999). To achieve suitable interventions, teacher training is advisable, in order to ensure that educators develop awareness, knowledge, and skills in multicultural issues and curriculum demands and materials. For the school psychologist, this is again an opportunity to consult and impart multicultural knowledge for prejudice-reduction programs. Collaborating with teachers on classroom lessons or participating in intergroup instruction or

prejudice reduction experiential exercises can be a service offered by the
school psychologist that will not only assist educators in program planning
but at the same time provide support for racial/ethnic advocacy and program
implementation. Some techniques recommended for teachers to put into
practice with their students to reduce prejudice (Ponterotto et al., 2006) are:

- Develop critical thinking skills.
- Utilize curricula and instructional techniques to reduce prejudice.
- Create a prejudice-free classroom and school environment.
- Use innovative instructional strategies that provide opportunities for coopera-
  tive learning.
- Create an environment free of prejudice and inequality. (see Ponterotto et al.,
  2006, pp. 165–179)

An examination of the effectiveness of the one-focus short-term prejudice
prevention programs indicates that many of the programs have been successful in reducing prejudice. However, caution is stressed due to some
research findings, which also point to an increase in prejudice or no effect at
all on intergroup relations (Stephan & Stephan, 1984; McGregor, 1993).
Apparently, studies on the effectiveness of prejudice reduction have failed to
examine the different types of intervention techniques that might be effective. Longitudinal research studies on school-based multicultural education
curricula and their effects on intergroup relations are lacking; consequently,
little is known about the lasting impact of these curriculum objectives on students (Sleeter & Grant, 1999).

School-Based Prejudice Reduction Interventions

Over the last several decades, several researchers (Ponterotto, Utsey, &
Pedersen, 2006; Gimmestad & de Chiara, 1982; Rooney-Rebeck & Jason,
1986; Pate, 1988) have developed various strategies for reducing prejudice.
This section reviews informative readings that describe several effective techniques for reducing prejudice and bias.

- Gimmestad, B. J., & de Chiara, E. (1982). Dramatic plays: A vehicle for prejudice
  reduction in the elementary school. *Journal of Education Research, 76*, 45–49.
  This article describes four plays about ethnic groups (blacks, Puerto Ricans, Jews,
  and Chinese), and related classroom activities to increase knowledge, improve
  attitudes about ethnic groups, and reduce prejudice.
- Pate, G. S. (1988). Research on reducing prejudice. *Social Education, 52*, 287–
  289. This article discusses various strategies for prejudice reduction
  (e.g., audiovisual strategies, films, drama, television, cognitive approaches, and
  cooperative learning approaches).

- Rooney-Rebeck, P., & Jason, L. (1986). Prevention of prejudice in elementary school students. *Journal of Primary Prevention, 7*, 63–73. This article advocates the use of cooperative group peer tutoring to improve interethnic relations among young children.
- Ponterotto, J. G., Utsey, S. O., & Pedersen, P. B. (2006). *Preventing prejudice: A guide for counselors, educators, and parents* (2nd ed.). Thousand Oaks, CA: Sage. Several chapters in this guidebook provide practical excercises for increasing multicultural awareness and prejudice reduction. Chapter 11 illustrates various exercises for improving race relations in elementary and middle schools. Chapters 12 and 13 provide strategies for race relations in high schools and on college campuses. Chapter 14 describes techniques for decreasing race relations in the community. The strategies suggested range from elementary cultural games for children to higher order thinking classroom debates, analysis of newspaper articles, and critical incidents that focus on real experiences or events.

When there is a need to increase school-based relationships with peers, Cohen and Fish (1993) recommend a national education project called *A World of Difference* that was created to increase awareness of prejudice and to protest against ethnic, religious, and racial bias. This involves an intensive teacher training aimed at the elimination of prejudice. The training program includes curriculum materials, videotapes, and support manuals. The *A World of Difference* project is tailored to the specific needs of the school. This teacher training project is an excellent opportunity for school psychologists to participate in and to advocate for prejudice reduction educational programs (further information can be obtained from the Anti-Defamation League of B'nai Brith, Department JW/AWOD, 823 United Nations Plaza, New York, NY 10017).

This chapter has highlighted the importance of prejudice reduction. However, its central aim has been to entice the nascent multicultural school psychologist to initiate, intervene in, and advocate for the implementation of prejudice reduction programs and strategies at the school and community level. In conjunction with the initial intention of imparting awareness and knowledge of the causes of prejudice, the review of racial/ethnic identity development models and the assessment of prejudice and didactic programs were examined specifically to encourage practitioners to see how these approaches hold a critical relationship to school-based clinical practice.

References

Aboud, F., & Doyle, A. B. (1996). Parental and peer influence on children's racial attitudes. *International Journal of Intercultural Relations, 20*, 371–383.
Aldarondo, F. (2001). Racial and ethnic identity models and their application: Counseling biracial individuals. *Journal of mental health counseling, 23*(3), 238–255.

Allport, G. W. (1954). *The nature of prejudice*. Reading, MA: Addison-Wesley.

American Psychological Association. (1992). *Ethical principles of psychologists and code of conduct*. Washington, DC: Author.

Atkinson, D., Morten, G., & Sue, D. W. (1983). *Counseling American minorities*. Dubuque, IA: William C. Brown.

Barbarin, O. A., & Gilbert, R. (1981). Institutional Racism Scale: Assessing self and organizational attributes. In O. A. Barbarin, P. R. Good, O. M. Pharr, & J. A. Siskind (Eds.), *Institutional racism and community competence* (pp. 147–171). Rockville, MD: National Institute of Mental Health, Center for Minority Group Mental Health Programs.

Banks, J. A. (1994). *An introduction to multicultural education* (3rd ed.). Boston: Allyn & Bacon.

Banks, J. A. (1995). *Multicultural education and the modification of racial attitudes*. In W. D. Hawley, & A. W. Jackson (Eds.), *Toward a common destiny* (pp. 315–339). San Francisco: Jossey-Bass.

Banks, J. A. (1997). *Educating citizens in a multicultural society*. New York: Teachers College Press.

Bieschke, K. J., Perez, R. M., & DeBord, K. A. (Eds.). (2007). *Handbook of counseling and psychotherapy with lesbian, gay, bisexual, and transgender clients* (2nd ed.). Washington, DC: American Psychological Association.

Bosacki, S. L. (2005). Religiosity in children and youth: Psychoeducational approaches. In C. L. Frisby, & C. R. Reynolds (Eds.), *Comprehensive handbook of multicultural school psychology* (pp. 611–650). Hoboken, NJ: John Wiley & Sons.

Burkard, A.W., Medler, B. R., & Boticki, M. A. (2001). Prejudice and racism. In J. G. Ponterotto, M. Casas, L. A. Suzuki, & C. M. Alexander (Eds.), *Handbook of multicultural counseling* (2nd ed., pp. 457–481). Thousand Oaks, CA: Sage.

Caplan, G., & Caplan, R. B. (1993). Mental health consultation and collaboration. Prospect Heights, IL: Waveland Press.

Cass, V. (1979) Homosexual identity formation: A theoretical model. *Journal of Homosexuality, 4*, 219–235.

Cassidy, T. (2000). Social background, achievement motivation, optimism and health: A longitudinal study. *Counseling Psychology Quarterly, 13*, 399–413.

Choney, S. K., Berryhill-Paapke, E., & Robbins, R. R. (1995). The acculturation of American Indians: Developing framework for research and practice. In J. G. Ponterotto, J. M. Casas, L. A. Suzuki, & C. M. Alexander (Eds.), *Handbook of multicultural counseling* (pp. 73–92). Thousand Oaks, CA: Sage.

Cochran, J. K., Beeghley, L., & Bock, E. W. (1988). Religiosity and alcohol behavior: An exploration of Reference Group Theory. *Sociological Forum, 3*(2), 256–276.

Cohen, J. J., & Fish, M. C. (1993). *Handbook of school-based interventions: Resolving student problems and promoting healthy educational environments*. San Francisco: Jossey-Bass.

Coleman, E. (1982) Developmental stages of the coming out process. In W. Paul, J. D. Weinrich, J. C. Gonsiorek, & M. E. Hotvedt (Eds.), *Homosexuality: Social, psychological, and biological issues*. Beverly Hills, CA: Sage.

Connelly, J. C., & Connelly, C. W. (1992). *School consultation: Practice and training* (2nd ed.). Boston: Allyn & Bacon.

Constantine, M. G., Richardson, T. Q., Benjamin, E. M., & Wilson, J. W. (1998). An overview of black racial identity theories: Limitations and considerations for future theoretical conceptualizations. *Applied and Preventive Psychology, 7,* 95–99.

Cross, W. E. Jr. (1971). The Negro to black conversion experience. *Black World, 20,* 13–27.

Cross, W. E. Jr. (1991). *Shades of black: Diversity in African-American identity.* Philadelphia: Temple University Press.

Cross, W. E., Jr. (1995). The psychology of Nigrescence: Revisiting the Cross model. In J. G. Ponterotto, J. M. Casas, L. A. Suzuki, & C. M. Alexander (Eds.), *Handbook of multicultural counseling* (pp. 93–122). Thousand Oaks, CA: Sage.

Dana, R. H. (Ed.). (2000). *Handbook of cross-cultural and multicultural personality assessment.* Mahwah, NJ: Lawrence Erlbaum.

Davidson, F. H., & Davidson, M. M. (1994). *Changing childhood prejudice: The caring work of the schools.* Westport, CT: Greenwood Press.

Devine, P. G. (1995). Prejudice and out-group perception. In A. Tesser (Ed.), *Advanced social psychology* (pp. 467–524). New York: McGraw-Hill.

Duckitt, J. H. (1991). The development and validation of a subtle racism scale in South Africa. *South African Journal of Psychology, 21,* 233–239.

Duckitt, J. (1992). *The social psychology of prejudice.* New York: Praeger.

Dunton, B. C., & Fazio, R. H. (1997). An individual difference measure of motivation to control prejudiced reactions. *Personality and Social Psychology Bulletin, 23,* 316–326.

Erickson, E. (1968). *Identity, youth and crisis.* New York: W. W. Norton.

Fassinger, R. E. (1998). Lesbian, gay, and bisexual identity and student development theory. In R. L. Sanlo (Ed.), *Working with lesbian, gay, bisexual, and transgender college students: A handbook for faculty and administrators* (pp. 13–22). Westport, CT: Greenwood Press.

Fassinger, R. E., & Miller, B. A. (1997). Validation of an inclusive model of sexual minority identity formation on a sample of gay men. *Journal of Homosexuality, 32,* 53–78.

Fischer, A. R., & DeBord, K. A. (2007). Perceived conflicts between affirmation of religious and sexual diversity. In K. J. Bieschke, R. M. Perez, & K. A. DeBord (Eds.), *Handbook of counseling and psychotherapy with gay, lesbian, bisexual, and transgender clients* (2nd ed., pp. 317–339). Washington, DC: American Psychological Association.

Fiske, S. T. (1998). Stereotyping, prejudice, and discrimination. In D. T. Gilbert, S. T. Fiske, & G. Lindsey (Eds.), *Handbook of social psychology* (Vol. 2, 4th ed.; pp. 357–411). New York: McGraw-Hill.

Frisby, C. L. (2005). The politics of multiculturalism in school psychology. In C. L. Frisby, & C. R. Reynolds (Eds.), *Comprehensive handbook of multicultural school psychology* (pp. 81–134). Hoboken, NJ: John Wiley & Sons.

Gimmestad, B. J., & de Chiara, E. (1982). Dramatic plays: A vehicle for prejudice reduction in the elementary school. *Journal of Education Research, 76,* 45–49.

Gollnick, D. M., & Chinn, P. C. (2006). *Multicultural education in a pluralistic society* (7th ed.). Upper Saddle River, NJ: Merrill Prentice Hall.

Gonsiorek, J. C. (2004). Reflections from the conversion therapy battlefield. *The Counseling Psychologist, 32,* 750–759.

Gurin, P., Peng, T., Lopez, G., & Nagda, B. (1999). Context, identity, and intergroup relations. In D. A. Prentice, & D. T. Miller (Eds.), *Cultural divides: Understanding and overcoming group conflict* (pp. 133–172). New York: Russell Sage Foundation.

Helms, J. E.. (1984). Toward a theoretical explanation of the effects of race on counseling. A black and white model. *The Counseling Psychologist, 12,* 153–165.

Helms, J. E. (1990). An overview of black racial identity theory. In J. D. Helms, ed., *Black and white racial identity: Theory, research, and practice* (pp. 9–32). New York: Greenwood Press.

Helms, J. E. (1995). An update of Helm's white and people of color racial identity models. In J. G. Ponterotto, J. M. Casas, L. A. Suzuki, & C. M. Alexander (Eds.), *Handbook of multicultural counseling* (pp. 181–198). Thousand Oaks, CA: Sage.

Helms, J. E. (2003). Racial identity in the social environment. In P. B. Pedersen, & J. C. Carey (Eds.), *Multicultural counseling in schools: A practical handbook* (pp. 44–58). Boston: Allyn & Bacon.

Helms, J. E., & Carter, R. T. (1990). Development of the white racial identity inventory. In J. E. Helms (Ed.), *Black and white racial identity: Theory, research, and practice* (pp. 67–80). New York: Greenwood Press.

Jacobs, J. H. (1992). Identity development in biracial children. In M. P. Root (Ed.), *Racially mixed people in America* (pp. 190–206). Thousand Oaks, CA: Sage.

Jones, J. M. (1997). *Prejudice and racism* (2nd ed.). New York: McGraw-Hill.

Jones, M. (2002). *Social psychology of prejudice.* Upper Saddle River, NJ: Prentice Hall.

Johnson, D. W., & Johnson, R. T. (1992a). Positive interdependence: Key to effective cooperation. In R. Hertz-Lazarowitz, & N. Miller (Eds.), *Interaction in cooperative groups* (pp. 174–199). New York: New York University Press.

Johnson, D. W., & Johnson, R. T. (1992b). Social interdependence and cross-ethnic relationships. In J. Lynch, C. Modgil, & S. Modgil (Eds.), *Cultural diversity in the schools* (Vol. II, pp. 179–190). London, UK: Falmer Press.

Johnson, D. W., Johnson, R. T., & Holubec, E. J. (1994). *The new circles of learning: Cooperative in the classroom and school.* Alexandria, VA: Association for Supervision and Curriculum Development.

Johnson, R., & Nagoshi, C. (1986). The adjustment of offspring of within-group and interracial/intercultural marriages: A comparison of personality factor scores. *Journal of Marriage and the Family, 48,* 279–284.

Kerwin, C., & Ponterotto, J. G. (1995). Biracial identity development: Theory and research. In J. G. Ponterotto, J. M. Casas, L. A. Suzuki, & C. M. Alexander (Eds.), *Handbook of multicultural counseling* (pp. 199–217). Thousand Oaks, CA: Sage.

Kich, G. K. (1992). The developmental process of asserting a biracial, bicultural identity. In M. P. P. Root (Ed.), *Racially mixed people in America* (pp. 304–317). Newbury Park, CA: Sage.

Kohlberg, L. (1969). Stage and sequence: The cognitive developmental approach to socialization. In D. A. Goslin (Ed.), *Handbook of socialization theory and research* (pp. 379–421). Chicago, IL: Rand McNally.

Kohlberg, L. (1981). *Essays on moral development*. New York: Harper & Row.

Kwan, K. L. K. (2001a). Models of racial and ethnic identity development: Delineation of practice applications. *Journal of Mental Health Counseling, 23*, 269–277.

Kwan, K.–L. K. (2001b). Counseling applications of racial and ethnic identity models: An introduction to the special issue. *Journal of Mental Health Counseling, 23*, 185–192.

Lantieri, L. (2001). *Schools with spirit*. Boston: Beacon Press.

Lewin, K. (1948). *Resolving social conflicts: Selected papers on group dynamics*. New York: Harper & Brothers.

Markus, H., & Nurius, P. (1986). Possible selves. *American Psychologist, 41*, 954–969.

Martines, D. (1993–1997). Clinical progress notes of Latino-American adolescents experiencing sexual identity emotional distress. Unpublished raw data.

Martines, D. (1993–2000). Clinical progress notes of psychological distress concerning adolescent racial/ethnic identity. Unpublished raw data.

Martines, D. (2003). Suggestions for training cross-cultural consultant school psychologists. *Trainers Forum, 23*, 5–13.

Martines, D. (2005, March). Teachers' perceptions of multicultural issues in psychoeducational settings. *Qualitative Report, 10*(1), 1–20.

Matute-Bianchi, M. E. (1986). Ethnic identities and patterns of school success and failure among Mexican-descent and Japanese-American students in a California high school: An ethnographic analysis. *American Journal of Education, 95*(1), 233–255.

McCarn, S. R., & Fassinger, R. E. (1996). Revisioning sexual minority identity formation: A new model of lesbian identity and its implications for counseling and research. *Counseling Psychologist, 24*, 508–534.

McConahay, J. B. (1986). Modern racism, ambivalence, and the modern racism scale. In J. F. Dovidio & S. L. Gaertner (Eds.), *Prejudice, discrimination, and racism* (pp. 91–125). Orlando, FL: Academic Press.

McGregor, J. (1993). Effectiveness of role playing and anti-racist teaching in reducing student prejudice. *Journal of Educational Research, 86*, 215–226.

Miller, D. B. (1999). Racial socialization and racial identity: Can they promote resiliency for African American adolescents? *Adolescence, 34*, 493–502.

Nelson, T. D. (2002). *The psychology of prejudice*. Boston: Allyn & Bacon.

Oskamp, S. (Ed.). (2000). *Reducing prejudice and discrimination*. Mahwah, NJ: Lawrence Erlbaum.

Oyserman, D. (1993). The lens of personhood: Viewing the self and others in a multicultural society. *Journal of Personality and Social Psychology, 65*(5), 993–1009.

Pate, G. S. (1988). Research on reducing prejudice. *Social Education, 52*, 287–289.

Pedersen, P. B., & Carey, J. C. (2003). *Multicultural counseling in schools: A practical handbook* (2nd ed.). Boston: Allyn & Bacon.

Phinney, J. S. (1990). Ethnic identity in adolescents and adults: Review of research. *Psychological Bulletin, 108*, 499–514

Phinney, J. S. (1992). The Multigroup Ethnic Identity Measure: A new scale for use with adolescents and young adults from diverse groups. *Journal of Adolescent Research, 7*, 156–176.

Phinney, J. S. (1993). A three-stage model of ethnic identity development in adolescence. In M. E. Bernal, & G. P. Knight (Eds.), *Ethnic identity: Formation and transmission among Hispanics and other minorities.* Albany, NY: State University of New York Press.

Phinney, J. S., & Kohatsu, E. L. (1997). Ethnic and racial identity development and mental health. In J. Schulenberg, J. L. Maggs, & K. Hurrelmann (Eds.), *Health risks and developmental transitions during adolescence* (pp. 420–443). New York: Cambridge University Press.

Phinney, J. S., & Rotheram, M. J. (Eds.). (1986). *Children's ethnic socialization: Pluralism and development.* Newbury Park, CA: Sage.

Ponterotto, J. G., Burkard, A., Rieger, B. P., Grieger, I., D'Onofrio, A. A., Dubuisson, A., et al. (1995). Development and initial validation of the Quick Discrimination Index (QDI). *Education and Psychological Measurement, 55,* 1016–1031.

Ponterotto, J., & Casas, H. (1987). In search of multicultural competence within counselor education programs. *Journal of Counseling and Development, 65,* 430–434.

Ponterotto, J. G., & Pedersen, P. (1993). *Preventing prejudice: A guide for counselors and educators.* Newbury Park, CA: Sage.

Ponterotto, J. G., Utsey, S. O., & Pedersen, P. B. (2006). *Preventing prejudice: A guide for counselors, educators, and parents.* Thousand Oaks, CA: Sage.

Poston, W. S. C. (1990). The biracial identity development model: A needed addition. *Journal of Multicultural Counseling and Development, 18,* 152–155.

Quintana, S. M. (1994). A model of ethnic perspective-taking ability applied to Mexican-American children and youth. *International Journal of Intercultural Relations, 18,* 419–448.

Quintana, S. M. (1998). Children's developmental understanding of ethnicity and race. *Applied and Preventive Psychology, 7,* 27–45.

Quintana, S., & Vera, E. (1999). Mexican American children's ethnic identity, understanding of ethnic prejudice, and parental ethnic socialization. *Hispanic Journal of Behavioral Sciences, 21,* 387–404.

Roberts, R. E., Phinney, J. S., Masse, L. C., Chen, Y. R., Roberts, C. R., & Romero, A. (1999). The structure of ethnic identity of young adolescents from diverse ethnocultural groups. *Journal of Early Adolescence, 19,* 301–322.

Rollins, D., & Riccio, C. A. (2005). The search for self: Racial/ethnic identity development. In C. L. Frisby & C. R. Reynolds (Eds.), *Comprehensive handbook of multicultural school psychology* (pp. 555–576). Hoboken, NJ: John Wiley & Sons.

Rooney-Rebeck, P., & Jason, L. (1986). Prevention of prejudice in elementary school students. *Journal of Primary Prevention, 7,* 63–73

Root, M. P. P. (1990). Disordered eating in women of color. *Sex Roles, 22*(7–8), 525–535.

Ruiz, A. S. (1990). Ethnic identity: Crisis and resolution. *Journal of Multicultural Counseling and Development, 18,* 29–40.

Sattler, J. M., & Hoge, R. D. (2006). *Assessment of children: Behavioral, social, and clinical foundations* (5th ed.). San Diego, CA: Jerome M. Sattler.

Selman, R. L. (1980). *The growth of interpersonal understanding: Developmental and clinical understanding.* San Diego, CA: Academic Press.

Shido, A., & Schroeder, M. (2002). Changing sexual orientation: A consumers' report. *Professional Psychology: Research and Practice, 33,* 249–259.

Sleeter, C. F., & Grant, C. A. (1999). *Making choices for multicultural educaton: Five approaches to race, class, and gender* (3rd ed.). Columbus, OH: Merrill.

Sodowsky, G. R., Kwan, K. L., & Pannu, R. (1995). Ethnic identity of Asians in the United States. In J. G. Ponterotto, J. M. Casas, L. A .Suzuki, & C. M. Alexander (Eds.), *Handbook of multicultural counseling* (pp. 123–154). Thousand Oaks, CA: Sage.

Stephan, W. (1999). *Reducing prejudice and stereotyping in the schools.* New York: Teachers College Press.

Stephan, W. G., & Stephan, C. W. (1984). The role of ignorance in intergroup relations. In N. Miller & M. B. Brewer (Eds.), *Groups in contact: The psychology of desegregation.* New York: Academic Press.

Stephan, W. G., & Stephan, C. W. (2000). An integrated threat theory of prejudice. In S. Oskamp (Ed.), *Reducing prejudice and discrimination* (pp. 23–44). Mahwah, NJ: Lawrence Erlbaum.

Sue, D. W., & Sue, D. (2003). *Counseling the culturally diverse: Theory and practice* (4th ed.). New York: Wiley.

Sue, S., & Sue, D. W. (1999). *Counseling the culturally different: Theory and practice.* New York: John Wiley & Sons.

Trulear, H. D. (2000). *Faith-based institutions and high-risk youth: First report to the field.* Philadelphia, PA: Public/Private Ventures.

Utsey, S. O., & Ponterotto, J. G. (1999). Validity studies: Further factorial validity assessment of scores on the Quick Discrimination Index (QDI). *Educational and Psychological Measurement, 59*(2), 325–335.

Van der Zee, K. I., & Van Oudenhoven, J. P. (2000). The Multicultural Personality Questionnaire: A multidimensional instrument of multicultural effectiveness. *European Journal of Personality, 14,* 291–309.

Van der Zee, K. I., & Van Oudenhoven, J. P. (2001). The Multicultural Personality Questionnaire: Reliability and validity of self and other ratings of multicultural effectiveness. *Journal of Research in Personality, 35,* 278–288.

Vandiver, B. J., Cross, W. E., Jr., Worrell, F. C., & Fhagen-Smith, P. E. (2002). Validating the Cross Racial Identity Scale. *Journal of Counseling Psychology, 49,* 71–85.

Van Knippenberg, D. (2000). Work motivation and performance: A social identity perspective. *Applied Psychology, 49,* 357–372.

Wax, M. L. (1984). Asocial philosophy and amoral social science. *Wisconsin Sociologist, 21*(4), 128–140.

Worthington, R. L., Savoy, H., Dillon, F. R., & Vernaglia, E. R. (2002). Heterosexual identity development: A multidimensional model of individual and group identity. *The Counseling Psychologist, 30,* 496–531.

Youngman, G., & Sadongei, M. (1974). Counseling the American Indian child. *Elementary school guidance and counseling, 8*(4), 273–277.

Youniss, J., McLellan, J. A., & Yates, M. (1999). Religion, community service, and identity in American youth. *Journal of Adolescence, 22,* 243–253.

Zanna, M. P., & Rempel, J. K. (1988). Attitudes: A new look at an old concept. In D. Bar-Tal & A. W. Kruglanski (Eds.), *The social psychology of knowledge* (pp. 315–334). New York: Cambridge University Press.

Annotated Bibliography

Bieschke, K. J., Perez, R. M., & DeBord, K. A (Eds.). (2007). *Handbook of counseling and psychotherapy with lesbian, gay, bisexual, and transgender clients* (2nd ed.). Washington, DC: American Psychological Association. *A comprehensive compiled text that balances research and theory with helpful applications to practice.*

Oskamp, S. (Ed.). (2000). *Reducing prejudice and discrimination.* Mahwah, NJ: Lawrence Erlbaum. *A well-researched text covering all aspects of prejudice and discrimination.*

Ponterotto, J. G., Utsey, S. O., & Pedersen, P. B. (2006). *Preventing prejudice: A guide for counselors, educators, and parents.* Thousand Oaks, CA: Sage. *A revised and expanded guide that provides the most current and extensive coverage of prejudice and racism. The guidebook also includes practical tools for combating prejudice development in children, adolescents, and adults.*

Stephan, W. (1999). *Reducing prejudice and stereotyping in the schools.* New York: Teachers College Press. *A good source of practical information and tools for reducing prejudice in school settings.*

Recommended Articles

The following articles are important to consider in this area:

Aboud, F. E., & Fenwick, V. (1999). Exploring and evaluating school-based interventions to reduce prejudice. *Journal of Social Issues, 55*(4), 767–786.

Beckstead, L., & Israel, T. (2007). Affirmative counseling and psychotherapy focused on issues related to sexual orientation conflicts. In K. J. Bieschke, R. M. Perez, & K. DeBord (Eds.), *Handbook of counseling and psychotherapy with lesbian, gay, bisexual, and transgender clients* (2nd ed., pp. 221–244). Washington, DC: American Psychological Association.

Gronsiorek, J. C. (2004). Reflections from the conversion therapy battlefield. *The Counseling Psychologist, 32,* 750–759.

Ponterotto, J. G., Catarina, I., Costa-Wofford, K., Brosbst, E., Spelliscy, D., Mendelsohn, J., Scheinholtz, J., & Martines, D. (2007). Multicultural personality dispositions and psychological well-being. *Journal of Social Psychology 147*(2), 119–135.

Shido, A., & Schroeder, M. (2002). Changing sexual orientation: A consumers' report. *Professional Psychology: Research and Practice, 33,* 249–259.

Van der Zee, K. I., & Van Oudenhoven, J. P. (2000). The Multicultural Personality Questionnaire: A multidimensional instrument of multicultural effectiveness. *European Journal of Personality, 14*, 291–309.

Van der Zee, K. I., & Van Oudenhoven, J. P. (2001). The Multicultural Personality Questionnaire: Reliability and validity of self and other ratings of multicultural effectiveness. *Journal of Research in Personality, 35*, 278–288.

Worthington, R. L., Savoy, H. B., Dillon, F. R., & Vernaglia, E. R. (2002). Heterosexual identity development: A multicultural model of individual and social identity. *The Counseling Psychologist, 30*, 496–531.

Useful Websites

Courage (and Courage International): www.couragerc.net. Courage is an apostolate of the Roman Catholic Church which ministers to same-sex attracted people and their families and significant others. This website includes links to a central office, resources such as books, tapes, videos, and a newsletter, plus guidelines to finding help at in-person chapter meetings, days of recollection, and retreats (in Spanish/French/Russian).

Exodus International: www.exodus-international.org. Exodus International is a Christian ministry serving students (www.ExodusYouth.net) and men and women who are experiencing same-sex attraction. Members receive support for their family and friends. There are links to articles, upcoming conferences, and finding a local ministry or counselor.

Evergreen International: http://evergreeninternational.org. Evergreen International is a complete resource founded by the Latter-Day Saints on same-sex attraction. The organization helps people who want to diminish attactions and overcome homosexual behavior. It is also a resource for their families, professional counselors, religious leaders, and friends. Articles, conferences, testimonies, and a reading list are available on the website's links.

One-By-One: http://oneby1.org. One-By-One is a Mormon ministry that offers conferences, seminars, resources, and testimonies to those in conflict with their sexuality.

Jonah: www.jonahweb.org. Jonah is dedicated to educating the worldwide Jewish community on same-sex attraction. The organization provides support groups, an online library, and rabbinical commentaries, and is also available in Spanish. There is a contact link that encourages interested viewers to seek futher resources and professional confidential assistance.

13

Giftedness and Diverse Students

Introduction to Giftedness and Cultural Considerations

It would be interesting to ask school psychologists in training, and in practice, how much knowledge or experience they have acquired servicing students who are gifted or talented. Although school psychology training has long focused on acquiring knowledge and skills in assessment, interventions, and consultation, much of the emphasis within these domains has been on children with particular exceptionalities. The broad category of students with exceptional needs is usually understood to be children and youth with disabilities, developmental handicaps, and behavioral or emotional problems. In effect, school psychologists are regularly anchored to servicing children and adolescents with specific learning disabilities, emotional and behavioral problems, and psychiatric disorders—all of which are commonly associated with "exceptionalities." As a general rule, gifted children or youth do not fit into the conventional identification of such exceptionalities, nor into the school curriculum, and in all likelihood are infrequently referred to school psychologists. Actually, few school psychologists have been trained in gifted education (Davis & Rimm, 2004). However, gifted and talented students also have special education needs, and school psychologists are in an ideal position to examine these needs.

The lack of emphasis on giftedness can be seen in documented data, which demonstrate that when school systems experience budgeting difficulties, special programs executed for gifted youth are often the first to be discontinued (Winner, 1997). Furthermore, since the early 1970s, dependent and independent government researchers have observed that gifted and talented programs have been available almost exclusively to Caucasian students (Mercer, 1973; Losen & Orfield, 2002; Ogbu, 1986; Wehmeyer & Schwartz, 2001). Minority students are undoubtedly overrepresented in special education and underrepresented in gifted programs. There are several reasons for this gross difference, ranging from biased referral to substandard assessment and eligibility practices. To this day, male students of African American, Hispanic, and Asian ethnicity maintain the highest classification rate of learning disabilities and constant school failure (Florence, 2007, cited in Bursztyn, 2007).

Although school psychologists typically are actively engaged in servicing children with challenging needs such as those mentioned above, awareness of factors involved in servicing intellectually and creatively gifted youngsters and adolescents is crucial to their professional practice. The following sections present an overview of assessment instruments, a view of giftedness from a culturally and ethnically diverse perspective, and traditional and emerging approaches to gifted education. The chapter is intended as a condensed guide for school psychologists to use when their services to the gifted are required. The work of Davis and Rimm (2004) is especially reviewed, given the authors' exemplary comprehensive text on the education of gifted and talented students.

Overview of Assessment Methods for Diverse Students

By definition, the federal government refers to *gifted* as "children who give evidence of high performance capability in areas such as intellectual, creative, artistic, leadership capacity, or specific academic fields, and who require services or activities not ordinarily provided by the school in order to fully develop such capabilities" (section 582, PL. 97-35, cited in Feldman, 2006, p. 342). Overall, giftedness has normally been linked to intelligence IQ tests scores over 120 and above. However, IQ scores should not be the sole identifiers of giftedness. In addition to standardized IQ tests, the assessment of giftedness should include alternative approaches (Groth-Marnat, 2003). Intelligence tests tap into specific domains such as verbal and mathematical abilities and logical reasoning, but fail to identify other domains of giftedness such as art and music or creative genius or talent. Typically, the identification of exceptionality in one particular domain can demonstrate giftedness. Therefore, children can demonstrate exceptionality in one domain and not necessarily manifest a "global giftedness" (Winner, 1997, 2000, cited in Vasta, Miller, & Ellis, 2004). Winner (1997) suggests several factors that contribute to giftedness:

- Giftedness derives from both nature and nurture.
- Parents and environmental forces do not cause or influence giftedness.
- There must be a biological component to giftedness because only some children manifest exceptional capacity for math, music, and art.
- Biology as a causal factor is insufficient without a supportive environment (e.g., help from parents, educators, and other helpful adults). (Winner, 1997, 2000, cited in Vasta et al., 2004)

Certainly the above suppositions strongly contribute to the identification and educational support of gifted children. However, it has been observed that having an extremely high IQ or an exceptional talent in a particular domain does not necessarily guarantee significant accomplishments or creativity. In fact, internal motivation, discipline, and environmental opportunities (particularly including suitable instructional methodology) are all preconditions for the successful blossoming of giftedness (Groth-Marnat, 2003). Moreover, there is a low correlation between high IQs and creativity (Amabile, 1983; Fuchs-Beauchamp, Kames, & Johnson, 1993; Sattler & Hoge, 2006). In any case, the newer psychometric measures such as the Stanford Binet-V (SB-V) and the Wechsler Intelligence Scale for Children IV (WISC-IV) have not overlooked gifted children. The SB-5 has a higher ceiling (IQ up to 175), whereas the WISC-IV has a "testing of the limits" procedure that permits psychologists to observe a child beyond the timed and formal standard instructions of the instrument. This is a significant advantage that can enable examiners to evaluate exceptional thinking abilities of gifted children (Van Ornum, Dunlap, & Shore, 2008).

Several theories on gifted children have emerged that provide important distinctions. A particularly important difference connected to giftedness is the study of creativity in children. Creativity is seen as having the ability to see things in a "novel" way, to have a special gift for creating new and original ideas or things—usually within the humanities. Creative adults can see things differently, and are able to look at unusual ideas and solutions to problems; thus it is their flexibility that allows them to seek new solutions, approaches, and/or opportunities (Sternberg & Lubart, 1992; Sternberg, Kaufman, & Pretz, 2002). Given this view of creativity in children, creativity is somewhat more challenging to predict. What can be observed in children is their ability to perform different tasks in unusual or different ways. But what constitutes unusual or novel ideas or responses? Vasta et al. (2004) discuss one approach which emphasizes the distinction between two types of thinking that have emerged, focusing on *convergent thinking* and *divergent thinking*. Vasta et al. (2004) offer definitions for both of these terms:

- *Convergent thinking* is a form of thinking whose goal is to discover the correct answer to problems with a definite solution—the form of thought emphasized on IQ tests.
- *Divergent thinking* is a form of thinking whose goal is to generate multiple possible solutions for problems that do not have a single correct answer—the form of thought hypothesized to be important for creativity. (p. 396)

Divergent thinking requires novelty ideas such as thinking of various possible interpretations to squiggle drawing. Squiggle tasks are used by researchers to measure divergent thinking in children and they help to observe individual differences in the ability for divergent thinking in childhood (Wallach, 1966). Vasta et al. (2004) stress that the demonstration of divergent thinking through the performance of such tasks does not necessarily predict creativity, since these tasks do not forecast the ability to actually bring about a creative product in the future. For children demonstrating abilities in artistic and musical creativity, additional measures apart from IQ tests should include: (a) a list of creative achievements; (b) the nomination of a qualified person; and (c) specific tests of creativity (Groth-Marnat, 2003, p. 190). In addition, alternative/informal assessment methods can include portfolios of exceptional examples of a child's creative masterwork (Van Ornum, Dunlap, & Shore, 2008). It appears that the conclusion reached regarding research on giftedness and creativity is that both can only thrive with environmental support.

A review of giftedness from a culturally diverse perspective indicates that gifted children from diverse cultural backgrounds and from low socioeconomic/ underprivileged families are in serious need of educational and emotional support from their teachers, school psychologists, and counselors. These children are rarely identified as gifted or talented, and usually receive only basic educational training (Davis & Rimm, 2004; Ford & Grantham, 2003). Several factors, such as culture, language differences, lack of family and peer reinforcement of intellectual and/or creative talents, and cultural bias in tests, usually contribute to their disproportionately small chance of being identified as gifted. This omission occurs across the major ethnic groups in the United States (i.e., African Americans, Hispanic Americans, Native Americans, and Asian Americans) (Davis & Rimm, 2004; Ford & Grantham, 2003).

Davis and Rimm (2004) rightly point out the importance of early identification of gifted disadvantaged and minority children and youth, and the need for adequate educational gifted programming. The authors summarize an important report, *No Gift Wasted: Effective Strategies for Educating*

Highly Able, Disadvantaged Students in Mathematics and Science (Alamprese & Erlanger, 1988) that reveals several noteworthy findings regarding disadvantaged gifted and talented students. The authors' recapped findings are reproduced below.

- Minority students are underrepresented in programs designed to serve gifted and talented students. Although minorities make up 30 percent of students enrolled in public schools, they represent less than 20 percent of the students selected for gifted and talented programs.
- Whereas students from low-income backgrounds comprise 20 percent of the student population, they make up only 4 percent of those students who perform at the highest levels on standardized tests (those who score at the 95th percentile or above).
- High school students from disadvantaged families (in which the mother did not complete high school) are less than half as likely to have participated in gifted and talented programs as more advantaged seniors.
- Disadvantaged students are far less likely to be enrolled in academic programs that can prepare them for college, and are about half as likely to take coursework in advanced math and science than more advanced students. Only 2 percent of high school seniors from poor families take calculus, whereas approximately 7 percent of those from more advantaged background do so. (Alamprese & Erlanger, 1988, cited in Davis & Rimm, 2004, p. 275)

Frasier (1990) notes that the IQ cutoff scores criteria for gifted programs exclude the potential identification of underprivileged and culturally diverse gifted students (and this includes many African Americans). Culturally diverse underprivileged children who may have low IQ and achievement scores (as a result of their disadvantaged backgrounds) most likely will not be identified as gifted. For these students, it is important to view their giftedness based on their "potential" (Davis & Rimm, 2004). In short, there is no doubt that inequalities exist, and that the identification and program placement of culturally diverse minority students—both the exceptionally challenged and the exceptionally gifted—is in need of educational reform.

An overview of assessment instruments for the identification of gifted and creative children and youth places emphasis on the need to assess the traditional domains of academic and cognitive abilities first. Any child perceived to have exceptional giftedness routinely undergoes a cognitive and academic evaluation. As already stated, high IQ test scores are one of the main criteria for identifying intellectual giftedness. For culturally diverse and underprivileged children, the IQ "cultural test bias" debate continues (Jensen, 1980; Frasier, Garcia, & Passow, 1995), and for many the use of psychometric cognitive measures is judged to be racially biased. The reliance on IQ test scores may suppress the observance of the genuine strengths and giftedness of culturally diverse children from deprived or dissimilar environments who may score within the average or below-average range of intellectual functioning, resulting in them not being identified as gifted. The same cultural bias difficulty has been observed in achievement tests. The conclusion reached appears to be that, although high IQ and achievement tests scores are good indictors of special types of giftedness, low test scores can totally eliminate the identification of giftedness in culturally diverse and underprivileged students.

Davis and Rimm (2004) describe the Skills Reinforcement Project (SRP) designed by Lynch and Mills (1990) to improve the academic achievement of 45 sixth graders identified with high potential. The selected group of students comprised a high proportion of African American and Hispanic Americans, in addition to children from low socioeconomic backgrounds. The SRP program proved to be effective. Nine high-potential students from SRP were accepted into gifted programs, as the authors state, "without recourse to affirmative action" (Davis & Rimm, 2004, p. 280). This example of effective interventions provides evidence that achievement test scores can be improved when appropriate programs are designed to increase the needed skills of high-potential gifted students who may not have scored highly in this area of assessment.

A crucial point to emphasize is that best practice calls for not "compacting" assessment results with just test scores, but rather should examine other types of intelligences (i.e., multiple intelligences, see Chapter 3) as well as use alternative informal methods of assessment such as dynamic (see Lidz, 2001) and portfolio assessment of exemplary work or curriculum based assessment (CBA) (see Chapter 2). The use of additional informal measures can lead to the identification of exceptional talents or creativity (e.g., artistic or scientific talent) which otherwise may not have been observed in a formal assessment.

Aside from intelligence and achievement tests, some useful identification methods are listed below.

- *Creativity tests*—These can be divergent thinking tests or personality and biographical inventories.
- *Teacher nominations*—These are used to recommend students for gifted programs.
- *Parent nominations*—Although infrequently used, these are important in obtaining information pertaining to a child's interests, hobbies, books read, remarkable accomplishments, special talents and opportunities, relationships, and special problems or needs.
- *Peer nominations*—These are considered good because peers can easily point out culturally gifted students due to peers' daily direct observations in the classroom. Some questions to ask are: Who is the smartest kid in the class? Who is best in math? Who has the best memory?

- *Self-nominations*—Self-motivated students with artistic, creative, scientific, and/or other interests and talents sometimes will initiate their own nominations for a special program. This type of nomination is almost compulsory at the junior and high school levels, since peer pressure often inhibits special talents.
- *Product nominations*—These are very helpful for examining the quality of special work a student has done (i.e., artwork, poetry, science projects, electronic or computer projects, dramatic talent, photography, and other uncommon works). (Davis & Rimm, 2004, pp. 90–95)

Additionally, rating scales have been developed for administration in collaboration with teachers, parents, peers, and self- and product nominations.

A review of assessment instruments for the identification of giftedness reveals that step-by-step plans, rating scales, and ability tests are used for identifying giftedness in preschoolers and secondary school students. For preschoolers, a three-step process for identifying intellectually gifted preschoolers includes:

1. informing parents and preschool teachers about the characteristics of gifted preschoolers and the availability of public programs in their state;

2. a general screening (which should include a parent and teacher questionnaire, brochure, and application form). The questionnaires require parents or teachers to rate the child on 45 different behaviors, some of which are and are not characteristics of gifted preschoolers, and to exemplify other outstanding behaviors exhibited by the preschooler;

3. an individual assessment, beginning with the Hess School Readiness Scale (Hess, 1975), a cognitive measure such as the Stanford Binet scale on which an IQ of 120 or higher is usually required (depending on the state regulation for acceptance into gifted program), and academic evaluation of math and reading skills (see Burns, Mathews, & Mason, 1990).

Early identification of gifted young children in kindergarten is recommended for appropriate interventions (Sankar-DeLeeuw, 2004).

Gifted children in middle and high school are evaluated for giftedness and talent following various similar procedures. Mindes (2007) provides a list of useful tests and rating scales to identify giftedness in children and youth from ages 6 to 18. Some of the suggested instruments follow.

1. The *Screening Assessment for Gifted Elementary Students—Primary* (SAGES-P—Corn & Johnson, 1992, Prufrock). The SAGES-P is administered for the evaluation of giftedness in children aged from 5 years to 8 years and 11 months. The SAGES-P comprises two sections: a reasoning subtest

and a general information subset. The reasoning subtest measures aptitude, and the general information subset measures achievement. Administration time is 30 minutes; the method is nonverbal, pencil and booklet.

2. The *Gifted Rating Scales* (Pfeiffer & Jarosewich, 2003, PsychCorp). These are norm referenced rating scales (for ages 4 to 6), developed from the existing theories of giftedness and federal and state rules concerning the definition of gifted and talented students (responses are in written form; 5–10 minutes' administration time).

3. *The Torrance Tests of Creative Thinking: Figural* (TTCT-F) (Torrance, 1998, Scholastic Testing Service). The TTCT-F has two sections that assess creative potential in various domains. The parts are: (a) the *Figural* section, which uses pictures to tap into creative thinking; and (b) the *Verbal* section, which evaluates thinking creatively through the use of words. Tests of thinking creatively with actions and movement are also available for age 3 to kindergarten. The Figural section can be administered in 30 minutes, the Verbal in 45 minutes. Both have nonverbal responses; administration is in booklet and pencil form.

4. *The Creativity Assessment Packet* (CAT) (William, 1980, Pro-Ed). The CAT comprises three instruments for identifying creativity: (a) the *Test of Divergent Thinking*; (b) the *Test of Divergent Feeling*; and (c) the *Williams Scale* (this third instrument is a rating scale). The six factors measured in the CAT packet are: fluency, flexibility, elaboration, originality, vocabulary, and comprehension. Administration time ranges from 25 to 30 minutes for each instrument; all have nonverbal responses; administration is in booklet and pencil form. (Mindes, 2007, pp. 389–390)

Table 13.1 presents Davis and Rimm's (2004) and Sattler and Hoge's (2006) recommended instruments for identifying and assessing gifted students. These instruments may be used by school psychologists, parents, teachers, and occasionally by the students themselves. Administration of only one instrument as the sole identifier of student giftedness is strongly discouraged. Practitioners are advised to use a multimodal method of identification and assessment, which may include rating scales, nomination procedures, and intelligence, achievement, and creativity tests.

Apart from the above measures, inventories are also available for the assessment of giftedness in secondary schools. Colangelo et al. (1996) give a detailed explanation of the PLAN inventory (American College Testing Program). Developed for tenth graders, the PLAN is useful for preparing students for appropriate high schools. This inventory measures high-level thinking skills,

Table 13.1   Instruments for Identifying and Assessing Giftedness

Instrument	Developers	Appropriate Ages	Description
Gifted and Talented Evaluation Scales (GATES)	Gilliam, Carpenter, & Christensen, (1996)	5–18 years	Five scales used by parents and teachers to assess intellectual ability, academic skills, leadership, creativity, and artistic talent; each scale takes 5–10 minutes.
Scales for Rating Behavioral Characteristics of Superior Students (rev. ed.) (SRBCSS)	Renzulli, Smith, White, Callahan, & Hartman (2000)	Grades 3–12	Ten scales used by teachers to assess: intellectual ability; creativity; motivation; leadership; artistic, musical, dramatic, and planning characteristics; communication-precision; and communication-expressiveness.
Gifted Evaluation Scale (2nd ed.) (GES-2)	McCarney & Anderson (1998)	5–18 years	Scale contains 48 items and is used by teachers to evaluate students' intellectual ability, creativity, specific academic ability, leadership, and ability in the performing or visual arts; takes about 15 minutes.
Achievement Identification Measure (AIM)	Rimm (1986)	School-aged children	A total of 77 items to be completed by parents to measure student academic motivation; versions are also available to be completed by students and teachers.
Frasier Talent Assessment Profile (F-TAP)	Frasier (1994; Frasier & Passow, 1994)	School-aged children	Examines 10 characteristics of gifted students: high motivation, special interests, communication talent, problem solving, memory, inquiry, insight, reasoning, imagination/creativity, and humor; fair assessment of minority groups.
Gifted Preschool Screening Packet	Burns, Mathews, & Mason (1990)	3 to 5 years	Parent and teacher questionnaires for rating preschoolers on 45 behaviors; provides parents and teachers with space to describe additional exceptional strengths of the child.

(Continued)

Table 13.1 (Continued)

Instrument	Developers	Appropriate Ages	Description
The PLAN inventory	American College Testing Program	Students in tenth grade	Intended to identify areas of exceptional academic performance; measures high-level thinking skills and use of judgment.
Purdue Academic Rating Scales (PARS)	Feldhusen, Hoover, & Sayler (1990)	Students in middle school and high school	Contains academic scales that measure math, science, English, social studies, and foreign languages; scales contain 15 items each and all items are rated on a five-point rating scale.
Purdue Vocational Rating Scales (PVRS)	Feldhusen (1997)	Students in middle school and high school	Vocational scales measuring agriculture, business and office, home economics, and trade and industrial; scales contain 15 items each and all items are rated on a five-point rating scale.

SOURCE: Sattler and Hoge (2006); Davis and Rimm (2004); Moon and Dixon (2006); National Research Center on the Gifted and Talented (NRC/GT).

such as problem solving, grasping implied meanings, drawing inferences, evaluating ideas, and making judgments within the domains of English, reading, mathematics and science.

The decision to use inventories, rating scales, or other measures for identifying giftedness, talented, or creativity lies with the practitioner and educator. In high schools, special talents or creativity may more easily be recognized because of the option of self-nomination by adolescents, which is often prompted by intrinsic motivation and a positive self-image as well as the development of special interests. School psychologists can encourage self-assessments, particularly with culturally/linguistically and ethnically diverse children and youth who may not be able to demonstrate their abilities and talents on the more conventional measures of giftedness. To reach cultural fairness in the identification of specific giftedness, creativity, or talents, culturally and ethnically diverse students will need school psychologists to advocate for them not only through the identification process, but in placement decisions for a suitable gifted program as well. Because of the respect for the profession of school psychology, practitioners can have a tremendous impact on the final considerations for placement of a gifted child. It is especially important for practitioners to recognize that the identification procedure used is central to gifted program acceptance. For this reason, it is crucial that school psychologists use multiple types of assessment instruments and informal methods that are culturally sensitive and unbiased. Involving teachers in the evaluative process is of utmost importance. Through collaborative joint effort, practitioners and educators can reach many gifted students who otherwise may not be identified.

As in any assessment, practitioners are cautioned regarding test selection. Reviewing tests' suitability, validity, and reliability are important essential factors to consider prior to instrument selection. Davis and Rimm (2004) suggest seeking information on validity and reliability on measures used in the identification of giftedness and creativity from the National Research Center on the Gifted and Talented at the University of Connecticut, Storrs.

Characteristics of Giftedness

Because of their giftedness and talents, exceptional children manifest distinct characteristics and can experience differences in their emotional and social development. However, the occurrence of emotional problems in gifted and ungifted children is probably the same (Pendarvis, Howley, & Howley, 1990; Schneider et al., 1989). Davis and Rimm (2004) summarize numerous recurrent characteristics of gifted students obtained from various sources. Their review reveals several more positive characteristics than negative ones. Some of the positive traits are:

- unusual alertness in infancy and later;
- early and rapid learning;
- superior language ability—verbally fluent, large vocabulary, complex grammar;
- superior analytic ability;
- efficient high-capacity memory;
- superior reasoning and problem-solving skills;
- the use of high-level thinking skills and efficient strategies;
- wide interests and interest in new topics;
- multiple capabilities;
- strong empathy, moral thinking, sense of justice, honesty, and intellectual honesty;
- strong internal control;
- independence, self-direction, capacity to work alone;
- imagination, creativeness, ability to solve problems;
- reflectiveness (Davis & Rimm, 2004, p. 33).

These are not the sole characteristics of gifted individuals, although these do summarize well some of the exceptionalities that can be signaled out in early development as well as in middle childhood and adolescence. However, Davis and Rimm's review also reveals negative characteristics of gifted children. Some of these are:

- interpersonal difficulties, due often to intellectual differences;
- underachievement, especially in uninteresting areas;
- nonconformity, sometimes in disturbing directions;
- perfectionism, which can be extreme;
- self-doubt, poor self-image;
- depression (Davis & Rimm, 2004, p. 33).

It is important to note that these traits are not observed in all gifted children and youth. Each individual may manifest different characteristics of giftedness. It is the responsibility of school psychologists and teachers to be aware that gifted children may react in unconventional ways due to their uniqueness, to the point of being perceived as emotionally disturbed. Actually, there is a risk that emotional problems could occur due to envious peers, apprehension, negative attitudes, unavailability of same intellectually gifted peers, and the lack of enriched school programs (Grossberg & Cornell, 1988). Gifted students also have been observed to respond better to psychosocial changes than other students (Robinson & Clinkenbeard, 1998). However, Rimm (2002) cautions that this observance is usually found in studies of moderately gifted children and may not accurately reflect those children who are intellectually gifted (high IQs of 160–179) or profoundly intellectually gifted children (IQs of 180+). Although negative correlations were found between gifted students and peer acceptance and relationships (Schneider, 1987), Rimm concludes that:

> Despite common wisdom and stereotypes to the contrary, exceptionally and profoundly advanced students do not show inherent social deficiencies more frequently than anyone else. It is the mismatch with the environments we afford them that isolates and discourages their efforts to relate to others. This situation is a responsibility we must all take seriously. (p. 27)

Nevertheless, it has been suggested that it would be helpful to apply a multicultural model of psychological assessment, the Multicultural Assessment Procedure (MAP) (see Chapter 2 for a description of MAP), that will aid in sounder comprehension of the social and emotional needs of gifted individuals (Levy & Plucker, 2003). Connecting MAP to giftedness is appropriate because, as the authors explain, giftedness is a "subculture," and individuals who are gifted and talented function in "multiple cultural contexts." This perspective can aid clinicians to work effectively with gifted individuals, since it is necessary to "accurately understand the interaction of the person's multiple cultural identities" (p. 229). Levy and Plucker (2003) present MAP for gifted and talented students by compiling four phases that guide the clinician to perform a sound multicultural assessment of a gifted person. The authors address several questions that should be asked during each phase of a *culturally gifted* evaluation. Some example questions are:

- What is the client's understanding of their talent?
- What other cultures does the client identify with (e.g., racial, ethnic, gender, religion)?
- How is giftedness viewed within the client's other cultural contexts?
- What is the family's understanding of giftedness?
- What expectations does the family have for the client?
- How is gifted viewed within the family's cultural context? (p. 235)

Additional recommendations suggest steps to take in interpreting the cultural data obtained, using psychological testing such as the Child Behavior Checklist (CBCL) (Achenbach, 1994), which measures social-emotional functioning and taps into different behaviors that have been endorsed frequently across diverse groups. Comparison of all cultural clinical information should be made with DSM-IV criteria (see Levy & Plucker, 2003 for further suggestions on MAP and cultural giftedness assessment).

Indeed, educators, counselors, and school psychologists are accountable for assuring not only that gifted children are identified early, but that recommendations for adequate program placement are followed through. Making suggestions for particularly enriched curricula or special gifted programs does not necessarily mean that this will actually take place. This is where the school psychologist can make a difference by taking influential advocacy steps that will ensure the gifted child will obtain adequate program placement. Advocacy opportunities come in various ways, such as providing parents with information on various gifted programs, requirements needed, how to follow the legal steps to take to ensure that the gifted child is given every opportunity to receive special educational services if difficulties are experienced, and seeking teacher collaboration in the evaluation and follow-up process.

Availability of Gifted Programs

Approaches to gifted education involve several program planning considerations. Educators and administrators are responsible for taking steps to help meet the educational needs of gifted and talented children and adolescents. Davis and Rimm (2004) discuss four main components of program planning. These are: (a) program philosophy and goals; (b) definition and identification; (c) instruction (students, personnel, location, and time considerations); and (d) program evaluation.

Program philosophy and goals are usually established through the forming of a gifted committee (an ideal opportunity for the school psychologist to join) that will determine what to include in the statement of the philosophy and goals/objectives for the proposed gifted program. Definition and identification delineates what is actually meant by gifted, talented, or creative. What criteria should be placed on grades, children with disabilities, and minority representations? How will students be identified? Instruction encompasses several areas. The needs of gifted students, and how best to meet their needs, are determined for the particular program. What school personnel will comprise the gifted committee, and which individuals will design, coordinate, and oversee the program? What teachers are qualified to teach in the program? The location of the gifted program (i.e., in a special class or a special school) is determined, based on the resources available. Time consideration involves deciding when the services will be available (e.g., in an after-class session, at weekends, over summer, or at another opportune time). As with all programs, a program evaluation plan should be decided. The important program evaluative questions are: How will student's knowledge base and high level cognitive increases be evaluated? Should the satisfaction of students and parents, or the effectiveness of instructional methodology, be given priority? (Davis & Rimm, 2004, p. 55). Program planning is a difficult undertaking, and there are several problematic areas, all of which can be traced to the four main components. These can range from the philosophy, rationale, and goals/objectives of the program to the types of gifts and talents to be addressed, the types of identification methods and criteria required for acceptance, to the availability of funds and the obtainable number of school psychologists, counselors, and other support services.

Various curriculum models have been developed for gifted children and adolescents. Davis and Rimm (2004, pp. 165–190) review 11 curriculum models that have very detailed practical suggestions and some models that are less detailed. Mainly, these curriculum models concentrate on incorporating various enrichment activities ranging from exploratory topics that focus on creativity, thinking skills, and communication skills to developing talents in visual and performing arts into the gifted program. Other enrichment activities included are for math, science, computer/internet, literature/writing, business/economics, and in social sciences/culture and language. These curriculum models are dedicated to encouraging the growth of giftedness and talent in children and adolescents within the classroom, with the aim of transcending the identified giftedness out of the classroom.

Affective-oriented curriculum models have also been created to address the special social/emotional needs of gifted children. Gifted students can be alienated socially because of their special intellectual exceptionalities. The transition from elementary to secondary school can be particularly difficult for the gifted student because of the tremendous need for social acceptance during adolescence. VanTassel-Baska (2006) has stressed the importance of enhancing the affective development of gifted adolescents by providing a curriculum that instructs specifically on the components of affective development. The author suggests that the Integrated Curriculum Model (ICM), which is recommended for cognitive development in several academic areas, can be used as a framework for structuring an affective development curriculum (VanTassel-Baska, Ries, Bass, Poland & Avery, 1998; VanTassel-Baska, Zuo, Avery, & Little, 2002). The ICM model posits three critical dimensions: (a) advanced content; (b) higher order thinking; and (c) focus on abstract concepts. Advanced content can be transferred to affective domains by applying the construct of emotional intelligence (EI) (see Chapter 3 on emotional intelligence) as a vehicle to challenge gifted students in their awareness of self and others. Higher order thinking and problem-solving skills are vital for improving the development of emotional intelligence, since EI is associated with metacognition and critical thinking. Abstract thinking can be used to improve affective development through the use of EI problem-based scenarios for motivating and challenging the gifted.

VanTassel-Baska (2006) explains that the use of EI lessons and strategies in a class curriculum is an important venue for the affective development of gifted students. Some of the author's presented sample lessons for EI enrichment are: *The Study of Emotion, Channeling Emotion to Promote Thinking, Developing and Applying Emotional Knowledge,* and *Regulation of Emotions.* Each lesson underlines the importance of "understanding emotions at levels that promote application of that understanding to improve human functioning in both cognitive and affective areas". Moreover, each EI lesson helps to exemplify the importance of having gifted students use their emotions to improve thinking as well as to stir up creative ways of responding to varied incentives or activities. In addition, EI lessons are useful for educators, counselors, and school psychologists to encourage gifted children and youth to use EI strategies in order to help understand themselves and others.

Sattler and Hoge (2006) stress that gifted children need programs which will match their abilities on both the cognitive and affective levels. The authors describe several types of programs offered by schools. Some of these are *pull-out groups, subject acceleration, grade skipping, magnet schools,* and *advanced placement* (AP) programs. Pull-out groups simply take gifted students out of the general education classroom and provide them with specialized instructional services. In the subject acceleration program, students are allowed into more advanced grades to continue learning a particular subject or sent to other institutions. Grade skipping allows gifted children to skip grades. Magnet schools are special schools established to offer gifted children and adolescents advanced courses or programs in specific areas such as science, information technology, or the performing arts. An AP program will let gifted students take college courses and examinations while still attending high school. In order to ensure that academically advanced children receive adequate education, it is recommended that they be placed in advanced grade levels. This is based on the standard placement according to competence theory.

Special Advice for the School Psychologist

Ultimately, school psychologists confronted with the assessment of an exceptionally gifted, creative, or talented child or adolescent will have to follow two main paths for adequate evaluation. First, they must diligently follow a sound culturally fair intellectual, social/emotional, and educational assessment (see Chapters 2, 3, and 4 for culturally fair assessment practices), in addition to the evaluation of any possible language-based factors affecting native and second language acquisition of cognitive and academic language proficiency (see Chapter 11). Second, and most essential to fairness, practitioners need to advocate for their gifted students regarding appropriate educational program placements. The latter will be more easily achieved if they have a good grasp of the main components of program planning for the gifted, together with knowledge of the distinctions between the educational planning of *acceleration* (offering a gifted child a standard curriculum that is advanced for their age) versus *enrichment* (designing richer and more diverse educational experiences within the curriculum). In addition to knowledge of the various gifted programs, awareness of the varied curriculum models will assist in making educational placement decisions and interventions (see Davis & Rimm, pp. 165–189).

Ethically, school psychologists are obligated to advocate for the identification of giftedness in children from various racial/ethnic and culturally and linguistically diverse children and youth. This type of advocacy can only be attained by following best practices in the assessment of giftedness. To attain this essential best practice, teachers and parents should be engaged in the assessment process.

Because teachers are often the first observers of giftedness in children, and are influential advocates, school psychologists can help in the identification of gifted and talented children by offering consultee-centered case consultation services whereby collaborative teacher-practitioner dyads are formed to identify characteristics of gifted and creative children and adolescents from culturally/linguistically and racial/ethnic diverse backgrounds. It is precisely through the efforts of consultant school psychologists that consultee-centered and group consultation services can be offered to advocate and impart knowledge pertaining to the understanding of diverse gifted students (see Chapter 8 on consultation). Through this consultative approach, both educators and consultant school psychologists can also educate minority and culturally diverse parents on gifted and talented identification and the availability of educational programs.

The influence teachers have in the decision to refer children to gifted and talented programs should not be forgotten. A student's ethnicity can, and has been known to, make a difference in a teacher's referral decision (see Elhoweris, Mutua, Alsheikh, & Holloway, 2005). Between 80 and 90 percent of teachers are middle-class Anglo American. In contrast, the majority of our student population are from culturally/linguistically diverse backgrounds (Cushner, McClelland, & Safford, 2003). This fact clearly implies that children's ethnicity can and may affect teacher's eligibility placement decisions for gifted and talented programs. Elhoweris et al. (2005) found "a potential link between teachers' bias against African American children and their underrepresentation in gifted and talented programs" (p. 30). In fact, in order to remedy the biased referral problem for children with disabilities and to increase appropriate referrals to gifted and talented programs, Grossman (1995, cited in Elhoweris et al., 2005) recommends that general education teachers' cultural knowledge be increased in order to reconstruct teacher attitudes. This is why disseminating knowledge of diverse cultures and ethnic groups may help promote non-biased opinions and aid teachers in the early identification of gifted children. Who is better suited than the school psychologist to take charge of this responsibility?

An additional vital recommendation for culturally fair assessment efforts also encompasses the final procedure of psychological report writing after an assessment of a gifted child has been completed. Chapter 7 discussed writing psychological and educational reports for culturally and linguistically diverse children, placing a strong emphasis on the interconnectedness between the steps taken in the assessment process and the writing of the psychological report. Thus the results obtained from a psycho-educational assessment become the written account (i.e., the psychological report). Adhering to the format and recommendations emphasized in Chapter 7, school psychologists who have identified unique exceptionalities in a child may include a special section in their psycho-educational report. Below are suggestions for specific headings and inclusion of information under each heading.

Formal Assessment of Giftedness

This section should include the results of formal measures used to identify giftedness. Name each instrument administered, then describe what it measures and the results obtained.

Informal Assessment of Giftedness

This section should continue to elaborate on the exceptionalities and talents observed through informal methods, such as portfolios, artwork, musical or kinesthetic (dance) talents (i.e., a repertoire of the child or adolescent's musical, art, drama achievements). Teacher inventories or observations (e.g., nominations) and peer/parent nominations, as well as self-assessment results should also be included. Any other informative methods used to provide evidence of the identified giftedness or talent (e.g., if consultee-centered teacher or parent consultation was helpful in the identification process, state the types of collaborative methods used for identification).

Social/Emotional Functioning

This section should include the child/student's emotional functioning based on the child's giftedness. Information regarding affective development (including self-concept) and peer and adult relationships are important components to include for determining the overall well being of the gifted child or youth identified.

Recommendation for Placement/Program

This section should outline curriculum and instructional recommendations; availability of gifted programs; and types of beneficial extracurricular activities for the gifted student.

Adherence to a multicultural assessment approach will enable the school psychologist to include varied formal and informal methods of assessment into the psychological report.

Finally, special consideration is necessary for gifted children and adolescents who may be learning disabled or have a specific disorder. School psychologists may encounter children who have a combination of both a disability and/or disorder, and are gifted. Children with learning disabilities who are gifted have manifested considerably weaker skills in decoding, spelling, visual discrimination, sequencing, spatial abilities, and in mathematics (Waldron & Saphire, 1992, p. 599).

Another special assessment consideration is the use of IQ tests with children who are gifted and have Attention Deficit Hyperactivity Disorder (ADHD). There is a possibility that school psychologists may not see ADHD patterns in the Wechsler tests if a child does exceptionally well on the digit span and mathematic subtests, thus decreasing the observance of a freedom from distractibility factor. To ensure that such a diagnostic error does not occur, it is suggested that a Stanford-Binet scale be utilized with children who may have high scores (e.g., the new SB-V) (Lovecky, 1999, p. 2; Lovecky & Silverman, 1998). Alternative assessment methods are also recommended for this population, to ensure accurate diagnosis. It is important that practitioners do not overlook the special needs of these "dual exceptionality" children (Lovecky, 1999, cited in Van Ornum, Dunlap, & Shore, 2008).

Lovecky (2004) gives special advice for psychologists to adhere to when servicing gifted children with ADHD, Asperger's Syndrome, and other learning deficits. First, psychologists who are not experienced with gifted children are advised to seek professional expertise in this area, or not to evaluate them. This applies to knowledge of assessment practice for giftedness in general and for giftedness with ADHD or Asperger's. Second, understand the importance of using tests with high ceilings in order to better observe strengths and weaknesses. The reason for this is that if low-ceiling tests are used, "the difference between strengths and weaknesses is compressed so it appears as if the child is not as different as he or she may really be. Recommendations based on faulty assessment of symptoms can be harmful to the child and family" (p. 463). Lovecky (2004) further advocates assessing the gifted child through the process method, "so that the child's own strengths are the measure of weakness rather than age-norm cutoffs" (p. 464).

Lastly, recommendations should be made based on the child's strengths and weaknesses, and suggestions should be made for the use of higher-order methods for compensatory growth. This is important because gifted children need to be stimulated, regardless of their particular weaknesses. Building on strengths is essential to maintain motivation in the gifted child or youth. Ultimately, the best assessment is really only attained directly by the clinician who, because of their clinical skills, can effectively administer the chosen instrument, observe the child, and interpret the results (Lovecky, 2004).

In the end, it is the school psychologist who can make a difference and change the course of a child's life through their clinical expertise and advocacy.

References

Achenbach, T. M. (1994). Child Behavior Checklist and related instruments. In M. E. Maruish (Ed.), *The use of psychological testing for treatment planning and outcome assessment* (pp. 517–549). Hillsdale, NJ: Lawrence Erlbaum.

Alamprese, J. A., & Erlanger, W. J. (1988). *No gifts wasted: Effective strategies for educating highly able, disadvantaged students in mathematics and science.* Washington, DC: Cosmos Corporation.

Amabile, T. M. (1983). *The social psychology of creativity.* New York: Springer-Verlag.

Burns, J. M., Mathews, F. N., & Mason, A. (1990). Essential steps in screening and identifying preschool gifted children. *Gifted Child Quarterly, 34*(3), 102–107.

Bursztyn, A. M. (2007). *The Praeger handbook of special education* (3rd ed.). New York: John Wiley & Sons.

Colangelo, N., Assouline, S. G., Cole, V., Cutrona, C., & Maxey, J. E. (1996). Exceptional academic performance: Perfect scores on the PLAN. *Gifted Child Quarterly, 40,* 102–110.

Corn, A. L.., & Johnson, S. (1992). *Screening assessment for gifted elementary students–primary edition.* Austin, TX: Pro-Ed.

Cushner, K., McClelland, A., & Safford, P. (2003). *Human diversity in education: An integrative approach* (4th ed.). New York: McGraw-Hill.

Davis, G. A., & Rimm, S. B. (2004). *Education of the gifted and talented* (5th ed). Boston, MA: Allyn & Bacon.

Dixon, F. A., & Moon, S. M. (2006) (Eds.). *The handbook of secondary gifted education.* Waco, TX: Prufrock.

Elhoweris, H., Mutua, K., Alsheikh, N., & Holloway, P. (2005). Effect of children's ethnicity on teachers' referral and recommendation decisions in gifted and talented programs. *Remedial and Special Education, 26*(1), 25–31.

Feldhusen, J. (1997). Educating teachers for work with talented youth. In N. Colangelo & G. Davis (Eds.), *Handbook of gifted education* (2nd ed., pp. 547–552). Boston: Allyn & Bacon.

Feldhusen, J. F., Hoover, S. M., & Sayler, M. F. (1990). *Identifying and educating gifted students at the secondary level.* Monroe, NY: Royal Fireworks Press.

Feldman, R. S. (2006). *Development across the life span* (4th ed). Upper Saddle River, NJ: Pearson/Prentice Hall.

Ford, D. Y., & Grantham, T. C. (2003). Providing access for culturally diverse gifted students: From deficit to dynamic thinking. *Theory into Practice, 23*(3), 217–226.

Frasier, M. M. (1990). The equitable identification of gifted and talented children. In B. Shade (Chair), *Issues in the education of gifted and talented minority children.* Symposium conducted at the annual meeting of the American Educational Association.

Frasier, M. M. (1994). *Traits, aptitudes, behaviors.* Athens, GA: Author.

Frasier, M. M., Garcia, J. H., & Passow, A. H. (1995). *A review of assessment issues in gifted education and their implications for identifying gifted minority students.* Storrs, CT: University of Connecticut, National Research Center on the Gifted and Talented.

Frasier, M. M., & Passow, A. H. (1994). *Towards a New Paradigm for Identifying Talent Potential*. (Research Monograph 94112). Storrs, CT: The National Research Center on the Gifted and Talented, University of Connecticut.

Fuchs-Beauchamp, D., Karnes, M. B., & Johnson, L. J. (1993). Creativity and intelligence in preschoolers. *Gifted Child Quarterly, 37*(3), 113–117.

Gilliam, J. E., Carpenter, B. O., & Christensen, J. R. (1996). *Gifted and Talented Evaluation Scales (Gates)*. Madrid: Psymtec.

Grossberg, I. N., & Cornell, D. G. (1988). Relationship between personality adjustment and high intelligence: Terman versus Hollingworth. *Exceptional Children, 55*, 266–272.

Grossman, P. L. (1995). Teachers' knowledge. In L. W. Anderson (Ed.), *International encyclopedia of teaching and teacher education* (2nd ed., pp. 20–24). London: Pergamon.

Groth-Marnat, G. (2003). *Handbook of psychological assessment*. New York: John Wiley & Sons.

Hess, R. J. (1975). *Hess school readiness scale*. Johnstown, PA: Mafex Associates.

Jensen, A. R. (1980). *Bias in mental testing*. New York: Free Press.

Kogan, N., & Wallach, M. A. (1966). Modification of a judgmental style through group interaction. *Journal of Personality and Social Psychology, 4*(2), 165–174.

Levy, J. J., & Plucker, J. A. (2003). Assessing the psychological presentation of gifted and talented clients: A multicultural perspective. *Counseling Psychology Quarterly, 16*(3), 229–247.

Lidz, C. S. (2001). An alternative approach to the identification of gifted culturally and linguistically diverse learners. *School Psychology International, 22*(1), 74–97.

Losen, D. J., & Orfield, G. (Eds.). (2002). *Racial inequity in special education*. Boston: Harvard Education Press.

Lovecky, D. V. (1999). *Gifted children with ADHD*. Providence, RI: Gifted Resource Center of New England.

Lovecky, D. V. (2004). *Different minds: Gifted children with ADHD, Asperger Syndrome, and other learning deficits*. Philadelphia, PA: Jessica Kingsley.

Lovecky, D. V., & Silverman, L. K. (1998). Gifted children with ADHD. Paper presented to the Panel of the NIH Consensus Development Conference on Diagnosis and Treatment of Attention Deficit Hyperactivity Disorder, Bethesda, MD.

Lynch, S., & Mills, C.J. (1990). The skills reinforcement project (SRP): An academic program for high potential minority youth. *Journal for the Education of the Gifted, 13*, 364–379.

McCarney, S. B., & Anderson, P. D. (1998). *The Gifted Evaluation Scale*. Columbia, MO: Hawthorne Educational Services.

Mercer, J. R. (1973). *Labeling the mentally retarded: Clinical and social system perspectives on mental retardation*. Berkeley, CA: University of California Press.

Mindes, G. (2007). *Assessing young children* (3rd ed.). Columbus, OH: Pearson/ Merrill Prentice Hall.

Moon, S. M., & Dixon, F. A. (2006). Conceptions of giftedness in adolescence. In F.A. Dixon & S. M. Moon (Eds.), *The handbook of secondary gifted education* (pp. 7–34). Waco, TX: Prufrock.

Naglieri, J. A. (2001). Understanding intelligence, giftedness and creativity using the PASS theory. *Roeper Review, 23*(3), 151–157.

Neihart, M., Reis, S. M., Robinson, N. M., & Moon, S. M. (Eds.). (2002). *The social and emotional development of gifted children: What do we know?* Waco, TX: Prufrock.

Ogbu, J. (1986). The consequences of the American caste system. In U. Neisser (Ed.), *The school achievement of minority children: New perspectives.* Hillsdale, NJ: Lawrence Erlbaum.

Pendarvis, E. D., Howley, A. A., & Howley, C. B. (1990). *The abilities of gifted children.* Englewood Cliffs, NJ: Prentice-Hall.

Pfeiffer, S. I., & Jarosewich, T. (2003). *Gifted rating scales.* San Antonio, TX: Psychological Corporation.

Renzulli, J. S., Smith, L. H., White, A. J., Callahan, C. M., & Hartman, K. F. (2000). *Scales for rating the behavior characteristics of superior students* (rev. ed.). Mansfield, CT: Creative Learning Press.

Robinson, A., & Clinkenbeard, P.R. (1998). Giftedness: An exceptionality examined. *Annual Review of Psychology, 49*, 117–139.

Rimm, S. B. (1986). *Underachievement syndrome: Causes and cures.* Watertown, WI: Apple.

Rimm, S. (2002). Peer pressures and social acceptance of gifted students. In M. Neihart, S. M. Reis, N. M. Robinson, & S. M. Moon (Eds.), *The social and emotional development of gifted children: What do we know?* (pp. 13–18). Waco, TX: Prufrock.

Sankar-DeLeeuw, N. (2004). Case studies of gifted kindergarten children: Profiles of promise. *Roeper Review, 26*(4), 192–207.

Sattler, J. M., & Hoge, R. D. (2006). Giftedness. In J. M. Sattler, & R. D. Hoge (Eds.), *Assessment of children: Behavioral, social, and clinical foundations* (5th ed., pp. 448–463). San Diego, CA: Jerome M. Sattler.

Schneider, B. H. (1987). *The gifted child in peer group perspective.* New York: Springer-Verlag.

Schneider, B. H., Clegg, M. R., Byrne, B. M., Ledingham, J. E., & Crombie, G. (1989). Social relations of gifted children as a function of age and school program. *Journal of Educational Psychology, 81*, 43–56.

Sternberg, R. J., Kaufman, J. C., & Pretz, J. E. (2002). *The creativity conundrum: A propulsion model of kinds of creative contributions.* New York: Psychology Press.

Sternberg, R. J., & Lubart, T. I. (1992). Buy low and sell high: An investment approach to creativity. *Current Directions in Psychological Science, 1*, 1–5.

Torrance, E. (1998). *Torrance Tests of Creative Thinking: Figural Test.* Bensenville, IL: Scholastic Testing Service.

VanTassel-Baska, J. (2006). A content analysis of evaluation findings across 20 gifted programs: A clarion call for enhanced gifted program development. *Gifted Child Quarterly, 50*(3), 199–210.

VanTassel-Baska, J., Ries, G., Bass, R., Poland, D., & Avery, L. (1998). A national study of science curriculum effectiveness with high-ability students. *Gifted Child Quarterly, 42*, 200–211.

VanTassel-Baska, J., Zuo, L., Avery, L. D., & Little, C. A. (2002). A curriculum study of gifted student learning in the language arts. *Gifted Child Quarterly, 46*, 30–44.

Vasta, R., Miller, S. A., & Ellis, S. (2004). *Child psychology* (4th ed.). Hoboken, NJ: John Wiley & Sons.

Van Ornum, W., Dunlap, L. L., & Shore, M. F. (2008). *Psychological testing across the* lifespan. Upper Saddle River: NJ, Pearson/Prentice Hall.

Waldron, K. A., & Saphire, D. G. (1992). Perceptual and academic patterns of learning-disabled/gifted students. *Perceptual and Motor Skills, 74*, 599–609.

Wehmeyer, M. L. & Schwartz, M. (2001). Disproportionate representation of males in special education services: Biology, behavior or bias? *Education and Treatment of Children, 24*, 28–45.

William, F. (1980). Creativity assessment packet. In S. L. Schurr (Ed.), *Dynamite in the classroom: A how-to handbook for teachers*. Columbus, OH: National Middle School Association.

Winner, E. (1997). *Gifted children: Myths and realities*. New York: Basic Books.

Winner, E. (2000). The origins and ends of giftedness. *American Psychologist, 55*, 159–169.

Annotated Bibliography

The following books are strongly recommended for increasing school psychologists' skills in several important areas of giftedness.

Davis, G. A., & Rimm, S. B. (2004). *Education of the gifted and talented* (5th ed.). Boston, MA: Allyn & Bacon. *This practical guide presents the best ideas and practices in the field of gifted education. From planning a sound gifted and talented program to the evaluation of a program, this leading text explores contemporary program models and problems of minority, disabled, and female gifted students. Chapters on creativity and teaching thinking skills—two concepts central to gifted education—help the reader to understand creative students, creative processes, and how to foster high levels of creative thinking.*

Dixon, F. A., & Moon, S. M. (Eds.). (2006). *The handbook of secondary gifted education*. Waco, TX: Prufrock. *This handbook is designed to help educational professionals interested in building effective and comprehensive educational opportunities for gifted secondary students. Topics include understanding the gifted adolescent, social/emotional issues, adolescent issues, best practices for curriculum and instruction and programming options (both school-wide and in specific subject areas), teacher education, and professional development.*

Lovecky, D. V. (2004). *Different minds: Gifted children with ADHD, Asperger Syndrome, and other learning deficits*. Philadelphia, PA: Jessica Kingsley. *This book reviews studies and provides actual cases that inform the reader of the latest thinking on this doubly different group of children. It will help the practitioner understand the gifted and is a practical guide for recognizing dual exceptionalities such as ADHD, AS, and learning deficits.*

Neihart, M., Reis, S. M., Robinson, N. M., & Moon, S. M. (Eds.). (2002). *The social and emotional development of gifted children: What do we know?* Waco, TX: Prufrock. *This text offers an examination of the essential topics teachers, parents, and researchers need to know about the social and emotional development of gifted children. The text includes chapters on peer pressure and social acceptance, resilience, delinquency, and underachievement.*

Recommended Articles

The following articles are important to consider in this area:
Kitano, M. K., & Lewis, R. B. (2005). Resilience and coping: Implications for gifted children and youth at risk. *Roeper Review, 27*(4), 200–205.
Uresti, R., Goertz, J., & Bernal, E. M. (2002). Maximizing achievement for potentially gifted and talented and regular minority students in a primary classroom. *Roeper Review, 25*(1), 27–31.

Useful Websites

National Association for Gifted Children: www.nagc.org
The National Foundation for Gifted and Creative Children: www.nfgcc.org
The National Research Center on the Gifted and Talented: www.gifted.uconn.edu/nrcgt.html
Center for Talented Youth—Johns Hopkins University: http://cty.jhu.edu
Summer Institute for the Gifted: www.giftedstudy.com
Advocacy for Gifted and Talented Education in New York State: www.agateny.com
Center for Gifted Education Policy: www.apa.org/ed/cgep.html
Council for Exceptional Children: www.cec.sped.org//AM/Template.cfm?Section=Home

Index

About the Author

Danielle Martines is Assistant Professor of psychology at Montclair State University in Upper Montclair, New Jersey and a licensed tri-lingual psychologist. She received her Professional Diploma and PhD in psychology from Fordham University, Lincoln Center Campus, New York with a specialization in bilingual school psychology and a Masters degree in School/Community Counseling from Long Island University, New York. Prior academic appointments include Assistant Professor of counseling psychology at City University of New York (CUNY) and Adjunct Professor at Manhattan College, the College of New Rochelle, and Fordham University.

Her professional priority is on quality multicultural psychology teaching for school, clinical, and counseling programs. She routinely teaches graduate level courses in cognitive assessment, school-based consultation methods, psychopathology, clinical interviewing, and the psychological aspects of disabling conditions, and supervises multi-ethnic school practicums and internships. As a multicultural scholar and trainer, she infuses multicultural competency training in all coursework and internships. She has authored and coauthored book chapters and articles for culturally and linguistically diverse student populations on academic and cognitive assessment, consultation, and culture and emotional intelligence. In addition to working with multi-ethnic individuals in her private practice, she has presented at a number of national and international conferences and provided consultation in the areas of diversity, multiculturalism, and culture and emotional intelligence.

About the Contributors

Natalio Extremera, Ph.D., is currently Professor of Organizational Behaviour at the Department of Social Psychology, University of Málaga, Spain. His doctoral dissertation examined the predictive validity of the emotional intelligence construct, following an EI ability model, on emotional well-being, interpersonal relationships, and occupational stress. He is a member of the Research Unit for Emotion and Cognition. He is the coauthor, with Dr. Fernández-Berrocal, of the book *Autocontrol Emocional* (2002), and has published several book chapters, as well as research articles, which have appeared in peer-reviewed journals. His recent research focuses on assessment issues in the field of emotional intelligence, particularly the impact of emotional intelligence on workplace context. He also teaches workshops on improving emotional intelligence abilities.

Pablo Fernández-Berrocal, Ph.D., is Psychology Professor at the University of Malaga and Director of the Emotion and Cognition Laboratory at the University of Malaga (Spain). He has published numerous articles in peer-reviewed scientific journals (e.g., *Behavioral and Brain Sciences, Cognition and Emotion, Personality and Individual Differences, Journal of Psychopathology and Behavioral Assessment*) and has authored many book chapters on various aspects of Emotional Intelligence. Additionally, he is a coauthor of the books *Corazones Inteligentes* (2002), *Autocontrol Emocional* (2002), *Desarrolla tu Inteligencia Emocional* (2004), and *Manual de Inteligencia Emocional* (2007). He is an experienced conference presenter on how to develop emotional intelligence.

Sara G. Nahari, Ph.D., is Associate Professor of the Graduate School of Education and Psychology at Touro College and Adjunct Associate Professor in the Graduate Program in School Psychology in Queens College, City University of New York. She received her doctorate from Fordham University, where she also received a Professional Diploma in bilingual school psychology and is a Nationally Certified School Psychologist. She was also Assistant Director of the Bilingual Psychological and Academic Assessment Support Center. Her entire career as teacher, guidance counselor, and psychologist in the New York City Public Schools was devoted to multicultural and bilingual issues. In 1992, she received the Bilingual Support Personnel of the Year Award of the New York State Association for Bilingual Education, and in 2004 she received the Fordham School of Education Alumni Achievement Award. She recently coedited the *Handbook on Multicultural School Psychology: An Interdisciplinary Perspective*. Her teaching, scholarly interests, and publications are related to multicultural assessment and parental involvement.